DISSERTATIONS IN PHILOSOPHY ACCEPTED AT AMERICAN UNIVERSITIES, 1861–1975

GARLAND REFERENCE LIBRARY
OF THE HUMANITIES
(VOL. 112)

DISSERTATIONS IN PHILOSOPHY ACCEPTED AT AMERICAN UNIVERSITIES, 1861–1975

Thomas C. Bechtle
Mary F. Riley

GARLAND PUBLISHING, INC. • NEW YORK & LONDON
1978

© 1978 by Thomas C. Bechtle and Mary F. Riley
All rights reserved

Library of Congress Cataloging in Publication Data
Bechtle, Thomas C
  Dissertations in philosophy accepted at American universities, 1861-1975.

  (Garland reference library of the humanities; v. 112)
  Includes index.
  1. Philosophy—Bibliography. 2. Dissertations, Academic—United States—Bibliography. I. Riley, Mary F., joint author. II. Title.
  Z7125.B38   [B72]   016.1   77-83392
  ISBN 0-8240-9835-8

Printed in the United States of America

CONTENTS

Preface vii
Obtaining Theses Listed xi
List of Abbreviations xiii
The Bibliography 1
Index 487

PREFACE

This bibliography is a record of dissertations which have been written over the past 115 years in 120 universities in the United States and Canada as a requirement for the award of the Ph.D. in philosophy.

The volume is arranged by author. As a rule, only those authors have been included whose dissertations are primarily concerned with philosophy and whose degrees have been earned in a department of philosophy. Some flexibility for inclusion, however, has been necessary in order to meet the problems posed by the inevitable number of variables and exceptions that any rule generates.

Prior to 1933, departmental disciplines were often more broadly based than today. In some universities, no structured department of philosophy existed. In others, some departments were interdisciplinary. It was not unusual, for example, to find philosophy and psychology studied in the same department. In each of these variant situations, decisions on inclusion of titles were based on the content of the dissertation. If it was essentially concerned with philosophical concepts, then it was included. If philosophy was secondary and another discipline was primary, as in the case of the Ed.D. or Th.D. degree, then it was omitted.

It was important, then, to study a variety of sources, to evaluate and cross-check lists and to verify each listing with the university at which the degree was granted.

The award of a doctorate for the study of philosophy in schools of theology presented a special problem. These dissertations were listed only when the Ph.D. in philosophy was awarded in cooperation with a university program. Schools whose chief function is the preparation of students for seminary or religious training were not included.

Preface viii

The techniques used in compiling this bibliography varied. For dissertations awarded prior to 1912, it was especially necessary to locate as many university lists as possible. We are indebted to Thomas R. Palfrey and Henry E. Coleman, Jr., for their *Guide to Bibliographies of Theses, United States and Canada,*[1] and to Ralph P. Rosenberg for his *Bibliographies of Theses in America.*[2] The former gave us some scope as to our research. After learning what published lists were available, we were able to evaluate our task. The latter amplified the Palfrey list.

We examined as many of the published lists as we were able to locate. Some were typed lists such as the material which was deposited at Columbia University Library by Ralph P. Rosenberg upon completion of his article. We are grateful to Eugene P. Sheehy, Head of the Reference Department at Columbia University Library, for allowing us to study the material.

After examining the published registers and abstracts of universities as they were available, we read commencement programs when we could and consulted the card catalogues of some universities.

In addition, the following lists of dissertations were consulted: *Comprehensive Dissertation Index, 1861–1972;*[3] *List of American Doctoral Dissertations Printed in 1912–1938;*[4] *Doctoral Dissertations Accepted by American Universities, 1933/34–1954/55;*[5] *American Doctoral Dissertations, 1955/56– ;*[6] *Dissertation Abstracts International;*[7] and the lists which appear annually in the *Review of Metaphysics*.

Where little or no information was available, we wrote to the Chairperson of a philosophy department and, if no response was received, to the Graduate Dean of the university in question.

It was only after all of our research was completed that we contacted the library of each institution and asked that our compilation be verified. This proved a critical juncture, for it was at this point that our listings became complete and accurate to a degree far beyond that of any of the printed sources we had consulted up to that time. For this attention to detail and accuracy, we are indebted to the Reference Librarians of all the institutions contacted.

We are also indebted at our own institution to Paul J. Reiss, Executive Vice President of Fordham University, who encouraged us to complete this work, to Anne M. Murphy, Director of Libraries at Fordham, whose generosity allowed us to pursue the research for this publication in the libraries of Fordham University, and to Joseph Vincie, who gave generously of his time and his knowledge of philosophy in the preparation of the index.

NOTES

1. Thomas R. Palfrey and Henry E. Coleman, Jr., *Guide to Bibliographies of Theses, United States and Canada* (Chicago: American Library Association, 1940).

2. Ralph P. Rosenberg, "Bibliographies of Theses in America," *Bulletin of Bibliography,* Part I, 18, No. 8 (1945), 181–82, and Part II, 18, No. 9 (1945), 201–203.

3. *Comprehensive Dissertation Index, 1861–1972* (Ann Arbor, Michigan: Xerox University Microfilms, 1973), 37 vols.
———*1973 Supplement, Author Index*, Vol. 5 (Xerox, 1974).
———*1974 Supplement, Author Index*, Vol. 5 (Xerox, 1975).
———*1975 Supplement, Author Index*, Vol. 5 (Xerox, 1976).

4. U.S. Library of Congress, *List of American Doctoral Dissertations Printed in 1912–1938* (Washington: Government Printing Office, 1913–1940). 26 vols.

5. *Doctoral Dissertations Accepted by American Universities, 1933/34–1954/55*, Nos. 1-22 (New York: H. W. Wilson, 1934–56).

6. *American Doctoral Dissertations, 1955/56–* (Ann Arbor, Michigan: Xerox University Microfilms, 1957–).

7. *Dissertation Abstracts International,* Vol. I, 1938– (Ann Arbor, Michigan: Xerox University Microfilms, 1938–).

OBTAINING THESES LISTED

Copies of many dissertations included in this work are available for purchase in microfilm or xerox form from Xerox University Microfilms, Ann Arbor, Michigan 48106. Where the authors have determined that copies can be so obtained, we have included for the reader's convenience the University Microfilms order number in the citation for each thesis. Abstracts for theses available for purchase (as well as for selected others) appear in the periodical *Dissertation Abstracts International* (1938–present). Should the reader wish to consult an abstract, he may obtain a volume-number-page citation for that abstract from *Comprehensive Dissertation Index, 1861–1972*, or from the annual supplements issued thereafter. For more specific information concerning the ordering of dissertations from University Microfilms, and for current prices and order forms, consult any recent number of *Dissertation Abstracts International*.

    Many of the theses listed in this bibliography are *not* available from University Microfilms but generally may be obtained either through interlibrary loan or by purchase of a copy produced by the university which granted the degree. A guide to the various lending and photoreproduction policies of universities in regard to dissertations is included in the prefatory pages of *American Doctoral Dissertations*. In addition, the interlibrary loans librarian at any research library will be able to assist the reader in determining the best possible method for obtaining a dissertation copy.

ABBREVIATIONS

CITED AS:

Alberta	University of Alberta Edmonton, Alberta Canada T6G 2E1
American U.	The American University Washington, D.C. 20016
Arizona	University of Arizona Tucson, Arizona 85721
Arizona St.	Arizona State University Tempe, Arizona 85281
Arkansas	University of Arkansas Fayetteville, Arkansas 72701
Berkeley	University of California Berkeley, California 94720
Boston Coll.	Boston College Chestnut Hill, Massachusetts 02167
Boston U.	Boston University Boston, Massachusetts 02215
Bowling Green	Bowling Green State University Bowling Green, Ohio 43402
Brandeis	Brandeis University Waltham, Massachusetts 02154
British Columbia	University of British Columbia Vancouver, British Columbia Canada V6T 1W5
Brown	Brown University Providence, Rhode Island 02912
Bryn Mawr	Bryn Mawr College Bryn Mawr, Pennsylvania 19010
Buffalo	State University of New York, Buffalo Buffalo, New York 14214
C.I.A.S.	California Institute of Asian Studies San Francisco, California 94110

Abbreviations xiv

C.U.N.Y	The City University of New York Graduate School and University Center New York, New York 10036
Cal., Davis	University of California, Davis Davis, California 95616
Cal., Irvine	University of California, Irvine Irvine, California 92664
Cal., S. Barbara	University of California, Santa Barbara Santa Barbara, California 93106
Cal., S. Cruz	University of California, Santa Cruz Santa Cruz, California 95060
Cal., S. Diego	University of California, San Diego La Jolla, California 92038
Calgary	University of Calgary Calgary, Alberta Canada T2N 1N4
Case	Case Western Reserve University Cleveland, Ohio 44105
Catholic U.	The Catholic University of America Washington, D.C. 20017
Chicago	University of Chicago Chicago, Illinois 60637
Cincinnati	University of Cincinnati Cincinnati, Ohio 45221
Claremont	Claremont Graduate School and University Center Claremont, California 91711
Colorado	University of Colorado Boulder, Colorado 80304
Columbia	Columbia University New York, New York 10027
Connecticut	University of Connecticut Storrs, Connecticut 06268
Cornell	Cornell University Ithaca, New York 14850
DePaul	DePaul University Chicago, Illinois 60604
Drew	Drew University Madison, New Jersey 07940
Duke	Duke University Durham, North Carolina 27706

Abbreviations

Duquesne	Duquesne University Pittsburgh, Pennsylvania 15219
Emory	Emory University Atlanta, Georgia 30322
Florida St.	Florida State University Tallahassee, Florida 32306
Fordham	Fordham University Bronx, New York 10458
Georgetown	Georgetown University Washington, D.C. 20007
Georgia	University of Georgia Athens, Georgia 30601
Harvard	Harvard University Cambridge, Massachusetts 02138
Hawaii	University of Hawaii Honolulu, Hawaii 96822
Illinois	University of Illinois Urbana, Illinois 61803
Illinois, Chi.	University of Illinois at Chicago Circle Chicago, Illinois 60680
Indiana	Indiana University Bloomington, Indiana 47405
Iowa	University of Iowa Iowa City, Iowa 52240
Iowa St.	Iowa State University Ames, Iowa 50010
Johns Hopkins	Johns Hopkins University Baltimore, Maryland 21218
Kansas	University of Kansas Lawrence, Kansas 66045
Laval	Université Laval Quebec City, Quebec Canada G1K 7P4
Loyola	Loyola University Chicago, Illinois 60611
M.I.T.	Massachusetts Institute of Technology Cambridge, Massachusetts 02139
McGill	McGill University Montreal, Quebec Canada H3C 3G1

Abbreviations xvi

McMaster	McMaster University Hamilton, Ontario Canada L8S 4L8
Manitoba	University of Manitoba Winnipeg, Manitoba Canada R3T 2N2
Marquette	Marquette University Milwaukee, Wisconsin 53233
Maryland	University of Maryland College Park, Maryland 20742
Massachusetts	University of Massachusetts Amherst, Massachusetts 01003
Miami	University of Miami Coral Gables, Florida 33124
Michigan	University of Michigan Ann Arbor, Michigan 48104
Michigan St.	Michigan State University East Lansing, Michigan 48223
Minnesota	University of Minnesota Minneapolis, Minnesota 55455
Missouri	University of Missouri Columbia, Missouri 65202
Missouri, K.C.	University of Missouri, Kansas City Kansas City, Missouri 64110
N.Y.U.	New York University New York, New York 10003
Nebraska	University of Nebraska Lincoln, Nebraska 68508
New Mexico	The University of New Mexico Albuquerque, New Mexico 87106
New School	New School for Social Research New York, New York 10011
Niagara	Niagara University Niagara University, New York 14109
No. Carolina	University of North Carolina Chapel Hill, North Carolina 27514
No. Dakota	University of North Dakota Grand Forks, North Dakota 58202
Northwestern	Northwestern University Evanston, Illinois 60201

Abbreviations xvii

Notre Dame	University of Notre Dame Notre Dame, Indiana 46556
Ohio St.	The Ohio State University Columbus, Ohio 43210
Ohio U.	Ohio University Athens, Ohio 45701
Oklahoma	University of Oklahoma Norman, Oklahoma 73069
Oregon	University of Oregon Eugene, Oregon 97403
Oregon St.	Oregon State University Corvallis, Oregon 97331
Ottawa	University of Ottawa Ottawa, Ontario Canada K1N 6N5
Penn St.	Pennsylvania State University University Park, Pennsylvania 16802
Pennsylvania	University of Pennsylvania Philadelphia, Pennsylvania 19104
Pittsburgh	University of Pittsburgh Pittsburgh, Pennsylvania 15213
Princeton	Princeton University Princeton, New Jersey 08540
Purdue	Purdue University Lafayette, Indiana 47907
R.P.I.	Rensselaer Polytechnic Institute Troy, New York 12181
Radcliffe*	Radcliffe College Cambridge, Massachusetts 02138
Rice	Rice University Houston, Texas 77001
Rochester	University of Rochester Rochester, New York 14627
Rockefeller	Rockefeller University New York, New York 10021
Rutgers	Rutgers, The State University New Brunswick, New Jersey 08903

*All Radcliffe College dissertations are stored in the archives of Harvard University.

Abbreviations xviii

S.M.U.	Southern Methodist University Dallas, Texas 75222
St. Bonaventure	St. Bonaventure University St. Bonaventure, New York 14778
St. John's	St. John's University Jamaica, New York 11432
St. Louis	St. Louis University St. Louis, Missouri 63103
Smith	Smith College Northampton, Massachusetts 01060
So. Illinois	Southern Illinois University Carbondale, Illinois 62901
Southern Cal.	University of Southern California Los Angeles, California 90007
Stanford	Stanford University Stanford, California 94305
Stony Brook	State University of New York at Stony Brook Stony Brook, New York 11790
Syracuse	Syracuse University Syracuse, New York 13210
Temple	Temple University Philadelphia, Pennsylvania 19122
Tennessee	University of Tennessee Knoxville, Tennessee 37916
Texas	University of Texas Austin, Texas 78712
Toronto	University of Toronto Toronto, Ontario Canada M5S 1A1
Tulane	Tulane University New Orleans, Louisiana 70118
U.C.L.A.	University of California, Los Angeles Los Angeles, California 90024
U. of Washington	University of Washington Seattle, Washington 98105
U.S. Int'l	United States International University San Diego, California 92131
Utah	University of Utah Salt Lake City, Utah 84112
Vanderbilt	Vanderbilt University Nashville, Tennessee 37302

Abbreviations

Virginia	University of Virginia Charlottesville, Virginia 22903
W. Ontario	University of Western Ontario London, Ontario Canada N6A 3K7
Washington U.	Washington University St. Louis, Missouri 63130
Waterloo	University of Waterloo Waterloo, Ontario Canada N2L 3G1
Wayne St.	Wayne State University Detroit, Michigan 48202
Wisconsin	University of Wisconsin Madison, Wisconsin 53706
Wm. & Mary	College of William and Mary Williamsburg, Virginia 23185
Yale	Yale University New Haven, Connecticut 06520
Yeshiva	Yeshiva University New York, New York 10033
York	York University Downsview, Ontario Canada M3J 1P3

- A -

1. Abbate, Fred J. Politics and principles: a critique of Michael Oakeshott's conception of rational conduct. Columbia, 1970. 71-6132

2. Abbot, Francis Ellingwood. The philosophy of space and time, and its relation to that of the conditioned and unconditioned. Accompanied by tables of cosmical and mental categories. Harvard, 1881.

3. Abbott, Myron James Edward. Anarchy and anarchism: Santayana on the nature of moral and political authority. Vanderbilt, 1974. 75-12759

4. Abbott, William Raymond. Sense experience in Spinoza's theory of knowledge. Ohio St., 1966. 66-9993

5. Abegg, Edmund Deats. Historical periodization: a trait-dominance theory. Columbia, 1969. 72-15560

6. Abel, George Ferdinand. The meaning and limits of mechanism. Yale, 1903.

7. Abel, Reuben. The philosophy of F.C.S. Schiller. New School, 1952.

8. Abelson, Raziel. An analysis of the concept of definition, and critique of three philosophical views concerning its role in knowledge. N.Y.U., 1957.
60-488

9. Abernethy, George L. The theory of social contract in England, 1642-1652. Michigan, 1936.

10. Abramov, Blanche Wohl. Geometrical structures in science. Indiana, 1973. 74-4655

11. Abrams, Natalie. Free-will and moral responsibility in the works of Charles Arthur Campbell. Columbia, 1972. 72-28005

12. Abrams, Russell Zachary. Convention, truth, and meaning. Yale, 1974. 75-11274

13. Achinstein, Peter Jacob. A study of confirmation theory. Harvard, 1961.

14. Ackerman, Phyllis. Essays on Hegel's *Phaenomenologie*. Berkeley, 1917.

15. Ackerman, Terrence Frank. The structure of practical reasoning and justification. Rochester, 1975.
75-22722

16. Ackermann, Robert John. Simplicity and the acceptability of scientific theories. Michigan St., 1960.
60-3405

17. Ackert, Paul Herman. The religious philosophy of Schleiermacher with a translation of his *Reden über religion*. Pittsburgh, 1957.
57-4242

18. Ackley, Sheldon Carmer. John Dewey's conception of shared experience as religious. Boston U., 1948.

19. Ackoff, Russell L. An experimental definition of personality. Pennsylvania, 1947.

20. Adamczewski, Zygmunt. The concept of satisfaction. Harvard, 1956.

21. Adams, Anne Donchin. Knowledge and the causal principle. Texas, 1970.
71-11506

22. Adams, Elie Maynard. An analysis of scientific explanation. Harvard, 1948.

23. Adams, Elizabeth. Aesthetic experience. Chicago, 1904.

24. Adams, Ernest Wilcox. Axiomatic foundations of rigid body mechanics. Stanford, 1956.
16011

25. Adams, George Plimpton. An interpretation and defence of the principle of idealism in metaphysics. Harvard, 1912.

26. Adams, John S. The aesthetics of pessimism: a study of the interrelation of Schopenhauer's ethics and his philosophy of art. Pennsylvania, 1935.

27. Adams, Marilyn McCord. The problem of God's foreknowledge and free will in Boethius and William Ockham. Cornell, 1967.
68-865

28. Adams, Norman Ratcliff. Schleiermacher's philosophy of freedom and his relation to the Leibnizian tradition. Syracuse, 1941.

29. Adams, Robert Merrihew. The modal argument for the ex-

istence of God. Cornell, 1969   69-13015

30. Adderley, Bertram R. Ownership and natural right. Georgetown, 1955.

31. Addis, Laird Clark, Jr. Gilbert Ryle's philosophy of mind. Iowa, 1964.   64-7900

32. Adelman, Howard. Rational explanation in history. Toronto, 1971.

33. Adelmann, Rev. Frederick Joseph. The rational appetite in the De fide orthodoxa of Saint John Damascene. St. Louis, 1955.

34. Adler, Ira N. Evil and theism: an analytic approach. N.Y.U., 1975.   75-22869

35. Adler, Jonathan Eric. Theories of induction: a guide and a critique. Brandeis, 1974.   74-27979

36. Adlerblum, Nima Hirschensohn. A study of Gersonides in his proper perspective. Columbia, 1926.

37. Ager, Tryg A. Kant's theory of representations: an interpretation of the metaphysical and transcendental deductions in the Critique of pure reason. Pittsburgh, 1970.   70-18361

38. Agnew, Priscilla Gregory. Hume's theory of consciousness and the idealist/realist interpretation of the Treatise. Claremont, 1975.   75-19660

39. Agonito, Rosemary Giambattista. Nervous systems, perception, and free persons. Syracuse, 1973.
        74-17556

40. Ahern, Dennis Michael. Hume on the evidential impossibility of miracles. Cal., Irvine, 1973.
        73-31430

41. Ahlén, Axel Carl Mauritz. Critics of utilitarianism within and without the movement. Minnesota, 1942.

42. Ahmad, M. Mobin. A restatement of the problem of the ultimate criterion of good. Chicago, 1969.

43. Ahrens, Olinde Kay. An evaluation of positivistic ethics. Nebraska, 1949.

44. Ahumada, Rodolfo. The philosophies of Antonio Caso and José Vasconcelos with special emphasis on their concepts of value. Southern Cal., 1963.   64-2559

45. Aichele, Ronald Guy. John Dewey's Democracy and educa-

tion: from a logical point of view. Missouri, 1971. 72-10570

46. Aiken, Henry David. The moral philosophy of David Hume. Harvard, 1943.

47. Aiken, Lillian W. The ethical theory of Bertrand Russell. Radcliffe, 1955.

48. Aikins, Herbert Austin. Hume's theory of causation. Yale, 1891.

49. Aitken, Frederick Malcolm. The concept of power in Nietzsche's ethics. Missouri, 1970. 70-20764

50. Akinpelu, Jones Adelayo. Moral education and moral objectivity. Columbia, 1970. 71-6133

51. Aklujkar, Ashok Narhar. The philosophy of Bhartrhari's Trikandi. Harvard, 1970.

52. Aklujkar, Vidyullekha. Primacy of linguistic units. British Columbia, 1973.

53. Alamshah, William H. John Dewey's ethical theory. Southern Cal., 1955.

54. Al-Azm, Sadik Jalal. The moral philosophy of Henry Bergson. Yale, 1961.

55. Albee, E. The beginnings of English utilitarianism. Cornell, 1894.

56. Albert, Ethel M. The philosophical consequences of modern physical theory. Wisconsin, 1949.

57. Albert, Sidney Paul. Esthetics and drama. Yale, 1939.

58. Albertson, Robert Grant. Values and the curriculum. Claremont, 1966. 68-4622

59. Albright, Gary Lewis. The concept of perspective in George Herbert Mead and Jose y Ortega y Gasset. Columbia, 1966. 66-12546

60. Albritton, Rogers Garland. A study of Plato's Philebus. Princeton, 1955. 20095

61. Alcalá, Francisco. Ortega y Gasset: la crisis de Europa vista a través de sus sistemas ideologicós (1902-1927). N.Y.U., 1971. 72-13333

62. Alderman, Harold Gordon. Heidegger and the overthrow of philosophy. Tulane, 1968. 68-15225

63. Al-Dijaili, Yehya S. An inquiry into the true relationship between Sufism and Islam. C.I.A.S., 1974.
    75-12699

64. Aldrich, Virgil Charles. A philosophy of meaning and fact. Berkeley, 1932.

65. Alexander, Hartley Burr. Problems of metaphysics and the meaning of metaphysical explanation; an essay in definitions. Columbia, 1901.

66. Alexander, Henry Aaron, Jr. Thomas Reid's defense of common sense. Berkeley, 1955.

67. Alexander, Hubert Griggs. The intelligibility of time. Yale, 1934.

68. Alexander, Jean Tangren. Norman Malcolm and dreaming and nonsense. Oregon, 1975.   76-15019

69. Alexander, John Gerald. An examination of the problem of physical determinism. Oregon, 1970.
    71-16798

70. Alexander, Joseph Davidson. A critique of representational thinking. Penn St., 1972.   73-13947

71. Alexander, Robert Eldon. The prospects for value-neutrality in the social sciences. Waterloo, 1970.

72. Algozin, Keith Warren. The common good as the key to Hobbes' civil philosophy. Marquette, 1967.
    68-474

73. Allaire, Edwin Bonar, Jr. A critical examination of Wittgenstein's *Tractatus*. Iowa, 1960.   60-4361

74. Allan, Denison Maurice. Purpose and causality: a study in the problem of body and mind. Harvard, 1926.

75. Allan, George James. A Whiteheadian approach to the philosophy of history. Yale, 1963.   71-18556

76. Alleman, George Merrin. A critique of some philosophical aspects of the mysticism of Jacob Boehme. Pennsylvania, 1932.

77. Allen, Allan J. Moral judgment and the concept of a universal imperative with special references to Kant. Indiana, 1967.   67-3642

78. Allen, Benjamin W.P. Epiphenomenalism in the moral philosophy of George Santayana particularly as it affects free will. Drew, 1953.

79. Allen, Diogenes. Faith as a ground for religious beliefs. Yale, 1965. 65-15002

80. Allen, Douglas Malcolm. The history of religions and Eliade's phenomenology. Vanderbilt, 1971.
72-3199

81. Allen, Elliott Bernard. The notion of being in Hervaeus Natalis. Toronto, 1958.

82. Allen, Estelle M. Meaning and methodology in Hellenistic philosophy. Chicago, 1936.

83. Allen, Harold Joseph. Teleology and the activity of natural systems. Columbia, 1955. 10166

84. Allen, James Thomas, Jr. An analysis of personal memory. Georgia, 1975. 76-13986

85. Allen, Jeffner Marie. Husserl and intersubjectivity: a phenomenological investigation of the analogical structure of intersubjectivity. Duquesne, 1973.
74-13186

86. Allen, Joseph Jerome. Self: a metaphysical theory. Tulane, 1973. 74-10682

87. Allen, Paul, III. A critical evaluation of the theories of moral justification of R.M. Hare and other selected twentieth-century philosophers. New School, 1975. 75-25441

88. Allen, Reginald Edgar. The status of soul in Plato's philosophy. Yale, 1958.

89. Allen, Sydney Earl, Jr. A study of the idea of revelation, with special reference to the thought of Paul Tillich and Karl Barth. Nebraska, 1964.
64-11922

90. Alles, Adam. Appetition in Leibniz and will in Schopenhauer. Yale, 1926.

91. Allinson, Robert Elliott. Five dialogues on knowledge and reality. Texas, 1972. 73-401

92. Allison, David Blair. Derrida's critique of Husserl: the philosophy of presence. Penn St., 1974.
74-28939

93. Allison, Henry Edward. Lessing and the enlightenment; a study of G.E. Lessing's philosophy of religion, and of its place within the context of eighteenth century thought. New School, 1964. 65-9097

94. Alluntis, Felix. The problem of expropriation. Catholic U., 1949.

95. Almeder, Robert Francis. The metaphysical and logical realism of Charles Sanders Peirce. Pennsylvania, 1969. 69-5601

96. Alston, William P. Internal relatedness and pluralism in the philosophy of Whitehead. Chicago, 1951.

97. Alton, Bruce Scott. An examination of the golden rule. Stanford, 1966. 67-4315

98. Alvino, James J. From 'cogito' to 'mitsein'-- the ontology of sociality. Boston Coll., 1975.
75-20695

99. Aman, Kenneth Joseph. Coherence in religious discourse. Yale, 1972. 72-22375

100. Ambrose, Alice. In defense of an external logic. Wisconsin, 1932.

101. Amendola, Amedeo. The ontology of St. Bonaventure. Duquesne, 1966.

102. Ameriks, Karlis Peter. Cartesianism and Wittgenstein: the legacy of subjectivism in contemporary philosophy of mind. Yale, 1973. 73-24934

103. Ames, Van Meter. The aesthetics of the novel. Chicago, 1924.

104. Ammerman, Robert Ray. The natures of concepts and images. Brown, 1956. 19517

105. Amundson, Ronald Arthur. Memory images and forms of memory. Wisconsin, 1975. 75-18580

106. Anacker, Stefan. Vasubandhu: three aspects. A study of a Buddhist philosopher. Wisconsin, 1970.
70-8257

107. Anagnostopoulos, Georgios. Some philosophical problems in Plato's early dialogues and the search for a method. Brandeis, 1971. 71-20320

108. Anastasia, Diane Doherty. Orthodox and Hegelian Marxism: a historical and critical study of two trends in contemporary Marxism. Boston U., 1975.
75-12236

109. Anderberg, Clifford William. The impact of evolution on Dewey's theory of knowledge and the critics of Dewey. Wisconsin, 1953.

110. Anderegg, Jerry Edward. The development of religious thought in Heine's work. Utah, 1973. 73-23106

111. Anderson, Alan Ross. A finitary system of logic. Yale, 1955.

112. Anderson, Albert Allan. The cognitive role of the arts. Boston U., 1971. 71-26382

113. Anderson, C. Alan. Horatio W. Dresser and the philosophy of new thought. Boston U., 1963. 64-389

114. Anderson, Clifford Earl. A study of social freedom. U. of Washington, 1974. 74-29366

115. Anderson, Cynthia. Supererogation and deontological ethics. Claremont, 1972. 72-30553

116. Anderson, Daniel Erwin. An objectificational theory of aesthetic value. Tulane, 1961. 61-3776

117. Anderson, Emerald Balboa. Semantic problems in Dewey's logic. Syracuse, 1966. 67-7055

118. Anderson, Ernest Paul. Some aspects of evaluative utterances and their justification. Connecticut, 1973. 73-24386

119. Anderson, Frederick Mitchell. John Dewey's critique of philosophies. Harvard, 1961.

120. Anderson, Fulton Henry. The influence of contemporary science on Locke's method and results. Toronto, 1920.

121. Anderson, Gerald Ray. Social development and the problem of self-determination (with special emphasis on the philosophies of Hegel and Marx). Northwestern, 1973. 74-7702

122. Anderson, James Clark. The transcendental deduction of body: an essay in the metaphysics of experience. Syracuse, 1975. 76-7694

123. Anderson, James Francis. Analogy: a study in Thomistic metaphysics. Toronto, 1940.

124. Anderson, John Joseph. Eros in Teilhard de Chardin: a study in the function of eros in the evolution of love-energy in ultimate Christian moral motivation. Fordham, 1971. 71-20154

125. Anderson, John Mueller. Structure and purpose. Berkeley, 1939.

126. Anderson, Kenneth Christian. Wilfrid Sellars and the theory of the given. Toronto, 1973.

127. Anderson, Leland Tyson, Jr. Wittgenstein and the logical possibility of immortality. Temple, 1972.
    72-17677

128. Anderson, Sr. M. Evangeline. The human body in the philosophy of St. Thomas Aquinas. Catholic U., 1953.

129. Anderson, Myron George. Language and ontology. Brown, 1959.
    59-4325

130. Anderson, Robert Fendel. Hume's first principles. Berkeley, 1963.
    64-5187

131. Anderson, Robert Milford, Jr. An essay in neuroepistemology. Minnesota, 1972.
    72-27721

132. Anderson, Susan Leigh. A philosophical analysis of the phenomenon of multiple personality in connection with the problem of personal identity. U.C.L.A., 1974.
    74-22973

133. Anderson, Thomas Charles. The object and nature of mathematical science in Aristotle and Thomas Aquinas: a comparison. Marquette, 1966.
    68-476

134. Anderson, Wallace Earl. Mind and nature in the early philosophical writings of Jonathan Edwards. Minnesota, 1961.
    61-4589

135. Anderson, Wilhelm. An orientation of Hume's moral philosophy. Chicago, 1932.

136. Andic, Martin Fedor. Mental images, appearances, and awareness. Princeton, 1967.
    67-13477

137. Andrade, Louis Edward. An examination of selected problems in philosophy and accounting. Nebraska, 1965.
    65-11413

138. Andre, Shane. The verification principle: its problems and development. Claremont, 1966.
    67-9537

139. Andrea, Anesti. The aesthetic of the early Nietzsche. Boston Coll., 1974.
    74-18258

140. Andrews, Charles Thomas. Action and bodily movement. No. Carolina, 1968.
    69-10133

141. Andriopoulos, Dimitri Zacharias. Issues and problems in contemporary Greek aesthetics. Buffalo, 1969.
    69-20559

142. Angel, Jay Leonard. Recursive grammars and the creative aspect of language use. British Columbia, 1974.

143. Angel, Roger Bernard. Relativity and covariance. McGill, 1970.

144. Angeles, Peter Adam. G.F. Stout's philosophy of animism. Columbia, 1959. 59-4051

145. Angell, Richard Bradshaw. Designata, language, and truth: a preface to a pragmatic rationalism. Harvard, 1954.

146. Angene, Lyle E. Reference and modality. Chicago, 1971.

147. Angier, Roswell Parker. The aesthetics of unequal division. Harvard, 1903.

148. Annas, Julia Elizabeth. Aristotle's criticism of Plato's theory of number. Harvard, 1973.

149. Annese, Thomas. Actions and the body. U.C.L.A., 1967. 68-6128

150. Annis, David Boyden. Knowledge and belief: the relation of the two concepts. Illinois, 1969. 70-781

151. Ansbro, John Joseph. Kierkegaard's critique of Hegel: an interpretation. Fordham, 1964. 64-13207

152. Anthony, Clifford Hugh. Language as a mirror of the world in Wittgenstein's *Tractatus*. W. Ontario, 1973.

153. Anton, Anatole Ben. Statements about power relations: a study of logical form. Stanford, 1973. 74-6443

154. Anton, John Peter. The doctrine of contrariety in Aristotle's philosophy of process: an essay on Aristotle's metaphysics of distributive being. Columbia, 1954. 8596

155. Anton, Peter. Empiricism and analysis. Indiana, 1961. 61-4418

156. Antz, Emma Louise. The self in the aesthetic experience. N.Y.U., 1930. 73-17688

157. Apostle, Hippocrates George. Aristotle's philosophy of mathematics. Harvard, 1943.

158. Appelbaum, David Marc. Critiques, virtues, and skepticism. Harvard, 1973.

159. Appleby, Peter Clare. A critical study of Peirce's philosophical theology. Texas, 1963.   64-6577

160. Aquila, Richard Emil. Intentionality. Northwestern, 1968.   69-1788

161. Aquino, Conrado P. Conflicting concepts of man and philosophies of education in relation to the Philippines. Georgetown, 1950.

162. Arapura, John Geeverghese. Radhakrishnan and integral experience. Columbia, 1960.   61-244

163. Arbaugh, George Evans. Value and ontology in contemporary British ethics. Iowa, 1959.   59-5694

164. Arbini, Ronald Anthony. The natural law tradition and its influence on Hobbes's concept of obligation. U. of Washington, 1961.   61-3975

165. Arbuckle, Gilbert B. A critique of the Thomistic doctrine of definition. Catholic U., 1962. 63-2067

166. Archer, Raymond Hardy. Hume and Sartre on the self. Rice, 1973.   73-21530

167. Ardagh, David William. Aquinas on happiness. U. of Washington, 1975.   75-28311

168. Arentz, Donald Walter. Aristotle's dialectical ethics. Syracuse, 1975.   76-7627

169. Arfa, Milton. Abraham Ibn Daud and the beginnings of medieval Jewish Aristotelianism with particular reference to the concept of substance in the *Emunah ramah*. Columbia, 1954.   8597

170. Armenti, Amedio William. Intuitionistic criticisms of the ethical theories of Bradley and Green. Michigan, 1959.   59-4877

171. Armetta, Paul Milo. Epistemological and axiological aspects of communication: as seen in the works of G.H. Mead, John Dewey, Hugh Duncan, Emile Durkheim, and Karl Popper. So. Illinois, 1975.   76-26927

172. Arms, Richard Allen. The notion of number and the notion of class. Pennsylvania, 1917.

173. Armstrong, Robert Cornell. Light from the East: studies in Japanese Confucianism. Toronto, 1914.

174. Armstrong, Robert Lawrence. Metaphysics in the development of British empiricism. Berkeley, 1962.

175. Arnaud, Richard Barry. Some metaphysical questions concerning individual things. Brown, 1969.
 70-8685

176. Arndt, Elmer J.F. The relation of value and being in the philosophy of Saint Thomas Aquinas. Yale, 1943.

177. Arner, Douglas Gene. Consciousness and reality. Michigan, 1955. 12539

178. Arneson, Richard James. John Rawls' theory of justice. Berkeley, 1975. 76-15100

179. Arnett, Willard Eugene. Beauty, art and reason: an examination of the artistic and aesthetic motivations in the philosophy of Santayana. Columbia, 1953. 6570

180. Arnold, Anthony P. Some ways moral judgment reflects personality. Chicago, 1973.

181. Arnold, Keith. Artefacts and change. No. Carolina, 1973. 74-5889

182. Arnold, Lloyd L., II. Aristotle's biological concepts and methods in the light of modern biology. Johns Hopkins, 1953.

183. Arnold, Robert Picher. An analysis and deduction of the categories of existence. Texas, 1970.
 71-11510

184. Aronson, Alan Ronald. Art and freedom in the philosophy of Jean-Paul Sartre. Brandeis, 1968.
 69-2043

185. Aronson, Jerrold Lloyd. Causation and scientific explanation. Wisconsin, 1967. 68-1076

186. Arras, John Dyer. A critique of existentialist ethics. Northwestern, 1972. 73-10177

187. Arrington, Robert Lee. The normative-descriptive dualism: a reconsideration. Tulane, 1966. 66-10750

188. Arrowood, Charles Flinn. The place of reflective thinking in the development and maintenance of moral values. Chicago, 1924.

189. Arthur, John Hugh. Systemic explanation and Marxian methodology. Vanderbilt, 1973. 73-25034

190. Artus, Walter W. The *Ars brevis* of Ramon Lull: a study. St. John's, 1967. 67-11446

191. Aschenbrenner, Karl Wilhelm. Aesthetic valuation and response. Berkeley, 1940.

192. Ascher, Anita Luria. Unity of thought and form in Plato's *Phaedrus*. Smith, 1942.

193. Ashbaugh, Anne Freire. Cosmology as philosophical myth: a reenactment of Plato's *Timaeus*. Duquesne, 1974. 74-21043

194. Ashby, Merrilee Hollenkamp. Truth and correspondence in mathematics. Michigan, 1970. 71-15081

195. Ashford, Moselle. Temperament and personality. Vanderbilt, 1941.

196. Ashley, Lawrence Raymond. Personal identity: historical and analytical considerations. Duke, 1973. 74-1119

197. Ashley, Myron Lucius. The nature of hypothesis. Chicago, 1901.

198. Ashmore, Jerome. Santayana's theories of art and aesthetics; an introductory study. Columbia, 1954. 8599

199. Ashmore, Robert B., Jr. The analogical notion of judgment in St. Thomas Aquinas. Notre Dame, 1966. 66-6564

200. Ashworth, Earline Jennifer. The *Logica Hamburgensis* of Joachim Jungius. Bryn Mawr, 1965.

201. Aspell, Patrick J. Thomistic critique of transsubjectivity in recent American realism. Catholic U., 1959.

202. Asquith, Peter Dean. Alternative mathematics and their status. Indiana, 1970. 71-6928

203. Atherton, Margaret Louise. Nativism. Brandeis, 1970. 70-24616

204. Atiyeh, George N. Avicenna's conception of miracles. Chicago, 1954.

205. Atkins, Robert Alan. Historical materialism as a bi-causal system. Berkeley, 1973.

206. Atkinson, Gary Michael. R.M. Hare's criticism of ethical naturalism. Duke, 1970. 70-23384

207. Attig, Thomas William. Cartesianism, certainty and
the 'cogito' in Husserl's <u>Cartesian meditations</u>.
Washington U., 1973. 74-13760

208. Atwell, John Everett. A critical exposition of Edmund
Husserl's first two logical investigations. Wisconsin, 1964. 64-13858

209. Auble, Joel Merritt. Two concepts of obligation.
Northwestern, 1971. 71-30732

210. Audi, Michael Nicholas. The interpretation of quantum
mechanics. Johns Hopkins, 1970. 73-12089

211. Audi, Robert Nemir. The explanation of human action
in common sense and contemporary psychology.
Michigan, 1968. 68-7552

212. Augros, Robert. Hume and the problem of the existence
of substance. Laval, 1974.

213. Augustin-Gabriel, Frère. La matière intelligible.
Laval, 1961.

214. Aune, Bruce Arthur. Sensations and human behavior: a
conceptual study. Minnesota, 1960. 60-2037

215. Austin, Eugene Munger. The ethics of the Cambridge
Platonists. Pennsylvania, 1935.

216. Austin, Harold J. 'Orientation to situation' in Talcott Parsons' concept of action. Chicago, 1975.

217. Austin, Stephen Spaulding. Kant's theory of apperception. Berkeley, 1974.

218. Auxter, Thomas Paul. Kant's moral teleology. Bryn
Mawr, 1973. 74-8947

219. Avey, Albert Edwin. An analysis of the process of
conceptual cognition. Yale, 1915.

220. Awerkamp, Donald Thomas. Emmanuel Lévinas: ethics
and politics. DePaul, 1974. 74-16466

221. Axelrod, Franklin Shepard. The principle of symmetry:
a study in the history and philosophy of scientific
method. Boston U., 1972. 72-25240

222. Axelsen, Diana Elna. A theory of linguistic force and
its application to language in poetry. Stanford,
1968. 69-17393

223. Axer, Rev. Engelbert. The knowledge of reality and

God according to Nicholas Berdyaev. Georgetown, 1948.

224. Axinn, Sidney. A study of Kant's philosophy of history. Pennsylvania, 1955. 13374

225. Ayim, Maryann Elizabeth. Peirce's view of the roles of reason and instinct in scientific inquiry. Waterloo, 1972.

226. Ayres, Clarence Edwin. The nature of the relationship between ethics and economics. Chicago, 1917.

227. Azar, Larry. The meaning of essence in the philosophy of Alfred North Whitehead. Toronto, 1953.

- B -

228. Babin, Arthur Eugène. The theory of opposition in Aristotle. Notre Dame, 1940.

229. Bach, Kent Preston. Two problems of perception. Berkeley, 1968. 69-14838

230. Bacheler, Muriel. Mysticism, an epistemological problem. Yale, 1915.

231. Bachrach, Jay Emil. The aesthetic object and its qualities: recent contributions from philosophical analysis. Columbia, 1967. 67-12235

232. Bacon, Sr. Barbara Ann. Hocking's theory of nuclear experience. St. Louis, 1969. 70-20365

233. Bacon, John Bennett. Being and existence: two ways of formal ontology. Yale, 1966. 66-14938

234. Bacon, Samuel Frederick. An evaluation of the philosophy and pedagogy of ethical culture. Catholic U., 1934.

235. Bagalay, John Earl, Jr. Authority and sovereignty in the modern state, with special emphasis on the American political system in the Revolutionary and constitutional periods prior to 1800. Yale, 1957.

236. Bagen, Rev. John J. The brotherhood of man in the philosophy of St. Thomas Aquinas. Catholic U., 1951.

237. Bahm, Archie J. An interpretation of the nature of presence and some implications of the interpretation. Michigan, 1933. 329

238. Bailey, James Lawrence. Ordinal numbers and the axiom of choice in Quine's New foundations. Harvard, 1962.

239. Bailey, Joan Eleanore. Is rational freedom possible? Yale, 1971. 72-16169

240. Bailey, John Altemus. The objectivity of moral and historical judgments: a comparison and contrast. Pittsburgh, 1970. 71-14485

241. Bailey, Kenneth Clinton. Use of scientific language in the validation of religious discourse. Minnesota, 1960. 60-3501

242. Bailiff, John Delaware. Coming to be: an interpretation of the self in the thought of Martin Heidegger. Penn St., 1966. 67-1908

243. Bails, Jerry Gwin. A study of the functional relationships between logic and pragmatics in polemic discourse. Missouri, K.C., 1960. 67-10096

244. Bainbridge, Robert. Evolution, education and the destiny of man. C.I.A.S., 1971. 74-16427

245. Baird, Robert Malcolm. John Dewey and Richard Brandt: a study in the justification of ethical principles. Emory, 1967. 67-14331

246. Bajema, Jacob. God as value-concept in contemporary American religious thought. Iowa, 1942.

247. Bakan, Mildred Blynn. An inquiry into the factuality of philosophical propositions. Ohio St., 1949.

248. Baker, Arthur Mulford. A final norm for morals and religion. Indiana, 1928.

249. Baker, Bruce French. On the possibility of the relation between existentialism and education. Northwestern, 1964. 64-12248

250. Baker, Clifford Henry. Reality in the works of Unamuno and Ortega y Gasset: a comparative study. Southern Cal., 1961. 61-6276

251. Baker, John Robert. Quantified modal logic and the problem of essentialism. Vanderbilt, 1973.
73-25036

252. Baker, Nancy Elizabeth. The concept of concept. Brandeis, 1971. 71-20321

253. Baker, Rannie Belle. The concept of a limited God in

recent personalism. Syracuse, 1933.

254. Baker, Richard R. The Thomistic theory of the passions and their influence upon the will. Notre Dame, 1941.

255. Baker, Robert B. Moore's realism and non-natural properties: an analysis of the metaphysics of Principia ethica. Minnesota, 1967. 68-7423

256. Baker, Thomas Nelson. The ethical significance of the connection between mind and body. Yale, 1903.

257. Baker, Virginia MacLynne Rudder. Linguistic and ontological aspects of temporal becoming. Vanderbilt, 1972. 73-14494

258. Bakewell, Charles Montague. Hegelianism and man; or, the problem of the one and the many from a modern standpoint. Harvard, 1894.

259. Bakst, James. A comparative study of philosophies of music in the works of Schopenhauer, Nietzsche, and Tolstoi. N.Y.U., 1942. 73-8417

260. Baldwin, Harold Westcott. The logic of reflexive refutations. Colorado, 1973. 74-12356

261. Baldwin, Robert Chester. Finality and value. Yale, 1932.

262. Balentine, William Lybrand. The concept. Pennsylvania, 1897.

263. Bales, Eugene Francis. Plotinus: a critical examination. Missouri, 1973. 74-18462

264. Bales, Royal Eugene. Act vs. rule-utilitarianism. Stanford, 1968. 69-8147

265. Balinsky, Margaret Anne. Plato's divided line. Rochester, 1973. 73-25790

266. Ballaine, Francis Knight. The relations between wisdom and science: illustrations of the history of a distinction. Columbia, 1936.

267. Ballard, Kaith Emerson. A refined utilitarian theory of obligation. Yale, 1961.

268. Ballew, Lynne Smith. Straight and circular: a study of imagery in Greek philosophy. Vanderbilt, 1975.
 76-15473

269. Balowitz, Victor Chaim. Personal identity and bodily identity. Columbia, 1969. 70-6935

270. Baltazar, Eulalia R. A critical examination of the methodology of The phenomenon of man. Georgetown, 1962.

271. Balz, Albert George Adam. Idea and essence in the philosophies of Hobbes and Spinoza. Columbia, 1918.

272. Bamford, Paul Vincent. The Kantian metaphysics of morals. No. Carolina, 1974. 75-15607

273. Bancroft, William Wallace. Joseph Conrad, his philosophy of life. Pennsylvania, 1931.

274. Banja, John Dennis. Ego and reduction: a key to the development of Husserl's phenomenology. Fordham, 1975. 76-17920

275. Banks, John Victor. Reference and reportage. Calgary, 1974.

276. Banner, William Augustus. Natural law and human rights: a critical exposition of a theory of just law. Harvard, 1947.

277. Bannerman, Lloyd Charles Francis. Spencer's philosophical interpretation of biological evolution. Toronto, 1962.

278. Banning, Cyrus Wayne. Are scientific laws rules? Michigan, 1965. 65-10924

279. Bar, Eugen Silas. The language of the unconscious according to Jacques Lacan. Yale, 1971. 71-28022

280. Barath, Desire. Thomas Aquinas' physics and the new sciences. Toronto, 1942.

281. Barbe, Carmen. La coutume dans la vie intellectuelle. Laval, 1968.

282. Barber, Kenneth Frank. Meinong's Hume studies: translation and commentary. Iowa, 1966. 67-2592

283. Barber, Richard Leslie. Logical possibility. Yale, 1950.

284. Barcan, Ruth Charlotte. A strict functional calculus. Yale, 1946.

285. Bardi, John Francis. Philosophy and the phenomenon of political obligation. Missouri, 1974. 75-20094

286. Bardsley, Beverly Jean. The soul as a self-moving motion: the synthesis of madness and sobriety in Plato's Phaedrus. Texas, 1975. 75-16634

287. Barford, Robert. The criticisms of the theory of forms in the first part of Plato's Parmenides. Indiana, 1970. 71-13534

288. Bargeliotes, Leonidas C. Pletho's philosophy of ethics. Emory, 1974. 74-23655

289. Barger, Bill Dale. Locke, substance and real essences. Claremont, 1972. 73-7226

290. Barglow, Ray Charles. Rationality in ethics and science. Berkeley, 1975.

291. Barker, Donald R. Becoming a Christian and assenting to assertions. Notre Dame, 1971. 71-21355

292. Barker, George Eldon. The concept of material substance in the Philosophy of Descartes (Volumes I and II). Purdue, 1975. 75-21084

293. Barker, John Anthony. A system of intensional logic. Tulane, 1967. 67-17897

294. Barker, Peter. Albert Einstein's philosophy of science: a preliminary study. Buffalo, 1975. 76-9027

295. Barker, Stephen Francis. Induction and hypothesis. Harvard, 1954.

296. Barkley, David W. Ideas of democracy in English and French philosophy during the enlightenment. Southern Cal., 1937.

297. Barnds, William Paul. Man's knowledge of God (as set forth in the philosophies of St. Thomas Aquinas and Frederick R. Tennant). Nebraska, 1949.

298. Barnes, Annette Nemore. Formal and non-formal requirements for notational and non-notational symbol systems. Brandeis, 1967. 67-16534

299. Barnes, Gerald Weygandt. Kant's doctrine of the highest good. Harvard, 1968.

300. Barnes, Kenneth Thomas. Identity, reference, and quantifying in. Massachusetts, 1972. 73-5523

301. Barnes, Mahlon Willis, Jr. Concept structure in Cassirer and Whitehead. Northwestern, 1961. 62-836

302. Barnett, Peter Herbert. Retreat from idealism: Emersonian themes in American religious philosophy. Columbia, 1970. 71-17464

303. Barnett, Samuel Roy. Martin Buber's doctrine of man. Purdue, 1972. 72-21155

304. Barnette, Ronald Lee. Explanation of human action. Cal., Irvine, 1972. 72-32334

305. Barnhart, Joe Edward. The religious epistemology and theodicy of Edward John Carnell and Edgar Sheffield Brightman: a study in contrasts. Boston U., 1964. 64-11656

306. Baron, Charles Hillel. Law and the fly-bottle: aspects of Professor Hart's jurisprudence of non-descriptive legal utterances. Pennsylvania, 1972. 73-13375

307. Barr, William Frank. A philosophical analysis of idealizations in science. Rochester, 1969. 70-2846

308. Barral, Mary Rose. Merleau-Ponty: the role of the body in interpersonal relations. Fordham, 1963. 63-5581

309. Barranda, Natividad Gatbonton. The concept of personhood in the thought of Martin Buber, Daisetz Suzuki, and Muhammad Iqbal. Claremont, 1969. 69-8931

310. Barrett, Clifford L. The metaphysical system of Charles Renouvier. Syracuse, 1926.

311. Barrett, Earl E. Types of religious certainty implied by Kant's treatment of the problem of God. Boston U., 1952.

312. Barrett, Robert Burke, Jr. C.I. Lewis's analytic method. Johns Hopkins, 1961.

313. Barrett, William. Aristotle's analysis of movement: its significance for its time. Columbia, 1938.

314. Barron, Rev. J. The idea of the absolute in modern British philosophy. Catholic U., 1929.

315. Barrow, George Alexander. The religious experience and historical revelation. Harvard, 1905.

316. Barry, Lawrence Elmer. Causality: a critique of Richard Taylor's theory. So. Illinois, 1970. 71-9969

317. Barry, Robert Michael. The epistemology of Talcott Parsons. Fordham, 1963. 63-5582

318. Bartky, Sandra Schwartz. A study of "Being" in the philosophy of Heidegger. Illinois, 1963. 64-6015

319. Bartlett, Edward Totterson, III. Aristotle and Ryle on pleasure. U. of Washington, 1970. 71-938

320. Barton, George Estes, Jr. The general aims of education determined by a method involving reflexion, postulation and synthesis. Ohio St., 1940.

321. Baseheart, Sr. Mary Catharine. The encounter of Husserl's phenomenology and the philosophy of St. Thomas in selected writings of Edith Stein. Notre Dame, 1960. 60-2670

322. Basham, Ronald Robert, Jr. The ontological argument: an exercise in logical analysis. No. Carolina, 1974. 74-26844

323. Bashier, Zakaria Imam. Temporalized modal syllogisms in Arabic logic with special reference to Avicenna and Al-Raqqad. Pittsburgh, 1973. 73-27141

324. Bashor, Philip Slosson. The philosophical structure and function of Plato's *Lysis*. Yale, 1956.

325. Basiline, Mary. The aesthetic motif from Thales to Plato. Colorado, 1921.

326. Basinger, David William. The miraculous. Nebraska, 1975. 76-13317

327. Baskow, Alan. Novel intuition: a philosophical defence of the existence of pre-linguistics apprehension. Yale, 1971.

328. Bass, Walter Arthur. Some difficulties in the theory of probability. Virginia, 1953. 7953

329. Bassen, Paul Conan. The private language argument and the argument of *Philosophical investigations*, paragraph 258. Berkeley, 1972.

330. Bassford, Harold A. Pain and perception. British Columbia, 1972.

331. Bastaki, Shafikah A.A. A reconstruction of Jonathan Edwards' volitional theory in the context of contemporary action theory: an examination of *Freedom of the will*. Pittsburgh, 1972. 73-13189

332. Bates, Stanley Pickett. Internalism and externalism: the status of motivation in moral theory. Harvard, 1973.

333. Bauer, Joachim. Modern notions of faith. Catholic U., 1930.

334. Baum, Bernard. The Baconian mind in early nineteenth century America. Michigan, 1942.   453

335. Baum, Maurice James. A comparative study of the philosophies of William James and John Dewey. Chicago, 1928.

336. Baum, Robert James. George Berkeley's philosophy of mathematics. Ohio St., 1969.   70-13977

337. Baumer, William Harry. The problem of meaning in religious language. Wisconsin, 1960.   60-5715

338. Baumgaertner, William. A study of definition. Laval, 1950.

339. Baumgarten, Elias. Merleau-Ponty's phenomenological reformulation of Freudian psychoanalysis. Northwestern, 1975.   76-11872

340. Baumrin, Bernard Herbert. The ethics of Sir David Ross and the epistemological foundations of ethical intuitionism. John Hopkins, 1961.

341. Bawn, John Grant. Ethics of the stoics. Pennsylvania, 1895.

342. Baxley, Thomas Frederick. Existence and quantification: the proper interpretation of the quantifiers. Florida St., 1969.   70-20058

343. Baxter, Anthony James. Individual responsibility and social control. Princeton, 1973.   74-9663

344. Baxter, Clayton Amos. Bosanquet's logic; a review of traditions and possibilities in the subject. Toronto, 1932.

345. Bayles, Michael Dale. Rule utilitarianism and an enlightened moral consciousness. Indiana, 1967.
     67-15063

346. Bayley, Francis C. The causes and evidence of beliefs: an examination of Hume's procedure. Columbia, 1936.

347. Bayley, James E. Self and personal identity in William James's *Principles of psychology*. Columbia, 1969.   70-6937

348. Baylis, Charles Augustus. Creative synthesis as a philosophical concept. Harvard, 1926.

349. Bazemore, Wallace Duncan. The elimination of the hiatus between the divine and the non-divine in the philosophy of Aurobindo. Stanford, 1969.
70-18376

350. Beach, John D. Necessitas quae est et materia. Laval, 1953.

351. Beaird, Charles Thomas. An analysis of distributive justice with special reference to the concept of profit. Columbia, 1971. 72-28012

352. Beal, Melvin Wyne. The Penser-signe problem and French empiricism; an examination of the epistemological function of signs in the work of three French empiricists /⎯Etienne Condillac, Destutt de Tracy, Maine de Biran_/. Rochester, 1970.
71-1368

353. Bealer, George Persson. A theory of qualities: a first-order extensional theory which includes a definition of analyticity, a one-level semantic method, and a derivation of intensional logic, set theory, and moral logic. Berkeley, 1973.

354. Beals, Lawrence Wilson. The problem of error. Harvard, 1933.

355. Beamer, Elbert Monroe. The Socratic image in Plato. Syracuse, 1972. 72-20310

356. Beanblossom, Ronald Edwin. The use of metaphor and analogy in Thomas Reid's epistemology. Rochester, 1971. 71-22283

357. Bear, Harry. The theoretical ethics of the Brentano school, a psychoepistemological approach. Columbia, 1955. 10781

358. Beard, Robert William. The concept of rationality in the philosophy of William James. Michigan, 1962.
63-313

359. Bearden, Elmer Holmes. Universals and individuals. U.C.L.A., 1949.

360. Beardslee, Claude Gillette. Arthur James Balfour's contribution to philosophy. Brown, 1931.

361. Beardsley, Monroe Curtis. The philosophy of determinism. Yale, 1939.

362. Beatty, Harry Alexander. Abstract terms and abstract entities. Stanford, 1969. 70-10424

363. Beatty, Joseph. A consideration of Plato's argument for justice in the Republic. Northwestern, 1972. 72-32376

364. Beatty, Richard Donohue. The logical foundations of Peirce's categories, 1867-85. Notre Dame, 1966. 67-13593

365. Beauchamp, Emmette William, III. The Kuhn-Popper debate. Texas, 1975. 75-25006

366. Beauchamp, Tom Lamar. Hume's theory of causation. Johns Hopkins, 1970. 72-28947

367. Beck, Lewis W. Synopsis: a study in the theory of knowledge. Duke, 1937.

368. Beck, Robert Nelson. Attacks on the Cartesian cogito. Boston U., 1950.

369. Beck, Victor Emmanuel. A translation of C.J. Boström's Philosophy of religion with a critical commentary. Boston U., 1947.

370. Becker, Edward Francis. Reference and translation: an examination of Quine's thesis of the radical indeterminacy of translation. Johns Hopkins, 1970. 70-20146

371. Becker, Lawrence C. On proving a man's responsibility. Chicago, 1965.

372. Beckett, William John. Probability, reasonable behavior, and reasonable belief. Brown, 1962. 63-1006

373. Becroft, Peter Brian. An attempt at a theory of mental dispositions and mental acts. U.C.L.A., 1953.

374. Bedan, David Edward. The concept of evolutionary progress in the context of contemporary philosophical naturalism. Notre Dame, 1970. 71-5521

375. Bedau, Hugo Adam, Jr. The concept of thinking. Harvard, 1961.

376. Bedell, Gary Louis. The logical foundations of metaphysics in the philosophy of F.H. Bradley. St. Louis, 1969. 70-20367

377. Beebe, Michael Douglas. A Gricean theory of reference. British Columbia, 1974.

378. Beebe, Rev. William Albert. Value and society: a study of the socio-moral thought of Ralph Barton Perry. Catholic U., 1969. 69-18577

379. Beebe-Center, John Gilbert. Affective habituation. Harvard, 1926.

380. Beehler, Rodger George. Moral life. Calgary, 1973.

381. Beelick, Donald James. Context and human actions. Ohio St., 1972. 73-1940

382. Beeson, Frederick Keplinger, II. J.L. Austin on statements and truth. Berkeley, 1975.

383. Beeson, Richard Wendell. The philosophy of symbolic interactionism. New Mexico, 1971. 72-13769

384. Beha, Sr. Helen Marie. Augustinian and Aristotelian elements in Matthew of Aquasparta's cognition theory. St. Bonaventure, 1960.

385. Behan, David Paul. Intentional action. Vanderbilt, 1967. 68-5382

386. Behling, Richard Wayne. Singular instantial sentences. So. Illinois, 1974. 75-103

387. Beierle, John David. Ockham's theory of consequences. Pennsylvania, 1957. 57-4845

388. Beis, Richard Hardy. Modern ethical relativism and the natural law theory of St. Thomas Aquinas. Notre Dame, 1964. 64-3337

389. Belaief, Gail. Spinoza's philosophy of law. Columbia, 1963. 64-9174

390. Belaief, Lynne. The ethics of Alfred North Whitehead. Columbia, 1963. 65-7437

391. Bélanger, Rev. Martin J. Le phénomene humain chez Jean Rostand. Catholic U., 1971. 71-17873

392. Belford, Jules. A physicalistic approach to the problem of other minds. Miami, 1970. 71-4314

393. Bell, James Alfred. Implementation of ethical norms. Boston U., 1969. 70-23131

394. Bell, Linda Ann. An analysis of moral judgment in connection with bad faith and inauthenticity in the early philosophy of J.-P. Sartre. Emory, 1973. 73-18520

395. Bellefleur, Michel. La signification du Loisir. Montreal, 1972.

396. Belnap, Nuel Dinsmore, Jr. The formalization of entailment. Yale, 1960.

397. Below, William A. The source of logical necessity. Cal., S. Barbara, 1975.

398. Belton, John H. Olympian-10, olympian-13, pythian-9 and the occasional nature of the pindaric epinician. Harvard, 1975.

399. Benacerraf, Paul. Logicism- some considerations. Princeton, 1960. 61-4511

400. Benard, Rev. Edmond P. The problem of belief in the writings of John Henry Newman, William James and St. Thomas Aquinas. Catholic U., 1950.

401. Benardete, José Amado. An essay on time: wherein a neglected argument for the prime mover is shown to be demonstrative. Virginia, 1954. 9632

402. Bendall, Lewis Kent. The philosophical foundations of intuitionism. Yale, 1960.

403. Bender, Frederic Lawrence. The origin and development of Marx's philosophical anthropology. Northwestern, 1969. 70-7

404. Bender, Joseph Earl. Moral qualities and intelligence according to St. Thomas. Catholic U., 1924.

405. Bender, Richard N. Prolegomena to the derivation of moral laws from psychological data. Boston U., 1952.

406. Benditt, Theodore Matthew. The concept of interest. Pittsburgh, 1971. 72-16561

407. Benedict, George Allen. The concept of continuity in Charles Peirce's synechism. Buffalo, 1973. 74-4382

408. Benedict, Mary Kendrick. Thought and being: a study in Mr. Bradley's metaphysics. Yale, 1903.

409. Benefiel, Patricia Anne. Religious experience as justification for belief in God. Stanford, 1975. 75-13486

410. Beneš, Václav Edvard. On the consistency of "New foundations." Princeton, 1953. 6789

411. Benfield, David William. The problem of defining knowledge. Brown, 1973. 74-2979

412. Benjamin, Abram Cornelius. The logical atomism of Bertrand Russell. Michigan, 1924.

413. Benjamin, Martin. Actions, movements, and identity. Chicago, 1970.

414. Benkert, Rev. Gerald. The Thomistic conception of an international society. Catholic U., 1942.

415. Bennett, Charles Andrew Armstrong. The cognitive value of the mystic experience. Yale, 1913.

416. Bennett, Daniel Clark. Action and the will. Stanford, 1959. 60-1351

417. Bennett, David. A study of persons. McGill, 1973.

418. Bennett, David Wells. The natural numbers from Frege to Hilbert. Columbia, 1961. 61-2655

419. Bennett, James Oliver. Necessary connection: a critique of Hume's analysis and its contemporary adherents. Tulane, 1972. 72-24392

420. Bennett, James R. Genius: an art of making new worlds. Chicago, 1972.

421. Bennett, John Beecher. Whitehead's philosophy of personal experience. Yale, 1969. 70-15676

422. Bennett, John Gates. On the nature of pictorial representation. Michigan, 1975. 75-20296

423. Bennett, Michael Ruisdael. Some extensions of a Montague fragment of English. U.C.L.A., 1974. 74-22937

424. Bennett, Rev. Owen. The nature of demonstrative proof. Catholic U., 1943.

425. Bennett, Philip William. The compatability of purposive and physical explanations. N.Y.U., 1972. 72-21493

426. Bennett, William John. Societal obligation. Texas, 1970. 72-2303

427. Benson, Paula Jann Erdwinn. The basis of the conflict between self-interest and duty in Henry Sidgwick's *Methods of ethics*. Colorado, 1971. 72-17242

428. Benson, Robert Lawrence. Fichte's original argument.
Columbia, 1974.   75-16099

429. Benson, Ronald Edward. The development of Schleiermacher's philosophy of religion in its cultural
context. Michigan St., 1970.   70-20435

430. Benson, Stephen Eric. A critique of John Dewey's
philosophical method in the light of an examination of his belief in the continuity of nature.
Colorado, 1970.   71-5868

431. Benson, Thomas L. The concept of "indoctrination":
a philosophical study. Johns Hopkins, 1975.
76-1580

432. Benton, Richard P. The aesthetics of Friedrich
Nietzsche: the relation of art to life. Johns
Hopkins, 1955.

433. Bentson, Henry Arthur. Roycean absolute with special reference to its religious significance.
N.Y.U., 1922.   73-20685

434. Berberelly, John C. The Greek sceptics and Sextus
Empiricus. Columbia, 1974.   75-18356

435. Berckman, Edward. The nature and function of hope
in the theatre of Bertolt Brecht. Chicago, 1972.

436. Berg, Edward Elling. L.S. Vygotsky's theory of the
social and historical origins of consciousness.
Wisconsin, 1970.   70-24782

437. Berger, Carol Alterkruse. Merleau-Ponty on the relations of body and soul. St. Louis, 1973.
74-4476

438. Berger, Fred Robert. Obligation and disobedience: a
study of the justification of civil disobedience
in the democratic state. Berkeley, 1969.
70-6060

439. Berger, George Kenneth. Time and thermodynamics.
Columbia, 1970.   71-17468

440. Berggren, Douglas Charles. An analysis of metaphorical meaning and truth. Yale, 1959.   68-7442

441. Bergmann, Frithjof H. Harmony and reason- an introduction to the philosophy of Hegel. Princeton,
1959.   60-4962

442. Bergmark, Robert Edward. Moral objectivism in W.R.
Sorley, W.D. Ross, A.C. Ewing, and A.C. Garnett.

Boston U., 1961. 61-710

443. Bergner, Jeffrey T. The epistemological origins of modern social science: 1870-1914. Princeton, 1973. 74-2313

444. Bergoffen, Debra B. The crisis of western consciousness: an interpretation of its meaning through an analysis of the temporal symbols of western culture. Georgetown, 1974. 74-16411

445. Berkowitz, Leonard Jay. The observational-theoretical distinction in the philosophy of science of logical empiricism. Johns Hopkins, 1975. 76-1562

446. Berleant, Arnold. Logic and social doctrine: Dewey's methodological approach to social philosophy. Buffalo, 1962. 62-3849

447. Berliner, Michael S. John Dewey's view of free-will. Boston U., 1971. 71-26385

448. Berlinski, David. The well-tempered Wittgenstein. Princeton, 1968. 69-2526

449. Bernard, Theos. Hatha yoga; the report of a personal experience. Columbia, 1944.

450. Bernard, Walter. The philosophy of Spinoza and Brunner. N.Y.U., 1933. 73-17723

451. Berndtson, Carl A.E. The problem of freewill in recent philosophy. Chicago, 1941.

452. Bernstein, Richard Jacob. John Dewey's metaphysics of experience. Yale, 1958.

453. Berofsky, Bernard Asher. Determinism. Columbia, 1963. 67-10363

454. Berquist, Duane H. Descartes and the way of proceeding in philosophy. Laval, 1964.

455. Berquist, Richard Harlow. The idea of the natural law in the writings of Giorgio Del Vecchio. Notre Dame, 1970. 71-5522

456. Berreckman, Carleton Arthur. Memory: a philosophical study. Northwestern, 1965. 66-2683

457. Berry, George David Wheaton. The semantics of truth and designation. Harvard, 1942.

458. Berry, Kenneth K. The problem of logical unity, as reflected in the logic of Aristotle. Virginia, 1939.

459. Bertling, Br. Hugh Martin. The political theory of St. Augustine. Loyola, 1941.

460. Bertman, Martin Allen. Hobbes: the natural and artifacted good. Syracuse, 1973. 74-10131

461. Bertocci, Peter A. The empirical argument for God in the thought of Martineau, Pringle-Patison, Ward, Sorley and Tennant. Boston U., 1935.

462. Bertoldi, Eugene F. Merleau-Ponty and the phenomenology of phenomenology. Waterloo, 1973.

463. Bertram, Maryanne Josephine. Subjectivity in the monism of Merleau-Ponty. Marquette, 1971. 72-5771

464. Bertsch, Jack Herman. An inquiry into the asymmetry and direction of time. Ohio St., 1968. 69-11608

465. Bestor, Thomas Wheaton. The things people do: solipsism and behavior. Oregon, 1973. 73-28577

466. Betz, Joseph Michael. The social self and self-correcting moral standards. Chicago, 1973.

467. Beversluis, Eric Henry. The concepts and rules of ethics. Northwestern, 1970. 71-10092

468. Beversluis, John. The connection between duty and happiness in Kant's moral philosophy. Indiana, 1972. 73-6487

469. Bhadra, Mrinal Kanti. A critical study of Sartre's ontology of consciousness. Oklahoma, 1971. 71-26541

470. Bhattacharya, Anima. Schopenhauer's pessimism and its foundations. Missouri, 1970. 71-8285

471. Bhattacharyya, Usha Rani. Our knowledge of the individual. Yale, 1955.

472. Bickel, William E. Camus, Marcuse and Skinner on the nature of man and the nature of society. Pittsburgh, 1974. 75-5113

473. Bickham, Stephen H. Moore, Ayer, and Austin on sense-data. So. Illinois, 1970. 71-2364

474. Bickley, Theodore Grant. Person and reality in the thought of Paul Tillich and Edgar S. Brightman. Boston U., 1971. 71-26386

475. Bidney, David. The idea of value and the metaphysics of Spinoza. Yale, 1932.

476. Biel, Joseph F. Method as a philosophical problem: an historical and critical study. DePaul, 1973. 73-28659

477. Bierman, Arthur Kalmer. Prall's aesthetics. Michigan, 1955. 12545

478. Bierstedt, Robert. Logic, language and sociology. Columbia, 1950. 1741

479. Bigelow, Leslie Cole. Direct knowledge and basic propositions. Harvard, 1952.

480. Bigger, Charles P., III. The nature of aesthetic judgment: an Augustinean interpretation. Virginia, 1951.

481. Bikson, Thomas Howard. The logical atomism of Bertrand Russell: a critical evaluation. Missouri, 1967. 68-284

482. Bikson, Tora Kay Lanto. Peirce's logic treated as semiotic. Missouri, 1969. 70-2960

483. Bilaniuk, Franziska Marie Therese. 'Weltanschauung' of Otto Flake with special reference to his view of Friedrich Nietzsche. Toronto, 1974.

484. Bildhauer, William Mathias. The reality of God: an investigation of the adequacy of Wittgensteinian fideism. Arizona, 1972. 73-12006

485. Bilek, George Edward. 'Transcendental psychology' in Kant's Critique of pure reason. Toronto, 1969.

486. Bill, Rev. Thomas Lee. The theory of nature in John Stuart Mill. St. Louis, 1963. 64-4231

487. Biller, Alan David. Whitehead's conception of speculative philosophy. Columbia, 1971. 71-23580

488. Biller, Sr. Mary Ann Catherine Siena. A re-examination of the definitions of vital processes, nutrition and growth: a problem in the philosophy of biology. St. John's, 1967. 67-11454

489. Billings, John Richard. J.S. Mill's defense of utilitarianism. Syracuse, 1967. 67-12054

490. Billings, Thomas Henry. The Platonism of Philo Judaeus. Chicago, 1915.

491. Bilsky, Manuel. The aesthetic theory of I.A. Richards. Michigan, 1951. 2574

492. Binkley, Robert Williams. Moral reasoning. Minnesota, 1958. 58-7391

493. Binkley, Timothy Glenn. Wittgenstein's language. Texas, 1970. 71-98

494. Binswanger, Harry. The biological basis of teleological concepts. Columbia, 1973. 76-15531

495. Binyon, Millard P. The virtues: a methodological study in Thomistic ethics. Chicago, 1947.

496. Birch, Thomas Harrison, Jr. Philosophical grammar: some elements of logical geography. Texas, 1969. 70-10752

497. Bird, Otto Allen. Mediaeval philosophic thought as reflected in the *Canzone d'amore* of Cavalcanti according to the commentary of Dinc del Garbo; text and commentary. Toronto, 1939.

498. Birmingham, Frank Pennell. Aristotle's concept of being in the *Posterior analytics*. Michigan, 1972. 72-29000

499. Biro, John Ivan. Meaning, speech acts and intentions. Syracuse, 1973. 74-17563

500. Birx, Harry James. Pierre Teilhard de Chardin's philosophy of evolution. Buffalo, 1971.

501. Bisbee, Eleanor. Instrumentalism in Plato's philosophy. Cincinnati, 1929.

502. Biser, Irwin. A general scheme for natural systems. Pennsylvania, 1938.

503. Bixler, Julius Seelye. Religion in the philosophy of William James. Yale, 1924.

504. Bjelland, Andrew George. The foundations of Bergson's metaphysics: an essay on Henri Bergson's early metaphysical dualism. St. Louis, 1970. 71-3250

505. Blachowicz, James Anthony. From ontology to praxis: a metaphilosophical inquiry into two philosophical paradigms. Northwestern, 1970. 71-1797

506. Black, Bryan Taylor. The critique of formalism. Waterloo, 1974.

507. Black, Edward J. A study of Aristotle's categories. Chicago, 1966.

508. Blackiston, Harry Spencer. A study in the ethics of the early romantic school in Germany. Pennsylvania, 1920.

509. Blackman, Rodney Jay. Commitment (explication of this term as applied to human activities.) Wisconsin, 1975.   75-18163

510. Blackstone, Richard Macartney. An examination of the philosophical methods of G.E. Moore. Brown, 1968.
                                                         69-9942

511. Blackstone, William Thomas. The ethics of Francis Hutcheson. Duke, 1958.

512. Blackwelder, Brent Francis. A refutation of the major arguments against ascribing rights to animals. Maryland, 1975.   76-3380

513. Blackwell, Richard J. Aristotle's theory of predication. St. Louis, 1954.

514. Blair, George Alfred. 'ENTEΛÉXEIA and 'ENÉPREIA in Aristotle. Fordham, 1964.   64-3572

515. Blair, Thomas Albert. Two evolutionary theories: neo-Darwinism and Teilhard de Chardin. St. John's, 1972.   72-21715

516. Blais, Martin. (Bro. Louis-Grégoire). La colère. Laval, 1964.

517. Blake, Ralph Mason. Hedonism in the light of modern discussions in the theory of value. Harvard, 1915.

518. Blanchard, Eric Summit. Describing systematic activities. Washington U., 1973.   74-13762

519. Blanchard, Milton Eugene. The negative principle in logic, mathematics, and ethics. Harvard, 1901.

520. Blanchet, Rev. Louis Emile. Deux enseignements sur l'infini. Laval, 1966.

521. Blanchette, Rev. Olivia A. The perfection of the universe in the philosophy of St. Thomas Aquinas. Laval, 1966.

522. Blankemeyer, Kenneth Joseph. Stevenson's theory of
emotive meaning in ethics. So. Illinois, 1974.
75-13229

523. Blankenship, John David. The theory of the soul in
Plato's metaphysics. Johns Hopkins, 1971.
71-29166

524. Blanshard, Brand. The nature of judgment. Harvard,
1921.

525. Blatz, Charles Val, III. "Ought" without "can".
Michigan, 1971. 71-23703

526. Blau, Joseph L. The Christian interpretation of the
cabala in the Renaissance. Columbia, 1944.

527. Blechman, Nathan. The philosophic function of value;
a study of experience showing the ultimate meaning
of evolution to be the attainment of personality
through culture and religion. N.Y.U., 1918.

528. Bledsoe, James P. The soul: an approach to the second definition. Laval, 1968.

529. Bleich, Judah David. Providence in late medieval Jewish philosophy. N.Y.U., 1974. 74-18139

530. Blewett, George John. The metaphysical basis of preceptive ethics. Harvard, 1900.

531. Blinderman, Charles S. T.H. Huxley's popularization
of Darwinism. Indiana, 1957. 57-3695

532. Blizek, William Lester. Toward an expressional aesthetic. Missouri, 1970. 71-8288

533. Block, Irving Leonard. Some epistemological problems
in Aristotle's theory of sense perception. Harvard,
1958.

534. Block, Jeffrey Edward. The role of powers in the philosophy of John Locke. Claremont, 1972.
72-26229

535. Blocker, Harry Eugene. An examination of problems involved in the ascription of emotive features to
works of art. Berkeley, 1966. 67-8529

536. Bl∅m, John Joseph. A systematic study of the mind-body relation according to Descartes. Columbia,
1974. 74-29567

537. Blose, Barry Llewellyn. Appearing and things. Columbia, 1969. 69-17574

538. Blote, Harold Carl. The concepts of nature and matter in early Greek philosophy. Chicago, 1927.

539. Bloustein, Edward Jerome. The legal philosophy of Hans Kelsen. Cornell, 1954. 10573

540. Bluestone, Natalie Suzanne Harris. Time and consciousness in Jean-Paul Sartre and William James. Johns Hopkins, 1963.

541. Blum, Alexendru. The logic of causality: a critical examination of some approaches. N.Y.U., 1968. 70-7391

542. Blum, Lawrence Alan. Some Kantian views regarding the moral significance of altruism and altruistic feeling. Harvard, 1974.

543. Blum, Roland Paul. Universalism and universalization in ethics. Berkeley, 1968. 69-14847

544. Blumberg, David Israel. 'Why should I be moral?': the problem of ultimate justification in ethics. Washington U., 1969. 70-10946

545. Blumenfeld, David Carl. The psychoanalytic concept of freedom. Berkeley, 1966. 66-15351

546. Blumenfeld, Jean Beer. Action and intention. Berkeley, 1973.

547. Blundo, Virginia Criscione. Jean-Paul Sartre's concept of bad faith: philosophical, literary, and psychological interpretations. Columbia, 1974. 74-15969

548. Blustein, Jeffrey Miles. Defense and revolution: toward a liberal theory of justified revolution. Harvard, 1974.

549. Blyth, John William. Whitehead's theory of knowledge. Brown, 1936.

550. Boardman, Rufus Norman. The significance of meaning in pragmatism and neo-realism. Chicago, 1919.

551. Boardman, William Giles. Hobbes' account of mind and knowledge. Columbia, 1954. 8607

552. Boardman, William Smith. Dualism vs. behaviourism: a false dichotomy in the philosophy of mind. Minnesota, 1967. 68-7278

553. Boas, George. An analysis of certain theories of

truth. Berkeley, 1917.

554. Boas, Marie. Robert Boyle and the corpuscular philosophy, a study of theories of matter in the seventeenth century. Cornell, 1949.

555. Boatright, John Raymond. Moral judgments and action. Chicago, 1972.

556. Bobik, Joseph. Saint Thomas on the individuation of bodily substances. Notre Dame, 1953. 10721

557. Bobonis, Guillermo Juan. Memory in Plato, Aristotle and Plotinus. Claremont, 1969. 69-14595

558. Bobrek, Edwin John. The philosophical heritage of Hubert Bonner. U.S. Int'l, 1971. 72-2277

559. Bode, B. The principle of _gratia gratum faciens_ in the ethics of Thomas Aquinas. Cornell, 1900.

560. Bode, James Richard. A logic for conditional statements. Ohio St., 1973. 73-26773

561. Bode, Roy R. A philosophy of courage. Catholic U., 1950.

562. Bodunrin, Peter Oluwambe. Plato and his contemporaries on the possibility of falsehood. Minnesota, 1971. 72-14273

563. Boër, Steven Ernest. Language games: an interpretation and critique of the later Wittgenstein's philosophy of language. (Volumes I and II.) Michigan, 1973. 73-24528

564. Bogaard, Paul Anthony. The philosophical implications of chemical combination. Emory, 1972. 72-32656

565. Bogdanski, Rev. Augustine A. The significance of Clement Baeumker in neo-scholastic philosophy. Marquette, 1938.

566. Bogen, James Benjamin. Aspects of the development of Wittgenstein's philosophy of language. Berkeley, 1968. 68-13886

567. Boggs, Charles Thomas. Nietzsche's polemic against Christianity. Texas, 1975. 75-16642

568. Bogholt, Carl M. John Dewey's views on philosophic method in his early writings, 1882-1903. Wisconsin, 1933.

569. Bogoslovsky, Boris Basil. The technique of contro-

versy; principles of dynamic logic. Columbia, 1929.

570. Bohan, James Charles, Jr. Vagueness: a critical examination of some traditional analyses. U. of Washington, 1970. 71-8460

571. Bohl, Frederick Robert, Jr. Davidson and Chisholm on events. Brown, 1972. 74-2982

572. Bohnert, Herbert Gaylord. The interpretation of theory. Pennsylvania, 1961. 61-3489

573. Bok, Sissela Ann. Voluntary euthanasia. Harvard, 1970.

574. Bokil, Shrinivas V. The problem of other minds and the development of solipsism in the 17th century (a study in the philosophy of Claude Brunet.) Rochester, 1967. 67-13612

575. Bole, Thomas James, III. Hegel's Science of logic as a transcendental ontology. Texas, 1973.
74-5198

576. Boler, John Francis. The structure of realism in the philosophy of Charles Sanders Peirce. Harvard, 1960.

577. Bolman, Frederick de W. Schelling: The ages of the world; translated with introduction and notes. Columbia, 1942.

578. Bolton, Martha Elizabeth Brandt. The distinction between primary and secondary qualities: a philosophical and historical study. Michigan, 1973.
74-3580

579. Bolton, Robert Harvey. Studies in Plato's Cratylus. Michigan, 1973. 74-3581

580. Bommarito, Bernard Angelo. The meaning of methodical reorientation of science and common sense in the thought of Bernard Lonergan. Fordham, 1972.
72-20553

581. Bonansea, Bernardino M. The theory of knowledge of Tommaso Campanella; exposition and critique. Catholic U., 1954.

582. Bond, Edward Jarvis. Moral obligation and human goodness. Cornell, 1964. 65-3712

583. Bond, Richard Ellison, Jr. A critical analysis of the concept of justice in Paul Tillich, Heinrich Rom-

men, and Walter Rauschenbusch. Yale, 1972.
72-28946

584. Bondeson, William Blaine. Plato and logos. Chicago, 1965.

585. Bonifacio, Armando Flores. The concept of rules: towards an analysis. Berkeley, 1968. 68-13887

586. Bonjour, Laurence Alan. Knowledge, justification, and truth: a Sellarsian approach to epistemology. Princeton, 1969. 70-14186

587. Bonnette, Dennis. St. Thomas on: "The per accidens necessarily implies the per se." Notre Dame, 1970. 71-5524

588. Boodin, John Elof. A theory of time. Harvard, 1899.

589. Bookstaber, Philip David. Postulates of perfectibility. Cincinnati, 1924.

590. Boone, Daniel Nathan. Fatalism: arguments and attitudes. Claremont, 1971. 71-29642

591. Boonin, Leonard George. The concept of a valid legal decision: a study in twentieth century legal philosophy. Columbia, 1963. 63-5947

592. Boorse, Christopher Lowell. Intentionality, linguistics, and the indeterminacy of translation. Princeton, 1972. 72-24668

593. Booth, Curtis Spence. Reflexive relations, limits, and defeasibility: a study in logic, semantics, and philosophic eccentricity. No. Carolina, 1958.
58-5931

594. Bordeau, Edward James. The practical idealism of John Dewey's political philosophy: an answer to some critics. Fordham, 1969. 70-11420

595. Bortz, William Kilmer. Authority and political obligation. Wisconsin, 1974. 75-2449

596. Bosche, Carol Marian. Plato's doctrine of quality: a metaphysical interpretation of Philebus 11A-16A. Yale, 1960.

597. Bossart, William Haines. The problem of self-knowledge. Northwestern, 1958. 59-199

598. Bossert, Philip Joseph. The origins and early development of Edmund Husserl's method of phenomenological reduction. Washington U., 1973. 73-24876

599. Botwinick, Aryen Isaac. Ethics, politics and epistemology: a study in the unity of Hume's thought. Princeton, 1973. 74-2314

600. Bouchard, Guy. Poetique du roman. Laval, 1973.

601. Boudreaux, Gregory Raymond. Freud's theory of personality and the concept of explanation in psychoanalysis. Duke, 1974. 75-6757

602. Boudreaux, Jack Christopher. A model-theoretic investigation of higher-order functional calculi. Notre Dame, 1975. 75-19922

603. Boudreaux, Michael Miles. Nothingness: the adventure of the for-itself. Missouri, 1973. 74-9909

604. Bouffard, Albert Edmund. Language and the ontological difference: Heidegger's quest for an experience with authentic language. Duquesne, 1970.
71-18147

605. Boughton, Jesse S. The idea of progress in Philo Judaeus. Columbia, 1932.

606. Bourdillon, Philip. Berkeley and Reid: an analysis of Reid's reaction to Berkeley's rejection of material substance. Rochester, 1972. 72-28726

607. Bourgeois, Patrick Lyall. Paul Ricoeur's hermeneutical phenomenology. Duquesne, 1970. 71-9053

608. Bourke, Laurence L. Tratus de tribus principus naturae of Antonius Andreae. St. Bonaventure, 1950.

609. Bourke, Vernon Joseph. Habitus as a perfectant of potency in the philosophy of St. Thomas Aquinas. Toronto, 1938.

610. Bouwsma, Oets Kolk. On difference in the criterion of F.H. Bradley. Michigan, 1928.

611. Bower, Gary Richard. Observation and determinism in quantum mechanics. Stanford, 1974. 74-26990

612. Bowers, David F. Hume and the neo-realists on causality: a study in a discarded concept. Princeton, 1932.

613. Bowie, Gordon Lee, Jr. The mind-body identity thesis. Stanford, 1971. 71-23488

614. Bowie, Norman Ernest. The problem of distributive justice. Rochester, 1968. 68-15822

615. Bowlden, Larry Smith. Excuses and moral obligation.
U. of Washington, 1968. 69-13540

616. Bowles, George McMillan. Did Plato believe in immanent universals? Stanford, 1970. 71-12858

617. Bowman, Andrew Lawrence. Meaning and nature: George H. Mead's theory of objects. Columbia, 1951.
2799

618. Bowman, Carroll Royce. Systematic morality: a study in the philosophy of Benedict Spinoza. Tulane, 1966. 66-10753

619. Bowman, Peter Allyn. Conventionality in distant simultaneity: its history and its philosophy. Indiana, 1972. 73-9755.

620. Bowne, Gwendolyn Duell. The development of the philosophy of logic from 1880 to 1908. Ohio St., 1963.
63-6231

621. Boxill, Bernard Romaric. A philosophical examination of black protest thought. U.C.L.A., 1971.
72-1467

622. Boyd, Richard Newell. A recursion-theoretic characterization of the ramified analytical hierarchy. M.I.T., 1970.

623. Boyer, Minor W. The extent of C.I. Lewis' Kantianism. Texas, 1953.

624. Boyle, Joan Mae. The process of discovery: Stephen C. Pepper's root-metaphor theory of philosophy. Catholic U., 1973. 73-21729

625. Boyle, Joseph Michael, Jr. The argument from self-referential consistency: the current discussion. Georgetown, 1970. 70-21277

626. Bracken, Harry McFarland. The early reception of Berkeley's immaterialism: 1710-1733. Iowa, 1956.
18521

627. Bradie, Michael Peter. Models and scientific realism. Hawaii, 1970. 71-12215

628. Bradish, Norman Conyers. John Sergeant: a seventeenth century critic of Locke. Northwestern, 1932.

629. Bradley, Denis John M. Transcendental critique and the possibility of a realistic metaphysics: a study in the philosophy of Joseph Marechal. Toronto, 1971.

630. Bradley, Duncan Lee. All the attributes of God: a study in method. So. Illinois, 1972. 72-28525

631. Bradley, Gerald Paul. The Freudian theories of anxiety: a phenomenological critique. Northwestern, 1970. 71-1803

632. Bradley, Raymond J. Selected problems concerning the natural law in Thomas Aquinas and in some of his modern commentators. Duquesne, 1973. 73-24082

633. Brady, Mthr. Cora E. The philosophy of creation in St. Bonaventure's Commentary on the sentences. Fordham, 1953.

634. Brady, F.I. Certitude. Georgetown, 1930.

635. Brady, Mthr. Gertrude Veronica. Basic principles of the philosophy of Jonathan Edwards. Fordham, 1951.

636. Brady, Ignatius Charles. The Liber de anima of William Vorillon: edition of text with an historical introduction and doctrinal studies. Toronto, 1948.

637. Brady, James B. The doctrine of mens rea: a study in legal and moral responsibility. Texas, 1970. 71-99

638. Brady, Rev. Jules Malachy. The function of the seminal reasons in Saint Augustine's theory of reality. St. Louis, 1949.

639. Brady, Sr. Marian. The philosophical basis of human values according to Thomistic principles. Catholic U., 1962. 63-1939

640. Brady, Mary L. John Dewey- philosophy as a methodology. Fordham, 1945.

641. Brady, Robby Ray. Theoretical limitations on scientific explanation. Claremont, 1975. 75-19661

642. Brady, Ronald Harold. Towards a common morphology for aesthetics and natural science: a study of Goethe's empiricism. Buffalo, 1972. 73-5084

643. Brahmachari, Mahanam B. The philosophy of Śrī Jīva Goswāmi (Vaisnava Vēdanta of the Bengal school). Chicago, 1937.

644. Bramann, Jorn Karl Roy. The problem of objectivity and ideology in the social sciences. Oregon, 1971. 72-8515

645. Brameld, Theodore Burghard. The rôle of acquiescence in Leninism. Chicago, 1931.

646. Brand, Myles Neil. Some systematic and extrasystematic considerations concerning the description of human actions. Rochester, 1967. 67-13613

647. Brandon, Melvin Joseph. F.H. Bradley's ethics of self-realization. St. Louis, 1972. 72-31457

648. Brandon, William Pew, Jr. Linguistic analysis, political science and political theory: some applications of contemporary Anglo-American philosophy to the study of politics and political theory. Duke, 1975. 75-29492

649. Brandt, Richard Booker. The problem of knowledge in Schleiermacher's philosophy. Yale, 1936.

650. Brantl, George Edward. The tragic commitment: an essay in existentialist metaphysics. Columbia, 1957. 57-2865

651. Bratman, Michael Edward. Thought, action and acting against one's better judgment. Rockefeller, 1974.

652. Braude, Stephen Edward. Tensed sentences. Massachusetts, 1972. 72-18257

653. Braun, Rev. William P. Monsignor Edward A. Pace, educator and philosopher. Catholic U., 1968. 69-9125

654. Braybrooke, David. Welfare, happiness, and the choice of policies. Cornell, 1953.

655. Breazeale, James Daniel. Toward a nihilist epistemology: Hume and Nietzsche. Yale, 1971. 71-28144

656. Brecht, Stefan Sebastian. The place of natural science in Hegel's philosophy. Harvard, 1959.

657. Bredenberg, Paul Arnold. Metaphysical foundations of the laws of thought. Yale, 1951.

658. Breen, Rev. Joseph S. Religion and secularism in the light of Thomistic thought. Catholic U., 1952.

659. Breidenbach, Francis J. The meaning of nature in Aristotle. St. Louis, 1953.

660. Brenkert, George Gilbert. Wants, prudence and morality. Michigan, 1971. 72-14814

661. Brennan, Bernard Patrick. The moral implications of James's pragmatism. Fordham, 1961.   61-1563

662. Brennan, Joseph Gerard. Thomas Mann's world. Columbia, 1942.

663. Brennan, Sr. M. Alethea. The origin of the rational soul according to St. Thomas. Catholic U., 1950.

664. Brennan, Robert Edward. A theory of abnormal cognitive processes according to the principles of St. Thomas Aquinas. Catholic U., 1925.

665. Brennan, Sr. Rose Emmanuella. The intellectual virtues. Catholic U., 1941.

666. Brennan, Rev. Walter Thomas F. Cosmogenesis as myth: a philosophic comparison and analysis of the Timaios of Plato and the Babylonian Enuma elish. DePaul, 1970.   72-7717

667. Brenner, William Henry. Faith and experience: a critical study of John Hick's contributions to the philosophy of religion. Virginia, 1970.
70-26585

668. Brentlinger, John Allen. The theory of forms in Plato's later dialogues. Yale, 1962.   70-16272

669. Bretall, Robert Walter. Prolegomena to a critical theory of value. Princeton, 1938.   2920

670. Bretscher, Theodore Adolph. Explanatory law in mechanistic and statistical reasoning. Cincinnati, 1932.

671. Brett, Axel. A critical approach to an esthetic theory. Illinois, 1923.

672. Brett, Nathan Chandler. The concepts of rule and action. Waterloo, 1972.

673. Brettler, Lucinda Ann Vandervort. The phenomenology of Adolf Reinach: chapters in the theory of knowledge and legal philosophy. McGill, 1973.

674. Brewster, Henry Webb. Sensation and intellection; their character and their function in the cognition of the real and the ideal. Minnesota, 1892.

675. Brewster, John M. A behavioristic account of the logical function of universals. Columbia, 1937.

676. Brewster, Leonard Earl. Time, logic, and what there

is. So. Illinois, 1971. 72-22493

677. Brezik, Victor Benjamin. Friendship and society; a study in Thomistic social philosophy. Toronto, 1944.

678. Bricker, George Barrett. The modal logic of induction. So. Illinois, 1970. 71-9975

679. Brickhouse, Thomas Campbell. Determinism and Aristotle's analysis of responsibility. Vanderbilt, 1974. 74-22163

680. Brickman, Benjamin. An introduction to Francesco Patrizi's Nova de universis philosophia. Columbia, 1942.

681. Bridges, Asa Paul. A defense of the argument from analogy for the existence of other minds. U.C.L.A., 1974. 75-1970

682. Bridges, Geoffrey. Petrus Thomae: identity and distinction. St. Bonaventure, 1957.

683. Bridges, Thomas William. The concept of meaning in Heidegger's Sein und zeit. Columbia, 1972.
    75-9319

684. Brief, Jean-Claude Wolfgang. The role of action and sensation in the construction of the object: Piaget revisited. Stanford, 1973. 74-6453

685. Brier, Robert Martin. The problem of backward causation. No. Carolina, 1970. 71-11675

686. Brimmer, Marvey Harter, II. Jules Lequier and process philosophy. Emory, 1975. 75-23677

687. Brinckerhoff, Robert Hamilton. Some ethical implications of Freudian and post-Freudian thought. Buffalo, 1969. 69-20582

688. Brinkley, Alan Burruss. The phenomenology of C.S. Peirce. Tulane, 1960. 60-5943

689. Brinton, Alan Paul. A contextual theory of singular terms. Minnesota, 1974. 75-12046

690. Brinton, Howard Haines. The philosophy of Jacob Boehme. Berkeley, 1926.

691. Briod, Marc Edouard. The primacy of discourse in determining the sense of Heidegger's authenticity: ground for a sensitive education. Northwestern, 1968. 69-6896

692. Bristol, John Roblin Murray. The nature and function of the moral sense in the ethical philosophies of Shaftesbury and Hutcheson. Toronto, 1970.

693. Britan, Halbert Hains. Ethics and aesthetics: their relation in pre-Kantian philosophy. Yale, 1902.

694. Britt, Patricia Marie. A logical analysis of subjunctive conditionals. U.C.L.A., 1959.

695. Brittan, Gordon Goodhue, Jr. Primary and secondary qualities. Stanford, 1966. 67-4325

696. Brock, Dan Willets. Political authority, morality and the possibilities of unanimity in political decision-making. Columbia, 1970. 71-6147

697. Brock, Jarrett Ernest. C.S. Peirce's logic of vagueness. Illinois, 1969. 70-13254

698. Brockelman, Paul Taylor. A phenomenological analysis of time. Northwestern, 1968. 69-1804

699. Brockhaus, Richard Roy. The relational theory of space: some metaphysical, epistemological and scientific considerations. Brown, 1971. 72-8088

700. Brockway, George Max. Leibniz, Hume, Kant and the contemporaries on the problem of evil. Wisconsin, 1973. 73-23055

701. Brodbeck, May Selznick. A critical examination of John Dewey's logic: the theory of inquiry. Iowa, 1947.

702. Brodeur, Charles Claude. The "object" in the psychology of perception. Toronto, 1967.

703. Brodhead, Brickley Burns. A comparison of the ethics of John Dewey and Frederick Nietzsche. Temple, 1956.

704. Brodie, Helen C. The limits of science: outline of logic and of the methodology of the exact sciences, by Leon Chwistek. Columbia, 1948.

705. Brodsky, Garrett Martin. John Dewey's theory of inquiry. Yale, 1961.

706. Brody, Boruch A. The rise of the algebra of logic. Princeton, 1967. 67-13483

707. Brody, Leon. The testing and analysis of certain types of verbal and non-verbal reasoning. Duke, 1937.

708. Brody, Sr. Mary Lou. An idealistic pragmatism: the development of the pragmatic element in the philosophy of Josiah Royce. Marquette, 1969.
70-11959

709. Brogan, Albert Perley. The problem of intrinsic value. Harvard, 1914.

710. Broido, Jonathan Dov. Generalization of model theoretic notions and the eliminability of quantification into modal contexts. Pittsburgh, 1974.
75-18226

711. Broiles, Rowland David. An analysis of Hume's arguments concerning the role of reason in moral decisions. Ohio St., 1963.   64-1244

712. Bromberger, Sylvain. The concept of explanation. Harvard, 1961.

713. Bronaugh, Richard Norton. Reason, person and community. An inquiry based on the moral philosophy of Arthur E. Murphy. Wisconsin, 1962.   63-635

714. Bronstein, Daniel Jay. Necessity, implication and definition. Harvard, 1933.

715. Brook, Richard J. Berkeley's philosophy of science. New School, 1972.   72-27865

716. Brooks, Richard Williams. The rope and the snake: an investigation of the concept of adhyasa (superimposition) in advaita vendanta. Minnesota, 1968.
69-1491

717. Brophy, John Mark. Benedict Spinoza: the enigma. Fordham, 1934.

718. Bross, Helen Hamilton. The problem of bifurcation in Whitehead's philosophy of science. Yale, 1952.

719. Bross, John Robert. The role of creativity in metaphysics and religion. Columbia, 1951. 3324

720. Brotherston, Bruce Wallace. Moral evil and the social conscience. Harvard, 1923.

721. Broudy, Harry Samuel. The metaphysical presuppositions of personal existence. Harvard, 1935.

722. Brough, John Barnett. A study of the logic and evolution of Edmund Husserl's theory of the constitution of time-consciousness, 1893-1917. Georgetown, 1970.   70-21278

723. Brouilette, Gérarda (Sr. Thérèse de Ste. Marie).
     L'âme comme principe du mouvement local d'après
     le "traité de l'âme" d'Aristote. Laval, 1965.

724. Broussard, Joseph Daphnis. Eternity in Greek and
     scholastic philosophy. Catholic U., 1963.
                                              63-7973

725. Brouwer, Frederick Earle. James Martineau: a study
     of an ethical position based upon motives. Yale,
     1961.

726. Brown, Alan W. The metaphysical society: Victorian
     minds in crisis, 1869-1880. Columbia, 1947.

727. Brown, Alward Embury. Selfhood: pure consciousness
     as the underlying form of the given. Harvard,
     1927.

728. Brown, Sr. Anthony Mary. Logica magistri Pauli Per-
     gulersis. St. Bonaventure, 1957.

729. Brown, Barry Francis. The being of accidents accord-
     ing to St. Thomas Aquinas. Toronto, 1966.

730. Brown, Charles Donald, Jr. Analyticity and synonymy
     within the framework of a theory of conceptual
     meaning. Missouri, 1969.   70-2964

731. Brown, Clifford William. The formal aesthetics of
     Adolph Zeising. Bryn Mawr, 1960.   60-6955

732. Brown, Delwin W. God and process: a study of the
     systematic theological alternatives in the process
     philosophy of Alfred North Whitehead. Claremont,
     1964.   66-3356

733. Brown, Geoffrey Wallace. The concept of psychologi-
     cal abnormality: a philosophical analysis of its
     normative commitments. Washington U., 1970.
                                              70-26848

734. Brown, Gladstone L. A Christian criticism of the
     philosophy of Karl Marx, with special reference to
     the problem of anthropology, philosophically and
     theologically understood. Drew, 1958.

735. Brown, Harold Chapman. The problem of the Kantian
     mathematical antimonies. Harvard, 1905.

736. Brown, Harold Irwin. A causal theory of perception.
     Northwestern, 1970.   71-1806

737. Brown, J.F. The doctrine of the freedom of the will

738. Brown, James Francis. Toward a phenomenology of affectivity. N.Y.U., 1974.   74-29956

739. Brown, Jerome Vincent. Divine illumination and the theory of knowledge in the philosophy of Henry of Ghent. Toronto, 1969.

740. Brown, John Howell. F.H. Bradley's theory of judgment (with special reference to *The principles of logic*.) Princeton, 1959.   59-5163

741. Brown, Lee Bateman. Deliberation and free agency. Northwestern, 1966.   66-13959

742. Brown, Ludlow Locke. Some contemporary attacks on the doctrine of universals. Buffalo, 1975.   76-9036

743. Brown, Malcolm Spencer. Plato's theory of knowledge and its mathematical background. Columbia, 1966.   68-11707

744. Brown, Mark Alan. The infinite divisibility of space and the geometry of spatial finitism. Syracuse, 1971.   71-23435

745. Brown, Paul Allen. The problem of musical meaning. Wisconsin, 1975.   76-2468

746. Brown, Peter Gilbert. Methodological problems in sociological studies of the city: reductionism, psychologism, verstehen. Columbia, 1969.   72-15564

747. Brown, Peter Irwin. J.S. Mill's *On liberty* and its relation to his utilitarianism. Harvard, 1965.

748. Brown, Peter McPherson. Toward the guidance of thought: the inductive logic of Rudolf Carnap. Wisconsin, 1973.   74-8993

749. Brown, S.H. "That which is perceived by the soul," being a dissertation on the analysis of propositions and a comparative study of the part propositional structures play in the metaphysical systems of Plato and Descartes. Radcliffe, 1928.

750. Brown, Stuart MacDonald, Jr. An exposition and criticism of Schleiermacher's religious philosophy. Cornell, 1942.

751. Brown, Walter Theodore. Studies in individualism. Harvard, 1912.

752. Brown, Wesley Miller. Rules and norms in John Stuart Mill's philosophy of science. Harvard, 1970.

753. Brown, William Richard. The last materialist: the ontology of George Santayana. Missouri, 1967.
68-3598

754. Browne, Benjamin J. Recent interpretations of Plato's social philosophy as fascistic. Boston U., 1952.

755. Browne, David Alister. Reasons, motives and causes. British Columbia, 1970.

756. Browne, Rev. Joseph W. An analysis and evaluation of Berkeley's doctrine on abstraction. Fordham, 1956.

757. Browne, Robert Charles. Some functional theories of religion and their philosophical bases: an essay in the integration of philosophy, religion and social science. Syracuse, 1959.   59-6296

758. Browne, Samuel Stanhope Stryker. The moral and the right. Harvard, 1944.

759. Browning, Grayson Douglas. Judgment and motivation in contemporary intuitionist ethics. Texas, 1958.
58-1644

760. Browning, Lorin Wayne. The open question argument in Moore and Hare. Michigan St., 1972.   72-22197

761. Browning, Robert Willard. Reason in ethics and morals: with special reference to the contributions of Hume and Dewey. Berkeley, 1947.

762. Brownstein, Donald Ian. Objects and their qualities. Minnesota, 1969.   70-5552

763. Broyer, John Albin. The ethical theory of George Herbert Mead. So. Illinois, 1967.   67-15857

764. Broyles, James Earl. The role of common sense in the empiricism of Charles Sanders Peirce. U. of Washington, 1964.   64-8771

765. Bruce, Charles Dawson. An investigation of self-deception. Michigan St., 1975.   75-20815

766. Bruening, William Harry. The naturalistic fallacy and value terms in ethics. Notre Dame, 1969.
69-18505

767. Brumbaugh, Robert Sherrick. The role of mathematics in Plato's dialectic. Chicago, 1942.

768. Brumm, Gordon Lee. Ethics with a linguistic starting point. Harvard, 1961.

769. Brunhumer, Walter Joseph. Ideas of evolution in German *Naturphilosophie*: Leibniz, Kant, Goethe. Northwestern, 1955. 13073

770. Brunk, Conrad Grebel. An examination of the nature of conscience and its claim to freedom. Northwestern, 1974. 75-7882

771. Bruno, John Favata. Rosmini's contribution to ethical philosophy. Columbia, 1916.

772. Brush, Brenda Margot. Psychology and sense-data. Michigan, 1961. 61-1724

773. Brushaber, George Karl. The realistic epistemology of George Dawes Hicks. Boston U., 1968. 69-3936

774. Bruteau, Beatrice. The reality and the value of the world in the philosophy of Sri Aurobindo. Fordham, 1969. 69-16215

775. Bruzina, Ronald Charles. Logos and Eidos: a study in the phenomenological meaning of "concept" according to Husserl and Merleau-Ponty. Notre Dame, 1966. 66-12142

776. Bryan, Robert Sedgwick. A defense of the possibility of objective aesthetics. Virginia, 1956. 17600

777. Bryant, David Charles. Pain, incorrigibility, and self-intimation. Michigan, 1974. 74-25162

778. Bryar, William J., Jr. St. Thomas and the existence of God: three interpretations. Chicago, 1950.

779. Bubacz, Bruce Stephen. An analysis of St. Augustine's inner-man as an enucleation of his epistemology. U. of Washington, 1973. 74-2199

780. Buchanan, Allen Edward. Autonomy, distribution, and the state. No. Carolina, 1975. 76-9224

781. Buchanan, Bruce Gardner. Logics of scientific discovery. Michigan St., 1966. 67-7525

782. Buchanan, Emerson. Aristotle's theory of being. Columbia, 1959. 59-6998

783. Buchanan, James Henry. Ground as unity and primordial

ground in the thought of Martin Heidegger. Penn
St., 1970. 71-21729

784. Buchanan, Patricia Ann Johnson. Philosophy and its
history: a study in historiography. Miami, 1975.
76-12825

785. Buchanan, Rupert Archer. Wittgenstein's discussion
of sensations. Duke, 1966. 67-6098

786. Buchanan, Scott Milross. Possibility. Harvard, 1925.

787. Buchcik, Anthony A. The concept of morals in the
philosophies of St. Augustine and John Dewey.
Chicago, 1955.

788. Bucher, Raymond John. The current urban academic
crisis: toward a solution according to Dewey's notion of the public. Fordham, 1970. 71-8700

789. Buchler, Justus. Charles Peirce's empiricism. Columbia, 1939.

790. Buck, Albert Francis. The concept of quantitative
equality. Harvard, 1906.

791. Buckenmeyer, Robert Eugene. The meaning of judicium
and its relation to illumination in the philosophical dialogues of Augustine. Southern Cal., 1967.
67-8005

792. Buckley, Eugene Carr. A philosophical treatise concerning certain mathematical aspects of the rule
of the majority. Notre Dame, 1969. 69-18506

793. Buckley, Rev. George M. The nature and unity of metaphysics. Catholic U., 1946.

794. Buckley, John Joseph, Jr. An experiential framework
for functional analyticity. Tulane, 1973.
73-25273

795. Buckley, Joseph Anthony. The dimensions of the real;
the metaphysical structure of the existent in the
philosophy of Jacques Maritain. Notre Dame, 1966.
66-12143

796. Bucklin, John Michael. On understanding constatives.
Oregon, 1973. 73-28582

797. Buckner, Michael D. An essay on human action. Chicago, 1975.

798. Budlong, Theodore Warren. Reference and belief. Cornell, 1973. 73-16095

799. Buehler, Walter E. The role of prudence in education. Catholic U., 1950.

800. Bueno, Anibal A. The meaning of meaning and the meaning of poetry. Emory, 1971.   71-22872

801. Buermeyer, Laurence Ladd. The phenomenology of thought. Princeton, 1919.

802. Bufford, Samuel Lawrence. Suzanne K. Langer's two theories of art. Texas, 1969.   70-10762

803. Buford, Thomas Oliver. The idea of creation in Plato, Augustine, and Emil Brunner. Boston U., 1963.
64-393

804. Bugbee, Henry Greenwood, Jr. The sense and the conception of being. Berkeley, 1947.

805. Bukala, Casimir Robert. Intersubjectivity in Sartre's dramatic philosophy. Boston Coll., 1970.
70-24597

806. Bunn, Robert James. Infinite sets and numbers. British Columbia, 1975.

807. Buonocore, Gloria Petra. An approach to linguistic signs and their designata. Yale, 1961.

808. Burbach, Maur Ralph. The theory of beatitude in Latin-Arabian philosophy and its initial impact on Christian thought. Toronto, 1944.

809. Burbridge, John William. Contingent truths of historical fact and eternal truths of reason: the challenge of Lessing's "Ditch" and the responses of Hegel and Schelling. Toronto, 1970.

810. Burch, George Bosworth. The epistemology of Bernard of Clairvaux. Harvard, 1939.

811. Burch, Robert William. On rules. Rice, 1969.
69-19269

812. Burdick, John Marshall. Knowledge, simplicity and discourse in Plato's Theaetetus. Wisconsin, 1968.
68-9060

813. Bures, Charles Edwin. A logical analysis of the definition and formation of scientific concepts. Iowa, 1939.

814. Burge, Charles Tyler. Truth and some referential devices. Princeton, 1971.   72-13732

815. Burge, Evan Laurie. Plato's concept of aitia.
Princeton, 1970. 70-14190

816. Burgener, Richard John Christian. The problem of
origin in a eudaemonist theory of beauty as illustrated in Shaftesbury and Hutcheson. Toronto, 1955.

817. Burger, Ronna Cheryl. Plato's Phaedrus: a defense
of a philosophic art of writing. New School, 1975.
75-25443

818. Burgess, Joseph Charles. Analyticity and arithmetic
in Kant and Frege. Buffalo, 1975. 75-18776

819. Burgh, Richard W. Punishment and respect for persons. Wisconsin, 1975. 75-23834

820. Burhenn, Herbert William Louis, Jr. Historical explanation: its philosophical description, its kinds, its religious uses. Yale, 1970.
71-16127

821. Burian, Richard M. Scientific realism, commensurability, and conceptual change: a critique of Paul Feyerabend's philosophy of science. Pittsburgh, 1971. 72-2138

822. Burk, Alan Caden. Intentional propositions 'de dicto' and 'de re' and non-propositional seeing.
Brown, 1973. 74-2988

823. Burk, Joseph Caden. The substantival and functional
theories of the concept. Princeton, 1939.
2924

824. Burke, Armand J. The significance of adjustment in
aesthetics. Chicago, 1923.

825. Burke, David Ronald. An examination of Jean-Paul
Sartre's conception of freedom. Michigan St.,
1965. 66-364

826. Burke, John Bruce. Philo and Alexandrian Judaism.
Syracuse, 1963.

827. Burke, John Patrick. The concept of world in Husserl's
transcendental phenomenology. Cal., S. Diego,
1974. 74-17704

828. Burke, John Robert. The nature and kinds of causal
relations according to William Ockham. Fordham,
1968. 68-11004

829. Burke, Richard J., Jr. George Herbert Mead and Harry Stack Sullivan: a study in the relations between philosophy and psychology. Chicago, 1959.

830. Burkett, John Howard. Descartes: a sympathetic reading. Texas, 1971. 72-11324

831. Burkhardt, Frederick H. Johann Gottfried Herder: God, some conversations; a translation with a critical introduction and notes. Columbia, 1940.

832. Burkhart, Anna Driver. The person in religion; an examination of Christianity's contribution to the history of thought. Pennsylvania, 1930.

833. Burkholder, Peter Manning. Recent uses of ethical models in epistemology. Tulane, 1965. 66-1545

834. Burks, Arthur Walter. The logical foundations of the philosophy of Charles Sanders Peirce. Michigan, 1941.

835. Burlage, Rev. Carl John. The proper object of metaphysics in the Latin text of Averroes. St. Louis, 1957. 58-4375

836. Burlingame, Charles Edward. On the logic of the 'seeing as' locution. Virginia, 1965. 66-3170

837. Burns, Emmett Carl, Jr. Love, power, and justice as central elements in a view of social change: a comparison and evaluation of the thought of Reinhold Niebuhr and Martin Luther King, Jr. Pittsburgh, 1974. 74-21677

838. Burns, Rev. Harry Robert. Hume's attitude towards religion. St. Louis, 1974. 74-24052

839. Burns, Rev. John V. Dynamism in the cosmology of Christian Wolff. Fordham, 1950.

840. Burns, Sr. Josephine. The early theory of human choice in the philosophy of Francisco Suarez. Marquette, 1968. 69-3311

841. Burns, Vincent L. Life- mechanistic or teleological? Pennsylvania, 1936.

842. Buroker, Jill Vance. The development of Kant's metaphysic of nature. Chicago, 1974.

843. Burr, John Roy. Three dimensions of philosophic intelligence: private, public and visional in the philosophies of Werner Fite, John Dewey, and George Santayana. Columbia, 1959. 59-4057

844. Burrell, David Bakewell. Analogy and philosophical language. Yale, 1965. 65-15020

845. Burrill, Donald Rex. The problem of moral authority in modern jurisprudence. Southern Cal., 1961. 62-1313

846. Burrington, Dale Eugene. The place of natural law in Protestant ethics: an examination of Emil Brunner's ethical theory. Johns Hopkins, 1964.

847. Burroughs, Joseph Alvin. Prudence integrating the moral virtues according to St. Thomas Aquinas. Catholic U., 1955.

848. Burrows, Constance. Some philosophical implications of three modern schools of psychology. Southern Cal., 1936.

849. Bursen, Howard Alexander. A philosophical investigation of machine theories of memory. Cornell, 1974. 75-6719

850. Burstein, Norman. Individuality. N.Y.U., 1974. 75-9642

851. Burt, Rev. Donald X. The state and religious toleration: aspects of the church-state theories of four Christian thinkers. Catholic U., 1960.

852. Burton, Charles Roderick. Locke's composition theory. Berkeley, 1953.

853. Burton, Marion LeRoy. The philosophical basis of Augustine's doctrine of sin. Yale, 1907.

854. Burton, Michael S. The role of time in Kant's metaphysic of experience. Claremont, 1971. 71-29657

855. Burton, Robert Glenn. Time, determinism and creativity. Northwestern, 1969. 70-18

856. Burtt, Edwin Arthur. The metaphysics of Sir Isaac Newton; an essay on the metaphysical foundations of modern science. Columbia, 1925.

857. Burwell, Convere Jones. The relation of Hegelian epistemology to the development of individuality. No. Carolina, 1937.

858. Busch, Thomas W. The role of *cogito* in the philosophy of Merleau-Ponty. Marquette, 1967. 68-479

859. Buschman, Charles Gibson Heisler. Experience, being, and physical science. Yale, 1974. 75-1343

860. Bush, John McKnight Brayton. Skepticism: a critical evaluation. U. of Washington, 1970. 71-8466

861. Bush, Merrill Eugene. The concept of substance in the light of gestalt theory. Cornell, 1939.

862. Bush, Wendell T. Avenarius and the standpoint of pure experience. Columbia, 1905.

863. Bushinski, Rev. Edward A. An introduction to the natural theology of John of St. Thomas. Fordham, 1958.

864. Bushman, Sr. Rita Marie. Right reason in Stoicism and in the Christian moral tradition up to Saint Thomas. St. Louis, 1947.

865. Bussey, Gertrude Carman. Typical recent conceptions of freedom. Northwestern, 1915.

866. Bussy, Rev. Joseph Gerard. Is existence a predicate? U. of Washington, 1957. 58-1075

867. Buswell, James O., Jr. The empirical method of Frederick Robert Tennant. N.Y.U., 1949. 1214

868. Butchvarov, Panayot Krustev. Prolegomena to a theory of relations. Virginia, 1955. 13829

869. Butler, Broadus Nathaniel. A pragmatic study of language and valuation. Michigan, 1952. 3727

870. Butler, Clark Wade. Negative feedback and the dialectic of Hegel. Southern Cal., 1970. 71-12376

871. Butler, Sr. Edward. Man's knowledge of God according to A.D. Sertillanges, O.P. Catholic U., 1968. 69-9144

872. Butler, Kenneth G. An exposition and critique of the logical structure and biological basis of the orthogenetic theory of Pierre Teilhard de Chardin. Ottawa, 1974.

873. Butler, Nicholas Murray. A study in the history of logical doctrine. Columbia, 1884.

874. Butler, Roy Willington, Jr. The epistemic status of religious symbols in the thought of Wilbur M. Urban. Boston U., 1966. 66-11291

875. Butler, William Allington. The ambiguities of equality: a study of the concept of equality in classical and contemporary political philosophy, and as interpreted by the United States Supreme Court under the chief justiceship of Earl Warren, 1954-1969. Harvard, 1971.

876. Butrick, Richard Porter, Jr. Carnap's explication of "analytic" and "meaning-of." Columbia, 1966.
67-5768

877. Butt, Samuel McC. The Greek city-state in the political philosophy of Bernard Bosanquet. Princeton, 1932.

878. Butterfield, Victor Lloyd. The ethical theory of William James. Harvard, 1936.

879. Butts, Robert E. Husserl's criticisms of Hume's theory of knowledge. Pennsylvania, 1957.
57-4243

880. Butts, William Henry. The problem of meaning in theological language. Columbia, 1971. 74-1472

881. Buzzelli, Donald Edward. The New list of categories: a study of the early philosophy of Charles Sanders Peirce. Fordham, 1974. 74-19639

882. Byer, Inez Vera Lord. Tillich's theory of God. Missouri, 1968. 69-3366

883. Byerly, Henry Clement. The ontological status of theoretical entities. Minnesota, 1967.
68-7285

884. Byler, Jacob Franklin. The epistemology of Locke, Berkeley and Hume. Pennsylvania, 1898.

885. Byles, William Esdaile. The educational philosophy of Louis Agassiz. N.Y.U., 1940. 73-3058

886. Bynagle, Hans Edward. Historians' questions and historical objectivity. Columbia, 1973.
73-28189

887. Byrd, Michael Evan. Quine on the philosophical foundations of epistemic logic. Cal., Irvine, 1972. 73-11645

888. Byrne, James W. Religious toleration: its background in the philosophy of John Locke. Fordham, 1957.

889. Byrne, Paul Michael. The doctrine of the soul in the

        Sapientiale of Thomas of York; study and text.
Toronto, 1956.

890. Byrne, Rodney Paul. Nomos and cosmos: Reichenbach's
explication of scientific language. Indiana, 1971.
72-6753

891. Byrnes, Richard Gabriel. The fallen soul as a Plotinian key to a better and fuller understanding of the character of time and history in the early works of Saint Augustine. Fordham, 1972.
73-4299

892. Bywater, William Glen, Jr. Dealing with aesthetic theory. Michigan, 1969.   70-14485

- C -

893. Cacoullos, Ann Rossettos. Rights and recognition: the theory of rights of Thomas Hill Green. Columbia, 1971.   74-8163

894. Cadieux, Jean André. The ontological status of fictional entities. Minnesota, 1975.   76-27790

895. Cadigan, Kathryn Adele. Neutrality in metaethics. Missouri, 1971.   72-10580

896. Cadwallader, Eva Hauel. Nicolai Hartmann's twentieth-century value Platonism. Indiana, 1972.
73-2694

897. Cady, Duane Lynn. Knowledge in Plato's Theaetetus. Brown, 1971.   72-8093

898. Cafagna, Albert Carl. Some steps toward the resolution of the holism-individualism controversy. Michigan, 1974.   75-10143

899. Caffrey, Mary Carol. Realism and knowledge according to William of Auvergne. Fordham, 1944.

900. Cahalan, John Charles. Necessary truths and philosophic method: a re-examination. Notre Dame, 1969.
69-12788

901. Cahill, Sr. Mary Camilla. The absolute and the relative in St. Thomas and in modern philosophy. Catholic U., 1939.

902. Cahn, Steven Mark. Fatalism: a philosophical study. Columbia, 1966.   69-15536

903. Caiazza, John Casto. Kuhn's theory of paradigms and the history of biology. Boston U., 1972.
72-25250

904. Cain, William Carner. The philosophy of Josiah Royce and its theological implications. Drew, 1928.

905. Caird, Alfred Page. The doctrine of quiddities and modes in Francis of Meyronnes. Toronto, 1948.

906. Cairns, Thomas Dorion. The philosophy of Edmund Husserl. Harvard, 1933.

907. Caldwell, Elizabeth F. The concept of finitude in Renouvier. N.Y.U., 1950.
73-21974

908. Caldwell, Hugh Harris. Science and liberal art. Virginia, 1960.
60-4594

909. Caldwell, Morley Albert. Does pragmatism involve indeterminism? Harvard, 1908.

910. Caldwell, Robert Lee. Reid and Hamilton on sense perception. U. of Washington, 1958.
58-3268

911. Calhoun, Edward Thomas Davidson. The form of the person in theoretic knowing. Yale, 1960.

912. Calhoun, Robert Lowry. An introduction to the philosophy of Thomas Davidson. Yale, 1923.

913. Califano, Joseph John. The problem of Kant's schemata in regard to the speculative sciences. St. John's, 1968.
69-4124

914. Callaghan, William Jerome. The philosophy of Francis Ellingwood Abbot. Columbia, 1958.
58-3215

915. Callahan, Daniel John. The uses of language: a study in the development of George Berkeley's thought. Harvard, 1965.

916. Callahan, Rev. Francis F. Philosophical method in Maurice Blondel. Fordham, 1956.

917. Callahan, John Leonard. A theory of esthetic according to the principles of St. Thomas Aquinas. Catholic U., 1927.

918. Callahan, Thomas Greylish. William Ockham and natural law. Michigan St., 1975.
75-27246

919. Callicott, John Baird. Plato's aesthetics and introduction to the theory of forms. Syracuse, 1972.
72-20314

920. Calvert, Carl Arthur. Relative identity: an examination of a theory by Peter Geach. U. of Washington, 1973. 73-22556

921. Calvert, Ernest R. The panpsychism of James Ward and Charles A. Strong. Boston U., 1942.

922. Camacho, Luis A. Pre-conceptual and pre-analytical inductive experience. Catholic U., 1973.
74-3498

923. Camele, Anthony Michael. Good reason in ethics: a critical evaluation. Marquette, 1972. 73-8263

924. Cameron, Evan William. On the inductive structure of works of art. Boston U., 1970. 70-22401

925. Caminiti, Francis Norman. Nicholas of Cusa: *Docta ignorantia*, a philosophy of infinity. Fordham, 1968. 69-2578

926. Camp, John Barton. Epistemological change as a basis of interpreting contemporary western culture, particularly in the arts of painting and music. Florida St., 1964. 65-295

927. Camp, Joseph Lee, Jr. Intentionality: two studies. Brown, 1967. 68-1442

928. Campbell, Sr. Arsenia M. The child and the beautiful. Niagara, 1937.

929. Campbell, Bertrand J. The problem of one or plural substantial forms in man as found in the works of St. Thomas Aquinas and John Duns Scotus. Pennsylvania, 1936.

930. Campbell, Charles Ray. The attack from behind: irony and Søren Kierkegaard's dialectic of communication. Syracuse, 1973. 74-8234

931. Campbell, James Ian. Logical positivism and religious statements. Notre Dame, 1965. 65-10075

932. Campbell, Lytle Blair. The ideology of egocentrism in seventeenth and eighteenth century France; some proponents and antagonists. Princeton, 1966.
66-13297

933. Campbell, Rex LeRoy. An examination of David Hume's philosophy of determinism. Utah, 1967. 67-11375

934. Campbell, Richmond Mullowny. The intelligibility of intrinsic value. Cornell, 1970. 70-16614

935. Campbell, William Edward. Causality: the scholastic view as compared with certain non-scholastic views. Pennsylvania, 1933.

936. Campbell, William Edward. Wittgenstein's picture theory of meaning. Washington U., 1973.
74-7035

937. Cancienne, Donald. The age of the universe. Laval, 1968.

938. Caner, Sarah Ann. The doctrine of man in the Salesian tradition, with special reference to the *Histoire littéraire du sentiment religieux en France* by Henri Bremond. Bryn Mawr, 1960. 61-6576

939. Canfield, John Vincent. The compatability of free will and determinism. Brown, 1962. 63-1009

940. Cangemi, Rev. Dominic. The Thomistic concept of the "vis cogitativa." Catholic U., 1951.

941. Cannavo, Salvatore. On the epistemological foundations of probability. N.Y.U., 1956. 59-1064

942. Canning, Jerry Warren. A logical analysis of criticisms directed at Freudian psychoanalytic theory. Maryland, 1966. 66-9277

943. Cannon, James Joseph, Jr. The development of logic in the Dominican school. Yale, 1961. 67-12530

944. Cantin, Sr. Eileen. Emmanuel Mounier's personalist view of history. Marquette, 1972. 73-8264

945. Cantin, Stanislas. H. Bergson et le problème de la liberté. Laval, 1949.

946. Cantwell, Rev. Peter W. Merleau-Ponty: towards a phenomenological psychology of real knowledge. Catholic U., 1966. 67-1247

947. Canty, John Thomas. Lesniewski's ontology and Godel's incompleteness theorem. Notre Dame, 1967.
67-13595

948. Capaldi, Nicholas. Judgment and sentiment in Hume's moral theory. Columbia, 1965. 65-9156

949. Capitan, William Harry. Doctrine and belief in poetry. Minnesota, 1960. 60-3502

950. Capiz, Pascual. Consent as a basis of political obligation in Locke, Rousseau, and Green. Chicago, 1950.

951. Caponigri, Aloysius Robert. Some aspects of the philosophy of Joseph de Maistre. Chicago, 1942.

952. Caputo, John David. The way back into the ground: an interpretation of the path of Heidegger's thought. Bryn Mawr, 1968. 69-9048

953. Capuzzi, Frank A. Socrates Manikos: an essay on the death of a hero-seer. Duquesne, 1972. 73-4669

954. Carafides, John L. The philosophy of reflection; an examination of Shadworth Hodgson's treatment of experience. Buffalo, 1971. 71-22558

955. Carandang, Amado Ilagen. Jean-Paul Sartre and his atheism. Notre Dame, 1966. 67-198

956. Carbonara, John Charles. Critical empiricism in C. Wright Mills. Buffalo, 1967. 67-10119

957. Card, Claudia Falconer. Retributive justice in legal punishment. Harvard, 1969.

958. Cardwell, Charles Evan. Representation and uncertainty: an essay on Pierre Duhem's philosophy of science. Rochester, 1972. 72-18806

959. Care, Norman Sydney. Action, explanation, and understanding. Yale, 1964. 65-1972

960. Carew, George Munda. The political philosophy of John Stuart Mill: a reconstruction of his principle of non-interference. Connecticut, 1975. 75-10610

961. Carey, Archibald, Jr. Richard Cumberland and the epistemology of ethics. Washington U., 1968. 68-5124

962. Carey, Sr. Helen. The importance of contemplation in Dewey's instrumentalism. Fordham, 1973. 74-2731

963. Carley, Leon Alanson. Mental, physical and moral delinquency and the courts. N.Y.U., 1915. 74-3376

964. Carlo, William Ernest. The doctrine of creation in Giles of Rome; a study of the relation of essence and existence in the creative act. Toronto, 1955.

965. Carloye, Jack Cloyd. Reason as a natural function in the philosophy of John Dewey. Illinois, 1960. 61-97

966. Carlson, Allen Arvid. The use of "reaction terms" in aesthetic judgments. Michigan, 1971.   71-23718

967. Carlson, Elliott Reinold. Concept shifts in science and Thomas S. Kuhn's The structure of scientific revolutions. Boston U., 1972.   72-25253

968. Carlson, George Radcliffe. A critical analysis of the concept 'moral.' Toronto, 1970.

969. Carlson, John William. Wittgenstein on language and philosophical understanding: a study of continuities in his thought. Notre Dame, 1970.   71-5526

970. Carlsson, Percy Allan. The theistic framework of Butler's ethics. Northwestern, 1961.   61-5298

971. Carmichael, Douglas. Order and human value. Indiana, 1954.   8781

972. Carmichael, Peter Archibald. The nature of freedom. No. Carolina, 1930.

973. Carmody, Michael F. References to Plato and the Platonici in the Summa theologiae of St. Thomas Aquinas. Pittsburgh, 1949.

974. Carnell, Edward John. The problem of verification in Søren Kierkegaard. Boston U., 1949.

975. Carnes, John Robb, Jr. An examination of the current status of natural law philosophy. Michigan, 1957.   58-892

976. Carnes, Ralph Lee. The Sapir-Whorf hypothesis: an analysis. Emory, 1965.   65-11505

977. Carnes, Robert Darrell. The analytic/synthetic distinction: a defense of its plausibility. Duke, 1965.   65-12982

978. Carney, James Donald. G.E. Moore's refutation of Berkeley's idealism. Nebraska, 1959.   59-4371

979. Carney, Rev. William J. Agent intellect and phantasm: their relationship in the teaching of St. Thomas and his commentators. Georgetown, 1949.

980. Carnicelli, Anthony. Patterns of aggressive comedy in the choruses of Aristophanes. Harvard, 1975.

981. Carnus, Juliette. The organization of matter in the eighteenth century French philosophy. Columbia, 1932.

982. Caron, James William Francis. Expression and scientific method in Descartes, Leibniz and Condillac. Toronto, 1969.

983. Carpenter, Elizabeth Teresa Galasso. A critical study of the emotive theory of ethics of A.J. Ayer. Nebraska, 1966. 66-7536

984. Carpenter, Rhys. The ethics of Euripides. Columbia, 1916.

985. Carpenter, Sandra Witt. Mead, Dewey and Wheelwright on scientific and expressive language. Claremont, 1970. 71-13676

986. Carpenter, Stanley Robert. The structure of technological action. Boston U., 1971. 71-26389

987. Carpino, Joseph J. A study of negation in Hegel. Fordham, 1960.

988. Carr, Charles Raymond, II. Illocutionary acts. Arizona, 1975. 76-1399

989. Carr, David Tredway. The awareness of persons and moral action. Yale, 1966. 66-14950

990. Carr, Edward Anderson Lindner. Resemblance, denotation, and depiction: an analysis of some conditions necessary for pictures to represent. Chicago, 1975.

991. Carr, Spencer David. Quine's theory of regimentation. Michigan, 1971. 71-15111

992. Carrier, David Stewart. Representation and expression in visual art. Columbia, 1972. 75-9323

993. Carrier, Leonard Samuel. The objects of perception and belief. Stanford, 1967. 67-11023

994. Carrington, William Thomas, Jr. Divine immutability revisited: the doctrine of St. Thomas Aquinas in the face of some contemporary challenges. Fordham, 1973. 73-16005

995. Carrithers, David Wallace. Joseph Glanvill and Pyrrhonic scepticism: a study in the revival of the doctrines of Sextus Empiricus in sixteenth and seventeenth century Europe. N.Y.U., 1972.
72-21497

996. Carroll, Marion Delia Crane. The principles of absolutism in the metaphysics of Bernard Bosanquet. Cornell, 1916.

997. Carroll, Robert Todd. The philosophy of Bishop Edward Stillingfleet in its seventeenth-century context. Cal., S. Diego, 1974. 74-19598

998. Carroll, Thomas Cyril, Jr. Causality and the theory of action. Cal., S. Barbara, 1975. 76-20503

999. Carson, Lewis Clinton. The object of knowledge: a dissertation on philosophical transcendence. Harvard, 1901.

1000. Carstens, Gustav Arnold. The relation of Qoheleth to contemporary Greek philosophy. N.Y.U., 1903.

1001. Carter, Curtis-Lloyd. Style, painting and language: a study of language-like features of painting. Boston U., 1971. 71-26390

1002. Carter, Hugh Sevier. The social theories of L.T. Hobhouse. Columbia, 1927.

1003. Carter, Kay Codell. George Berkeley's views on linguistic meaning. Cornell, 1968. 68-15710

1004. Carter, Richard Burnett. Descartes' notion of body. Columbia, 1967. 70-23426

1005. Carter, Robert Edgar. A study of intrinsic value in G.E. Moore and C.I. Lewis. Toronto, 1969.

1006. Carter, Walter Baillie. The status of universals in Locke, Berkeley and Hume. Toronto, 1953.

1007. Carter, William Randolph. On disproving causal claims by appeal to logical relations. Virginia, 1968. 68-18183

1008. Cartwright, Helen Rollins Morris Benkard. Classes, quantities, and non-singular reference. Michigan, 1964. 64-6661

1009. Cartwright, Nancy Lynn Delaney. A philosophical analysis of the concept of mixture in quantum mechanics. Illinois, Chi., 1971. 72-4352

1010. Cartwright, Richard Lee. Logical constructions. Brown, 1954. 9810

1011. Casassa, Charles Stephen. The political thought of Francisco de Vitoria. Toronto, 1946.

1012. Case, Edward M. A critique of the formative thought underlying Francis Suarez's concept of being. Catholic U., 1959.

1013. Casebier, Allan Frank. Style terms in the languages of the art critic and the art historian. Michigan, 1969. 70-14486

1014. Casey, Rev. Donald Patrick. Croce on liberty: societal and individual tensions. St. Louis, 1972. 72-23915

1015. Casey, Edward Scott. Poetry and ontology: a study of poetic imagination, poetic language, and the imaginary. Northwestern, 1967. 67-15202

1016. Casey, John Francis. Refutation and argument in philosophy: a metaphilosophical inquiry. Fordham, 1975. 75-18880

1017. Casey, John Perry, Jr. Knowledge, belief, and evidence. Iowa, 1975. 75-23022

1018. Casey, Joseph Thomas. The primacy of metaphysics. Catholic U., 1936.

1019. Cashman, Tyrone McNally. Man's place in nature according to Blaise Pascal. Columbia, 1974. 74-28485

1020. Caso, Allen D. Passion and spirit in man: a study in the philosophy of Malebranche. Fordham, 1972. 73-1469

1021. Caspar, Sr. George Marie. Gabriel Marcel's metaphysics of integral human experience. Notre Dame, 1968. 69-4057

1022. Casper, Dennis John. Being and predication in Plato's *Sophist*. Illinois, 1972. 73-17144

1023. Cassel, Herbert William. Religious concepts and conceptual change. Temple, 1973. 73-18679

1024. Cassidy, John Henry. The simplicity of scientific theories measured. Rochester, 1975. 75-22732

1025. Cassidy, John Robert. Logic and determinism: a history of the problem of future contingent propositions from Aristotle to Ockham. Bryn Mawr, 1965. 66-1530

1026. Cassidy, Rev. Laurence Lavelle. The infinite consciousness of man according to Nicholas of Cusa. Fordham, 1968. 68-11005

1027. Cassidy, Robert C.F. Thought and freedom: a study of ontic, introspective and empirical concepts of freedom. Princeton, 1971. 72-2694

1028. Cassin, Chrystine Elizabeth. The origin and development of Bertrand Russell's theory of descriptions. Florida St., 1968. 69-11286

1029. Castañeda, Hector Neri. The logical structure of moral reasoning. Minnesota, 1954. 8447

1030. Castell, Alburey. Mill's logic of the moral sciences: a study of the impact of Newtonism on early nineteenth-century social thought. Chicago, 1931.

1031. Castiglione, Robert Louis. The reality of the past: a comparison of the philosophies of Alfred North Whitehead and Paul Weiss. Catholic U., 1971. 71-29235

1032. Castoe, Walter Paul. The metaphysical value of the doctrine of 'the spiritual life' in the philosophy of Rudolf Eucken. Cincinnati, 1930.

1033. Castonguay, Charles Ernest. Meaning and existence in mathematics: on the use and abuse of the theory of models in the philosophy of mathematics. McGill, 1971.

1034. Castonguay, Jean-Louis. La liberté de l'individu dans la société politique chez Harold J. Laski. Montreal, 1974.

1035. Castro, Matilde. The respective standpoints of psychology and logic. Chicago, 1907.

1036. Casullo, Albert Francis. The appeal to inconceivability in claims to a priori knowledge. Iowa, 1975. 76-13367

1037. Catalano, Joseph S. The education of substantial forms according to St. Thomas Aquinas. St. John's, 1962.

1038. Catan, John Richard. The relation between soul and separate mind in Aristotle. Toronto, 1965.

1039. Catania, Francis Joseph. Divine infinity according to Albert the Great's commentary on Lombard's Sentences. St. Louis, 1959. 60-324

1040. Caton, Charles Edwin. A description and evaluation of the method of the ordinary-language philosophers and its doctrinal basis. Michigan, 1956. 57-2866

1041. Caton, Hiram Pendleton, III. The mastery of nature and wisdom: an essay on the means and end of Descartes' design. Yale, 1966. 66-14953

1042. Cattermole, George Berger. A critical survey of the philosophy of C.I. Lewis. Stanford, 1974.
74-20180

1043. Caulfield, Joseph. Practical ignorance. Laval, 1951.

1044. Causey, Robert Louis. Derived measurement and the foundations of dimensional analysis. Berkeley, 1967. 68-43

1045. Cauvel, Martha Jane. The critic, "Blest with a poet's fire": Alexander Gerard's interpretation of genius, taste, and aesthetic criticism. Bryn Mawr, 1962. 63-2382

1046. Cavalconte, Charles C. Leonardo da Vinci's contributions to science and technology. St. John's, 1971. 72-31014

1047. Cavanagh, Rev. Patrick Edmund. The doctrine of assent of John Henry Newman. Notre Dame, 1964.
64-10492

1048. Cavarnos, Constantine Peter. The classical theory of relations. Harvard, 1948.

1049. Cavell, Marcia Schmid. Aesthetic concepts: the place of reason in criticism. Harvard, 1969.

1050. Cavell, Stanley Louis. The claim to rationality: knowledge and the basis of morality. Harvard, 1961.

1051. Caws, Peter James. The functions of definition in modern physical science. Yale, 1956.

1052. Cebik, LeRoy Bruce. Colligation and history: a study in the relation of the use of concepts to problems in the philosophy of history. Nebraska, 1967. 68-738

1053. Cederblom, Jerry Bruce. A development of C.I. Lewis' theory of the foundations of ethics. Claremont, 1973. 73-6166

1054. Celarier, James LeRoy. Aristotle's _Physica_ and Plato's _Parmenides_. Pennsylvania, 1960. 60-3632

1055. Cell, Edward Charles. Analytic philosophy and assertions about God. Princeton, 1964. 64-9450

1056. Ceniza, Claro Rafols. Some basic presuppositions of classical philosophy. Syracuse, 1974. 75-13967

1057. Centore, F. Floyd. Robert Hooke's contributions to mechanics: a study in seventeenth century natural philosophy. St. John's, 1968. 69-4130

1058. Cerf, Walter Hyman. Spirit and world: prolegomena to a philosophy of art. Princeton, 1941. 2927

1059. Cernic, David G. The unfolding of the person through the four historical conceptions of being. Fordham, 1970. 71-8702

1060. Chabot, Sr. Marie-Emmanuel. Le concept de nature chez Ciceron. Laval, 1959.

1061. Chacon, Roger Jose. Plato's theory of punishment. Harvard, 1958.

1062. Chaffee, John H. The psychoanalytic concept of the unconscious: a phenomenological critique. N.Y.U., 1972. 72-31067

1063. Chaffin, Bill Mack. A critical analysis of Ryle's concept of self-knowledge. Arkansas, 1972. 72-29656

1064. Chakrabarti, Chandana. A critical appraisal of James' doctrine of pure experience. Buffalo, 1975. 76-1432

1065. Chakrabarti, Kisor Kumar. A study of the logic of Gotama. Buffalo, 1975. 75-18781

1066. Chambers, Connor John, Jr. Henri Bergson and the reality of the physical world. St. Louis, 1970. 71-3252

1067. Chambers, Lawson Powers. Idea and ideal. Harvard, 1916.

1068. Chambers, Winifred Morphew. Clinical interpretations and the debate over the scientific acceptability of psychoanalysis. Chicago, 1975.

1069. Champagne, Ronald Oscar. A formalization of the dialectical development of intelligence. Fordham, 1974. 74-19642

1070. Champawat, Narayan Singh. On the concept of an observation language. U.C.L.A., 1969. 69-19480

1071. Chan, Benjamin Chun Piu. The development of neo-Buddhist thought in modern China as represented in the philosophy of Hsiung Shih-li: the identi-

fication of reality and function. Temple, 1968.
69-14076

1072. Chan, Wing Tsit. An abstract of the philosophy of Chuang Tzŭ. Harvard, 1929.

1073. Chandler, Albert Richard. Plato's theory of ideas studied in the light of Husserl's theory of universals. Harvard, 1913.

1074. Chandler, Hugh Storer. The possibility of definition. Cornell, 1964. 65-3716

1075. Chandler, Kenneth Clark. Realism without dualism: an examination of Dewey's non-dualistic realism. Texas, 1973. 74-5210

1076. Chandler, Robert Woodward. Ethical relativism in the light of contemporary American theories. Columbia, 1953. 5183

1077. Chang, Wipzie Shionyu. The significance and some limitations of Hegel's ethics. Michigan, 1919.

1078. Chang, Yen-Ling. The citizen-statesman, or a Whiteheadian politic: an essay on importance. Texas, 1975. 76-8006

1079. Chang Chen-Tong, Aloysius. Le Tao et les contraires. Laval, 1968.

1080. Chao, Stephen Shyong. Existential themes in Confucianism. DePaul, 1974. 74-23648

1081. Chao, Yuen Ren. Continuity: a study in methodology. Harvard, 1918.

1082. Chapin, Wallace Torrey. Evolutionary ethics. Princeton, 1890.

1083. Chapman, Emmanuel. St. Augustine's philosophy of beauty. Toronto, 1934.

1084. Chapman, Frank Miller. The concept of the sublime. Harvard, 1931.

1085. Chapman, Harmon Marbold. The transcendental standpoint and method. Harvard, 1933.

1086. Chappell, Vere Claiborne. The philosophy of process. Yale, 1958.

1087. Charlson, Price Ellsworth. Aesthetic formalism. Berkeley, 1960.

1088. Charron, William Cletus. An exposition and analysis of William James' views on the nature of man. Marquette, 1966. 68-480

1089. Chase, Alston S. The formal approach: prolegomenon to a theory of justice. Princeton, 1967. 68-8911

1090. Chastain, Charles. Reference and context. Princeton, 1973. 74-2317

1091. Chatalian, George. Proofs of the external world. Harvard, 1968.

1092. Chateaubriand, Oswaldo. Ontic commitment, ontological reduction, and ontology. Berkeley, 1971.

1093. Chatterjee, Dipankar. Morality and liberation in the philosophies of Samkara and the Bhagavad gita. U. of Washington, 1975. 76-17427

1094. Chaves, Eduardo O.C. David Hume's philosophical critique of theology and its significance for the history of Christian thought. Pittsburgh, 1972. 73-5005

1095. Chekola, Mark Gregory. The concept of happiness. Michigan, 1974. 75-655

1096. Chellas, Brian Farrell. The logical form of imperatives. Stanford, 1968. 69-13933

1097. Ch'en, Ching-Pan Joseph. Confucius as a teacher; philosophy of Confucius with special reference to its educational implications. Toronto, 1940.

1098. Chen, Ellen Marie. Tao, nature, man: a study of the key ideas in the Tao te ching. Fordham, 1966. 66-13498

1099. Chen, Te. Dewey's concept of moral good. So. Illinois, 1969. 70-426

1100. Cheney, David Ross. Some methodological prolegomena to moral philosophy. Miami, 1971. 72-12900

1101. Cheney, James Elwood. The concept of desire. Wisconsin, 1974. 74-18923

1102. Cheng, Andrew Chih-Yi. Hsüntzu's theory of human nature and its influence on Chinese thought. Columbia, 1928.

1103. Cheng, Chung-Ying. Peirce's and Lewis' theories of

induction. Harvard, 1964.

1104. Cheng, Hsueh-Li. An expository and critical study of Madhyamika philosophy from Chinese sources. Wisconsin, 1974. 75-5925

1105. Cherbonnier, Edmond La Beaume. Freedom and time: a study in some recent contributions to the problem. Columbia, 1951. 3328

1106. Chervin, Ronda DeSola. The process of conversion in the philosophy of religion of Søren Kierkegaard. Fordham, 1967. 68-3684

1107. Chethimattam, Rev. John Britto. Consciousness and reality according to the principles of Sri Ramanuja. Fordham, 1968. 68-11007

1108. Chiaraviglio, Lucio. Abstraction and temporality: a study of Whitehead's metaphysics. Emory, 1961. 62-25

1109. Chiariello, Michael V., Jr. An examination of radicalism as a theory of rationality in social philosophy. Boston U., 1973. 73-23470

1110. Chidsey, Harold Russell. The metaphysical bases of religion in the light of recent philosophy. Harvard, 1920.

1111. Chihara, Charles Seiyo. On mathematical discovery. U. of Washington, 1960. 60-4280

1112. Child, Arthur Henry. The problems of the sociology of knowledge: a critical and philosophical study. Berkeley, 1939.

1113. Child, James William. The ontological commitment of physical theories. Indiana, 1967. 68-7210

1114. Childress, Marianne Miller. The morally good as ontologically perfective. St. Louis, 1960.
 61-744

1115. Chin, Yueh Liu. The political theory of Thomas Hill Green. Columbia, 1920.

1116. Chin Lee, Grace. Social individualism, a systematic treatment of the metaphysics of George Herbert Mead. Bryn Mawr, 1940.

1117. Chinn, Ewing Y. A critical appraisal of the prevalent model of scientific explanation. Southern Cal., 1966. 67-5293

1118. Chinnock, Eugénie. Plato's educational views: a comparative study of the Republic and the Laws. N.Y.U., 1940.   73-3072

1119. Chisholm, Roderick Milton. The basic propositions of empirical knowledge. Harvard, 1942.

1120. Choquette, Anne Marie Imelda. Saint Augustine's doctrine of sense knowledge. Toronto, 1944.

1121. Choron, Jacques. Death as motive and motif of philosophical thought with special consideration of Schopenhauer. New School, 1960.

1122. Chrisman, John Michael. A study of two major Thomistic attempts to reconcile stable intelligibility with evolutionary change. Toronto, 1971.

1123. Christ, Paul Sydney. The psychology of the active intellect of Averroes. Pennsylvania, 1926.

1124. Christensen, Darrel Elvyn. Some implications for the doctrine of God of Hegel's concept of thought as meditation. Southern Cal., 1965. 65-9969

1125. Christensen, Ferrel Marvin. A defense of temporal 'becoming.' Indiana, 1971.   72-9967

1126. Christenson, Thomas Joseph. An analysis of the role of value experience in a theory of valuation. Yale, 1968.   68-11170

1127. Christodoulides, Efstathios Haralambos. An analysis of the historical basis of humanism and its relation to modern educational theory. Texas, 1973. 73-25988

1128. Christodoulou, Marie Nicholas. An examination of the concept of community in Plato's political theory. Cornell, 1952.

1129. Christy, Arthur. The Orient in American transcendentalism. Columbia, 1932.

1130. Christy, Lowell Frederick, Jr. The philosophy of Peter Pan: growing up, growing old, coming home. Cal., S. Cruz, 1975.   76-13014

1131. Chu, Chi-hsien. A study of the development of Sun Yat'sen's philosophical ideas. Columbia, 1950.
1837

1132. Churchill, James Spencer. Martin Heidegger: Kant and the problem of metaphysics, translated with

an introduction and notes. Indiana, 1960.
60-2805

1133. Churchill, Jordan Maurice. Moral judgment and self-knowledge. Columbia, 1956. 19235

1134. Churchill, Robert Paul. Civil disobedience: definition and justification. Johns Hopkins, 1975.

1135. Churchill, William. The tendency toward idealism in recent scientific conceptions of matter. Yale, 1901.

1136. Churchland, Paul Montgomery. Persons and P-predicates. Pittsburgh, 1969. 70-5344

1137. Churchman, Charles W. Towards a general logic of propositions. Pennsylvania, 1938.

1138. Churgin, Gershon A. Royce's theory of knowledge, an analytical exposition. Johns Hopkins, 1941.

1139. Cioffari, Vincent. Fortune and fate from Democritus to St. Thomas Aquinas. Columbia, 1935.

1140. Cipollone, Anthony P. Ethical elements in the philosophy of Paul Ricoeur. DePaul, 1974.
74-23649

1141. Cisek, Robert Alexander. The problem of individuation. Buffalo, 1974. 75-16502

1142. Clack, Robert Jerold. Analysis and ontology: a study of reconstructionism in the early philosophy of Bertrand Russell. No. Carolina, 1964.
65-14321

1143. Claghorn, George Stuart. Aristotle's criticism of Plato's Timaeus. Pennsylvania, 1953. 4916

1144. Claiborne, John Hogan, IV. A Freudian theory of laughter. Tennessee, 1971. 72-5424

1145. Clancy, Bonnie Ruth Aarons. Thought at an impasse: a case study of philosophical mysticism. Michigan, 1971. 72-4842

1146. Clapp, James G. Locke's conception of the mind. Columbia, 1937.

1147. Clark, Ann Kramer. Implications of metaphor or for the sake of the word: an Aristotelian critique and an Augustinian reconstruction. Texas, 1973.
74-5215

1148. Clark, David William. The structure of Ockham's moral doctrine. Loyola, 1973. 73-23140

1149. Clark, Frances Benbow. Pascal's concept of the heart. Yale, 1962.

1150. Clark, George Alfred. Perceptual value and the new estheticism. Pennsylvania, 1950. 8916

1151. Clark, Gordon Haddon. Empedocles and Anaxagoras in Aristotle's De anima. Pennsylvania, 1929.

1152. Clark, James Wilfred. Wolfgang Koehler's conception of direct experience. Michigan, 1957. 58-393

1153. Clark, John Alden. The ground of moral obligation. Harvard, 1935.

1154. Clark, John Philip. The social and political philosophy of William Godwin. Tulane, 1974. 75-2926

1155. Clark, Leonard Walter. The moral and political philosophy of David Hume. Yale, 1967. 68-4842

1156. Clark, Mthr. Mary Twibill. Augustine, first philosopher of freedom. Fordham, 1955.

1157. Clark, Orville Verdell. Aesthetics and the failure of art. Penn St., 1968. 69-14497

1158. Clark, Ralph William. The universal in the philosophy of Saint Thomas Aquinas. Colorado, 1971. 72-3636

1159. Clark, Robert Charles. Action and behavior in the theories of Talcott Parsons. Columbia, 1971. 72-10425

1160. Clark, Romane Lewis. An analysis of certain forms of negation employed in theory of knowledge. Iowa, 1952. 4056

1161. Clarke, Bowman Lafayette. An approach to the problem of language and natural theology. Emory, 1961. 62-26

1162. Clarke, David Sterling, Jr. An interpretation of Charles Peirce's category of firstness. Emory, 1963. 64-9402

1163. Clarke, Desmond M. The role of experience in Descartes' scientific method. Notre Dame, 1974. 74-9263

1164. Clarke, Dolores Marie. Moral dispositions in Kant's ethics. Notre Dame, 1974. 74-20562

1165. Clarke, Eunice A. An examination of George Herbert Mead's concept of the self as seen through the themes science, evolution, emergence and time. Pennsylvania, 1972. 73-1367

1166. Clarke, Francis Palmer. The intellect in the philosophy of St. Thomas. Pennsylvania, 1928.

1167. Clarke, Stanley Gordon. Emotion. Duke, 1969. 69-16750

1168. Clarke, Thompson Morgan. The nature of traditional epistemology. Harvard, 1962.

1169. Clatterbaugh, Kenneth Charles. The problem of individuation. Indiana, 1967. 67-3661

1170. Clayton, Marcus McLean, Jr. A critical study of four principal theories in Brand Blanshard's philosophical system. Emory, 1967. 68-4478

1171. Cleary, Thomas F. Sayings and doings of Pai-Chang Huai-Hai, Ch'an master of great wisdom. Harvard, 1975.

1172. Clegg, Jerry Stephen. On critical opinion. U. of Washington, 1962. 62-6584

1173. Clément, André. La conception du hasard chez Lévy Bruhl et la critique qui en fit Bergson. Laval, 1954.

1174. Clement, William Carl. An analysis of the concept of structure. Berkeley, 1952.

1175. Clements, Tad Sherridan. A critical examination of the premises of humanism. Buffalo, 1962. 62-3850

1176. Clifford, John Edward. Tense and tense logic. U.C.L.A., 1971. 72-3171

1177. Clift, Daniel Kennedy. A prosopography to the speeches of Cicero: historical figures before 80 B.C. Harvard, 1975.

1178. Clifton, Charles Thomas. An examination of the realist appeal to common sense. Cincinnati, 1935.

1179. Clive, Geoffrey H. The connection between ethics and religion in Kant, Kierkegaard, and F.H. Bradley. Harvard, 1953.

1180. Close, Frederick Phelps. Seminar on Tillich: the
relationship between philosophy and theology in
the thought of Paul Tillich. Texas, 1975.
76-14425

1181. Clough, Rosa T. Looking back at futurism. Columbia,
1942.

1182. Clouser, Karl Danner. Ernest Cassirer's concept of
myth as a symbolic form. Harvard, 1961.

1183. Clouser, Roy Anthony. Transcendental critique, ontological reduction, and religious belief in the
philosophy of Herman Dooyeweerd. Pennsylvania,
1972. 73-1369

1184. Coady, Sr. M. Anastasia. The phantom according to
the teaching of St. Thomas. Catholic U., 1932.

1185. Cobb, Robert Allan. The Cartesian principle of self-
evidence and Merleau-Ponty's thesis that "I am my
body." Toronto, 1974.

1186. Cobb, Veda Alison. Language and ontologies in Aristotle's *Categories*. Boston Coll., 1975.
75-20699

1187. Cobb, William. Attitudes. Yale, 1972. 73-14100

1188. Cobb, William Small, Jr. The relationship between
internal and social justice in Plato's *Republic*.
Vanderbilt, 1966. 66-8046

1189. Cobitz, Joseph Lester. The method of analysis in the
philosophy of Russell and Moore. Harvard, 1948.

1190. Coburn, Robert Craig. Concerning the justification
of memory-beliefs. Harvard, 1958.

1191. Cocchiarella, Nino Barnabas. Tense logic: a study
of temporal reference. U.C.L.A., 1966.
66-9326

1192. Cockayne, Charles Alexander. The relation of Spinoza to Hobbes. Yale, 1908.

1193. Cocutz, John Theodore. Kant's theory of self. Yale,
1950.

1194. Coder, David Allen. The identity thesis of mind and
body. Cornell, 1968. 69-5751

1195. Cody, Arthur Burrell. *Quid ius?*: an examination of
the claims made concerning the nature of valid law
and a new one advanced. Berkeley, 1961.

1196. Coe, William Jerome. Metaphilosophy and absolute presuppositions. Penn St., 1967. 68-11974

1197. Coffa, José Alberto. Foundations of inductive explanation. Pittsburgh, 1973. 74-6770

1198. Coffey, Daniel James. Leopoldo Zea and a problem-solving approach to philosophy. Northwestern, 1971. 71-30763

1199. Coffey, Patrick Joseph. Personal and impersonal moral reasoning. St. Louis, 1967. 68-1215

1200. Coffin, Charles M. John Donne and the new philosophy. Columbia, 1937.

1201. Coffin, Francis Howells. Santayana: a liberal and sceptical materialist. Columbia, 1955. 10171

1202. Coffin, Peter Robinson. Philosophy, education, and value: a philosophic study. Brown, 1960. 62-5737

1203. Cogan, James Ennis. Essay on phenomenological ontology: on description and analysis. Rice, 1971. 71-26276

1204. Cogan, Marc Roland. The role of the speeches in Thucydides' History of the Peloponnesian war. Chicago, 1974.

1205. Cogan, Robert. Some applications of recent logical theory to the problem of non-existence. Syracuse, 1972. 72-20318

1206. Cogell, Wayne Clifford. The foundations of Russell's philosophy of value. Missouri, 1969. 70-2973

1207. Coggin, Walter A. The role of the will in personality development. Catholic U., 1954.

1208. Cohen, Barry Frederick. A critical analysis of Sterling Lamprecht's theory of causality. Buffalo, 1971. 72-10485

1209. Cohen, Carl. The philosophical foundations of legal responsibility. U.C.L.A., 1955.

1210. Cohen, Cynthia Bachner. The logic and ontology of Ian Ramsey's theory of religious language. Columbia, 1970. 73-16192

1211. Cohen, Felix Solomon. The valuation of law. Harvard, 1929.

1212. Cohen, George. The categories of J.S. Mill. Columbia, 1967. 68-8572

1213. Cohen, Gordon Douglas. Mind-body identity, incorrigibility and conceptual revision. Loyola, 1973. 73-23141

1214. Cohen, Howard Samuel. Explanation in history: theory and practice. Harvard, 1971.

1215. Cohen, Margaret Linda. Three theories of obligation. Pittsburgh, 1975. 75-21749

1216. Cohen, Mark Nathan. The concept of space in Kant's Critique of pure reason: differences in the role of space in the aesthetic and analytic of the two editions of the Critique. C.U.N.Y., 1975. 75-19983

1217. Cohen, Maurice Herbert. Plato's use of ambiguity and deliberate fallacy: an interpretation of the implicit doctrines of the Charmides and Lysis. Columbia, 1963. 64-2741

1218. Cohen, Mendel Fisher. Determinism and human action. Illinois, 1961. 61-4277

1219. Cohen, Morris Raphael. Kant's doctrine as to the relation between duty and happiness. Harvard, 1906.

1220. Cohen, Saul Marc. Incorrigibility, avowals, and the concept of unconscious desire. Cornell, 1967. 67-12335

1221. Cohen, Sheldon Marc. Ethical naturalism and real definition. Northwestern, 1970. 71-1818

1222. Cohen, Stephen. A general theory of blaming. Chicago, 1974.

1223. Cohen, Ted. The grammar of taste. Harvard, 1972.

1224. Cohen, William Howard. A Rilkean aesthetics of poetry: a new interpretation of Rilke's Sonnets to Orpheus. So. Illinois, 1970. 71-2372

1225. Cohn, Priscilla. The idea of the nothing in the philosophy of Martin Heidegger. Bryn Mawr, 1969.

1226. Colacurcio, Robert Eugene. The perception of excellency as the glory of God in Jonathan Edwards: an essay towards the epistemology of discernment. Fordham, 1972. 73-1470.

1227. Cole, Herbert Brockett. The relevance of the intention of the artist to art criticism. Minnesota, 1973. 73-25590

1228. Cole, Richard. Possibilities. Chicago, 1962.

1229. Coleman, Donald Allan. In search of the laws of action. Columbia, 1965. 66-6926

1230. Coleman, Earle Jerome. Philosophy of painting by Shih-T'ao: a translation and exposition of his Hua-P'u (Treatise on the philosophy of painting.) Hawaii, 1971. 72-10163

1231. Coleman, Francis Jerome. An essay concerning critical reasoning. Johns Hopkins, 1963.

1232. Coleman, John. The concept of equality as held by Thomas Jefferson. Pittsburgh, 1934.

1233. Coleman, Michael Dixon. Beyond Sartre: toward a phenomenology of evolving consciousness. Cal., S. Barbara, 1972. 75-11490

1234. Coleman, Samuel. Reason in tradition: the political philosophy of Michael Oakeshott. Columbia, 1966. 66-12552

1235. Coleman, Winson. Knowledge and freedom in the political philosophies of Plato and Aristotle. Chicago, 1950.

1236. Collier, Kenneth William. An essay in epistemic logic. Pittsburgh, 1971. 72-13427

1237. Collinge, William Joseph. Faith and reason: Augustinian and analytic approaches. Yale, 1974. 75-15296

1238. Collingwood, Francis Joseph. The theory of being in Summa de bono (Book II) of Ulrich of Strasbourg: philosophical study and text. Toronto, 1952.

1239. Collins, Ardis Bea. The doctrine of being in the Theologia Platonica of Marsilio Ficino with special reference to the influence of Thomas Aquinas. Toronto, 1968.

1240. Collins, Arthur William. The logical structure of explanatory argument with special reference to history. Columbia, 1959.

1241. Collins, Edward Joseph. "Mundus est fabula" or the context and development of Descartes' scientific thought. Harvard, 1971.

1242. Collins, Gladys E. The principle of the best in the metaphysics of Leibniz. Radcliffe, 1937.

1243. Collins, James D. The Thomistic philosophy of the angels. Catholic U., 1944.

1244. Collins, Marie Taylor. Some modern conceptions of natural law. Cornell, 1919.

1245. Collins, Paul Weidner. The logic of functional analysis in anthropology. Columbia, 1964.
67-10354

1246. Collins, Robert Emmett. Eternity and time as predicated of God, angels, and men. Marquette, 1970.
71-5294

1247. Collinson, John. The structure of Berkeley's empiricism in The principles. Johns Hopkins, 1953.

1248. Colloque, Orrok. The concept of purpose; a philosophical thesis. N.Y.U., 1904. 74-3380

1249. Colman, George Tilden. Certain movements in England and America which influenced the transition from the ideals of personal righteousness of the 17th century to the modern ideals of social service. Chicago, 1915.

1250. Colter, Larry Wear, Jr. Propositions (argument that concept of a proposition is a theoretical one). Illinois, 1974. 75-11782

1251. Colucci, Robert Joseph. The meaning of history in the thought of Nietzsche. Penn St., 1971.
72-13837

1252. Colver, Anthony Wayne. Evidence and point of view in the writing of history. Harvard, 1957.

1253. Commenator, George Edward. Phenomenology of love in Max Scheler. Boston Coll., 1970. 70-24599

1254. Compton, John Joseph. Creativity and value. Yale, 1953.

1255. Conacher, Desmond J. Conceptions of pleasure in the pre-Socratic philosophers. Chicago, 1951.

1256. Condon, William Stephen. The Freudian model of human nature. Pittsburgh, 1962. 63-2421

1257. Confrey, Eugene Anthony. The appearance of inconsistency in J.S. Mill's reconciliation of liberty and equality. Yale, 1963. 67-11944

1258. Congdon, Howard Krebs. The principle of sufficient reason and the cosmological argument. Purdue, 1970. 70-18617

1259. Conger, George Perrigo. Theories of macrocosms and microcosms in the history of philosophy. Columbia, 1922.

1260. Congleton, Ann. Spinoza, Kierkegaard, and the eternal particular. Yale, 1962.

1261. Conkling, Mark Leslie. B.F. Skinner: a philosophical analysis. Oklahoma, 1974. 75-15252

1262. Conlan, Rev. F. Allan. A critique of the neo-naturalistic philosophy of religion of Henry Nelson Wieman in the light of Thomistic principles. Catholic U., 1958.

1263. Conley, Peter Vincent. The development of the notion of hermeneutics in the works of Bernard J. Lonergan, S.J. Catholic U., 1973. 73-21096

1264. Conlon, James Joseph. An interpretation of Nietzsche's overman. Marquette, 1975. 76-16874

1265. Conlon, William Joseph. The history of the problem of unicity and plurality of substantial form especially in the writings of Giles of Rome. St. John's, 1974. 75-3240

1266. Connell, Richard J. An exposition of St. Albert's De natura logicae. Laval, 1951.

1267. Connelly, George Edward. The existence and natures of God in the philosophy of Alfred North Whitehead. St. Louis, 1962. 64-3736

1268. Connelly, Kentigern. The role of self-experience in personality theory: a study of the Allport-Bertocci debate. Ottawa, 1974.

1269. Connelly, Robert Joseph. Negative prehension in Whitehead. St. Louis, 1970. 70-20377

1270. Connely, John Bradley. An analysis of the philosophical beliefs implicit within general semantics and their relevance for educational theory. Southern Cal., 1970. 70-23150

1271. Conner, Orville Glendon. Plato's theory of soul. Harvard, 1957.

1272. Connolly, James Denis. Thomas Hobbes and his recent

   critics. Pittsburgh, 1967.   68-6118

1273. Connolly, John Matthew. Action. Harvard, 1971.

1274. Connolly, William Richard, Jr. The given and the <u>a priori</u>: some issues in the epistemology of C.I. Lewis. Michigan St., 1973. 74-6024

1275. Connor, Joseph Gerard. The Jesuit college and electivism: a study in the philosophy of American education. Georgetown, 1959.

1276. Conover, Charles Eugene. The source of validity of moral obligation. Cincinnati, 1943.

1277. Conroy, David Loram. Plato's early theory of knowledge. Massachusetts, 1974. 75-6004

1278. Conroy, Graham Patrick. Language and morals in Berkeley's philosophy. Berkeley, 1957.

1279. Conway, David Alton. Religious faith: some contemporary views. Princeton, 1967. 68-2469

1280. Conway, Rev. James I. The nature of Cartesian realism. Fordham, 1952.

1281. Conway, Rev. Pierre Hyacinthe. Essays on immortality. Laval, 1946.

1282. Cook, Daniel Joseph. The role of language in Hegel's philosophy. Columbia, 1968. 69-9182

1283. Cook, Edward McLean. The deficient cause of moral evil according to St. Thomas. Catholic U., 1962. 63-255

1284. Cook, Gary Alan. The self as moral agent: a study in the philosophy of George Herbert Mead. Yale, 1966. 66-4889

1285. Cook, John Webber. An essay on Russell's conception of an ideal language. Nebraska, 1960. 60-4499

1286. Cook, Joyce Mitchell. A critical examination of Stephen C. Pepper's theory of value. Yale, 1965. 65-15025

1287. Cook, Monte Lee. Acts and objects: Malebranche and Arnauld on ideas. Iowa, 1971. 71-22013

1288. Cook, Sandra Bornholdt. Designators and reference: a causal theory of names. Wayne St., 1975. 76-10932

1289. Cooke, Reginald. The practical philosophy of F.E. Beneke. Wisconsin, 1915.

1290. Cooke, Roger Marvin. Non-objectivity in classical mechanics: an essay in the foundations of mechanics from the viewpoint of Heinrich Hertz. Yale, 1974.   75-1346

1291. Cooke, Vincent Michael. Wittgenstein's use of the private language discussion. Wisconsin, 1971.
   71-23293

1292. Cooley, John Cleveland. Mind and the new positivism. Yale, 1934.

1293. Cooney, Patrick Brian. The development of Cartesian metaphysics: Descartes, Malebranche and Geulincx. McGill, 1972.

1294. Coons, John Warren. The concept of control in John Dewey's philosophy. Iowa, 1933.

1295. Cooper, Barton Charles. An examination of the ethics of Francis Hutcheson. Berkeley, 1956.

1296. Cooper, Bryant Syme. The philosophy of Sir Oliver Lodge. Vanderbilt, 1934.

1297. Cooper, David E. A critique of John Rawls' theory of social justice. Waterloo, 1972.

1298. Cooper, John Madison. Plato's *Theaetetus*. Harvard, 1967.

1299. Cooper, William Frazier. Romero's theory of value. Indiana, 1967.   67-15077

1300. Cope, James Raymond. Religion and the dialectical materialism of Karl Marx. Ohio St., 1937.

1301. Copeland, Edith Ayres. Some ethical aspects of logical theory. Chicago, 1921.

1302. Copeland, John Wilson. Green, Bradley, and Sidgwick on ultimate good. Cornell, 1953.

1303. Copilowish, Irving Marmer. The logical paradoxes from 1897 to 1904. Michigan, 1948.

1304. Coppenger, Mark Thomas. A defense of phenomenalism. Vanderbilt, 1974.   74-22167

1305. Corbo, Claude. Les théories epistemologiques et sociales de T.B. Veblen (1857-1929); clefs pour une lecture de Veblen. Montreal, 1973.

1306. Corcoran, Rev. Albert C. Godefredi de Fontibus, quaestiones disputatae de vertutibus. Fordham, 1946.

1307. Corcoran, James Patrick. Hegel's philosophy of history. Illinois, 1974. 75-11783

1308. Corcoran, John Patrick, Jr. Generative structure in two-valued logics. Johns Hopkins, 1963.

1309. Cordero, Ronald Anthony. Gauthier, Stevenson, and practical reasoning. Illinois, 1969. 70-823

1310. Cording, Richard Arnold. Sartre's theory of freedom. Missouri, 1969. 69-16067

1311. Corea, Pater Vincent. The will and its freedom in the thought of Plato, Aristotle, Augustine and Kant. Boston U., 1961. 61-1099

1312. Corello, Anthony Vincent. Structures of the field of consciousness: a study of part-whole organization in William James' epistemology. New School, 1970. 71-10619

1313. Corish, Denis Joseph. Temporal order: a preliminary investigation of certain aspects, consistent with common usage, of a logic of time. Boston U., 1973. 73-23471

1314. Corliss, Richard Lee. A theory of contextual implication and its application to an analysis of religious belief. Illinois, 1968. 69-1321

1315. Cormier, Ramona Theresa. Toynbee and the problem of historical knowledge. Tulane, 1960. 60-6479

1316. Cornay, David Bruce. Evidence, temporalization, and transcendence: presence in a phenomenological ontology. Tulane, 1974. 75-2928

1317. Cornett, Linda Bowdoin. The undermining effects of Kant's psychological theory upon his ethics. Emory, 1970. 70-22879

1318. Cornett, Robert Arnold. Individualism in the ethics of Elijah Jordan. Illinois, 1953. 5953

1319. Cornman, James Welton. Linguistic reference and the mind-body problem. Brown, 1960. 62-5737

1320. Corr, Charles Anthony. Order and method in Christian Wolff's philosophy. St. Louis, 1966. 67-2944

1321. Corrado, Michael Louis. Modality de re and the problem of essentialism. Brown, 1970.   71-13852

1322. Corrigan, Mthr. Mary. A translation and a study of the Aristotelian sources of the Summa totius logicae Aristotelis. Fordham, 1934.

1323. Cortes Osorio, Alberto. Identity in quantum mechanics. Indiana, 1971.   72-6762

1324. Cory, Charles Edward. An examination of the doctrines of Hegel, especially their bearing upon the spiritual interests of man. Yale, 1905.

1325. Cosby, Gordon Grant. The moral reasons for legal excuses. Michigan, 1975.   75-20320

1326. Cosens, Grayson V. The nature and function of myth in the philosophies of Ernst Cassirer, Susanne K. Langer, and H.B. Alexander. Southern Cal., 1957.

1327. Costello, Edward Blair. The problem of evil in Plotinus, Leibniz and Aquinas. Northwestern, 1959.
60-425

1328. Costin, William Wilberforce. Introduction to the genetic treatment of the faith-consciousness in the individual. Johns Hopkins, 1908.

1329. Coté, André. La logique de la première opération. Laval, 1961.

1330. Cotton, David Avery Heath. Law in the Old Stoa and its antecedents. Southern Cal., 1968. 68-7177

1331. Cotton, James Harry. The finite self in the philosophy of Josiah Royce. Princeton, 1931.

1332. Coulson, William Rodney. Client-centered therapy and the nature of man. Notre Dame, 1964.   64-7959

1333. Coulter, Chan Lowell. Language and analysis in the philosophy of David Hume. Harvard, 1960.

1334. Courtney, Charles Edgar, Jr. Phenomenology and theism: Henry Duméry's proposal. Northwestern, 1965.
65-12062

1335. Cousins, Ewert Hilary. The notion of the person in the De trinitate of Richard of St. Victor. Fordham, 1966.   66-13497

1336. Cousins, Rev. Joseph D. Analysis of the epistemological and metaphysical background and import of the Protagorean relativity of sense impression. Duquesne, 1938.

1337. Coutant, Victor. Alexander of Aphrodisias: commentary on Book IV of Aristotle's Meteorologica. Columbia, 1936.

1338. Coval, Samuel Charles. Some limitations and expansions of the linguistic method in aesthetics. No. Carolina, 1957.

1339. Cowan, Joseph Lloyd. On explanations of the foundations of logic. Chicago, 1959.

1340. Cowan, Thomas Anthony. Criminal mind as criminal behavior. Pennsylvania, 1932.

1341. Cowling, Donald John. Augustine's theory of knowledge. Yale, 1909.

1342. Cox, Azizah al-Hibri. A defense of standard deontic logic. Pennsylvania, 1975. 76-3159

1343. Cox, Chana Berniker. Leibniz's philosophy of space. Columbia, 1971. 74-29576

1344. Cox, David F. Karl Marx's philosophy of value. Boston U., 1953.

1345. Cox, George Clarke. The philosophy of Richard Avenarius. Harvard, 1910.

1346. Cox, James William. An analysis of Paul Ricoeur's philosophy of the will and voluntary action. Vanderbilt, 1973. 73-25040

1347. Cox, Rev. John F. A Thomistic analysis of social order. Catholic U., 1943.

1348. Cox, Kendall Boice. Hume's theory of moral judgments in the Treatise. Michigan, 1963. 63-6892

1349. Cox, Ronald Ray. The phenomenology of relevance: a critical grounding of Schutz's theory of the life-world. Texas, 1971. 72-11333

1350. Coyne, Anthony Moncrief. Mathematical truth. No. Carolina, 1974. 74-26863

1351. Coyne, Margaret Urban. A critical study of two models for speech act analysis. Northwestern, 1975. 76-11880

1352. Cragg, Robert Cecil. Collingwood's logic of question and answer; a study of its logical and philosophical implications, and of its bearing on historical method. Toronto, 1948.

1353. Craig, Alastair Nicol. Matter and structure. Columbia, 1951.   2529

1354. Craighead, Houston Archer, Jr. Process and being: the concept of God in the philosophies of Charles Hartshorne and Paul Tillich. Texas, 1970.   70-18219

1355. Crane, Esther. The place of hypothesis in logic. Chicago, 1917.

1356. Cranford, William Ivy. Historical theories of perception. Yale, 1895.

1357. Cranor, Carl Forrest. Respect for persons. U.C.L.A., 1971.   72-11879

1358. Cranston, Mildred Welch. The teleclogical argument in the Gifford Lectures. Boston U., 1930.

1359. Crawford, Albert Berry. Privacy, morality, and self-interest. So. Illinois, 1968.   69-6259

1360. Crawford, Dan Duvall. Gustav Bergmann's theory of perception. Pittsburgh, 1972.   72-22452

1361. Crawford, David Robert. Manifestations and interpretations of alienation from the self. DePaul, 1972.   72-31243

1362. Crawford, Donald Wesley. Kant's aesthetics. Wisconsin, 1965.   65-10594

1363. Crawford, Jeffrey William. Essentialism and possible worlds. Wayne St., 1975.   75-25233

1364. Crawford, John Forsyth. The relation of inference to fact in Mill's logic. Chicago, 1913.

1365. Crawford, Patricia Ann. The concept of a physical object- its role in thought and language. Minnesota, 1959.   60-916

1366. Crawford, William Rex. The freeman's morals: a critique of the philosophy of Remy de Gourmont. Pennsylvania, 1926.

1367. Creary, Lewis Graham. The pragmatic justification of induction: a critical examination. Princeton, 1969.   70-8357

1368. Creath, John Richard. Science, syntax, and semantics: an examination of the philosophy of language of

Rudolf Carnap. Pittsburgh, 1975.   75-21750

1369. Creed, Isabel P. A critical study of the philosophy of logic and theory of meaning of recent positivism. Berkeley, 1936.

1370. Creegan, Robert F. Human individuality, philosophically considered. Duke, 1939.

1371. Creel, Richard Earl. Dewey's theory of the common good. So. Illinois, 1969.   70-7272

1372. Creer, Leland Morrison. A defense of the covering law theory of historical explanation. Utah, 1966.
66-8084

1373. Creighton, J.E. The will; its structure and mode of action. Cornell, 1892.

1374. Crem, Theresa. A commentary on the *Rhetoric* of Aristotle- Book I, chapter 1-2. Laval, 1958.

1375. Cremer, Peter Simon. Moral individualism. Berkeley, 1972.

1376. Crenshaw, Floyd Dale. The cosmological approach to theism: a study in contemporary British philosophy. Vanderbilt, 1964.   64-10550

1377. Cress, Donald Alan. Descartes and his encounter with the sceptical dragon. Marquette, 1972.
73-8269

1378. Cresswell, John Reginald. The position of value in the philosophical system of S. Alexander. Cornell, 1926.

1379. Crichton, John Willison. The principles of living beings: an exploratory essay. Michigan, 1965.
65-5289

1380. Crimmel, Henry H., Jr. Verbalism and nihilism. Chicago, 1960.

1381. Crissman, Paul. The moral philosophy of John Dewey. Northwestern, 1930.

1382. Critelli, Ida JoAnn. The political good in the philosophy of John Locke. Marquette, 1965.
67-3626

1383. Crittenden, Charles Christopher. Referring and existence. Cornell, 1964.   64-13827

1384. Crocker, David Alan. A Whiteheadian theory of intentions and actions. Yale, 1970.   70-25254

1385. Crocker, John Lawrence. Necessity and unrevisability. Harvard, 1970.

1386. Crocker, Sylvia Mae Fleming. Ontology and the ontological argument. Missouri, 1969.   69-16068

1387. Crockett, Campbell. The problem of universals. Cincinnati, 1949.

1388. Croddy, William Stephen. Meaning in oral communication. Brown, 1970.   71-13853

1389. Crom, Scott Edward. Collingwood and metaphysics. Yale, 1952.

1390. Cronan, Rev. Edward P. The dignity of a human person. Catholic U., 1950.

1391. Cronin, Francis Raymund. Complexity-consciousness in Teilhard de Chardin. Fordham, 1971.
                                                 71-20158

1392. Cronin, Rev. John F. Cardinal Newman: his theory of knowledge. Catholic U., 1935.

1393. Cronin, Timothy John. Objective being, in Descartes' thought and in a source of Descartes. Toronto, 1956.

1394. Cronk, George Francis. George Herbert Mead on time and action. So. Illinois, 1971.   72-10246

1395. Cronkhite, Roland Frederick. The metaphysics of love in contemporary existentialism with special emphasis on Jean-Paul Sartre. Catholic U., 1970.
                                                 71-12496

1396. Cronquist, John. Hare and prescriptivism. Stanford, 1972.   73-4485

1397. Crooks, Ezra Breckenridge. Religion as experience. Harvard, 1910.

1398. Crosby, April Evalyn. Some ethical obligations of liberal arts college professors. Vanderbilt, 1974.
                                                 75-1131

1399. Crosby, H. Lamar, Jr. Thomas of Bradwardine: his Tractatus de proportionibus and its significance for the development of mathematical physics. Columbia, 1953.

1400. Crosson, Frederick James. Presence and subjectivity. Notre Dame, 1956. 17752

1401. Crow, Carolyn D. Belief. Bryn Mawr, 1967.

1402. Crowell, Edward Floyd. On the ambiguity of "obligation." U. of Washington, 1967. 67-14163

1403. Crowley, Sr. Margaret Ellen. The notion of nature in the corpuscular philosophy of Robert Boyle. Marquette, 1970. 71-5296

1404. Crowley, William A. The logic of the early Greek physicians. Chicago, 1917.

1405. Crumbine, Nancy Jay. The same river twice: a critique of the place of eros in the philosophy of Kierkegaard. Penn St., 1972. 73-13962

1406. Cua, Antonio So. Richard Price and contemporary ethical intuitionism. Berkeley, 1958.

1407. Cudahy, Brian James. A prologue to some theories on causality. St. Bonaventure, 1962.

1408. Cudmore, Ann Kreilkamp. Language as Wittgenstein's way of life. Boston U., 1973.

1409. Culbertson, James Thomas. The place of the sense world in physical theory. Yale, 1940.

1410. Culhane, Sr. Marietta. A philosophical clarification of the contemporary concept of self-identity. Georgetown, 1973. 74-14920

1411. Cullen, Bernard Anthony. Hegel's unsuccessful quest for harmony. Michigan, 1975. 76-9377

1412. Cullen, John Charles. The unity of René Le Senne's philosophy. St. Louis, 1974. 74-24063

1413. Culp, Cordie Jacob. The ethical idea of renunciation. N.Y.U., 1914. 73-17806

1414. Cummens, John Albert. Self-knowledge and historical consciousness. So. Illinois, 1972. 72-28532

1415. Cumming, Robert J. The psychological structure of Descartes' moral philosophy. Chicago, 1950.

1416. Cummings, Philip Wilbur. Hegel's *Logic* as a critique of the logical theories of his predecessors. Pittsburgh, 1972. 73-1644

1417. Cummins, Phillip Daniel. Pierre Bayle's critique of matter and its impact on modern philosophy. Iowa St., 1961. 61-5557

1418. Cummins, Robert Charles. Programs and theories of behavior. Michigan, 1970. 71-23728

1419. Cummins, William Joseph. Plato's theory of human motivation. Emory, 1975. 75-23680

1420. Cunningham, Francis James. Eros and eidos: Plato's inchoate theory of creativity. Fordham, 1974. 74-19645

1421. Cunningham, Frank. Some contributions of Morris R. Cohen to American philosophy. Boston U., 1951.

1422. Cunningham, Frank Arthur. Objectivity in social science. Toronto, 1970.

1423. Cunningham, Henri-Paul. Biologie et finalité. Laval, 1971.

1424. Cunningham, Holly Estil. Three types of logical theory. Chicago, 1918.

1425. Cunningham, Sr. Miriam Ann. Certitude and the philosophy of science. Catholic U., 1960.

1426. Cunningham, Robert L. The Aristotelian notion of nature. Laval, 1951.

1427. Cunningham, Stanley Byrne. The significance of St. Albert the Great's De bono in early thirteenth-century moral philosophy. Toronto, 1965.

1428. Cunningham, Suzanne M. Language and intersubjectivity in the phenomenology of Edmund Husserl. Florida St., 1972. 72-27910

1429. Cunningham, William. The basis of realism. Catholic U., 1912.

1430. Cupples, Brian William. Explanation in science. W. Ontario, 1973.

1431. Curley, Edwin Munson. Spinoza's metaphysics: an interpretation. Duke, 1963. 64-4732

1432. Curley, Thomas Vincent. Peirce's search for a method. Fordham, 1968. 69-2588

1433. Curran, Charles Arthur. An analysis of a process of therapy through counselling and its implications for a philosophy of personality. Ohio St., 1944.

1434. Curran, Thomas Joseph. The teachability of virtue according to Plato. Southern Cal., 1969.
69-17877

1435. Curran, William Stephen. Logical form and explanatory models. Texas, 1974. 74-24845

1436. Currey, Earnest C. The concept of man as the basis of morality: a critical study of some philosophical attempts to ground morality on the essence of man. N.Y.U., 1973. 74-13318

1437. Currie, Bethia S. God and matter in early Stoic physics. New School, 1971. 72-4029

1438. Currie, Cecil. Ernst Troeltsch's philosophy of history. Harvard, 1946.

1439. Curtis, Barry Alan. Principles of practical reasoning. Harvard, 1975.

1440. Curtis, Carl Harold. A reexamination of F.H. Bradley's critique of relations. Southern Cal., 1975.
76-5238

1441. Curtler, Hugh Mercer, Jr. Subjectivism, objectivism and certain tendencies in current British and American ethical theory. Northwestern, 1964.
65-3254

1442. Cushman, Herbert Ernest. The historical development of the concepts of causality. Harvard, 1897.

1443. Cutler, Anna Alice. The influence of aesthetical considerations upon Kant's theory of knowledge. Yale, 1896.

1444. Cutter, Walter Airey. The philosophy of religion in America since 1900. Duke, 1933.

1445. Cwi, David. William James's "pure experience" philosophy: genesis and criticism. Johns Hopkins, 1973. 74-10404

1446. Czajkowski, Casimir J. The theory of private property in John Locke's political philosophy. Notre Dame, 1941.

1447. Czerwionka, Felicia Emily. The self in William James' psychology. Notre Dame, 1974. 74-8893

- D -

1448. Daams, Gerritt. Competing loyalties and practical decisions. Columbia, 1952.

1449. Dady, Sr. Mary Rachael. The theory of knowledge of Saint Bonaventure. Catholic U., 1939.

1450. Daher, Adel Hussein. God, factuality and necessity. N.Y.U., 1967. 68-6054

1451. Dahl, Leif Nelson. Marcuse on the individual in the advanced industrial society. So. Illinois, 1974. 75-109

1452. Dahl, Norman Olav. An examination of the principle that "ought" implies "can." Berkeley, 1971.

1453. Daise, Benjamin. Kierkegaard's pseudonymous works. Texas, 1973. 74-5225

1454. Dakin, Arthur H., Jr. The supernatural in the religious philosophy of Baron Friedrich von Hügel. Princeton, 1933.

1455. Dale, Robert Donald. Generic statements: a critical examination of some recent theories. Berkeley, 1973. 74-15306

1456. Daley, James William. Freud and moral philosophy. Northwestern, 1966. 67-4213

1457. Daley, John B. The Christian explanation of the problem of suffering. Niagara, 1936.

1458. D'Alfonso, Joseph. Some metaphysical implications of the category of potentiality. Boston U., 1942.

1459. Daling, John Thomas. The theory of perception of Thomas Reid, an exposition and re-evaluation. Michigan, 1943.

1460. Dalkey, Norman Crolee. The plurality of language structures. U.C.L.A., 1942.

1461. Dallery, Arleen Beberman. On the loss of the other in existence and philosophy. Yale, 1969. 70-15690

1462. Dallery, Robert Carleton. Philosophy as integrative

speech: studies in Plato and Merleau-Ponty, with an appendix: a translation of Maurice Merleau-Ponty's L'Oeil et l'esprit. Yale, 1968.
69-13096

1463. Dalrymple, Edwin Stuart, III. On Hegel's doctrine of the notion as universality, particularity and individuality. Yale, 1974. 75-1349

1464. Dalrymple, Houghton B. Experience and knowing: an introduction to a theory of knowledge. Texas, 1955.

1465. Dalton, Peter Cornelius. Conscious states. Rochester, 1973. 73-14802

1466. Daly, Sr. Jeanne Joseph. The metaphysical foundation of free will as a transcendental aspect of the act of existence in the philosophy of St. Thomas Aquinas. Catholic U., 1958.

1467. Daly, Br. John Emmanuel. Orestes A. Brownson and transcendentalism. Fordham, 1955.

1468. Daly, Richard Timon, Jr. Applications of the mathematical theory of linguistics. Washington U., 1970. 71-11031

1469. Damhorst, Rev. Donald Edward. Social norms and Protestant ethics: the ethical views of Reirhold Niebuhr and H. Richard Niebuhr. St. Louis, 1963.
64-4239

1470. D'Amico, Robert. Consciousness and history: phenomenological and structuralist philosophies of the human sciences. Buffalo, 1974. 75-7740

1471. D'Amour, Donald Henry. Aristotle on heroes. Notre Dame, 1971. 71-27753

1472. D'Amour, Gene Albert. Political theory as a science or ethical theory as the hard core of a scientific research program. Minnesota, 1971. 72-5519

1473. Dana, Edmund Trowbridge. The true, the right, and the good. Harvard, 1912.

1474. Dancy, Russell Mather. Possibility and eternity in Aristotle. Harvard, 1966.

1475. D'Angelo, Edward. Soft and hard determinism. Buffalo, 1966. 65-12107

1476. Daniel, Sr. Marion Agnes. Josiah Royce: the embodiment of the American experience in community.

Fordham, 1970.   71-8707

1477. Daniels, George Harrison, Jr. Baconian science in
      America, 1815-1845. Iowa, 1963.   64-3360

1478. Danielson, Peter Andrew. The justification of pro-
      perty rights. Toronto, 1975.

1479. Danner, Edwin R. Leibniz and the present view of
      freedom. American U., 1931.

1480. Dannhauser, Werner J. Nietzsche's image of Socrates.
      Chicago, 1971.

1481. Danto, Arthur Coleman. Acts and histories. Colum-
      bia, 1953.   6596

1482. D'Arienzo, William A. "Don Quijote de la Mancha":
      a study of the political philosophy of Cervantes.
      New School, 1970.   71-12836

1483. Darlington, James Henry. Philosophy of Immanuel
      Kant. Princeton, 1884.

1484. Darlington, Jared Lloyd. A priori probability and
      inductive estimation. Yale, 1957.

1485. Darmstadter, Howard Michael. W.V.O. Quine on trans-
      lation. Princeton, 1967.   68-8916

1486. Darnoi, Rev. Dennis N. Kenedy. Edward von Hartmann's
      metaphysics of the unconscious: a historical study
      and an evaluation on the basis of Aristotelian
      and Thomistic principles. Catholic U., 1964.
                                                 64-12487

1487. Darwall, Stephen Leicester. Reason, self-regard, and
      morality. Pittsburgh, 1972.   73-16339

1488. Das, Parimal. Foundations for guidance in Indian
      philosophical and social thought. Columbia, 1950.
                                                     1840

1489. Dashiell, John Frederick. The philosophical status
      of values. Columbia, 1913.

1490. Dauenhauer, Bernard Peter. Some uses of the concept
      of causality in theories of explanation. Tulane,
      1968.   68-15241

1491. Dauer, Francis Watanabe. Criteria and the inner life.
      Harvard, 1970.

1492. Daugert, Stanley M. The philosophy of Thorstein Veblen. Columbia, 1950.

1493. Daugherty, Donald Hayes. Truth in art: an analysis of the types of truth-judgment used in aesthetic criticism. Ohio St., 1930.

1494. Davenport, Charles Kidder. Neural integration in relation to the environment. Yale, 1929.

1495. Davenport, Manuel Manson. A critical study of the value and ethical theory of C.I. Lewis made by reference to current psychological theories of perception. Illinois, 1957.   58-4376

1496. David, Gerald Lee. Logical positivism, the mind-body problem and immortality. Yeshiva, 1974.
   75-20589

1497. David, Keith Raymond. Percept and concept in William James. So. Illinois, 1969.   70-7273

1498. Davidson, Donald Herbert. Plato's *Philebus*. Harvard, 1949.

1499. Davidson, Henry N. Ucken's philosophy: foundation of characteristic religion. N.Y.U., 1908. 73-20699

1500. Davie, William Eugene. Prudence. Cal., Irvine, 1969.   70-279

1501. Davies, Arthur Ernest. A critical examination of Hume's psychology of knowledge. Yale, 1898.

1502. Davies, Henry. Origen's theory of knowledge. Yale, 1896.

1503. Davies, Rev. Julian A. Some problems of will in ordinary language philosophy. Fordham, 1970.
   71-8708

1504. Davies, Samuel Harry. Some aspects of the concept of substance. Michigan, 1932.

1505. Davis, Arthur P. Isaac Watts, his life and works. Columbia, 1943.

1506. Davis, Bernard Eugene, Jr. Notion of protomeaning. M.I.T., 1968.

1507. Davis, Charles C., Jr. An investigation concerning the Hilbert-Sierpinski logical form of the axiom of choice. Notre Dame, 1973.   74-49

1508. Davis, Clarence George. Obligation and aspiration

in ethics. Indiana, 1962. 63-3813

1509. Davis, Devra. Conceptualizations of religion and science in some writings of Emmanuel Kant and Auguste Comte. Chicago, 1972.

1510. Davis, Helen Edna. Tolstoy and Nietzsche; a problem in biographical ethics, with a forward by John Dewey. Columbia, 1929.

1511. Davis, John Barnabas. The Hermeneutics of Baconian tradition: a study of Barfield's poetical semantic. Penn St., 1973. 74-20913

1512. Davis, John Whitney. Imagism in Locke, Berkeley, and Hume. Boston U., 1957. 57-2521

1513. Davis, John William. Value and individuality: an inquiry into the worth of the human person. Emory, 1959. 59-3530

1514. Davis, Lawrence Howard. The concepts of action and agency. Michigan, 1969. 70-14496

1515. Davis, Merrill C. The concept of transcendence in the philosophy of Alfred North Whitehead. Chicago, 1963.

1516. Davis, Michael Peter. The duality of soul in Plato's Philebus. Penn St., 1974. 75-19742

1517. Davis, Michael Stuart. Representation and consent: an inquiry into the foundations of political obligation. Michigan, 1972. 72-29026

1518. Davis, Philip Edward. The Cartesian and Spinozistic theories of time. Yale, 1955.

1519. Davis, Ralph Marchant. Some philosophic problems of the sense of touch. Oregon, 1957. 67-16155

1520. Davis, Richard Slaton. Whitehead's moral philosophy. Washington U., 1971. 71-27321

1521. Davis, Robert Evan. The meaning and validity of religious language. Nebraska, 1958. 58-3766

1522. Davis, Stephen Thane. Faith and evidence: an epistemological study of the nature of religious faith. Claremont, 1970. 71-13682

1523. Davis, Steven. Illocutionary acts and transformational grammar. Illinois, 1968. 68-12100

1524. Davis, Thomas Duncan. Sartre: without complaints or

excuses. Michigan, 1975. 75-29204

1525. Davis, William Hatcher. The philosophy of C.S. Peirce. Rice, 1965. 65-10323

1526. Davison, Joanne Letitia. The shaping of a seventeenth century Confucian philosopher: the thought and environment of Li Yung. Stanford, 1974.
74-20185

1527. Davitt, Rev. Thomas Edwin. The relation between the concept of law and the philosophy of intellect and will. St. Louis, 1950.

1528. Dawson, Rev. William Francis. A study in emotivism with an Aristotelian response. Notre Dame, 1968.
68-9416

1529. Day, Abbyann. The <u>Concordantia</u> <u>veritatis</u> attributed to Benedict of Assignano: text and study. Toronto, 1953.

1530. Day, Rev. Francis T. The concept of being in the metaphysics of Suarez. Fordham, 1951.

1531. Day, Sebastian J. Intuitive cognition: a key to the significance of the later scholastics. St. Bonaventure, 1947.

1532. Day, Thomas Franklin. Israel's messianic consciousness. Syracuse, 1916.

1533. Day, Thomas Paul. The role of the <u>Lebenswelt</u> in the later philosophy of John Wild. St. Bonaventure, 1973. 73-24342

1534. Daye, Douglas Dunsmore. Metalogical studies in sixth-century Buddhist proto-metalogic from the Sanskrit and Chinese texts of the Nyayapravesa: or unpacking ordinary Sanskrit. Wisconsin, 1972.
72-31526

1535. Dayton, Eric Brian. Desire and practical reason. W. Ontario, 1973.

1536. Deal, Thomas W. Ernst Cassirer's philosophy of history. So. Illinois, 1970. 71-9982

1537. Dean, Thomas Jackson. The logic of language and persons: a methodological introduction to the interpretive metaphysics of Heidegger. Columbia, 1968.
69-12960

1538. Deangelis, William James. The empiricists' theory of the will. Cornell, 1970. 71-1052

1539. Debbins, William. The philosophy of R.G. Collingwood. Syracuse, 1959. 59-2661

1540. DeBenedictus, Matthew M. The social thought of St. Bonaventure. Catholic U., 1946.

1541. DeBlois, Austen Kennedy. The present stage and tendency of philosophy in America. Brown, 1889.

1542. DeBoe, Cornelius M. The distinction between the primordial and consequent natures of God in the philosophy of Professor Alfred North Whitehead. Princeton, 1939. 571

1543. De Boer, Cecil. Space-time and conpresence: a critical discussion of the philosophy of S. Alexander. Michigan, 1929.

1544. De Boer, Jesse. A critical study of Bergson's theory of change, duration and causality. Harvard, 1942.

1545. De Boer, Lawrence Paul. Valuation and judgments in metaphysics and religion: a study of the philosophy of Alfred North Whitehead. Columbia, 1967. 67-14037

1546. De Bow, Robert Shallcross. The idealism of Berkeley. Pennsylvania, 1890.

1547. De Brabander, Rev. René Firman. The immanent philosophy and transcendent religion: Henry Duméry's philosophy of Christianity. Georgetown, 1965. 65-15130

1548. Debrock, Guy J. *Sache und sage*: the development of the problem of language in Hegel's early philosophy. Boston Coll., 1973. 73-16440

1549. Debus, Ute Irmgard. A critical analysis of Husserl's *Ideen* *I*. Johns Hopkins, 1971. 71-29194

1550. DeCesare, Richard Angelo. A comparative evaluation of the social self in the philosophies of George Herbert Mead and Gabriel Marcel. Boston Coll., 1968. 69-9824

1551. Dechert, Charles R. Thomas More and society: a study in renaissance thought. Catholic U., 1952.

1552. Deck, John Norbert. Nature as contemplation in Plotinus. Toronto, 1960.

1553. Deckert, Marion George. Some criticisms of the application to English of a Quinian definition of logical truth. Chicago, 1969.

1554. De Coursey, Sr. M. Edwin. The theory of evil in the metaphysics of St. Thomas and its contemporary significance. Catholic U., 1948.

1555. Deeken, Alfons Theodor. Ethics and history in Max Scheler. Fordham, 1973. 74-2736

1556. Deetz, Stanley Albert. Essays on hermeneutics and communication research. Ohio U., 1973.
73-25740

1557. DeGeorge, Richard Thomas. Solitude and communion: a study of their meaning and relation in human existence. Yale, 1959.

1558. DeGrood, David Harry. An examination of the category of essence from the pre-Socratics to Locke. Buffalo, 1966. 68-12108

1559. DeGruchy, Raymond Paul. Ready-made facts and meaning: a critique of realist theories of truth. Waterloo, 1972.

1560. DeHaven, Steven Lee. Intensionality and intentionality. Toronto, 1971.

1561. Deininger, Whitaker Thompson. Historical analysis in America: a selective appraisal of some recent types. Columbia, 1953. 4564

1562. Deitsch, Martin. The logic of criteria with special application to mental predicates. Michigan, 1969.
69-17990

1563. DeKoninck, Thomas. Les contraintes et l'immaterialité de l'intelligence. Laval, 1971.

1564. De Kryger-Monsman, Diana. The conception of the self in absolute idealism with special reference to the philosophy of Mary W. Kalkins. Johns Hopkins, 1934.

1565. Delacruz, Enrique Buado, Jr. Presupposition: towards an analysis. U.C.L.A., 1974. 74-24629

1566. DeLacy, Estelle Allen. Meaning and methodology in Hellenistic philosophy. Chicago, 1935.

1567. deLaguna, T. de L. The relation of ethics to evolution. Cornell, 1901.

1568. Delaney, Cornelius Francis. Mind and nature in Cohen,

Woodbridge and Sellars. St. Louis, 1968.
68-14063

1569. Delaney, Howard Raymond. The doctrine of four term analogy in Aristotle. St. Louis, 1959.
60-328

1570. DeLange, David Leroy. Three theories of free action. Brown, 1971. 72-8104

1571. deLarge, Percy Lee. Empirical method in science and philosophy. Chicago, 1928.

1572. Delattre, Edwin Jules. Objectivity and the passive knower. Texas, 1970. 70-18222

1573. De la Vega, Rev. Francis J. Social progress and happiness in the philosophy of St. Thomas Aquinas and contemporary American sociology. Catholic U., 1949.

1574. Del Carril, Mario Federico. Types, tokens and subjects. Minnesota, 1974. 74-17240

1575. Delehant, Sr. M. Dunstan. The role of quality in the philosophy of St. Thomas Aquinas. Catholic U., 1950.

1576. Delfini, Alexander F.M. Genesis and structure of H. Marcuse's social philosophy. Buffalo, 1974.

1577. DeLillo, Nicholas Joseph. On logical definability: an investigation into the theory of logical definability and several of its consequences. N.Y.U., 1971. 71-28529

1578. Della Penta, Clement Joseph. The social value of hope in modern social thought and Thomas Aquinas. Catholic U., 1942.

1579. Dellasala, John Anthony. A resemblance theory of universals. N.Y.U., 1973. 74-13320

1580. DeLong, Howard. The development of R.G. Collingwood's theory of history. Princeton, 1960. 61-1983

1581. DeLong, Russell Victor. The concept of personality in the philosophy of Ralph Barton Perry. Boston U., 1940.

1582. DeLuca, Anthony James. Freud's contribution to a philosophy of religion. Fordham, 1971.
71-26963

1583. De Lucca, John. Immediacy and immutability: a study

in the theory of knowledge. Ohio St., 1955.
15825

1584. De Maio, Arthur Anthony. The idea of the absolute, according to Benedetto Croce. St. John's, 1967.
68-3822

1585. Demand, Nancy Hobbs. Plato's concept of law in the later dialogues. Pennsylvania, 1965. 65-13320

1586. DeMarco, Donald Thomas. The nature of the relationship between the mathematical and the beautiful in music. St. John's, 1969. 70-1357

1587. DeMarco, Joseph Peter. The nature and function of the concept of the community in the early and later thought of C.S. Peirce. Penn St., 1969.
70-19403

1588. DeMatteis, Philip Breed. Individuality and the social organism: the controversy between Max Stirner and Karl Marx. So. Illinois, 1972. 73-6198

1589. Demecs, Desiderio Dezsö. A critical analysis of Georg Lukács' social philosophy of art. Buffalo, 1965. 65-10153

1590. Demopoulos, William George. On the possibility structure of physical systems. W. Ontario, 1974.

1591. Demos, Raphael. The definition of judgment. Harvard, 1916.

1592. Demura, Teizaburo. The nature of religious truth. Harvard, 1912.

1593. Denecke, Rev. Charles J. The role and importance of self-existence in the science of metaphysics. Georgetown, 1945.

1594. De Nicolas, Antonio T. Four-dimensional man: the implicit philosophy of the Rgveda. Fordham, 1971.
71-20159

1595. Denise, Theodore Cullom. The social writings of the philosopher Bertrand Russell. Michigan, 1955.
12196

1596. Dennehy, Raymond Leo. The subject as the metaphysical ground of Maritain's personalism. Toronto, 1973.

1597. Dennen, Rev. Gerard F. The vision of truth in the doctrine of Saint Augustine. Fordham, 1955.

1598. Denty, Michael William. Reminders of God: on the uses of argument in religious discourse. Notre Dame, 1975.　75-27985

1599. De Nys, Martin J. The Hegelian sources of Marx' concept of man. Loyola, 1973.　74-16940

1600. De Olaso, Ezequiel. Leibniz and Greek scepticism. Bryn Mawr, 1969.

1601. De Paoli, Donald Angelo. Freedom and mutuality. Fordham, 1971.　71-20160

1602. Derden, James Kirwin, Jr. Analyticity and scientific theories with special reference to the work of Rudolf Carnap. Toronto, 1971.

1603. Desen, Wilfred Désiré. The ontology of Jean-Paul Sartre: essay of systematization and critique. Harvard, 1951.

1604. Desharnais, Rev. Richard Paul. The history of the distinction between God's absolute and ordained power and its influence on Martin Luther. Catholic U., 1966.　67-1251

1605. Deshpande, Madhav Murlidhar. Kaundabhatta on the philosophy of nominal meaning. Pennsylvania, 1972.　72-25563

1606. De Silva, Manikku Wadu Padmasiri. A study of motivational theory in early Buddhism with reference to the psychology of Freud. Hawaii, 1967.　67-13693

1607. Desjardins, Paul Jacques Roy Dit. The form of Platonic inquiry. Yale, 1959.

1608. Desjardins, Rosemary. The rational enterprise: *Logos* in Plato's *Theaetetus*. Pennsylvania, 1975.　76-3162

1609. Desmonde, William H. Self-actualization: loving and strategic. Columbia, 1951.

1610. De Sousa Pernes Bon, Ronald. Categories, translation, and linguistic theory. Princeton, 1966.　67-7383

1611. Dethlefs, Ferris Henry. Descriptive meanings. Harvard, 1953.

1612. Detrixhe, Wylene Rae Wisby. God and evil: the theistic dilemma. Vanderbilt, 1973.　74-1337

1613. Detsch, Richard Ralph. Georg Trakl: a search for oneness. Colorado, 1971. 71-5884

1614. Deutsch, Eliot Sandler. Approaches to mysticism: a study of the interpretations of Rudolph Otto, Evelyn Underhill, Sri Aurobindo. Columbia, 1960. 60-2447

1615. Devereux, Anne Rogers. Der vorgriff (the pre-apprehension of being) and the religious act in Karl Rahner. Georgetown, 1973. 74-1427

1616. Devine, Philip Edwards. The very idea of an ontological argument. Berkeley, 1972.

1617. Devitt, Michael James. The semantics of proper names: a causal theory. Harvard, 1972.

1618. DeVos, Peter Allen. Metaphysics, science, and certainty: a study of some key Cartesian notions. Brown, 1973. 74-3000

1619. Devrnja, Milutin P. The conceptions of human existence in the early works of F.M. Dostoevskii. Buffalo, 1972. 72-27243

1620. Dewan, John Lawrence. The doctrine of being of John Capreolus; a contribution to the history of the notion of esse. Toronto, 1967.

1621. Dewart, Leslie Sutherland. The development of Karl Pearson's scientific philosophy. Toronto, 1954.

1622. Dewey, Ernest Wayne. Thorstein Veblen's general theory of valuation. Texas, 1954.

1623. Dewey, John. Psychology of Kant. Johns Hopkins, 1884.

1624. Dewey, Malcolm Howard. Herder's relation to the aesthetic theory of his time; a contribution based on the fourth critical Wäldchen. Chicago, 1918.

1625. Dewey, Robert Eugene. Operationalism as an epistemological theory of meaning. Harvard, 1949.

1626. Dewhurst, David William. The unconscious. Cornell, 1971. 72-13152

1627. Dewing, Arthur Stone. Negation and intuition in the philosophy of Schelling. Harvard, 1905.

1628. Dewitz, Ludwig Richard. The role of the hereafter in ancient Israel. Johns Hopkins, 1960.

1629. DeWolf, Lotan H. Premises of the arguments concerning the immortality in thirty Ingersoll lectures (1896-1934). Boston U., 1935.

1630. Diamadopoulos, Peter. Aristotle on accountability and responsibility: Ethica nicomachea book Γ, i-v. Harvard, 1957.

1631. Dicker, Georges. Knowing and coming-to-know in Dewey's theory of knowledge. Wisconsin, 1969.
70-3512

1632. Dickie, George Thomas. A critical interpretation and evaluation of the main features of the moral sense philosophy of Francis Hutcheson as presented in his Inquiry, essay, and illustrations with an analysis of the previous criticism of these features. U.C.L.A., 1959.

1633. Dickinson, Frank. Dualism and functionalism. Chicago, 1929.

1634. Dickoff, James William. Analytic ethics: from Moore to Good as an external mode. Yale, 1962.

1635. Didoha, Michael. Conceptual distortion and intuitive creativity (a study of the role of knowledge in the thought of Nicholas Berdyaev.) Georgetown, 1969. 70-4630

1636. Diefenbeck, James Allen. The nature of historical knowledge. Harvard, 1950.

1637. Diehl, Frank. An historical and critical study of radical behaviorism as a philosophical doctrine. Johns Hopkins, 1932.

1638. Dietl, Paul Joseph. Explanation and action: an examination of the controversy between Hume and some of his contemporary critics. Indiana, 1964.
65-3474

1639. Dietrichson, Paul. Freedom and responsibility. Yale, 1955.

1640. Dietz, R.P. Conrad. Ortega y Gasset on idealism. Laval, 1970.

1641. DiFederico, Gabriel Joseph. The ontological argument: Anselm's intention. St. John's, 1970.
71-9527

1642. Diggs, Bernard J. Love and being: an investigation into the metaphysics of St. Thomas Aquinas. Columbia, 1947.

1643. DiGiovanna, Joseph J. Linguistic phenomenology: philosophical method in J.L. Austin. Notre Dame, 1972.　　　　　　　　　　　　　　　　　72-26803

1644. DiGiovanni, Giorgio. Contingency: its foundation in Hegel's logic of becoming. Toronto, 1970.

1645. Di Lascia, Alfred Paul. Don Luigi Sturzo: a study in transcendental historical relativism. Fordham, 1968.　　　　　　　　　　　　　　　　68-11012

1646. Diller, Elliot Van Nostrand. The concept of feeling in the religious philosophy of Schleiermacher. Harvard, 1934.

1647. Dillhoff, Frank C. How is scholastic logic facing modern logic? Pittsburgh, 1951.

1648. Dillick, Sidney. The political philosophy of John Dewey. Toronto, 1942.

1649. Dillon, David A. An inquiry into the notion of Christian philosophy. Laval, 1950.

1650. Dillon, James Patrick. Idea and object in the philosophy of Josiah Royce. Boston Coll., 1969.
　　　　　　　　　　　　　　　　　　　　　70-3371

1651. Dillon, Martin Conboy. Merleau-Ponty's ontology. Yale, 1970.　　　　　　　　　　　　　　　70-25085

1652. Dilworth, David Augustine. The Platonism-pragmatism polarity in Whitehead's thought. Fordham, 1963.
　　　　　　　　　　　　　　　　　　　　　63-5588

1653. Di Muccio, Mary-Jo. A relevant concept of individual freedom and responsibility in contemporary democratic society in relation to the thinking of John Dewey. U.S. Int'l, 1970.　　　　　　　70-22353

1654. Dinan, Stephen Anthony. Causality and consciousness in Sartre's theory of knowledge. Marquette, 1973.
　　　　　　　　　　　　　　　　　　　　　74-18223

1655. Di Nardo, Rev. Ramon Albert. The unity of the human person. Catholic U., 1962.

1656. Di Norcia, Vincent Joseph. Inquiry and development in Bernard Longergan's Insight. Toronto, 1969.

1657. Dionne, Gérard. La crainte et l'éducation. Laval, 1972.

1658. Diorio, Joseph Anthony. Ethics, actions and things: a cross-cultural analysis of the ontological foundations of moral deliberation. Columbia, 1973.　　　　　　　　　　　　　　　73-28200

1659. Di Piazza, Joseph Salvatore. Amnesic aphasia and Goldstein's holistic method: an epistemological study. Toronto, 1973.

1660. Dipre, Gilio Louis. The language-games of Wittgenstein: a prologomenon to a metaphysics of being. St. Bonaventure, 1969.　　　　　　　　70-11268

1661. Divine, Thomas Mark. Natural rights: their scope and limits. Columbia, 1973.　　　　74-29582

1662. Dixon, John Edward. Reason and sympathy in Hume's *Treatise*. British Columbia, 1974.

1663. Dmochowski, Henry W. The moral philosophy of David Hume and the 'is-ought' question. N.Y.U., 1974.
　　　　　　　　　　　　　　　　　　　75-9651

1664. Doan, Frank Carleton. Pluralism and the moral life. Harvard, 1904.

1665. Doan, Frank Mellor. Emergence and organized perspectives; a study in the philosophy of George Herbert Mead. Toronto, 1952.

1666. Dobos, Arthur Anthony. Simplicity in scientific theory: a case history approach. St. Louis, 1972.
　　　　　　　　　　　　　　　　　　　74-4501

1667. Dodson, George Rowland. The idea of the good in Plato. Harvard, 1903.

1668. Doherty, John J. The concept of man in Communist philosophy. Catholic U., 1955.

1669. Dolan, John Michael. Translation and meaning: an examination of Quine's translational indeterminacy hypothesis. Stanford, 1968.　　　　69-13945

1670. Dolan, Rev. Joseph Vincent. Natural law and modern jurisprudence. Laval, 1959.

1671. Dolan, S. Edmund. The resolutive and compositive modes. Laval, 1948.

1672. Dollard, Rev. Stewart Edward. Bergsonian metaphysics and God. St. Louis, 1934.　　　176

1673. Dolson, C.N. The philosophy of Friedrich Nietzsche. Cornell, 1899.

1674. Dombro, Rev. Richard J. The two supreme Newmanic realities. Fordham, 1958.

1675. Dommeyer, Frederick C. Four pragmatic theories of meaning. Brown, 1937.

1676. Domotor, Zoltan. Probabilistic relational structures and their applications. Stanford, 1969.
70-01519

1677. Donaghy, Hugh Kevin. The logic of "ought." Toronto, 1972.

1678. Donahue, Rev. Eugene Leo. The path from believing to knowing in Hegel. St. Louis, 1968. 69-334

1679. Donaldson, George Leo. Hume's theory of relations. Syracuse, 1970. 70-24072

1680. Donaldson, Gerald Aaron. Prolegomenon to a juristic philosophy of sovereignty and political authority. Virginia, 1969.

1681. Donaldson, James. Hegel's dialectic and the motion of motion. Laval, 1965.

1682. Doney, Willis Frederick, Jr. Berkeley and material objects. Princeton, 1949. 10883

1683. Donnell, Franklin Hunkins, Jr. An essay on thinking and imagining. Princeton, 1960. 60-4978

1684. Donnellan, Keith Sedgwick. C.I. Lewis and the foundations of necessary truth. Cornell, 1961.
61-6744

1685. Donnelly, John Joseph Patrick. Søren Kierkegaard's Teleological suspension of the ethical: a reinterpretation. Brown, 1970. 71-13858

1686. D'Onofrio, John Francis. An examination of the redundancy theory of truth. Syracuse, 1972.
73-7718

1687. Donohue, Kevin E. Reflection and faith in Søren Kierkegaard. Catholic U., 1973. 73-12464

1688. Donohue, Rev. Thomas Christopher. Warfare and justice in sixteenth century scholasticism. St. Louis, 1960. 61-747

1689. Donoso, Anton Edward. The relationship between comcom sense and science according to John Dewey. Toronto, 1960.

1690. Donovan, Sr. M. Annice. The henological argument for the existence of God in the works of St. Thomas. Notre Dame, 1946.

1691. Donovan, Rickard John. Social epistemology of Josiah Royce. Fordham, 1970. 71-8709

1692. Doody, John Anthony. Scientific realism and instrumentalism: an analysis of the concepts of description and explanation. Notre Dame, 1974. 74-20044

1693. Dooley, Patrick Kiaran. "Humanism" in the philosophy of William James. Notre Dame, 1969. 70-7887

1694. Doppelt, Gerald David. The characterization of phenomenalist statements in theories of knowledge. Johns Hopkins, 1969. 72-16857

1695. Doran, Sr. M. Verda Clare. On the goodness of created things. Laval, 1947.

1696. Dordick, Webb Lee. An examination of Whitehead's doctrine of causal efficacy. Buffalo, 1971.

1697. Dore, Clement Joseph, Jr. Hallucinations: an epistemological study. Harvard, 1961.

1698. Dorff, Elliot Nelson. The right and the good. Columbia, 1971. 74-8169

1699. Dorman, Laurence Michael. David Hume and the miracles controversy: 1749-1800. Cal., S. Diego, 1973. 74-1367

1700. Dorman, Neil Allen. Generalization in ethics. Wisconsin, 1967. 67-12418

1701. Dornenburg, Noreen Susan. Psychic distance and contemporary art. Yale, 1973. 74-10667

1702. Doron, Pinchas. Nehemiah Kalomiti's *War of truth*; edited with introduction, exposition, and notes. N.Y.U., 1975. 76-10163

1703. Dorrough, Douglas Charles. A prolegomenon to some future considerations of the notion of analogy. No. Carolina, 1964. 65-9004

1704. Dorter, Kenneth Neil M. The doctrine of recollection in Plato's *Phaedo*. Penn St., 1967. 68-8682

1705. Dorval, Georgette. Expositio definitionis pulchri

a s. Thoma traditae. Laval, 1940.

1706. Doss, Seale Robert. Words and facts: an examination of the correspondence theory of truth. Berkeley, 1966. 67-8550

1707. DosSantos, Sueli Mendes. A proof of the formal correctness of an instructional system interpreter. Stanford, 1975. 75-6839

1708. Dotterer, Ray Harbaugh. The argument for a finitist theology. Johns Hopkins, 1917.

1709. Doty, E. William. The metaphysical basis of music. Michigan, 1936.

1710. Doty, Ralph Edward, Jr. Early academic critique of the stoic criterion of truth. Columbia, 1973. 76-29294

1711. Doty, Stephen Charles. Heidegger's Kant-interpretations: throught re-trieve to dialogue. DePaul, 1973. 73-28660

1712. Doucet, Marcel. Dispute de Maxime le Confesseur avec Pyrrhus; introduction, texte critique, traduction et notes. Montreal, 1973.

1713. Doudna, Roger Blaisdell. The justification of poetry. Kansas, 1973. 73-30806

1714. Dougherty, Charles J. Phenomenological critiques of empiricism: a study in the philosophies of Husserl and Peirce. Notre Dame, 1975. 75-19930

1715. Dougherty, George V. The moral basis of social order according to St. Thomas. Catholic U., 1941.

1716. Dougherty, Jude P. Recent American naturalism: an exposition and critique. Catholic U., 1960.

1717. Dougherty, Rev. Kenneth F. The subject, object and method of the philosophy of nature according to St. Thomas Aquinas. Catholic U., 1951.

1718. Douglas, George Halsey. Croce's aesthetic and theory of culture in The philosophy of spirit. Illinois, 1968. 68-12108

1719. Dove, Kenley Royce. Toward an interpretation of Hegel's Phänomenologie des geistes. Yale, 1965. 65-15031

1720. Dowd, Mthr. Ruth. St. Bernard's contribution to

philosophy. Fordham, 1956.

1721. Downes, Chauncey B. Husserl's theory of other minds: a study of the Cartesian meditations. N.Y.U., 1963. 64-6458

1722. Downey, Br. Leo Robert. Life, reason and history in the philosophy of Ortega y Gasset. Fordham, 1961. 61-1567

1723. Downey, Michael Eugene. Language about God: analytic, synthetic, or synthetic a priori. Georgetown, 1975. 75-24479

1724. Downing, George Dowell, III. Freud's concept of unconscious mind. Yale, 1969. 71-13795

1725. Downing, Thomas Edward. Constructions of epistemic verbs. Stanford, 1973. 73-30386

1726. Doxsee, Carll Whitman. Hume's relation to Malebranche. Princeton, 1916.

1727. Doyle, James Fender. Natural justice in politics and law. Yale, 1964.

1728. Doyle, John Patrick. The metaphysical nature of the proof for God's existence according to Francis Suarez, S.J. Toronto, 1966.

1729. Doyle, Sr. Mary Antoinette. Nature and naturalism in George Santayana. St. Louis, 1960. 61-748

1730. Draghi, Robert A. The negative judgment. Catholic U., 1966. 67-1253

1731. Drake, Durant. The problem of things in themselves. Columbia, 1910.

1732. Drange, Theodore Michael. Type crossings. Cornell, 1963. 63-8121

1733. Draughton, Wells Earl. Kuhn, Feyerabend, and the development of scientific knowledge. N.Y.U., 1971. 72-13349

1734. Dreher, John Hugo. A study of human action. Indiana, 1971. 72-6769

1735. Dreher, John Paul. The metaphysical bases of Spinoza's ethical and political thinking. Chicago, 1961.

1736. Dreisbach, Donald Fred. An account of religious revelation. Northwestern, 1970. 71-1833

1737. Drengson, Alan Rodney. Self-deception. Oregon, 1971. 72-14723

1738. Drennen, Donald Arthur. The oppositionist character of Nicholas Berdyaev's philosophy. Fordham, 1959.

1739. Dresser, Horatio Willis. The element of irrationality in the Hegelian dialectic. Harvard, 1907.

1740. Dretske, Frederick Irwin. Space, time and substance: a philosophical inquiry. Minnesota, 1960.
60-5594

1741. Dreyfus, Hubert Lederer. Husserl's phenomenology of perception: from transcendental to existential phenomenology. Harvard, 1964.

1742. Driscoll, Donald Joseph. Types of permanence in the philosophies of Anaximander and Pythagoreanism. New School, 1972. 72-27868

1743. Driscoll, Rev. John M. Situation ethics and the practical validity of universal moral principles. Catholic U., 1964. 64-12490

1744. Driscoll, Leo Cornelius. Methodology of Charles Sanders Peirce. Fordham, 1964. 64-8576

1745. Drouin, Rev. Paul-Émile. Étude comparée de Saint-Thomas d'Aquin et de Suarez sur la question de l'entitatif et de l'intentionnel. Laval, 1951.

1746. Drumin, William Arthur. The corpuscular philosophy of Robert Boyle: its establishment and verification. Columbia, 1973.

1747. Drummond, John Joseph. Presenting and kinaesthetic sensations in Husserl's phenomenology of perception. Georgetown, 1975. 76-6184

1748. Drury, George. Contemporary rhetoric: a possible contribution to problems of language and valuation. Chicago, 1958.

1749. D'Souza, Mervyn Cajetan. Gandhi's model of man and non-violence. St. Louis, 1973. 74-24

1750. DuBois, Rev. Ronald Lee. Reason in ethics: a Whiteheadian perspective. St. Louis, 1971. 71-21381

1751. Du Bose, Louisa Shannon. The concept of possibility in C.I. Lewis' epistemology. Bryn Mawr, 1958.
59-1002

1752. Dubray, Charles A. Theory of physical dispositions. Catholic U., 1905.

1753. Dubrule, Diane Elizabeth. Divine infinity in the writings of Henry of Ghent. Toronto, 1968.

1754. Dubs, Homer H. The philosophy of Hsuntze; ancient Confucianism as developed in the philosophy of Hsuntze. Chicago, 1925.

1755. Ducasse, Curt John. The fallacy of counteraction, and its metaphysical significance. Harvard, 1912.

1756. Duclow, Donald F. The learned ignorance: its symbolism, logic and foundations in Dionysius the Aeropagite, John Scotus Eriugena and Nicholas of Cusa. Bryn Mawr, 1974.   75-8280

1757. Duda, William Leonard. Constructive functions in the syntax of languages, machines, and cortex. Yale, 1957.

1758. Dudeck, Caroline Verna. Hegel's concept of freedom as it develops in The phenomenology of mind. Bryn Mawr, 1974.   75-8281

1759. Duerlinger, James Peter. Aristotle's logic. Wisconsin, 1966.   66-9901

1760. Duerr, Howard John. The world-ground and the world-order. No. Carolina, 1953.

1761. Dufault, Wilfred J. L'apriorisme dans les termes de la science expérimentale. Laval, 1949.

1762. Duffy, Rev. John A. A philosophy of poetry based on Thomistic principles. Catholic U., 1944.

1763. Duggan, Timothy John. Thomas Reid's theory of empirical evidence. Brown, 1957.   58-4377

1764. Duhrssen, Alfred. Genesis and structure of an intersubjective world. Chicago, 1957.

1765. Dukelow, Owen Warner. Herbert Butterfield: the epistemology of a working historian. Minnesota, 1960.
                    60-5596

1766. Dukes, Edward Norman. Alexander Sermoneta's commentaries on Heytesbury and Strode: a contribution to late medieval logic in England and Italy. Columbia, 1973.   73-28203

1767. Dumontet, Georges. Morality and religion in the

        philosophy of Henri Bergson. Harvard, 1944.

1768. Dunbar, Donald Rhodes. The concrete universal in the philosophy of F.H. Bradley. Boston U., 1965.
65-11225

1769. Duncan, Elmer Hubert. Kierkegaard and value theory: a study of the three spheres of existence. Cincinnati, 1962.
62-4777

1770. Duncan, Roger Bruce. The role of the concept of philia in Plato's Dialogues. Yale, 1969.
70-2724

1771. Dundon, Stanislaus John Sherman. Philosophical resistance to Newtonianism on the continent, 1700-1760. St. John's, 1972.
72-21719

1772. Dunham, Albert Millard. The concept of tension in philosophy. Chicago, 1933.

1773. Dunham, Barrows. A study in Kant's aesthetics; the universal validity of aesthetic judgments. Princeton, 1933.

1774. Dunham, Bradford. Elementary logic as an instrument for concept construction. Harvard, 1950.

1775. Dunham, James Henry. Freedom and purpose; an interpretation of the psychology of Spinoza. Pennsylvania, 1913.

1776. Dunlap, John Timlin. Models and modality. Georgia, 1972.
72-34067

1777. Dunlap, Lowell Alverson, Jr. Sense, nonsense, and senselessness: an essay in the continuity of the thought of Ludwig Wittgenstein. Marquette, 1972.
73-8270

1778. Dunlop, Charles E.M. An analysis of dreaming. Duke, 1972.
73-19474

1779. Dunn, Sr. Dorothy Ann. The problem of dualism in John Dewey. St. Louis, 1966.
67-2948

1780. Dunn, E. Catherine. The concept of ingratitude in renaissance English moral philosophy. Catholic U., 1947.

1781. Dunn, Jon Michael. The algebra of intensional logics. Pittsburgh, 1966.
67-5554

1782. Dunn, Oliver Charles. A study of Bergson's theory of morality. Cornell, 1937.

1783. Dunne, Sr. Mary Rachel Carrin. Kierkegaard and Socratic ignorance: a study of the task of a philosopher in relation to Christianity. Notre Dame, 1970. 71-5534

1784. Dunphy, William Berchman. The doctrine of causality in the *Quaestiones in metaphysicam* of Peter of Auvergne. Toronto, 1953.

1785. DuRand, Clifford Darwin. Participatory democracy. Florida St., 1974. 75-6318

1786. Durant, William James. Philosophy and the social problem. Columbia, 1917.

1787. Dusek, Rudolph Valentine. The implications of the Duhemian argument for the social sciences. Texas, 1972. 73-18419

1788. Duska, Ronald Felix. The justification of ethical principles. Northwestern, 1971. 71-30789

1789. Dutton, Denis L. Art and anthropology: aspects of criticism and the social studies. Cal., S. Barbara, 1975.

1790. Dutton, John Dale. Ethical and legal theory in the United States: a comparative study. Pennsylvania, 1956. 17223

1791. Duzy, Br. E. Stanislaus. The philosophy of social change. Catholic U., 1944.

1792. Dworkin, Gerald Bob. The nature and justification of coercion. Berkeley, 1966. 66-15383

1793. Dyche, Eugene Inglish. The life and works, and philosophical relations, of John (Janus Junius) Toland. Southern Cal., 1944.

1794. Dye, James Wayne. Unity in duality: an examination of the metaphysics of Nicolas Berdyaev. Tulane, 1960. 60-5944

1795. Dyke, Charles Eugene. Political duties and their limits. Brown, 1966. 67-2234

1796. Dykhuizen, George. The conception of God in the philosophy of Josiah Royce: a critical exposition of its epistemological and metaphysical development. Chicago, 1934.

1797. Dykstra, Vergil Homer. An examination of Stephen Toulmin's theory of morals. Wisconsin, 1953.

- E -

1798. Eames, Samuel Morris. Some methodological problems in John Dewey's theory of valuation. Chicago, 1958.

1799. Earle, William. Thought and its object. Chicago, 1952.

1800. Earle, William James. James' stream of thought as a point of departure for metaphysics. Columbia, 1969.   70-6961

1801. Earls, Kevin John. A commentary of Nietzsche's Zarathustra (Parts I-III). Duquesne, 1974.
    75-14321

1802. Early, Thomas Howard. Creativity and value: an elucidation of the metaphysical status of value in Whitehead's philosophy. Boston Coll., 1972.
    72-21420

1803. Earman, John. Some aspects of temporal asymmetry. Princeton, 1968.   69-10493

1804. East, Simon-Pierre. La méthode en biologie selon le premier livre du: De partibus animalium d'Aristote. Laval, 1959.

1805. Easterling, Marvin Leon. Hume's theory of moral judgment. Illinois, 1958.   59-501

1806. Eastman, Lucius Root, Jr. The logic of entailment. Texas, 1969.   69-21805

1807. Eastman, William. A critical discussion of Russell's neutral monism. Brown, 1956.   19321

1808. Easton, Loyd D. Does the understanding of wholes require both analysis and synopsis? Boston U., 1942.

1809. Easton, Stewart Copinger. Roger Bacon and the search for universal knowledge; a reconsideration of the life and work of Roger Bacon in the light of his own stated purposes. Columbia, 1950.   1845

1810. Eaton, Howard Ormsby. The Austrian philosophy of values. Wisconsin, 1928.

1811. Eaton, Marcia May Muelder. The use of the concept of intention in the explanation of literature. Stanford, 1967. 68-11289

1812. Eaton, Ralph Monroe. The method of induction. Harvard, 1917.

1813. Ebenreck, Clyde William. The relationship between atheism and the philosophy of man in the philosophy of Karl Marx. Catholic U., 1972. 72-22672

1814. Eberenz, James H. The concept of sovereignty in four medieval political philosophers: John of Salisbury, St. Thomas Aquinas, Egidius Colonna, and Marsilius of Padua. Catholic U., 1968.
69-8907

1815. Eberle, Rolf Arthur. Nominalistic systems: the logic and semantics of some nominalistic positions. U.C.L.A., 1965. 66-218

1816. Eberly, Paul Franklin. John Wesley's philosophy of religion. Syracuse, 1934.

1817. Ebersole, Frank B. Biology and the theory of knowledge: an analytical method for the theory of knowledge, and its relation to biological laws. Chicago, 1947.

1818. Ebert, Edgar P. The philosophy of Posidonius on philosophy. Ohio St., 1946.

1819. Echelbarger, Charles Gary. Wilfrid Sellars' philosophy of mind. Ohio St., 1969. 70-14008

1820. Eckoff, William Julius. Kant's inaugural dissertation of 1770 /_De mundi sensibilis_/, tr. into English with an introduction and discussion. Columbia, 1893.

1821. Eckstein, Jerome. Interestedness and non-interestedness: two approaches to knowledge. Columbia, 1961. 61-1073

1822. Economos, Judith Jarrard. The identity thesis. U.C.L.A., 1967. 67-12220

1823. Eddins, Berkley Branche. The role of value-judgments in the philosophies of history of Oswald Spengler and Arnold J. Toynbee. Michigan, 1961.
61-6345

1824. Eddy, Janice Orion Brandwie. Two investigations in aesthetics. Florida St., 1970. 71-6999

1825. Edel, Abraham. Aristotle's theory of the infinite. Columbia, 1934.

1826. Edelson, Thomas Harold. Prescriptive determination in ethical and non-ethical language. Berkeley, 1974.

1827. Edgar, Earl Eugene, Jr. The formal conditions of an empirical ethics. Cincinnati, 1940.

1828. Edgar, William John. Logic and intuition: an essay on necessity. Syracuse, 1972. 73-7720

1829. Edge, Hoyt Littleton. Epiphenomenalism and Rorty's theory of identity. Vanderbilt, 1970. 70-24859

1830. Edison, George. Ethic of means. Toronto, 1942.

1831. Edlow, Robert Blair. Galen on ambiguity: an English translation of Galen's De captionibus (On fallacies) with introduction and commentary. Pennsylvania, 1972. 73-1384

1832. Edwards, Edward Paul. The logic of moral discourse. Columbia, 1951. 3535

1833. Edwards, James Creighton. Persuasion and discovery: a study of Wittgenstein's philosophy. No. Carolina, 1972. 73-4815

1834. Edwards, Kenneth Creighton. Method and paradox. Georgia, 1974. 75-23756

1835. Edwards, Paul E. Lewis Mumford's search for values. American U., 1970. 70-24273

1836. Edwards, Rem Blanchard. Freedom, responsibility, and obligation. Emory, 1962. 62-6000

1837. Edwards, Sandra Stanton. Medieval theories of distinction. Pennsylvania, 1974. 74-22834

1838. Edwards, William F. The logic of Iacopo Zabarella (1533-1589). Columbia, 1960. 61-247

1839. Effler, Roy R. John Duns Scotus and the principle "Omne quod movetur ab alio movetur." St. Bonaventure, 1962.

1840. Efros, Israel Isaac. The problem of space in Jewish mediaeval philosophy. Columbia, 1917.

1841. Egan, Edmund Joseph. Moral irreversibility as incarnate value in the situational context. Fordham, 1973. 74-2740

1842. Egan, Howard Thomas. Gassendi's view of knowledge: a study of the epistemological basis of his logic. Fordham, 1975.   75-18883

1843. Egan, Martin Kieran. Myth and history. Cornell, 1972.   73-343

1844. Eggan, Lloyd Arthur. On the thesis that common nouns are names, and the question of extension determination. Wisconsin, 1975.   75-23840

1845. Eggerman, Richard Wayne. The generalization principle in ethics. Illinois, 1970.   71-14735

1846. Eggleston, Sr. Mary Frederick. Some effects of the theory of evolution on the philosophy of religion. Notre Dame, 1934.

1847. Egyed, Bela Imre. Reference and intensionality; an essay on Quine's philosophy of logic. McGill, 1968.

1848. Ehman, Robert Ray. The objective reality of the principles of reason. Yale, 1961.

1849. Ehrcke, William Frederick. Theories of belief. Calgary, 1973.

1850. Ehrlich, Leonard Harry. Karl Jaspers' philosophy of science. Yale, 1960.

1851. Eisenberg, Allan Mark. The function of the intentional body in Merleau-Ponty's *Phenomenology of perception*. Columbia, 1974.   75-7492

1852. Eisenberg, Paul David. Duties to oneself: leading arguments concerning them from Kant to the present and a new defence of them. Harvard, 1967.

1853. Eisenstadt, Michael. The philosophy of Xenophanes of Colophon. Texas, 1970.   72-2330

1854. Ekman, Rosalind. The problem of Akrasia: a test for the adequacy of metaethical theories. Brown, 1962.   63-1017

1855. Elbert, Rev. Edmund J. A Thomistic study of the psychology of human character. Catholic U., 1956.

1856. Elbert, John Aloysius. Newman's conception of faith prior to 1845; a genetic presentation and synthesis. Cincinnati, 1932.

1857. Elbrecht, Joyce Fondren. Philosophy as a repetitive cosmogonic act. Tulane, 1967.   68-4032

1858. Elder, Crawford Latterner, III. Towards a revised Hegelian theory of nature. Yale, 1975.
76-11511

1859. Elder, Lucius Walter. A criticism of some attempts to rationalize tragedy. Pennsylvania, 1913.

1860. Eleazar, José M. Xavier Zubiri: his fundamental moral concepts. Fordham, 1953.

1861. Elevitch, Bernard. The critical idealism of Léon Brunschvicg. Columbia, 1961. 61-5462

1862. Elfstrom, Gerard Alan. The import of moral being in John Rawls' Theory of justice. Emory, 1975.
76-12178

1863. Elgin, Catherine Zincke. Reference and meaning: a tractarian analysis of incommensurable representational systems. Brandeis, 1975. 75-15101

1864. Elias, Julius. Fredrich Schiller: the poet as philosopher. Columbia, 1963. 64-2744

1865. Elkin, W.B. Hume, the relation of the Treatise of human nature, Book I, to the Inquiry of human understanding, Ch. I-VIII. Cornell, 1894.

1866. Ellard, George. Science and ideology in Karl Marx. Yale, 1973. 73-25201

1867. Ellin, Joseph. George Herbert Mead's philosophy of mind. Yale, 1962.

1868. Ellington, James W. The communicability of aesthetic feeling: an application of Kant's Critique of aesthetic judgment to the fine arts. Chicago, 1958.

1869. Elliott, Herschel Hugh. The epistemological meaning of verified scientific constructs. Yale, 1950.

1870. Elliott, Richard Lee. The hypothesis of creative evolution in the philosophy of Charles Sanders Peirce. New Mexico, 1974. 75-5892

1871. Ellis, Frank Richard. Hume's theory of nature. St. Louis, 1962. 64-3740

1872. Ellis, Matt Locke. John Dewey's theory of value. Yale, 1933.

1873. Ellis, Ralph David. Human and transcendental subjectivity: the problem of self-alienation. Duquesne, 1975. 76-13117

1874. Ellis, Willis Davis. Gestalt psychology and meaning. Berkeley, 1930.

1875. Elliston, Frederick Allen. 'Mitsein' in Sein und zeit: towards a phenomenology of social existence. Toronto, 1975.

1876. Elveton, Roy Owen. The concept of the phenomenon. Northwestern, 1967. 68-3174

1877. Ely, Stephen Lee. The conception of God as developed by contemporary American philosophers. Wisconsin, 1938.

1878. Emblom, William John. The theory of reality in the philosophy of R.G. Collingwood. Illinois, 1962. 62-2904

1879. Embree, Lester Eugene. The 'true philosophy' in Hume's Treatise. New School, 1972. 72-27870

1880. Emch, Arnold Frederick. The Logica demonstrativa of Girolamo Saccheri. Harvard, 1934.

1881. Emge, Walter George. A critique of 'power': the role of descriptive, teleological and normative concepts in politics. Yale, 1969. 70-16263

1882. Emmett, Kathleen Ann. Talking about seeing: an examination of some aspects of the Ayer-Austin debate on the sense-datum theory. Ohio St., 1973. 74-10953

1883. Emmons, Donald C. The brain process theory of mind: a critical analysis. Chicago, 1963.

1884. Emmons, Douglas Lloyd. The paradox of man in the philosophy of John Dewey. Oklahoma, 1970. 71-12566

1885. Engel, Elizabeth Sidney. Plato on rhetoric and writing. Yale, 1973. 73-25202

1886. Engel, Eva Johanna. Carl Philip Moritz: a study of his ethical and aesthetic concepts. Cornell, 1954. 9745

1887. Engel, Saul Morris. The philosophy of language in Hobbes and Locke; a comparative study. Toronto, 1959.

1888. Engelbrecht, Helmuth C. Johann Gottlieb Fichte. Columbia, 1933.

1889. Englebretsen, George Francis. Sommers' tree theory,

　　　　possibility and existence. Nebraska, 1971.
　　　　　　　　　　　　　　　　　　　　71-19481

1890. Englehardt, Hugo Tristram, Jr. The categorial relation of mind and body. Texas, 1969. 70-10784

1891. Engler, Barbara Orchard. The concept of knowledge in the thought of Sigmund Freud. Drew, 1967.
　　　　　　　　　　　　　　　　　　　　67-14372

1892. Engles, Sr. Mary Francisca. The evaluation of the standard of morality in modern ethical theories. St. Louis, 1931.

1893. English, Jane Elizabeth. Beyond observation: the nature of scientific theories. Harvard, 1974.

1894. English, Parker Thomas. Empiricistic philosophical stories. W. Ontario, 1974.

1895. Ensley, Francis G. The naturalistic interpretation of religion by John Dewey. Boston U., 1938.

1896. Enteman, Willard Finley. A philosophic critique of the economic concept of profit maximization. Boston U., 1965.　　　　　　　　　　　65-11218

1897. Epp, Ronald Harry. Katharsis in the early Platonic dialogues and its cultural antecedents. Buffalo, 1971.　　　　　　　　　　　　　　　　71-22561

1898. Epstein, Fanny Lechter. The identity approach to the mind-body problem: a critical examination. Boston U., 1971.　　　　　　　　　　　71-26404

1899. Erde, Edmund Lyman. Philosophy and science, Wittgenstein and Chomsky: an examination of the current theory of innate ideas. Texas, 1970.
　　　　　　　　　　　　　　　　　　　　70-18227

1900. Erdos, Edward. Space, time, and the mathematical continuum: a criticism of the ability of set-theoretical models to adequately account for the nature of spatial and temporal extension. N.Y.U., 1975.　　　　　　　　　　　　　　　75-28527

1901. Ericksen, Ephraim. The psychological and ethical aspects of Mormon group life. Chicago, 1918.

1902. Erickson, Carl Gustaf. The meaning of consciousness. Yale, 1922.

1903. Erickson, Stephen Anthony. The metaphysician as constructive thinker: an interpretation of Heidegger's thought. Yale, 1964.

1904. Erlandson, Douglas Kent. The concepts of memory: a study in the philosophy of psychology. Johns Hopkins, 1973. 73-28395

1905. Erlichson, Herman. Interpretation and models in the philosophy of quantum mechanics. Columbia, 1968. 71-17578

1906. Erlinghagen, Rev. Helmut. Moral, personal responsibility: its conditions and limitations. Fordham, 1953.

1907. Ermatinger, Charles Joseph. The coalescent intellective soul in post-Thomistic debate. St. Louis, 1963. 64-4244

1908. Ernest, Stephen Thomas. The naturalism of Frederick J.E. Woodbridge: man and nature in the pursuit of happiness. Fordham, 1973. 74-2742

1909. Erpenbeck, James Richard. The relation of pragmatism and realism in the philosophy of C.S. Peirce. Notre Dame, 1965. 65-14609

1910. Erwin, Edward James. The concept of meaninglessness. Johns Hopkins, 1968. 69-21101

1911. Eshelman, Larry James. Persons, robots and self-deception: a philosophical analysis of psychological defense mechanisms. Waterloo, 1973.

1912. Esheté, Andreas. The social structure of freedom. Yale, 1971. 71-16232

1913. Eshleman, Martin. The relation of aesthetic and ethical values. Yale, 1940.

1914. Eslick, Leonard J. Scientific abstraction and the unity of essence. Virginia, 1939.

1915. Espinoza, Miguel Adolfo. Dynamics of multivocal sentences. Washington U., 1974. 75-6591

1916. Esposito, Joseph Louis. An examination of category-relativism. N.Y.U., 1970. 71-2285

1917. Estall, Henry Martyn. Studies in the philosophy and psychology of Franz Brentano. Cornell, 1938.

1918. Estep, Myrna Lynne. A study in pedagogical epistemology: the relation between theoretical and procedural knowing. Indiana, 1975. 76-2807

1919. Estrada, Charles Joseph. Freedom and the personality in the thought of André Gide, Albert Camus and

Fyodor Dostoevsky. Fordham, 1965. 65-9508

1920. Etzwiler, Lyle James. John Baconthorpe's relation to Averroism. Toronto, 1969.

1921. Evans, Cedric. The ethical philosophy of G.E. Moore and W.D. Ross. Cornell, 1938.

1922. Evans, Charles Stephen. Subjective justifications of religious belief: a comparative study of Kant, Kierkegaard, and James. Yale, 1974. 75-1356

1923. Evans, Clyde Henry. Quantum theory and the independent existence of physical objects. Michigan St., 1971. 71-31194

1924. Evans, Daniel Luther. Realism and reality (a study of new realism from the standpoint of axiology.) Ohio St., 1923.

1925. Evans, James Willis, Jr. Heraclitus and Parmenides as moral philosophers. Yale, 1970. 70-25261

1926. Evans, Joseph J. Regulative pure reason, reflective judgment, and the culmination of Kant's ethics. Bryn Mawr, 1974.

1927. Evans, Joseph William. Development of Thomistic principles in Jacques Maritain's notion of society. Notre Dame, 1951. 5268

1928. Evans, Lawrence Chambers. Scepticism in the philosophy of George Santayana. Utah, 1966. 66-4360

1929. Evans, Melbourne. Principles and methods of physical thought: a study in the philosophy and science of ancient and early modern times. Berkeley, 1948.

1930. Evans, Meredydd. Perception and common sense in the writings of Thomas Reid. Princeton, 1955. 13690

1931. Evans, Robert Howard. The decline and revival of critical realism. Pittsburgh, 1967. 68-4432

1932. Evans, Robert Rees. John Toland's pantheism: a revolutionary ideology and enlightenment philosophy. Brandeis, 1965. 65-14419

1933. Evans, William. Belief and art. Chicago, 1935.

1934. Everett, Charles W. The education of Jeremy Bentham. Columbia, 1932.

1935. Everett, Millard Spencer. Utilitarianism as a universal morality. Chicago, 1929.

1936. Everett, Walter Goodnow. Greek scepticism. Brown, 1895.

1937. Everson, Thomas Edward. Separability and substance in Aristotle's metaphysics. Johns Hopkins, 1973.
73-28396

1938. Ewen, Frederick. The prestige of Schiller in England, 1788-1859. Columbia, 1932.

1939. Ewer, Mary A. A survey of mystical symbolism. Columbia, 1933.

1940. Exdell, John Baron. Social contract and the common good. Texas, 1973. 74-5234

1941. Ezorsky, Gertrude. Truth as a warranted performance: a synthesis of John Dewey's and P.F. Strawson's concepts of truth. N.Y.U., 1961. 66-9681

- F -

1942. Faaborg, Robert Winslow. Ayer, Austin, and the argument from illusion. Iowa, 1972. 72-26673

1943. Faber, Richard Nathaniel. Category-mistakes. Michigan, 1975. 65-10951

1944. Facione, Peter Arthur. The theory of meaning as intention. Michigan St., 1971. 72-8668

1945. Fackenheim, Emil Ludwig. Substance and perseity in mediaeval Arabic philosophy, with introductory chapters on Aristotle, Plotinus and Proclus. Toronto, 1945.

1946. Factor, Ralph Lance. Ostension and the problem of qualitative abstraction. Georgia, 1970.
71-3729

1947. Fafara, Richard John. The notion of the "idée efficace" in the philosophy of Nicolas Malebranche. Toronto, 1975.

1948. Fagin, Charles Joseph. The doctrine of the divine ideas in the _Summa de bono_ of Ulrich of Strasbourg; text and philosophical introduction. Toronto, 1948.

1949. Fagot, Anne M. Causal vs. teleological explanation

of behavior. Stanford, 1971. 72-11546

1950. Fahrnkopf, Robert Leroy. Wittgenstein on universals. British Columbia, 1973.

1951. Fain, Haskell. Some moral and methodological problems in the social sciences. Berkeley, 1956.

1952. Fair, Frank Kenneth. The logic of some which- and whether- questions. Georgia, 1971. 72-10951

1953. Fairbanks, Matthew Jerome. C.S. Peirce and nineteenth century positivism. Notre Dame, 1961. 61-3728

1954. Fairchild, David Lawrence. Merleau-Ponty and Austin: a study in philosophical method. Northwestern, 1972. 72-32427

1955. Fales, Evan M. The structure of explanations. Temple, 1974. 74-28222

1956. Falk, Arthur Eugene, Jr. A many-sorted ontology and the progress of science: an interpretation of Whitehead's early philosophy of nature as a proposal for language reform. Yale, 1966. 66-6887

1957. Fallico, Arturo Biagio Luciano. A critical interpretation of the aesthetics of Benedetto Croce. Northwestern, 1941.

1958. Fallon, Timothy Patrick. The notion of truth in Herveus Natalis. Toronto, 1967.

1959. Fan, Kuang Tih. Wittgenstein's conception of philosophy. Hawaii, 1967. 68-11924

1960. Fandozzi, Phillip Robert. The Heideggerian perspective on nihilism: a critique of modern technology through its manifestations in literature, philosophy and social thought. Hawaii, 1974. 75-5036

1961. Farber, Marvin. Phenomenology as a method and as a philosophical discipline. Harvard, 1925.

1962. Farber, Paul Lawrence. Buffon's concept of species. Indiana, 1970. 71-06846

1963. Farley, Mthr. Elizabeth Howlin. The efficacy of secondary causes in the doctrine of Saint Thomas Aquinas. Fordham, 1955.

1964. Farley, Gerard Clifford. The role of possibility in conception and judgment. Fordham, 1969. 70-11429

1965. Farooqi, Waheed Ali. A spiritual interpretation of reality in the light of Berkeley's immaterialism. Michigan St., 1966. 67-7538

1966. Farre, George Lincoln. The structure of explanatory statements in classical physics. Johns Hopkins, 1960.

1967. Farrell, Daniel Michael. Paying the penalty: the role of punishment in theories of justified civil disobedience. Rockefeller, 1974.

1968. Farrugia, Rev. Edward George. Did Bergson's moral thinking undergo radical development? St. Louis, 1972. 74-4510

1969. Faruki, Mohamed Zudhi Taji. The universal categories of Charles Sanders Peirce. Indiana, 1957. 58-5066

1970. Faruqi, Isma'il Ragi A., el. On justifying the good. Indiana, 1953. 4373

1971. Fassiotto, Marie-Jose. L'humanisme pragmatique de Jean Meslier. Berkeley, 1974.

1972. Fathi, Karim Matta. John Stuart Mill's theories of universals in relation to his different theories of universal propositions. Wisconsin, 1956. 19084

1973. Faurot, Jean Hiatt. The realism of Thomas Reid. Toronto, 1946.

1974. Fauser, Rev. John Joseph. The theory of freedom in William James. St. Louis, 1967. 68-1218

1975. Faust, William Floyd. The ethical significance of the abnormal in human experience. Ohio St., 1935.

1976. Fay, Charles. Saint Thomas' modification of Boethius' doctrine on being, goodness and participation. St. Louis, 1956.

1977. Fay, Cornelius. The theory of immediate perception among twentieth century scholastic philosophers with special emphasis on the contributions of Domet de Vorges and Léon Noel. Columbia, 1955. 15626

1978. Fay, Rev. Thomas Aquinas. Heidegger on logic: an encounter of his thought with Wittgenstein. Fordham, 1971. 71-20165

1979. Faysse, Patrick. Le contradictoriel. Laval, 1975.

1980. Feagin, Susan Louise. General criteria in aesthetic theories. Wisconsin, 1975. 75-20762

1981. Feagins, Carroll Spurgeon. Critiques of pacifism by some American and British philosophers since 1914. Northwestern, 1954. 1C294

1982. Feehan, Rev. Stephen Stanislaus. Substance, reason and intuition in Spinoza. St. Louis, 1970. 71-21386

1983. Feehan, Rev. Thomas D. An analysis of lying and some thoughts on its moral evaluation. Brown, 1970.

1984. Feeley, Thomas. The function of touch. Laval, 1965.

1985. Feenberg, Andrew Lewis. The dialectics of theory and practice. Cal., S. Diego, 1972. 73-10971

1986. Feinberg, Joel. Naturalism and liberalism in the philosophy of Ralph Barton Perry. Michigan, 1957. 58-1399

1987. Feinberg, Walter. A comparative study of the social philosophies of John Dewey and Bernard Bosanquet. Boston U., 1966. 66-11305

1988. Feld, Michael Edward. The derivation of "ought" from "is." Brown, 1973. 74-3011

1989. Feld, Norbert R. The persistence of realism in the modern scientific interpretations of nature. Catholic U., 1954.

1990. Feldman, Fred Albert. Some problems concerning identity. Brown, 1969. 70-8714

1991. Feldman, Richard Harold. Non-propositional analyses of belief. Massachusetts, 1975. 75-27513

1992. Feldman, Richard Joseph. Legal realism and the rule theory of law. Washington U., 1971. 72-9331

1993. Feldman, Seymour Nat Oscar. Ernst Cassirer's Theory of the concept. Columbia, 1963. 64-5547

1994. Feldman, William Taft. The fundamental motivation in the philosophy of John Dewey. Johns Hopkins, 1932.

1995. Feldstein, Leonard Charles. The norms of science: an evaluation of the views of Meyerson, Duhem and Peirce. Columbia, 1957. 57-2867

1996. Fell, Albert Prior. The aesthetic relevance of the

artist's intention. Columbia, 1963.   64-1562

1997. Fell, Gilbert Samuel. Person and community: an appraisal of the Roycean social ideal. Temple, 1969.   69-19954

1998. Fell, Joseph Phineas, III. A critique of Jean-Paul Sartre's theory of emotion. Columbia, 1963.
65-7444

1999. Felt, Rev. James Wright. Whitehead's early theory of scientific objects. St. Louis, 1965.
65-14639

2000. Fendrich, Roger Paul. Experience and explanation: Dewey's metaphysics and theory of inquiry. Texas, 1971.   72-15753

2001. Fenton, Norman E. Father. Leibniz's doctrine on space. Chicago, 1969.

2002. Ferguson, Ann. Some philosophical problems concerning action and desire. Brown, 1965.   65-13648

2003. Ferguson, Sr. Jane Frances. The philosophy of equality. Catholic U., 1942.

2004. Fernandez-Castaneda, Rev. Jaime. W.E. Hocking on the will to power and the state. St. Louis, 1969.
70-20383

2005. Ferrara, Taddeo Nazareno. The role of reason or the meaning of "intelligere" in the works of Anselm of Canterbury. Fordham, 1971.   71-26968

2006. Ferrara, Vincent James. The role of art in Hegel's philosophy. Fordham, 1969.   69-16218

2007. Ferrari, Leo. The origin of the state according to Plato. Laval, 1958.

2008. Ferree, Rev. William F. The act of social justice in the philosophy of St. Thomas Aquinas and in the encyclicals of Pope Pius XI. Catholic U., 1942.

2009. Ferriols, Rev. Roque. The "psychic-entity" in Aurobindo's The life divine. Fordham, 1959.

2010. Fethe, Charles B. Indeterminism and acting on reason. N.Y.U., 1970.   70-21829

2011. Fetzer, James Henry. Propensities of frequencies: a study in the logic of concept formation. Indiana, 1970.   71-6848

2012. Feuer, Lewis Samuel. The philosophical analysis of space and time. Harvard, 1935.

2013. Ficarra, Francis Thomas. Collingwood's New leviathan. Illinois, 1962. 62-595

2014. Field, Hartry Hamlin. Reference, truth and meaning. Harvard, 1972.

2015. Field, Jeffrey Michael. Revolution and tradition in Descartes' philosophy of science. Michigan, 1974. 75-684

2016. Fielder, John Herbert. The concepts of matter and emanation in the philosophy of Plotinus. Texas, 1970. 71-11532

2017. Figen, Abraham. An evaluation of the moral philosophy of J.N. Findlay. N.Y.U., 1968. 69-7949

2018. Filer, Malva Esther. Self-identity and the other in Unamuno. Columbia, 1966. 66-12561

2019. Finch, Henry Leroy, Jr. The Greek idea of limitation; an interpretation of the Greek ethos and of Plato's philosophy in relation to it. Columbia, 1951. 3337

2020. Fine, Arthur I. The issue of epistemological realism in the theory of quantum mechanical measurement. Chicago, 1963.

2021. Fine, Gail Judith. Plato and acquaintance. Harvard, 1975.

2022. Fingarette, Herbert. The influence of knowledge upon behavior. U.C.L.A., 1949.

2023. Fink, Joel Steven. A critique of relevance in education. Boston U., 1972. 72-25271

2024. Fink, Joseph L. A critique of the philosophy of pragmatism in the light of scholastic philosophy, with special reference to the nature of truth. Niagara, 1935.

2025. Finkelstein, Henry Albert. Prolegomena to a philosophy of technics; historical and critical studies of man's control of nature. Pennsylvania, 1940.

2026. Finkelstein, Robert Joseph. The regularity theory: causation and production. Columbia, 1969. 70-6970

2027. Finkelstein, Rona Glassman. The empirical identity

theory of mind and brain: an examination and evaluation. Rochester, 1964.   64-11272

2028. Finn, James Patrick, Jr. Ethics and etiquette. Duquesne, 1974.   74-21039

2029. Finnegan, Rev. Owen Edward. An historical and metaphysical study of natural law theory applied to questions of freedom of expression in the United States. Michigan St., 1965.   66-6122

2030. Finocchiaro, Maurice Anthony. The problem of explanation in historiography of science. Berkeley, 1969.   70-6099

2031. Firth, Roderick. Sense-data and the principle of reduction. Harvard, 1943.

2032. Fischer, Gilbert Richard. A study in the philosophy of Husserl. Chicago, 1962.

2033. Fischer, Kurt Rudolf. Franz Brentano's philosophy of *Evidenz*. Berkeley, 1964.   64-9013

2034. Fischer, Norman Arthur. Alienation, reification, and the labor theory of value: the philosophical basis of Marx's economics. U. of Washington, 1975.   76-17467

2035. Fischer, Thomas Grier. Innatism in contemporary psychology. Texas, 1974.   74-24857

2036. Fiser, Karen Beth. The problem of privacy and the "private language argument." Virginia, 1972.   72-33359

2037. Fisher, Donald. The concept of value. Harvard, 1913.

2038. Fisher, James George, Jr. The distinction between substance and principal attribute in Descartes. Georgetown, 1974.   74-16412

2039. Fisher, John Andrew. On being guided by a rule: some reflections on a conceptual problem in Chomsky's theory of syntax. Minnesota, 1971.   72-5526

2040. Fisher, John J. On the definition of good. Pennsylvania, 1952.

2041. Fisher, Rev. Luke. Social leadership according to Thomistic principles. Catholic U., 1943.

2042. Fisher, Mitchell S. Robert Boyle, devout naturalist;

a study in science and religion in the seventeenth century. Columbia, 1946.

2043. Fisher, Rosemary Fitzpatrick. Man and freedom in Jean-Paul Sartre: two stages in his thought. St. Louis, 1972.   72-23931

2044. Fishman, Stephen Michael. The epistemology of G.H. Lewes. Columbia, 1967.   67-10580

2045. Fisk, Milton Thomas. An essay on time. Yale, 1958.

2046. Fismer, Arnold W. Relation of morality and religion. N.Y.U., 1899.   73-20718

2047. Fitch, Frederic Brenton. A system of symbolic logic which avoids the paradoxes without a theory of types. Yale, 1934.

2048. Fitch, Gregory Werner. Necessity and contingency in Leibniz. Massachusetts, 1974.   75-6027

2049. Fitch, Robert Elliot. Voltaire's philosophic procedure. Columbia, 1935.

2050. Fite, Warner H. The meaning of subjective and objective. Pennsylvania, 1894.

2051. Fitts, Sr. Mary Pauline. John Locke's theory of meaning: an exposition and critique. Catholic U., 1960.

2052. Fitzgerald, Desmond James. The unity of man in Descartes: a study of Descartes' treatment of a medieval and Renaissance problem. Berkeley, 1954.

2053. Fitzgerald, Gisela. The language of private sensations: Russell in light of Wittgenstein's private language remarks. Purdue, 1973.   74-15157

2054. Fitzgerald, Sr. Janet Anne. A study of Alfred North Whitehead's method of extensive abstraction as a mathematical model. St. John's, 1971. 71-20712

2055. Fitzgerald, John Joseph. Peirce's theory of signs as the foundation for his pragmatism. Tulane, 1962.   62-6475

2056. Fitzgerald, Paul Peter. The truth about tomorrow's sea fight. Harvard, 1967.

2057. Fitzgibbon, John Francis. The origin of ideas according to the Latin Avicennian tradition. Notre Dame, 1956.   18074

2058. Fitzgibbon, John Paul William. The philosophy of poetic symbolism- medieval and modern. Georgetown, 1958.

2059. Fitzgibbons, Robert Edward. R.S. Peters on the logic of justifying educational politics. Boston U., 1972. 72-25272

2060. Flaccus, Louis William. Analysis of moral evaluation. Harvard, 1904.

2061. Flanagan, Rev. Joseph Francis. The basic patterns of human understanding according to Bernard Lonergan. Fordham, 1967. 67-11490

2062. Flanigan, Sr. Thomas Marguerite. Collingwood on the nature of metaphysics. St. Louis, 1964. 64-13461

2063. Flay, Joseph Charles. Hegel and Dewey and the problem of freedom. Southern Cal., 1965. 65-9972

2064. Fleck, Leonard Michael. G.H. Mead's pragmatic theory of knowledge. St. Louis, 1975. 76-863

2065. Fleckenstein, Norbert J. A critique of John Dewey's theory of the nature and the knowledge of reality in the light of the principles of Thomism. Catholic U., 1954.

2066. Fleetwood, Arthur Hugh. Cognitive, conative, and affective mental states: a project in philosophical taxonomy. Michigan, 1969. 70-14520

2067. Fleming, Neal Bond. Hocking's philosophy of the human self. Boston U., 1941.

2068. Fleming, Robin Sherwood. Patterns of scientific change: the acid-base research tradition. Virginia, 1975. 76-6

2069. Flemming, Arthur Henry. Egoism in Spinoza. U.C.L.A., 1975. 76-8991

2070. Fleshman, Arthur Cary. The metaphysics of education. N.Y.U., 1910. 74-3385

2071. Fletcher, James Erving. The orienting reflex as an index of program content attention value: a paradigmatic study. Utah, 1971. 71-16173

2072. Fletcher, James John. Generalization in art criticism and the role therein of paradigmatic aesthetic objects. Indiana, 1973. 74-352

2073. Flores, Albert William. Materialism: a critical e-
valuation of the various attempts to defend this
thesis from the problem presented by the phenomenal properties of sensations. Ohio St., 1974.
74-24323

2074. Flory, Paul M. The principle of teleology in the
philosophy of Wilhelm Dilthey. Cornell, 1934.

2075. Floss, Simon William. An outline of the philosophy
of Antoine-Augustin Cournot. Pennsylvania, 1940.

2076. Flower, Elizabeth F. The changes and their causes
in the editions of Sidgwick's Methods of ethics.
Pennsylvania, 1939.

2077. Flower, Robert John. The mathematical/ontological
conditions kinematic 'mathisis': a study of Plato's Theatetus. Syracuse, 1973. 74-8254

2078. Flynn, Bernard Charles. Sartre's doctrine of freedom: the development of Sartre's philosophy from
ontology to philosophical anthropology. Duquesne,
1967.

2079. Flynn, John David. An interpretation and defense of
physicalist psychology. Columbia, 1973.
74-12711

2080. Flynn, Rev. John Vincent. The development of Kant's
theory of sensation. Fordham, 1945.

2081. Flynn, Rev. Thomas J. Empirical and metaphysical
proofs for the immortality of the human soul.
Fordham, 1956.

2082. Flynn, Thomas Robert. "We are all assassins": Jean-
Paul Sartre and the problem of collective responsibility. Columbia, 1970. 73-27336

2083. Foa, Pamela Susan Paola. The know-know thesis and
conclusive evidence. Stanford, 1973. 73-20475

2084. Fodor, Jerry Alan. The uses of "use," a study in the
philosophy of language. Princeton, 1960.
60-4987

2085. Fogel, Philip H. Metaphysical elements in sociology.
Princeton, 1904.

2086. Fogelin, Robert John. The definition of ethical
terms. Yale, 1960.

2087. Fogg, Walter Larry. Experience and order in Blanshard
and Whitehead. Boston U., 1963. 63-6570

2088. Fohr, Samuel Denis. Faith and rationality. Michigan, 1968.　　　　　　　　　　　　　69-12095

2089. Foldstrom, John Harold. The experience of the self in the philosophy of Maine de Biran. Northwestern, 1969.　　　　　　　　　70-6461

2090. Foley, Rev. Leo M. A critique of the philosophy of being of Alfred North Whitehead in the light of Thomistic philosophy. Catholic U., 1946.

2091. Foley, Sr. M. Thomas Aquin. Authority and personality development according to St. Thomas Aquinas. Catholic U., 1956.

2092. Foley, Michael Alan. H.L.A. Hart on ascriptivism and legal responsibility. So. Illinois, 1973.　　　　　　　　　　　　74-6198

2093. Foley, Richard Francis. The desire theory and metaethics. Brown, 1975.

2094. Føllesdal, Dagfinn Kare. Referential opacity and modal logic. Harvard, 1961.

2095. Folse, Henry Joseph, Jr. Metaphysical implications of elementary quantum mechanics. Tulane, 1972.　　　　　　　　　　　　72-24404

2096. Fontaine, Rev. Raymond G. The doctrine of separable accident in the philosophy of Saint Thomas. Catholic U., 1950.

2097. Fontaine, William T.V. Fortune, matter and providence; a study of Ancius Severinus Boethius and Giordano Bruno. Pennsylvania, 1936.

2098. Fontana, Vincent V. Causality and time: a study in the relationship between causality and temporal sequence. Fordham, 1971.　　　71-20168

2099. Fontinelli, Eugene. The participation theory of being in the philosophy of Josiah Royce. Fordham, 1957.

2100. Foo, Thoong-sien. Method in moral judgment- an intercultural analysis. Columbia, 1950. 1848

2101. Forbes, Jesse F. Plato's idea of God. N.Y.U., 1894.

2102. Forcheimer, Estelle. Kant's religion within the bounds of pure reason. N.Y.U., 1919.

2103. Ford, James Adams. The problem of introspection with specific reference to Broad and Ryle. Toronto, 1970.

2104. Ford, Lewis Stanley. The ontological foundation of
Paul Tillich's theory of the religious symbol.
Yale, 1963.   65-6506

2105. Forderhase, Earl Duane. A study of the concept of a
finite god in the philosophies of William James
and Alfred North Whitehead. Oklahoma, 1973.
                                               74-4013

2106. Foreman, Robert Alvin. A critique of prescriptivism.
Syracuse, 1974.   75-13982

2107. Forest, Ilse. Creation versus process. Yale, 1939.

2108. Forgie, James William, Jr. Is existence a property?
Cornell, 1968.   69-5758

2109. Forguson, Lynd Wilks. Perception and justification:
a conceptual study. Northwestern, 1964.
                                               65-3262

2110. Fornasari, Rev. Archimedes. Reality as a solidarity
of creative process: a critical interpretation of
Whitehead's *Category of the ultimate*. Catholic
U., 1969.   69-18575

2111. Forrester, James William. An examination of the
second part of Plato's *Parmenides*. Johns Hopkins,
1968.   68-16416

2112. Forrester, Mary Gore. A re-examination of the arguments from illusion and hallucination. Johns
Hopkins, 1969.   70-11782

2113. Forsman, Rodger Ernest. Austin Farrer's notion of
apprehension: an analysis and appraisal of his
claim to knowledge of substance. Toronto, 1974.

2114. Fort, William E. A philosophical examination of
some contemporary theories of history. Duke, 1933.

2115. Fortenbaugh, William Wall. Aristotle's concept of
deliberate choice. Pennsylvania, 1964.
                                               65-1363

2116. Forthman, William Hunter. The reasonable over-belief. U.C.L.A., 1965.   66-229

2117. Fortier, Théodore. On friendship: its nature, kinds
and effects. Laval, 1972.

2118. Fosnot, Pearl Beatrice. Tradition and change in
John Dewey's social philosophy. Boston U., 1940.

2119. Foss, Laurence. Substance as a category of descriptive metaphysics. Notre Dame, 1968.   69-4063

2120. Foster, Alfred Leon. Formal logic in finite terms. Princeton, 1931.

2121. Foster, Hague Doyen. Intuitive conceptualization and the relativity of space, time, and motion. Chicago, 1966.

2122. Foster, Lawrence. Hume's theory of moral judgments. Pennsylvania, 1966.   67-7837

2123. Foster, Lynn Vasco. Constructionalism and the contemporary mind-body identity debate. Brandeis, 1971.   71-30127

2124. Foster, Marguerite Herzik. Mind as the function of symbols. U.C.L.A., 1941.

2125. Foster, Thomas Rowland. The Russell-Leibniz definition of identity: some problems. Ohio St., 1974.
74-24324

2126. Fotion, Nicholas George. Descriptive versus committive analysis: a contrast in two basic approaches to the analysis of ordinary value discourse. No. Carolina, 1957.

2127. Foulk, Gary Joe. The non-naturalist criticisms of private psychological naturalism. Oregon, 1966.
67-1855

2128. Foust, Conald George. Crisis and meaning in priests. Emory, 1972.   72-32664

2129. Fowler, George B. Intellectual interests of Englebert of Admont. Columbia, 1947.

2130. Fox, Claude Lawrence. A critique of R.G. Collingwood's metaphysics. Colorado, 1975.   76-3901

2131. Fox, Marvin. Moral fact and moral theory: a study of some methodological problems in contemporary ethics. Chicago, 1950.

2132. Fox, Michael Allen. Explanation and the unconscious. Toronto, 1970.

2133. Fox, Rev. Robert James. Limitation of warfare according to the just war theory. Catholic U., 1963.   64-351

2134. Foxx, Robert Gray. Erewhon and free-will revisited. U. of Washington, 1965.   65-15377

2135. Fraenckel, Carl Hartwig. Hegel, Croce, and Gentile.
Harvard, 1928.

2136. Francis, Leslie Ann Pickering. Impartiality and the
justification of moral principles. Michigan,
1974.   75-690

2137. Francis, Richard P. The doctrine of natural selection in John Dewey's value theory. Notre Dame,
1964.   64-10494

2138. Francisco, Edward Allen. Wants and acts: logical,
causal, and material connections. Purdue, 1974.
74-26711

2139. Francoeur, Br. Robert Alfred. The people in the social role of the Church according to Lamennais.
Notre Dame, 1958.   58-870

2140. Frank, James Paterson. An interpretation of the
Freudian theory of human nature and its relation
to ethics. Northwestern 1964.   64-5837

2141. Frank, Robert Worth. Dean Inge's interpretation of
mysticism. Northwestern, 1934.

2142. Frank, Tamar Zahava. Al-Kindî's Book of definitions:
its place in Arabic definition literature. Yale,
1975.   76-13710

2143. Franke, James Paul. The justification of punishment:
an examination of some aspects of the retributiv-
ist theory of punishment. Vanderbilt, 1963.
68-17969

2144. Frankel, Charles. The faith of reason; the idea of
progress in the French Enlightenment. Columbia,
1948.

2145. Frankel, Henry Robert. Examination of Harré's analysis of models, powers and natures, and their
role in scientific explanation. Ohio St., 1975.
75-19436

2146. Frankena, William. Recent intuitionism in British
ethics. Harvard, 1937.

2147. Frankfurt, Harry G. The essential objectivity of
what is known. Johns Hopkins, 1954.

2148. Franklin, Samuel Floyd. The content of individualism
as presented by typical modern thinkers. N.Y.U.,
1925.   73-17871

2149. Franks, Thomas Harbinson, Jr. Sartre's concept of

sincerity. Michigan, 1971. 72-14867

2150. Fránquiz, José Antonio. Borden Parker Bowne's treatment of the problem of change and identity. Boston U., 1940.

2151. Franz, Rev. Edward Q. The Thomistic doctrine on the possible intellect. Catholic U., 1950.

2152. Frary, Rev. Joseph Palmer. The ontological argument in modern debate. Fordham, 1972. 73-1476

2153. Frazier, Allie Mitchell. The concept of the self in the metaphysics of Charles Arthur Campbell. Boston U., 1963. 63-6566

2154. Fredrickson, Owen P. The psychology of ownership. Catholic U., 1954.

2155. Free, Lincoln Forrest. The philosophical and educational views of Henri Bergson. N.Y.U., 1939.

2156. Freed, Robert Bruce. Two competing models of the mind: an argument for mentalism. Berkeley, 1966. 66-8312

2157. Freedman, Benjamin. Principle and purpose: two kinds of legal consistency. C.U.N.Y., 1975. 75-21521

2158. Freeman, David Hugh. A comparative study of the relationship between philosophy and theology as exemplified by representatives of neo-Augustinianism, neo-Thomism, and neo-existentialism. Pennsylvania, 1958. 58-1841

2159. Freeman, Donald Dale. Radical evil and original sin: Kant's doctrine of freedom in existential perspective. Drew, 1969. 69-18622

2160. Freeman, Eugene. The categories of Charles Peirce. Chicago, 1937.

2161. Freeman, James Beaumont. Algebraic semantics for modal and relevant predicate logics. Indiana, 1973. 74-354

2162. French, F.C. The concept of law in ethics. Cornell, 1892.

2163. French, Sr. Mary Anne. Creation in Saint Thomas: a metaphysical study. St. Louis, 1962. 64-3741

2164. French, Peter Andrew. Rules, practices, and forms of life. Miami, 1971. 72-12899

2165. French, Stanley George. Concepts, meaning and meta-ethics. Virginia, 1959.   59-4220

2166. Freppert, Rev. Lucan Raymond. The basis of norality according to William Ockham. St. Bonaventure, 1961.

2167. Fretz, Raymond Morris. The philosophic background of college biology textbooks. Niagara, 1941.

2168. Friberg, Hans D. Love and justice in political theory: a study of Augustine's definition of the commonwealth. Chicago, 1945.

2169. Frick, Ivan Eugene. A study of the objective and subjective aspects of selfhood in the thought of Alfred North Whitehead. Columbia, 1959.   60-8

2170. Fried, Marlene Gerber. Marx's historical materialism and the problem of explanation in history. Brown, 1972.   73-2263

2171. Friedman, Joel Irwin. The set theory of proper classes. U.C.L.A., 1966.   66-12843

2172. Friedman, Kenneth Stephen. Statistical thermodynamics and the foundations of probability. M.I.T., 1972.

2173. Friedman, Marilyn Ann. The explanation of human behaviour in terms of its rationality. W. Ontario, 1974.

2174. Friedman, Michael Lee. Foundations of space-time theories. Princeton, 1972.   73-18757

2175. Friedman, Robert Malcolm. The ontology of Maurice Merleau-Ponty. Columbia, 1972.   75-12311

2176. Friedman, William Hillel. Some issues raised by the deductive logic of John Stuart Mill. Virginia, 1970.   70-26605

2177. Friel, Rev. George Q. Punishment, in the philosophy of St. Thomas Aquinas, and among some primitive peoples. Catholic U., 1939.

2178. Fries, Horace S. The development of Dewey's utilitarianism. Wisconsin, 1934.

2179. Friquegnon, Marie-Louise. Religious vision: truth and metaphor. N.Y.U., 1974.   74-18158

2180. Frisch, Joseph C. Extension and comprehension in

logic. Laval, 1968.

2181. Fritts, Frank. The concept of equality in its relation to a principle of political obligation. Princeton, 1914.

2182. Fritz, Anita D. An estimate of the influence of Malebranche upon the philosophy of Berkeley. Bryn Mawr, 1950.

2183. Fritz, Charles A., Jr. Bertrand Russell's construction of the external world. Columbia, 1950.
1849

2184. Fritzky, Ferdinand Joseph. Aesthetic preference for abstract designs as a function of their perceived complexity. Princeton, 1964.

2185. Froelich, Thomas Joseph. The intersubjective structure of subjectivity in Merleau-Ponty. Duquesne, 1975. 76-13120

2186. Froman, Wayne Jeffrey. Merleau-Ponty: language and the act of speech. Fordham, 1975. 76-4118

2187. Fromm, Georg Heinrich. The anti-rational critique of Kant's philosophy among his contemporaries: Jacobi, Hamann, Herder, Aenesidemus-Schulze. Brandeis, 1966. 67-459

2188. Fry, Samuel Thomas. An examination of some ontological problems from the point of view of the philosophy of Franz Brentano. Brown, 1974.
75-9152

2189. Fry, Stanley Aaron. Self-realization: a moral paradigm. R.P.I., 1975. 76-3695

2190. Frye, Albert Myrton. A study in ethics. Berkeley, 1930.

2191. Frye, Marilyn Powell. Meaning and illocutionary force. Cornell, 1969. 70-5794

2192. Frye, Robert Edward. Pragmatism in recent non-pragmatic systems: Santayana, Bergson, Whitehead. Indiana, 1956. 19461

2193. Fu, Wei-Hsun. Contemporary ethical autonomism: a critical study of Sartre and Hare. Illinois, 1969.
70-849

2194. Fuchs, Alan Edward. Hedonism and the concept of pleasure. Harvard, 1973.

2195. Fuchs, Rev. Oswald. The psychology of habit according to William Ockham. St. Bonaventure, 1950.

2196. Fuchs, Wolfgang Walter. Phenomenology and the metaphysics of presence: an essay in the philosophy of Edmund Husserl. Penn St., 1971. 72-9462

2197. Fuehrer, Mark Lawrence. The development of Kant's moral theology (in the Religion within the limits of reason alone.) Minnesota, 1974. 74-17245

2198. Fullinwider, Robert King. A critique of empiricism in recent ethical theory. Purdue, 1970.
70-18644

2199. Fulmer, Gilbert Everett. Wittgenstein, relativism, and reason. Rice, 1972. 72-26409

2200. Fulton, James A. The elements of causation. Brown, 1970. 71-13865

2201. Fulton, James Street. Five theories of truth. Cornell, 1934.

2202. Fulton, William Howard. On the vindication of induction: an attempt to complete the Reichenbach-Salmon program of vindicating induction. Minnesota, 1971. 72-14297

2203. Fumerton, Richard Anthony. Phenomenalism (examination of epistemological pressures toward a phenomenalistic analysis.) Brown, 1974. 75-9153

2204. Funchion, Kevin Paul. Russell, Strawson, and the king of France. Toronto, 1974.

2205. Fung, William Y. The theory of values in emergent evolution. N.Y.U., 1944. 73-17882

2206. Fung, Yu Lan. A comparative study of life's ideals; the way of decrease and increase, with interpretations and illustrations from the philosophies of the East and the West. Columbia, 1924.

2207. Funk, Roger L. Ethics and emotion; a study in the philosophy of Max Scheler. Northwestern, 1969.
70-58

2208. Funt, David. Diderot's esthetics. Columbia, 1966.
67-823

2209. Furgeson, Earl Hubert. The philosophical problem of political liberty with special reference to the social philosophy of Jean Jacques Rousseau. Boston U., 1939.

2210. Furry, William Davis. The aesthetic experience: its nature and function in epistemology. Johns Hopkins, 1907.

2211. Furth, Montgomery Thomas. On concept and object: Frege and a problem of universals. Berkeley, 1964. 64-13002

2212. Fuska, Michael Jan. Logic, language and the free will defense. Georgetown, 1975. 76-16324

2213. Fuss, Peter Lawrence. The structure of Royce's ethical theory. Harvard, 1962.

- G -

2214. Gaa, James Clyde. On the moral autonomy of science. Washington U., 1975. 76-14056

2215. Gadow, Sally Adair Metcalf. The relation of form and content in Hegel's Phenomenology of spirit. Texas, 1975. 76-8032

2216. Gagnon, Sr. Lorraine Marie. An analysis and evaluation of the role of symbol and semblance in the philosophy of art of Susanne K. Langer. Notre Dame, 1971. 71-27757

2217. Gagnon, Maurice. Le rationalisme de Descartes. Laval, 1968.

2218. Gahringer, Robert Ervin. The principle of self-criticism in practical reason. Harvard, 1953.

2219. Gale, George Daniel. The physicist as philosopher. Cal., Davis, 1971.

2220. Gale, Richard Milton. Time in analytic philosophy. N.Y.U., 1961. 62-1500

2221. Galgan, Gerald Joseph. The self and society in the thought of Henry David Thoreau. Fordham, 1971. 71-26969

2222. Galis, Leon. The 'rules of use' theory as a semantic theory of meaning. No. Carolina, 1966. 67-986

2223. Gallagher, Donald Arthur. The Scio me esse of Saint Augustine and the Cogito ergo sum of René Descartes. Marquette, 1944.

2224. Gallagher, Idella Jane. Moral obligation in the

philosophy of Henri Bergson. Marquette, 1963.
65-94

2225. Gallagher, Kenneth T. The philosophical method of Gabriel Marcel. Fordham, 1958.

2226. Gallagher, Thomas Austin. The contemporary status of the notion of existence and its limitation in Thomistic metaphysics. Catholic U., 1958.

2227. Gallagher, William J. Whitehead's theory of the human person. New School, 1974.   74-26962

2228. Galligan, Edward Michael. Plato and the philosophy of language. Indiana, 1965.   65-10823

2229. Galliher, Herbert Parrish. A theory of Lebesgue measure in an extension of basic logic. Yale, 1952.

2230. Gallup, John Richard. The primary meanings of the Latin word Modus. Laval, 1963.   63-6872

2231. Gambatese, Rev. Angelus. The commentary of William of Ockham on Aristotle's Perihermenias, /with_7 Part two, commentary on the Perihermenias, /Latin text_7. Notre Dame, 1966.   67-200

2232. Gambino, Richard. Concepts of mental disorder and criminal responsibility in law. N.Y.U., 1968.
68-13118

2233. Gamble, Harold Franklin. Analogy arguments for other minds. Washington U., 1974.   75-6594

2234. Gamertsfelder, Walter Sylvester. Thought, existence, and reality as viewed by F.H. Bradley and Bernard Bosanquet. Ohio St., 1920.

2235. Gandy, Daniel Ross. Karl Marx's philosophy of history: a new interpretation. Texas, 1967.
67-14829

2236. Gangadean, Ashok Kumar. Time, truth and logical determinism. Brandeis, 1971.   71-20330

2237. Ganguly, Rev. Theotonius Amal. Purush and prakrti (self and nature): a philosophical appraisal of Patanjala-Samkhya-Yoga. Notre Dame, 1951.
5270

2238. Gannon, Sr. Mary Ida. The active theory of sensation in Plotinus and St. Augustine. St. Louis, 1952.

2239. Gans, Steven Lawrence. An analysis of the philosophical methodology of Martin Heidegger. Penn St., 1967.   68-11984

2240. Ganz, Carole Ann Alpert. Events. Stanford, 1969.   70-18409

2241. Ganz, Joan Safran. Rules: a systematic study. Pennsylvania, 1967.   67-12744

2242. Garber, Daniel Elliot. A theory of justification. Harvard, 1975.

2243. Garber, Helen Lisa. A comparative study of Plato and Tagore in relation to esthetic education. N.Y.U., 1940.   73-3147

2244. Garcia-Fidalgo, Manuel. A critical examination of the identity theory. Miami, 1971.   71-19856

2245. Garcia-Gomez, Jorge. Living reason: the groundwork for a theory of reason in the philosophy of Ortega y Gasset. New School, 1971.   72-4032

2246. Gardner, James R. The role of experience and value in naturalistic and personalistic thought as represented by the philosophies of Clarence Irving Lewis and Edgar Sheffield Brightman. Illinois, 1953.   5230

2247. Gardner, Michael Roland. Indeterminacy of translation, quantum logic, and necessary truth. Harvard, 1971.

2248. Gardner, Ralph Ahiga. A philosophical examination of measurement in physics. Duke, 1942.

2249. Gardner, Romaine Luverne. Theonomous ethics: a study in the relationship between ethics and ontology in the thought of Paul Tillich. Columbia, 1966.   69-15547

2250. Garelick, Herbert Myron. Spinoza's absolute presupposition. Yale, 1958.

2251. Garey, Sr. Mary Jocelyn. Measure in the eternity of God and in created durations. Laval, 1946.

2252. Garfinkel, Alan Jay. Explanation and individuals. Harvard, 1975.

2253. Garland, William Jay. Whitehead's concept of actuality. Johns Hopkins, 1966.   66-12491

2254. Garner, Richard Thomas. The use of reasons in ethics and aesthetics. Michigan, 1965.   66-5073

2255. Garnier, Horatio Knight. John Stuart Mill and the philosophy of mediation. Columbia, 1919.

2256. Garrett, Richard George. A Jamesian metaphysics of morals. Columbia, 1971. 72-10433

2257. Garrett, Roland William. Dewey's metaphysics. Columbia, 1970. 71-17490

2258. Garrett, Walter Eugene. Antoine Augustin Cournot's theory of historical explanation. Columbia, 1967. 67-10585

2259. Garrity, Robert John. Finality in the philosophy of Henri Bergson. Duquesne, 1964.

2260. Garside, Bruce Allen. Aristotle's concept of nature as specific activity of function and its use in the Nicomachean ethics. Claremont, 1965. 67-9544

2261. Garside, Christine Allen. Strawson's Individuals: Part one. Claremont, 1967. 68-4624

2262. Garson, James Warfield. The logics of space and time. Pittsburgh, 1969. 70-11812

2263. Garver, John Newton. Grammar and criteria. Cornell, 1965. 65-12398

2264. Garvey, Charles Michael. Substance and being in Books four and five of the Sapientiale of Thomas of York: study and texts. Toronto, 1952.

2265. Garvey, Edwin Charles. St. Thomas' interpretation of Aristotle on the questions of creation and God. Toronto, 1937.

2266. Garvey, Sr. Mary P. Saint Augustine: Christian or neo-Platonist? From his retreat at Cassisiacum until his ordination at Hippo. Marquette, 1939.

2267. Garvin, Lucius. Propositions and facts. Brown, 1933.

2268. Garvin, Ned Stewart. Analysis in Russell: its ontological and epistemological foundations. Boston U., 1975. 75-13

2269. Garvin, Rev. Thomas Robert. The individual and society and John Dewey. St. Louis, 1971. 72-23935

2270. Gaskins, Richard Hill. An examination of Hegel's dialectical method. Yale, 1971. 72-16324

2271. Gatto, Edo Peter. The doctrine in the opusculum, De natura generis, attributed to St. Thomas Aquinas. Toronto, 1962.

2272. Gatzke, Ken Walter. Objectivity and aesthetic judgment in the philosophy of Frank Sibley. Illinois, 1974. 75-310

2273. Gauss, Charles Edward. The aesthetic theories of French artists, 1855 to the present. Johns Hopkins, 1941.

2274. Gavin, William Joseph. An aesthetic approach to the philosophy of William James. Fordham, 1970. 71-8714

2275. Gean, William David. The concept of emotion. Berkeley, 1972.

2276. Geary, Andrew C. Marxist-Hegelian dialectics. Laval, 1949.

2277. Gedalecia, David. Wu Ch'eng: a neo-Confucian of the Yüan. Harvard, 1971. 71-30156

2278. Geddes, Leonard Robert. The foundations of morality. Cal., S. Diego, 1968. 68-11840

2279. Geels, Donald Eugene. False beliefs and possible states of affairs. Indiana, 1974. 75-8940

2280. Geffen, M. David. Faith and reason in Elijah del Medigo's Behinat ha-dat and the philosophic backgrounds of the work. Columbia, 1970. 71-6175

2281. Geiger, Joseph Roy. Some religious implications of pragmatism. Chicago, 1916.

2282. Geisler, Norman Leo. Religious transcendence: some criteria. Loyola, 1970.

2283. Gelber, Sidney. The philosophy of John Grote. Columbia, 1954. 8664

2284. Gelinas, Elmer Thomas. The relation between life and existence: a study of vivere viventibus est esse as found in Thomas Aquinas. Toronto, 1954.

2285. Geller, Leonard Raymond. The wayfaring self: a study of Gabriel Marcel's philosophy of man. Texas, 1971. 72-11349

2286. Gellman, Jerome I. Non-existence, modalities, and Anselm's ontological argument. Wayne St., 1970. 71-405

2287. Gelpi, Rev. Donald Louis. Emerson's philosophy of
      religious experience. Fordham, 1970. 71-8715

2288. Gelven, Charles Michael. Martin Heidegger's theory
      of fundamental ontology. Washington U., 1966.
      66-11870

2289. Genauer, Marvin. The treatment of homicide in the
      Talmud. U. of Washington, 1970. 71-16947

2290. Genco, Peter. Verification, falsification and the
      language of Christian theism. N.Y.U., 1970.
      71-2291

2291. Gendin, Sidney. Theories of punishment and the idea
      of criminal responsibility. N.Y.U., 1965.
      66-8561

2292. Gendlin, Eugene T. The function of experiencing in
      symbolization. Chicago, 1958.

2293. Gendreau, Francis Richard. The realism of William
      James. Boston Coll., 1974. 74-19217

2294. Gendron, Bernard Louis. The materialist conception
      of man: a critical investigation. Notre Dame,
      1967. 67-13597

2295. Genova, Anthony C. The transcendental principles of
      synthetic unity in the critical philosophy of Im-
      manuel Kant. Chicago, 1965.

2296. Genova, Judith. An approach to Wittgenstein's meta-
      physics. Brandeis, 1970. 70-24630

2297. Gentry, George Vincent. Sensible appearance and phys-
      ical reality: a critical study of some phases of
      Broad's sensum theory. Chicago, 1931.

2298. Geoghegan, William Davidson. Varieties of Platonism
      in contemporary religious thought; with special
      reference to W.R. Inge, P.E. More, A.E. Taylor,
      William Temple, A.N. Whitehead and George Santay-
      ana. Columbia, 1951. 2533

2299. Georgacarakos, George N. A study in the modal exten-
      sions of Lewis' S4. Missouri, 1973. 74-18532

2300. Georgalis, Nicholas. Indeterminacy of translation
      and intended interpretation. Chicago, 1974.

2301. George, Rev. Francis Eugene. Society and experience:
      a critical examination of the social philosophies
      of Royce, Mead and Sellars. Tulane, 1969.
      70-24521

2302. George, Richard John. The role of points in Hume's analysis of space. Notre Dame, 1965. 65-6786

2303. George, Rolf Armin. The problems of the infinite and the continuum in some major philosophical systems of the Enlightenment. Michigan St., 1961. 61-2693

2304. Geran, Juliana. Alfred North Whitehead on the ontological principle: a critique of early modern epistemology in Process and reality. Chicago, 1974.

2305. Gerber, David Albert. Gratuitous argument: an analysis of criticisms of the linguistic constructions of John Austin, Russell, Ayer, and Carnap. Texas, 1970. 72-2337

2306. Gerber, William. The domain of reality. Columbia, 1946.

2307. Gerhard, William A. Infra-rational knowledge and the intellectual virtue of prudence. Notre Dame, 1948.

2308. Gerlach, Allen Meyer. Hartshorne's conception of God. Harvard, 1951.

2309. Gerlach, Muriel Wood Winet. Interval measurement of subjective magnitudes with subliminal differences. Stanford, 1957. 58-4378

2310. Germain, Paul. La génération et la corruption des mixtes. Laval, 1952.

2311. Gerraughty, Roddy Francis. The role and treatment of poetry in Plato's Republic. Penn St., 1974. 74-28955

2312. Gerrity, Bro. Benignus. St. Thomas' doctrine of substantial form, and of the relations between this doctrine and certain problems and movements of contemporary philosophy. Catholic U., 1937.

2313. Gerry, Rev. Joseph J. Kierkegaard: the problem of transcendence; an interpretation of the stages. Fordham, 1959.

2314. Gerson, Lloyd Philip. The unity of Plato's Parmenides. Toronto, 1975.

2315. Gerson, Oscar. Mental association. Pennsylvania, 1898.

2316. Gerstein, Louis Coleman. On the conception of God

in the philosophy of Maimonides and St. Thomas
Aquinas. N.Y.U., 1943. 73-17888

2317. Gert, Bernard. The moral philosophy of Thomas Hobbes.
Cornell, 1962. 62-5824

2318. Gervasi, Julian Anthony. The philosophy of Michele
Federico Sciacca. Notre Dame, 1965. 65-11114

2319. Gettier, Edmund Lee, III. Bertrand Russell's theories of belief. Cornell, 1961. 61-6747

2320. Gettner, Alan Frederick. Analytic truth in the philosophies of Quine and the later Wittgenstein.
Columbia, 1971. 72-10435

2321. Geuras, Dean Peter. An analysis of memory. Colorado, 1972. 73-1773

2322. Geuss, Raymond. Persons and selves. Columbia, 1971.
74-17862

2323. Gewirth, Alan. Marsilius of Padua and medieval political philosophy. Columbia, 1951.

2324. Geyer, Denton Loring. The pragmatic theory of truth as developed by Peirce, James and Dewey. Illinois, 1914.

2325. Geyer, George Edwin, Jr. The nature and content of first philosophy in the text of Ibn Ruschd's Great commentary on Book twelve of Aristotle's Metaphysics. Marquette, 1967. 68-485

2326. Ghobar, Ash. Abstract entities. Wisconsin, 1959.
59-3189

2327. Gianelli, Arthur Francis. A study of the electromagnetic field theory of James Clerk Maxwell from the standpoint of a modified realist view of the nature of scientific theory. St. John's, 1970.
71-9528

2328. Giannoni, Carlo Borromeo. Conventionalism in logic.
Pittsburgh, 1966. 66-13473

2329. Gibbard, Allan Fletcher. Utilitarianisms and coordination. Harvard, 1971.

2330. Gibbens, Helen Paxton. Berkeley and Wittgenstein: some correlations. Oklahoma, 1970. 70-21829

2331. Gibson, David Eugene. Hans-Georg Gadamer's hermeneutic as a critique of historical reason. Rice, 1968. 68-15623

2332. Gibson, Joan McIver. Anthony Ashley Cooper, third earl of Shaftesbury: aesthetic theory and its implications for skepticism and a doctrine of wit, humor, and ridicule. Cal., S. Diego, 1974.
74-17706

2333. Gibson, Mary B. Behind the veil of ignorance: a dim view. A critical study of Rawls's Theory of justice. Princeton, 1975. 76-18246

2334. Gibson, Mary Sheila O'Neill. Time and the metaphysics of finite being. Toronto, 1972.

2335. Gibson, Roland Leonard. Time and eternity. Claremont, 1970. 71-13691

2336. Giegengack, Sr. Mary Elizabeth. Can God be experienced? A study in the philosophy of religion of William Ernest Hocking. Georgetown, 1972.
72-22771

2337. Gienapp, Ruth Anne. The monism of Ernst Haeckel. Cornell, 1969. 69-5021

2338. Gier, Nicholas Francis, Jr. Heidegger and the ontological "differenz": a historical-philosophical analysis. Claremont, 1972. 73-6169

2339. Giere, Ronald Nelson. Prediction and confirmation. Cornell, 1968. 68-15720

2340. Gieschen, Donald Werner. C.D. Broad's philosophy of logic. Minnesota, 1962. 63-1211

2341. Gietz, William Arnold. Toward a cognitive theory of ethics. Rochester, 1974. 74-22582

2342. Giffin, John J. The interpretation of the two Thomistic definitions of certitude. Laval, 1954.

2343. Giglio, Rev. Charles Joseph. Freedom of self-determination in Saint Thomas and contemporary western thought. Catholic U., 1964. 64-10749

2344. Giguere, John Arthur. Bertrand Russell's theory of empiricism: an analysis of his later works. Marquette, 1970. 71-5298

2345. Giguere, Robert J. The social value of public worship according to Thomistic principles. Catholic U., 1950.

2346. Gilbert, Joseph. Universalizability and generalization argument in ethics. N.Y.U., 1969.
70-3069

2347. Gilbert, Michael A. A logical analysis of relevance. Waterloo, 1974.

2348. Gilbert, Neal Ward. Concepts of method in the Renaissance and their ancient and medieval antecedents. Columbia, 1956. 16809

2349. Gilbert, Thomas Endor. Utilitarianism and distributive justice. Massachusetts, 1973. 7L-8595

2350. Gilbertson, Mark Orland. Knowledge and the concept of the future. Southern Cal., 1974. 74-21473

2351. Giles, James Earl. A contemporary interpretation of William James's will-to-believe argument. Fordham, 1971. 71-26972

2352. Gillan, Garth Jackson. Logos and symbol: an essay in the phenomenology of operative language. Duquesne, 1966.

2353. Gillespie, Norman Chase. Fundamental moral principles: Kant, Singer, and Lyons. Wisconsin, 1970. 71-3458

2354. Gilligan, Bernard Benedict. Philosophy and psychiatry. Fordham, 1956.

2355. Gillman, Neil Gardner. Gabriel Marcel on religious knowledge. Columbia, 1975. 75-27415

2356. Gillon, Rev. James A. Hegel's *Phenomenology of mind*: a critical commentary. Notre Dame, 1975. 75-13091

2357. Gilman, Richard C. The general metaphysics of William Ernest Hocking. Boston U., 1952.

2358. Gilmour, John Calvin. Analogical generalization and Whitehead's panpsychism. Emory, 1966. 66-8653

2359. Gilpin, Robert Crafton. An examination of some expressive theories of ethical judgment. Wisconsin, 1955.

2360. Gimbel, Barbara E. Freud's theory of mind and meaning. Bryn Mawr, 1949. 7296

2361. Gimigliano, Anthony James. The ethical and political thought of Giovanni Gentile. Columbia, 1961. 61-3881

2362. Gináscol, Frederick H. Mediaeval origins of modern philosophy and science. Texas, 1952.

2363. Ginet, Carl Allen. Reasons, causes, and free will. Cornell, 1961. 61-1428

2364. Ginsberg, Mitchell Dobkin. Belief: its conceptual and phenomenological structure. Michigan, 1967. 68-7607

2365. Ginsberg, Robert Ernest. Social contract and the elimination of war. Pennsylvania, 1966. 67-3071

2366. Ginzburg, Benjamin. The doctrine of essence in the philosophy of Spinoza. Harvard, 1926.

2367. Gioscia, Victor Joseph. Plato's image of time: an essay in philosophical sociology. Fordham, 1963. 63-5592

2368. Girgus, Samuel Bruce. Against the grain: the achievement of John Hersey. New Mexico, 1971.

2369. Girill, Terry Robert. Scientific micro-reductive explanations. Berkeley, 1973.

2370. Girvetz, Harry Kenneth. Valuation and moral progress. Berkeley, 1938.

2371. Gish, Delbert R. The problem of a rational good. Boston U., 1943.

2372. Given, Philip Lombard. The juristic person: a problem in the philosophy of law. Harvard, 1927.

2373. Givner, David Aaron. A study of George Berkeley's theory of linguistic meaning: with a discussion of Locke's account of language and a consideration of the relevance of their philosophies of science. Columbia, 1959. 59-4062

2374. Glanville, John J. Verification in the philosophy of nature. Notre Dame, 1950.

2375. Glass, Ronald Johnson. Leibniz and perception. Ohio St., 1972. 73-2002

2376. Glathe, Alfred Bouligny. Hume's theory of the passions and of morals: a study of his theory of the imagination in books II and III of the Treatise. Berkeley, 1947.

2377. Gleason, Rev. Robert Walter. The objective good for the person. Fordham, 1948.

2378. Glenn, John Deavenport, Jr. Kant's doctrine of aesthetic ideas. Yale, 1968. 69-8354

2379. Glick, Daryl John. Freedom, density, and philosophy:
an examination of Blondel's L'action. Notre Dame,
1969.   69-18510

2380. Glickman, Jack Bennett. J.L. Austin's theory of
speech acts. N.Y.U., 1972.   72-21507

2381. Glicksman, Marjorie. The concept of existenz in contemporary German philosophy. Radcliffe, 1935.

2382. Glidden, David Kenneth. The Epicurean theory of knowledge. Princeton, 1971.   72-2709

2383. Glidden, Jocelyn Cheney. Hume on superstition. Colorado, 1969.   69-19537

2384. Glidewell, Richard Alfred. Material man: a study of
mental predicates, robots, and consciousness. So.
Illinois, 1974.   75-13270

2385. Glossop, Ronald John. A critical analysis of some
aspects of Charles L. Stevenson's ethical theory.
Washington U., 1960.   60-4686

2386. Glouberman, Seymour. Examples and necessity. Cornell, 1972.   72-23665

2387. Glowienka, Emerine Frances. The Christian metaphysics of Gerard Smith, S.J. Marquette, 1973.
                                         73-27525

2388. Gluck, Samuel Emanuel. The ethical development of
managerial responsibility. Columbia, 1960.
                                         60-5090

2389. Glymour, Clark Noren. Theories: an examination of
the logical empiricist philosophy of science.
Indiana, 1970.   70-10258

2390. Goble, Louis Frank. A coherence theory of meaning.
Pittsburgh, 1968.   68-7842

2391. Gochnauer, Myron Louis. Analysis of knowledge. W.
Ontario, 1973.

2392. Godar, James Patrick. An evaluation of W.T. Stace's
views on explanation and their role in his interpretation of mystical experience. Marquette,
1969.   70-11963

2393. Godbey, John William, Jr. Mental images and imaging
experiences. Duke, 1974.   75-2381

2394. Godbout, Robert Maurice. R.G. Collingwood's theory
of action and duty: a systematic restatement.

Kansas, 1974. 75-6187

2395. Godcharles, Charles A. Some contemporary political theories philosophically considered. Duke, 1937.

2396. Godow, Rew Arnold, Jr. A philosophical analysis of behavioristic psychology with special emphasis on theoretical and methodological questions concerning behavior therapy. Illinois, 1974. 75-315

2397. Godsey, Raleigh Kirby. Relation and substance in the metaphysics of Alfred North Whitehead. Tulane, 1969. 70-6397

2398. Goe, George. Empiricism and geometry in Hobbes and Locke. Columbia, 1959. 59-3100

2399. Goedecke, Walter R. Rights, interests, and the Constitution: the jurisprudence of Mr. Justice Stephen Johnson Field. Chicago, 1958.

2400. Goff, Edwin Leroy. The teaching and learning of virtue. Boston Coll., 1974. 74-18740

2401. Goff, Robert Allen. The language of method in Wittgenstein's Philosophical investigations. Drew, 1967. 67-14374

2402. Gohdes, Clarence Louis Frank. The periodicals of American transcendentalism. Columbia, 1931.

2403. Goheen, John David Maclay. The problem of matter and form and the De ente et essentia of Thomas Aquinas. Harvard, 1935.

2404. Goicoechea, David L. The equivalence of the existential and the religious in Kierkegaard. Loyola, 1972.

2405. Golawski, Bernard. The philosophy of the atonement or reconciliation. Case, 1949.

2406. Goldberg, Bruce Charles. Physicalism; some considerations. Princeton, 1964. 65-2131

2407. Goldberg, Bruce Lawrence. A phenomenological approach to the question of certainty. Colorado, 1973. 73-23251

2408. Goldberg, Fred Ivan. Empiricism and necessary truth. Brandeis, 1969. 70-12216

2409. Goldblatt, David Ian. Wittgenstein, rules and logical necessity. Pennsylvania, 1972. 72-25578

2410. Goldenson, Robert Myar. The concept of intuition. Harvard, 1941.

2411. Goldfarb, Warren David. On decision problems for quantification theory. Harvard, 1975.

2412. Golding, Martin Philip. Community, covenant, and reason: a study in Jewish legal philosophy. Columbia, 1959.   59-3101

2413. Goldinger, Milton Benjamin. The moral justification of punishment. Ohio St., 1965.   66-6259

2414. Goldman, Alan Harris. Implications of Piaget for a philosophy of perception. Columbia, 1972.
    72-31211

2415. Goldman, Alvin Ira. Action. Princeton, 1965.
    65-6376

2416. Goldman, Holly Martin Smith. The generalization principle in ethics. Michigan, 1972. 73-11125

2417. Goldman, Michael. A consideration of some theories of ontological commitment. Brown, 1969.
    70-8718

2418. Goldman, Steven Louis. An essay on intersubjectivity. Boston U., 1971.   71-26416

2419. Goldner, Sanford. The language of pragmatism. U.C.L.A., 1941.

2420. Goldshur, David. Cognitive domains in the philosophies of Descartes and Spinoza. U.C.L.A., 1941.

2421. Goldstein, Leon Jay. Form, function and structure: a philosophical study concerning the foundations of theory in anthropology. Yale, 1954.

2422. Goldstein, Signe Barbara Burke. The concept and the significance of the model in physics. Columbia, 1969.   70-6979

2423. Goldstone, Peter Jay. Human nature and political philosophy. Wisconsin, 1968.   69-918

2424. Goldthwait, John Turner. Kant's pre-critical esthetic: a study, together with a translation into English, of Kant's Observations on the feeling of the beautiful and sublime. Northwestern, 1957.
    57-4846

2425. Goldworth, Amnon. The utilitarianism of Jeremy Bentham as a social decision method. Stanford, 1960.
    60-3803

2426. Golightly, Cornelius Lacy. Thought and language in Whitehead's categorial scheme. Michigan, 1941.

2427. Gomberg, Paul. The ambiguity of 'possible' in skeptical arguments. Harvard, 1972.

2428. Gomes, Gabriel Joseph. Foundations of ethics in Walter Burleigh's commentary on Aristotle's Nicomachean ethics. Columbia, 1973.   73-26610

2429. Gonda, Joseph P. Politikē technē in Protagoras: 309-338. Penn St., 1975.   76-26827

2430. Gondin, William R. Prefaces to inquiry; a study in the origins and relevance of modern theories of knowledge. Columbia, 1941.

2431. Gonsalves, Rev. Milton Albert. Scheler's phenomenology of free decision. Fordham, 1974. 74-19659

2432. Gonso, Raymond Milton. The science of ethics and theory of personality of Charles Bernard Renouvier. Ohio St., 1936.

2433. Gonzales, Crescens. Imperfectio et peccatum veniale. Laval, 1941.

2434. Gonzalez, Rev. Carlos Ignacio. J.J. Rousseau, metaphysician of human nature. St. Louis, 1970.
   71-21390

2435. Gooch, Paul William. Socratic paradox in Plato: a study in virtue, knowledge and related concepts in Plato's Dialogues. Toronto, 1970.

2436. Goode, Terry Michael. Neo-regularism and causal historical explanation. Wayne St., 1972.
   73-12518

2437. Goodell, Willard Arthur. Behaviorism and teleology. Yale, 1921.

2438. Goodman, Donald Franklin. Freedom, the person, and community: Berdyaev and the Marxist leaven. Fordham, 1967.   68-3691

2439. Goodman, Harvey Louis. Heidegger's aesthetic theory: truth and the work of art. Tennessee, 1974.
   75-11168

2440. Goodman, Henry Nelson. A study of qualities: an essay in elementary constructional theory. Harvard, 1941.

2441. Goodman, Russell Brian. Some psychological phenomena

and the nature of perception. Johns Hopkins,
1971.   72-16911

2442. Goodpaster, Kenneth Edwin. Prescriptivism and neo-
naturalism in ethical theory. Michigan, 1973.
73-24572

2443. Goodrum, Craig Randall. The rationality of actions.
Texas, 1974.   75-4375

2444. Goodwin, Robert Peter. The metaphysical pragmatism
of Charles Sanders Peirce. Georgetown, 1958.

2445. Goodwin, William Francis. Knowledge and existence
in the philosophy of George Santayana. Berkeley,
1949.

2446. Goosens, William Kenneth. The logic of experimentation. Stanford, 1970.   71-19690

2447. Gordon, Alexander Duff. Implications of logical
positivism for ethical theory. Nebraska, 1963.
64-2620

2448. Gordon, Kate. Psychology of meaning. Chicago, 1903.

2449. Gordon, Lee DeWayne. Immediacy and private language
in the problem of other minds. Texas, 1971.
72-11352

2450. Gordon, Martin L. The rationalism of Jacob Anatoli.
Yeshiva, 1974.   74-23549

2451. Gordon, Robert Morris. The argument from similar
cases in moral discourse. Columbia, 1965.
66-6933

2452. Gordon, William Sherman. The problem of verification of religious beliefs. Texas, 1973.
73-26008

2453. Gordy, Michael Louis. Features of consciousness
fundamental to selfhood. Texas, 1970. 71-11541

2454. Gore, William. Imagination in Spinoza and Hume.
Chicago, 1901.

2455. Gorfinkle, Joseph Isaac. The eight chapters of Maimonides on ethics (<u>Shemonah perakim</u>), a psychological and ethical treatise. Columbia, 1909.

2456. Gorospe, Rev. Vitaliano Rebuldela. Moral obligation
in John Dewey's ethical naturalism. St. Louis,
1962.   64-3742

2457. Gorovitz, Samuel. Deductive models for causal explanation. Stanford, 1963. 64-5579

2458. Gorr, Michael John. The structure of human action. Brown, 1975. 76-15639

2459. Goss, Martha J. Concepts of reality and the utilization of imagination. Stanford, 1971.

2460. Gosselin, Marcelle. Le droit naturel. Laval, 1967.

2461. Gotesky, Rubin. Logic as an independent science. An examination of E. Husserl's conception of pure logic in the Prolegomena zur reinen logik, first volume of the Logische untersuchungen. N.Y.U., 1939. 73-17906

2462. Gotshalk, Dilman Walter. The problem of mind and objects; the philosophies of Samuel Alexander and Ernst Cassirer. Cornell, 1927.

2463. Gotshalk, Richard Allan. What is philosophy? Northwestern, 1957. 57-4847

2464. Gotterbarn, Donald William. Hume's theory of relations. Rochester, 1971. 72-715

2465. Gotthelf, Allan Stanley. Aristotle's conception of final causality. Columbia, 1975. 75-12360

2466. Gottlieb, Dale Victor. Use of formal systems in logic and mathematics. Brandeis, 1970.
70-24632

2467. Gottlieb, Roger S. "The existing individual and the will-to-power": a comparison of Kierkegaard's and Nietzsche's answers to the question: What is it to make a transition from one value system to another? Brandeis, 1975. 75-24801

2468. Goudge, Thomas Anderson. The theory of knowledge in Charles S. Peirce. Toronto, 1937.

2469. Gouinlock, James Sturges. Metaphysics and value theory: a study in the moral philosophy of John Dewey. Columbia, 1969. 70-6980

2470. Gould, Carol Cirelle. Authenticity and being-with others: a critique of Heidegger's Sein und zeit. Yale, 1971. 72-16327

2471. Gould, James Adams. The independent origin of pragmatism in France, Germany, and the United States. Michigan, 1954. 7654

2472. Gould, Josiah Bancroft, Jr. The philosophy of Chrysippus. Johns Hopkins, 1962.

2473. Gould, William Edward. The philosophy of Boris Chicherin; from practice to theory. Yale, 1970.
71-16244

2474. Gourevitch, Victor. The *Philosophy of life* of Wilhelm Dilthey. Chicago, 1956.

2475. Govier, G.R. A study of transcendental arguments. Waterloo, 1971.

2476. Gowen, Howard Burnham. Beyond the limits of nihilism: an analysis of the works of Albert Camus. Florida St., 1961.   61-5643

2477. Gowen, Julie. Philosophy and comparative religion. Wisconsin, 1972.   73-10713

2478. Goyette, Charles Edgar, Jr. Self-evidence, truth criterion and concept: its methodological and metaphysical nature. U.C.L.A., 1956.

2479. Gozdowski, Edward William. Concepts, objectivity, and time: an interpretation of the analytic of principles in Kant's *Critique of pure reason*. Notre Dame, 1974.   74-25428

2480. Grabau, Richard Fred. Existence and truth in the philosophy of Karl Jaspers. Yale, 1953.
70-24052

2481. Graber, Glenn Campbell. The relationship of morality and religion: language, logic and apologetics. Michigan, 1972.   72-29065

2482. Grady, Joseph Elmer. An existential approach to the ethical problem of decision. DePaul, 1971.
72-7719

2483. Grady, Sr. Mary-Rita. Time, the form of the will: an essay on Josiah Royce's philosophy of time. Georgetown, 1973.   74-1432

2484. Graeser, Andreas. Plotinus and the Stoics. Princeton, 1970.   71-1605

2485. Graff, James Allan. Moral agency. Brown, 1963.
64-1973

2486. Graham, George Albert. The identities of persons. Brandeis, 1975.   75-24802

2487. Graham, Joseph Martin. Secondary causal influx according to Saint Thomas Aquinas. Notre Dame, 1962. 62-2297

2488. Graham, William Clarence. Strawson's concept of a person. Toronto, 1969.

2489. Grajewski, Rev. Maurice J. The formal distinction of Duns Scotus. Catholic U., 1944.

2490. Gram, Moltke Stefanus. Two theories of the a priori. Indiana, 1966. 66-14825

2491. Gramlich, Francis W. Symbolism and meaning. Princeton, 1936.

2492. Grandstrand, Karen Lynn. Ifs, cans, and the compatibilist thesis. Minnesota, 1973. 74-10506

2493. Grandy, Richard Edward. On formalization and formalistic philosophies of mathematics. Princeton, 1968. 68-9680

2494. Grandy, William Norman. Empirical method in its application to religious epistemology with reference to the writings of D.C. Macintosh and H.N. Wieman. Northwestern, 1951.

2495. Grange, Joseph. Tragic value in the thought of Alfred North Whitehead. Fordham, 1970. 71-8718

2496. Grannum, Stanley Everton. The metaphysics of the self involved in the thought of James Ward, Frederick R. Tennant, and Mary W. Calkins. Boston U., 1948.

2497. Granrose, John Thomas. The implications of psychological studies of conscience for ethics. Michigan, 1966. 67-1749

2498. Grant, Brian Eric James. Wittgenstein on pain and privacy. Cal., Irvine, 1968. 69-754

2499. Grantham, Emily Virginia. Personality and society. Columbia, 1972.

2500. Grassi, Carlo Albert. The doctrine of creation in the Sapientiale of Thomas of York; study and text. Toronto, 1952.

2501. Grassi, Joseph Gerald. The political philosophy of Benedetto Croce. Buffalo, 1960. 60-4313

2502. Grassian, Victor David. Criminal responsibility and the mentally ill offender. U.C.L.A., 1970. 70-21530

2503. Gravander, Jerry Wallace. Newton's New theory about light and colors and the hypothetico-deductive account of scientific method: scientific practice contra philosophic doctrine. Texas, 1975.
75-16676

2504. Gravely, James William. Heidegger and metaphysics: an attempt to found a dialogue. Tulane, 1974.
74-20756

2505. Graves, John Cowperthwaite. The conceptual foundations of contemporary relativity theory. Princeton, 1969.
70-14211

2506. Gray, Bonnie Jean. An interpretation of the moral philosophy of David Hume: how to derive 'ought' from 'is.' Syracuse, 1973.
74-8258

2507. Gray, Christopher Berry. The methodology of Maurice Hauriou. Catholic U., 1970.
70-23672

2508. Gray, Henry David. Emerson; a statement of New England transcendentalism as expressed in the philosophy of its chief exponent. Columbia, 1905.

2509. Gray, Jesse G. Hegel's Hellenic ideal. Columbia, 1941.

2510. Gray, Paul Dennis. A defense of P.F. Strawson's theory of self. Ohio St., 1970.
71-7466

2511. Gray-Smith, Rowland. God in the philosophy of Schelling. Pennsylvania, 1933.

2512. Grean, Stanley. Shaftesbury's philosophy of religion and morals: a study in enthusiasm. Columbia, 1961.
61-5463

2513. Greco, Joseph V. The dialectic of the early Stoics. Catholic U., 1970.
70-22692

2514. Green, Garrett Douglas. Positive religion in the early philosophy of the German idealists. Yale, 1971.
72-16328

2515. Green, Gervase. The concepts of evolution and mechanism. Yale, 1897.

2516. Green, James Lloyd. The legal philosophy of Alf Ross. Columbia, 1968.
69-409

2517. Green, Michael Barry. A study of the conceptual connections between thinking, feeling, and emotions, and an analysis of some emotional reactions which are based on unsound thinking. U.C.L.A., 1972.
73-1698

2518. Green, Osborne Harvey, Jr. Criteria, incorrigibility, and feelings. Vanderbilt, 1966. 66-10980

2519. Green, Thomas Franklin. Thomas Reid's theory of sensation and perception. Cornell, 1953.

2520. Green, Rev. Thomas Henry. The idea of novelty in Peirce and Whitehead. Notre Dame, 1968.
69-4066

2521. Green, Willard Poole. Collective responsibility. Temple, 1975. 75-28221

2522. Greenberg, Arthur Richard. Reid on scepticism, idealism, and perceptual knowledge. Iowa, 1973.
74-16629

2523. Greenberg, Robert Sidney. P.F. Strawson's theory of reference. Chicago, 1966.

2524. Greenberg, Sidney. The infinite in Giordano Bruno, with a translation of his *Dialogue concerning the cause, principle and one*. Columbia, 1950.

2525. Greene, Alice B. The religious uses of silence. Columbia, 1938.

2526. Greene, Diana Scesny. 'Peri Phiseos': on being and the world. The development of metaphysics from Thales to Parmenides. Colorado, 1975. 75-23602

2527. Greene, James Peter. The relation of science to common sense in the philosophy of John Dewey. Notre Dame, 1971. 72-5127

2528. Greene, Murray. Hegel's notion of pre-conscious mind. New School, 1962.

2529. Greene, Robert Alan. Substance, mind and the categories: an Aristotelian theory of language. Colorado, 1974. 75-3785

2530. Greenlee, Douglas Arthur. The sign theory of C.S. Peirce. Columbia, 1964. 67-10375

2531. Greenman, Martin A. Whitehead's theory of meaning. Chicago, 1950.

2532. Greenspan, Patricia S. Derived obligation: some paradoxes escaped. Harvard, 1972.

2533. Greenstein, Harold. Philosophy, science and human behavior. N.Y.U., 1968. 68-13120

2534. Greenwell, James Richard. The morality of abortion.

Arizona, 1975. 76-1404

2535. Greenwood, Robert Lawrence. G.E. Moore's theory of perception. Miami, 1968. 70-1217

2536. Greenwood, Walter Robert. Current naturalism and Christian theism. Drew, 1927.

2537. Greer, Melvin Emal. Triumph of the spirit: Royce's theory of the one and the many. Tulane, 1963.
64-1810

2538. Gregor, Mary Jeanne Irish. Kant's applied ethics; a study of the application of the categorical imperative in the Tugendlehre of the Metaphysik der sitten. Toronto, 1957.

2539. Gregory, Carlton Herbert. The problem of descriptive religious statements with special reference to the thought of Paul Tillich. Brown, 1959.
59-4343

2540. Gregory, Donald Rex. Existence and necessity: some new considerations on the ontological argument for the existence of God. Vanderbilt, 1972.
73-1618

2541. Gregory, Raymond. A study of Locke's theory of knowledge. Ohio St., 1917.

2542. Gregory, Thomas Maclay. The imperative function of an ethical judgment. Pennsylvania, 1958.
58-1843

2543. Greif, Gary Francis. St. Thomas' method of establishing the subject of metaphysics; a modern reconstruction. Toronto, 1965.

2544. Grenoble, Arthur Bultmann. Hedonism reconsidered: a critical examination of Hilliard's axiology and its implications for ethical theory. Tulane, 1973. 74-10687

2545. Grewe, Rudolf. On Ackermann's set theory. U.C.L.A., 1966. 66-7130

2546. Grier, Philip Todd. Contemporary Soviet ethical theory. Michigan, 1973. 74-3635

2547. Griesbach, Marcellus Frederick. The relationship between temporal and spiritual powers in John of Paris and James of Viterbo; a study of early fourteenth century Thomistic political philosophy. Toronto, 1956.

2548. Griffin, James Philip. Foundations of ethical value in the philosophy of Roy Wood Sellars and William Temple. Boston U., 1966. 66-11299

2549. Griffin, John J. The interpretation of the two Thomistic definitions of certitude. Laval, 1950.

2550. Griffiss, James Edward, Jr. A study of the principle of negativity in the philosophy of Hegel. Yale, 1962.

2551. Griffith, Stephen Ray. Personal identity. Pittsburgh, 1973. 73-27179

2552. Griffith, William Byron. Problems about infinity: Wittgenstein's contributions. Yale, 1963.

2553. Griffith, William James. G.E. Moore's concept of analysis and its relation to metaphysics. Brown, 1973. 74-3019

2554. Griffiths, Leslie Morris Samuel. A logical analysis of I.M. Crombie's position on the theology and falsification debate. Nebraska, 1968. 69-17324

2555. Grill, Michael A. Descartes: a re-interpretation of his metaphysics and science. Kansas, 1975. 76-16727

2556. Grimes, William Van, Jr. The language of practical discourse. No. Carolina, 1969. 70-3237

2557. Grimm, Robert Henry. Subject-predicate sentences. Duke, 1963. 63-6998

2558. Grimm, Rodolfo Ahumada. The philosophies of Antonio Caso and José Vasconcelos with special emphasis on their concepts of value. Southern Cal., 1963.

2559. Grimm, Ruediger Hermann. Knowledge and power: Nietzsche's will to power as an epistemological principle. Boston Coll., 1974. 74-19723

2560. Griner, Robert Homer. The method of presupposition: a significant a priori. Yale, 1962.

2561. Grisez, Germain. Basic oppositions in logical theory. Chicago, 1959.

2562. Griswold, H.D. Brahman; a study in the history of Indian philosophy. Cornell, 1900.

2563. Grob, Leonard Max. The renewal of philosophy: a study of the thought of Sartre and Levinas. Penn St., 1975. 75-22680

2564. Grontkowski, Christine Rosenbauer. The priority of the scientific image: an investigation of Wilfred Sellars' ontological commitments. Fordham, 1969.
69-16221

2565. Gross, Barry Roy. The concept of imagination. Toronto, 1966.

2566. Gross, Mason Welch. The problem of the nature of knowledge, considered with special reference to the work of the Vienna circle and related thinkers. Harvard, 1938.

2567. Gross, Sidney Abbe. Santayana's theory of knowledge from The life of reason through Realms of being. Tulane, 1967.
67-17917

2568. Gross, Walter Elliot. The American Philosophical Society and the growth of science in the United States, 1835-1850. Pennsylvania, 1970.
71-19230

2569. Grosser, Elmer Joseph. St. Thomas Aquinas and the Politics of Aristotle. Toronto, 1954.

2570. Grossman, Morris. Santayana as dramatist and dialectician: a critical estimate made with the help of unpublished manuscripts. Columbia, 1960.
60-3077

2571. Grossman, Neal Kenneth. The problem of measurement in quantum mechanics: a critical survey. Indiana, 1971.
71-17444

2572. Grossman, Ross M. Expression and works of art. Wisconsin, 1971.
71-9172

2573. Grossmann, Reinhardt Siegbert. Meaning, ontology, and intensional contexts. Iowa, 1958. 58-2961

2574. Grosso, Michael Anthony. Death and the myth of the true earth in Plato's Phaedo. Columbia, 1971.
72-19126

2575. Grover, Dorothy Lucille. Topics in propositional quantification. Pittsburgh, 1970.   71-10550

2576. Grover, Robinson Allen. The concept of political control. Brown, 1969.   70-8729

2577. Groves, John Lawrence. The influence of Heidegger in Latin-American philosophy. Boston U., 1960.
60-3451

2578. Grow, Ann Elizabeth. The will and individuality in

Josiah Royce. Fordham, 1972. 73-1479

2579. Gruender, C. David. A study of the place of sensation in knowledge. Wisconsin, 1957. 57-4244

2580. Gruenenfelder, John Bernard. Plato's theory of scientific knowledge in the later dialogues. Notre Dame, 1961. 61-3730

2581. Grugan, Arthur Anthony. Thought and poetry: language as man's homecoming. A study of Martin Heidegger's question of being and its ties to Friedrich Holderlin's experience of the holy. Duquesne, 1972. 73-4665

2582. Grunbaum, Adolf. The philosophy of continuity: a philosophical interpretation of the metrical continuum of physical events in the light of contemporary mathematical conceptions. Yale, 1951.
70-23046

2583. Grunebaum, James O. An analysis of the concept of interest. Chicago, 1970.

2584. Grunewald, Robert Nichol. An exposition of John Dewey's concept of the problematic situation and an appraisal of that concept from the standpoint of the Ames demonstrations in perception. Claremont, 1964. 66-3333

2585. Grunstra, Bernard Richard. The nature of the measrement activity. Pennsylvania, 1963. 63-7049

2586. Gruzalski, Bart Karl. Act utilitarianism and utilitarian generalization: the equivalence thesis. Maryland, 1974. 75-7330

2587. Guerrieri, Daniel Joseph. Towards a fundamental understanding of the future: an essay on the identity of being and the future. Duquesne, 1971.
72-9862

2588. Guerry, Thomas Herbert, III. Correspondence, "true," and "truth." No. Carolina, 1972. 73-4830

2589. Guilfoil, James Daniel. The epistemology of C.D. Broad. Marquette, 1970. 71-5299

2590. Guinan, Sr. St. Michael. On love. Laval, 1951.

2591. Guiniven, John Joseph. Mathematical ontology in Aristotle. Massachusetts, 1975. 76-5338

2592. Guleserian, Theodore. Abstract entities and the semantics of philosophy. Yale, 1963.

2593. Gulick, Walter Brooks. Kant's idea of metaphysics: from ontology through empirical and transempirical systems to authentic existence. Claremont, 1974. 74-20101

2594. Gull, Richard Arthur. A problem of analysis. Iowa, 1968. 68-16807

2595. Gulliver, Julia Henrietta. The substitutes for Christianity proposed by Comte and Spence; dialectic of Plato. Smith, 1888.

2596. Gumz, Frederick August. A philosophical analysis of theological language. Toronto, 1961.

2597. Gunderson, Keith Robert. Mentality and machines (essays on mechanistic philosophy.) Princeton, 1963. 64-2682

2598. Gunderson, Martin Louis. Berkeley's idealism. Cornell, 1974. 74-24235

2599. Gunter, Addison Yancey, III. The unity of intuition and the understanding in Bergson. Yale, 1963.

2600. Gupta, Amitabha. On truth as correspondence. Georgia, 1973. 74-4806

2601. Gupta, Bina. The conception of the self in Hume and Buddhism. So. Illinois, 1975. 76-3311

2602. Gurland, Robert H. The problem of induction: is it a pseudo-problem. N.Y.U., 1971. 72-13366

2603. Gurney, John Orson, Jr. Rules of acceptance and the body of scientific knowledge. Wisconsin, 1974. 74-18934

2604. Gurr, Rev. John Edwin. The principle of sufficient reason in some scholastic systems, 1750-1900. St. Louis, 1955.

2605. Gustafson, Donald Franklin. The structure of A.N. Whitehead's speculative philosophy. Texas, 1961. 62-509

2606. Gustafson, Rev. Gustaf J. The theory of natural appetency in the philosophy of St. Thomas Aquinas. Catholic U., 1944.

2607. Gustafson, James Walter. Causality and freedom in Jonathan Edwards, Samuel Alexander and Brand Blanshard. Boston U., 1967. 67-13314

2608. Gustason, William Whitby. Negation and assertion in

Frege and the *Tractatus*. Michigan, 1968.
68-13319

2609. Gutas, Dimitri. Greek wisdom literature in Arabic translation: a study in the literary transmission of popular ethics. Yale, 1974. 75-15305

2610. Guthrie, Edwin Ray, Jr. The paradoxes of Mr. Russell, with a brief account of their history. Pennsylvania, 1912.

2611. Guthrie, George Paul. Kant and Ritschl: a study in the relation between philosophy and theology. Chicago, 1962.

2612. Guthrie, Kenneth Sylvan. Numenius of Apamea, the father of neo-platonism: works, biography, message, sources and influence. Columbia, 1917.

2613. Gutierrez, Claudio. Epistemology and economics: contribution to the logical analysis of economic theory. Chicago, 1966.

2614. Gutierrez, Florentino Rosaire. De republica secundum Franciscum de Vitoria. Laval, 1941.

2615. Gutmann, James. Schelling: of human freedom. Columbia, 1936.

2616. Gutting, Gary Michael. The logic of discovery in theoretical physics. St. Louis, 1968. 69-348

2617. Gutwirth, Marc Raphael. Hesiod and his view of man. Harvard, 1963.

2618. Guy, Alfred Hugh, Jr. The ethics of the *Tractatus*. Georgia, 1973. 74-4807

2619. Guyer, Paul David. Criteria for judgment: Kant and the problem of taste. Harvard, 1974.

2620. Guzikowski, Maximilian E. A philosophy of liberalism according to Thomistic principles. Catholic U., 1950.

2621. Guzzetta, John Frederick. An analysis of arguments for and against sex education in the schools. Buffalo, 1973. 73-5114

2622. Gyorgy, John. Faith and social progress: prospective and retrospective social evolution conceived as progressive faith manifestation. Harvard, 1907.

- H -

2623. Haag, Alvin Samuel. Some German influences in American philosophical thought from 1800 to 1850. Boston U., 1939.

2624. Haas, Kenneth Eugene. A concept of ends-means relations for value theory. Syracuse, 1969.
70-10347

2625. Haber, Theodore Adam. Elements for a theory of practice. Yale, 1970. 71-16247

2626. Habermehl, Lawrence LeRoy. Value in the evolutionary world views of Samuel Alexander, C. Lloyd Morgan, and Pierre Teilhard de Chardin. Boston U., 1967.
67-13274

2627. Habib, Wadad. The uniqueness and intelligibility of value. Bryn Mawr, 1951.

2628. Hachey, Sr. Mary Mercedes. An investigation and evaluation of two interpretations of St. Thomas' doctrine on the objectivity of the concept. Notre Dame, 1957. 20220

2629. Hacker, Edward Albert. Idealism, realism and the ego-centric predicament. Buffalo, 1961.
61-4858

2630. Hackler, Chris. Political obligation. No. Carolina, 1975. 76-20030

2631. Hackmann, Emil Edward. The concepts of myth, philosophy, and history, in the demythologizing theology of Rudolf Bultmann. Nebraska, 1963.
64-2622

2632. Hackstaff, Lawrence Howard. The status of the laws of thought and their function in systems. Yale, 1958.

2633. Haddox, John Herbert. Reasons for the importance of a philosophical study of some of the basic principles of the living world. Notre Dame, 1959.
59-4208

2634. Haden, James Coke. Kant and the problem of space. Yale, 1953.

2635. Hadgopoulos, Demetrius John. Aristotle's theory of the demonstrative syllogism. Wayne St., 1974.
75-13325

2636. Hadley, Robert Francis. Convention and the intensional concepts. British Columbia, 1973.

2637. Hadreas, Peter James. Merleau-Ponty: on perception. Berkeley, 1975.

2638. Haentzchel, A. The sources of assurance. Wisconsin, 1929.

2639. Hagen, Fred William. A critical examination of some recent conceptions of the nature of metaphysics. U. of Washington, 1959.
59-5462

2640. Hagen, John Richard. Models for metaphor. Texas, 1974.
75-4381

2641. Hagensick, Paul Wandell. Galileo's views on falling bodies: the logic of scientific laws. Wisconsin, 1954.

2642. Hagerty, Cornelius. The problem of evil. Catholic U., 1911.

2643. Haggerty, William John, Jr. Realism in the philosophy of Orestes A. Brownson. Boston U., 1960.
60-3452

2644. Hahn, Lewis Edwin. A contextualistic theory of perception. Berkeley, 1939.

2645. Hahnfeld, John Henry. Paul Tillich and the significance of human existence. Penn St., 1971.
72-19314

2646. Haight, David Frederick. The transcendental ontology of P.F. Strawson: an interpretation and defense. Northwestern, 1968.
69-6933

2647. Hailperin, Theodore. A set of axioms for logic. Cornell, 1943.

2648. Haines, Byron Linwood. Moral principles and moral relevance: a critique of Singer's Generalization in ethics. U. of Washington, 1966.
67-2158

2649. Haines, Randolph James. The value theory of John Dewey and ecological values. Yale, 1975.
75-24546

2650. Haines, Wayne Thomas. An appraisal of Karl Jaspers and Karl Löwith: their views of history. DePaul,

1972.   72-31244

2651. Haist, Gordon Keith, Jr. The creation of values,
      with special reference to Raymond Polin. So. Il-
      linois, 1974.   75-116

2652. Halbasch, Keith Edward. Bertrand Russell's early
      philosophy of language. Illinois, 1969.
                                              70-13338

2653. Halberstadt, William Harold. The aesthetics of
      Francis Hutcheson and David Hume. Illinois, 1955.
                                              15216

2654. Halbrook, Stephen Porter. The Marx-Bakunin contro-
      versy: intellectual origins, 1844-1870. Florida
      St., 1972.   72-23003

2655. Haley, Sr. Mary Alice. Mathematics and method in
      Leibniz's metaphysics. St. Louis, 1971.
                                              72-5291

2656. Halfter, Joy Isolde. Performatives: what they are
      and how they mean. Stanford, 1972.   73-4504

2657. Hall, Granville Stanley. The perception of space.
      Harvard, 1878.

2658. Hall, Harrison Belding. Scepticism and perceptual
      faith. Northwestern, 1973.   74-7753

2659. Hall, James Herrick, Jr. God-talk. No. Carolina,
      1964.   65-4012

2660. Hall, James Walker. Self-prediction and free will.
      Johns Hopkins, 1975.

2661. Hall, Michael. G.E. Moore's "Proof of an external
      world." Colorado, 1972.   73-18567

2662. Hall, Richard Baxter. Morality and reasons for ac-
      tion. U.C.L.A., 1973.   73-13141

2663. Hall, Richard John. The nature of mathematical
      truth. Princeton, 1963.   64-2685

2664. Hall, Robert William. An analysis of individualism
      in the philosophy of Plato. Harvard, 1953.

2665. Hall, Ronald Lavon. The structure of inquiry: a stu-
      dy in the thought of Michael Polanyi. No. Caro-
      lina, 1973.   74-5922

2666. Hallberg, Fred William. The empirical status of Car-
      tesian dualism. (Volume I: The problem of sen-

tience; Volume II: The problem of sapience.)
Minnesota, 1969.   70-15735

2667. Hallen, Barry. Boldness and caution in the methodology and social philosophy of Karl Popper.
Boston U., 1970.   70-23136

2668. Hallen, Patricia Ann. The philosophical problem of relation in the philosophies of Aristotle, Aquinas and Hegel. Boston U., 1970.   70-23137

2669. Haller, Elsa Linda. Does Karl Jaspers' "Philosophie" justify his indictment of the German people in 1945? Michigan, 1958.   58-7724

2670. Hallie, Philip Paul. Maine de Biran and the doctrines of Locke, Berkeley and Hume. Harvard, 1953.

2671. Halpern, Robert I. C.I. Lewis' conception of the given and the problem of epistemic justification. C.U.N.Y., 1975.   75-20520

2672. Halpin, Sr. Marlene. The origin of the first principle. Catholic U., 1963.   64-354

2673. Hamburg, Carl H. Symbol and reality. Columbia, 1958.

2674. Hamby, James Harold. Kant on moral anthropology.
St. Louis, 1973.   74-4516

2675. Hamilton, Catherine Sears. David Hume's contributions toward a theory of historical knowledge.
Yale, 1951.

2676. Hamilton, Clarence. Psychological interpretation of mysticism. Chicago, 1914.

2677. Hamilton, James Brooke, III. The individuality and/or sociality of morality: prospects for resolving this controversy within the framework of contemporary ordinary language analysis. Emory, 1972.
72-32667

2678. Hamilton, James Edward. A comparison of the moral theories of Charles Finney and Asa Mahan. Buffalo, 1972.   73-5117

2679. Hamilton, James Raleigh. Quine's revival of ontology. Texas, 1974.   74-14701

2680. Hamilton, Paul James. The problem of defining 'art' and 'artistic value.' Vanderbilt, 1975.
76-15488

2681. Hamilton, Wayne Bruce. Søren Kierkegaard's conception of temporality. McGill, 1972.

2682. Hamlin, Howard Phillips, Jr. A critical evaluation of John Locke's philosophy of religion. Georgia, 1972. 73-5705

2683. Hammer, Louis Zellig. Philosophical implications of the poetic art. Yale, 1960.

2684. Hammerschmidt, William Warner. Time in Whitehead. Cornell, 1940.

2685. Hammett, Jenny Lee Yates. Existential conceptions of death: Heidegger, Tillich, Rilke. Syracuse, 1973. 74-8262

2686. Hammond, Albert Larphier. Anti-intellectualism in present philosophy. Johns Hopkins, 1924.

2687. Hammond, Francis. Conception de la société dans la sociologie de Gabriel de Tarde. Laval, 1944.

2688. Hammond, John Luther. Perry, Dewey, C.I. Lewis, and critics of ethical naturalism. Stanford, 1965. 65-12786

2689. Hammond, Percy Malcolm. Philosophical implications of indeterminacy and their effects on the doctrines of freedom, chance, and God. Boston U., 1949.

2690. Hampsch, George Harold. Some aspects of the Marxist notion of classless society. Notre Dame, 1963.

2691. Hamrick, William Seaton. Body space and time in the philosophies of Whitehead and Merleau-Ponty. Vanderbilt, 1971. 71-29301

2692. Han, Yu-Shan. The meaning of experience in the thought of John Dewey. Boston U., 1929.

2693. Hanagan, John Joseph. The contribution of Robert Kilwardby to thirteenth-century thought on the doctrine of relation. Toronto, 1973.

2694. Hancock, Roger Nelson. Kant's political philosophy. Yale, 1956.

2695. Handwerk, Patricia Ann. An investigation of the concept of action. Ohio St., 1968. 69-11644

2696. Handy, Rollo Leroy. The philosophic critique of naturalistic ethics. Buffalo, 1954. 8438

2697. Hanen, Marsha Pearlman. Examination of adequacy
conditions for confirmation. Brandeis, 1970.
70-17121

2698. Haney, Sr. Dorothy Ann. Linearism, cyclicism, and
development in Hegel's philosophy of history.
Catholic U., 1969. 69-16328

2699. Hanink, James Gee. Persons, rights, and the problem
of abortion. Michigan St., 1975. 75-27269

2700. Hanke, John Warren. The ontological status of the
work of fine art in the aesthetics of Maritain.
Indiana, 1967. 67-15102

2701. Hanks, Donald Kirk. The performatory theory of
truth. Tulane, 1970. 70-24524

2702. Hanly, Charles Mervyn Taylor. The nature of freedom
in the philosophy of Sartre; a critical study by
means of a comparison with psychoanalytic theory.
Toronto, 1964.

2703. Hanly, Kenneth Ralph. Fatalism. Oregon, 1967.
67-16163

2704. Hanna, Joseph Ford. The methodology of the testing
of learning models, with applications to a new
stimulus discrimination model of two-choice behavior. Berkeley, 1966. 66-3608

2705. Hanna, Maurice. Justificationalism versus non-just-
ificationalism in philosophy: a critique of the
theory of rationality in Karl Popper and W.W.
Bartley III. Southern Cal., 1969. 69-13061

2706. Hannaford, Robert Varlan. A critical study of F.H.
Bradley's Ethical studies. Columbia, 1955.
15630

2707. Hannaford, William Edward, Jr. The identity theory
of J.J.C. Smart. Colorado, 1972. 73-1779

2708. Hanpeter, F. Oliver. John Locke and the corpuscular
theory. Duke, 1975. 75-29504

2709. Hansen, Chad Deloy. Philosophy of language and logic in ancient China. Michigan, 1972. 73-11139

2710. Hansen, Forest Warnyr. Music, feeling, and meaning:
a study of four theories. Johns Hopkins, 1967.
70-14814

2711. Hansen, James Edwin. The dialectic of 'praxis' in
Karl Marx's Das kapital. Buffalo, 1971. 72-222

2712. Hansing, Ovidia. Motives and the moral judgment. Northwestern, 1936.

2713. Hanson, Clifford Tange. The concepts of right and ought in the philosophies of G.E. Moore, Sir William David Ross and A.C. Ewing. Nebraska, 1955. 12749

2714. Hanson, Harry A. The democratic ideal in the thought of India. Boston U., 1944.

2715. Hanson, William Herbert. Logistic systems that formalize the distinction between analyticity and factual truth. Yale, 1965. 65-9681

2716. Hantz, Harold D. The biological motivation in Aristotle. Columbia, 1939.

2717. Hapke, Rodelia Josephine. Willard Van Orman Quine: translational indeterminacy. Stanford, 1974.

2718. Har, Kyung-Durk. A digest, classification, and critical examination of certain social laws. Harvard, 1928.

2719. Harangi, László. Some philosophical aspects of cosmology. Pittsburgh, 1958. 58-2026

2720. Harap, Louis. Poetry and philosophical truth. Harvard, 1932.

2721. Hardeman, Thomas Patterson. The philosophy cf Lucius Annaeus Seneca. Illinois, 1956. 16398

2722. Harder, Allen James. Scientific methodology and the growth of knowledge. Indiana, 1971. 72-9976

2723. Harder, Robert Lincoln, Jr. Copernicus, Galileo, and ideal conditions. Columbia, 1956. 19243

2724. Hardgrave, Hannah. A theory of film criticism. Chicago, 1971.

2725. Hardin, Clyde Lawrence. 'Sense-datum,' sense-data, and phenomenalism. Princeton, 1958. 58-7847

2726. Hardwick, Charles Sidney. Language learning and language games in Wittgenstein's later work. Texas, 1967. 67-14834

2727. Hardwig, John Robert. Autonomy and rationality in moral decisions. Texas, 1975. 75-16681

2728. Hardy, Helen Lorena McArthur. Causality in emergent evolution. Toronto, 1958.

2729. Hare, John Edmund. Aristotle's theories of essence. Princeton, 1975. 76-20362

2730. Hare, Pater Hewitt. G.H. Mead's metaphysics of sociality. Columbia, 1965. 65-13950

2731. Hargrove, Eugene Carroll. Wittgenstein and ethics. Missouri, 1974. 75-20119

2732. Hargrove, John Lawrence. A study in the philosophy of law of Jeremy Bentham. Harvard, 1965.

2733. Haring, Ellen Stone. Substantial form in Aristotle's Metaphysics. Radcliffe, 1959.

2734. Harkenrider, Edward W. The relation of the virtue of justice to personality. Catholic U., 1952.

2735. Harkness, Georgia Elma. The philosophy of Thomas Hill Green, with special reference to the relations between ethics and the philosophy of religion. Boston U., 1923.

2736. Harm, Rudolph Henry. Phillips Brooks; a study of his understanding of the nature and development of the moral and intellectual life of man. N.Y.U., 1970. 71-13646

2737. Harman, Gilbert Helms. Skepticism and the definition of knowledge. Harvard, 1964.

2738. Harmer, Evelyn Saunders. Thomas Hobbes: a defense of the rational base of political power. Brandeis, 1971. 71-30131

2739. Harmon, Frances B. The social philosophy of the St. Louis Hegelians. Columbia, 1943.

2740. Harmse, George Edward. Freedom: the principle of existence. Virginia, 1953. 7967

2741. Harnish, Robert Michael. Studies in logic and language. M.I.T., 1972.

2742. Haroutunian, Joseph. Piety versus moralism. Columbia, 1932.

2743. Harper, Mary-Angela. A study of the metaphysical problem of intersubjectivity. Georgetown, 1967. 67-9464

2744. Harper, William Arthur. Human revolt: a phenomenological description. Southern Cal., 1971. 71-12392

2745. Harper, William Leonard. Counterfactuals and representations of rational belief. Rochester, 1974.
74-22587

2746. Harrah, David. An analysis of communication. Yale, 1954.

2747. Harrell, Jean Gabbert. Esthetic continuity; a study in musical value. Columbia, 1950.   1855

2748. Harries, Karsten. In a strange land:an exploration of nihilism. Yale, 1962.   67-9640

2749. Harriman, Charles Jessup. The role of metaphor in cognition: self-reference, iconicity, and simple natures. New Mexico, 1972.   73-8369

2750. Harrington, Rev. John. The contemporary philosophy of security in the light of the scholastic theory of divine providence. Catholic U., 1952.

2751. Harrington, John Beattie. William James's theory of religious knowledge. Princeton, 1953.
6810

2752. Harrington, Kathleen Wilson. Frederick J.E. Woodbridge and the naturalistic interpretation of Plato. Emory, 1971.   72-3027

2753. Harrington, Michael Louis. Whitehead's theory of propositions. Emory, 1972.   73-12180

2754. Harris, Benjamin Malcolm. The metaphysical basis of religion. Brown, 1923.

2755. Harris, Charles Edwin, Jr. Wittgenstein's criticism of ostensive explanation. Vanderbilt, 1964.
65-1807

2756. Harris, Charles Reginald Schiller. The place of Duns Scotus in mediaeval thought. Princeton, 1923.

2757. Harris, David Adrian. The analogous conception of being: a study in dialectical idealism. Catholic U., 1974.   75-16533

2758. Harris, Donald Frederick. A categorial approach to George H. Mead's concept of the self. Columbia, 1974.   74-28503

2759. Harris, Henry Silton. The social philosophy of Giovanni Gentile. Illinois, 1954.   7849

2760. Harris, James Franklin, Jr. Analyticity and the *a*

priori: some traditional theories, recent objections, and alternative suggestions. Vanderbilt, 1966.   66-10984

2761. Harris, James Roland. Knowledge, emotion and the individual's freedom. Temple, 1971.   71-31085

2762. Harris, Leonard. Racism and the materialist anthropology of Karl Marx. Cornell, 1974.   74-24238

2763. Harris, Marquis Lafayette. Some conceptions of God in the Gifford lectures during the period 1927-29. Ohio St., 1933.

2764. Harris, Robert Taylor. The liberalism of John Stuart Mill. Harvard, 1949.

2765. Harris, William Glen. Teleology in the philosophy of Joseph Butler and Abraham Tucker. Pennsylvania, 1941.

2766. Harrison, Bernard Joseph. Meaning and understanding: an essay in the philosophy of language. Michigan, 1961.   61-6361

2767. Harrison, Craig Royston. 'Time' in the physical world. Stanford, 1967.   67-17433

2768. Harrison, Frank Russell, III. Concerning the possibility of a general theory of analogy. Virginia, 1961.   61-4545

2769. Harrison, Max H. Hindu monism and pluralism. Columbia, 1932.

2770. Harrison, Stanley Martin. Man's glassy essence: an attempt to construct a theory of person based on the writings of Charles Sanders Peirce. Fordham, 1971.   71-26975

2771. Hart, Alan. The synthetic epistemology of Herbert Spencer. Pennsylvania, 1965.   66-4618

2772. Hart, Charles Aloysius. The Thomistic theory of mental faculties. Catholic U., 1930.

2773. Hart, James. Hedwig Conrad-Martius' ontological phenomenology. Chicago, 1972.

2774. Hart, James Bruce. The Marxist critique of ethics. Waterloo, 1975.

2775. Hart, Wilbur Dyre. Wittgenstein, philosophy, logic and mathematics. Harvard, 1969.

2776. Harter, Edward Darcy. A study of 'hexis' and dispositional properties in Aristotle. Illinois, 1972. 73-17235

2777. Hartjes, John F. The critique of the 'given' in Wilfrid Sellars and Edmund Husserl. Catholic U., 1974. 74-19467

2778. Hartley, John Joseph Leo. The philosophy of Maurice Merleau-Ponty: a philosophy of form. Toronto, 1970.

2779. Hartman, David. Thought and action in Maimonides: a study in the relationship of the individual and the community. McGill, 1973.

2780. Hartman, Donald Terry. The methodology of psychology. Michigan, 1972. 73-6843

2781. Hartman, Edwin Mitman, II. Aristotle on soul and body. Princeton, 1969. 70-8368

2782. Hartman, James Barclay. A Gestalt theory of musical perception. Northwestern, 1959. 59-4803

2783. Hartman, Richard Otis. Aspects of personality as key analogical factors in the metaphysics of Leibniz and Schopenhauer. Boston U., 1963. 63-5909

2784. Hartman, Robert Schirokauer. Can field theory be applied to ethics? Northwestern, 1946.

2785. Hartman, Thomas Hayes. Signs and things. Rochester, 1975. 75-15206

2786. Hartmann, Henry Gottlieb. Locke, a constructive realist. Columbia, 1912.

2787. Hartshorne, Charles. An outline and defence of the argument for the unity of being in the absolute or divine good. Harvard, 1923.

2788. Hartt, Joel. An examination of Bertrand Russell's philosophy of politics. N.Y.U., 1974. 74-29991

2789. Harvanek, Rev. Robert Francis. The philosophy of creation of St. Gregory of Nyssa. Fordham, 1944.

2790. Harvey, Horace Hale, III. Decision theory in the good life: mathematical, logical, ethical and other tools and techniques as aids for making ethical-moral decisions. Tulane, 1969. 70-6401

2791. Harvey, Peter John. Aristotle on truth with respect

to incomposites. Michigan, 1975.   76-9415

2792. Harvey, Rudolf. Liberty under historical liberalism. Catholic U., 1941.

2793. Harvey, Samuel Patrick. A general line of argument against philosophical skepticism. No. Carolina, 1975.   75-29034

2794. Harvey, Warren. Hasdai Cresca's critique of the theory of the acquired intellect. Columbia, 1973.   74-1488

2795. Harward, Donald West. The distinction in the Tractatus between saying and showing. Maryland, 1970.   71-25272

2796. Haserot, Francis Samuel. The logic of being. Harvard, 1935.

2797. Hashimoto, Rentaro. Process and finality in Hegel. Fordham, 1963.   64-2416

2798. Haslett, David Warner. The fundamental moral imperative: an interpretation of C.I. Lewis' theory of moral rightness. Minnesota, 1970.   71-18740

2799. Hassel, Rev. David John. Method and scientia in St. Augustine: a study of Books VIII to XV in his De trinitate. St. Louis, 1963.   64-4250

2800. Hassol, Milton David. A critique of the 'good reasons school' of ethical analysis. Columbia, 1966.   67-5783

2801. Hatch, Leon Stanley, Jr. Free will and determinism in Moore, Nowell-Smith and Austin. Boston U., 1969.   69-18418

2802. Hater, Rev. Robert James. Psycho-philosophy of the human person. (Gordon W. Allport's dynamic theory of human personality, with special emphasis on the philosophical implications derived from the study of his approach to man.) St. John's, 1967.   68-3823

2803. Hathaway, Ronald Fred. Hierarchy and the definition of order in the letters of Dionysius: historical and interpretive studies in later Neoplatonism, with Migne text, translation and notes. Brandeis, 1965.   65-14423

2804. Hattiangadi, Jagdish N. Notes on the theory of rationality. Princeton, 1970.   71-14380

2805. Haugness, Norman. Contextual elements in ethical judgments. So. Illinois, 1968. 69-1745

2806. Hauptli, Bruce Worthing. From myth to metaphor: a study of W.V. Quine's epistemological realism. Washington U., 1974. 74-22522

2807. Hausheer, Herman. St. Augustine; diversity of historical streams due to the cross-currents in the thought and life of St. Augustine. Iowa, 1922.

2808. Hausman, Alan Michael. Goodman's ontology. Iowa, 1966. 66-7208

2809. Hausman, Carl Ransdell. Creativity in art. Northwestern, 1960. 60-4761

2810. Hausman, David Baer. A critical examination of H.H. Price's philosophy of perception as presented in Perception. Iowa, 1971. 71-30442

2811. Hausser, Harry E. Hegel's philosophy of art. Chicago, 1955.

2812. Haver, Ronald John. Aristotle and the third man. Pittsburgh, 1973. 73-16344

2813. Hawi, Sami Salim. Naturalism and mysticism in Ibn Tufayl. Buffalo, 1972.

2814. Hawkins, Benjamin Sanford, Jr. Frege and Peirce on properties of sentences in classical deductive systems. Miami, 1971. 72-12876

2815. Hawkins, David. A causal interpretation of probability. U.C.L.A., 1941.

2816. Haworth, Lawrence Lindley. The practical philosophies of John Dewey and Elijah Jordan. Illinois, 1952. 3998

2817. Hay, Gerald Conrad, Jr. Maritain's theory of poetic knowledge: a critical study. Catholic U., 1964. 64-11084

2818. Hay, William H. A philosophical analysis of particular ethical statements. Illinois, 1943.

2819. Hayes, Frank Ambrose. Platonic elements in Spinoza's theory of method. Indiana, 1956. 57-3696

2820. Hayes, Rev. Justin Donald. Moral conscience in the thought of Saint Bonaventure. St. Louis, 1955.

2821. Hayes, Sr. Mary Dolores. Various group mind theories

viewed in the light of Thomistic principles. Catholic U., 1942.

2822. Hayes, Sr. Patricia. An analysis of Kant's use of the term 'metaphysics.' Georgetown, 1974.
74-26431

2823. Hayes, Victor Clarence. Myth, reason and revelation: perspectives on and a summary-translation of three books from Schelling's Philosophy of mythology and revelation. Columbia, 1970. 73-8951

2824. Hayes, William Henry. French aesthetic theories, 1700-1750. Berkeley, 1967. 67-11630

2825. Haymond, William Stanley. Hume's theory of sense perception. St. Louis, 1959. 60-337

2826. Hayner, Paul Collins. History and historical ontology in Schelling's philosophical development. Columbia, 1950. 1745

2827. Haynes, David Nathan. John Rawls' theory of justice as fairness. U. of Washington, 1973. 74-15576

2828. Haynes, Peter Frederic Ronald. The possibilities of imagination. Calgary, 1972.

2829. Haynes, Richard Pierce. Plato's theory of forms and the self-predication assumption. Illinois, 1962.
62-2921

2830. Haynes, Thomas Morris. Institutional theories of law: Hauriou and Jordan. Illinois, 1949.
1547

2831. Hays, Lloyd Daniel. The ethical intuitionism of Richard Price. Michigan St., 1966. 67-7546

2832. Hazard, Paul-Alfred. The passion of shame in the teachings of Freud and Aquinas. Laval, 1970.

2833. Hazelton, Roger. The relation between value and existence in the philosophies of Nicolai Hartmann and Alfred North Whitehead. Yale, 1937.

2834. Hazelton, William Dean. Reidentifying persons. No. Carolina, 1971. 72-18408

2835. Headley, Leal Aubrey. The concept of purpose. Harvard, 1916.

2836. Healy, Margaret Mary. Freedom and determinism in the philosophy of Thomas Hobbes. Bryn Mawr, 1969. 70-10009

2837. Heanue, James Edward, Jr. Introduction to the English edition of Meinong's Über annahmen with selections from the translation: On assumptions. Southern Cal., 1973.   7L-920

2838. Hearn, Thomas Kermit, Jr. The objectivism of Hume's ethics. Vanderbilt, 1965.   66-23

2839. Heath, L.R. The concept of time in science and philosophy; a study of its development and application. Radcliffe, 1927.

2840. Heath, Rev. Thomas R. Aristotelian influence in Thomistic wisdom: a comparative study. Catholic U., 1956.

2841. Hébert, Thomas. La connaissance du singulier matériel selon Jean de Saint Thomas. Laval, 1948.

2842. Hecht, Rev. Francis Torrens. Self-evidence of God's existence in some theologians, 1650-1750. St. Louis, 1954.

2843. Heck, James Arthur. The logos idea and human thought. Drew, 1927.

2844. Hecker, Judith Katz. Reason and responsibility: an explanatory translation of "Kitab al-tawlid" from "al-mughni fi abwab al-tawhid wa-l-'adl" by Qadi 'Abd Al-Jabbar Al-Hamadhani, with introduction and notes. Berkeley, 1975.   75-26538

2845. Heckman, Henry John. A critical examination of R.M. Hare's prescriptive universalism. Ohio St., 1967.   67-10900

2846. Hedman, Carl Gordon. The explanation of actions. Columbia, 1970.   71-17501

2847. Hefelbower, Samuel Gring. The relation of John Locke to English deism. Harvard, 1914.

2848. Heffner, David James. Marx on the relations between nature and man. St. Louis, 1973.   74-24085

2849. Hegstrom, Victor Harald. Schopenhauer and ancient Hindu philosophy: a comparative study in pessimism. Yale, 1894.

2850. Heidelberger, Herbert. Knowledge and certainty: a study in epistemic logic. Princeton, 1962.   63-4119

2851. Heil, John Ferguson. The identity theory of mind. Vanderbilt, 1970.   70-24869

2852. Heiman, Ambrose J. The *esse* of creatures in the doctrine of Jean Quidort; study and texts. Toronto, 1949.

2853. Heimbeck, Raeburne Seeley. Theology and meaning: a critique of metatheological skepticism. Stanford, 1963. 65-1

2854. Heimsath, Star McDaniel. Whitehead's conception of God. Yale, 1941.

2855. Hein, Hilde Stern. Theories of aesthetic inspiration. Michigan, 1961. 61-2757

2856. Hein, Karl Friedrich, Jr. The phenomenological structure of fictional worlds. Florida St., 1972. 72-21316

2857. Heinecken, Martin John. The absolute paradox in Søren Kierkegaard. Nebraska, 1942.

2858. Heinen, Sr. Julitta. A critique of Hare's theory of moral judgment. Catholic U., 1975. 75-21535

2859. Heintz, John William. Subjects and predicables. Duke, 1965. 66-86

2860. Heintz, Lawrence Leroy. Duty, obligation, and moral ought: a commitment theory of obligation. Cal., S. Barbara, 1975. 76-9884

2861. Heiser, Basil Herman. The status of metaphysics according to John Duns Scotus. Toronto, 1941.

2862. Heiser, John Herbert. The identity of intellect and intelligible in the philosophy of Plotinus. St. Louis, 1973. 74-24086

2863. Heizer, Ruth Bradfute. A critique of Karl Popper's solution to the problem of induction. Indiana, 1971. 71-29574

2864. Held, Virginia Potter. The public interest and individual interests. Columbia, 1968. 72-1323

2865. Heller, Bernard. Stoic elements in the philosophy of Spinoza. Michigan, 1932.

2866. Hellman, Geoffrey Paul. Steps in the theory of radical translation. Harvard, 1973. 75-26051

2867. Helm, Bertrand Paul. Systemic relations and valuation: the problem of internal and external relations. Tulane, 1966. 67-3846

2868. Helm, Robert Meredith. A critique of the ethics of philosophical idealism. Duke, 1950.

2869. Helsel, Paul R. The concept of *nous* in early Greek philosophy. Southern Cal., 1935.

2870. Helstrom, Kenneth L. The problem of moral reasoning. Kansas, 1973. 74-12570

2871. Hemmendinger, David. Husserl's phenomenological program: a study of evidence and analysis. Yale, 1973. 73-26295

2872. Hendel, Charles William. Studies in the philosophy of David Hume. Princeton, 1917.

2873. Henderson, Edgar Herbert. Critical realism: an historical study. Harvard, 1937.

2874. Henderson, Edward Hugh. Two metaphysical theories of the self: C.A. Campbell and A.M. Farrer. Tulane, 1967. 67-17922

2875. Henderson, Thomas Greenshields. Essence, matter, and nature in the philosophy of Santayana. Harvard, 1939.

2876. Henderson, Toliver Young, Jr. Moral justification. Texas, 1964. 64-11801

2877. Hendley, Brian Patrick. Wisdom and eloquence: a new interpretation of the *Metalogicon* of John of Salisbury. Yale, 1967. 67-7021

2878. Hendry, Herbert Edward. Expressive completeness. Michigan St., 1966. 66-8455

2879. Henke, Frederick. A study in the psychology of ritualism. Chicago, 1910.

2880. Henle, Paul. Implication considered in the light of the laws of abstract systems. Harvard, 1933.

2881. Henle, Robert John. Saint Thomas and Platonism; a study of the *Plato* and *Platonici* texts in the writings of Saint Thomas. Toronto, 1954.

2882. Henley, Kenneth Irvin. On constructing morality. Virginia, 1972. 72-33365

2883. Hennessy, Rev. James E. The background, sources, and meaning of divine infinity in St. Gregory of Nyssa. Fordham, 1963. 63-5594

2884. Henry, Carl F.H. The influence of personalistic

idealism on the theology of Augustus H. Strong. Boston U., 1949.

2885. Henry, Margaret Young. The relation of dogmatism and scepticism in the philosophical treatises of Cicero. Columbia, 1925.

2886. Henry, Maureen Diane. The development of civil theology in modern political theory: from the fall to the parousia. Notre Dame, 1974.   74-17428

2887. Henry, Wesley Leroy. A study of David Hume versus his eighteenth-century English contemporaries on the question of natural theology. Vanderbilt, 1974.   74-22171

2888. Henry, Wilbert Cameron. The analysis of knowledge in John Stuart Mill and William Whewell. Toronto, 1958.

2889. Henson, Donald Allen. Mystical states of consciousness: an examination of their nature and interpretation. Purdue, 1972.   73-15814

2890. Henson, Richard Goodrich. Philosophy and the ordinary uses of words. Yale, 1957.   70-14456

2891. Hentrich, John James. The private self in Heidegger and the search for genuine community. Yale, 1975.   75-24553

2892. Hentz, George L. Monistic movement. N.Y.U., 1916.

2893. Henze, Donald Frank. The work of art. Wisconsin, 1954.

2894. Hepp, Maylon Harold, Jr. A critical examination of G.E. Moore's theory of knowledge and philosophic method. Brown, 1939.

2895. Herbenick, Raymond Michael. C.S. Peirce and contemporary theories of the systems concept and systems approach to problem-solving and decision-making: an introductory essay on systems theory in philosophical analysis. Georgetown, 1968.   69-2715

2896. Herbert, Gary Bruce. Human nature and the dialectic of desire in the philosophy of Thomas Hobbes. Penn St., 1972.   73-20089

2897. Herbert, Robert Troy. John Locke's problem of personal identity. Nebraska, 1962.   62-2681

2898. Hereford, Thomas Graham. The significance of "imaginative contexts" in analytical and speculative philosophy. Virginia, 1962.   62-5923

2899. Herman, Arthur Ludwig. The problem of evil and Indian thought. Minnesota, 1970.   71-8159

2900. Herman, Daniel Jacques. Finality in the philosophy of Henri Bergson. Northwestern, 1968. 69-1845

2901. Herman, Stephen Jay. Clearness and distinctness in Descartes. Massachusetts, 1975.   75-16561

2902. Hermann, Robert Martin. The relevance of recent educational criticism to the thought of John Dewey. Pittsburgh, 1962.   63-2429

2903. Herr, Judith Lauren. A philosophy of theatricality: a phenomenological description of the aesthetic structures in the arts of performance. Florida St., 1971.   72-271

2904. Herring, Frances White. Ryle's revolt against dualism: an evaluation of Gilbert Ryle's The Concept of mind. Berkeley, 1956.

2905. Herrmann, Jesse. A criticism of some deterministic systems in their relation to practical problems. Princeton, 1914.

2906. Herschorn, Arnold. A theory of meaning. Princeton, 1972.   73-9615

2907. Hersh, Thomas Ross. Hallucinations. U.C.L.A., 1971.   72-2825

2908. Hershbell, Jackson Paul. A commentary on the fragments of the poem of Parmenides. Harvard, 1964.

2909. Hertz, Joseph Herman. Ethical system of James Martineau. Columbia, 1894.

2910. Hertz, Richard Alan. Rules and language: a philosophical study of linguistic communication. Pittsburgh, 1967.   68-202

2911. Hertzberg, Lars Henrik. Explanations of conduct; a philosophical treatise. Cornell, 1970.   71-7363

2912. Herx, Frederick Charles. The problem of illumination in St. Bonaventure and St. Thomas Aquinas: during the period 1250-1259. Notre Dame, 1961.   61-3731

2913. Herzberger, Hans George. Contextual analysis. Princeton, 1961.   61-4785

2914. Hess, Peter Hans. Certain questions related to the freedom-determinism problem. Brown, 1971.
72-8127

2915. Hester, Joseph Parks Robinson. A metaethical examination of the question "why be moral?" Georgia, 1973. 73-31898

2916. Hester, Marcus Baxter. An analysis of the meaning of poetic metaphor. Vanderbilt, 1964. 64-8072

2917. Hester, William. A critical examination of the philosophy of Charles Bernard Renouvier, with particular reference to his metaphysics. Duke, 1947.

2918. Hetzler, Florence M. An introduction to the philosophy of nature: the commentary of St. Thomas Aquinas on Book one of the Physics of Aristotle. Fordham, 1959.

2919. Heuser, Patricia Ann. Woodbridge, critic of modern philosophy. Columbia, 1950. 2344

2920. Hewins, Patrick Thomas. Rationality in science. Calgary, 1972.

2921. Heysham, Theodore. St. Augustine and his philosophy-especially freedom of will. Pennsylvania, 1898.

2922. Hibben, John Grier. Relation of ethics to jurisprudence. Princeton, 1893.

2923. Hickey, Thomas James. A systems approach to the logic of justification in ordinary language. Georgetown, 1975. 75-21628

2924. Hickman, Larry Allen. Logical second intentions: late scholastic theories of higher level predicates. Texas, 1971. 72-11354

2925. Hicks, Joe Harold. Divine and human subjectivity in Kant. Yale, 1969. 70-2741

2926. Higginbotham, James Taylor. Some problems in semantics and radical translation. Columbia, 1973.
74-12724

2927. Higgins, David Jeremiah. Possibility in Peirce and Heidegger: a propaedeutic for synthesis. Missouri, 1968. 68-12494

2928. Higgins, Edward Francis. A critique of John Dewey's theory of the concrete moral good in the light of the philosophy of St. Thomas Aquinas. St. John's, 1974. 75-3254

2929. Hilden, William. 'Exist' is not a predicate: a dogma of analytic philosophy. Nebraska, 1972.
73-15368

2930. Hiley, David Ranald. Mind-body identity, materialism and psychological explanation. Georgia, 1972.
73-5711

2931. Hill, A.R. The epistemological function of the "thing in itself" in Kant's philosophy. Cornell, 1895.

2932. Hill, Charles Leander. An exposition and critical estimate of the philosophy of Philip Melanchthon. Ohio St., 1938.

2933. Hill, Christopher Surleau. On the mysteries of belief. Harvard, 1972.

2934. Hill, David. Perceptual episodes. Chicago, 1975.

2935. Hill, James Franklin. Universalizability and prescriptivity: a critical evaluation of the moral philosophy of R.M. Hare. Georgia, 1974.
75-8154

2936. Hill, James Joseph. The outside figure of the inside form: the origins and implications of a thirteenth century idea. Johns Hopkins, 1966.

2937. Hill, Knox C. Philosophic method and theory of art in Croce and Dewey. Chicago, 1954.

2938. Hill, Myles Eugene. The philosophical aspects of the Newberry Medal Award books, 1922-1971. Arizona St., 1974.
74-9886

2939. Hill, Patrick Joseph. The structure of agreement and disagreement: a dialogical study of the uses of philosophical reason. Boston U., 1969.
69-18438

2940. Hill, Richard Ray. Philosophical skepticism and the logic of enquiry. Colorado, 1972.
73-1783

2941. Hill, Roscoe Earl. Excuses, 'could not,' and criminal responsibility. Chicago, 1968.

2942. Hill, Sharon Bishop. Ideal observer theories in ethics. Harvard, 1968.

2943. Hill, Thomas English, Jr. An examination of some of Kant's formulations of the categorical imperative. Harvard, 1966.

2944. Hill, Walker Hawes. Peirce and Dewey and the spectator theory of knowledge. Wisconsin, 1938.

2945. Hillenbrand, Martin J. Power and morals. Columbia, 1949.

2946. Hillesheim, James Walter. Nietzsche's philosophy of education: a critical exposition. Southern Cal., 1968. 68-7186

2947. Hilliard, Albert L. The forms of value: the extension of a hedonistic axiology. Columbia, 1950.

2948. Hillman, Owen N. A critical study of the philosophy of Emile Meyerson. Brown, 1934.

2949. Hiltner, John. Four basic problems in Max Scheler's moral philosophy. Nebraska, 1932.

2950. Hinchcliff, George David. Technology and dehumanization. DePaul, 1974. 74-23651

2951. Hinchcliff, John Clarence. The logic of mystery: an analysis based on some contemporary philosophies. Drew, 1969. 70-1090

2952. Hinderer, Drew Elliott. Music analysis and the genuine instance problem. Michigan, 1975.
75-20366

2953. Hines, John Nicholas, III. A theory of society. Emory, 1972. 72-25937

2954. Hinman, Lawrence Michael. Nietzsche's philosophy of play. Loyola, 1975. 75-22352

2955. Hinman, Willis S. Literary quotations and allusions in the Rhetoric, Poetics, and Nicomachean ethics of Aristotle. Columbia, 1935.

2956. Hinners, Richard Caswell. Martin Heidegger's conception of the question: "What is the meaning of to-be?", in Sein und zeit. Toronto, 1955.

2957. Hinrichs, Gerard. Critical theory of the general introduction course to philosophy. Southern Cal., 1940.

2958. Hinshaw, Virgil Goodman, Jr. An enquiry into the factual basis of human knowledge. Princeton, 1945. 703

2959. Hirsch, Eli. Essence and identity. N.Y.U., 1971.
71-24752

2960. Hirschbein, Ronald Lee. The application of Henry

Wieman's concept of creative interchange to problems of value theory. Syracuse, 1970. 71-10931

2961. Hissey, Richard James. Russell's early realism. York, 1972.

2962. Hitchcock, David Lancelot. The role of myth and its relation to rational argument in Plato's dialogues. Claremont, 1974. 74-20103

2963. Hitterdale, Larry Joe. Verbal propositions in J.S. Mill's logic. Johns Hopkins, 1972. 72-24968

2964. Hivale, Bhaskar Pandurang. Religious consciousness and the idea of God in contemporary occidental philosophy. Harvard, 1928.

2965. Hiz, Henry Thadeus. An economical foundation for arithmetic. Harvard, 1948.

2966. Ho, Hsiu-Hwang. Some semantical problems in deontic logic and imperative logic. Michigan St., 1969. 70-15053

2967. Hoagland, Sarah Lucia. The status of common sense, G.E. Moore and L. Wittgenstein: a comparative study. Cincinnati, 1975. 75-22587

2968. Hoban, Rev.James H. The Thomistic concept of person with some social, political and educational implications. Catholic U., 1939.

2969. Hobbs, A. Hoyt. Sensory integration in Aristotle and Berkeley. Brandeis, 1971. 71-30132

2970. Hobbs, Grimsley T. Personality and self in the views of Francis Herbert Bradley and Bernard Bosanquet. Duke, 1955.

2971. Hobbs, William Gordon. Abductive inference: its conception and justification in transcendental philosophy. No. Carolina, 1975. 75-29036

2972. Hochberg, Gary Mitchell. Kant's theory of obligation. Brown, 1971. 72-8129

2973. Hochberg, Herbert Irving. An examination of the philosophy of W.V. Quine. Iowa, 1954. 10216

2974. Hockenos, Warren Joseph. An examination of Reductio ad absurdium and Argumentum ad hominem arguments in the philosophies of Gilbert Ryle and Henry W. Johnstone, Jr. Boston U., 1968. 68-18091

2975. Hocking, Richard B. O'Reilly. Space and intersubjectivity: the formal and value aspects of space. Yale, 1935.

2976. Hocking, William Ernest. The elementary experience of other conscious being in its relations to the elementary experiences of physical and reflexive objects. Harvard, 1904.

2977. Hockney, Donald James. Certainty and objective statements: an examination of C.I. Lewis's theory of empirical knowledge. Cornell, 1966.
66-5514

2978. Hocutt, Max Oliver. The logical foundations of Peirce's theory of values. Yale, 1960.

2979. Hodapp, Paul Francis. Responsibility and deontology. Washington U., 1970. 71-11039

2980. Hodder, Alfred LeRoy. The metaphysics of the specious present. Harvard, 1897.

2981. Hodge, Elizabeth J. A prolegomenon to a theory of responsibility. N.Y.U., 1975. 75-22892

2982. Hodge, Frederick A. John Locke and formal discipline. Virginia, 1911.

2983. Hodge, John Laurent. A philosophical basis of pacifism. Yale, 1968. 69-8366

2984. Hodges, Donald Clark. Ethics and manners. Columbia, 1954. 8688

2985. Hodges, Michael Pahlow. Quine on "ontological commitments." Virginia, 1967. 67-17602

2986. Hoekstra, Raymond. The negative judgment: its place in theory of knowledge and metaphysics. Michigan, 1929.

2987. Hoffman, Joshua. An outline of a defense of a compatibilist position on the free will and determinist debate. Brandeis, 1972. 72-32103

2988. Hoffman, Kurt. Existential philosophy: a study of its past and present forms. Harvard, 1949.

2989. Hoffman, Lester Victor. Crucial issues in explanation: the content, scope, and method of the nomological theory. Harvard, 1970.

2990. Hoffman, Robert. Language, minds, and knowledge. N.Y.U., 1968. 69-7959

2991. Hoffman, Robert Lewis. The concept of emergence: an historical and conceptual analysis. Tulane, 1974.
74-20762

2992. Hoffman, Steven Alan. Conscious states, neurophysiological processes and the principle of complementarity. Colorado, 1975. 75-23607

2993. Hoffman, William Michael. The centrality of freedom for Kant's critical thought. Massachusetts, 1972.
73-6683

2994. Hoffmann, William Edward, Jr. Perception and signs. Georgia, 1971. 72-10975

2995. Hoffmaster, Charles Barry. Justification and the judicial decision. Minnesota, 1975. 76-14905

2996. Hofstadter, Albert A. Locke and scepticism. Columbia, 1935.

2997. Hogan, Charles Alfred. The problem of perception. Berkeley, 1932.

2998. Hogan, Rev. Joseph E. The virtue of prudence in the social philosophy of St. Thomas. Catholic U., 1951.

2999. Hogan, Richard Alan. Plato's *Charmides*: a translation and commentary. Purdue, 1974. 74-26723

3000. Hohler, Thomas P. The I and the not-I: transcendental intersubjectivity in Fichte's early philosophy. Duquesne, 1972. 72-29451

3001. Holahan, Thomas Randall. An interpretation of Fichte's notion of 'feeling': as the pure form of intuition grounding a transcendental doctrine of the elements of both practical and theoretical knowledge. Yale, 1972. 73-14340

3002. Hole, George T. Aesthetic perception: a philosophical analysis. Rochester, 1968. 68-15837

3003. Holland, William Louis. Psychological explanation: a critical study of analogical behaviorism. Yale, 1965. 65-15058

3004. Hollenbach, Sr. Mary William. The nature of the intellectual and moral virtues and their various relationships. Notre Dame, 1960. 60-2672

3005. Hollencamp, Rev. Charles. Causa causarum. Laval, 1946.

3006. Hollinger, Robert. The naturalist-conventionalist dispute about classification. Wisconsin, 1972.
72-24883

3007. Holloway, Rev. Alvin Jacob. The transformation of Stoic themes in St. Augustine. Fordham, 1966.
66-7093

3008. Holly, William John. Program-resistant aspects of knowing-that and knowing-how. Cal., Irvine, 1975.
76-13861

3009. Holman, Emmett Lou. The epistemic status of sense perception. Maryland, 1973.
73-28859

3010. Holman, Sr. M. John. Nature-imagery in the works of St. Augustine. Catholic U., 1932.

3011. Holmer, Paul L. Kierkegaard and the truth: an analysis of the presuppositions integral to his definition of the truth. Yale, 1946.
66-37

3012. Holmes, Arthur. The decay of rationalism. Pennsylvania, 1908.

3013. Holmes, Arthur Frank. The realistic argument in twentieth century English and American philosophy. Northwestern, 1957.
57-4848

3014. Holmes, Bernard George. The Anselmian problem; its various interpretations and a suggested solution. Toronto, 1946.

3015. Holmes, Edward Alonza, Jr. The idea of incarnation in Hegel's philosophy of history. Emory, 1963.
63-6719

3016. Holmes, Eugene C. Social philosophy and the social mind: a study of the genetic methods of J.M. Baldwin, G.H. Mead and J.E. Boodin. Columbia, 1942.

3017. Holmes, Larry. Charles S. Peirce and scientific metaphysics. Harvard, 1962.

3018. Holmes, Richard Hood. Husserl's transcendental turn. Washington U., 1972.
73-5044

3019. Holmes, Robert Lawrence. John Dewey's ethics in the light of contemporary metaethical theory: an analysis and interpretation of his account of the nature of moral judgments. Michigan, 1961.
61-6367

3020. Holmes, Roger Wellington. Gentile's *Sistema di logica*. Harvard, 1933.

3021. Holmstrom, Nancy Christina. Identities, states, and the mind-body problem. Michigan, 1970.
71-15181

3022. Holschuh, Albrecht. Utopismus im werk Ingeborg Bachmanns: eine thematische untersuchung. Princeton, 1965.

3023. Holt, Dennis Charles. A critical examination of at least three arguments to the incompatibility of foreknowledge and free will. Oregon, 1975.
76-5174

3024. Holthaus, Reuben Simon Henry. Berkeley's criterion of truth. Boston U., 1946.

3025. Holther, William B. Some logical terms in the conversational language. U.C.L.A., 1946.

3026. Holtrop, Elton. Edwards' conception of the will in the light of Calvinistic philosophy. Case, 1948.

3027. Holtz, David Adrian. The emergence of the American aesthetic statement in the nineteenth century: James Jackson Jarves. New Mexico, 1972.

3028. Holtzman, Joan Hirsch. Two classes of emotions: affects and attitudes. Columbia, 1972. 76-16358

3029. Holveck, Eleanore Walkowski. Edmund Husserl's concept of the ego in the *Cartesian meditations*.
No. Carolina, 1970. 71-11708

3030. Holveck, John E. Aquinas' interpretation and use of Aristotle's theory of matter. Duquesne, 1973.
73-24514

3031. Holzman, Richard Marc. "...To endeavor peace...": an examination of the moral and civil philosophy of Thomas Hobbes. Johns Hopkins, 1973.
74-10418

3032. Hong, Kilo. Problems of interpretation in modern arts. M.I.T., 1975.

3033. Hood, Webster Franklin. A Heideggerian approach to the problem of technology. Penn St., 1968.
69-5556

3034. Hook, Sidney. The metaphysics of pragmatism, with an introductory word by John Dewey. Columbia, 1927.

3035. Hooker, Clifford Alan. The secondary qualities and systematic philosophy. York, 1970.

3036. Hooker, John Norman, Jr. Essentialism and transworld identity. Vanderbilt, 1974. 75-1138

3037. Hooker, Michael Kenneth. Descartes on himself and his body. Massachusetts, 1973. 74-8601

3038. Hoopes, James Barnard. An interpretation of Plato's Euthyphro. Vanderbilt, 1967. 68-5389

3039. Hoople, Ross Earle. The treatment of solipsism in realsim and absolute idealism; an essay in contemporary epistemology. Syracuse, 1928.

3040. Hoover, Hardy. The philosophy of George Santayana. Harvard, 1929.

3041. Hopkins, Edwin Elwell. Wilfrid Sellars' analysis of physical modality: in search of an argument. Duke, 1971. 72-31572

3042. Hopkins, Jasper Stephen, Jr. Epistemological foundations of R.G. Collingwood's philosophy of history. Harvard, 1963.

3043. Hopkins, Rev. John Vincent. Urban on the form of philosophical intelligibility. St. Louis, 1963. 64-4252

3044. Hopper, Stanley R. The ground of contemporary heresy concerning man: an essay in comparative criticism exploratory of the Christian doctrine of man. Drew, 1936.

3045. Hopson, Ronald Clark. The role of scientific explanation in a general theory of inductive inference. Rochester, 1972. 72-28758

3046. Hopwood, Victor George. A critique of objective standards in poetic judgment. Toronto, 1950.

3047. Horak, Richard Alan. Causal explanation: interpretation of its function and structure. Toronto, 1974.

3048. Horgan, Terence Edward. Microreduction and the mind-body problem. Michigan, 1974. 74-25221

3049. Horne, Herman Harrell. The history and philosophy of the problem of sin. Harvard, 1899.

3050. Horosz, William. A philosophical critique of Reinhold Niebuhr's doctrine of man. Buffalo, 1957. 57-4849

3051. Horowitz, Louise Schwartz. Criteria of personal

identity. Columbia, 1969. 69-17594

3052. Horrigan, Rev. Alfred F. Metaphysics as a principle of order in the university curriculum. Catholic U., 1944.

3053. Horrigan, Sr. Anita. Moral standards and social organization. Catholic U., 1953.

3054. Horter, George Cash. Empiricism versus rationalism; the search for truth. Pennsylvania, 1899.

3055. Horton, Walter Marshall. The philosophy of Abbé Bautain. Columbia, 1926.

3056. Horwitz, Gertrude Rivka. Speech and time in the philosophy of Franz Rosenzweig. Bryn Mawr, 1963. 64-6773

3057. Hoskyn, Fred Percy. The rationalism of Malebranche. Yale, 1927.

3058. Hosler, Douglas Evertt. The place of rationality in explanation. Pittsburgh, 1970. 71-17688

3059. Hospers, John. Meaning and truth in the arts. Columbia, 1946.

3060. Hough, Ronald Fredrick. The cognitive status of scientific theories. Ohio St., 1970. 70-26305

3061. Houghton, Rev. Giles K. Merleau-Ponty: the genesis of objectivity in natural perception. Catholic U., 1970. 70-22732

3062. Houghton, Harold. Aurobindo and Whitehead: a comparative and critical study of supermind and creativity. C.I.A.S 1975. 76-8237

3063. Houlgate, Laurence Davis. Knowledge, action, and responsibility. U.C.L.A., 1967. 67-9886

3064. Houlihan, Sr. Elizabeth Marie. Metaphysical necessity in St. Thomas and its historical foundations. Fordham, 1954.

3065. Houlihan, Sr. Teresa. From vagueness and confusion toward clarity and distinctness in human knowledge. A comparison between Aristotle and Piaget. Laval, 1970.

3066. Howald, John Thomas. Dietrich Bonhoeffer and the hypothesis of the future. Penn St., 1968.
69-5558

3067. Howard, Delton Thomas. John Dewey's logical theory.
       Cornell, 1916.

3068. Howard, Deryl Johnson. Science, causation, and be-
       havior. No. Carolina,1974.   75-4829

3069. Howard, Michael Stuart. Objects and social context
       in some language-games: a study in Wittgenstein's
       later philosophy. Cornell, 1975.   76-8169

3070. Howard, Richard Charles. From philosophy to politi-
       cal economy: Karl Marx and the theory-praxis prob-
       lem. Texas, 1970.   71-11558

3071. Howard, Vernon Alfred. The academic compromise on
       free will in nineteenth century American philoso-
       phy: a study of Thomas C. Upham's A philosophical
       and practical treatise on the will (1834). In-
       diana, 1965.   65-10841

3072. Howard, Wendell T. A critical study of Peirce's theo-
       ry of perceptual judgment. Texas, 1955.

3073. Howe, Clarence Smith. Ernst Cassirer's Toward a log-
       ic of the humanities: a translation with critical
       introduction. Columbia, 1960.   60-1593

3074. Howe, Leroy Thomas. Existence as a perfection: a
       reconsideration of the ontological argument.
       Yale, 1965.   65-15061

3075. Howell, David Howard. Internalism and externalism
       in moral philosophy. Stanford, 1964. 65-2878

3076. Howell, Robert Charles. Transcendental arguments.
       Michigan, 1967.   67-15637

3077. Howell, Thomas Joseph. Indices in perception and
       indices in logic. Brown, 1960.   62-5748

3078. Howells, Edmund Gibson. Hume and teleology: a back-
       ground study of Hume's interest in the argument
       from design. Stanford, 1975.   76-5742

3079. Howey, Richard Lowell. A critical examination of
       Heidegger's and Jaspers' interpretations of
       Nietzsche. Southern Cal., 1969.   69-19375

3080. Howie, John. Creativity in the thought of William
       Ernest Hocking and Henry Nelson Wieman. Boston
       U., 1965.   65-11240

3081. Hoy, David Couzens. Poetics and hermeneutic: the
       methodology of interpretation. Yale, 1972.
                                             72-22388

3082. Hoy, Joyce Beck. Between history and God: hermeneutics and the possibility of theological language. Yale, 1973. 73-16783

3083. Hoy, Ronald Casey. Time and the mental: an examination of Broad's and Husserl's theories of temporal consciousness. Pittsburgh, 1973. 74-18421

3084. Hoyt, Harold Baldwin. The concept of the dehumanization of man in the philosophy of Gabriel Marcel. Oklahoma, 1970. 70-22990

3085. Hsu, Pao-chien. Ethical realism in Neo-Confucian thought. Columbia, 1933.

3086. Hsuang, Joseph Ran-Fun. East-west cultural systems. A Chinese translation. C.I.A.S., 1974.
74-24547

3087. Hu, Suh. The development of the logical method in ancient China. Columbia, 1922.

3088. Huang, Siu-Chi. Lu Hsiang-Shan, a twelfth century Chinese idealist philosopher. Pennsylvania, 1944.

3089. Huber, Curtis Edward. A critical comparison of the views of C.D. Broad and Gilbert Ryle on the concept of self-knowledge. Wisconsin, 1961.
62-4693

3090. Huddart, Bonita Jean. Time and becoming in the cosmology of *Process and reality*. Yale, 1963.

3091. Huddlestun, Bernard P. Augustine's *Confessions* X-XI. Catholic U., 1972. 73-1340

3092. Hudlin, Edward Warrington. The poetics of the cinema. Columbia, 1973. 76-16359

3093. Hudson, James. The doctrine of the actual occasion in Whitehead. Boston U., 1946.

3094. Hudson, James Leonard. Logic, language, and intensional objects: an essay in the philosophy of logic. Johns Hopkins, 1972. 72-19453

3095. Hudson, Jay William. The treatment of personality by Locke, Berkeley, and Hume: a study, in the interests of ethical theory, of an aspect of the dialectic of English empiricism. Harvard, 1908.

3096. Hudson, Yeager. Metaphysical causality in the philosophies of Brand Blanshard, Roy Wood Sellars, and John Laird. Boston U., 1965. 65-11231

3097. Huertas-Jourda, José. On the threshold of phenomenology: a study of Edmund Husserl's Philosophie der arithmetik. N.Y.U., 1969.   70-2470

3098. Huetter, Rev. Norbert J. The eidetic existentialism of St. Thomas. Fordham, 1952.

3099. Huff, Douglas Lee. General terms. Missouri, 1974.
   75-20122

3100. Huff, George Alan. Geometry and formal linguistics. Stanford, 1973.   73-14910

3101. Huff, Thomas Peycke. Hume on moral obligation. Rice, 1968.   68-15630

3102. Huggett, William John. Charles Peirce's search for a method. Toronto, 1954.

3103. Hughes, Gerald Joseph. Blaming for actions done in ignorance. Michigan, 1970.   71-4644

3104. Hughes, Lynn Elizabeth Swanson. Metaphor in the moral philosophy of Iris Murdoch. Buffalo, 1974.

3105. Hughes, Sr. M. Cosmas. The intelligibility of the universe in the philosophy of St. Thomas Aquinas. Catholic U., 1946.

3106. Hughes, Roderick P., III. The notion of the ethical in Kierkegaard. Notre Dame, 1973.   73-12072

3107. Hughes, Walter Dominic. Law in quintessence: according to St. Thomas and Suarez. St. John's, 1972.
   72-21722

3108. Hugly, Philip Grandjean. The problem of other minds. Berkeley, 1965.   66-3616

3109. Hull, Richard Thompson. The role of the principle of acquaintance in contemporary disputes over the relation of mental, perceptual, and physical. Indiana, 1971.   72-6791

3110. Hullett, James Neal. C.I. Lewis and world order; a critical analysis of Lewis on the given, the concept, and the a priori in Mind and the world order. Brandeis, 1967.   67-16556

3111. Humber, James Michael. A critical analysis of C.J. Ducasse's theory on causality. Buffalo, 1970.
   71-6081

3112. Humbert, Earl Rudisill. Moral language, grading, and the prescriptivist program. Yale, 1959.

3113. Hume, Robert Ernest. (a) The pantheism of the Upanishads. (b) A translation of the principal Upanishads. Yale, 1901.

3114. Hummer, Harry David. The ideas of God in the British neo-Hegelians. Drew, 1931.

3115. Humphrey, Christopher Carter. The deductive justification of scientific theories as refutation of known alternatives. U. of Washington, 1967.
68-3854

3116. Humphrey, Ted Bradley. Kant's theory of sensible intuition for ontological dualism. Cal., S. Diego, 1969.
69-9232

3117. Humphreys, Willard Charles, Jr. Anomalies and scientific theories. Yale, 1966.
67-88

3118. Humphries, Barbara Marie. Some recent discussions of necessity and analyticity. Harvard, 1967.

3119. Humphries, Jill. Automata theory as a model of biological replication, adaptation and evolution. Waterloo, 1973.

3120. Hungerman, Sr. Marie Gabriel. Berkeley and Newtonian natural philosophy. St. Louis, 1960.
61-754

3121. Hunt, Rev. Ben B. The nature and significance of the One that follows Being in the philosophy of St. Thomas Aquinas. Catholic U., 1950.

3122. Hunt, DeRay Louis. Some of the relations between Descartes and Locke. Toronto, 1940.

3123. Hunt, Sr. Michael Mary. Time in the philosophy of Maurice Merleau-Ponty. Catholic U., 1969.
69-16885

3124. Hunt, Terence James. Is morality essentially social? Vanderbilt, 1971.
72-3218

3125. Hunt, Walter Murray, Jr. An examination of some problems about the nature of "moral" situations and their role in ethics. Indiana, 1973.
74-377

3126. Hunter, Bruce Anthony. Empiricism and the foundations of empirical knowledge. Brown, 1975.
76-15643

3127. Hunter, John Arden. John Wisdom's psychoanalytical model of philosophy. Wisconsin, 1971. 72-2015

3128. Huntley, Martin Adrian. Implicature and semantic theory. Minnesota, 1972.   73-10577

3129. Huntress, Erminie G. The phenomenology of conscience. Radcliffe, 1937.

3130. Hurlbutt, Robert Harris, III. Science and theology in eighteenth-century England. Berkeley, 1953.

3131. Hurley, Patrick Joseph. Methodology in the writings of A.N. Whitehead. St. Louis, 1973.   74-4527

3132. Hurrell, Paul Manson. A program for analysis of empirical meaning in religious expressions. Michigan, 1961.   61-6368

3133. Hurst, Albert S. The ontological value of the moral ideal. Yale, 1905.

3134. Hurst, William James. The self in the philosophy of Merleau-Ponty. Fordham, 1974.   74-25055

3135. Hurwitz, Gerald Quincy. A defense of Kant's ethics and metaphysics against Moore's early criticism. Johns Hopkins, 1968.   71-2953

3136. Husain, Martha. The question "What is being?" in Aristotle: his reformulations and answers. Waterloo, 1973.

3137. Husik, Isaac. Messer Leon's commentary upon the Vetus logica. Pennsylvania, 1903.

3138. Hussong, Hazel May. An analysis of group conflict. Pennsylvania, 1931.

3139. Hustwit, Ronald Earl. What is the meaning of religious language? Texas, 1970.   70-18254

3140. Hutcheson, Richard Ervin Joseph. Whitehead's theory of causation. Harvard, 1962.

3141. Hutchinson, James William. America: a region of the soul. New Mexico, 1975.   76-7958

3142. Hutchison, Percy Adams. Logical and psychological problems in poetic criticism. Harvard, 1904.

3143. Hyde, William H. Wittgenstein and criteria. Cal., S. Barbara, 1975.

3144. Hyland, Drew Alan. Eros and philosophy: a study of Plato's Symposium. Penn St., 1965.   66-8726

3145. Hynes, J. Gordon. Idealistic and Stoic backgrounds

of the philosophy of the apostle Paul. N.Y.U.,
1937. 73-3206

3146. Hyslop, James Hervey. The problem of space. Johns Hopkins, 1887.

- I -

3147. Iannone, Abel Pablo. Character traits. Wisconsin,
1975. 75-20773

3148. Ichimura, Shohei. Nagarjuna's philosophy of Sunyata and his dialectic. Chicago, 1972.

3149. Idziak, Janine Marie. God and emotions. Michigan,
1975. 75-29249

3150. Ihara, Craig Kei. Two concepts of supererogation. U.C.L.A., 1972. 73-10434

3151. Ihde, Don. Paul Ricoeur's phenomenological methodology and philosophical anthropology. Boston U.,
1964. 64-11623

3152. Iino, David Norimoto. Coherence in Hartmann's Ethik. Boston U., 1941.

3153. Immerwahr, John Raymond. Thomas Reid's theory of perception. Michigan, 1972. 72-29098

3154. Inagaki, Bernard R. The constitution of Japan and the natural law. Catholic U., 1955.

3155. Ingardia, Richard. F.H. Bradley's doctrine of judgment as a metaphysical problem. Colorado, 1971.
72-17269

3156. Ingham, Gerald Charles. Sellars' theory of universals and particulars. Brown, 1974. 75-9181

3157. Ingham, Harrington Vose. Fiction, truth, and reference. Southern Cal., 1974. 75-1064

3158. Inglis, Rev. Brian Desmond. Philipp Frank's philosophy of scientific knowing. Marquette, 1970.
71-5303

3159. Ingram, Robert Richard. The logical roles of modifiers in English. Claremont, 1972. 72-30542

3160. Inman, Floyd Albert. Metamathematics and the philosophy of formal languages. Boston U., 1971.
71-26426

3161. Innis, Robert Edward. The logic of consciousness: an examination of M. Polanyi's model of mind. Fordham, 1971. 71-20173

3162. Inouye, Shina. Leibniz and Fichte on the nature of will. Yale, 1927.

3163. Iobst, Philip Kirschman. The normative philosophy of Roy Wood Sellars: a critical examination. Buffalo, 1975. 76-1447

3164. Iorio, Dominick Anthony. The notion of intelligible extension in Nicolas Malebranche. Fordham, 1966. 66-7094

3165. Iredell, Francis Raymond. The problem of the self: an epistemological study of the reality and nature of the self-conscious experience. Harvard, 1937.

3166. Ireland, Michael Peter. Intentions. Toronto, 1972.

3167. Irish, Loomis C. Human nature and the arts. The aesthetic theory of Henry Home, Lord Kames. Columbia, 1961. 61-5468

3168. Irvine, Charles Crawford. Institutions and institutional change. Princeton, 1942.

3169. Irwin, John Paul. On categories and types. Syracuse, 1968. 68-13835

3170. Irwin, Terence Henry. Theories of virtue and knowledge in Plato's early and middle dialogues. Princeton, 1973. 73-18764

3171. Iseminger, Gary Hudson. Action, policies and principles. Yale, 1961.

3172. Isenberg, Arnold. The metaphysics of immediate experience. Harvard, 1935.

3173. Isner, Dale W., Jr. Understanding "understanding" through representation and reasoning. Pittsburgh, 1975. 75-21758

3174. Israel, David Joel. Quine and the naturalization of epistemology. Berkeley, 1974.

3175. Iverson, Sherwin Louis. Entailment: C.I. Lewis and the paradoxes of strict implication. Buffalo, 1972. 73-5127

3176. Ivry, Alfred L. Moses of Narbonne's treatise, The perfection of the soul. Partial edition with translation and notes. Brandeis, 1963. 64-3073

- J -

3177. Jack, Henry Howard. The moral philosophy of Adam Smith. Harvard, 1955.

3178. Jacklin, Rev. Edward G. The problem of individuation in St. Thomas Aquinas. Fordham, 1950.

3179. Jacklin, Phillip Drummond. Certainty and criteria of truth. Yale, 1968. 68-14845

3180. Jackson, Arthur F. Can one man teach another: a comparative analysis of treatments in Plato, Aristotle, Augustine, Aquinas, Buber and Lonergan. Boston Coll., 1973. 73-32471

3181. Jackson, Howard Oliver. A critical analysis of Gottlob Frege's philosophy of language. Berkeley, 1967. 68-10343

3182. Jackson, Joseph Hollister. A philosophical analysis of individual ethical opinions. Brown, 1940.

3183. Jacobs, Norman. Ethical relativity. N.Y.U., 1939. 73-17949

3184. Jacobs, William Clayton. Consciousness of moral obligation. Pennsylvania, 1896.

3185. Jacobs, William Samuel. Einai and existence in Aristotle. Ohio St., 1974. 74-24348

3186. Jacobson, Fritz. A sketch of the development of speculative thought in Sweden. Yale, 1889.

3187. Jacobson, John Howard, Jr. Meaning and meaninglessness in natural and artificial languages. Yale, 1957.

3188. Jacobson, Paul Kenneth. From speech to logos: an interpretation of Merleau-Ponty's philosophy of language. Duquesne, 1975. 76-13119

3189. Jacoby, Paul Joseph. "Common sense" in epistemology. Notre Dame, 1942.

3190. Jacot, Robert Edgard. Existentialism, naturalism, and the theory of history. Northwestern, 1973. 73-30620

3191. Jaeger, Robert A. Seeing. Cornell, 1971. 71-22981

3192. Jaffa, Harry Victor. Thomism and Aristotelianism; a study of the <u>Commentary</u> of St. Thomas Aquinas on the <u>Nicomachean ethics</u> of Aristotle. New School, 1951.

3193. Jaffe, Haym. Natural law as controlled but not determined by experiment. Pennsylvania, 1932.

3194. Jaffe, Raymond. The pragmatic conception of justice. Berkeley, 1953.

3195. Jager, Ronald Albert. Moore and necessity. Harvard, 1964.

3196. Jaggar, Alison Mary. On communication in philosophy: a study of the problems involved in the re-expression of theoretical philosophical statements. Buffalo, 1970. 71-7177

3197. Jaggar, Charles Albert. Value of realism as a philosophy. Princeton, 1888.

3198. Jamali, Naseem Zia. Personal identity and DNA theory. N.Y.U., 1975. 76-10181

3199. Jamalpur, Bahram. God and man: a historical and critical comparison of Ibn Sina and Molavi within the esoteric Iranian tradition of Islamic philosophy. Notre Dame, 1970. 71-5542

3200. James, Edward Warren. Concerning the failure of some attempts to preserve entailment. Southern Cal., 1970. 71-7715

3201. James, Gene Gray. Ralph Barton Perry's theory of value: a critical analysis. No. Carolina, 1969. 70-3259

3202. James, Patricia Ann. Decidability in the logic of subordinate proofs. Yale, 1962.

3203. James, Ralph Emerson, Jr. The function of the relationship between the abstract and the concrete in Charles Hartshorne's treatment of some traditional Christian doctrines. Drew, 1965. 65-11329

3204. James, Theodore Earle. <u>De primo et ultimo instanti</u>: Petri Alboini Mantuani, edited with an introduction, analysis and notes. Columbia, 1968. 71-17590

3205. James, Walter Thomas. The philosophy of Noah Porter (1811-1892). Columbia, 1951. 2823

3206. Jameton, Andrew Lang. Testimony and evidence: the social foundation of knowledge. U. of Washington, 1972. 73-3731

3207. Jamieson, John Clarence. Semantical theory and analyticity. Kansas, 1973. 74-12580

3208. Janik, Allan Stanley. Uncle Ludwig's book on ethics: Wittgenstein's *Tractatus* reconsidered. Brandeis, 1970. 71-20334

3209. Janik, Linda Gardiner. The concept of truth in the historical theory of the Italian renaissance. Brandeis, 1973. 73-32389

3210. Jannusch, Bruce A. A re-evaluation of H.H. Price's theory of perception. So. Illinois, 1970. 71-10009

3211. Jaques, Robert Shepherd. Action; logical, metaphysical and normative in Maurice Blondel. Toronto, 1938. 62

3212. Jaquette, William Alderman, III. Value, nothingness and Jean-Paul Sartre. Missouri, 1969. 70-2995

3213. Jardine, John Gonsalves, Jr. Towards a metaphysics of community: a critical study of John Dewey's social philosophy. Tulane, 1974. 75-11898

3214. Jarrett, Charles Edwin. A study of Spinoza's metaphysics. Berkeley, 1974.

3215. Jarrett, James Louis, Jr. The cognitive value of poetry. Michigan, 1948.

3216. Jarvis, Rev. Edward A. The conception of God in the later Royce. Ottawa, 1973. 74-780

3217. Jarvis, Judith. Necessity and meaning. Columbia, 1959. 59-4069

3218. Jascalevich, Alexander A. Three conceptions of mind, their bearing on the denaturalization of the mind in history. Columbia, 1926.

3219. Javier, Benjamin P. The *a priori* factor in the logic and psychology of Marechal's critical philosophy. Fordham, 1956.

3220. Jayne, Edward Stanley. The theory of mediation and its critical applications. Buffalo, 1971.

3221. Jeffery, Harriet M. Berkeley's philosophy in Britain and America, 1800 to the present: a study of revived interest and revised interpretations. Colorado, 1942.

3222. Jeffko, Walter George. John Macmurray's logical form of the personal: a critical exposition. Fordham, 1970. 70-20122

3223. Jeffrey, Richard Carl. Contributions to the theory of inductive probability. Princeton, 1957.
58-7851

3224. Jellema, William Harry. The philosophy of Josiah Royce. Michigan, 1923.

3225. Jen, Hua. Three types of phenomenalism in contemporary philosophy. Harvard, 1947.

3226. Jenkins, Iredell. The elements of aesthetic recognition and judgment. Virginia, 1937.

3227. Jennings, Richard Charles. Rationalism and mentalism in Cartesian linguistics. Washington U., 1968. 69-8999

3228. Jensen, Alfred Dewey. Perspective, paradox and predestination. Texas, 1970. 71-143

3229. Jensen, Henning. Motivation and the moral sense in Francis Hutcheson's ethical theory. Harvard, 1969.

3230. Jensen, Jack Winfield. Prescriptivism, descriptivism and the purpose of morality. Boston U., 1975.
75-20993

3231. Jentz, Arthur Henry, Jr. Ethics in the making: the genesis and nature of ethical theory in the philosophy of Alfred North Whitehead. Columbia, 1965.
65-13959

3232. Jessup, Bertram Emil. Relational value meanings. Berkeley, 1939.

3233. Jetté, Emile. La perception chez Bergson. Laval, 1943.

3234. Jewell, Robert Dean. The problem of justifying deduction. Brown, 1965. 65-13660

3235. Jha, Krishna Mohan. An inquiry into A.J. Ayer's theory of meaning and truth. Toronto, 1966.

3236. Jha, Ram Chandra. The Vedantic and the Buddhist concept of reality as interpreted by Samkara and Nagarjuna. C.I.A.S., 1972. 73-32475

3237. Joannides, Peter. Neutral monism in Mach. Cornell, 1955. 10745

3238. Jobe, Evan Kermit. The nature of time. Indiana, 1973. 74-382

3239. Jobes, James William, Jr. On revealing: an examination of some questions concerning art as a source of knowledge. Virginia, 1967. 67-17605

3240. Johanning, Jon Carl. The perception of persons: a comparison of recent approaches to the problem of other minds. Yale, 1966. 67-3449

3241. Johanson, Arnold Edwin. Philosophy and the limits of doubt. Yale, 1969. 70-2748

3242. Johnsen, Bredo Christoffer. Knowledge and induction in Bertrand Russell's Human knowledge. Harvard, 1972.

3243. Johnson, Allison Heartz. Actual entities: a study of A.N. Whitehead's theory of reality. Toronto, 1937. 61

3244. Johnson, Arthur Lee. Religion in the age of reason: a philosophical study of the religious views of David Hume. Nebraska, 1973. 74-12993

3245. Johnson, Baylor Laurence. Sights and sounds: a study of Nelson Goodman's aesthetics. Northwestern, 1974. 74-28654

3246. Johnson, Charles Wayne. Formal aspects of neural modeling. Michigan St., 1971. 71-31233

3247. Johnson, Conrad Derrall. The use of fundamental norm theories in distinguishing between the legal and non-legal. Michigan, 1969. 70-4109

3248. Johnson, Dan Collins, Jr. The meaning and justification of ethical statements. Kansas, 1971. 71-27158

3249. Johnson, David Eugene. The ontology of presupposing: a critical examination of the philosophy of P.F. Strawson. Iowa, 1965. 66-3448

3250. Johnson, David Martel. A formulation model of perceptual knowledge: the outline and defense of a judgmental theory of perception. Yale, 1969. 69-15990

3251. Johnson, Donald Hanlon. Norman O. Brown's theory of symbolic consciousness: towards a new politics.

Yale, 1971. 71-28184

3252. Johnson, Edith Henry. Argument of Aristotle's metaphysics. Columbia, 1906.

3253. Johnson, Eleanor Margaret. The essential nature of trueness. Boston U., 1939.

3254. Johnson, Frederick Alfsen. Non-linguistic theories of truth. Ohio St., 1970. 71-18029

3255. Johnson, George. The arithmetical philosophy of Nicomachus of Geraso. Pennsylvania, 1911.

3256. Johnson, Harold J. Nature, knowledge, and convention in the philosophy of Hobbes. Chicago, 1958.

3257. Johnson, John Prescott. The problem of value apprehension. Northwestern, 1959. 60-441

3258. Johnson, Lawrence Eugene. Propositions, facts, related "entities," and truth. Cal., S. Diego, 1970. 71-26573

3259. Johnson, Major Lanius, Jr. A contribution toward a non-substantial theory of time. Brown, 1971. 72-8133

3260. Johnson, Mary Helgren. Some philosophical problems of accounts of motion. U. of Washington, 1967. 68-3855

3261. Johnson, Oliver Adolph. The right and the good in ethics. Yale, 1951.

3262. Johnson, Paul Jerald. Hobbes's concept of natural law and obligation. Johns Hopkins, 1969. 69-21086

3263. Johnson, Ralph Henry. The concept of existence in the Concluding unscientific postscript. Notre Dame, 1972.

3264. Johnson, Richard Clark. A preface to a metaphysics of value. Harvard, 1950.

3265. Johnson, Roger Bruce Cash. Metaphysics of knowledge; being an examination of T.H. Green's theory of reality. Princeton, 1900.

3266. Johnson, William Hallock. Free-will problem in modern thought. Columbia, 1902.

3267. Johnston, Charles Hughes. A psychological study of the mutual influence of feelings. Harvard, 1905.

3268. Johnston, Dale Allen. An American anarchist: an analysis of the individualist anarchism of Benjamin R. Tucker. New Mexico, 1973. 74-10351

3269. Johnston, Herbert Leo. Mediaeval teachings on the morality of usury. Toronto, 1938.

3270. Johnston, Julia Marie. Descartes and the liberty of indifference: an essay on Cartesian method. Bryn Mawr, 1965. 66-1535

3271. Johnston, Pat Hanna. Some extensions of counterpart theory and possible worlds framework with respect to counterfactuals and causal modalities. Cincinnati, 1972. 72-31738

3272. Johnstone, Henry Webb, Jr. A grammar of the sense-datum language. Harvard, 1950.

3273. Jolin, Stephen Towne. What philosophy is for Gabriel Marcel. Marquette, 1970. 71-20734

3274. Joly, Ralph Phillip. The human person in a philosophy of education. Catholic U., 1961. 62-275

3275. Jones, Adam Leroy. Early American philosophers. Columbia, 1898.

3276. Jones, Charles Edwin. The theory of truth as subjectivity in Kierkegaard, compared with theories of truth in Blanshard and Ayer. Arkansas, 1973. 73-27390

3277. Jones, David Clifford. The hypothesis of value. Texas, 1974. 74-24879

3278. Jones, David Henry. Freud's theory of moral conscience. Harvard, 1963.

3279. Jones, Frederick Beresford. Plato's contributions to legal philosophy. Penn St., 1974. 74-21010

3280. Jones, George, Jr. A critical examination of the religious and moral thought of Reinhold Niebuhr. Brown, 1961. 63-1437

3281. Jones, Hardy Eugene. Kant's principle of personality. Wisconsin, 1970. 71-303

3282. Jones, Howard. Phronesis in Heraclitus. Indiana, 1970. 71-6864

3283. Jones, Jack William. Personalistic tendencies in the thought of Josiah Royce. Boston U., 1968. 68-18136

3284. Jones, Jere Jene. On the distinction between religiousness "A" and religiousness "B" in the <u>Concluding scientific postscript</u> of Søren Kierkegaard. Nebraska, 1971. 71-19494

3285. Jones, Marc E. George Sylvester Morris: his philosophical career and theistic idealism. Columbia, 1948.

3286. Jones, Martin Monroe. The categorial concept of emergence in the philosophy of George H. Mead. Tulane, 1969. 70-24528

3287. Jones, Michael Paul. George Herbert Mead's perspectival theory of consciousness, perception, and knowledge. Texas, 1973. 73-26026

3288. Jones, Michael Thomas. Intentionalist and conventionalist solutions to problems of reference in the philosophy of language. Ohio St., 1973. 74-3213

3289. Jones, Olin McKendree. Empiricism and intuitionism in Reid's common sense philosophy. Columbia, 1927.

3290. Jones, Ozro T., Jr. The meaning of the "moment" in existential encounter according to Kierkegaard. Temple, 1962. 63-238

3291. Jones, Royce Paul. C.S. Peirce on intuition and instinct. Oklahoma, 1972. 73-9160

3292. Jones, Thomas Evan. Relation of moral judgments to freedom. Johns Hopkins, 1964.

3293. Jones, William Alexander. The development of the social philosophy of Jean-Paul Sartre. Notre Dame, 1970. 71-5544

3294. Jones, William Benjamin. The Carnap-Hempel analysis of scientific theories: a study of its internal difficulties. Vanderbilt, 1974. 75-1140

3295. Jones, William Ronald. Sartre's philosophical anthropology in relation to his ethics: a criticism of selected critics. Brown, 1969. 70-8739

3296. Jones, William T. Kant's theory of moral freedom. Princeton, 1937.

3297. Jordan, Elijah. The constitutive and regulative principles in Kant. Chicago, 1911.

3298. Jordan, James Augustus, Jr. A concept of self and

value from Whitehead and its implications for education. Emory, 1958. 59-459

3299. Jordan, James Nicholas. Hume's account of the conception of physical objects. Texas, 1966.
66-7341

3300. Jordan, Robert Woodrow. Ethics and aesthetics in Plato's philosophy. Harvard, 1950.

3301. Joseph, Audrey Benderman. Artistic vision and the metaphysical imagination: toward a phenomenology of aesthetic consciousness. New Mexico, 1974.
75-18635

3302. Jost, Lawrence John. Ethical naturalism: a contemporary category with ancient application. Toronto, 1973.

3303. Joubert, Rev. Gerard. Qualities of citizenship in St. Thomas. Catholic U., 1941.

3304. Jourdain, Alice. The role of created goods in the philosophy of St. Augustine. Fordham, 1949.

3305. Joy, Glenn Clarence. Pierre Duham: physical theory, experiment, and conventionalism. Texas, 1970.
71-145

3306. Juarez-Paz, Rigoberto. Studies in twentieth century Spanish philosophy. Minnesota, 1958. 59-1277

3307. Jubin, Brenda Lu. Some parts and aspects of F.H. Bradley's metaphysics. Yale, 1973. 74-11751

3308. Judy, Rev. Albert Glenn Norbert. Robert Kilwardby: De ortu scientiarum. A critical edition. Toronto, 1973.

3009. Juffras, Angelo. Hume's theory of meaning. Columbia, 1969. 70-18820

3310. Julia-Marie, Sr. Self love and human society. Laval, 1952.

3311. Jung, Robert William. The aesthetics of José Ortega y Gasset. Illinois, 1966. 66-12357

3312. Junkersfeld, Sr. M. Julienne. The Aristotelian-Thomistic conception of chance. Notre Dame, 1945.

3313. Justice, John Keith, Jr. Inductive rationality. Texas, 1975. 75-24893

3314. Justin, Gale D. Kant and Berkeley. Chicago, 1972.

- K -

3315. Kachi, Yukio. Language and reality in Plato's theory of characters. Princeton, 1970. 70-19784

3316. Kadankavil, Kurian T. Metaphysical and epistemological pluralism in Mundakopanishad. Fordham, 1974. 74-25058

3317. Kading, Daniel. The examination of some contemporary subjective ethical theories. Cornell, 1949.

3318. Kadish, Mortimer Raymond. Toward a theory of decision. Columbia, 1950. 1865

3319. Kadosh, David. Motion, place, void and the elements. Yeshiva, 1969. 69-21012

3320. Kaelin, Eugene Francis. Alain, aesthetician: an essay in the philosophy of art. Illinois, 1954. 9093

3321. Kagey, Rudolf. F.H. Bradley's logic. Columbia, 1931.

3322. Kahane, Howard. Six inductive problems. Pennsylvania, 1962. 62-4310

3323. Kahl, Harry Russell. The philosophical works of Helmholtz: the philosophy and epistemology of the German scientist. Columbia, 1951. 2826

3324. Kahn, Rev. Eric Earl. Saint Bonaventure's Collationes in hexaemeron: a translation of five lectures, with an introduction and commentary. St. Louis, 1962. 64-3744

3325. Kahn, Joseph. Spinoza's idea of God. N.Y.U., 1904.

3326. Kahn, Journet David. A Thomistic theory of emotion. Notre Dame, 1956. 15405

3327. Kahn, Lina. Metaphysics of the supernatural as illustrated by Descartes. Columbia, 1918.

3328. Kahn, Sholom Jacob. Taine's historical criticism; a study in science and aesthetic judgment. Columbia, 1950. 1771

3329. Kahoe, Walter. Vitalism, mechanism, and racial memory. Pennsylvania, 1949.

3330. Kain, Philip Joseph. Schiller, Hegel, Marx and the aesthetic ideal of ancient Greece. Cal., S. Diego, 1974. 74-27561

3331. Kainz, Howard Paul, Jr. The self-reflection of consciousness in Hegel's phenomenology. Duquesne, 1968.

3332. Kaiser, Charles Hillis. Physical causality in the light of recent developments in physical theory. Harvard, 1934.

3333. Kaiser, Denny Nolan. Language, law, and morals. Michigan, 1964. 64-8179

3334. Kajevich, Rev. Stojiljko Ned. Nikolay Berdyaev's theory of uncreated freedom and its metaphysical origins. DePaul, 1975. 75-19893

3335. Kalal, Leonard Anthony. A critique and defense of the representational theory of measurement. Colorado, 1972. 72-25182

3336. Kalas, John William. Three theories of religious experience: Otto, Tennant and Santayana. Columbia, 1962. 62-5184

3337. Kalberer, Augustine Anthony. Saint Thomas' notion of order. Toronto, 1946.

3338. Kalif, George. Metaphysics of the self. Harvard, 1933.

3339. Kalikow, Theodora June. Konrad Lorenz's ethological theory, 1927 to 1943: history and philosophical critique; sources of misleading animal-human comparisons. Boston U., 1974. 74-14214

3340. Kalin, Jesse Gene. Ethical egoism and the universalization requirement. Berkeley, 1969. 7C-6132

3341. Kalin, Martin Gregory. Kant's theory of transcendental propositions. Northwestern, 1970. 71-1887

3342. Kalish, Donald. The role of propositions in philosophical logic, with special reference tc the philosophy of Bertrand Russell. Berkeley, 1949.

3343. Kalita, Dwight Kenton. They call it Christianity, I call it consciousness: a theological correlation of Paul Tillich and R.W. Emerson. Bowling Green, 1972. 72-27220

3344. Kallen, Horace Meyer. Notes on the nature cf truth.

Harvard, 1908.

3345. Kalosieh, William Peter. Mystery as knowledge in the philosophy of Gabriel Marcel. Fordham, 1975.
75-18888

3346. Kamali, Sabih Ahmad. The concept of human nature in Hujjat Allah al-Bālighah and its relation to Shah Waliullah's doctrine of fiqh. McGill, 1959.

3347. Kamber, Richard. A study of the relationship between philosophy and literature. Claremont, 1975.
75-16236

3348. Kamins, Herbert. Aesthetic claims: a criticism of Collingwood's, Lewis's, and Richard's theories, and an alternative analysis of critical evaluations. Cornell, 1955. 11907

3349. Kaminsky, Jack. The philosophy of George Henry Lewes. N.Y.U., 1950. 73-22132

3350. Kamler, Howard Frederick. The concept of emphatic understanding. Michigan, 1971. 71-23782

3351. Kamoski, Liudomir Edward. Function. Cornell, 1969.
70-514

3352. Kamp, Johan Anthony Willem. Tense logic and the theory of linear order. U.C.L.A., 1968.
69-1111

3353. Kanda, Rev. John Robert. Certain intellectual operations and the neo-scholastic manuals. Georgetown, 1959.

3354. Kane, Sr. Ann Virginia. Truth and political freedom according to Thomistic principles. Catholic U., 1950.

3355. Kane, Francis Ignatius. Heidegger's "sein" and linguistic analytic objections. Georgetown, 1975.
77-6182

3356. Kane, Robert Hilary. Intentionality and language: an approach to the philosophy of mind. Yale, 1964.

3357. Kane, Rev. William J. The philosophy of relation in the metaphysics of St. Thomas. Catholic U., 1958.

3358. Kang, Wook. G.H. Mead's concept of rationality: a study in philosophical anthropology. Columbia, 1970. 71-17510

3359. Kannwischer, Arthur. Psychology and ethics in John Stuart Mill's Logic. Pittsburgh, 1952.

3360. Kanter, Samuel Israel. The Nuremberg trials, a test case for jurisprudence. Ohio St., 1971.
71-27493

3361. Kantonen, Taito Almar. The influence of Descartes on Berkeley. Boston U., 1931.

3362. Kantor, Jacob Robert. The functional nature of the philosophical categories. Chicago, 1917.

3363. Kaplan, Abraham. The language of value: a study in pragmatics. U.C.L.A., 1942.

3364. Kaplan, David Benjamin. Foundations of intensional logic. U.C.L.A., 1964.
64-8563

3365. Kaplan, Martin Harold. Collage itself. Stanford, 1975.

3366. Kaplan, Robert Stephen. A structural analysis of Santayana'a philosophy of religion. Columbia, 1966.
67-797

3367. Kappy, Ellen Gail. Truth and the justification of belief: a study in the epistemology of William James. Wisconsin, 1972.
72-23746

3368. Karlin, Eli. Freedom and its presuppositions: a metaphysical inquiry. Yale, 1947.

3369. Karp, David Jacob. General ontology. M.I.T., 1975.

3370. Kasachkoff, Tziporah F. Theories of punishment. N.Y.U., 1972.
73-11721

3371. Kashiyama, A.S. Historicity in Karl Jaspers' thinking: its practical structure present in a correlation between his thinking and historic consciousness. Alberta, 1975.

3372. Kaslusis, Thomas Patrick. Action performs man: the meaning of the person in Japanese Zen Buddhism. Yale, 1975.
76-14592

3373. Kassel, Frank. Relativity and the critical philosophy. Pennsylvania, 1926.

3374. Kasten, Vance Robert. A concept of violence. Michigan, 1971.
72-14909

3375. Kates, Carol Ann. Language and no-thingness. Tulane, 1968.
69-3804

3376. Kates, Lawrence Robert. The psycho-physical identity thesis. Maryland, 1971. 72-1640

3377. Katterhenry, Edwin A. A critique of Aristotle's doctrine of the mean. Cincinnati, 1939.

3378. Kattsoff, Louis O. Postulational methods. Pennsylvania, 1934.

3379. Katuin, Gerald Albert. A comparison of methods in science and philosophy. Chicago, 1923.

3380. Katz, Jerrold Jacob. The problem of induction and its dissolution. Princeton, 1960. 60-5010

3381. Katz, Joseph. Plotinus' search for the good. Columbia, 1951.

3382. Katz, Marvin Charles. Trends toward synthesis in the philosophy of Robert S. Hartman. So. Illinois, 1966. 67-3164

3383. Katzner, Louis Isaac. An analysis of the concept of justice. Michigan, 1968. 69-12149

3384. Katzoff, Charlotte Pearlberg. The object of knowledge in the philosophy of Solomon Maimon and its relationship to the thing in itself in Kant's *Critique of pure reason*. Columbia, 1971. 72-1338

3385. Kauber, Peter George. William James's ethics of belief. Buffalo, 1972. 72-27258

3386. Kauffman, Alvin H. Elan vital, nisus, and creativity as treated in the thought of H. Bergson, S. Alexander, and A.N. Whitehead. Boston U., 1952.

3387. Kaufman, Arnold Saul. Liberalism in transition: the political philosophy of Leonard Trelawny Hobhouse. Columbia, 1955. 15633

3388. Kaufman, Steven Andrew. Ontological relativity. Pennsylvania, 1975. 76-3181

3389. Kaufman, William Elliot. The relation of man to the world in the philosophy of John Wild. Boston U., 1971. 71-26429

3390. Kaufmann, Rev. Leo Bernard. Predication and reality in Plato. St. Louis, 1957. 58-4379

3391. Kaufmann, Walter Arnold. Nietzsche's theory of values. Harvard, 1947.

3392. Kavaloski, Vincent Carl. The vera causa principle: a historico-philosophical study of a metatheoretical concept from Newton through Darwin. Chicago, 1974.

3393. Kavanaugh, John Francis. Whole and part in Hegel, Marx, and Marcuse. Washington U., 1973.
74-13778

3394. Kavka, Gregory Stephen. Moral ideals. Michigan, 1973.
74-15774

3395. Kawabe, Jiroku. The development of Confucianism in Japan under the influence of the philosophy of Shushi. Yale, 1904.

3396. Kay, Stanley Broughton. Kant on the existence of God: from the Beweisgrund to the critical philosophy. Ohio St., 1966.
67-2466

3397. Ke, Li. Some epistemological implications of modern physical science. Southern Cal., 1953.

3398. Keane, Sr. Ellen Marie. The equation of subjectivity and truth in Kierkegaard's Postscript. Notre Dame, 1965.
65-14610

3399. Keane, Helen Virginia. Knowledge by connaturality in St. Thomas Aquinas. Marquette, 1966.
67-3630

3400. Kearley, Carroll Clay. The non-Eleatic concept of being in the works of José Ortega y Gasset. Notre Dame, 1965.
65-11115

3401. Kearney, Chester Milton. Two neglected aspects of the truth situation. Chicago, 1931.

3402. Kearney, John Kevin. The ethical significance of Kant's aesthetics. Bryn Mawr, 1972.
73-5894

3403. Kearney, Rev. William Francis. Cassirer's Mirandola. Laval, 1946.

3404. Kearns, John Thomas. Lesniewski, language, and logic. Yale, 1962.

3405. Kearns, Thomas J. Continuity in Galileo Galilei's New science. Catholic U., 1967.
67-15437

3406. Kearns, Thomas Rost. Vagueness. Wisconsin, 1968.
69-940

3407. Keating, James W. The function of the philosopher in American pragmatism. Catholic U., 1953.

3408. Keating, Sr. Mary William. The relation between the proofs for the existence of God and the real distinction of essence and existence in St. Thomas Aquinas. Fordham, 1962. 63-210

3409. Keaton, Alvin Eugene. The philosophical significance of cybernetics. Oklahoma, 1969. 70-2317

3410. Kedl, George Kent. Each according to its own kind. Oregon, 1970. 71-10747

3411. Keegan, Francis Lauren. The development of Jacques Maritain's conception of Christian philosophy: 1910-1929. Notre Dame, 1959. 60-1126

3412. Keehley, Jay Taylor. The resolution of models in the natural sciences as types of metaphors. Florida St., 1974. 75-4773

3413. Keeler, Rev. Leo William. The problem of error from Plato to Descartes: an historical study. St. Louis, 1933.

3414. Keen, Clive Nigel. Naturalism, skepticism and reason in Hume's *Treatise*. McMaster, 1975.

3415. Keen, Tom Clifton. George Herbert Mead's social theory of meaning and experience. Ohio St., 1968. 68-15339

3416. Keenan, Brian Michael. Political reality: an essay in political theory. Waterloo, 1974.

3417. Keene, Carol Ann Mary. F.H. Bradley's theory of self. St. Louis, 1970. 70-20401

3418. Keeton, Morris Teuton. The philosophy of Edmund Montgomery. Harvard, 1938.

3419. Keezer, Philip Willard. Temporal and valuational dimensions of the image of man held by campus religious and parareligious leaders. Ohio St., 1973. 74-10984

3420. Kegley, Charles William. The doctrines of the absolute and of God in the philosophy of N.O. Lossky. Northwestern, 1943.

3421. Kegley, Jacqueline Ann Kovacevic. Josiah Royce's theory of knowledge. Columbia, 1971. 72-20047

3422. Keim, Robert Gordon. An investigation of epistemic preferability. Brown, 1971. 72-8138

3423. Keleher, James Francis. A philosophy of cooperation.

Columbia, 1948.

3424. Kellenberger, Bertram James. Some problems of religious belief and religious knowledge. Oregon, 1967. 67-10784

3425. Keller, Chester Z. An examination of L.T. Hobhouse's conception of morals in evolution with special reference to cultural anthropology. Southern Cal., 1956.

3426. Keller, Marcia Lynn. The movement left: dialectics of violence and love. Yale, 1971. 72-17132

3427. Kelley, David Christopher. The evidence of the senses. Princeton, 1974. 75-23214

3428. Kelley, Michael Harry. Methodological problems of logical probability. Wisconsin, 1969. 69-22411

3429. Kellner, Douglas Mackay. Heidegger's concept of authenticity. Columbia, 1973. 73-28222

3430. Kellner, Marc Edward. Civil disobedience in democracy: a philosophical justification. Washington U., 1973. 73-24890

3431. Kells, Lucas Carlisle. Typical methods of thinking in science and philosophy. Columbia, 1910.

3432. Kelly, Charles John. The presuppositions of John Stuart Mill's theory of names and propositions. Notre Dame, 1969. 69-12790

3433. Kelly, Derek Arthur. The role of examples in philosophical reasoning. Boston U., 1969. 69-18765

3434. Kelly, Eugene. Max Scheler and phenomenology. N.Y.U., 1971. 72-3089

3435. Kelly, Frank Joseph, Jr. The historicism of José Ortega y Gasset. Oklahoma, 1973. 73-23945

3436. Kelly, Gertrude Rose. A study of transcendental arguments. Waterloo, 1971.

3437. Kelly, James Patrick. The continuation between the human sense powers and the human speculative intellect according to St. Thomas Aquinas. St. John's, 1963.

3438. Kelly, John C. Laws and the explanation of intentional actions. Chicago, 1969.

3439. Kelly, John Emory. The notion of love in Plotinus

and its relation to knowledge. Catholic U., 1970.
71-11068

3440. Kelly, John Michael. The animistic materialism of William Pepperell Montague. Toronto, 1948.

3441. Kelly, Sr. M. James Therese. An examination of Eric Gill's philosophy of art. Notre Dame, 1962.
63-292

3442. Kelly, Matthew John. The interpretation of St. Thomas Aquinas of *Physics* 191a 7-8:"The underlying nature is known by analogy." Notre Dame, 1963.
63-7326

3443. Kelly, Br. Pascal. An analysis of the proper senses in the philosophy of St. Thomas Aquinas. Fordham, 1952.

3444. Kelly, Patrick. Cognition, the given, and the quest for certainty in empirical knowledge. Emory, 1966.
67-212

3445. Kelson, Jacob Coleman. Nature, selves, and universals. Harvard, 1928.

3446. Kelvington, James Robert. A developmental concept of responsibility in the light of some modern and contemporary philosophers. Duquesne, 1966.

3447. Kemerling, Garth Leroy. John Locke and mind/body dualism. Iowa, 1974.
75-1211

3448. Kempner, Martin Lewis. The concept of meta-ethical impartiality. Brandeis, 1972.
72-17990

3449. Kendall, Edward Gridley. The place of experience in cognition: a thesis defended against the claims of Kant. Yale, 1899.

3450. Kendzierski, Lottie H. The Aristotelian physics and the problem of creation in the thirteenth century. Fordham, 1945.

3451. Kenevan, Phyllis Berdt. Time, consciousness, and the ego in the philosophy of Sartre. Northwestern, 1969.
70-86

3452. Kennard, Kenneth Clifton. Whitehead's contribution to contemporary discussion of the nature of metaphysics. Northwestern, 1966.
66-14004

3453. Kennedy, Bart Franklin. An interpretation of Alfred North Whitehead's theory of eternal objects. Tulane, 1973.
74-10692

3454. Kennedy, Gail. The psychological empiricism of John Stuart Mill. Columbia, 1928.

3455. Kennedy, Leonard Anthony. Abstraction and illumination in the doctrine of St. Albert the Great. Toronto, 1958.

3456. Kennedy, Rev. Paul Vincent. A philosophical appraisal of the modernist gnosticism of Nicholas Berdyaev. St. Louis, 1936.   192

3457. Kennedy, Ralph Clarence, III. On solving the new riddle of induction: a study of Nelson Goodman's theory of projectibility. Berkeley, 1975.
76-15254

3458. Kennedy, Robert Emmet, Jr. Destutt de Tracy and the origins of "ideology." Brandeis, 1973.

3459. Kennedy, Samuel Joseph. Conscience: its nature and role in moral activity, according to St. Thomas Aquinas. Notre Dame, 1963.   63-7327

3460. Kenney, Rev. Wilton Henry. John Locke and the Oxford training in logic and metaphysics. St. Louis, 1959.   60-339

3461. Kennick, William E. A methodological approach to metaphysics, with special reference to the philosophies of Aristotle, Hume, Dewey, and Whitehead. Cornell, 1952.

3462. Kennington, Richard. On the intention of Descartes' Meditations. New School, 1966.

3463. Kenny, Dumont F. A philosophical analysis of the reorientation program in Germany. Chicago, 1953.

3464. Kent, Beverley E. Logic in the context of Peirce's classification of the sciences. Waterloo, 1975.

3465. Kent, Edward Allen. Duties in rem: a new property theory. Columbia, 1966.   66-6939

3466. Kent, Ernest Daryl. The ethics of Thomas Hill Green. Columbia, 1954.   8697

3467. Kent, William J. Purpose and activity. Johns Hopkins, 1974.   75-12956

3468. Kent, William P. The political philosophy of John Dewey. Chicago, 1950.

3469. Kerins, Rev. James. The social role of self control. Catholic U., 1943.

3470. Kerner, George. Some recent ethical theories and the performatory approach to moral language. Harvard, 1960.

3471. Kerns, Thomas A., Jr. Altered states of consciousness: a philosophical analysis of their psychological, ontological, and religious significance. Marquette, 1973. 73-27510

3472. Kerr, Donna Hanneman. Listening and speaking: asymmetries. Columbia, 1973. 73-29844

3473. Kerr, Stanley Roy. Transcendental arguments: an essay on P.F. Strawson's metaphysics. Yale, 1972. 72-17133

3474. Kerr, William Osborne, Jr. An examination of John Herman Randall, Jr.'s philosophy of religion. Buffalo, 1969. 70-17341

3475. Kersten, Frederick Irving. Husserl's investigations toward a phenomenology of space. New School, 1964. 65-1108

3476. Kerstetter, William E. John Locke's conception of freedom. Boston U., 1943.

3477. Kesling, Jerrel. Meaning and reality: a study of Max Weber's theory of science. Penn St., 1974. 75-10792

3478. Kessler, Hubert. Basic factors in the growth of mind and self, analysis and reconstruction of G.H. Mead's theory. Illinois, 1940.

3479. Kessler, Warren Leslie. The problem of attributes in Spinoza. Wisconsin, 1969. 71-12694

3480. Ketchum, Richard Jennings. Truth and being in Plato's Sophist. Pennsylvania, 1971. 71-26038

3481. Ketels, Luther Henry. The philosophy of Thomas Hill Green. Drew, 1926.

3482. Ketner, Kenneth Laine. An essay on the nature of world views. Cal., S. Barbara, 1972. 73-8116

3483. Kett, Merriellyn. Moore and Russell's refutation of Bradley's idealism. DePaul, 1973. 73-28662

3484. Kevane, Rev. Eugene. An Augustinian philosophy of education for American Catholic schools. Catholic U., 1962. 63-1943

3485. Keyes, Anne Marie. The philosophy operative in contemporary humanistic psychology: knowing and willing in Allport, Maslow and Rogers. Marquette, 1975. 76-8642

3486. Keyes, Rev. Charles Don. From nihilism to comedy: a phenomenological and systematic study in the philosophy of religion. Duquesne, 1968.

3487. Keys, Mereld D. An examination of formalism as a general aesthetic theory. Claremont, 1967. 68-10516

3488. Keyser, Robert. Skepticism of David Hume. N.Y.U., 1892. 75-02803

3489. Keyt, David Alan. C.I. Lewis's theory of meaning. Cornell, 1955. 15019

3490. Keyworth, Donald Roland. The status of theological first principles according to Hume and Kant. Ohio St., 1958. 58-542

3491. Khan, Abraham Habibulla. The treatment of the theme of suffering in Kierkegaard's works. McGill, 1973.

3492. Khatchadourian, Haig A. The coherence theory of truth: a critical evaluation. Duke, 1956.

3493. Khoobyar, Helen. On thinking: a Heidegger-Dewey comparison for philosophy of education. Berkeley, 1973.

3494. Kibens, Maija. The Chomskyan paradigm and semantic creativity. Michigan, 1973. 74-3655

3495. Kidder, Joel Holloway. Methods, principles, and knowledge in the ethical philosophy of Henry Sidgwick. Pittsburgh, 1968. 69-12831

3496. Kielkopf, Charles Francis. An examination of Ludwig Wittgenstein's Remarks on the foundations of mathematics. Minnesota, 1962. 63-4302

3497. Kiernan, William Edward. At-homeness in a changing world: the relationship between change-meaning-intentionality in the philosophy of John Dewey. Fordham, 1974. 74-19666

3498. Kiesau, Robert Frank. A double-aspect theory of the mental and the material. Syracuse, 1972. 72-20345

3499. Kilgore, William Jackson. Alejandro Korn's interpretation of creative freedom. Texas, 1958. 59-168

3500. Killeen, Sr. Mary Vincent. Man in the new humanism. Catholic U., 1934.

3501. Killeen, Rev. Sylvester M. The philosophy of labor in St. Thomas. Catholic U., 1939.

3502. Kim, Chin-Tai. The structure of historical explanation. Harvard, 1965.

3503. Kim, Choon Sup. Dialectical method. Columbia, 1952.
3685

3504. Kim, Ha Poong. Locke's political theory: a reconsideration of its systematic unity. Boston U., 1964. 64-11629

3505. Kim, Ha Tai. The influence of the doctrine of the will in post-Kantian idealism upon the philosophy of Josiah Royce. Southern Cal., 1950.

3506. Kim, Hee-Jin. The life and thought of Dōgen. Claremont, 1965. 67-9513

3507. Kim, Hong-woo. Phenomenology and political philosophy: a study of the political implications of Husserl's account of the life-world. Georgia, 1975. 76-13963

3508. Kim, Jaegwon. Explanation, prediction and retrodiction: some logical and pragmatic considerations. Princeton, 1962. 63-530

3509. Kim, Sang-Ki. The problem of the contingency of the world in Husserl's phenomenology. Buffalo, 1973.
74-4416

3510. Kim, Tae-Kil. Naturalism and emotivism: some aspects of moral judgments. Johns Hopkins, 1960.

3511. Kimball, Robert Howard. Thought and speech. Yale, 1974. 75-15314

3512. Kimber, Robert B. Alfred Döblin's godless mysticism. Princeton, 1965. 65-13147

3513. Kimble, James P., Jr. Reflexive arguments in philosophy. Texas, 1966. 66-7342

3514. Kimmel, John Edward. The distinction between moral and non-moral principles. Johns Hopkins, 1970.
71-16729

3515. Kimmel, Larry Dean. A critical appraisal of the moral philosophy of David Hume. Texas, 1968.
68-16106

3516. Kimpton, Lawrence Alpheus. The problem and method of the critical philosophy. Cornell, 1935.

3517. Kinderlehrer, Jacqueline Bunn. Aesthetic and non-aesthetic properties. Minnesota, 1974.
75-12096

3518. King, (first name unknown). Differentiation of the religious consciousness. Chicago, 1904.

3519. King, Edward George. The concept of spiritual substance in the empiricist philosophy of George Berkeley. Notre Dame, 1965. 65-14611

3520. King, James Timothy, Jr. The development of Hume's moral philosophy from 1740-1751: the relationship of the *Treatise* and the second *Inquiry*. Notre Dame, 1967. 68-776

3521. King, Jessie Charles, Jr. Moral responsibility, excusing conditions, and the problems of freedom. Harvard, 1967.

3522. King, John Lewellyn. Induction, confirmation and explanation. Wisconsin, 1973. 73-21005

3523. King, John Michael. Functionalistic explanations of behavior. Cal., Davis, 1974. 75-8340

3524. King, Kendall Cross. Realism in contemporary political theory. Michigan, 1960. 60-6895

3525. King, Thomas Wayne. Thinking, freedom and intersubjectivity in the philosophy of Merleau-Ponty. New Mexico, 1971. 72-8352

3526. King, William Lewis. Methods of meaning-analysis in ethics: Moore, Stevenson, and Ziff. Stanford, 1967. 68-15066

3527. King-Farlow, John. Future truth: some metaphysical puzzles. Stanford, 1960. 60-6738

3528. Kingston, George Frederick. The foundations of faith; a study in levels of belief with suggestions as to corresponding stages in individual and social development. Toronto, 1923.

3529. Kinney, Sr. Cyril Edwin. A critique of the philosophy of George Santayana in the light of Thomistic principles. Catholic U., 1942.

3530. Kinney, Laurence F. Hypostasis in Plotinus. Virginia, 1936.

3531. Kinzel, Sr. Margaret Mary. The metaphysical basis of certain principles of the religious life in the light of Thomistic principles. Catholic U., 1960.

3532. Kipnis, Kenneth. Concept and convention: an essay on the making of sense. Brandeis, 1972.
72-32104

3533. Kirby, Brian Samuel. On supposing: a study in the logic of knowledge, belief and imagination. Duke, 1970. 71-10388

3534. Kirby, Gerald Joseph. Law in the writings of John of Salisbury and St. Thomas Aquinas. Toronto, 1936.

3535. Kirby, John D. Sociality and individuality as phases of ethical change. Texas, 1952.

3536. Kirby, Ronald Vernon. The other minds quandary. Berkeley, 1966. 67-8588

3537. Kirk, John Robert. Cognitive and valuational factors in scientific research. U.C.L.A., 1951.

3538. Kirk, Robert Elefter. Intermediate logics and equational classes of Brouwerian algebras. M.I.T., 1972.

3539. Kirkpatrick, Robert Thomas. Reflection and intentionality. Northwestern, 1956. 57-1382

3540. Kirmani, Sanaullah. A section from the logic of Avicenna's *Danish nameh-e ala'i* text with translation, analysis, and notes: a contribution to the history of logic. Michigan St., 1974. 75-14765

3541. Kirn, Arthur Gilbert. An interpretation of Thomistic freedom according to Gustav Siewerth. Toronto, 1968.

3542. Kirscher, John C. Stuart Hampshire's argument against determinism: a critical evaluation. Princeton, 1967. 68-2491

3543. Kirshbaum, Harold Reis. Toward an understanding of the causal relation: a critique, expansion, and inversion of regularity theories of causation. Berkeley, 1973.

3544. Kirven, Robert Hoover. Emanuel Swedenborg and the revolt against deism. Brandeis, 1965. 65-14424

3545. Kishinami, Tsunezo. The development of philosophy

in Japan. Princeton, 1914.

3546. Kisiel, Theodore Joseph. Toward an ontology of crisis. Duquesne, 1962.

3547. Kissin, Peter Petrell. Negation in natural language. Wisconsin, 1969. 70-3585

3548. Kitch, Ethel May. The origin of subjectivity in Hindu thought. Chicago, 1914.

3549. Kitchel, Mary Jean. Walter Burley's doctrine of the human intellect: a study with an edition of selected texts. Toronto, 1974.

3550. Kitchener, Richard Frank. Explanation in psychology. Minnesota, 1970. 71-8170

3551. Kitcher, Patricia Williams. The problem of personal identity. Princeton, 1974. 75-20640

3552. Kitcher, Philip Stuart. Mathematics and certainty. Princeton, 1974. 74-17467

3553. Kiteley, Murray James. Indirect discourse and modal composition. Minnesota, 1959. 59-6025

3554. Kivy, Peter Nathan. The seventh sense: a study in eighteenth-century British aesthetic theory. Columbia, 1966. 66-12574

3555. Klass, Walter K. Faith and reason in Kant's philosophy. Yale, 1939.

3556. Klauder, Rev. Francis J. The intrinsic nature of good and evil according to St. Bonaventure. Fordham, 1953.

3557. Klausner, Neal William. Knowing and being in the philosophy of C.A. Strong. Yale, 1941.

3558. Kleinman, Lowell. Imagining. N.Y.U., 1972.
73-31215

3559. Klein, Barbara Von Eckardt. Conceptions of sensory experience and mind-body identity. Case, 1974.
75-5064

3560. Klein, Charles F.A. Which is the true system of philosophy? Syracuse, 1884.

3561. Klein, Dennis D. Dimensions of culture in the thought of Bernard Lonergan. Boston Coll., 1975.
75-21278

3562. Klein, John Theodore. The concept of person in Strawson and Hampshire. Boston U., 1969. 69-18710

3563. Klein, Mary Katherine McKeon. The concept of political freedom in Hannah Arendt. Boston U., 1973. 73-23493

3564. Klein, Peter David. The revolt against sense-data; a defense of the sense-data framework. Yale, 1966. 67-101

3565. Klein, Theodore Ernest, Jr. The world as horizon: Husserl's constitutional theory of the objective world. Rice, 1967. 67-13092

3566. Kleiner, Scott A. The concept of force and the explanatory efficacy of Newtonian mechanics. Chicago, 1968.

3567. Kleinman, Jacqueline Agnew. Public/private- the education of Søren Kierkegaard. Ohio St., 1971. 72-4538

3568. Kleinman, Robert Maurice. World-models: an inquiry into the philosophical implications of physical cosmology. Columbia, 1964. 65-7367

3569. Kleinz, Rev. John P. The theory of knowledge of Hugh of St. Victor. Catholic U., 1944.

3570. Kleis, Sander J. Brightman's idea of God. Indiana, 1961. 61-4455

3571. Klemke, Elmer Daniel. An examination of the epistemology of G.E. Moore. Northwestern, 1960. 60-4768

3572. Klenk, Virginia H. Wittgenstein's philosophy of mathematics. Pittsburgh, 1972. 73-4999

3573. Kleppner, Amy Morrissey. The relevance of moral judgments to the critical evaluation of literature. Columbia, 1960. 60-3095

3574. Kliger, George. Radical realism, sense-contents and ontology: a critical examination of some aspects of Tadeusz Kotarbinski's philosophy. Minnesota, 1967. 68-7343

3575. Kline, George Louis. Spinoza in Soviet philosophy. Columbia, 1950. 2484

3576. Kline, Rev. Robert Reeves. The present status of value theory in the United States. Georgetown, 1959.

3577. Klopke, John Robert. Malebranche's theory of natural judgment. Toronto, 1961.

3578. Kloss, Waldemar. The place of Desiserius Erasmus in the history of philosophy. Harvard, 1908.

3579. Klubertanz, George Peter. The vis cogitativa according to St. Thomas Aquinas; sources and doctrine. Toronto, 1947.

3580. Kluge, Eike-Henner Wendelin. Functions and things: an essay in the metaphysics of Frege and Wittgenstein. Michigan, 1968. 69-2335

3581. Knaack, Jay Amos. Rational self-interest. N.Y.U., 1973. 74-1913

3582. Knapke, Othmar. A history of the theory of sensation from St. Augustine to St. Thomas. Catholic U., 1915.

3583. Knasas, John Francis. An analysis and interpretation of the Tertia via of St. Thomas Aquinas. Toronto, 1975.

3584. Knight, Jack Carey. The nature of moral and legal rights. Miami, 1975. 75-25417

3585. Knight, Minerva Shelburne. The free will problem: analyzed from the standpoint of recent philosophy and science. Iowa, 1935.

3586. Knight, Rachel. The truth values of the mysticism of George Fox; a study in the sources of religious insight. Iowa, 1919.

3587. Knight, Samuel Robinson. A Thomistic interpretation of Aristotle's theory of universals. Virginia, 1954. 9651

3588. Knight, Thomas Stanley. Beyond Parmenides: the problem of non-being. An ontological essay developing some implications of Plato's distinction between absolute and relative non-being. Syracuse, 1956.
16655

3589. Knoblock, John H. Method and theory in comparative studies of the formative stages of civilizations. Florida St., 1962. 62-4618

3590. Knodell, Preston Gilbert, Jr. The development of scientific theory as exemplified in astronomical discovery. Catholic U., 1969. 69-20297

3591. Knox, Israel. The aesthetic theories of Kant, Hegel,

and Schopenhauer. Columbia, 1937.

3592. Knox, John, Jr. Can we still believe in correspondence? An attempted vindication of the correspondence theory of truth in the face of contemporary challenges. Yale, 1961. 65-7556

3593. Kobelja, Carl D. Metaphysical presuppositions of the ego-centric predicament in the operational analysis of P.W. Bridgman. Marquette, 1972.
73-8281

3594. Koch, Adrienne. The philosophy of Thomas Jefferson. Columbia, 1943.

3595. Koch, Donald Frederick. John Dewey's psychology of ethics. Claremont, 1967. 68-10517

3596. Koch, Harold Christian. The background and development of Santayana's philosophical thought. Temple, 1957.

3597. Koch, Philip John. A theory of obligation. U. of Washington, 1970. 71-16965

3598. Kocourek, Roman-A. Rationalization in mathematics. Laval, 1946.

3599. Koecher, Karel Frantisek. Ideology, philosophy, and science. Columbia, 1970. 71-17514

3600. Koehl, Richard Arthur. A study of the philosophy of common sense. Wisconsin, 1962. 63-663

3601. Koehle, Eckhard J. Personality; a study according to the philosophies of value and spirit of Max Scheler and Nicolai Hartmann. Columbia, 1941.

3602. Koehler, Conrad James. Method, meaning, and ontological controversies. So. Illinois, 1969.
70-434

3603. Koehn, Donald Robert. Peirce's explanation of the validity of synthetic inference in the "Illustrations of the logic of science." Illinois, 1969.
70-13383

3604. Koenen, Sr. Jane. Human operations and their finalities in Saint Thomas Aquinas. St. Louis, 1959.
60-342

3605. Koestenbaum, Peter. Freedom as the basis of truth and reality in Russell's positivism and Stace's mysticism. Boston U., 1958.

3606. Koethe, John Louis, Jr. Sceptical arguments and certainty. Harvard, 1973.

3607. Kohák, Erazim Václav. Evil and the Christian symbol of salvation. Yale, 1958.

3608. Kohanski, Alexander S. Nicolai Onufreievich Lossky's theory of knowledge; a presentation and a critical analysis. Vanderbilt, 1936.

3609. Kohl, Marvin Seymour. The problem of vagueness: a study in the relations of words and the world. N.Y.U., 1966. 68-10113

3610. Kohls, Henry H. Some factors in our knowledge of existence compared with teachings of Aquinas. Georgetown, 1953.

3611. Kohnky, Frances. Subjective element in mysticism. Cincinnati, 1912.

3612. Kohs, Samuel Calmin. Intelligence measurement; a psychological and statistical study based upon the block-design tests. Stanford, 1923.

3613. Kolb, David Alan. Conceptual pluralism and rationality. Yale, 1972. 72-29742

3614. Kolb, Robert West, Jr. The intentionality of sensation. No. Carolina, 1974. 75-15658

3615. Kolenda, Konstantin. The authority of moral appeal. Cornell, 1953.

3616. Koller, Alice Ruth. The concept of emotion: a study of the analyses of James, Russell, and Ryle. Radcliffe, 1960.

3617. Koller, John M. The metaphysical bases and implications of Indian social ideals in traditional India, Gandhi and Aurobindo. Hawaii, 1966.
67-13703

3618. Koller, Kerry Joseph. Christianity and philosophy according to Kierkegaard's Johannes Climacus. Notre Dame, 1975. 75-19942

3619. Kollmann, Edward Charles. Studies in the modern theory of imagination with especial reference to its historical development from the Renaissance to Kant. Harvard, 1950.

3620. Kolumban, Olga Maria Markus. The ontological basis of realism and symbolism in art. Penn St., 1965.
66-8733

3621. Kondoléon, Theodore J. Exemplary causality in the philosophy of St. Thomas Aquinas. Catholic U., 1967. 67-15446

3622. Konecky, Stanley Jay. A discussion concerning the normative and descriptive elements of ethical valuation theory. Rochester, 1973. 73-25819

3623. Konecsni, Johnemery. Meta-biology and its relation to meta-science. N.Y.U., 1971. 73-21127

3624. Konrad, Armin Richard. The justification of a moral argument: the anti-naturalists and Kant. Emory, 1968. 68-15752

3625. Konvitz, Milton Ridvas. Meaning and value; a study in the axiology of S. Alexander. Cornell, 1933.

3626. Konyndyk, Kenneth John, Jr. Austin's objections to the argument from illusion. Wayne St., 1970. 71-430

3627. Kooy, Vernon Eugene. God and nature in John Scotus Erigena- an examination of the neoplatonic elements and their Greek patristic sources in the ontological system of John Scotus Erigena. Claremont, 1972. 72-26240

3628. Kopelman, Loretta Criden. Intentionality and physicalism. Rochester, 1966. 66-10808

3629. Koppelman, Walter Harold. The philosophy of legal functionalism: a critical evaluation of the thought of Felix S. Cohen. Columbia, 1969. 72-15579

3630. Kordig, Carl Robert. Meaning invariance and scientific change. Yale, 1969. 70-16289

3631. Korgen, Reinhard Lunde. Operationally defined magnitudes in the language of science. Harvard, 1945.

3632. Korn, Eugene Barry. Groundwork of a logic of obligation. Columbia, 1973. 73-26619

3633. Korsak, Ronald Alexander. On the justification of induction. Utah, 1972. 72-21372

3634. Korsmeyer, Carolyn Wilker. Aesthetic form: formal beauty and the problem of relativism in the theories of Hutcheson and Kant. Brown, 1972. 73-2301

3635. Korth, Robert George. Transcendental illusions. Calgary, 1974.

3636. Koslow, Arnold. Changes in the concept of mass from Newton to Einstein. Columbia, 1965. 65-9164

3637. Kosman, Louis Aryeh. The Aristotelian backgrounds of Bacon's *Novum organum*. Harvard, 1964.

3638. Kosok, Michael. The dialectic of consciousness in Hegel's phenomenology of the spirit. Columbia, 1964. 65-4576

3639. Kossel, Clifford George. The problem of relation in the philosophy of Saint Thomas Aquinas. Toronto, 1945.

3640. Kostman, James Philip. Aristotle's energeia-kinesis distinction: studies on action and change. Stanford, 1974. 74-27047

3641. Kottman, Karl Augustinus. Law and apocalypse: the moral thought of Luis de León (1527?-1591). Cal., S. Diego, 1970. 70-23288

3642. Kotzin, Rhoda Hadassah. Language and formalization. Yale, 1960.

3643. Koury, James Lawrence. The question of the justifiability of Aristotle's *Nicomachean* doctrine of "eudaimonia." Johns Hopkins, 1975. 76-8536

3644. Kowalski, James George. Lesniewski's ontology extended with the axiom of choice. Notre Dame, 1975. 75-27770

3645. Kozel, Sr. Constance Mary. A study of love as a perfective of the human person. Catholic U., 1967. 67-7324

3646. Kozy, John, Jr. Rational realism- a philosophy of common sense. Penn St., 1963. 63-6304

3647. Kraemer, William S. Hobhouse's theory of the rational good and its critics. N.Y.U., 1942. 73-20744

3648. Kramer, F.F. Sources of gnosticism. Colorado, 1896.

3649. Kramer, Richard Neil. The ontological foundations of negatives. Indiana, 1953. 6444

3650. Kraus, Rev. Donald William. Toward a realistic theory of moral value: a constructive study of Perry, Vives and T.V. Smith. St. Louis, 1959. 60-343

3651. Kraus, Elizabeth Muir. Thought before it hardens: a

study in the evolutionary philosophy of Charles
Sanders Peirce. Fordham, 1970.   71-8722

3652. Kraus, Richard James. Free individual in a free society: the philosophy of Justice William O. Douglas. Fordham, 1971.   71-26979

3653. Kraushaar, Otto Frederick. Lotze's theory of knowledge. Harvard, 1933.

3654. Krausz, Michael. A critique of R.G. Collingwood's theory of 'absolute presuppositions.' Toronto, 1969.

3655. Kraut, Richard. Two studies in classical Greek moral philosophy. Princeton, 1969.   70-14220

3656. Krc, Melvyn Paul. Plato's distinction between knowledge and opinion. Wisconsin, 1973.   73-15974

3657. Krebbs, Norman Adelbert. Plato's errant cause. U. of Washington, 1971.   71-28433

3658. Krecz, Charles Alex. Fact and particular: a study in basic ontology. Texas, 1975.   75-24897

3659. Kreeft, Peter John. A study of wonder in Plato and Augustine. Fordham, 1966.   66-13520

3660. Kreilkamp, Karl. The metaphysical foundations of Thomistic jurisprudence. Catholic U., 1939.

3661. Kreilkamp-Cudmore, Ann. Language as Wittgenstein's way of life. Boston U., 1973.   73-14134

3662. Krell, David Farrell. Nietzsche and the task of thinking: Martin Heidegger's reading of Nietzsche. Duquesne, 1971.   72-9865

3663. Kremer, Elmar Joseph. Malebranche and Arnauld: the controversy over the nature of ideas. Yale, 1961.
      66-7687

3664. Krentz, Arthur Alfred. Being, not-being, appearing and the nature of Sophistry: some neglected aspects of Plato's *Sophist*. Waterloo, 1972.

3665. Kresge, Elijah Everett. Kant's doctrine of teleology. Pennsylvania, 1913.

3666. Kress, Jerry Ralph. The problem of synonymy. Michigan, 1967.   67-17800

3667. Kretchmar, Robert Scott. A phenomenological analysis of 'Other' in sport. Southern Cal,1971.71-12397

3668. Kretschmann, Philip Miller. Aristotle on gravitation. Princeton, 1929.

3669. Kretzmann, Norman J.K. Semiotic and language analysis in the philosophies of the Enlightenment. Johns Hopkins, 1953.

3670. Krikorian, Yervant Hovhannes. The concept of mechanism. Harvard, 1933.

3671. Krimerman, Leonard Isaiah. The utilitarianism of John Stuart Mill: a reconstruction. Cornell, 1964. 65-4159

3672. Krimm, Hans Heinz. Common-sense conceptions of causality. Johns Hopkins, 1960.

3673. Krimsky, Sheldon. The nature and function of Gedankenexperimente in physics. Boston U., 1970.
70-22397

3674. Krishna, Purushotman Muthu. The political philosophy of Sri Aurobindo; an exposition and assessment of the integral system of a leading Indian thinker. New School, 1963.

3675. Kristensen, Juhl-Bagge. The relevance of Søren Kierkegaard's existentialism to a philosophy of education. Buffalo, 1970.

3676. Kristiansen, Magne Warren. Relationships between the later writings of Ludwig Wittgenstein and their readers. Yale, 1974. 75-1374

3677. Krohn, William Otterbein. The ethics of modern pessimism. Yale, 1889.

3678. Krois, John Michael. Ernst Cassirer's philosophy of symbolic forms and the problem of value. Penn St.,1975. 76-17182

3679. Kronman, Anthony Townsend. Autonomy and interaction in the social thought of Max Weber. Yale, 1972.
73-14568

3680. Kroyer, John Wilson. To be flesh: an inquiry into the basic dimensions of a theory of emotion. Berkeley, 1966. 66-15423

3681. Krummel, Richard Frank. Neitzsche und der Deutsche geist: ausbreitung und wirkung des Neitzscheschen werkes im Deutschen sprachraum bis zu seinem todesjahr. Ein schrifttumsverzeichnis der jahre 1867-1900. (German text.) Kentucky, 1971.
71-25901

3682. Krusé, Cornelius Francis. An analytical study of pessimism, especially as exemplified by its modern types. Yale, 1922.

3683. Krutzen, Rudolph Wilhelm. Explanation in history, Duke, 1968. 69-11945

3684. Kubara, Michael Philip. Plato's normative psychology. Waterloo, 1974.

3685. Kubitz, Oskar Alfred. Development of John Stuart Mill's system of logic. Illinois, 1931.

3686. Kubly, Harold Edward. State sovereignty and international morality. Wisconsin, 1936.

3687. Kubrin, David Charles. Providence and the mechanical philosophy: the creation and dissolution of the world in Newtonian thought. A study of the relations of science and religion in seventeenth century England. Cornell, 1968.

3688. Kudo, Tozaburo. The ethics of Confucius. Yale, 1903.

3689. Kuehl, James Robert. Phenomenology of imaging. Northwestern, 1968. 69-1874

3690. Kuflik, Arthur. The relevance of community rules: three case studies. Princeton, 1973. 74-9698

3691. Kugel, Peter. Logics of discovery. Harvard, 1973.

3692. Kuhn, Alvin Boyd. Theosophy, a modern revival of ancient wisdom. Columbia, 1931.

3693. Kuhns, Richard Francis, Jr. Perception, understanding and style: a study in the foundations of criticism developed from an examination of artistic creativity and appreciation. Columbia, 1955. 15743

3694. Kulstad, Mark Alan. Leibniz's expression thesis. Michigan, 1975. 75-29268

3695. Kultgen, John H., Jr. Philosophic principles in chemical explanations: Boyle, Lavoisier and Mendeleev. Chicago, 1952.

3696. Kundargi, Gundu Narayan. Broad's theoretical approach to ethics. So. Illinois, 1968. 69-1750

3697. Kung, Joan Rajala. Some aspects of Aristotle's treatment of necessity. Pennsylvania, 1973. 73-24171

3698. Kunkel, Francis Leo. A critical study of Graham

Greene. Columbia, 1959.   59-2855

3699. Kunkel, Joseph Charles. Aristotle's categories: a
      developmental study of the logic-real relation-
      ship. St. Bonaventure, 1969.   70-11267

3700. Kunt, Sevin. Hegel's phenomenology and value con-
      cepts. So. Illinois, 1966.   67-3166

3701. Kunz, Robert M. A critical examination of the radi-
      cal empiricism of William James. Buffalo, 1953.
                                             5445

3702. Kunze, Robert W. The origin of the self: a presenta-
      tion of the philosophy of Levinas from the stand-
      point of his criticism of Heidegger. Penn St.,
      1974.   75-9796

3703. Kuo, Dah-Chuen. The impact of science on Dewey's
      ethics. So. Illinois, 1969.   70-435

3704. Kupfer, Joseph Harris. Bishop Berkeley's rule-utili-
      tarianism. Rochester, 1971.   72-735

3705. Kupfer, Lillian. Greek foreshadowing of modern meta-
      physical and epistemological thought. N.Y.U.,
      1901.   73-17990

3706. Kurban, Mulhim Ibrahim. Meaning and confirmability.
      Princeton, 1954.   9431

3707. Kuring, Adolf. The sensory and intellectual factor
      of knowledge in Aristotle. Chicago, 1925.

3708. Kurtz, Paul W. The problems of value theory. Col-
      umbia, 1952.

3709. Kurtzman, David Robert. Structural properties of norm-
      ative ethical theories. Maryland, 1966. 66-9294

3710. Kuykendall, Eleanor Hope. John L. Austin's theory of
      knowledge. Columbia, 1966.   67-5788

3711. Kuypers, Mary Shaw. Studies in the eighteenth centu-
      ry background of Hume's empiricism. Columbia, 1931.

3712. Kvart, Igal. Counterfactuals. Pittsburgh, 1975.
                                             76-5454

3713. Kvitko, David. A philosophic study of Tolstoy.
      Columbia, 1927.

3714. Kyburg, Henry Ely, Jr. Probability and induction in
      the Cambridge school. Columbia, 1955. 12311

- L -

3715. Labrie, Robert. Commentaire du traité du temps d'Aristote. Laval, 1952.

3716. LaCentra, Walter J. Freedom and society in Jacques Maritain. St. John's 1964.

3717. Lacey, Trammell Calhoun, Jr. Happiness and duty: a critique of utilitarianism. U. of Washington, 1967.   67-14186

3718. Lachs, John. A critical examination of Santayana's philosophy of mind. Yale, 1961.

3719. Lackey, Douglas Paul. Temporal asymmetry and indeterminism. Yale, 1970.   70-26175

3720. Lackner, Vincent Frederick. Alfred North Whitehead's conception of scientific method. Toronto, 1962.

3721. Lacock, Darrell Dexter. The political philosophy of Bernard Bosanquet. Yale, 1967.   67-8389

3722. LaCorte, John Joseph. A critical analysis of the dialectical philosophy of William Temple. Southern Cal., 1970.   70-26524

3723. La Croix, Richard Ray. An examination of the relationship between Proslogian II and Proslogian III: are there two arguments for the existence of God in the Proslogian? Minnesota, 1970.   71-8174

3724. Lacy, William Larry. An inquiry into the nature of mental acts. Virginia, 1963.   64-716

3725. Lad, John Francis. On intuition, evidence, and unique representation. Stanford, 1973.
   73-14921

3726. Ladd, John. An essay toward a definition of practical reason. Harvard, 1948.

3727. Lademan, William D. Friedrich Nietzsche's philosophy of the free spirit. Fordham, 1957.

3728. Ladenson, Robert Franklin. The concept of decision. Johns Hopkins, 1969.   70-14808

3729. Lafferty, Theodore Thomas. The logical and epistemological implications of the theory of perspectives. Chicago, 1928.

242

3730. Lahey, John Lee. Egoism and the concept of morality. Miami, 1973. 73-25922

3731. Lai, Tyrone Tai Lun. Infinitesimals and the infinite universe: a study of the relation between Newton's science and his metaphysics. Cal., S. Diego, 1972. 73-23169

3732. Lake, Charles D. The possibilities and limitations of visual art as understood by Susanne K. Langer for the expression of Christian truth as understood by H. Richard Niebuhr. Chicago, 1972.

3733. Laks, Hyman Joel. Limits of authority in the legal system of Judaism. Pennsylvania, 1974. 75-2751

3734. Laky, Rev. John J. A study of George Berkeley's philosophy in the light of the philosophy of St. Thomas. Catholic U., 1951.

3735. Lally, Br. A. Victor. Interpretation of personality in several schools of the "New psychology." Fordham, 1935.

3736. Lalor, Juvénal. The notion of limit. Laval, 1944.

3737. LaLumia, Joseph R. Philosophy and psychology in Emile Meyerson's investigations. Cornell, 1951.

3738. Lamb, James Walter. Fundamental concepts in the theory of rule-sets. Brown, 1972. 73-2305

3739. Lamb, Roger Edward. Two epistemological dogmatists: Reid and Moore. Rochester, 1966. 66-6860

3740. Lambert, Garth Roderick. A study of Aristotle's concepts of moral and intellectual education in the context of modern educational theory. Toronto, 1975.

3741. Lambert, Joseph Frederick. A logical analysis of Tolman's theory of learning. Michigan St., 1956. 59-2638

3742. Lambert, Richard Thomas. Man's knowledge of his soul in St. Thomas Aquinas. Notre Dame, 1971. 71-27763

3743. Lambert, Rev. Roger. La voie d'invention dans les physiques d'Aristote. Laval, 1966.

3744. Lambros, Charles Homer. The logical positivists' doctrine of necessary truth. Harvard, 1973.

3745. Lamm, Herbert. The relation of concept and demonstration in the ontological argument. Chicago, 1940.

3746. Lamm, Norman. The study of _Torah_ _lishmah_ in the works of R. Hayyim of Volozhin. Yeshiva, 1966.
66-12086

3747. Lammiman, Forrest Boyd. The concept of a virtue. Yale, 1975.
75-26744

3748. Lamont, Corliss. Issues of immortality. Columbia, 1932.

3749. Lampel, Clare. Linguistic analysis in ethics: a study of the moral philosophy of R.M. Hare. Columbia, 1960.
60-3686

3750. Lampert, Laurence Albert. The views of history in Nietzsche and Heidegger. Northwestern, 1971.
71-30868

3751. Lamprecht, Sterling Power. The moral and political philosophy of John Locke. Columbia, 1918.

3752. Lamy, Jean Maurice. Marx, interprête de l'atomisme antique de Hegel à Epicure. Montreal, 1973.

3753. Landers, James Russel. The political thought of Han Fei. Indiana, 1972.
72-21394

3754. Landes, Margaret Winifred. A comparison between Bergson's doctrine of intuition and Royce's doctrine of interpretation. Yale, 1923.

3755. Landesman, Bruce Michael. The obligation to obey the law: an essay on law, social institutions, and morality. Michigan, 1971.
72-4919

3756. Landesman, Charles, Jr. The concept of form in four philosophies of logic. Yale, 1959.

3757. Landon, Charles Cecil. Reality and Plato: a criticism of the idealistic interpretation of Plato on the nature of the real. Harvard, 1954.

3758. Landrum, George Roy. Predicating existence and the ontological argument. Wayne St., 1971.
71-29759

3759. Lane, Elizabeth Bobette. The notion of "Meaningless" in contemporary philosophy of language. Yale, 1940.

3760. Lane, Robert Cravens. The theory of mimesis in the
Republic, the Statesman and the Laws of Plato.
Fordham, 1971. 71-20175

3761. Lanfear, Jimmy Ray. An analysis of Wittgenstein's
locution "meaning as use." Rice, 1968.
68-15636

3762. Lang, Berel. The cognitive significance of art.
Columbia, 1961. 61-3449

3763. Langan, William J. An existential analysis of Saint
John of the Cross. Northwestern, 1969.
70-6489

3764. Langbauer, Delmar N. Sanatana Dharma and modern
philosophy; a study of Indian and Whiteheadian
thought. Claremont, 1970. 71-13711

3765. Lange, John Frederick. In defense of ethical naturalism; an examination of certain aspects of the
naturalistic fallacy, with particular attention
to the logic of the open question argument.
Princeton, 1963. 64-1330

3766. Langer, Monika Mechthilde. Violence in the philosophy of Merleau-Ponty. Toronto, 1973.

3767. Langerak, Edward A. Orienting oneself rationally:
Kant's constructive philosophy of religion.
Princeton, 1972. 72-29797

3768. Langham, Derald George. Genesa: an attempt to develop a conceptual model to synthesize, synchronize, and vitalize man's interpretation of universal phenomena. U.S. Int'l, 1969. 70-12914

3769. Langiulli, Nino Francis. Possibility and existence:
a study of Nicholas Abbagnano's ontology. N.Y.U.,
1973. 74-13348

3770. Langley, Raymond Joseph. Hume's logic of the imagination. Fordham, 1965. 65-14175

3771. Langley, Rev. Wendell Edward. Berthier's Memories
de Trevoux (1745-1762): Fideism and the problem
of method. St. Louis, 1960.

3772. Lango, John Wesley. Whitehead's ontology. Yale,
1969. 70-2757

3773. Langton, Stuart. Social alienation and education.
Boston U., 1969. 69-18724

3774. Lanigan, Joseph Francis. An investigation into the human knowledge of the singular. Notre Dame, 1956. 15675

3775. Lapan, Arthur. The significance of James' essay. Columbia, 1936.

3776. LaPara, Nicholas Anthony. Law, inference and modality. Pittsburgh, 1970. 70-19495

3777. LaPierre, Michael John Joseph. The objective concept; a study in the noetical theory of Gabriel Vasquez (d.1604). Toronto, 1957.

3778. Lardner, Sr. Mary Denise. The notion of person as self-transcendence in Bernard Lonergan. Boston Coll., 1970. 70-25584

3779. Largo, Gerald Andrew. The concept of community in the writings of John Macmurray: a study of John Macmurray's concept of community for Roman Catholic liturgy. N.Y.U., 1971. 72-11466

3780. Larkin, Sr. Miriam Therese. A study of language in the philosophy of Aristotle. Notre Dame, 1965. 65-11116

3781. Larmi, Oliver Julian. Plato on the unknowability of sensibles. Pennsylvania, 1971. 71-26044

3782. Larochelle, Joseph. La solidarité humaine selon l'enseignement des derniers souverains pontifes. Laval, 1948.

3783. Larrabee, Harold Atkins. The philosophical foundations of the social theory of Henri de Saint-Simon. Harvard, 1925.

3784. Larrabee, Mary Jeanne. Static and genetic phenomenology: a study of two methods in Edmund Husserl's philosophy. Toronto, 1974.

3785. Larsen, Allan Warren. The difference between the psychical and physical in the philosophy of Nicolai Hartmann. Duquesne, 1971. 72-9866

3786. Larsen, Robert Edwin. The relation between logic and ontology: with special reference to Morris R. Cohen. Minnesota, 1957. 57-3273

3787. Larson, Lawrence Wesley. Self-knowledge and the unconscious. Stanford, 1967. 68-11316

3788. Larson, Sue Howard. Practical implication: some problems in the logic of assertion. Stanford, 1962. 63-2726

3789. LaRue, Daniel Wolford. Type studies in the methods of escape from subjectivism. Harvard, 1911.

3790. Lascola, Russell Anthony. The role of relativity in Berkeley's philosophy. Southern Cal., 1970. 70-16873

3791. Lashchyk, Eugene M. Scientific revolutions: a philosophical critique of the theories of science of Thomas Kuhn and Paul Feyerabend. Pennsylvania, 1969. 70-7819

3792. Laska, Peter Jerome. Kant's theory of the moral will. Rochester, 1970. 70-17889

3793. Laskey, Dallas. Practical reason in the moral philosophy of Henry Sidgwick. Harvard, 1961.

3794. Latta, Betsy Carol Postow. A conciliatory approach to morals. Yale, 1970. 70-26177

3795. Laudan, Larry Lynn. The idea of a physical theory from Galileo to Newton: studies in seventeenth-century methodology. Princeton, 1966. 66-9620

3796. Laudier, Rev. Robert Edward. The meaning of person in George Holmes Howison's philosophy. Marquette, 1968. 69-3319

3797. Lauer, Rosemary Zita. Voltaire's constructive deism. St. Louis, 1958. 59-906

3798. Lauter, Herman Alfred. On Reichenbach's analysis of scientific laws. U.C.L.A., 1967. 68-224

3799. Lavely, John Hillman. Prolegomena to philosophy of history. Boston U., 1950.

3800. Lavere, Joseph. The political principles of John Locke. Laval, 1956.

3801. Lavers, Enoch Cook. The moral philosophy of Richard Price and its influence. Being a study in ethics both critical and appreciative of his chief work: A review of the principal questions and difficulties in morals. N.Y.U., 1909. 73-22203

3802. Lavine, Thelma Z. The naturalistic approach to theory of knowledge. Radcliffe, 1939.

3803. Lawler, Rev. Donald David. The moral judgment in contemporary analytic philosophy. St. Louis, 1959. 60-346

3804. Lawler, James M. The metaphysics of death in the philosophy of Maurice Blondel. Chicago, 1971.

3805. Lawrence, Edwin George. Aristotle's theory of definition. Wisconsin, 1972.   72-22102

3806. Lawrence, John Shelton. A.N. Whitehead's panpsychical theory of the individual existent. Texas, 1964.   64-11807

3807. Lawrence, Nathaniel Morris. The development of Whitehead's epistemology. Harvard, 1949.

3808. Lawrence, Roy Frederick. Motives, intentions, and actions. Berkeley, 1966.   67-8596

3809. Lawrence, William H. The influence of German on Scottish philosophy. N.Y.U., 1893.   74-1233

3810. Lawry, Edward George. Fidelity and the age of suspicion: an essay on the relationship of value and knowledge. Texas, 1971.   72-15795

3811. Lawry, John Field. A defense of epistemological monism. Harvard, 1960.

3812. Lawson, James Sharp. Art as a stimulus to the religious consciousness. Toronto, 1931.

3813. Lazara, Vincent Anthony. The realist-instrumentalist controversy in quantum mechanics. Arizona, 1973.   74-2003

3814. Lazaron, Hilda R. Gabriel Marcel, the dramatist. Columbia, 1959.   59-2856

3815. Lazarus, Frederick Kumar. The metaphysics of Rāmānuja and Bowne. Boston U., 1957.   57-3274

3816. Lazerowitz, Morris. Judgment, propositions and knowledge. Michigan, 1936.

3817. Leach, Frederick Harold. The concept of transcendence in modern philosophy. Toronto, 1939.

3818. Leach, James John. Historical explanation and value-neutrality. Michigan St., 1965.   66-406

3819. Lean, Martin. Sense-perception and matter: a critical analysis of C.D. Broad's theory of perception. Columbia, 1953.

3820. Lear, George Andrew, Jr. Self-development. Cornell, 1970.   71-1068

3821. Leatherman, Roger Lee. An empirical study of attitudes and values in a university faculty. Michigan, 1963. 64-847

3822. Leavenworth, May Belle. Dewey's theory of the self and its role in his theory of ethics. C.U.N.Y., 1975. 76-1484

3823. Leblanc, Hugues. Two calculi of individuals: an essay on the nominalistic foundations of ontology. Harvard, 1948.

3824. Leblanc, Joseph. Droit des parents dans l'éducation des enfants. Laval, 1928.

3825. Le Bosquet, John Edwards. True and false in miracle. Harvard, 1907.

3826. LeBoutillier, Cornelia Geer. Religious values in the philosophy of emergent evolution. Columbia, 1936.

3827. Leckie, George G. Kant's architectonic. Virginia, 1933.

3828. LeClair, Sr. M. St. Ida. Utopias and the philosophy of St. Thomas Aquinas. Catholic U., 1941.

3829. Le Cocq, Rhoda P. The radical thinkers: Martin Heidegger and Sri Aurobindo. C.I.A.S., 1969.

3830. Ledden, Joseph E. The nature of philosophical problems. Brown, 1946.

3831. Lee, Donald Clark. The history of philosophy and the idea of progress: a study in the historiography of philosophy. Cal., S. Diego, 1971.
71-30356

3832. Lee, Donald Soule. Creativity and control in the scientific method. Yale, 1961.

3833. Lee, Edward Nicholls. The concept of the "image" in Plato's metaphysics /with_/ appendix: Studies in the text of Timaeus 48E-52D. Princeton, 1964.
65-2141

3834. Lee, Harold Newton. Perception and aesthetic value. Harvard, 1930.

3835. Lee, James Joseph. The person as dialectic: Freud's contribution to a philosophy of man. Fordham, 1974. 74-25117

3836. Lee, Kwang-Sae. A critical study of Kant's views on scientific methodology and the modality of scientific laws. Yale, 1966. 66-13892

3837. Lee, Myung-Hyun. The later Wittgenstein's reflection on meaning, language and forms of life. Brown, 1974. 75-9197

3838. Lee, Otis Hamilton. The unknowable as a metaphysical concept. Harvard, 1930.

3839. Lee, Richard Thompson. Whitehead's theory of the self. Yale, 1962. 64-11902

3840. Lee, Tien-Ming. The logic of philosophico-linguistic analysis. Chicago, 1975.

3841. Leeb, La Verne Maria Shelton. The coherence and historical pictures of reference on the nature of reference. Minnesota, 1975. 75-27167

3842. Lefebvre, Rev. Reginald Raymond. Lenin's materialism: an evaluation of the philosophical basis of Russian communism. St. Louis, 1936. 193

3843. LeFevre, Perry D. The nature of personal existence. Chicago, 1951.

3844. Legault, Henri. Le Marxisme et la critique de la religion. Laval, 1944.

3845. Leggett, Richard C. The methodological significance of the unity of consciousness in Fichte's theoretical Wissenschaftslehre. Tennessee, 1975.
75-18969

3846. Lehman, Hugh Stephen. Function statements in biology. Harvard, 1963.

3847. Lehmann, Scott. A first order logic of knowledge and belief. Chicago, 1970.

3848. Lehmann, William Henry, Jr. The philosophic foundation of Luther's ethics. Loyola, 1968.

3849. Lehocky, Daniel Leroy. Reasons, causes, and agency. Wisconsin, 1972. 72-23748

3850. Lehrer, Keith Edward. Ifs, cans, and causes. Brown, 1960. 62-5755

3851. Leiber, Justin. On the notion that "work of art" is "indefinable." Chicago, 1967.

3852. Leibowitz, Constance. The value of human life.
N.Y.U., 1973. 74-13353

3853. Leichti, Terence Mark. Some problems concerning individuation of persisting objects. U.C.L.A., 1975. 75-22644

3854. Leidecker, Kurt Friedrich. The noetical terminology in the Upanishads and Bhagavad Gītā. Chicago, 1927.

3855. Leiser, Burton M. Custom and its relation to law. Brown, 1968.

3856. Leisey, Robert George. The search for the neaning of truth in the philosophy of Karl Jaspers. Toronto, 1974.

3857. Leiss, William Carl. The domination of nature.
Cal., S. Diego, 1969. 70-12851

3858. Leitch, Andrew. Laws, rules, and principles, their sense and value for conduct. Yale, 1919.

3859. Leites, Edmund. Conscience and self-love in Joseph Butler's ethics. Harvard, 1972.

3860. Leith, Thomas Henry. Popper's views of theory formation compared with the development of post-relativistic cosmological models. Boston U., 1963.
63-6564

3861. Lemieux, Albert Arby. The theory of knowledge according to Francesco Suarez. Toronto, 1945.

3862. Lemmer, Rev. Jerome George. The problem of the plurality of substantial forms in a compound as treated by St. Albert the Great. St. Louis, 1937.
200

3863. Le Moine, Roy Emanuel. The anagogic theology of Wittgenstein's *Tractatus*. Florida St., 1972.
72-27922

3864. Lemon, Frank M. Recent American humanism: an exposition. American U., 1937.

3865. Lemos, Ramon. A critical exposition of Green's *Prolegomena to science*. Duke, 1955.

3866. Lennon, Joseph Luke. The nature of experience and its role in the acquisition of scientific knowledge according to the philosophy of St. Thomas Aquinas. Notre Dame, 1954. 10728

3867. Lennon, Thomas Michael. The problem of intentionality in recent analytic philosophy. Ohio St., 1968. 68-15348

3868. Lentz, Oscar H. Pragmatism and logical positivism: a critical examination of the scientific foundations. Texas, 1955.

3869. Lenz, John William. Hume's skepticism and the experimental method of reasoning. Yale, 1953.

3870. Lenzen, Victor Fritz. Outlines of a science of phenomenology, with special reference to meaning and truth. Harvard, 1916.

3871. Leonard, Henry Siggins. Singular terms. Harvard, 1931.

3872. Leonard, Linda Schierse. An existential analysis of detachment. Duquesne, 1966.

3873. Leplin, Jarrett. The concept of an *ad hoc* hypothesis. Chicago, 1972.

3874. Lerner, Eric Joseph. The emotions of self-deception. Cornell, 1975. 75-27038

3875. Lerner, Michael P. Justification for democracy: the Marxist perspective. Berkeley, 1972.

3876. Lescoe, Francis Joseph. The theory of the first principle in the *Summa de bono* of Ulrich of Strasbourg: philosophical study and text. Toronto, 1949.

3877. Lesher, James Hunter. *Gnosis* and *episteme* in Plato's *Theaetetus*: a study in Plato's later epistemology. Rochester, 1967. 67-8962

3878. Leslie, Charles Whitney. The religious philosophy of William James. Harvard, 1945.

3879. Leslie, Robert J. The epicureanism of Titus Pomponius Atticus. Columbia, 1950.

3880. Lessing, Alfred. Meaning and value in music: a study of the problem and theories of musical aesthetics. Yale, 1962. 68-4088

3881. Lessing, **Arthur**. Man is Freedom: a critical study of the conception of human freedom in the philosophies of Heidegger and Sartre. Tulane, 1966.
66-10766

3882. Leue, William Hendrichs. Metaphysical foundations
for a theory of value in the philosophy of A.N.
Whitehead. Harvard, 1952.

3883. Levensky, Mark Alan. Direct awareness. Michigan,
1966. 67-8296

3884. Levensohn, Stephen Bernard. The development of political theology from Alexander the Great to Jean
Bodin. Florida St., 1962. 62-4619

3885. Levi, Albert W. A study in the social philosophy of
John Stuart Mill. Chicago, 1938.

3886. Levi, Don Simeon. Finite controllability. Harvard,
1964.

3887. Levi, Isaac. Positivism and realism in the epistemology of Moritz Schlick. Columbia, 1957.
57-2868

3888. Levin, David Michael. A critique of Edmund Husserl's
theory of adequate and apodictic evidence. Columbia, 1967. 68-5611

3889. Levin, Leonard Samuel. Deriving a theological position from mind-body interactionism. Brandeis,
1973. 73-32396

3890. Levin, Michael Eric. Wittgenstein's philosophy of
mathematics. Columbia, 1969. 70-7017

3891. Levine, Andrew. Democracy and community: the significance of Kenneth Arrow's general possibility
theorem for democratic theory. Columbia, 1971.
72-1350

3892. Levine, David. The Bustan al-ukul by Nathaniel ibn
al-Fayyumi, edited and translated from an unique
manuscript in the library of Columbia University.
Columbia, 1902.

3893. Levine, David Lawrence. Plato's Charmides: on the
political and philosophical significance of ignorance. Penn St., 1975. 76-10753

3894. Levine, Stephen King. Art and being in the philosophy of Martin Heidegger: an interpretation and
critique of Der ursprung des kunstwerkes. New
School, 1968. 68-15768

3895. Levinger, Lee Joseph. The causes of anti-Semitism
in the United States. A study in the group and
sub-group. Pennsylvania, 1925.

3896. Levinson, Jerrold. Properties, qualities, and categoriality. Michigan, 1974.   75-10215

3897. Levinson, Joel Herbert. In defense of the postulation elimination theory of the mind-body problem. Rochester, 1973.   73-25825

3898. Levinstein, Irwin B. The human world of Homer, Herodotos, and Isokrates: the presentation of identity in ancient Greece. Chicago, 1973.

3899. Levison, Arnold Boyd. Proof and the case-by-case procedure. Virginia, 1959.   59-4233

3900. Levitsky, Ihor A. The concept of measurement in the social sciences. Duke, 1948.

3901. Levy, Edwin, Jr. Interpretations of quantum theory and Soviet thought. Indiana, 1969.   70-7475

3902. Levy, Robert Jay. Carnap and the explication of empiricism. Duke, 1970.   71-10391

3903. Levy, Solomon E. The problem of causal contingency: the meaning of intensionality in physical theory. Southern Cal., 1954.

3904. Levy, Steven Robert. Knowledge and communication. U.C.L.A., 1974.   74-22953

3905. Lewis, Allison L. A critical examination of three contemporary aesthetic theories. Duke, 1961.   62-1998

3906. Lewis, Benjamin Franklin. The concept of "meaning in history." Cincinnati, 1961.   61-5227

3907. Lewis, Charles MacDonald. Logical analysis and theological language: an interpretation. Vanderbilt, 1967.   67-7456

3908. Lewis, Charles Wesley, Jr. Sense or nonsense: the ontological argument for the existence of God in the thought of Charles Hartshorne. Georgia, 1973.   73-31916

3909. Lewis, Clarence Irving. The place of intuition in knowledge. Harvard, 1910.

3910. Lewis, David Kellogg. Conventions of language. Harvard, 1967.

3911. Lewis, Donald F. The notion of time in the cosmology of A.N. Whitehead. So. Illinois, 1970.   71-10023

3912. Lewis, Douglas Edward. Moore's realism. Iowa, 1964.
65-482

3913. Lewis, Earl Errington. The theory of perception in the philosophy of G.F. Stout. Toronto, 1939.

3914. Lewis, Gordon Russell. Faith and reason in the thought of St. Augustine. Syracuse, 1959.
59-2665

3915. Lewis, Harry Anthony. Criteria, theory and knowledge of other minds. Stanford, 1966. 67-7940

3916. Lewis, John Underwood. Man's natural knowledge of the eternal law. Marquette, 1966. 67-3631

3917. Lewis, Leicester Crosby. The philosophical principles of French modernism. Pennsylvania, 1925.

3918. Lewis, Olin A. Metaphysic of experience of Shadworth H. Hodgson. Drew, 1951.

3919. Lewis, Randy Lynn. Descartes and Malebranche: a structural history. Texas, 1975. 76-14486

3920. Lewis, Thomas Albert. Judgment as belief. Johns Hopkins, 1910.

3921. Leys, Wayne Albert Risser. Needs and values in religion. Chicago, 1930.

3922. Li, Gwan-yuen. A study of *wei* (doing) and *wu wei* (non-doing) in Lao-tzŭ's *Tao tê ching*. New School, 1950.

3923. Li, Kwang-wu. An examination of the ethics of L.T. Hobhouse. Wisconsin, 1952.

3924. Li, Tu. S.C. Pepper's concept of metaphysics as the theory of world hypotheses. So. Illinois, 1974.
75-127

3925. Liao, Wen Kwei. Morality versus legality: historic analysis of the motivating factors of sccial conduct. Chicago, 1931.

3926. Libby, Margaret S. The attitude of Voltaire to magic and sciences. Columbia, 1935.

3927. Li Brize, James A. A study in the philosophy of labor. Buffalo, 1963. 64-2730

3928. Licht, Robert Arthur. The teachings of nature and soul in Aristotle's *Nicomachean ethics*. Penn St., 1975. 76-10755

3929. Lichtenberg, Benjamin. Ethical and anthropological problems of the biological revolution. Fordham, 1973. 74-2749

3930. Lichtenbert, Robert Henry. A revised principle of polarity, with applications to aesthetics. Tulane, 1975. 76-13595

3931. Lichtman, Richard. The cognitive significance of art. Yale, 1957. 65-9858

3932. Liddell, Anna Forbes. The logical relationship of the philosophy of Hegel to the philosophies of Spinoza and Kant. No. Carolina, 1924.

3933. Liddell, Brandan Edwin Alexander. Motives and intentions. Michigan, 1961. 61-2768

3934. Liddy, Roy Balmer. The relation of science and philosophy. Toronto, 1915.

3935. Lieb, Irwin Chester. Logical form. Yale, 1953.

3936. Liggett, George A. The philosophy of Spencer, Huxley and Bain, is the philosophy of unqualified materialism. N.Y.U., 1895.

3937. Lilienkamp, Paul Frederick. Liberation in recent Marxist theory. So. Illinois, 1970. 71-2388

3938. Lilje, Gerald Wade. Katz-Fodor semantics and problems in the philosophy of language. Illinois, 1970. 71-5166

3939. Limper, Peter Frederick. Value and the individual in the philosophies of Whitehead and Peirce. Yale, 1975. 75-26748

3940. Lin, Po-chen. A critical analysis of Albert Schweitzer's philosophy of civilization with special reference to his ethical conception of reverence for life. Southern Cal., 1953.

3941. Lincicome, David Van Cleave. Evaluative semantics. Washington U., 1971. 71-19820

3942. Lincourt, John M. Precursors in American philosophy of George Herbert Mead's theory of emergent selfhood. Buffalo, 1972. 73-5142

3943. Lind, Richard Walfred. In defense of beauty: a phenomenological analysis of the hedonics of perception. Southern Cal., 1971. 72-6082

3944. Lindberg, Luther Eugene. The relationship of educational philosophy to the issues of confirmation in the Lutheran churches in the United States in the middle of the 20th century. Boston U., 1969.
69-18772

3945. Lindemann, Sr. Kathryn M. A clarification of the meaning of 'social philosophy' through an examination and clarification of the extension of the domain of social philosophy. Michigan St., 1975.
75-27294

3946. Linden, George William. The philosophy of art of Samuel Alexander. Illinois, 1956. 19844

3947. Lindermayer, Eric Roy. Jean-Paul Sartre: original choice. Columbia, 1974. 75-7519

3948. Lindgren, John Ralph. Adam Smith's theory of the ultimate foundations of commercial society. Marquette, 1963. 65-99

3949. Lindley, Samuel Edward. The risks of freedom- an introduction to the philosophy of Karl Jaspers, with translations. Cornell, 1953.

3950. Lindley, Thomas F., Jr. The philosophical presuppositions of Thomas Jefferson's social theories. Boston U., 1952.

3951. Lindner, Theodore G. The psychological necessity of St. Paul's conversion. Ohio St., 1949.

3952. Lindon, Luke James. The notion of human virtue according to Saint Thomas Aquinas. Toronto, 1954.

3953. Lineback, Richard Harold. The place of the imagination in Hume's epistemology. Indiana, 1963.
64-490

3954. Linehan, Daniel F. A criticism of Kant's synthetic a priori judgments. Columbia, 1888.

3955. Linehan, Rev. James C. The rational nature of man with special reference to the effects of immorality on the intellect according to Saint Thomas: a metaphysical study. Catholic U., 1937.

3956. Linenbrink, Mary Cecilia. A synthesis of Pierre Teilhard de Chardin's views on the origin and development of consciousness. Colorado, 1969.
70-5869

3957. Link, Henry Charles. The determination of value in instinct. Yale, 1916.

3958. Link, Mae M. Kierkegaard's way to America: a study in the dissemination of his thought. American U., 1951.

3959. Linnell, John S. Berkeley's criticism of abstract ideas. Minnesota, 1954. 8126

3960. Linsky, Bernard. Natural kinds and natural kind terms. Stanford, 1975. 76-5760

3961. Linsky, Leonard. A study in meaning: the interchangeability of expressions in non-existential contexts. Berkeley, 1948.

3962. Linwood Mead, Harvey. The middle science of astronomy. Laval, 1974.

3963. Liotta, James French. Mill and Cassirer on meaning and reference. So. Illinois, 1972. 72-28538

3964. Lipkin, Robert J. Reasons: studies in the nature of the explanation and justification of actions. Princeton, 1974. 75-20644

3965. Lipman, Matthew. Problems of art inquiry. Columbia, 1953. 8719

3966. Lipman, Wynona Moore. Attitudes of Diderot toward primitivism. Columbia, 1953. 5199

3967. Lipschutz, Susan Barbara Strauss. Participatory democracy. Michigan, 1969. 70-14582

3968. Lipton, Charles Lewis. The general nature and significance of Hegel's Logic; an essay in dialectics. Toronto, 1942.

3969. Lipton, Michael Robin. Quine's criterion of ontological commitment. M.I.T., 1974.

3970. Lisska, Anthony Joseph. Role of phantasms in Aquinan perceptual theory. Ohio St., 1971. 71-27511

3971. List, Hugo Karl. Approach to a definition of leisure. Michigan St., 1966. 67-7571

3972. List, Peter Charles. The theory of sense-data in twentieth century British philosophy. Michigan St., 1969. 70-15073

3973. Litke, Robert Frederick. Intentional rule-guided language conduct. Michigan, 1974. 74-25254

3974. Litman, Alexander. Cicero's doctrine of nature and man. Columbia, 1930.

3975. Little, Ivan Lee. The validity of knowledge in the sociology of knowledge. Nebraska, 1953.

3976. Littlefield, Loy Deane. Time and the temporal. Northwestern, 1968. 69-1884

3977. Liu, King Shu. The thought of Lao-Tze, its origin, content, and development. Northwestern, 1915.

3978. Liu, Kwok Chiu. The problem of meaning in contemporary American & British philosophy. Wisconsin, 1925.

3979. Liu, Shu-Hsien. A critical study of Paul Tillich's methodological presuppositions. So. Illinois, 1966. 67-3169

3980. Livergood, Norman David. The principle of activity in Marx's dissertation and its influence on his thought. Yale, 1962.

3981. Livingston, Donald Wilson. A study of the idea of history in Hume's metaphysics. Washington U., 1968. 69-9001

3982. Lizotte, Aline. Le fait social dans les théories sociologiques contemporaines. Laval, 1970.

3983. Llamzon, Benjamin Sembrano. Esse as first actuality in Bañez. St. Louis, 1962. 64-3750

3984. Llewellyn, Robert Reed. Alfred North Whitehead's analysis of metric structure in Process and reality. Vanderbilt, 1971. 71-29308

3985. Lloyd, Alfred Henry. Freedom. Harvard, 1893.

3986. Lloyd, Warren Estelle. The concept of self. Yale, 1898.

3987. Locke, Alain LeRoy. The problem of classification in the theory of value. Harvard, 1918.

3988. Locke, John Goodwin. The social genesis and character of universals. Chicago, 1923.

3989. Lockquell, Rev. Clément. La génération temporelle de la sagesse chez les poètes-théologiens et les premiers physiologues. Laval, 1942.

3990. Lockridge, Thomas Francis. Philosophical problems of historical explanation. Brown, 1973. 75-12476

3991. Loeb, Louis Edward. Causal theories. Princeton, 1975. 75-23220

3992. Loemker, Leroy Earl. The criticism of idealism by G.E. Moore and R.B. Perry. Boston U., 1931.

3993. Loew, Cornelius Richard. The development of the idea of estrangement in Hegel's early writings. Columbia, 1951. 3433

3994. Loewenberg, Jacob. The genesis of Hegel's dialectical method. Harvard, 1911.

3995. Loewer, Barry Monroe. Knowledge, names, and necessity. Stanford, 1975. 76-5763

3996. Loftin, Robert W. The problem of explanation in history. Florida St., 1969. 70-3823

3997. Loftsgordon, Donald Rice. Retributive morality and its alternatives. Columbia, 1959. 59-1492

3998. Loftus, Br. Arthur Austin. The works and the mystical theology of William of St. Thierry. Fordham, 1940.

3999. Logan, Carrie Elizabeth. The psychology of Schopenhauer in its relation to his system of metaphysics. N.Y.U., 1902. 73-22231

4000. Logan, John Daniel. The Aristotelian concept of Physis. Harvard, 1896.

4001. Logan, John Frederick. The blue guitar: a semantic study of poetry. Texas, 1962. 62-4854

4002. Lohkamp, Rev. Richard Joseph. The meaning and significance of Charles S. Peirce's On a new list of categories. Notre Dame, 1970. 71-19081

4003. Lomasky, Loren Eric. Plantinga on God and other minds: an examination of inductive apologetics. Connecticut, 1975. 76-1682

4004. Lombard, Lawrence Brian. Quotations and quotation marks: semantical considerations. Stanford, 1974. 74-27054

4005. Lombardi, Joseph Laurence. The ethics of distribution: three methods of appraisal. N.Y.U., 1975. 75-28560

4006. Londis, James John. The relation between reason and religious experience in the philosophical theology of Nels F.S. Ferré, John Hick, and John E. Smith. Boston U., 1973. 73-23498

4007. Lonergan, Rev. Martin Joseph. Gabriel Marcel's phenomenology of incarnation. Georgetown, 1970.
7C-26652

4008. Long, David Wesley. Michael Polanyi's theory of knowledge. Florida St., 1967.   67-14453

4009. Long, Douglas Clark. The argument from analogy for the existence of other minds. Harvard, 1963.

4010. Long, Jerome Bowman. Dewey and pragmatism: towards a true conception of values in process. Fordham, 1962.   62-3770

4011. Long, Marcus. The relation between the logical theories of Lotze, Bosanquet and Dewey; a study in the morphology of knowledge. Toronto, 1940.

4012. Long, Thomas Aquinas. Wittgenstein, criteria and private experience. Cincinnati, 1965. 65-12920

4013. Long, Wilbur Harry. The philosophy of Charles Renouvier and its influence on William James. Harvard, 1927.

4014. Longacre, Frederick Lawson. A theory of morality enforcement. N.Y.U., 1975.   75-28562

4015. Longino, Helen Elizabeth. Inference and discovery. Johns Hopkins, 1973.   76-8492

4016. Longley, Peter Macdonald. Hume's logic- ideas and inference. Minnesota, 1968.   69-6828

4017. Longwood, Walter Merle. The ends of government in the thought of Reinhold Niebuhr and Jacques Maritain: a study in Christian social ethics. Yale, 1970.   70-16299

4018. Lonnes, Jerome LeRoy. The ethical theory of Richard Price. Emory, 1969.   69-17719

4019. Loptson, Peter James. Cartesian essentialism. Pittsburgh, 1972.   73-13198

4020. Lor, Aaron Arieh. Processes in Judaism: Ahad Ha-Am and Mordecai M. Kaplan. C.I.A.S., 1975.
75-19908

4021. Lord, Catherine. The cognitive import of art (with reference to Kant's theory of aesthetic judgment). Indiana, 1959.   59-4017

4022. Lorenz, Daniel Edward. The theology of Kant. Columbia, 1891.

4023. Lorenz, Helene Schell. Hierarchic man: philosophy and the individual in the work of Maurice Merleau-Ponty. Tulane, 1971. 71-27295

4024. Lorimer, Frank. The growth of reason; a study of the rôle of verbal activity in the growth of the structure of the human mind. Columbia, 1929.

4025. Losasso, Rosemarie. Selk-knowledge: a dialectic of silence and expression. Fordham, 1974. 74-19670

4026. Losoncy, Thomas Anthony. The nature of the intellectual soul in the teachings of Giles of Rome. Toronto, 1972.

4027. Lossee, John Price, Jr. A comparison of methodological principles basic to the quantum mechanics of Bohr and Heisenberg, the metaphysics of Emmet, and the theology of Tillich. Drew, 1961. 61-3844

4028. Loughran, Rev. Thomas Joseph. Efficient causality and extrinsic denomination in the philosophy of St. Thomas Aquinas. Fordham, 1969. 70-11438

4029. Loux, Michael Joseph. Aristotle and Ockham: a study in categories. Chicago, 1968.

4030. Louzecky, David James. Reasons, actions, and beliefs. Wisconsin, 1975. 75-19077

4031. Love, Howard Louis. Gerald Heard's natural theology in relation to the philosophy of Henri Bergson. Boston U., 1962. 62-3613

4032. Love, Julian Price. The Johannine philosophy of life. Cincinnati, 1930.

4033. Lovell, David Gilbert. Social determinism. Wisconsin, 1975. 75-19078

4034. Lover, Robert Edmund. An alternative logic. Case, 1972. 72-18706

4035. Lovin, Keith Harold. Legal positivism and morality. Rice, 1971. 71-26316

4036. Lovitt, Charles William. Sartre's use of Genet. Columbia, 1965. 66-6942

4037. Lowe, Victor August. Conceptions of nature in the philosophical systems of Whitehead, Russell, and Alexander. Harvard, 1935.

4038. Lowenstam, Steven. The typological death of Patroklos. Harvard, 1975.

4039. Lowenstein, Marc. Personal identity. Rochester, 1975. 75-22753

4040. Lowenthal, David. An inquiry into the moral foundation of Montesquieu's De l'ésprit des lois. New School, 1953.

4041. Lowery, Ellen Forst. Relationship: a typology of views. Cal., S. Cruz, 1973. 73-32499

4042. Lowinger, Armand. The methodology of Pierre Duhem. Columbia, 1941.

4043. Lowry, Ann Plamondon. The ontological status of the mathematicals. Emory, 1968. 69-5238

4044. Lowry, Atherton Clark. The world of Merleau-Ponty. Fordham, 1973. 73-16022

4045. Lowry, Jon William. The ontological status of value. Emory, 1969. 70-5748

4046. Lu, Martin Wu-chi. Language and reality in the later Russell. So. Illinois, 1973. 73-23700

4047. Luban, David Jay. The misuse of objectivity in the foundations of politics, language, and knowledge. Yale, 1974. 75-15331

4048. Lubin, Melvin. Deontology and the moral life: the ethical writings of H.A. Prichard, W.D. Ross, E.F. Carritt, and C.D. Broad. Columbia, 1952.
3902

4049. Lubow, Neil Bruce. The mind-body identity theory. U.C.L.A., 1974. 74-18780

4050. Lucas, Eldon Ray. Some aspects of Kant's philosophy of mathematics. Johns Hopkins, 1962.

4051. Lucas, George. Agnosticism and religion; an analysis of Spencer's religion of the unknowable. Catholic U., 1895.

4052. Lucas, Gerald Morton. Whewell's philosophy of the inductive sciences. Columbia, 1956. 17067

4053. Lucas, Raymond Earl, Jr. Empirical certainty. Tulane, 1967. 67-17930

4054. Lucash, Frank S. Gustav Bergmann's method and ontology. So. Illinois, 1970. 71-2389

4055. Luce, David Randall. Causal relations between mind and body: a new formulation of the mind-body problem. Michigan, 1957. 58-1428

4056. Luce, Robert Edward. A comparative study of certain basic categories in the philosophies of Leibniz and Whitehead. Harvard, 1940.

4057. Lucey, Kenneth Gerald. Some approaches to an ontology of properties. Boston U., 1973. 73-14158

4058. Lucier, Ruth Ellen Miller. Critical realism and the appearance problem: a commentary on the critical realism of G. Dawes Hicks and on options for its further development in the views of D.M. Armstrong and Roderick Chisholm. Maryland, 1972.
73-18254

4059. Luckenbach, Sidney Albert. From logical positivism to logical empiricism and hypercritical realism: the philosophy of science of Herbert Feigl. Pittsburgh, 1969. 70-5378

4060. Luckhardt, Charles Grant. Does 'thinking one ought' entail action? Emory, 1973. 73-18526

4061. Lucks, Rev. Henry Albert. The philosophy of Athenagoras; its sources and value. Catholic U., 1936.

4062. Ludman, Earl A. A priori concepts and Kant's aims in the transcendental deduction. Chicago, 1972.

4063. Ludwig, Gerald Alton. Right and duty and their relation to contiguous ethical concepts. DePaul, 1974.
74-23652

4064. Ludwig, Jan Keith. The logic of function statements. Johns Hopkins, 1971. 71-29155

4065. Luebke, Neil Robert. Paul Tillich's philosophy and theology of history. Johns Hopkins, 1968.
68-10572

4066. Luecke, Richard H. God and contingency in the philosophies of Locke, Clarke, and Leibniz. Chicago, 1955.

4067. Lugg, Andrew Maxwell. Deterministic systems. Michigan, 1974. 75-10220

4068. Lugo, Elena. José Ortega y Gasset's sportive sense of life: his philosophy of man. Georgetown, 1967. 68-1894

4069. Luizzi, Vincent L. A naturalistic theory of justice:
a critique of C.I. Lewis' ethics. Pennsylvania,
1973. 73-24179

4070. Lund, David Herbert. Private language, the egocentric outlook, and the nature of mind. Minnesota,
1972. 73-10604

4071. Lunnon, Margot Florence. Towards a theory of the
emotions. Berkeley, 1975. 76-15291

4072. Luqueer, Frederic Ludlow. Hegel as educator. Columbia, 1896.

4073. Lurie, Yuval. The correspondence thesis. Cornell,
1973. 73-18357

4074. Luther, Arthur Richard. Existence as dialectical
tension: a study of the philosophy of W.E. Hocking. Marquette, 1966. 68-491

4075. Luty, Carl E. Phenomenology and cosmology: the discordant harmony of Plato's *Philebus*. Penn St.,
1974. 75-10813

4076. Luxembourg, Lilo Katrin. Francis Bacon and Denis
Diderot: philosophers of science. Columbia, 1965.
65-13968

4077. Lycan, William G. Persons and the identity theory.
Chicago, 1970.

4078. Lynam, Gerald J. The good political ruler according
to St. Thomas Aquinas. Catholic U., 1953.

4079. Lynch, Jarman. Perspectives in relation to activity
as substance. Chicago, 1928.

4080. Lynch, John Edward. The theory of knowledge of Vital
du Four (c.1260-1327). Toronto, 1965.

4081. Lynch, John Joseph, Jr. Metaphysical and epistemological presuppositions of H. Weyl's conception
of mathematics. Fordham, 1961. 61-1573

4082. Lynch, Lawrence Edward Michael. The doctrine of the
non-coeternity of ideas in John the Scot. Toronto, 1940.

4083. Lynes, John Walter. Descartes, Hintikka, and the
Cogito. Illinois, 1970. 71-14852

4084. Lyon, Quinter Marcellus. Three typical views of
progress. Ohio St., 1933.

4085. Lyons, Alexander. Shaftesbury's ethical principle of adaptation to universal harmony. N.Y.U., 1909.
74-3404

4086. Lyons, Daniel D. A critique of absolute individualism. Chicago, 1967.

4087. Lyons, David Barry. Utilitarian generalization. Harvard, 1963.

4088. Lyons, Rev. James W. A philosophical critique of certitude according to Newman. Loyola, 1975.
75-14518

4089. Lyons, Rev. Lawrence F. Material and formal cause in the philosophy of Aristotle and St. Thomas. Catholic U., 1958.

4090. Lyons, Leonard Stephen. Counterfactuals and truth conditioning. Brown, 1969.   70-8755

4091. Lyons, Richard Gerald. The influence of Hegel on the philosophy of education of William Torrey Harris. Boston U., 1964.

- M -

4092. Mabe, Alan Ray. The relationship of law and morality in democratic theory. Syracuse, 1971. 72-6598

4093. McAlister, Linda L. The development of Franz Brentano's ethics. Cornell, 1969.   70-3767

4094. McAllister, Alan P. Metaphysical propositions: the views of Brand Blanshard and Charles Hartshorne. Toronto, 1975.

4095. McAllister, Rev. Joseph B. St. Thomas opusculum- De occultis operibus naturae. Catholic U., 1939.

4096. McAllister, Winston K. The compatibility of psychological hedonism and utilitarianism. Michigan, 1947.

4097. McArthur, Robert Paul. Truth-value semantics for tense logic. Temple, 1972.   73-8878

4098. McArthur, Ronald. The universale in preadicando and the universale in causando. Laval, 1963.

4099. McAuliffe, Sr. Agnes Teresa. Some modern non-intellectual approaches to God. Catholic U., 1934.

4100. McBride, Frank Abbott. The later Wittgenstein's conception of teaching. Michigan St., 1972.
72-30006

4101. McBride, William Leon. The concept of fundamental change in law and society. Yale, 1964.
65-1937

4102. McCabe, Russell Tyler. The origin and role of the categories in experience and inquiry (a comparison of the theories of Kant and Peirce.) No. Carolina, 1973.
73-26209

4103. McCall, Raymond Joseph. Necessity, analogy and the historical position of Spinoza. Fordham, 1941.

4104. McCall, Rev. Robert Edward. The reality of substance. Catholic U., 1956.

4105. McCalmont, Peter Wells. Metaphysics, conceptual relativism, and the construction of reality. Brown, 1973.
74-3051

4106. McCann, Edwin William. Locke's theory of essence. Pennsylvania, 1975.
76-3191

4107. McCann, Hugh, Jr. Basic actions, trying and overt movements. Chicago, 1972.

4108. McCarthy, Charles Raymond. The political philosophy of Orestes A. Brownson. Toronto, 1962.
63-6990

4109. McCarthy, Donald James. Free choice and liberty according to Thomas Bradwardine. Toronto, 1965.

4110. McCarthy, George Edward. The social anthropology of Hegel and Marx. Boston Coll., 1972.
72-22910

4111. McCarthy, Harold Edwards. Problems in aesthetic evaluation. Berkeley, 1947.

4112. McCarthy, James Duvall. Duty and interest in Butler's moral theory. Ohio St., 1970.
70-19340

4113. McCarthy, Jeanette E. Effect of a memory aid upon concept attainment: a developmental study. Loyola, 1968.

4114. McCarthy, John W. The naturalism of Samuel Alexander. Columbia, 1948.

4115. MacCarthy, Mark Michael. On methodological individualism. Indiana, 1975.
75-23483

4116. McCarthy, Michael Halpin. Psychologism, an historical and critical study. Yale, 1971.   71-17030

4117. McCarthy, Michael Henry. Kant's justification of freedom. Toronto, 1973.

4118. McCarthy, Thomas Anthony. Husserl's phenomenology and the theory of logic. Notre Dame, 1968.
69-4071

4119. McCaskill, David George. Conceptual schemes and the revolt against the foundation theory of knowledge. Wayne St., 1972.   73-12567

4120. Maccia, Elizabeth Steiner. A critical analysis of teleological explanation in biology. Southern Cal., 1957.

4121. McClain, Edward Ferrell. Paul Taylor's theory of justification. So. Illinois, 1969.   70-7300

4122. McClatchey, John Blackford. On defining knowledge as justified true belief. Georgia, 1973. 73-31922

4123. McCleary, Richard Calverton. Existential thinking in America, 1918-1941: the advent of a style. Yale, 1961.

4124. McClennen, Edward Francis. Justice as an object of rational decision. Johns Hopkins, 1968.
68-16445

4125. McClintock, James Alfred. The pragmatic spirit in modern English and American theism. Drew, 1934.

4126. MacClintock, Stuart. John of Jandun and the problem of Latin Averroism. Columbia, 1951.   3361

4127. McClintock, Thomas Lamb. An examination of ethical relativism. Wisconsin, 1962.   63-604

4128. McClure, George Tarrence. An inquiry into the meaning of "presuppose." Ohio St., 1958. 58-3441

4129. McClure, Matthew Thompson. A study of the realistic movement in contemporary philosophy. Columbia, 1912.

4130. McClurg, Jack. A philosophical study of the biological theories of Aristotle, Darwin, and Weismann. Chicago, 1961.

4131. McCluskey, Rev. John Joseph. Theology and "disclosure models": an interpretation and critique of Ian Ramsey's writings. Notre Dame, 1969.
69-13508

4132. McCluskey, Marilyn F. Faith and human life according to William James. Loyola, 1972.   73-16824

4133. McCollough, Joe Lawrence. Zeno, extension, and the problem of method. Emory, 1970.   70-22887

4134. McConnell, Frederick W. Experience and idealism as treated by Berkeley, Kant, and James Ward. Boston U., 1952.

4135. McConnell, Ray Madding. The ground of moral obligation. Harvard, 1908.

4136. McConnell, Terrance Callihan. Moral dilemmas and ethical consistency. Minnesota, 1975. 76-14932

4137. McCool, Rev. Gerald A. The historical sources of the image and likeness of God in the anthropology of Saint Augustine. Fordham, 1956.

4138. McCormack, Elizabeth Jane. F.H. Bradley's philosophy of man. Fordham, 1966.   67-11493

4139. McCormack, Eric David. Frederick Matthias Alexander and John Dewey; a neglected influence. Toronto, 1958.

4140. McCormick, Charles Wesley. The ethics of Homer. N.Y.U., 1898.

4141. McCormick, Peter Neely. Privileged access and a hypothetical construct theory of mental states. Michigan, 1973.   74-15799

4142. McCoy, Charles. Ludwig Feuerbach and the formation of the Marxian revolutionary idea. Laval, 1953.

4143. McCracken, Charles James. The reception of Malebranche's philosophy in Britain. Berkeley, 1969.   70-13107

4144. McCreary, John Kenneth. Recent developments in the philosophy of religion. Toronto, 1944.

4145. McCrimmon, Mary F. The classical philosophical sources of Bernardus Sylvestris. Yale, 1953.

4146. McCrimmon, Mitchell Drew. Foundations of operant behavior theory. W. Ontario, 1975.

4147. McCue, Rev. Edward Charles. Theophany: a study of the nature of God and his manifestations from the works of Joannes Scotus Erigena, ninth century Irish philosopher. St. Louis, 1934.

4148. McCullough, Ernest John. The theory of motion in Saint Albert the Great. Toronto, 1971.

4149. McCullough, Laurence Bernard. The early philosophy of Leibniz on individuation: a study of the <u>Disputatio metaphysica de principio individui</u>. Texas, 1975. 76-14494

4150. McCurdy, John Derrickson. Imaginal perception. Penn St., 1970. 71-16637

4151. McCurdy, William Jarvis. The concept of the object in the positivistic philosophy. Harvard, 1932.

4152. McCurley, Henry Hawkins, Jr. Aristotle: metaphysics and method. Georgia, 1974. 75-8186

4153. McCutchen, Duval T. Technique for democracy. Pennsylvania, 1938.

4154. McDade, Jesse Nathaniel. Frantz Fanon: the ethical justification of revolution. Boston U., 1971. 71-26446

4155. McDermott, Agnes Charlene Senape. The assertoric and model propositional logic of the Pseudo-Scotus. Pennsylvania, 1964. 65-1377

4156. McDermott, John Donovan. John Dewey: ethical inquiry and the psychological standpoint. Notre Dame, 1969. 69-18513

4157. McDermott, John J. Experience is pedagogical: the genesis and essence of the American nineteenth century notion of experience. Fordham, 1959.

4158. McDermott, Robert A. Radhakrishnan's comparative philosophy. Boston U., 1969. 70-4679

4159. MacDonald, Audrey. Peirce's philosophy of mind. Texas, 1963. 64-92

4160. MacDonald, Rev. Charles Raymond. The role of negation in knowledge. Laval, 1965.

4161. MacDonald, Douglas Malcolm. Reason in action or spirit detached: an examination of the compatability of the life of reason and the spiritual life in Santayana's philosophy. Vanderbilt, 1971. 71-20296

4162. McDonald, Joseph B. The art of agriculture according to the teaching of St. Thomas. Laval, 1959.

4163. MacDonald, Lauchlan Donald. A critical estimate of the writings of John Grote. Boston U., 1950.

4164. McDonald, Michael Francis. Duties to oneself. Pittsburgh, 1972. 73-13197

4165. MacDonald, Ralph James Joseph. Gregory of Rimini and notitia simplex. Toronto, 1946.

4166. MacDonald, Robert. Critique of the modern social theories of conscience in the light of an intellectualistic ideal. N.Y.U., 1910. 74-1247

4167. McDonald, Rev. William J. The social value of property according to St. Thomas Aquinas. Catholic U., 1939.

4168. McDonnell, James Kevin. Religion and ethics in the philosophy of William of Ockham. Georgetown, 1971. 71-30354

4169. McDonough, Richard Michael. Wittgenstein and the law of the excluded middle. Cornell, 1975.
76-9551

4170. Maceda, Rev. Hernando M. Theory of optimism and plenitude: St. Thomas and Leibniz (an interpretation.) Fordham, 1953.

4171. McElroy, Elliott Watson. The nature of experience and the role of God: Whitehead's response to Hume. Georgia, 1972. 73-5737

4172. McElroy, Howard C. Bentham's educational policies. Pittsburgh, 1939.

4173. McEvilly, Walter Wayne. Music and metaphysics. Southern Cal., 1963. 64-2587

4174. McEvoy, Paul Poynter. The philosophy of Neils Bohr. M.I.T., 1972.

4175. McEwen, William Peter. Whitehead's metaphysical interpretation of the meaning and growth of a human individual. Boston U., 1940.

4176. McFadden, Rev. Charles J. A metaphysical study of the philosophy of dialectical materialism. Catholic U., 1938.

4177. McFarland, John Anthony. Moore's and Russell's critiques of F.H. Bradley. Brandeis, 1971.
71-30138

4178. McFarlane, William Hugh. Philosophy and common sense: a neo-scholastic appraisal of a conflict in contemporary philosophy. Virginia, 1957. 57-4246

4179. McGann, Rev. Thomas F. Suarez and personalism. Fordham, 1956.

4180. McGee, Charles Douglas. C.I. Lewis' theory of sense meaning. Harvard, 1957.

4181. McGee, Ellen F. An American approach to the problem of evil: a study of the history of its development and its articulation as a philosophy by William James. Fordham, 1969. 69-16230

4182. McGill, Vivian Jerould. Universals and substances. Harvard, 1925.

4183. McGill, William Marcus. Reason, faith, and the problem of evil in the thought of Edgar S. Brightman and Nels F.S. Ferre. Boston U., 1974. 74-20394

4184. McGilp, Ian Findlay. The unity of Plato's political thought. British Columbia, 1974.

4185. McGilvary, Evander Bradley. The principle and the method of the Hegelian dialectic, a defence of the dialectic against its critics. Berkeley, 1897.

4186. McGilvray, James Alasdair. Time and knowledge: an inquiry into the "now." Yale, 1968. 69-8387

4187. McGinley, John Willard. The question of life in Heidegger's *Being and time*. Boston Coll., 1971. 71-16861

4188. McGinn, Robert Eugene. The concept of prestige: a philosophical analysis with applications to political argument. Stanford, 1969. 70-10485

4189. McGinnis, James Brown, III. Freedom and its realization in Gandhi's philosophy and practice of nonviolence. St. Louis, 1974. 75-26286

4190. McGinnis, Thomas Michael. Julian Huxley's evolutionary ethics: its account of the ethical ought. St. Louis, 1971. 72-23971

4191. McGovern, Rev. Thomas. The division of logic. Laval, 1957.

4192. McGowan, Robert Lee. Sympathy and conscience: a study of Adam Smith's ethical theory. Emory, 1963. 64-178

4193. McGowan, William Herron. Berkeley's general theory of signs. Johns Hopkins, 1957.

4194. McGrade, Arthur Stephen. Public religion- a study of Hooker's "polity" in view of current problems. Yale, 1961. 69-15740

4195. McGrath, Charles F. Gregory of Nyssa's doctrine on knowledge of God. Fordham, 1964. 64-13222

4196. McGreal, Ian P. The meaning of moral obligation. Brown, 1947.

4197. MacGregor, Rev. Philip S. Spinoza and religious philosophy. Fordham, 1952.

4198. McGregor, Robert Mar. "Aesthetic", broadly and narrowly speaking: an examination of the psychological approach to a general theory of art. Michigan, 1970. 71-15236

4199. MacGuigan, Mark Rudolph. The best form of government in the philosophy of St. Thomas Aquinas. Toronto, 1957.

4200. MacGuigan, Maryellen. The foundations of sexuality: Maurice Merleau-Ponty's conception of sexuality and its place in his philosophy. Ottawa, 1975.

4201. McGuigan, Sr. St. George. The nominalism and realism in Abelard. Fordham, 1939.

4202. McGuire, Jerry Carter. Value philosophy and contemporary cinema. Southern Cal., 1966. 66-5488

4203. McGuire, Richard Randolph. Realism and subjectivism: G.E. Moore and C.I. Lewis. Buffalo, 1974. 75-7774

4204. Machado, Rev. Michael A. The category of depth in the philosophy of Gabriel Marcel. Duquesne, 1963.

4205. Machamer, Peter K. Points about observation in science. Chicago, 1972.

4206. Machan, Tibor Richard. Human rights: a metaethical inquiry. Cal., S. Barbara, 1971. 72-25038

4207. Machina, Kenton Frank. Borderline cases, a problem in predicating. U.C.L.A., 1968. 69-5333

4208. Machle, Edward Johnstone. Mysticism and realism in the philosophical systems of Nyāya-Vaiśeṣika, James Bissett Pratt, and Friedrich, Baron von Hügel. Columbia, 1952. 4219

4209. Macho, Rev. Thomas. Freedom and necessity in St. Augustine. Fordham, 1961. 61-1574

4210. McInerny, Ralph. The existential dialectic of Søren Kierkegaard. Laval, 1954.

4211. McIntire, Russel Martin, Jr. Some implications of Jean-Paul Sartre's concept of consciousness for a theory of human action. Vanderbilt, 1972. 73-14522

4212. McIntire, Walter Oscar. Current theories in the psychology of instinct in their social applications. Harvard, 1914.

4213. McIntyre, Rev. Clarence Cameron. The modern idea of God among American Protestant theologians. Fordham, 1933.

4214. McIntyre, Jane Lipsky. New perspectives on Locke and personal identity. Stanford, 1973. 73-14941

4215. McIntyre, Ronald Treadwell. Husserl and referentiality: the role of the Noema as an intensional entity. Stanford, 1970. 71-12947

4216. Mack, Eric. A theory of natural rights. Rochester, 1973. 73-25830

4217. Mack, Robert D. The appeal to immediate experience; philosophic method in Bradley, Whitehead and Dewey. Columbia, 1945.

4218. MacKay, Alfred Farnum. Speech acts. No. Carolina, 1967. 68-6749

4219. MacKay, Donald Sage. Mind in the Parmenides; a study in the history of logic. Columbia, 1924.

4220. Mackay, I. Hegel's philosophy of mind. Cornell, 1901.

4221. McKay, Paul L. The religious aspect of the philosophy of Josiah Royce. N.Y.U., 1945. 73-8683

4222. McKay, Thomas James. Essentialism and quantified modal logic: Quine's argument and Kripke's semantics. Massachusetts, 1974. 74-25915

4223. McKee, Patrick Leo. The sense-datum in hallucinatory seeing. Maryland, 1971. 72-1665

4224. McKeldin, James Reese. Theories of the cyclic in certain ancient philosophies. Pittsburgh, 1957. 57-1747

4225. McKenna, Rev. Terence Patrick. The logic of religious language; a second-order study of Christian language and of the key role within it of the Via negativa. Toronto, 1968.

4226. McKenna, William Anthony. Roman Ingarden: ontology and idealism. Northwestern, 1975.   75-29706

4227. McKenney, John L. The problem of a science of ethics in the philosophies of John Dewey and Bertrand Russell. Ohio St., 1952.   58-4837

4228. MacKenzie, Ann Wilber. An analysis of purposive behavior. Cornell, 1972.   72-26349

4229. MacKenzie, Nollaig. Empiricism, verification, and reduction, with special reference to the role of non-universal necessary truths in the work of Strawson and Shoemaker. Cornell, 1972.
   72-26350

4230. McKeon, Charles K. A study of the Summa philosophiae of the Pseudo-Grosseteste. Columbia, 1949.

4231. McKeon, Richard Peter. The philosophy of Spinoza; the unity of his thought. Columbia, 1928.

4232. McKeough, Michael John. The meaning of the rationes seminales in St. Augustine. Catholic U., 1926.

4233. McKeown, Cecil Garland Stewart. A study in perception. Princeton, 1953.   6822

4234. Mackey, Louis Henry. The nature and the end of the ethical life according to Kierkegaard. Yale, 1954.

4235. Mackey, Rev. Robert R. The role of prudence in the act of obedience according to St. Thomas. Fordham, 1957.

4236. McKian, John Daniel. The limits of natural knowledge according to St. Thomas Aquinas. Loyola, 1940.

4237. McKim, Vaughn Richard. Human action and a scientific image of man. Yale, 1966.   66-13905

4238. MacKinnon, Flora Isabel. Philosophical writings of Henry More. Toronto, 1924.

4239. McKirachan, John C. The temporal and the eternal in the philosophy of Thomas Hill Green. Princeton, 1939.

4240. McKirahan, Richard Duncan, Jr. Aristotle's theory of demonstrative science. Harvard, 1973.

4241. Macklin, Ruth Chimacoff. Theory of action. Case, 1969. 69-9354

4242. McKnight, Stephen Alen. Cassirer, Toynbee, and Voegelin's conceptions of the intelligible field of historical study. Emory, 1972. 72-25942

4243. McKown, Delos Banning. The classical Marxist critiques of religion: Marx, Engels, Lenin, Kautsky. Florida St., 1972. 72-31412

4244. McLane, Henry Earl, Jr. Kierkegaard's use of the category of repetition: an attempt to discern the structure and unity of his thought. Yale, 1961.

4245. McLaren, Robert Bruce. A study of philosophy curriculum dissonance in selected colleges and universities in California. Southern Cal., 1972. 72-11939

4246. McLaren, Ronald Eugene. The doctrine of convention. Yale, 1965. 65-15074

4247. McLarty, Furman G. Conscience and the ethical oecumene: a study in the moral philosophy of stoicism. Duke, 1935.

4248. McLaughlin, Andrew. Objectivity and theoretical perspectives in science. Buffalo, 1969. 69-20566

4249. McLaughlin, John Farrell. Subject-predicate and logical form. Brandeis, 1973. 73-15454

4250. McLaughlin, Louise Elizabeth. Idealistic tendencies in some recent naturalism. Boston U., 1949.

4251. McLaughlin, Robert James. Abstraction as constitutive of science according to Aristotle and Saint Thomas Aquinas. Toronto, 1965.

4252. McLaughlin, Robert Michael. Theoretical entities and philosophical dualisms: a critique of instrumentalism. Indiana, 1967. 67-15132

4253. McLaughlin, Wayman Bernard. The relation between Hegel and Kierkegaard. Boston U., 1958. 58-3111

4254. McLaughlin, William James. Analogy and other minds. Michigan, 1968. 69-12181

4255. MacLean, Charles Fraser. A critique of John Stuart Mill's examination of Hamilton's philosophy. Yale, 1866.

4256. McLean, Rev. George F. Man's knowledge of God according to Paul Tillich, a Thomistic critique. Catholic U., 1958.

4257. McLean, Jeanne Priley. Immediate experience and the problem of expression: a study in the philosophy of Bergson. Loyola, 1975. 75-22359

4258. McLean, William Donald. Morris R. Cohen and the liberal temper: a philosopher's conception of liberalism. Michigan, 1971. 72-14941

4259. MacLellan, Thomas M. The moral virtues which rectify the exercise of the speculative life. Laval, 1958.

4260. McLelland, Reginald Franklin. Everett Hall and categorial systems. Georgia, 1973. 73-31926

4261. McLendon, Hiram James. The causal theory of perception. Harvard, 1950.

4262. MacLennan, Simon Fraser. Impersonal judgment, its nature, origin and significance. Chicago, 1896.

4263. MacLeod, William John. Some interrelations between the psychology and philosophy of William James. Boston U., 1948.

4264. McMahan, Knight Warner. The ethical development of Friedrich Nietzsche. Harvard, 1937.

4265. McMahon, Deanna Bernice Stein. David Hume's philosophy of religion: a study based on his theories of meaning, identity, and natural propensities. Wisconsin, 1972. 72-31547

4266. McMahon, Francis E. The humanism of Irving Babbitt. Catholic U., 1931.

4267. McMahon, Rev. George J. The order of procedure in the philosophy of nature. Laval, 1959.

4268. McMahon, Joseph John. Bergson's theistic evolutionism. St. John's, 1975. 76-2995

4269. McMahon, Martin Brian. Bertrand Russell's two ontologies. Wisconsin, 1972. 72-13981

4270. McMahon, Sr. Mary Roberta. *Separatio* in recent Thomism. St. Louis, 1963. 64-4260

4271. McMahon, Br. Patrick. The concept of matter in the metaphysics of Henri Bergson. St. Louis, 1965.
65-14652

4272. McMahon, William Edward. Hans Reichenbach's philosophy of grammar. Notre Dame, 1970. 71-5550

4273. McManus, Rev. Charles J. The notion of being according to Thomas de Vio Cardinal Cajetan. Fordham, 1947.

4274. McManus, Rev. Ora Roland. The concept of the personal in the writings of John Macmurray. Catholic U., 1967. 67-7325

4275. MacMillan, Donald. William James' philosophy of religion, with specific reference to his philosophy of mind. Toronto, 1962.

4276. McMorrow, George J. A metaphysical study on the individual and the person. Notre Dame, 1940.

4277. McMurrin, Sterling M. Positivism and the logical meaning of normative value judgments. Southern Cal., 1946.

4278. McNabb, James Randolph, Jr. C.I. Lewis and the foundations of practical reason. Buffalo, 1973.
74-4426

4279. McNally, Patrick Henry. The unity and consistency of the Nicomachean ethics. Boston Coll., 1975.
75-9718

4280. McNaughton, Robert Forbes, Jr. On establishing the consistency of systems. Harvard, 1951.

4281. MacNeil, Eileen M. Conflict versus communication: the social philosophy of Walter P. Reuther. Fordham, 1973. 73-16023

4282. McNitt, Harold Austin. John Dewey's democratic liberalism: its philosophical foundations. Michigan, 1956. 57-2179

4283. McNulty, Thomas Michael. Realism in physics. Minnesota, 1970. 71-8185

4284. McNutt, Walter S. Is the pragmatic theory of knowledge compatible with serious religious faith? Cincinnati, 1922.

4285. Macomber, William Burns. The phenomenological notion of truth in Hegel and Heidegger. Toronto, 1963.

4286. McPeck, John Edward. A logic of discovery: lessons from history and current prospects. W. Ontario, 1973.

4287. MacPhail, Malcolm Leod. Educated men and the church. Harvard, 1912.

4288. McPheeters, Colin Allen. Early moral standards of Kentucky and Missouri. Chicago, 1916.

4289. MacPherson, Jessie Hall Knox. The dilemma of realism; a study of the theory of knowledge in the philosophy of G.E. Moore. Toronto, 1944.

4290. McPherson, Mary Patterson. Transcendence and freedom in the philosophy of F.H. Bradley. Bryn Mawr, 1969.   70-10013

4291. MacQueen, David John. The notion of superbia in the works of St. Augustine with special reference to the De civitate Dei. Toronto, 1958.

4292. Macquesten, Rockwood. Higher criticism, the philosophical outgrowth of Spinosism. N.Y.U., 1893.
                                                              73-20754

4293. McRae, Farquhar D. Spencer's moral theory. N.Y.U., 1896.   73-20768

4294. McRae, Robert. The relation of John Stuart Mill's logic to his metaphysics and epistemology. Johns Hopkins, 1946.

4295. McSweeney, Rev. Alan J. Truth and society according to St. Thomas Aquinas. Catholic U., 1943.

4296. McTighe, Thomas Paul. God and physics in Galileo and Descartes. St. Louis, 1955.

4297. MacVannel, John Angus. Hegel's doctrine of the will. Columbia, 1896.

4298. McWaters, Roger Warren. The concept of a miracle. Minnesota, 1974.   74-26210

4299. McWilliams, Rev. James A. The bearing of the integral composition on the essential composition of bodies. St. Louis, 1930.

4300. Madden, Edward H. An examination of Gestalt theory. Iowa, 1950.

4301. Madden, Robert E. Husserl and the problem of hidden reason: intentionality as accomplishing life. Duquesne, 1973.   74-13191

4302. Madigan, Patrick Sarsfield. The political philosophy of Samuel Pufendorf. Tulane, 1972.   73-2203

4303. Magel, Charles R. An analysis of Kierkegaard's philosophic categories. Minnesota, 1960. 61-614

4304. Magid, Carolyn Hope. Experience and the foundations of knowledge. Princeton, 1974. 75-6656

4305. Magid, Henry M. English political pluralism; the problem of freedom and organization. Columbia, 1941.

4306. Magnus, Bernd. Heidegger and Nietzsche's doctrine of eternal recurrence. Columbia, 1967. 70-23451

4307. Magrish, James L. A philosophical basis for judicial thinking. Cincinnati, 1957. 57-4245

4308. Magruder, James Edward. C.I. Lewis's philosophy of action. So. Illinois, 1973. 74-6274

4309. Maguire, Rev. James J. The philosophy of modern revolution. Catholic U., 1943.

4310. Mahajan, Satinder Nath. A comparative study of the main theories of justification of political authority. Hawaii, 1969. 70-19510

4311. Mahan, Walter Basil. The relation of the right to the good in recent ethical theory. Chicago, 1923.

4312. Mahan, Wayne Wilbur. Dislocations in the system and method of Paul Tillich's Systematic theology. Texas, 1967. 67-8125

4313. Maher, Michael J. We are: an essay on the meaning of intersubjectivity in the philosophy of Gabriel Marcel. Duquesne, 1973. 74-13188

4314. Mahoney, Edward Patrick. The early psychology of Agostino Nifo. Columbia, 1966. 67-801

4315. Maier, Josef. On Hegel's critique of Kant. Columbia, 1939.

4316. Maitland, Jeffrey Algert. Kantian issues in contemporary aesthetics. Minnesota, 1971. 72-5549

4317. Majchrzak, Rev. Colman J. A brief history of Bonaventurianism. Catholic U., 1957.

4318. Major, D.R. The principle of teleology in the critical philosophy of Kant. Cornell, 1896.

4319. Majors, Troy Edwin. The problem of the disjunction between thought and existence. Northwestern, 1967. 67-15283

4320. Makinde, Moses Akinola. John Stuart Mill's theory of logic and scientific method as a rejection of Hume's scepticism with regard to the validity of inductive reasoning. Toronto, 1975.

4321. Makkreel, Rudolf Adam. Wilhelm Dilthey's concept of the imagination. Columbia, 1966. 67-802

4322. Malament, David Baruch. Some problems concerning the causal structure of space-time. Rockefeller, 1975.

4323. Malcolm, John Finlay. Plato's conception of moral knowledge. Princeton, 1961. 62-1896

4324. Malcolm, Norman Adrian. The nature of necessary propositions. Harvard, 1940.

4325. Malhotra, Ashok Kumar. Nausea: an expression of Sartre's existential philosophy. Hawaii, 1969. 70-9973

4326. Mâlik, Charles Habib. The metaphysics of time in the philosophies of A.N. Whitehead and M. Heidegger. Harvard, 1937.

4327. Malinas, Gary Adrian. Intentionality and reference. Washington U., 1968. 68-17195

4328. Malino, Jonathan Wolf. Ontological commitment and semantics. Columbia, 1975. 76-13126

4329. Malinovich, Stanley. Morality as reasoning about the concept of man. N.Y.U., 1967. 68-6083

4330. Mallin, Samuel Barry. Merleau-Ponty's metaphysical epistemology. Toronto, 1974.

4331. Mallory, John William. The problem of tragedy in Nietzsche's early reflections. Northwestern, 1970. 71-10157

4332. Malone, Michael Emerson. The fundamental difference problem in the theory of action. Texas, 1972. 73-477

4333. Malone, Robert Wilcox. Events: their identity and individuation. Miami, 1971. 72-12886

4334. Maloney, James. The formal constituent of a sin of commission. Laval, 1946.

4335. Maloney, Rev. William. Individualism: extreme and moderate. Catholic U., 1951.

4336. Ma'luf, Fakhri B. The a priori in science according to the philosophy of Meyerson. Michigan, 1943.

4337. Maly, Kenneth R. The mittence of being and the task of thinking: a placing of the question of language. Duquesne, 1971.   72-12037

4338. Mamo, Plato Salvator. The notion of the self in the writings of Plotinus. Toronto, 1967.

4339. Manahan, W. The epistemological function of the ideas in Kant's philosophy. Cornell, 1898.

4340. Mandelbaum, Maurice H., Jr. Historical relativism in recent philosophy of history. Yale, 1936.

4341. Mandelberg, Alan David. Science, social science and new ideas- an essay in the philosophy of discovery. Oregon, 1971.   71-23120

4342. Mandina, Francis P. The natural theology of Michele Federico Sciacca considered in its positive and historical aspects. Fordham, 1953.

4343. Maner, Ernest Walter. Priority in perceptual individuation. Boston U., 1975.   74-26460

4344. Manheimer, Ronald J. Kierkegaard and the education of historical consciousness. Cal., S. Cruz, 1973.   74-17390

4345. Manicas, Peter Theodore. The concept of the individual in philosophies of William Graham Sumner, William James, Josiah Royce, and Lester Ward. Buffalo, 1963.   63-5876

4346. Manier, August Edward. The meaning of Nature in the philosophy of Leibniz. St. Louis, 1961.   61-6477

4347. Manley, James Carhart. Reasons in aesthetics. Michigan, 1972.   73-11197

4348. Manley, Michael Francis. God, his nature and existence according to the Sapientiale of Thomas of York; text and study. Toronto, 1952.

4349. Mann, Jesse Aloysius. Existential import and the Aristotelian syllogistic. Catholic U., 1958.

4350. Mann, Louis Leopold. Social ethics of the Talmud. Yale, 1919.

4351. Mann, William Edward. The logic of Saint Anselm's ontological argument. Minnesota, 1971.
72-365

4352. Manniello, Br. Andrew. The ontological status of intentionality in the philosophy of Maurice Merleau-Ponty. Fordham, 1974.
74-19715

4353. Mannoia, Vincent James, Jr. Whitehead's ontological principle: a defense and interpretation. Washington U., 1975.
75-4767

4354. Mannolini, Carol Ann. Toward a philosophy of feminism: a matter of androgyny. So. Illinois, 1975.
76-3329

4355. Manns, James William. Universality and objectivity in aesthetic judgment. Boston U., 1972.
72-25305

4356. Manor, Ruth. Conditional forms: assertion, necessity obligation and commands. Pittsburgh, 1971.
72-13432

4357. Mansbridge, Christopher. On the possibility of apprehending God in contemporary British philosophy. Notre Dame, 1973.
73-12069

4358. Manship, Winfield Scott. Kant and Schleiermacher on knowledge and faith. Yale, 1901.

4359. Mantautas, Vaidievutis Andrious. Meister Eckhart's mysticism and its place in the history of western philosophy. Fordham, 1968.
69-2597

4360. Manzo, Rev. Marcellus Peter. The philosophy of Valeriano Magni. Fordham, 1941.

4361. Mappes, Thomas A. Inductive reasoning and moral reasoning: parallel patterns of justification. Georgetown, 1973.
74-14930

4362. Marantz, Frederick. The aesthetics of Wilhelm von Humboldt: reflected through selected essays and letters. Columbia, 1969.
70-7028

4363. Marbourg, W. Denver. Action and bodily motion. Kansas, 1971.
72-32905

4364. Marchal, Joseph Howard. The concept of system: elements of a formal approach. Washington U., 1971.
71-19823

4365. Marchand, Jean-Paul M. The temporal character of experience in the philosophy of A.N. Whitehead. Fordham, 1974.
74-19672

4366. Marcil, Rev. George. Efficient causality in the philosophy of John Duns Scotus. Catholic U., 1965. 66-8812

4367. Marcil-Lacoste, Louise. The epistemological foundations of the appeal to common sense in Claude Buffier and Thomas Reid. McGill, 1974.

4368. Marcolongo, Francis Jeremiah. Aristotle- Aquinas- Ockham: a comparative study of three approaches in metaphysics and their philosophical significance for understanding the medieval contribution to the scientific revolution. Cal., S. Diego, 1971. 72-12784

4369. Marcotte, J. Normand. Matter and knowledge. Laval, 1945.

4370. Margolis, Joseph Zalman. The art of freedom: an essay in ethical theory. Columbia, 1953. 6669

4371. Marhenke, Paul. A relativistic theory of perception, being a solution of the problem of perception on the basis of the relativity of space and time. Berkely, 1928.

4372. Marie de Lourdes, Mthr. Étude et commentaire critique sur l'Enquiry concerning human understanding de Hume. Laval, 1944.

4373. Marien, Rev. Francis Joseph. God in the personalism of Borden Parker Bowne. St. Louis, 1956.

4374. Mark, Thomas C. Spinoza's theory of truth. Columbia, 1970.

4375. Markle, Gilbert Scott. Conceptual revision and the identity theory. Yale, 1968. 69-8389

4376. Marks, Charles Emil. Private language. Cornell, 1972. 73-9353

4377. Marks, Robert W. The philosophic faith of Benjamin Paul Blood, a study of the thought and times of an American mystic. New School, 1953.

4378. Marlies, Michael W. A re-examination of Mill's "utilitarianism" in the context of his philosophy of science. Brandeis, 1973. 73-32398

4379. Marlin, Randal Robert Alexander. Morality and the criminal law: some problems concerning intention, foresight and responsibility. Toronto, 1973.

4380. Marling, Rev. Joseph Maria. The order of nature in the philosophy of St. Thomas Aquinas. Catholic U., 1934.

4381. Marmura, Michael Elias. The conflict over the world's pre-eternity in the Tahāfuts of al-Ghāzali and Ibn Rushd. Michigan, 1959. 59-4955

4382. Maron, Melvin Earl. The meaning of the probability concept. U.C.L.A., 1951.

4383. Marquand, Allan. The logic of the Epicureans. Johns Hopkins, 1880.

4384. Marquis, Donald Bagley. Scientific realism and the antinomy of external objects. Indiana, 1970. 70-22836

4385. Marra, William A. Our knowledge of objects through themselves and as themselves. Fordham, 1952.

4386. Marras, Ausonio. Intentionality and mental acts. Duke, 1967. 68-5228

4387. Marsh, James Leonard. Hegel and Kierkegaard: a dialectical and existential contrast. Northwestern, 1971. 71-30881

4388. Marshall, Charles William. The theory of functions and objects, and of sense and reference, with special attention to the writings of Gottlob Frege. Cornell, 1952.

4389. Marshall, Donald Kainer. The restoration of logic in Thomas Reid. Chicago, 1939.

4390. Marshall, Ernest Clare. An explication of William James' neutral monism and some applications to his pragmatism. Ohio St., 1970. 71-18050

4391. Marshall, George John, Jr. Can human nature change? A tentative response in the light of the positions of Dewey, Sartre, and their critics. Georgetown, 1975. 76-11651

4392. Marshall, G. A study of the ethical system of Jean Marie Guyau. Radcliffe, 1910.

4393. Marshall, John, Jr. A defense of libertarianism. Yale, 1967. 68-5182

4394. Marshall, John M. Martin Heidegger and Medard Boss: dialogue between philosophy and psychotherapy. Oklahoma, 1974. 75-15265

4395. Marshall, John Paul. An existential encounter with experimentalism. Nebraska, 1975. 76-2037

4396. Marshall, Linda Edith. The garments of philosophy: a study of philosophical myth in the twelfth century. Toronto, 1974.

4397. Marshall, Margaret. The place of the faculty theory in educational psychology. Fordham, 1933.

4398. Marshall, Norman Arthur. Evidence, inference and perceptions. Oregon, 1970. 70-21571

4399. Marshall, Troward Harvey. A study of the origins of Hegel's philosophy of religion. Harvard, 1910.

4400. Martel, Jean-Paul. Le *Metalogicon* de Jean de Salisbury: structure rhétorique. Montreal, 1974.

4401. Martin, Bernard. The philosophical anthropology of Paul Tillich. Illinois, 1961. 61-1643

4402. Martin, Edwin Alexander, Jr. Quantifying into opaque contexts: may we or may we not? M.I.T., 1968.

4403. Martin, George Arthur. An interpretative principle for understanding Kierkegaard. Notre Dame, 1969. 69-18512

4404. Martin, Herbert. Cognition and the absolute, or, the possibility of knowing God. Yale, 1905.

4405. Martin, James August. Conceptual analysis and criterial change. Michigan, 1969. 69-18054

4406. Martin, Jerry Lee. Knowledge of other minds: some problems in the logic and epistemology of scepticism. Northwestern, 1970. 71-1910

4407. Martin, John Neil. Sortal presupposition: a study of category mistakes, their logic, and importance. Toronto, 1973.

4408. Martin, Joseph Ramsey, Jr. The causes and objects of emotions. Virginia, 1967. 67-17611

4409. Martin, Michael Lou. Psychoanalysis and scientific methodology. Harvard, 1962.

4410. Martin, Norman Marshall. Sheffer functions and axiom sets in m-valued logic. U.C.L.A., 1952.

4411. Martin, Raymond Frederick. Causation. Rochester, 1968. 68-9386

4412. Martin, Rex. Collingwood's critique of the concept of human nature. Columbia, 1967.

4413. Martin, Richard Milton. A homogeneous system for formal logic. Yale, 1941.

4414. Martin, Robert Lazarus. A semantic analysis of the liar paradox. Yale, 1965. 65-15077

4415. Martin, Robert M. Seeing: an argument that visual images are evidence for facts about the external world. Michigan, 1971. 72-14936

4416. Martin, Seymour Guy. Maimon's development of Kant with special reference to the aesthetic. Pennsylvania, 1910.

4417. Martin, Stuart B. The notion of error in Descartes' theory of the embodied self. Fordham, 1958.

4418. Martin, Vincent M. Nicholas of Cusa on God and the creature. Laval, 1948.

4419. Martin, William Oliver. On the nature of truth. Harvard, 1934.

4420. Martinez, Mthr. M. Louise. Recta ratio according to Saint Thomas Aquinas. St. Louis, 1950.

4421. Martinich, Aloysius Patrick. Reference and the axiom of existence: an essay in the philosophy of language. Cal., S. Diego, 1973. 73-19779

4422. Martire, Joseph Edmund. The logic of depiction and the logic of description: an analysis of "the picture theory" of the Tractatus and its criticisms in the Philosophical investigations. Georgetown, 1974. 74-21648

4423. Martos, Joseph. Bernard Lonergan's theory of transcendent knowledge. DePaul, 1973. 73-19068

4424. Marx, Werner. The meaning of Aristotle's "ontology." New School, 1953.

4425. Marzec, Michael Joseph. The nature of explanation in seventeenth-century science. Southern Cal., 1973. 74-932

4426. Masi, Evelyn Ann. Mill's method of moral inquiry. Radcliffe, 1956.

4427. Masiello, Ralph J. The intuition of being according to the metaphysics of St. Thomas Aquinas. Catholic U., 1955.

4428. Maslanka, John Stanley. The interrelationship of being and language in Heidegger's thought. Boston Coll., 1974. 75-13654

4429. Maslow, Alexander Parfeni. A study in Ludwig Wittgenstein's Tractatus lo philosophicus. Berkeley, 1934.

4430. Mason, Charles Wesley. The value-philosophy of Alfred Edward Taylor. N.Y.U., 1973. 73-19949

4431. Mason, David R. A study of time in the philosophies of Alfred North Whitehead and Martin Heidegger with implications for a doctrine of providence. Chicago, 1973.

4432. Mason, Ernest Douglas. Alain Locke's philosophy of value: an introduction. Emory, 1975. 76-1626

4433. Mason, Gabriel R. Spinoza and Schelling. N.Y.U., 1911. 73-20759

4434. Mason, Homer Eugene. The concept of a morally responsible person: a study of non-cognitivism in ethics. Harvard, 1957.

4435. Mason, Perry Carter. Ontic commitment and abstract entities in the philosophy of Wilfrid Sellars. Yale, 1968. 69-13359

4436. Massey, Gerald Jay. The philosophy of space. Princeton, 1964. 64-9460

4437. Massie, David Milton. A philosophical essay on the logic of terms. Columbia, 1971. 74-8200

4438. Mates, Benson. The logic of the Old Stoa. Berkeley, 1948.

4439. Mathers, Donald Murray. Historical knowledge in the philosophy of R.G. Collingwood. Columbia, 1953. 8729

4440. Mathers, Robert Leslie. The nature of logical necessity: an examination of a contemporary controversy. U.C.L.A., 1959.

4441. Mathers, Ruth Anna Hall. The interpretation of theoretical statements. U.C.L.A., 1961.

4442. Matheson, Gordon Ford. The concept of analyticity. Yale, 1954.

4443. Mathews, Bernard Reese, Jr. Hume's theory of sympathy. Johns Hopkins, 1968. 68-16444

4444. Mathews, Paul Luke. A study of the literary background and the methodology of Saint Thomas' Commentary on the Posterior analytics of Aristotle. St. Louis, 1958. 59-909

4445. Mathias, Thomas Rowley. Bonaventurian ways to God through reason. St. John's 1970. 70-25593

4446. Mathur, Dinesh Chandra. The significance of "qualitative thought" in Dewey's philosophy of art. Columbia, 1955. 15639

4447. Matilal, Bimal Krishna. The Navya nyāya doctrine of negation. Harvard, 1965.

4448. Matin, Abdul. The correspondence theory of truth and the Austin-Strawson debate. Toronto, 1969.

4449. Matross, Gerald N. T.H. Green and the concept of rights. Kansas, 1972. 73-11924

4450. Matsen, Herbert Stanley. Alessandro Achillini, 1463-1512, and his doctrine of "universals" and "transcendentals." Columbia, 1969. 70-17033

4451. Matson, Wallace Irving. De re publica. Berkeley, 1949.

4452. Mattea, James. The philosophical implications of Jean Piaget's theory of mental operations. Marquette, 1973. 73-27511

4453. Mattern, Charles David. Personal freedom within the third antinomy. Pennsylvania, 1940.

4454. Mattern, John Walter. The problem of a monistic ontology. Yale, 1959.

4455. Mattern, Ruth Marie. Locke on the essence of powers of soul. Princeton, 1975. 76-20781

4456. Matthews, Gareth Blanc. An interpretation and critique of the concept of the inner man in the epistemology of St. Augustine. Harvard, 1961.

4457. Matthews, Robert J. Interpretation and understanding: an essay in philosophical metacriticism. Cornell, 1974. 75-1442

4458. Mattingly, Rev. Basil M. De principiis naturae of St. Thomas Aquinas: a critical edition. Notre Dame, 1957. 22142

4459. Mattingly, Richard Edward. Direct realism: an account of the relation between experience and knowledge. Texas, 1971. 72-11379

4460. Mattingly, Susan Shotliff. Whitehead's theory of eternal objects. Texas, 1968. 69-6182

4461. Mattoon, Carolyn Orr. Kantian perspectives of the self. Yale, 1970. 70-25111

4462. Maue, James Brooks. Value and obligation: an integration of the theories of Ralph Barton Perry, C.I. Lewis, Dewitt Parker, and Charles L. Stevenson. Southern Cal., 1960. 60-5482

4463. Maurer, Armand Augustine Arthur. Ockham's interpretation and criticism of the formalism of Duns Scotus. Toronto, 1947.

4464. Mauzey, Jesse V. Montaigne's philosophy of human nature. Columbia, 1933.

4465. Mavrodes, George Ion. The concept of a direct experience of God. Michigan, 1961. 61-6394

4466. Maxwell, Douglas Vance. Substance and *a priori* knowledge: a Spinozan epistemology. Toronto, 1974.

4467. Maxwell, Peter J. Possibility as a principle in Leibniz's thought. Marquette, 1967. 68-492

4468. May, Joseph Austin. Kant's concept of geography and its relation to recent geographical thought. Toronto, 1968.

4469. May, William Eugene. The reality of matter in the philosophy of Henri Bergson. Marquette, 1968. 69-3321

4470. Mayberry, Thomas Calvin, Jr. An examination of typical criticisms of sense-datum theories. U. of Washington, 1960. 60-4291

4471. Maydole, Robert Edwin. Many-valued logic as a basis for set theory. Boston U., 1973. 73-14162

4472. Mayeaux, Anne Russell. A phenomenology of woman. Emory, 1975. 76-1627

4473. Mayeda, Sengaku. The Upadeśasāhasrī of Śankarācārya, critically edited with introduction. Pennsylvania, 1961. 61-3576

4474. Mayer, Fred. A critical examination of the metaphysical foundation of Schopenhauer's voluntarism. Southern Cal., 1944.

4475. Mayer de Berncastle, John Robert Andrew. The temporalistic implications of the Socinian doctrine of divine knowledge and some of its historical anticipations. Emory, 1961. 63-2233

4476. Mayeroff, Milton. John Dewey's concept of the unification of the self: an exposition and critique. Columbia, 1961. 61-3893

4477. Mayers, Eugene David. Some modern theories of natural law. Columbia, 1956. 20061

4478. Mayers, Ronald Burton. The problem, meaning and function of "transcendence" in a social ethic with particular reference to the social ethics of John Dewey and Reinhold Niebuhr. Syracuse, 1972. 72-20357

4479. Mayfield, Paul McCune. Knowledge and being in Plato's Republic. Johns Hopkins, 1975. 76-1526

4480. Mayfield, William Hollingsworth. Platonism and Christianity in the work of Paul Elmer More. Indiana, 1953. 6446

4481. Maynard, Sr. M. Francis. The structure of the human act according to Saint Thomas Aquinas. Marquette, 1941.

4482. Maynard, Patrick Lee. A study of depiction. Cornell, 1970. 71-13812

4483. Mayo, David James. "Art" and related concepts: a logical analysis. Pittsburgh, 1970. 70-17994

4484. Mayo, Stephan Thomas. Aftermath of the absolute: a study of contingency in the phenomenology of Maurice Merleau-Ponty. Fordham, 1974. 74-19675

4485. Mayo, Thomas Franklin. Epicurus in England (1650-1725.) Columbia, 1934.

4486. Mays, Morley. The attributes of Spinoza's treatment of God. Virginia, 1949.

4487. Meacham, William Paul. A phenomenological description of the self. Texas, 1971. 72-19630

4488. Mead, Edward H. The ideological foundations of medieval art. Southern Cal., 1936.

4489. Means, Blanchard William. The problem of a scale in value. Yale, 1932.

4490. Measell, James Scott. Development of the concept of analogy in philosophy, logic, and rhetoric to 1850. Illinois, 1970. 71-14867

4491. Mechanic, Janevive Nadler. Cournot's probabilism.
Columbia, 1959.   59-2865

4492. Meckler, Lester. The sign-analysis of meaning and
language. U.C.L.A., 1951.

4493. Meehan, Rev. Francis X. Efficient causality in Aristotle and in St. Thomas. Catholic U., 1940.

4494. Meerbote, Ralf Herbert. Kant's transcendental skepticism. Harvard, 1970.

4495. Megill, Kenneth Alden. The community as a democratic principle in Marx's philosophy. Yale, 1966.
66-13909

4496. Mei, Tsu-Lin. Towards a foundation for a logic of
grammars. Yale, 1962.   69-16879

4497. Mei, Yi-Pao. The ethical and political philosophy
of Motse. Chicago, 1927.

4498. Meier, Carl Wagner. Kant's second analogy: a reconstruction. Duke, 1972.   72-23242

4499. Meier, Frederick William. A translation of Erwin
Panofsky's Idea, with a critical introduction.
Duke, 1933.

4500. Meier, Klaus Volker. Authenticity and sport: a conceptual analysis. Illinois, 1975.   76-6870

4501. Meier, Menachem. A critical edition of the Sefer ta
amey ha-mizwoth (Book of reasons of the commandments) attributed to Isaac Ibn Farhi, Section I-
Positive commandments; with introduction and
notes. Brandeis, 1974.   74-28002

4502. Meiklejohn, Donald Waldron. The relation between
ethical and intellectual judgments in the philosophy of John Dewey. Harvard, 1936.

4503. Meilach, Michael David. Religious encounter and the
philosophy of organism: suggestions for a Whiteheadian ontology. Fordham, 1971.   71-20182

4504. Meiland, Jack W. Studies in the explanation of action. Chicago, 1962.

4505. Meisler, Richard Allen. Evolution: a theory system.
Columbia, 1966.   66-8526

4506. Melber, Jehuda. Hermann Cohen's philosophy of Judaism. Yeshiva, 1968.   68-5576

4507. Melchert, Norman Paul. An examination of the physical realism of Roy Wood Sellars. Pennsylvania, 1964. 64-10406

4508. Melden, Abraham Irving. Belief and the analysis of propositions. Berkeley, 1938.

4509. Melekian, Yervant Elia. The doctrine of the superman in the philosophy of Nietzsche. Iowa, 1915.

4510. Mellema, Gregory Frank. Multiple quantifiers and restricted range in epistemic logic. Massachusetts, 1974. 75-6057

4511. Mellican, Robert Eugene. History, society, and the person: the thought of Don Luigi Sturzo. Loyola, 1971. 71-28133

4512. Mellick, David Chester. The metaphysics of behavior. Ohio St., 1973. 74-3257

4513. Mellor, Stanley Alfred. Individualism in German thought, with special reference to Nietzsche and Schopenhauer. Harvard, 1909.

4514. Melnick, Arthur. Self-consciousness in the philosophy of Kant. Chicago, 1970.

4515. Melrose, James A. A genetic view of consciousness. Wisconsin, 1929.

4516. Melvin, Margaret Georgiana. The abstract idea in English empiricism. Bryn Mawr, 1921.

4517. Melzer, John H. An examination of critical monism. Vanderbilt, 1937.

4518. Melzer, Yehuda. Analysis of the concept of just war. Columbia, 1973. 76-15546

4519. Mendenhall, Vance. Les foyers de la reflexion: une introduction a l'étude de la méthode Nabertienne. Ottawa, 1975.

4520. Menges, Matthew C. The concept of univocity regarding the predication of God and creature according to William Ockham. St. Bonaventure, 1952.

4521. Menkiti, Ifeanyi Anthony. Collective responsibility. Harvard, 1974.

4522. Menza, Victor George. Poetry and the techne theory: an analysis of the Ion and the Republic, Bks. III and X. Johns Hopkins, 1972. 73-12159

4523. Menzel, Paul Theodore. The role of ideals in determining moral obligations. Vanderbilt, 1971.
71-29314

4524. Merrill, Daniel Davy. The theory of logical constants. Minnesota, 1962. 62-3093

4525. Merrill, Gary Howard. A semantically closed theory of truth. Rochester, 1974. 74-14408

4526. Merrill, Kenneth Rogers. Whitehead's theory of givenness. Northwestern, 1963. 64-2506

4527. Merrington, Ernest Northcroft. The metaphysical problem of personality: a critical and constructive study in the light of recent thought. Harvard, 1905.

4528. Messenger, Theodore Ives, Jr. On formulating theories of universals. Johns Hopkins, 1962.

4529. Mester, Richard Arnold. The concrete embodiment of thirdness in the philosophy of Charles S. Peirce. Penn St., 1971. 72-19351

4530. Mesthene, Emmannuel George. Some views about the nature of intelligibility. Columbia, 1963.
64-11306

4531. Metrick, Dennis Lawrence. The problem of being in Royce. Penn St., 1968. 69-9790

4532. Metzel, Nancy Lou Davis. "Lived space": a critical introduction to Eugene Minkowski's "Lived time." Northwestern, 1973. 73-30664

4533. Metzgar, John Newton, Jr. Marxist philosophy in Lucien Goldmann. Northwestern, 1975. 75-29708

4534. Metzger, Kenneth Hughes. An analysis of the leading conceptual confusions in George Berkeley's *An essay towards a new theory of vision*. Nebraska, 1968. 68-18026

4535. Metzger, Robert S. John Locke: a reappraisal of some critical points in his philosophy. Columbia, 1958. 58-2700

4536. Meyer, Charles Richard. Entrenchment and comparative projectability: prospects for inductive logic. Washington U., 1973. 73-24895

4537. Meyer, Herbert Heinrich. A critical study of Max Scheler's philosophical anthropology in its relation to his phenomenology. Boston U., 1972.
72-25308

4538. Meyer, Leroy Nelson. Ontological commitment, quantification, and ontology. Virginia, 1975.
76-29

4539. Meyer, Marilyn. Ralph Cudworth's philosophical system. Columbia, 1952. 3688

4540. Meyer, Robert Kenneth. Topics in modal and many-valued logics. Pittsburgh, 1966. 66-13878

4541. Meyerhoff, Hans. Types of ethical premises. U.C.L.A., 1942.

4542. Meyers, Douglas Edmond. Hobbes's concept of obligation. Berkeley, 1973.

4543. Meyers, Robert George. Belief and truth in Charles Peirce. Buffalo, 1966. 66-7981

4544. Meyn, Henning Ludwig. Husserl's transcendental logic and the problem of its justification. Brown, 1971. 72-8156

4545. Mezes, Sidney Edward. Pleasure and pain defined. Harvard, 1893.

4546. Mezz, Gilbert S. A thread from alienation to the absurd. Arizona St., 1974. 75-494

4547. Mfoulou, Jean. Ideology and nation building: the Tanzanian case. Boston U., 1974. 74-14219

4548. Micallef, Paul. The morality of legalized abortion. Laval, 1972.

4549. Miceli, Rev. Vincent Peter. The life of communion and community in the philosophy of Gabriel Marcel. Fordham, 1961. 62-1034

4550. Michael, Emily Poe. The early logic of C.S. Peirce. Pennsylvania, 1973. 73-24194

4551. Michael, Frederick Seymour. Meaning in metaphors: an essay in semantic analysis. Pennsylvania, 1973. 73-24195

4552. Michael, Sally Jean. An examination of the role of natural belief in David Hume's philosophy of religion. Harvard, 1968.

4553. Michalos, Alexandros Charles. Probability and degree of confirmation: a study of the disagreement between Karl Popper and Rudolf Carnap from 1934 to 1964. Chicago, 1965.

4554. Michel, Virgil. The critical principle of Orestes A. Brownson. Catholic U., 1918.

4555. Michelsen, John Magnus. Santayana's theory of symbolic knowledge. U. of Washington, 1970.
71-1002

4556. Michener, Norah Evangeline. The integral humanism of Jacques Maritain as related to his philosophy of the person. Toronto, 1953.

4557. Mickunas, Algis. Human action and its ontological context: the correlation of subjective activity and the activity of things. Emory, 1969.
69-19612

4558. Midy, Godefroy. Ralph Waldo Emerson's philosophy of the person. Fordham, 1971. 71-26981

4559. Miedzianogora, Myriam. Gilbert Ryle and Jean-Paul Sartre: a comparative study of two theories of mind. Columbia, 1965. 65-13975

4560. Miel, Jan. Pascal as theologian, an interpretation based on the Écrits sur la grace. Princeton, 1965.

4561. Mihalich, Joseph C. The notion of value in the existentialism of Jean-Paul Sartre. Georgetown, 1965. 65-6992

4562. Mijuskovic, Ben Lazare. The simplicity, unity, and identity of thought and soul from the Cambridge Platonists to Kant: a study in the history of an argument. Cal., S. Diego, 1972. 72-33081

4563. Mikula, Donald Max. The concept of the moral self in Dewey's ethical theory. So. Illinois, 1967.
67-15865

4564. Milburn, Myra Ellen Moss. Benedetto Croce's two theories of truth: a critical discussion and evaluation. Johns Hopkins, 1966. 66-5230

4565. Millard, Richard Marion, Jr. The place of value in Whitehead's thought. Boston U., 1950.

4566. Millen, Herbert. Bahya Ben Asher: the exegetical and ethical components of his writings. Yeshiva, 1974. 74-23552

4567. Miller, Arthur Ronald. Intentions and consequences: toward a theory of act-description. Michigan St., 1975. 76-5606

4568. Miller, Bruce Lee. Principles, rules and cases: the logic of judicial decisions. Case, 1970.
7C-25893

4569. Miller, Clyde Lee. A commentary on Plato's Protagoras. Yale, 1974. 75-1385

4570. Miller, David. Emergent evolution and the scientific method. Chicago, 1932.

4571. Miller, David Lee. Value and some key but unfinished doctrines in Whitehead's philosophy. So. Illinois, 1969. 70-7303

4572. Miller, Douglas James. The justifiability cf civil violence: the moral dialectic and depiction of violent resistance in a democracy. Claremont, 1972. 72-30576

4573. Miller, Eddie Le Roy. A critical analysis cf the philosophical fragments of Epicharmus. Southern Cal., 1965. 68-5871

4574. Miller, Edward Leonard. An essay on agency and rights. Rochester, 1972. 72-28777

4575. Miller, Fred Dycus. Aristotle's account of being and truth. U. of Washington, 1971. 71-28449

4576. Miller, George William, Jr. The development of empirical realism. Texas, 1962. 62-4856

4577. Miller, Harlan Bingham. Machinery and intelligence. Virginia, 1965. 66-3199

4578. Miller, Hugh. The psychology of arithmetic. Harvard, 1927.

4579. Miller, Irving. Significance of the mathematical element in the philosophy of Plato. Chicago, 1904.

4580. Miller, James Edwin, III. From Marx to Sartre. Brandeis, 1975. 75-24825

4581. Miller, James Robert, Jr. Sense and transcendence: a study in Johann Georg Hamann's philosophy of language. Tulane, 1967. 67-17933

4582. Miller, James V. An inquiry into Plato's treatment of wealth. Boston U., 1955.

4583. Miller, James Wilkinson. Critical realism. Harvard, 1927.

4584. Miller, Jerome Aloysius. The irrefutability of metaphysical truths. Georgetown, 1973. 74-14441

4585. Miller, John Franklin, III. Meaning, verification, and religious knowledge. N.Y.U., 1969.
70-27256

4586. Miller, John William. The definition of the thing. Harvard, 1922.

4587. Miller, Keith Bruce. The relation of moral ideology to dynamic moral philosophy. Southern Cal., 1963.
64-1070

4588. Miller, Larry. Finitary proofs. Chicago, 1970.

4589. Miller, Leonard Gordon. Some problems concerning the justification of moral rules. Cornell, 1954.

4590. Miller, Mary Boat. The logic of indeterminacy in quantum mechanics. Brown, 1961. 63-1449

4591. Miller, Mitchell Hooper, Jr. Irony, mediation, and philosophical statesmanship: a study of Plato's Statesman. Buffalo, 1972. 73-5148

4592. Miller, O.W. The Kantian thing-in-itself; or, the creative mind. Cincinnati, 1926.

4593. Miller, Paul John William. The concept of existence in the thirteenth-century philosophy. Harvard, 1951.

4594. Miller, Richard Warner. Charles S. Peirce's theory of probability. Illinois, 1970. 70-21018

4595. Miller, Richard William. Solipsism and language in the writings of Wittgenstein. Harvard, 1975.

4596. Miller, Robert Grace. The notion of the agent intellect in Saint Albert the Great. Toronto, 1938.

4597. Miller, Robert John. The problem of substantial form in the early writings of St. Thomas Aquinas. Toronto, 1955.

4598. Miller, Veronica Ann. The paradox of the reformed subjectivist principle in Whitehead's philosophy. Tulane, 1970. 70-24538

4599. Miller, Wesley Carrol. Education and the emerging Humanist movement. Ohio St., 1971. 72-4581

4600. Miller, Willard Marshall. C.S. Peirce on the philosophy of history. Illinois, 1969. 70-13424

4601. Miller, William Arthur. Kant's realisms. Ohio St., 1972. 73-11542

4602. Miller, William Peter. Metaphysical pluralism and some implications for a theory of space and time. Yale, 1967. 68-5187

4603. Millikan, James Dean. Heidegger, time, and self-transcendence. Yale, 1966. 66-13912

4604. Millikan, Ruth Garrett. Empirical identity. Yale, 1969. 70-2770

4605. Millman, Arthur Behr. Foundations for a rationale of scientific development. Chicago, 1974.

4606. Milmed, Bella Kussy. Kant's theory of knowledge and current philosophical issues. N.Y.U., 1959. 74-12899

4607. Milne, Gretchen Elizabeth. Søren Kierkegaard: philosophy by indirection. Texas, 1964. 64-11819

4608. Milo, Ronald Dmitri. Aristotle on practical knowledge and weakness of will. U. of Washington, 1962. 63-3129

4609. Min, Anselm Kyongsuk. The speculative foundation of religion: a study in Hegel's transcendental metaphysics. Fordham, 1974. 74-25070

4610. Minahan, John Patrick, Jr. The metaphysical misunderstanding of Wittgenstein's *Tractatus*. Georgetown, 1970. 70-21287

4611. Minas, James Sayer. On the construction of propositional calculi. Illinois, 1963. 64-550

4612. Minh, Rev. Nguyen-Duc. Natural philosophy and Einstein's concept of space. St. John's, 1968. 68-4121

4613. Mink, Louis Otto, Jr. Knowledge of the past. Yale, 1952.

4614. Minner, Charles Ben. The concept of value in nineteenth-century naturalism. Harvard, 1930.

4615. Minnich, John W. The antagonism between the intuitive and discursive in Schopenhauer. Claremont, 1974. 75-12748

4616. Minogue, Brendan Patrick. Cartesian optics: a test case for the partial interpretationist's account of models. Ohio St., 1974. 75-3146

4617. Mins, Henry F., Jr. Materialism, the scientific bias. Columbia, 1935.

4618. Minton, Arthur Jerry. J.L. Austin's theory of speech acts. Cincinnati, 1972. 72-31740

4619. Miracchi, Silvano. Russell: negative facts and ontology. Iowa, 1972. 72-17586

4620. Miron, Rev. Cyril Harry. The problem of altruism in the philosophy of Saint Thomas. Catholic U., 1939.

4621. Mischel, Theodore. R.G. Collingwood's philosophy of art. Columbia, 1958. 58-2701

4622. Mish 'Alani, James Karam. Objects, names and variables: an investigation in the theory of designation. Brown, 1961. 63-1450

4623. Mishkin, Paul Alan. The equation of knowledge with certainty. Boston Coll., 1974. 74-18260

4624. Mishra, Krushna Prasad. Principle in contemporary moral philosophy; an enquiry into the concept of principle in the moral philosophy of R.M. Hare, K. Baier, and M.G. Singer. Toronto, 1967.

4625. Missett, James R. Man as other-directed: speech and sexuality. St. John's, 1973. 73-29969

4626. Missner, Marshall. Chomsky's concept of implicit knowledge. Chicago, 1970.

4627. Mitchell, Arthur. Freedom and intuition in Henri Bergson's philosophy. Harvard, 1910.

4628. Mitchell, Donald William. Rudolf Otto and a philosophy of religious crisis. Hawaii, 1972.

4629. Mitchell, Thomas. Modern theories of the nature and function of ideals. Chicago, 1922.

4630. Mitchell, William H., Jr. The implicit prospective dimension of the symbol in the early works of Freud, 1893-1900. Duquesne, 1973. 74-5841

4631. Mitias, Michael Hanna. A critique of ethical theory from a Whiteheadian standpoint. Waterloo, 1971.

4632. Mitros, Rev. Joseph. The philosophy of religion of Edgar Sheffield Brightman. Fordham, 1955.

4633. Miyuki, Mokusen. An analysis of Buddhist influence on the formation of the Sung Confucian concept of Li-Ch'i. Claremont, 1964. 66-3378

4634. Mize, Johnny Melvyn. The influence of Kant's moral argument on three British personal idealists: A.S. Pringle-Pattison, W.R. Sorley, C.C.J. Webb. Southern Cal., 1973. 73-31657

4635. Modrak, Deborah Karen. The perception interpretation of the Aristotelian practical syllogism. Chicago, 1974.

4636. Moennig, Hans Dressel. Studies in the philosophy of Franz Brentano. Iowa, 1966. 67-16822

4637. Moga, Michael David. Intersubjectivity: a Heideggerian reflection. Tulane, 1970. 70-24540

4638. Mohan, Pandiri Krishna. Gandhi's idea of non-violence. So. Illinois, 1972. 72-24365

4639. Mohan, Rev. Robert P. A Thomistic philosophy of civilization and culture. Catholic U., 1948.

4640. Mohr, Rev. John Patrick. Self-referential language and the existence of God in the philosophy of Hegel. Georgetown, 1974. 74-26433

4641. Molina, Fernando Romero. Whitehead's realism in relation to the problem of perception. Yale, 1959. 67-3736

4642. Moline, Jon Nelson. Ethical justification and knowledge. Duke, 1964. 64-11742

4643. Momeyer, Richard Warren. Pleasure and sensation. U. of Washington, 1970. 71-1005

4644. Monagle, John Francis. Friendship in Aristotle and St. Thomas Aquinas: its relation to the common good. St. Louis, 1973. 74-4553

4645. Monahan, Arthur Patrick. The doctrine of being in Peter of Auvergne's Quaestiones in metaphysicam. Toronto, 1953.

4646. Monahan, Edward Joseph. The doctrine of human liberty and free will in John Buridan's Quaestiones super decem libros Ethicorum Aristotelis ad Nicomachum. Toronto, 1953.

4647. Monast, Joseph Horace, III. Evidence, common sense, and metaphysical systems: the philosophical methodology of Stephen C. Pepper. Tulane, 1975. 75-23289

4648. Mondadori, Fabrizio Giulio. Modal semantics and determinate names. Harvard, 1972.

4649. Moneta, Giuseppina Chiara. The identity of the logical proposition: a study in genetic phenomenology. New School, 1969. 70-7657

4650. Monfort, Kirk Harry. Quine's argument for indeterminacy of translation. Stanford, 1973. 74-6516

4651. Monk, Robert Andrew. The objectivity of scientific observation. Cornell, 1973. 74-10884

4652. Monroe, D.S. Warner. The vital impulse as a basis for mortality: a critical development of Bergson's position. U. of Washington, 1947.

4653. Monsma, Peter H. Karl Barth's idea of revelation. Columbia, 1937.

4654. Monson, Charles Horold, Jr. Common good in the political philosophy of Locke, Green, and Perry. Cornell, 1952.

4655. Montague, Rev. Michael Joseph. Secondary causality in the act of will-to-end in the writings of Saint Thomas Aquinas. St. Louis, 1953.

4656. Montague, Phillip Thomas. Evaluative reasoning and its relation to inductive reasoning. Stanford, 1966. 67-4409

4657. Montague, Richard Merritt. Contributions to the axiomatic foundations of set theory. Berkeley, 1957.

4658. Montague, William Pepperell, Jr. An introduction to the ontological implicates of practical reason. Harvard, 1898.

4659. Montgomery, George Redington. The distinctions between theology and philosophy. Yale, 1901.

4660. Montgomery, Martha Barber. The place of ethical disagreement in ethical theory: emotivism versus the genetic tradition of Baldwin, Piaget and Kohlberg. Pennsylvania, 1971. 72-17399

4661. Montgomery, Sharon Burke. Value statements and corrigibility. Pennsylvania, 1972. 73-13441

4662. Montgomery, William R.Hammond. A critical study of Alfred North Whitehead's philosophy of education in the light of its historical, biographical, and metaphysical backgrounds. Toronto, 1960.

4663. Monticone, George Thomas. Linguistic critique of religion. Calgary, 1974.

4664. Moody, Ernest Addison. The logic of William of Ockham. Columbia, 1935.

4665. Moody, Harry Richardson, Jr. Participation and perfection in Meister Eckhart's doctrine of man. Columbia, 1973.   73-28489

4666. Moody, Raymond Avery, Jr. The meaning of proper names. Virginia, 1969.   70-4817

4667. Mooney, Edward Fiske. Gesture, commitment, and vision: generative roots of human being. Cal., S. Barbara, 1969.

4668. Moor, Donald Robert. The "use" theory of meaning. Oregon, 1975.   76-15048

4669. Moor, Gulliume. Ontological realism: a critique of Gustav Bergmann. Northwestern, 1971.   71-30898

4670. Moor, James Haller. Computer consciousness. Indiana, 1972.   73-6504

4671. Moore, Addison W. Functional versus the representational theories of knowledge in Locke's essay. Chicago, 1898.

4672. Moore, Asher Martin. The relation of sense-data to physical objects: the nature of the problem in the light of the theory of logical constructs. Harvard, 1948.

4673. Moore, Brooke Noel. Anti-phenomenalist theses in Strawson's argument for the basicness of material bodies. Cincinnati, 1973.   73-24847

4674. Moore, Charles Alexander. Moral obligation and its metaphysical foundation. Yale, 1932.

4675. Moore, Edward Carter. Metaphysics and pragmatism in the philosophy of C.S. Peirce. Michigan, 1950.
     1939

4676. Moore, Harold Francis. Instrumentalism and the assessment of social importance. Fordham, 1971.
     71-20183

4677. Moore, Jared Sparks. The metaphysical problem of relation considered as a category in a system of synthetic transcendentalism. Harvard, 1905.

4678. Moore, John Bruce. On retributive justifications of punishment. Harvard, 1965.

4679. Moore, John Clayton. An investigation of selected American-Negro philosophies of art: a basis for formulating Negro literary aesthetic thought within the American aesthetic syndrome. Syracuse, 1970.   71-10952

4680. Moore, John Morrison. Theories of religious experience; with special reference to James, Otto and Bergson. Columbia, 1938.

4681. Moore, John Thomas. Locke's concept of faith. Kansas, 1970.   71-13341

4682. Moore, Mark Anthony. Can a theory of ethical intuitionism be defended? Tennessee, 1973. 73-20023

4683. Moore, Rev. Philip. The works of Peter of Poitiers. Catholic U., 1936.

4684. Moore, Robert Edward. Spencer's naturalistic theory of ethics. Pennsylvania, 1969.   70-7836

4685. Moore, Ronald Melville. A critical study of Kelsen's theory of legal norms. Columbia, 1971.
     74-12743

4686. Moore, Stanley Williams. The metaphysical theory of the state in Hobbes, Rousseau, and Hegel. Berkeley, 1941.

4687. Moore, Theodore McGinnes. The background of Edmund Burke's theory of the sublime. Cornell, 1933.

4688. Moore, V.F. The ethical aspects of Lotze's metaphysics. Cornell, 1900.

4689. Moore, Willis. Meaning and language. Berkeley, 1937.

4690. Morais, Herbert M. Deism in eighteenth century America. Columbia, 1934.

4691. Moran, James Anthony. Martin Buber's _I and thou_: an interpretive study. Fordham, 1971.   71-20184

4692. Moran, John Henry. Ludwig Wittgenstein's philosophical therapy. Fordham, 1962.   63-213

4693. Moran, Jon Stephen. Religious selfhood in the philosophies of Josiah Royce and G.H. Mead. Tulane, 1972.   72-24417

4694. Moran, Lawrence P. Permanence and process; a philosophical investigation into the foundations of the law of energy conservation. Catholic U., 1951.

4695. Moran, Vincent Jerome. The relation of Brownson to the philosophy of Kant. Toronto, 1954.

4696. Morano, Donald Victor. A phenomenology of guilt. Northwestern, 1968. 69-1897

4697. Moravcsik, Julius Matthew Emil, Jr. Meaning and being in the Sophist and the Parmenides. Harvard, 1959.

4698. Morawetz, Bruno. The epistemology of John Norris. Toronto, 1963. 64-7120

4699. Morawetz, Thomas Hubert. The nature of moral reasoning and its relationship to law. Yale, 1969. 70-16310

4700. Morden, Michael James. Paying attention as a mental action. Columbia, 1972. 73-9036

4701. Moreland, John M. Projectibility and randomness. Claremont, 1973. 73-22781

4702. Moreland, Marc Marion. Development of the concept of individualism with reference to the work of Roger Williams. Toronto, 1937.

4703. Morelli, Mario Frank. Fairness and political obligation. Washington U., 1971. 72-9359

4704. Morency, Robert. L'action selon Jean de St.-Thomas. Laval, 1945.

4705. Morewedge, Parviz. A study in Ibn Sina and sulfism. U.C.L.A., 1969. 70-14308

4706. Morgan, Charles Grady. Explanation and the evaluation of hypotheses: formal language accounts. Johns Hopkins, 1970. 70-26705

4707. Morgan, Douglas N. Photography and philosophy: an essay on the esthetics of a new art medium. Michigan, 1948. 1065

4708. Morgan, George Allen, Jr. The philosophy of Wilhelm Dilthey. Harvard, 1930.

4709. Morgan, John Daniel. Towards a metaphysics of value: a critical study of the axiological implications of the metaphysics of Saint Thomas Aquinas. Southern Cal., 1966. 67-415

4710. Morgan, Kathryn Pauly. Merleau-Ponty's critique of Descartes: an evaluation. Johns Hopkins, 1973. 74-10435

4711. Morgan, Morris Jonathan. Macintosh's criticism of personalism. Boston U., 1945.

4712. Morgan, William Sacheus. Causation: a treatise of the general problem together with a detailed exposition and criticism of Kant's theory. Yale, 1895.

4713. Morgareidge, Clayton Clarke. The nature, function, and acquisition of concepts. Duke, 1965. 66-1379

4714. Morgenbesser, Sidney. Theories and schemata in the social sciences. Pennsylvania, 1956. 57-4850

4715. Morick, Harold. Wittgenstein's attack on the privileged access view of thoughts and feelings. Columbia, 1966. 69-15575

4716. Morick, Sandra Harding. On Quine and the foundations of knowledge. N.Y.U., 1973. 74-16849

4717. Morillo, Carolyn R. Santayana's presupposition theory of knowledge: a critical examination in the light of some contemporary analyses. Michigan, 1965. 66-5101

4718. Morison, Paul G. An introduction to the general empirical method. Chicago, 1954.

4719. Morkovsky, Sr. Theresa Clare. Freedom in Henri Bergson's metaphysics. St. Louis, 1966. 67-2960

4720. Morlan, George. America's heritage from John Stuart Mill. Columbia, 1936.

4721. Morris, Bertram. An analysis of the aesthetic experience and of the aesthetic judgment as reflecing upon a general theory of values. Cornell, 1934.

4722. Morris, Charles William, Jr. Symbolism and reality: a study in the nature of the mind. Chicago, 1925.

4723. Morris, Daniel Joseph. The *Liberum arbitrium* according to St. Thomas Aquinas. Toronto, 1936.

4724. Morris, Frank Edward. The problem of externality with special reference to the philosophy of Bernard Bosanquet. Yale, 1916.

4725. Morris, Henry David. Standards for reinterpretation. Pennsylvania, 1974. 75-2763

4726. Morris, John Martin. Types of certainty in the foundations of the sciences in the philosophy of René Descartes. Michigan St., 1968. 69-5919

4727. Morris, Phyllis Ada Sutton. Sartre's concept of a person. Michigan, 1969. 69-18064

4728. Morrison, James Carlton. Meaning and truth in Wittgenstein's *Tractatus*. Penn St., 1964. 64-13414

4729. Morrison, John Joseph. A definition of mathematics. Notre Dame, 1951. 5274

4730. Morrison, Mabel Margaret. The idealistic theory of relations. Toronto, 1928.

4731. Morrison, Ronald Philip. Man and the world: Heidegger and his interpretation of Kant. Emory, 1975. 76-1629

4732. Morrison, Roy Dennis, II. Ontology and naturalism in the philosophies of John Herman Randall, Jr., and Paul Tillich. Chicago, 1972.

4733. Morriston, Barbara Wine. Husserl on other minds. Northwestern, 1974. 74-28694

4734. Morriston, Charles Wesley. Phenomenology and the problem of the external world. Northwestern, 1972. 73-10261

4735. Morrow, Frank Aaron, Jr. Pragmatic paradoxes. Michigan, 1964. 64-12651

4736. Morse, James K. Jedidiah Morse, a champion of New England orthodoxy. Columbia, 1939.

4737. Morse, Warner Alden, Jr. Legal insanity. Chicago, 1972.

4738. Morsink, Johannes. Science and dialectic in Aristotle: a philosophical study of the *Generation of animals*. Wisconsin, 1975. 75-8225

4739. Morton, Bruce Newcomb. Some problems in the philosophy of music. Rochester, 1972. 72-18828

4740. Morton, Edmund William. The doctrine of *ens commune* in St. Thomas Aquinas. Toronto, 1954.

4741. Morton, John Adam. Adam's thesis. Princeton, 1972. 72-24690

4742. Morton, John Duncan. An analytical examination of the classical problem of acrasia. Toronto, 1973.

4743. Morton, Joseph. The development of Plato's theory of sense perception. Johns Hopkins, 1968.
68-16451

4744. Mosedale, Frederick Edward. Instrumentalism, words, and philosophical explanations of language. Oregon, 1974.
74-26552

4745. Moser, Shia. The concept of ethical relativism. Buffalo, 1958.
58-1948

4746. Mosher, David Lewis. The concept of truth in St. Augustine's theory of knowledge. Texas, 1965.
65-8076

4747. Moskoff, Eugene Alexander. The Russian philosopher Chaadayev, his ideas and his epoch. Columbia, 1937.

4748. Mosley, Albert Gene. Perspectives on the Kuhn-Popper debate: new directions in epistemology. Wisconsin, 1975.
75-18609

4749. Mosmann, Charles John, Jr. Common sense and its use in philosophy. Columbia, 1954.
8739

4750. Mossner, Ernest Campbell. Bishop Butler and the age of reason. Columbia, 1936.

4751. Mothershead, John Leland. On the possibility of an objective moral standard. Harvard, 1938.

4752. Mothersill, Mary. Lewis and Stevenson: a critical comparison of two theories of value. Radcliffe, 1954.

4753. Motoda, Joseph Sakanoshin. Confucianism. Pennsylvania, 1895.

4754. Motora, Yuzero. Exchange, considered as the principle of social life. Johns Hopkins, 1888.

4755. Mott, Thomas Hezekiah, Jr. Ethical theory and non-naturalism. Yale, 1956.

4756. Moulton, Eben Sears. An analysis of John Rawls' A theory of justice. Vanderbilt, 1974.
74-22185

4757. Moulton, Janice Marie. Are causal contexts referentially opaque. Chicago, 1972.

4758. Moulton, John Russell. The logic of interpretation. Berkeley, 1966.
66-3661

4759. Mourant, John Arthur. The physiocratic conception of natural law. Chicago, 1940.

4760. Mourelatos, Alexander Phoebus Dionysius. The philosophy of Parmenides. Yale, 1964. 65-1977

4761. Moutafakis, Nicholas James. A logic of imperatives. N.Y.U., 1969. 70-7409

4762. Mouton, David L. Some problems in the philosophical analysis of thinking. Chicago, 1964.

4763. Mouw, Richard S. The identification of behavior and the problem of other minds. Chicago, 1971.

4764. Mowry, David Newell. Factual memory: an analysis of its meaning and logic. Boston U., 1974. 74-14220

4765. Mucklow, Neale Harmon. The Cartesian circle. Cornell, 1963.

4766. Mudge, Evlyn Leigh. Sense-feeling complexes conditioning the God-experience. Iowa, 1916.

4767. Muehlmann, Robert George. Prichard's philosophy of perception. Iowa, 1968. 69-8780

4768. Mueller, Ian Bisset. The relationship of the generalized continuum hypothesis and the axiom of choice to the Von Neumann-Bernays-Godel axioms for set theory. Harvard, 1964.

4769. Mueller, Iris Wessel. Mill and French thought, being a study of the influence of French thought on the development of John Stuart Mill's political and social philosophy. Illinois, 1954. 10526

4770. Mueller, Robert William. A critical examination of Martin Buber's criticisms of Søren Kierkegaard. Purdue, 1974. 74-26754

4771. Mugerauer, Robert William, Jr. The autonomy of literature: toward the reconciliation of the intrinsic and extrinsic dimensions with special reference to the works of Northrop Frye and Yvor Winters. Texas, 1973. 74-5295

4772. Muir, David George. Plato's aesthetics, his positive theory of the arts. Syracuse, 1971. 72-6608

4773. Muir, John Wallace. A critical study of the ethics of P.H. Nowell-Smith. Georgia, 1970. 71-13098

4774. Mulder, Robert Frederick. The concept of miracles. Brown, 1971. 72-8178

4775. Mulhern, John Joseph. Problems of the theory of predication in Plato's *Parmenides*, *Theaetetus* and *Sophista*. Buffalo, 1970.   71-6096

4776. Mulhern, Mary Margaret. Aristotle's theory of predication: the *Categoriae* account. Buffalo, 1970.   71-15039

4777. Mullahy, Bernard I. Thomism and mathematical physics. Laval, 1947.

4778. Mullally, Joseph P. The *Summulae logicales* of Peter of Spain. Columbia, 1945.

4779. Mullane, Donald Thomas. Aristotelianism in St. Thomas. Catholic U., 1929.

4780. Mullane, Harvey Paul. An examination of Freud's metapsychology. Cincinnati, 1964.   64-11974

4781. Mullaney, James V. The natural terrestial end of man. Fordham, 1954.

4782. Mullatti, Laxman Channappa. The Navya-Nyaya theory of inference. British Columbia, 1972.

4783. Mullen, John Douglas. The explication of the concept of individual preference. Boston U., 1972.   72-25312

4784. Mullen, Sr. Mary Dominica. Essence and operation in Thomistic and in modern philosophy. Catholic U., 1941.

4785. Mullen, Wilbur H. A comparison of the value theories of E.S. Brightman and A.N. Whitehead. Boston U., 1955.

4786. Muller-Thym, Bernard Joseph. The establishment of the university of being in the doctrine of Meister Eckhart of Hochheim. Toronto, 1938.

4787. Mullett, Sheila Ann Mason. A critical analysis of the claim that some judgments of psychotherapy are moral judgments. Purdue, 1972.   72-31233

4788. Mullin, Richard Patrick, Jr. The place of metaphysics in the moral universe of William James. Duquesne, 1973.   74-13190

4789. Mullins, Warren James. The political philosophy of David Hume. Berkeley, 1958.

4790. Mulvaney, Robert Joseph. The development of Leibniz's concept of justice. Emory, 1965.   65-11508

4791. Mulvihill, Josephine Folk. The American new realist concept of substance with special reference to the substantiality of the self or ego. St. Louis, 1932. 170

4792. Munday, Daniel Peter. Godfrey of Fontaine's theory of knowledge. Toronto, 1938.

4793. Mundy, Judith Curry. The law of the conditioned restudied. Virginia, 1970. 70-26592

4794. Munevar, Gonzalo. Radical knowledge: an essay on the nature of scientific understanding. Berkeley, 1975.

4795. Munitz, Lenore Bloom. A prologue to a theory of value. Bryn Mawr, 1948. 1293

4796. Munitz, Milton K. The moral philosophy of Santayana. Columbia, 1939.

4797. Munk, Arthur William Philip. Roy Wood Sellars' criticisms of idealism. Boston U., 1945.

4798. Muñoz-Colberg, Magda. An evaluation of Auguste Comte's theory of inequality. Georgetown, 1965. 65-4121

4799. Munsat, Stanley Morris. The concept of memory. Michigan, 1965. 66-14561

4800. Munson, James Ronald. The science of science: a critical examination of John Stuart Mill's philosophy of science. Columbia, 1967. 67-14070

4801. Munster, Ralf F.W. The development of ethics in the philosophy of Max Scheler; a study in personalistic phenomenology. Duke, 1952.

4802. Murchland, Bernard Gerald. Alienation: the problem and some philosophical antecedents. Buffalo, 1968. 63-11543

4803. Murdoch, John Emery. Geometry and the continuum in the fourteenth century: a philosophical analysis of Thomas Bradwardine's *Tractatus de continuo*. Wisconsin, 1957. 57-3697

4804. Murphey, Murray G. The synechism of Charles Sanders Peirce. Yale, 1954.

4805. Murphree, Idus Laviga. Evolution: from cosmic progress to human reconstruction. The concepts of evolution and progress in the works of Spencer, Tylor, Lubbock, Morgan, and Veblen. Columbia, 1953. 6676

4806. Murphree, Wallace Allgood. The status of the mental: a Whiteheadian response to Armstrong's materialiam. Vanderbilt, 1972. 72-26117

4807. Murphy, Arthur Edward. The metaphysics of space-time. Berkeley, 1926.

4808. Murphy, Edward John. The legal philosophy of Elijah Jordan: a critical examination. Tulane, 1973. 73-25296

4809. Murphy, Frances Harder. The place of moral responsibility in the philosophies of Whitehead and Peirce. Brown, 1940.

4810. Murphy, Frank Joseph. Ethical egoism. Purdue, 1971. 71-20511

4811. Murphy, James Maurice. Positivism in England: the reception of Comte's doctrines, 1840-1870. Columbia, 1968. 69-15698

4812. Murphy, Jeffrie Guy. Kant's philosophy of moral right: a critical examination of its teleological foundations. Rochester, 1966. 66-6862

4813. Murphy, John Peter. Descartes' decision to doubt. Texas, 1968. 69-6194

4814. Murphy, Joseph Samson. The theory of universals in eighteenth century British empiricism. Brandeis, 1961. 62-1211

4815. Murphy, Rev. Laurence Thomas. The role of nature and connaturality in moral philosophy according to St. Thomas Aquinas. Notre Dame, 1964. 64-10497

4816. Murphy, Rev. Richard Timothy. Phenomenology and the dialectic: a study of pre-reflexive consciousness in the phenomenological theories of Husserl, Sartre and Merleau-Ponty. Fordham, 1963.

4817. Murray, Michael Edward. Modern philosophy of history: its origin and destination. Yale, 1968. 69-8395

4818. Murray, Rev. Michael V. The theory of distinctions in the metaphysics of Francis Suarez. Fordham, 1945.

4819. Mursell, James Lockhart. Descartes' theory of space. Harvard, 1918.

4820. Murungi, John Justo. Two views of history: a study of the relation of European and African culture. Penn St., 1970. 71-21780

4821. Murungi, Robert Wallace. Bertrand Russell's theory of neutral monism. Columbia, 1967. 67-14071

4822. Murzynski, Joan Marie. Different approaches to number. Laval, 1974.

4823. Muses, Charles Arthur. Dionysius Andreas Freher: an inquiry into the work of a fundamental contributor to the philosophic tradition of Jacob Boehme. Columbia, 1951. 2844

4824. Muska, Rudolph Charles. Antithetical religious conceptions in Kierkegaard and Spinoza. Michigan St., 1960. 61-1189

4825. Mussard, Richard Ream. Frege's theory of the foundations of language. So. Illinois, 1969.
70-7305

4826. Mutch, William James. The mental states of the Hebrew prophets. Yale, 1894.

4827. Muyskens, James Leroy. Religion based on hope. Michigan, 1971. 72-14952

4828. Myatt, Rodney Thomas. A critical examination of R.S. Peters' conception of education. N.Y.U., 1973.
74-12853

4829. Myers, Charles Mason. The role of determinate and determinable modes of appearing in perception. Michigan, 1954. 8389

4830. Myers, Charles Raymond. Silence and the unspoken: a study of the modes of not speaking. Texas, 1975.
75-24928

4831. Myers, David Benton. Marx's dialectical critique. Texas, 1972. 73-7606

4832. Myers, Edward De Los. The Platonism of John Smith: with a comparative study of the doctrines of the other so-called Cambridge Platonists. Princeton, 1931.

4833. Myers, Francis Milton. Conflicting philosophies of democracy. Wisconsin, 1944.

4834. Myers, Gerald Eugene. An analysis of propositional attitudes; a linguistic approach. Brown, 1954.
9832

4835. Myers, Henry Alonzo. An introduction to the timely and synoptic elements of metaphysics, illustrated by the logic (synoptic element) and history (timely element) of the conceptions of perspectives and the metaphysical object appearing in the logos of Heraclitus, the attributes and substance of Spinoza, the perspectival monads of Leibniz, the categories and absolute of Hegel, and the concepts and intuition of Bergson. Cornell, 1933.

4836. Myers, Joseph Rawley. Social distance according to St. Thomas Aquinas. Catholic U., 1955.

4837. Myers, Orvil Floyd. The significance of the mathematical element in the philosophy of Bertrand Russell. Chicago, 1926.

4838. Myers, Robert Edward. Studies in method and religion in Hume's *Science of human nature*. Ohio St., 1968.   68-15362

4839. Myhill, John Renfred. A semantically complete foundation for logic and mathematics. Harvard, 1949.

4840. Myro, George. In defense of a modest mentalism. Harvard, 1969.

- N -

4841. Nabe, Clyde Milton. Max Scheler on phenomenology and man's place in the cosmos. Purdue, 1975.   76-567

4842. Nacpil, Emerito P. Paul Tillich's doctrine of the fall; a theological interpretation of the problem of existence. Drew, 1961.   61-6574

4843. Nagel, Ernest. On the logic of measurement. Columbia, 1931.

4844. Nagel, Thomas. Altruism. Harvard, 1963.

4845. Nagy, Elizabeth Virginia. The moral self in terms of behavior. Yale, 1923.

4846. Nagy, Paul Joseph. The doctrine of experience in the philosophy of Jonathan Edwards. Fordham, 1968.   68-11022

4847. Nahm, Milton Charles. The aesthetic response; an antinomy and its resolution. Pennsylvania, 1932.

4848. Naify, James Frederick. Arabic and European occasionalism: a comparison of Al-Ghazali's occasionalism and its critique by Averroes with Malebranche's occasionalism and its criticisms in the Cartesian tradition. Cal., S. Diego, 1975.
75-22184

4849. Najarian, Nevart. The epistemological presuppositions of communication. Boston U., 1940.

4850. Najm, Sami Majid. The theory of value: an introduction to philosophical intelligibility. Yale, 1962.

4851. Nakashima, Rikizo. Kant's doctrine of the thing-in-itself. Yale, 1889.

4852. Nakhnikian, George. Plato's theory of empirical knowledge. Harvard, 1949.

4853. Nammour, Jamil Daoud. Problems about language and the world: family resemblances and common properties. Oregon, 1969. 70-2533

4854. Narayana-Moorty, Jagarlapudi Sree Rama Lakshmi. Problems of self-knowledge. Berkeley, 1973.

4855. Narbutas, Jonas V. The spirit of faith seeking understanding in Royce's philosophy. Fordham, 1969. 70-11444

4856. Nardo, Gaetano John. The aesthetics of Benedetto Croce: a critical evaluation of its terminology and internal consistency. (Parts I-IV). N.Y.U., 1956. 57-1748

4857. Nardone, Henry F. St. Thomas Aquinas and the condemnation of 1277. Catholic U., 1963. 63-7980

4858. Narveson, Anne Churchill Humphrey. The problem of privacy in Locke's philosophy of language. Harvard, 1967.

4859. Narveson, Jan Fredrick. The structure of utilitarian ethics. Harvard, 1961.

4860. Nash, Elwin Peter Whitwell. Esse actuale; the problem of existence and individuality in Giles of Rome. Toronto, 1948.

4861. Nash, Ronald Herman. St. Augustine's theory of knowledge. Syracuse, 1964. 65-3426

4862. Nasr, Waddah Nassim. John Rawls' arguments for the feasibility of his theory of justice: a study of

the relationships between normative and empirical considerations in accounts of the nature of moral and political obligation. Minnesota, 1975.
75-21119

4863. Nasser, Alan George. The ontological argument and the problem of evil. Indiana, 1972. 72-15923

4864. Natanson, Harvey Burt. Spinoza's metaphysics: a new interpretation. Nebraska, 1953.

4865. Natanson, Maurice Alexander. A critical analysis of the foundations and phenomenological structure of the ontology of Jean-Paul Sartre. Nebraska, 1950.

4866. Nathan, George John. Hume's Genuine theism and religion. Toronto, 1972.

4867. Nathanson, Stephen Lewis. Scepticism and concept possession. Johns Hopkins, 1969. 69-21073

4868. Natoli, Grace Mary. The actualism of Giovanni Gentile and its critique by Michele Federico Sciacca. Fordham, 1973. 73-16025

4869. Naughton, E. Russell. Freedom in education according to Thomistic principles. Catholic U., 1950.

4870. Nauman, St. Elmo Harry, Jr. The social philosophies of Søren Kierkegaard and Nikolai Frederik Severin Grundtvig. Boston U., 1969. 69-18758

4871. Nauss, Edward John. Foundations of the analysis of evaluative language. Yale, 1960.

4872. Navia, Luis Eduardo. The problem of the freedom of the will in the philosophy of Schopenhauer. N.Y.U., 1972. 72-21528

4873. Navickas, Juozas-Leonas. The moral philosophy of Lossky. Fordham, 1958.

4874. Naylor, Andrew. The concept of remembering. Chicago, 1966.

4875. Neale, Philip Whitby. The self in Whitehead, Bradley and Hume in the light of their doctrines of internal and external relations. Vanderbilt, 1975.
76-112

4876. Neblett, William Richards, Jr. Some views on moral obligation. U.C.L.A., 1968. 68-16564

4877. Nedzynski, Thomas George. The logical problem of existential import. Catholic U., 1974. 74-19473

4878. Needleman, Jacob. The role of the existential a priori in the work of Ludwig Binswanger. Yale, 1961.

4879. Neely, Frank Wright. The metaphysics of action. Yale, 1967. 68-13185

4880. Neff, Emery. Carlyle and Mill, mystic and utilitarian. Columbia, 1924.

4881. Negley, Glenn Robert. The categories of political analysis. Chicago, 1940.

4882. Nehamas, Alexander. Predication and the theory of forms in the Phaedo. Princeton, 1971. 72-14159

4883. Neidorf, Robert Allen. Bifurcation and events: a study in Einstein, Russell, and Whitehead. Yale, 1959.

4884. Neill, Thomas, Jr. The significance of acknowledgment. Yale, 1972. 72-22516

4885. Nelkin, Norton. Perception and language. Kansas, 1969. 69-21558

4886. Nell, Onora Sylvia. Universalizability. Harvard, 1969.

4887. Nelson, Alvin Fredolph. The nature and significance of moral feelings. Ohio St., 1942.

4888. Nelson, Burt. Theories, laws and scientific explanation. Wisconsin, 1959. 59-5805

4889. Nelson, Everett John. An intensional logic of propositions. Harvard, 1929.

4890. Nelson, Herbert James. Blondel on Kant: a key to L'action of 1893. Buffalo, 1969. 70-17351

4891. Nelson, John C. Some comments on the identity conditions for material objects. Chicago, 1970.

4892. Nelson, John O. Philosophical theories of memory. Cornell, 1951.

4893. Nelson, John Thomas. Religious freedom and the public order in a pluralistic society. St. John's, 1969. 70-10563

4894. Nelson, Ralph Carl. Jacques Maritain's conception of "moral philosophy adequately considered." Notre Dame, 1961. 61-739

4895. Nelson, Ralph Waldo. The role of faith in Kant's philosophy. Chicago, 1931.

4896. Nelson, Raymond J. Peirce's theory of knowledge. Chicago, 1949.

4897. Nelson, Sherwood Mathis. The role of history in the political philosophy of R.G. Collingwood. Berkeley, 1954.

4898. Nelson, William Newell, III. The principle of fair play. Cornell, 1972. 73-10131

4899. Nemerson, Steven Samuel. Philosophical and legal foundations of strict liability. C.U.N.Y., 1973. 73-21052

4900. Nemetz, Anthony A. Art in St. Thomas Aquinas. Chicago, 1953.

4901. Nephew, Albert Henry, II. Philosophy is theology: the nature and function of philosophy according to John Macmurray. Marquette, 1970. 71-5309

4902. Nesher, Dan. An analysis of Spinoza's political philosophy. Brandeis, 1972. 72-32114

4903. Netzky, Ralph Marc. A new approach to the nature of time. Northwestern, 1969. 70-128

4904. Neufeld, Elmer. Psychoanalysis, science, and morality: a critique of the ethical theory of Erich Fromm in some comparison to Louis Feuer and Karen Horner. Chicago, 1973.

4905. Neujahr, Philip Joseph. Persons as subjects of experience. Yale, 1973. 73-28310

4906. Neumaier, John Joseph. Bertrand Russell's social philosophy and its relation to logic, ethics, and sociology. Minnesota, 1954. 13369

4907. Neustaedter, Marcus. Experience; the rise and development of the concept in the history of philosophy. N.Y.U., 1906. 74-3409

4908. Neville, Michael Richard. Kant's theory of aesthetic pleasure. Johns Hopkins, 1970. 71-16737

4909. Neville, Robert Cummings. A theory of divine creation. Yale, 1963.

4910. Nevins, Stanley A. The form of the personal as model for speaking about God. Fordham, 1973. 73-16026

4911. Nevins, William M. Ethical relations of church and state. Georgetown, 1933.

4912. Newbold, William Romaine. Prolegomena to a theory of belief. Pennsylvania, 1891.

4913. Newburger, Stanley Wyman. Lalande's theories of induction and experimentation. Columbia, 1956.
16289

4914. Newby, James Allen. The problem of validation. Southern Cal., 1975. 75-6432

4915. Newell, James David. The philosophy of Henry Sidgwick. Maryland, 1975. 75-8419

4916. Newgarden, Arthur Albert. A general approach to aesthetic experience. Buffalo, 1963. 64-2731

4917. Newhall, David Havens. Phenomenological analysis of the structure of the moral situation. Princeton, 1948. 10981

4918. Newhall, Jannette. The influence of William James on Georg Wobbermin's psychology and philosophy of religion. Boston U., 1931.

4919. Newman, Frederick Delano. Explanation and explaining in history. Stanford, 1963. 63-6434

4920. Newman, Herbert Lee. Individuality in Bosanquet's philosophy of society and religion. Boston U., 1939.

4921. Newman, Jay Alan. An examination of humanistic relativism. York, 1971.

4922. Newman, Josephine Kathleen. Changing perspectives in Brownson's philosophical thought. Toronto, 1971.

4923. Newman, Nancy Dorothy. 'To perceive is to have a sensation': a study in the philosophy of perception of the seventeenth-century and eighteenth-century. Princeton, 1974. 75-23229

4924. Newton, Robert D. A conception of the public. Columbia, 1957. 25150

4925. Neyer, Joseph. Ethics and sociology: a study in Durkheim and French neo-positivism. Harvard, 1942.

4926. Ni, Tsing-Yuan. A study in classical Taoism with special reference to cosmology and anthropology. Southern Cal., 1938.

4927. Nichipor, Walter Norman. The text of Herodian's history. Harvard, 1975.

4928. Nicholas, Sr. Joan Dunston. Bergson's theory of the unity of the person. St. Louis, 1973. 74-24125

4929. Nichols, Kenneth Edward. The concept of choice. Massachusetts, 1973. 73-14662

4930. Nichols, Rodney Ralph. Being and symbol in Paul Tillich. Missouri, 1974. 75-16033

4931. Nicholson, Graeme Alexander. The ontological difference: a study in Heidegger. Toronto, 1968.

4932. Nicholson, John Angus. Some aspects of the philosophy of L.T. Hobhouse. Toronto, 1925.

4933. Nicholson, Linda J. Karl Marx and human action. Brandeis, 1975. 75-24829

4934. Nicholson, Susan Tefft. Abortion and the Roman Catholic church. Pittsburgh, 1975. 75-21762

4935. Nickel, James Wesley. On the notions of cognitive and noncognitive meaning. Kansas, 1968. 68-17432

4936. Nickles, Thomas Jacob. The structure and interrelationships of physical theories. Princeton, 1969. 70-14230

4937. Nicol, Carl Conrad Wernle. The influence of functions and occupations. Chicago, 1916.

4938. Nicolson, Margaret Erskine. A comparative study of the ethics of Spinoza and Nietzsche. Yale, 1924.

4939. Nielsen, Harry A. An essay on induction. Nebraska, 1955. 12760

4940. Nielsen, Kai E. Justification and morals. Duke, 1955.

4941. Niemeyer, Sr. M. Fredericus. The one and the many in the social order. Catholic U., 1951.

4942. Niemi, Gunnar Wayne. Modality and self reference. Michigan, 1970. 71-4694

4943. Nietmann, William D. A philosophical principle for interpreting psychological data and theory. Boston U., 1943.

4944. Nietmann, William Frederick. Metaphysics and approaches to making sense: ordinary language philosophy and existential phenomenology. Claremont, 1968. 63-18281

4945. Nikander, Viljo Kustaa. Berkeley's Siris. Harvard, 1935.

4946. Nilson, Donald Richard. Quantum logic, quantum probability, and quantum measurement: a philosophical perspective on the quantum theory. Indiana, 1972. 73-14614

4947. Nisbet, Arthur Lee. A comparative analysis of Herbert Marcuse's and John Dewey's conceptions of freedom. Buffalo, 1974. 75-1506

4948. Nishiyama, Yuji. The structure of a proposition. M.I.T., 1974.

4949. Nissen, Bruce Allen. Moral means and ends in social change: Dewey and Marxism. Columbia, 1975. 75-18425

4950. Nissen, Lowell Allen. John Dewey's theory of inquiry and truth. Nebraska, 1962. 63-2407

4951. Noah, Aris. Singular terms and predication. Brandeis, 1973. 73-32401

4952. Noble, Cheryl Neel. Justification and judgment in Dewey's theory of value. Rochester, 1973. 73-25840

4953. Nobo, Jorge Luis. Extension and solidarity: a study of the fundamental thesis of Whitehead's philosophy of organism. Texas, 1973. 74-24925

4954. Nochlin, Philip. A critical exposition of Russell's philosophical logic. Columbia, 1955. 12458

4955. Nolan, Paul F. Saint Thomas and the unconscious mind. Catholic U., 1953.

4956. Nolan, Philip Jerome. Platonism in the Essais of Montaigne. Cornell, 1953.

4957. Nolting, Frederick Ernest, Jr. Certainty, truth and probability: a study in epistemology. Virginia, 1942.

4958. Noonan, John T. Banking and the scholastic analysis of usury. Catholic U., 1951.

4959. Noonan, Mark Luke. Transcendence and community: a reflection in the philosophy of Josiah Royce. Fordham, 1971. 71-20185

4960. Noone, John Bernard, Jr. The form and meaning of knowledge in mathematical-physics. Fordham, 1954.

4961. Nordenhaug, Theodore Davis. Schleiermacher's philosophy of religion: a reconstruction. Johns Hopkins, 1968. 68-10574

4962. Nordquist, Roger Frank. Emil Brunner on the province of reason. Yale, 1966. 66-13924

4963. Nordstrom, Louis Douglas. Sartre and evil: a study of Saint Genet: actor and martyr. Columbia, 1973. 76-29301

4964. Noren, Stephen Joel. Smart's identity theory and the mind-body problem. Massachusetts, 1968. 69-11569

4965. Noreña, Carlos Garcia. Juan Luis Vives: a humanistic conception of philosophical knowledge. Cal., S. Diego, 1967. 67-12355

4966. Norman, Jack. Events and semantic theories. Pittsburgh, 1974. 74-20827

4967. Normile, Michael Christopher. Individual and society: Dewey's reconstruction and resolution. Georgetown, 1975. 76-11662

4968. Norris, Donald Carl. A critique of Whitehead's theory of consciousness. Boston U., 1972.
72-25314

4969. Norris, Louis W. The criticism of the concept of substance by the six American neo-realists. Boston U., 1937.

4970. Norris, Orland Otway. A behaviorist account of individuation. Chicago, 1927.

4971. Norris, Stephen Edward. Aspects of action descriptions. Pittsburgh, 1972. 73-13252

4972. Norton, Bryan George. Linguistic frameworks and ontology: a study in the meta-ontology of Rudolf Carnap. Michigan, 1970. 71-15251

4973. Norton, David Fate. From moral sense to common sense: an essay on the development of Scottish common sense philosophy, 1700-1765. Cal., S. Diego, 1966. 66-11782

4974. Norton, David Lloyd. Transcendental imagination: a post-Kantian appraisal. Boston U., 1968.
68-18079

4975. Norton, Edwin Lee. The concepts of harmony and organism in ethics. Harvard, 1900.

4976. Norton, Rita Nolan. Foundations for an adequate criterion of paraphrase. Pennsylvania, 1965.
65-13364

4977. Norton, William Joseph, Jr. Bishop Butler: moralist and divine. Columbia, 1939.

4978. Nosich, Gerald Matthew. Scientific theories in transition: sameness and change of meaning. Illinois, Chi., 1973.
74-4645

4979. Novak, David. Suicide and morality in Plato, Aquinas and Kant. Georgetown, 1971.
72-30355

4980. Noval, Martin. The unconscious in Freud and Breton. Waterloo, 1973.

4981. Novalis, Peter N. Adequate translation: a critique of W.V. Quine's indeterminacy thesis. Johns Hopkins, 1974.
75-12969

4982. Nowotny, Sr. Joan. Gabriel Marcel's philosophy of hope. Toronto, 1974.

4983. Nozick, Robert. The normative theory of individual choice. Princeton, 1963.
64-6279

4984. Nucho, Fuad N. The meaning of freedom in the philosophy of Nicolas Berdyaev. Temple, 1962.

4985. Nugent, Francis Raymond. The nature and properties of immanent action; an essay in peripatetic philosophy. Notre Dame, 1961.
61-740

4986. Nugent, Rev. James B. The fundamental theistic argument in the metaphysical doctrine of Saint Thomas Aquinas. Catholic U., 1960.

4987. Null, Gilbert T. Noetic processes of identification experienced in carrying out the method of physical science. New School, 1974.
74-21373

4988. Nunn, William Albert, III. The location of pain. Virginia, 1967.
68-3116

4989. Nusenoff, Ronald Elliot. A Neofregean theory of the informative functioning of singular terms. Ohio St., 1975.
76-3510

4990. Nussbaum, Erich. Cosmology: a study in appearance. Virginia, 1949.

4991. Nussbaum, Martha Louise Craven. Aristotle's De motu animalium. Harvard, 1975.

4992. Nute, Donald Elmer, Jr. Identification and demonstrative reference. Indiana, 1974. 74-13532

4993. Nutting, Willis Dwight. The problem of transcendence in the philosophy of Joseph Geyser. Iowa, 1933.

4994. Nys, Pierre Emile. Body and soul: the center of metaphysics? Georgetown, 1961.

- O -

4995. Oakes, Guy Brown. On the possibility of a science of social relations. Cornell, 1968. 69-7295

4996. Oakes, Robert Aaron. Presentationalism vs. representationalism: a critical examination of the historical dispute concerning the immediacy of perceptual knowledge. Pennsylvania, 1966.
66-10653

4997. Oaklander, Lester Nathan. The ontology of C.D. Broad's The mind and its place in nature. Iowa, 1973. 74-16672

4998. Oastler, John Alan Lindsey. The problem of the certainty of perceptual knowledge claims. N.Y.U., 1969. 69-21268

4999. Oberdiek, Hans Fredrick. The moral relevance of motives, intentions, and actions. Wisconsin, 1965. 65-4824

5000. Oberlander, George Edward. Reflection and Husserl's transcendental-phenomenological epoché. Texas, 1972. 73-495

5001. O'Briant, Walter Herbert. Gottfried Wilhelm Leibniz: General investigations concerning the analysis of concept and truths. A translation and an evaluation of its sugnificance and place in Leibniz's logic and metaphysics. Emory, 1966. 67-215

5002. O'Brien, Astrid Marie. The meaning of resolution as a reflective method in the philosophy of Thomas Aquinas. Fordham, 1975. 75-18930

5003. O'Brien, Sr. Consilia. The antecedents of being; an analysis of the concept de nihilo in St. Thomas' philosophy. Catholic U., 1939.

5004. O'Brien, George Dennis. Meaning and fact: a study in the philosophy of Wittgenstein. Chicago, 1961.

5005. O'Brien, Gerald Damien. A concept of man in the humanist tradition. U.S. Int'l, 1971. 71-19095

5006. O'Brien, Rev. Gerard Charles. Neoplatonism and the marriage doctrine of the early Augustine. Fordham, 1974. 74-19679

5007. O'Brien, James F. The concept of nature in philosophy and physics. Catholic U., 1952.

5008. O'Brien, Robert Charles. The achievement of selfhood and the life of reason in the Ethics of Spinoza. Fordham, 1968. 69-2602

5009. O'Brien, Robert James. Ego, self, and person: a study in Sartre's phenomenological psychology and ontology. Cal., S. Cruz, 1971. 73-14465

5010. O'Brien, Thomas S. The principle of finality in the philosophy of St. Thomas Aquinas. Fordham, 1957.

5011. O'Brochta, Thomas Francis. The metaphysical basis of human freedom according to Alfred North Whitehead. Loyola, 1973. 73-23153

5012. O'Callaghan, Jeremiah Joseph. Walter of Chatton's doctrine of intuitive and abstractive knowledge; study and text. Toronto, 1949.

5013. O'Callaghan, Rev. Louis Thomas. The function of reflection in the psychology of Saint Thomas Aquinas. Fordham, 1948.

5014. O'Callaghan, William Jude. The constitution of created composite being in Liber de summo bono, (Book IV, Tract II, 1-8) of Ulrich of Strasbourg, O.P.: philosophical study and text. Marquette, 1970. 72-5783

5015. Ochs, Carol Rebecca Blumenthal. The ontological argument in Descartes, Spinoza and Leibniz. Brandeis, 1968. 69-2059

5016. Ockenga, Harold J. Poverty as a theoretical and practical problem of government in the writings of Jeremy Bentham and the Marxian alternative. Pittsburgh, 1939.

5017. O'Connell, Sr. M. Marguerite. The relation between solitude and social action as lived and taught by Saint Bernard. Notre Dame, 1949.

5018. O'Connell, Richard Allan. The structure of meaning and knowledge. Wayne St., 1974.   74-29839

5019. O'Connor, Daniel Denis. Intentionality and the phenomenology of human awareness. Yale, 1961.

5020. O'Connor, Dennis Thomas. The structure of behavior: an analysis and critique. St. Louis, 1972.
74-4557

5021. O'Connor, Rev. Edward M. Potentiality and energy. Catholic U., 1939.

5022. O'Connor, Finbarr William. Other things not being equal: from equality by procedure to equality of result. Pennsylvania, 1975.   76-3207

5023. O'Connor, John J. Philosophical aspects of communication. Catholic U., 1953.

5024. O'Connor, John Joseph. Dewey's logical theory: some clarifications and criticisms. Columbia, 1952.
4228

5025. O'Connor, John Morris, III. The epistemological foundations of John Locke's moral and political philosophy. Harvard, 1965.

5026. O'Connor, Maurice J. Responsibility to moral life. Catholic U., 1903.

5027. O'Connor, Patrick D. Human nature, pragmatism, and democracy: an interpretation of John Dewey. U.S. Int'l, 1972.   72-10521

5028. O'Connor, Paul Ernst. Epistemic seeing and objectivity. Washington U., 1975.   75-21732

5029. O'Connor, Robert Francis. The social philosophy of Ortega y Gasset. Texas, 1975.   75-16717

5030. O'Connor, William Patrick. The concept of the human soul according to St. Augustine. Catholic U., 1921.

5031. O'Connor, Rev. William Richard. St. Thomas Aquinas and the natural desire for God. Fordham, 1943.

5032. Odell, Stanley Jack. Incorrigibility and the foundations of empirical knowledge. Illinois, 1967.
68-8187

5033. O'Donnell, Rev. Clement Maria. The psychology of St. Bonaventure and St. Thomas Aquinas. Catholic U., 1936.

5034. O'Donnell, James Reginald. The De bono et malo of William of Auvergne; edition of text with introduction and analytical studies. Toronto, 1946.

5035. O'Driscoll, Lyla Hamilton. Toward a theory of natural rights. U.C.L.A., 1974.   74-29273

5036. Oei, Lee Tjiek. Hu Shih's philosophy of man as influenced by John Dewey's instrumentalism. Fordham, 1974.   74-19681

5037. Oelschlaeger, Max Frederick, II. A philosophical critique of historical causation. So. Illinois, 1973.   74-6234

5038. O'Flaherty, James C. The linguistic foundations of Hamann's concept of unity. Chicago, 1951.

5039. O'Flynn, Sheila. The first two meanings of "rational process" according to the exposition in Boethius' De trinitate. Laval, 1955.

5040. Ogilvy, James Angus. Relations. Yale, 1968.   69-8399

5041. O'Grady, Donald Arthur. A metaphysics of beauty. Notre Dame, 1959.   59-4410

5042. O'Hara, Rev. Christopher Edward. The relationship between philosophy and theology in the ontologism of Vincenzo Gioberti. Fordham, 1949.

5043. O'Hara, Sr. M. Kevin. The connotations of wisdom according to St. Thomas Aquinas. Catholic U., 1956.

5044. O'Hare, Rev. Joseph Aloysius. The meaning of action in the phenomenology and logic of Hegel. Fordham, 1968.   68-11024

5045. O'Hare, William Timothy. The significance of "need" in the philosophy of Karl Marx. Marquette, 1973.   74-18235

5046. Okadigbo, Chuba. On Hegel's treatment of Egypt. Catholic U., 1973.   73-22763

5047. O'Keefe, Rev. Martin D. The search for control: a study of the origins of the thought of Empedocles and Heraclitus. Michigan St., 1969.   69-20902

5048. O'Keefe, Raymond J. Reasoning about God and reasoning about man. Princeton, 1968. 69-2774

5049. O'Kelley, Thomas Augustus. A quaternary notation applied to the problems of minimization and the detection of symmetry in Boolean functions. Florida St., 1968. 72-13550

5050. Okolo, Rev. Chukwudum Barnabas. Self as an individual in Dewey-- a philosophic inquiry. Catholic U., 1973. 73-19023

5051. Okrent, Mark Benjamin. Knowledge and freedom: the compatibility of morality and absolute idealism. Yale, 1972. 72-33028

5052. Olafson, Frederick Arlan. Appearance and transcendence: a study of the physicalistic theory of mind. Harvard, 1951.

5053. O'Laughlin, Sr. Mary Dositheus. A treatise on the imagination. Niagara, 1939.

5054. Oldenquist, Andrew George, Jr. Moral rules. Ohio St., 1962. 63-75

5055. Olds, Glenn A., Jr. An inquiry concerning the nature of moral insight. Yale, 1948.

5056. Olds, Marianne E. The nature and function of the logical constructions of Bertrand Russell. Radcliffe, 1952.

5057. O'Leary, Conrad John. The substantial composition of man according to St. Bonaventure. Catholic U., 1931.

5058. O'Leary, James Francis. Aristotle's *Poetics* read as a reply to the Platonic indictment of poetry. Syracuse, 1971. 72-6611

5059. O'Leary, Paul Thomas. Peirce's conception of belief. Toronto, 1973.

5060. Olela, Henry. The rationale for an African philosophy: a critical examination of the African cosmological views with some reference to the Luo beliefs. Florida St., 1971. 72-13551

5061. Olewiler, Betty Jane. Whitehead's philosophy of language and the Whorf hypothesis. Johns Hopkins, 1971. 71-29157

5062. Olguín, Manuel. The controversy of free will in British philosophy. Berkeley, 1946.

5063. Olin, Doris Finkel. Thomas Reid's theory of sensation and perception. Cornell, 1971. 71-27393

5064. Olive, Don Hilliard. Contemporary analytical thought and language about God. Tulane, 1975. 75-23290

5065. Oliver, George Benjamin. Relevance of linguistic theory to philosophy: a study of transformational theory. Northwestern, 1967. 68-3208

5066. Oliver, James Willard. Pragmatics and probabilities. Harvard, 1949.

5067. Oliver, William Donald. The concept and the thing. Wisconsin, 1936.

5068. Olivier, Ann. Maritain's creative intuition and its relation to his earlier and later epistemological thought. Catholic U., 1971. 71-24227

5069. Olmstead, Wendy Raudenbush. An examination of the relations between thought and perception with reference to Homer, the Pythagoreans, Heraclitus, Plato, and Aristotle. Chicago, 1974.

5070. Olscamp, Paul James. A Berkeleyan analysis of the uses of language in ethics. Rochester, 1962. 62-6669

5071. Olsen, Richard Ellison. Logical necessity: a critical examination of conventionalist and related theories of necessary truth. Brown, 1971. 72-8159

5072. Olshewsky, Thomas Mack. Intentions and oppositions: an organon for axiological inquiry. Emory, 1964. 65-8500

5073. Olson, Alan Melvin. Transcending and transcendence in Karl Jaspers' philosophy of existenz. Boston U., 1973. 74-14223

5074. Olson, Raymond E. Hobbes's logical conventionalism. Johns Hopkins, 1955.

5075. Olson, Robert Goodwin. A naturalistic theory of ethics. Michigan, 1958. 58-3718

5076. Oltman, John McCuish. Translation and determinate meaning. Texas, 1974. 74-24917

5077. O'Mahony, Rev. Timothy J. Individuation in the philosophy of Nicolaus Cusanus. Fordham, 1947.

5078. O'Malley, Joseph James. Material being and scientific knowledge according to Pierre Duhem. Marquette, 1965. 68-494

5079. O'Meara, William Joseph. The unity of Duns Scotus' thought. Toronto, 1933.

5080. O'Meara, William Martin. Speculative reason and religious experience in Whitehead. Loyola, 1969.

5081. O'Neil, Brian Edgar. Epistemological direct realism in Descartes' philosophy. Berkeley, 1968. 68-10387

5082. O'Neil, Br. Campion. The notion of essence in some neoplatonic writings of St. Thomas Aquinas. Catholic U., 1967. 67-17143

5083. O'Neil, Charles Joseph. The structure and foundation of prudence in Aristotle. Toronto, 1939.

5084. O'Neil, Richard Alan. A reformulation and defense of the is-ought gap. Vanderbilt, 1972. 73-14526

5085. O'Neill, Kevin David. Kierkegaard's attempt at a balanced philosophy of religion. Yale, 1967. 68-5194

5086. O'Neill, Rev. Reginald F. The meaning of our world as seen by St. Bonaventure in the light of exemplary causality. Fordham, 1952.

5087. O'Neill, William Edwin. On models in the knowledge of nature. Boston Coll., 1970. 70-24607

5088. Onwuanibe, Richard Chibikodo. An ethical inquiry on Frantz Fanon's revolutionary humanism: a critique of the use of violence. Georgetown, 1975. 76-16455

5089. Onyewuenyi, Rev. Innocent Chilaka. The relation of reason and faith in Hegel's philosophy of religion. Duquesne, 1970. 70-21268

5090. Oppenheim, Rev. Frank Mathias. Royce's mature idea of general metaphysics. St. Louis, 1962. 64-989

5091. Opper, Jacob. The cosmological basis of western culture, 1600-1900 A.D.: concomitants of the natural sciences in the musical, literary, and graphic arts. Florida St., 1970. 71-7082

5092. O'Reilly, Peter. Sancti Thomae de Aquino Expositio super librum Boetii De hebdomadibus; an edition and a study. Toronto, 1960.

5093. Orenduff, Jess Michael. A system of truth-valued modal logic. Tulane, 1972. 73-12057

5094. Orens, Irving P. Foundations of inductive geometry. Virginia, 1934.

5095. Orenstein, Alex. Existence and the particular quantifier. N.Y.U., 1972. 72-21530

5096. Organ, Troy Wilson. An index to Aristotle. Iowa, 1941.

5097. Orlebeke, Clifton James. Plato's theory of natural law. Harvard, 1963.

5098. Ornstein, Jack Hervey. A critique of the mind-brain identity theory and a defense of a multi-aspect theory of the mind. Cal., S. Diego, 1970.
71-7980

5099. Osborn, Andrew D. The philosophy of Edmund Husserl in its development from his mathematical interests to his first conception of phenomenology in Logical investigations. Columbia, 1934.

5100. Osborn, Velva Jeanne. Judgment and feeling in the aesthetic theory of Bernard Bosanquet. Illinois, 1965. 65-11848

5101. Osborne, Charles Henry. A response to Austin on "real." Virginia, 1973. 73-32453

5102. Osborne, Clifford Pierson. The problem of change in Greek science. Chicago, 1931.

5103. Osborne, William A. The evolutionary humanism of Teilhard de Chardin. New School, 1965.
66-3961

5104. Oscanyan, Frederick Stone. Mr. F.H. Bradley's theory of logic: an essay on The principles of logic. Yale, 1969. 70-2783

5105. Osgniach, Rev. Augustine John. The scholastic doctrine of the four principal categories. U. of Washington, 1926.

5106. O'Shea, Robert S. Truth of being through knowledge by connaturality. Catholic U., 1956.

5107. Osterle, John. The problem of meaning. Laval, 1941.

5108. Ostheimer, Rev. Anthony Leo. The family; a Thomistic study in social philosophy. Catholic U., 1939.

5109. Ostien, Philip Alan. The reduction of theories. Pennsylvania, 1972.   73-1426

5110. O'Sullivan, Joan Gabriel. Existentialism and phenomenology as a basis for philosophy of history. Boston U., 1971.   71-26461

5111. O'Sullivan, Maureen. Paul Ramsey's just war theory. Manitoba, 1972.

5112. Otake, Masaru Victor. A study of Japanese taste with An observation concerning Furyu and the structure of Iki by Kuki Shuzo. Syracuse, 1956. 57-2180

5113. Otis, Eugène. Les théories de l'évolution. Laval, 1944.

5114. O'Toole, Rev. Christopher J. The philosophical theory of creation in the writings of St. Augustine. Catholic U., 1944.

5115. O'Toole, Rev. Edward J. The mind-body problem in contemporary schools of language analysis. Fordham, 1959.

5116. O'Toole, Frederick Joseph. Qualities and powers in the corpuscular philosophy of Robert Boyle. Cal., Davis, 1972.   73-8342

5117. Otten, Daniel Joseph. Reason and religion in Santayana. St. Louis, 1971.   72-5316

5118. Otto, Abbe John. The commentary of St. Thomas on Book I of the Ethics. Laval, 1952.

5119. Otto, Herbert Roderick. Steps toward a system of translation from ordinary discourse into an applied logic. Pennsylvania, 1968.   69-152

5120. Otto, M.C. Some logical implications of causation. Wisconsin, 1911.

5121. Ouren, Dallas Victor Lie. HaMILLton: Mill on Hamilton-- a re-examination of Sir William Hamilton's philosophy. Minnesota, 1973.   74-10559

5122. Outland, Ronald Wayne. Thought and time in Hegel's Phenomenology. Tennessee, 1975.   75-26730

5123. Outlaw, Lucius Turner, Jr. Language and the transformation of consciousness: foundations for a her-

meneutic of black culture. Boston Coll., 1972.
72-24053

5124. Overholt, William A. Reason and the nonrational in Lovejoy, Montague, and Tsanoff. Boston U., 1951.

5125. Overvold, Gary Eldon. Husserl and the science of philosophy. Claremont, 1966.   67-9521

5126. Owen, Derwyn Randulph Grier. Meaning, metaphysics, and symbolism. Toronto, 1942.

5127. Owen, William A. Whitehead's philosophy of science and the concept of substance. Georgetown, 1964.

5128. Owens, Francis X.J. A study of natural and humanistic motivations in thirteen cases of religious conversion. Georgetown, 1955.

5129. Owens, Rev. Thomas J. The problem of interpersonal relationships as posed in contemporary thought. Fordham, 1952.

5130. Owsley, Richard Mills. The moral philosophy of Karl Jaspers. Indiana, 1960.   60-6314

5131. Ozar, David Thomas. The concept of owning. Yale, 1974.   75-1387

5132. Ozar, Lorraine Audrey Lubawy. Learning and teaching: a philosophical formulation and critique of Skinnerian education. Fordham, 1974.   74-25074

- P -

5133. Pacheco, Armando C. Plato's conception of love. Notre Dame, 1942.

5134. Pacheco, Emanuel Albert. Does saying so make it so? An examination of John Searle's doctrine of assertions and abberations. Oregon, 1973.   73-28628

5135. Packard, Dennis Jay. Six papers on choice theory. Stanford, 1974.   74-27075

5136. Packer, Mary N. Porter. Cicero's presentation of Epicurean ethics, a study based primarily on De finibus I and II. Columbia, 1938.

5137. Packman, Laila Jenson. A critical analysis of some naturalistic solutions of the mind-body problem. Iowa, 1938.

5138. Paderón, Eduardo San Juan. The theory of the moral sense in Shaftesbury: an approach to his concepts of virtue and man. Fordham, 1972.   73-1488

5139. Padgett, Jack Francis. The concept of personality in William Temple's philosophy. Boston U., 1959.   59-3471

5140. Page, Benjamin Bakewell. The Czechoslovakian reform movement, 1963-68: a problem in the theory of socialism. Florida St., 1970.

5141. Pageler, John Charles. The soul and time: first principles of modern métaphysical speculation as represented in the thought of Martin Heidegger. Claremont, 1966.   68-10561

5142. Pahel, Kenneth Ronald. Stephen Pepper's ethical empiricism and recent critics of naturalism. Illinois, 1965.   65-11849

5143. Pahi, Biswambhar. Studies in implicational calculi. Yale, 1966.   66-13928

5144. Paige, Rupert Douglas. The concept of sense-data. Nebraska, 1963.   64-779

5145. Pailthorp, Charles Norman. Causes, reasons, and knowings. Pittsburgh, 1967.   68-6121

5146. Painter, Jack Whitfield. A semiotic approach to some problems and theories in the interpretation of metaphors. Emory, 1961.   62-6007

5147. Pait, James Albert. The influence of Descartes on seventeenth-century English philosophy. Virginia, 1941.

5148. Pak, Hisung. Subjectivism and intuition (a theory of the given). Michigan, 1937.

5149. Palacios, Gonzalo T. The notion of freedom in the political philosophy of Simon Bolivar. Catholic U., 1970.   70-22690

5150. Palmer, Oran Walker, Jr. History as thought process taught by the philosophical method. Claremont, 1967.   68-10530

5151. Palmer, Richard David. Locke's doctrine of representative perception. Ohio St., 1970.   71-7534

5152. Palmieri, Lucien Eugene. An examination of the principle of verification. Wisconsin, 1953.

5153. Palter, Robert M. Philosophy and theories of relativity. Chicago, 1952.

5154. Paluch, Stanley John. Philosophical inquiry into the language and methodology of history. Alberta, 1966.

5155. Palyi, Raissa. K.N. Leontiev and his theory of aestheticism. Chicago, 1954.

5156. Pampusch, Sr. Anita Marie. Isaac Newton's notion of scientific explanation. Notre Dame, 1972.
72-16270

5157. Pan, Cedric Hung-chao. Nietzsche's philosophy in Buddhist perspectives. So. Illinois, 1973.
74-6235

5158. Panaro, Gerald Paul. Personal knowing: some implications for the philosophy of religion. Boston Coll., 1975.

5159. Pancheri, Lillian Unger. The atomism of Pierre Gassendi: ontology for the new physics. Tulane, 1972. 72-24419

5160. Panichas, George Emanuel. The liberal theory of property. Arizona, 1975. 76-2546

5161. Panish, Theodore Michael. Phenomenology and the human body. Missouri, 1970. 71-8374

5162. Panush, Irving. An analysis of C.I. Lewis' general theory of value and obligation as it relates to esthetics. Michigan, 1958. 58-3719

5163. Panzl, Barbara Carol Lax. Art and the horizon of the opaque. Penn St., 1967. 68-12000

5164. Pap, Arthur. The *a priori* in physical theory. Columbia, 1946.

5165. Papageorgopoulos, Nenos A. The language of tragedy: an essay on the tragic form by means of a critical analysis of Susanne K. Langer's theory of expression. Penn St., 1973. 74-16055

5166. Paparella, Benedict Anthony. Sociality and sociability: a philosophy of sociability according to St. Thomas Aquinas. Catholic U., 1955.

5167. Papay, Joseph Louis. The concept of non-being in Plato and in his predecessors and contemporaries. Fordham, 1957.

5168. Pape, Leslie Manock. The naturalistic ethics of John Dewey. Chicago, 1930.

5169. Pappas, George Sotiros. Some perceptual and epistemic features of sense-data. Pennsylvania, 1974.
74-22890

5170. Paradis, André. Un temoin nouveau de la tradition onirocritique Artemidorienne: le Liber Zachelis in solutione sompniorum (ms. Gdansk 2224). Edittion critique et analyse des sources. Montreal, 1972.

5171. Paradis, Gilles. Le comique. Laval, 1971.
73-1218

5172. Parejko, James E. Nietzsche's nihilism. So. Illinois, 1969.
70-7307

5173. Parent, William Allan. Mill's conception of the Summum bonum. Brown, 1970.
71-17138

5174. Park, Désirée. Berkeley's theory of notions. Indiana, 1968.
68-11424

5175. Park, Dorothy Gwendolyn. The objectivity of value: a study of the ethics of Nicolai Hartmann. Nebraska, 1937.

5176. Park, Mary Isabel. A study of the philosophical basis of Leibniz' optimism. Yale, 1904.

5177. Park, Ynhui. An ontological interpretation of the concept of "expression" in the philosophy of Merleau-Ponty. Southern Cal., 1970.
71-7731

5178. Park, Young Sik. Wittgenstein's version of verifiability in the Tractatus. Emory, 1975.
75-23684

5179. Parker, Bernard Street. Thomas de Bungeye's commentary on the first book of Aristotle's De Caelo. /Portion of text in Latin./ Tulane, 1968.
68-15260

5180. Parker, Clarence Monroe, Jr. Francisco Romero's "theory of man." Oklahoma, 1973.
73-23956

5181. Parker, DeWitt Henry. The nature and object of historical knowledge. Harvard, 1908.

5182. Parker, Francis Howard. Identity of percept and object in recent American realism. Harvard, 1949.

5183. Parker, George Frederick. Duration and method in the philosophy of Henri Bergson. Pittsburgh, 1959.
59-4461

5184. Parker, Harold Leftridge. C.I. Lewis' ethical theory based upon his conceptions of the good and the right. Emory, 1967.
67-14341

5185. Parker, Richard Barron. Moral injustice. Chicago, 1968.

5186. Parker, Richard Burl. The theory of relations in Russell's metaphysics. U. of Washington, 1973.
74-2223

5187. Parker, Steven Hugh. Is the practice of clinical psychology experimental? Purdue, 1975.
76-574

5188. Parker, Willis Allen. Pluralism and irrationalism in the philosophy of William James. Harvard, 1912.

5189. Parkhurst, Helen Huss. Recent logical realism. Bryn Mawr, 1917.

5190. Parks, William. The influence of Scottish sentimentalist ethical theory on Thomas Jefferson's philosophy of human nature. Wm. & Mary, 1975.
75-19108

5191. Parrill, Lloyd Ellison. The concept of humor in the pseudonymous works of Søren Kierkegaard. Drew, 1975.
75-28991

5192. Parry, Richard David. The agent's knowledge of his own action. No. Carolina, 1968.
69-10190

5193. Parry, William Tuthill. Implication. Harvard, 1932.

5194. Parsons, Barbara Ann. The importance of man in Whitehead's philosophy. Tulane, 1970. 70-24547

5195. Parsons, Charles Dacre. On constructive interpretation of predicative mathematics. Harvard, 1961.

5196. Parsons, Kathryn Joan Pyne. The criteriological theory of meaning: an exposition and critique. Stanford, 1967.
68-11336

5197. Parsons, Terence Dwight. The elimination of individual concepts. Stanford, 1966.
66-14709

5198. Pasch, Alan. Some problems in recent empiricism. Princeton, 1955.
13719

5199. Pascual, Ricardo R. A logical analysis of fictionalism with respect to the theory of truth. Chicago, 1939.

5200. Pashman, Louis Jonathan. The genetic fallacy. N.Y.U., 1970. 72-9782

5201. Paske, Gerald Howard. Moral education. Wisconsin, 1964. 64-13913

5202. Paskow, Alan. Novel intuition: a philosophical defense of the existence of prelinguistic apprehension. Yale, 1971. 71-31093

5203. Pasotti, Robert Neil. Giambattista Vico and the psychology of history. Columbia, 1964. 64-9198

5204. Passel, Howard Samuel. Justifying basic principles. No. Carolina, 1975. 76-9279

5205. Passell, Dan. Hume on probability. Stanford, 1964. 65-2893

5206. Pastin, Mark Joseph. The logic of evidence. Harvard, 1973. 76-16889

5207. Patel, Ramesh Nath. A constructive critique of the foundations of philosophy. New Mexico, 1970. 71-9284

5208. Paternoster, Bruce. Modeling and the relation of normal science to a paradigm theory. Yale, 1973. 73-29234

5209. Paterson, Antoinette Mann. Knowledge and virtue in Giordano Bruno. Buffalo, 1966. 66-12123

5210. Paterson, George Morton. Radical kenosis: a study of the referential base of religious language. Toronto, 1971.

5211. Patrick, George Thomas White. The fragments of the work of Heraclitus of Ephesus on nature. Johns Hopkins, 1888.

5212. Pattantyus, Rev. John Emeric. Justice as a political virtue in Aristotle. Catholic U., 1969. 70-8600

5213. Patten, Steven Crain. Kant's response to Hume on the unity of mind. U. of Washington, 1974. 75-4033

5214. Patterson, Charles Henry. Problems in logic. Nebraska, 1924.

5215. Patterson, E.R. Romantic elements in Hegel's philosophy. Radcliffe, 1914.

5216. Patterson, Herbert Parsons. An extension of the "pure experience" philosophy of William James. Yale, 1913.

5217. Patterson, Richard Allen. Plato's image theory of participation. Pennsylvania, 1975.   76-3209

5218. Patton, Carl, Jr. The state and the person in the thought of Alberdi and Caso. Boston U., 1957.
57-2522

5219. Patton, Thomas Edgington. An examination of reference. Harvard, 1959.

5220. Paul, Anthony Martin. Figurative language. Johns Hopkins, 1969.   69-13497

5221. Paul, Jean Miriam. Realism versus nominalism. Minnesota, 1971.   72-14351

5222. Paul, Jeffrey Elliott. Individualism, holism, and human action: an investigation into social scientific methodology. Brandeis, 1974.   74-16832

5223. Paul, John Philip. An analysis and evaluation of Henri Poincare's cosmology, epistemology, and philosophy of science. Marquette, 1969.
70-11969

5224. Paul, Richard William. Logic as theory of validation: an essay in philosophical logic. Cal., S. Barbara, 1968.   70-2068

5225. Paul, Wilford Noel. The religious views of John Stuart Mill. New Mexico, 1972.   73-1552

5226. Paul, William Wright. Paul Tillich's interpretation of history. Columbia, 1959.   59-3124

5227. Pauley, Edward Haven. The correspondence theory of truth in twentieth century analytic philosophy. Boston U., 1969.   69-18426

5228. Paullin, William Theodore. The datum of knowledge; Das gegebene in the translation from Kant to Fichte. Pennsylvania, 1904.

5229. Paulsen, David Lamont. Comparative coherency of Mormon (finitistic) and classical theism. Michigan, 1975.   75-8090

5230. Paulsen, David Warren. Dispositional concepts and causal properties. Stanford, 1970. 71-19743

5231. Paulson, Stanley Lowell. Rylean explanations of behavior. Wisconsin, 1968. 69-974

5232. Pauly, Thomas Erwin. Reichenbach's philosophy of the topology of time. St. Louis, 1970. 70-20414

5233. Pauson, Marian LaGarde. A study of the sublime. Tulane, 1965. 66-1564

5234. Pax, Clyde Victor. The approach to God in the thought of Gabriel Marcel. Notre Dame, 1962. 62-5583

5235. Paxson, Thomas Dunning, Jr. Ethics in Plato's early dialogues: ethical non-naturalism and the inadequacy of popular values. Rochester, 1970. 71-1417

5236. Payer, Pierre Joseph. The doctrine of prudence in the writings of Albert the Great. Toronto, 1969.

5237. Payne, Michael Anthony. The necessary relation between law and morals in Lon L. Fuller's The morality of law. Georgia, 1972. 73-5759

5238. Payne, Wilfred G. The logic of science. Wisconsin, 1930.

5239. Payzant, Geoffrey Barss. Art invention as discovery and elaboration. Toronto, 1960.

5240. Peach, William Bernard. The ethics of Richard Price. Harvard, 1951.

5241. Peal, Sr. Janet M. Contemplation in the natural ethics of Thomas Aquinas. St. John's, 1968. 68-11258

5242. Peale, John Stafford. The theory of belief. No. Carolina, 1974. 75-15687

5243. Pearl, Leon. The rationalist moral argument of Richard Price. N.Y.U., 1957. 58-4381

5244. Pearl, Philip David. William Whewell's conception of the philosophy of science. New School, 1966. 67-4764

5245. Pearson, John Grant Lundy. Scepticism and action; a study of sceptical principles and their relation to systematic thought. Toronto, 1943.

5246. Pecharroman, Ovid. Nature and moral man in the philosophy of Baron d'Holbach. Fordham, 1974.
74-25076

5247. Peck, William Dayton. On autonomy: the primacy of the subject in Kant and Kierkegaard. Yale, 1974.
74-25760

5248. Peckham, George Williams. Logic of Bergson's philosophy. Columbia, 1917.

5249. Pederson, LaMoyne Lloyd. An investigation of the forms and defenses of teleological ethical theories, with emphasis on the ethical theory of Brand Blanshard. Southern Cal., 1970.   71-7733

5250. Peery, Rebekah Smith. An interpretation of personal love founded on the phenomenological ontology of Martin Heidegger. Vanderbilt, 1974.   75-1150

5251. Pegis, Anton Charles. The problem of the soul in the thirteenth century; the threefold graduation. Toronto, 1931.

5252. Peikoff, Sylvan Leonard. The status of the law of contradiction in classic logical ontologism. N.Y.U., 1964.   65-1658

5253. Peiros, Sherri. Kierkegaardian parody. Cal., S. Cruz, 1974.   75-12022

5254. Pell, Orlie Anna Haggerty. Value-theory and criticism. Columbia, 1930.

5255. Pelletier, Francis Jeffry. Some problems of non-singular reference: a logic for sortal, mass, and adverbial terms. U.C.L.A., 1971.   72-5856

5256. Pelletier, Yvan. La connaissance confusé, principe et fondement permanent du bien achève de l'intelligence speculative. Laval, 1975.

5257. Peltz, Richard W. Ontological principles in discussions of literary criticism. Chicago, 1953.

5258. Pemberton, Harrison Joseph, Jr. The problem of personal identity with special reference to Whitehead and Bergson. Yale, 1953.

5259. Pence, Gregory Eugene. A critical examination of John Rawls' *A theory of justice*. N.Y.U., 1974.
75-9684

5260. Penet, Sr. Mary Emil. Property and right in representative Catholic moralists of the thirteenth to seventeenth centuries. St. Louis, 1951.

5261. Penick, John Jacob. Wittgenstein on sensory pyrrhonism. No. Carolina, 1975. 75-29062

5262. Penn, Stuart Lee. The ethical relativism of Edward Westermarck. Yale, 1957.

5263. Penna, James Vincent. The problem of the soul and its powers in the De anima of William of Auvergne. Toronto, 1971.

5264. Pennepacker, Joseph S. The body-mind problem in James Ward's philosophy. Boston U., 1937.

5265. Pennock, Gilbert Lee. The consciousness of communion with God; a study in the psychology of religion. N.Y.U., 1919. 73-18089

5266. Penrose, Stephen Beasley Linnard. The reputation and influence of Francis Bacon in the seventeenth century. Columbia, 1935.

5267. Pepper, George B. The concept of man in theoretical anthropology. Fordham, 1958.

5268. Pepper, Stephen Coburn. A theory of value in terms of stimulus and response. Harvard, 1916.

5269. Perillat, Robert Joseph. St. Thomas Aquinas on the principle of subsistence. Notre Dame, 1958.
58-7100

5270. Perkins, Edward Moreland, Jr. A study of cognition: a psychological approach. Harvard, 1953.

5271. Perkins, Lisa Haenlein. The concept of "good moral character" in naturalization proceedings. Columbia, 1967. 67-12271

5272. Perkins, Raymond Keller, Jr. Meaning and acquaintance in the early philosophy of Bertrand Russell. Duke, 1973. 74-7559

5273. Perkins, Robert Lee. Kierkegaard and Hegel: the dialectical structure of Kierkegaard's ethical thought. Indiana, 1965. 65-10875

5274. Perlis, Donald Richard. Ackermann's set theory and related topics. N.Y.U., 1972. 72-21532

5275. Perlmutter, Martin. A critical examination of justification theory. Illinois, 1974. 75-398

5276. Perloff, Michael Norman. Agents and their reasons for actions. Pittsburgh, 1975. 76-366

5277. Perotti, James L. The problem of God in Heidegger.
      Duquesne, 1969.

5278. Perreiah, Alan Richard. Is there a doctrine of sup-
      position in the Logica magna? Indiana, 1967.
                                                67-15146

5279. Perrier, Joseph Louis. The revival of scholastic
      philosophy in the nineteenth century. Columbia,
      1909.

5280. Perrin, Ronald Fredric. Max Scheler's concept of the
      person: towards a radical humanism. Cal., S.
      Diego, 1971.   71-24598

5281. Perry, Charles Milton. Tappan's contribution to
      American philosophy and culture. Michigan, 1911.

5282. Perry, Charner Marquis. The genesis and operation
      of moral judgments: a study of British theories
      from Hobbes to Adam Smith. Chicago, 1926.

5283. Perry, David Louis. The concept of pleasure. Ber-
      keley, 1963.   63-5541

5284. Perry, James Frederic. On the significance of prax-
      iology for the study of education. Indiana, 1972.
                                                72-30440

5285. Perry, John Richard. Identity. Cornell, 1968.
                                                68-16760

5286. Perry, Ralph Barton. The life of reflection and
      energy: an ethical defense of the common morality
      of freedom, duty, and goodness. Harvard, 1899.

5287. Perry, Reginald Carman. The conflict of idealism
      and realism in Pringle-Pattison's philosophy.
      Toronto, 1945.

5288. Perry, Thomas Daniel. A theory of reasoning in eth-
      ics. Columbia, 1966.   69-15576

5289. Petale-Amato, John. Ernst Cassirer's theory of cul-
      ture. Fordham, 1974.   74-25077

5290. Peterfreund, Sheldon Paul. Three current theories
      of value. Pennsylvania, 1948.   2787

5291. Peterkin, John Manion. Proving the existence of God:
      inference or intuition? A study of the cosmologi-
      cal theism of E.L. Mascall. Marquette, 1974.
                                                74-22300

5292. Peters, Curtis Harold. Immanuel Kant on hope. Washington U., 1975. 76-14081

5293. Peters, Francis Edward. Aristoteles Arabus, the oriental translations and commentaries on the Aristotelian corpus. Princeton, 1961. 62-1900

5294. Peters, Selton Luke. A dualistic materialist theory of mind. Brown, 1975. 76-15692

5295. Petersen, Frithjof Ragnar. The philosophy of American political pluralism. Columbia, 1954.
8753

5296. Peterson, Forrest Harold. The study of power in the philosophies of Hegel and Marx. Georgetown, 1960.

5297. Peterson, John Francis. Logical atomism and the realsim-nominalism issue: a critique of contemporary atomism from the viewpoint of classical realism. Indiana, 1965. 65-10876

5298. Peterson, Paul Kermit. Meaning and wish fulfillment: an analysis of Freud's explanation of dreaming. Minnesota, 1972. 73-10620

5299. Peterson, Philip Leslie. A property instance theory of particulars. Duke, 1963. 63-7510

5300. Peterson, Sandra Lynne. The Masker paradox. Princeton, 1969. 70-8385

5301. Peterson, Sven Richard. William James: the formative years, 1842-1884. Columbia, 1954. 8754

5302. Petock, Stuart Jay. Kant and Collingwood on aesthetic experience. Cincinnati, 1971. 72-7527

5303. Petrick, Eileen Bagus. Heidegger on nihilism and the finitude of philosophy. Penn St., 1973.
74-16063

5304. Petrick, Joseph Anthony. Peirce on Hegel. Penn St., 1972. 73-20114

5305. Petrie, Hugh Gilbert. Rote learning and learning with understanding. Stanford, 1965. 66-2604

5306. Petriz, Margaret M. The philosophy of anger in relation to the virtues in the philosophy of St. Thomas Aquinas. Catholic U., 1953.

5307. Petti, Fred Charles. Method and metaphysics in the philosophy of Descartes. Boston Coll., 1973.
73-16441

5308. Pettit, Tupper Fleet. Judgment and the concept of time. N.Y.U., 1970. 71-2328

5309. Petty, Benjamin Aby. The definition of category in Aristotle, Kant, and Bowne. Boston U., 1961. 61-709

5310. Petty, Orville Anderson. The interpretation of the Meno of Plato. Yale, 1915.

5311. Peyton, John David. Explanations of behavior: a critical examination of Charles Taylor's philosophy of psychology. Pittsburgh, 1969. 69-12517

5312. Pezzolo, Peter Eugene. A contribution to the interpretation of Marxian theory. Yale, 1973. 73-29239

5313. Pfaff, Roland Leonard. Bullough's 'psychical distance', the aesthetic attitude, and appreciation of theater and film. Michigan, 1974. 74-25294

5314. Pfeffer, Rose. The tragic view in Nietzsche's philosophy. Columbia, 1963. 67-10356

5315. Pfeifer, David Elmer. The Summum bonum in the philosophy of C.S. Peirce. Illinois, 1971. 72-12337

5316. Pfeiffer, Raymond Smith. Pragmatism in the epistemology of Willard Van Orman Quine. Washington U., 1974. 75-14910

5317. Pfeiffer, Walter Mark. The Cratylus: Plato's investigation of names. Toronto, 1971.

5318. Pfunter, Carl Herman. An examination of the extent of philosophical dependence, methodological and metaphysical, of John Dewey on Charles Peirce. Georgetown, 1967. 68-1899

5319. Pham-Van-Long, Joseph. La spiritualité de l'âme humaine. Laval, 1958.

5320. Phelps, Sr. Mary. Rationes seminales in Jacobus de Viterbio. St. Louis, 1975. 75-26302

5321. Phelps, Moses Stuart. Title of dissertation unknown. Yale, 1874.

5322. Philip, Edward Parkinson. Scientific method, behavioral science, and rationality. Columbia, 1975. 75-27454

5323. Philippoussis, Jean. Le mythe philosophique: recherche et expression du sens de l'homme. Montreal, 1974.

5324. Philips, Michael Lawrence. Toward an adequate theory of mental language. Johns Hopkins, 1971.
71-21035

5325. Philipson, Morris H. C.G. Jung's theory of symbolism as a contribution to aesthetics. Columbia, 1959.
60-24

5326. Phillips, Alan Martin. The theory of intuition in Plato's Republic. Michigan St., 1969. 69-20914

5327. Phillips, Bernard. Being and process: a study in two philosophies. Yale, 1940.

5328. Phillips, George Blanchard. The concept of possible worlds in Leibniz's system. Harvard, 1920.

5329. Phillips, Herbert Joseph. The status of sense data. U. of Washington, 1933.

5330. Phillips, John Noble. Types of analytic truth. No. Carolina, 1955.

5331. Phillips, Mark A. The common sense philosophy of G.E. Moore. Loyola, 1970.

5332. Phillips, Rilla Mary. Time, freedom and self-consciousness in the philosophies of Karl Jaspers and Nicolas Berdyaev. Bryn Mawr, 1961.
62-5095

5333. Philp, Joseph Howard. The principle of individuation in the philosophy of Josiah Royce. Yale, 1916.

5334. Piatt, Douglas Ayres. Mind and nature. Chicago, 1925.

5335. Picard, Rev. Guy. La causalité accidentelle dans la nature. Laval, 1966.

5336. Picard, Maurice. Values, immediate and contributory, and their interrelation. N.Y.U., 1919.
74-1270

5337. Piccone, Paul. The philosophy of Antonio Banfi and European Marxism. Buffalo, 1970.   71-7207

5338. Pierce, Christine Margaret. The role of natural law in contemporary theories of legal procedural rights with special reference to problems in generality. Syracuse, 1969.   70-10379

5339. Pierce, Edgar. The aesthetics of simple forms. Harvard, 1895.

5340. Pierce, Ellis Ernest. De natura Dei. Drew, 1931.

5341. Pietersma, Henry. Edmund Husserl's concept of philosophical clarification; its development from 1887 to 1913. Toronto, 1962.

5342. Piggush, James Ralph. Peter Winch and the philosophy of the social sciences: a critical analysis. Notre Dame, 1974. 74-14250

5343. Pigors, Paul John William. The ethics of personality. Harvard, 1927.

5344. Pike, Nelson Craft. Hume on personal identity. Harvard, 1963.

5345. Pillote, Joyce Elaine Henricks. An analysis of morality. Michigan, 1969. 70-4167

5346. Pincoffs, Edmund Lloyd. The justification of legal punishment. Cornell, 1957. 57-3275

5347. Pingel, Martha Mary. An American utilitarian; Richard Hildreth as a philosopher, with selections from his published and unpublished works. Columbia, 1949.

5348. Pinkard, Terry Paul. The foundations of transcendental idealism: Kant, Hegel, Husserl. Stony Brook, 1975. 75-16203

5349. Pinkham, Gordon Nye. Case studies of scientific contributions. Berkeley, 1973. 74-10710

5350. Pinsky, Leonard Orville. Form and content in theory of knowledge since Kant. Iowa, 1952. 4098

5351. Pinto, Robert Charles. Sensory experience and ultimate evidence. Toronto, 1973.

5352. Pippin, Robert Buford. Kant and the problem of transcendental philosophy: unity and form in the Critique of pure reason. Penn St., 1974.
 75-9824

5353. Pisaneschi, Sr. Janet Irene. Chauncey Wright's philosophy of science. St. Louis, 1972. 72-23997

5354. Pitcher, George Willard. Illocutionary acts: an analysis of language in terms of human acts. Harvard, 1957.

5355. Pitt, Jack Arthur. Philosophical analysis and the critical philosophy of history. Yale, 1957.

5356. Pitt, Joseph Charles. An analysis of Wilfrid Sellars' theory of justification as explanation. W. Ontario, 1972.

5357. Pixler, Paul Wellington. The metaphysics of Wilbur M. Urban. Boston U., 1958. 58-3116

5358. Pizante, William Arthur. The concept of value in Whitehead's philosophy. Johns Hopkins, 1962.

5359. Place, James Gordon. Merleau-Ponty's philosophy of painting: a metaphysics of painting. So. Illinois, 1971. 72-10285

5360. Plantinga, Alvin Carl. Ethics and metaphysical naturalism. Yale, 1958.

5361. Plantinga, Cornelius A. The personalist philosophies of William Stern and Philipp Kohnstamm. Duke, 1940.

5362. Plantinga, Theodore. Understanding as the basis for historical inquiry in the later philosophy of Wilhelm Dilthey. Toronto, 1975.

5363. Platt, David Sellers. The religious claim to knowledge: critical remarks on natural theology. Pennsylvania, 1958. 58-3369

5364. Platt, Thomas Walter. Spencer and James on mental categories: a re-evaluation in light of modern biology. Pennsylvania, 1967. 67-7870

5365. Pletcher, Galen Kenneth. Mysticism and knowledge. Michigan, 1971. 72-4953

5366. Plochman, George K. Nature and the living creature in four theories of biology. Chicago, 1950.

5367. Pluhar, Werner Schrutka. Insentience, morality, and sensitivity. Michigan, 1973. 73-24656

5368. Poetker, Joseph Leonard. A theory of epistemic appraisal terms. No. Carolina, 1970. 71-11736

5369. Pohle, William Baldwin. Studies in the physical theory of Plato's Timaeus. Princeton, 1969.
 69-14429

5370. Poitras, Jean-Guy. L'expositio symboli dans la littérature Latine du moyen-âge occidental. Montreal, 1972.

5371. Polansky, Ronald Mark. Aristotle's understanding of human affectivity. Boston Coll., 1974. 74-19224

5372. Pole, Nelson. The meaning of terms employed in scientific languages and the problem of induction. Ohio St., 1971. 71-22523

5373. Politella, Joseph. Plationism, Aristotelianism, and Cabalism in the philosophy of Leibniz. Pennsylvania, 1938.

5374. Politis, Constantine. Analytic and synthetic sentences. Columbia, 1959. 60-1603

5375. Polkowski, William Allen. The evidential value of religious experience for the existence of God. Michigan, 1971. 72-4954

5376. Pollock, John Leslie. Analyticity and implication. Berkeley, 1965. 65-13564

5377. Pollock, Lansing. Reciprocity in moral theory. Chicago, 1970.

5378. Pollock, Robert Channon. The doctrine of rectitude in St. Anselm. Toronto, 1932.

5379. Polonoff, Irving Ivan. Kant's early writings. Yale, 1953.

5380. Pols, Edward Joseph, Jr. The idea of freedom in the metaphysics of Whitehead. Harvard, 1949.

5381. Pomedli, Rev. Michael M. Heidegger and Freud: the power of death. Duquesne, 1972. 72-29455

5382. Pomerance, Irwin. The moral utopianism of Georges Sorel. Columbia, 1950. 1889

5383. Poole, Cyril Francis. A critical examination of Hobhouse's theory of knowledge. Toronto, 1957.

5384. Popkin, Richard Henry. The neo-intuitionist theory of mathematics and logic. Columbia, 1950. 1890

5385. Poppen, Jacob. Relation of faith and certainty. Princeton, 1896.

5386. Porreco, Rocco E. The place of economics in the philosophical hierarchy. Catholic U., 1949.

5387. Portman, Stephen Gregory. The problem of values and Jean-Paul Sartre's existential psychoanalysis. New Mexico, 1971. 72-3996

5388. Portnoy, Julius. A psychology of art creation. Pennsylvania, 1942.

5389. Portnoy, Mark Barry. Self-deception. Calgary, 1973.

5390. Poser, Steven Kenneth. Meaning and communication. Calgary, 1973.

5391. Pospesel, Howard Andrew. The existence of propositions. No. Carolina, 1967. 68-6756

5392. Post, John Frederic. The logic of presupposition. Berkeley, 1968. 69-10366

5393. Postow, Betsy Carol. A conciliatory approach to morals. Yale, 1970.

5394. Posy, Carl J. The intuitionistic continuum and the mathematical a priori. Yale, 1971. 71-31098

5395. Potok, Herman Harold. The rationalism and skepticism of Solomon Maimon. Pennsylvania, 1965.
66-292

5396. Pott, William H. Modern ethics. Columbia, 1886.

5397. Pott, William Sumner Appleton. Chinese political philosophy. Virginia, 1925.

5398. Potter, Elizabeth Faye. Kant's doctrine of threefold synthesis. Rice, 1974. 74-21320

5399. Potter, Jean Alice. Theories of symbol and analogy in religious cognition. Yale, 1954.

5400. Potter, Karl Harrington. Raghunātha's Padārthattvanirūpana (On what words refer to): a study in Navya-nyāya metaphysics. Harvard, 1955.

5401. Potter, Nelson Thomas, Jr. Maxims and the application of the categorical imperative. Johns Hoplins, 1969. 69-21067

5402. Potter, Suzanne Elizabeth. A study of the Regulae de sacra theologia of Alan of Lille. Columbia, 1972. 74-29643

5403. Potter, Rev. Vincent George. Peirce's ontological pragmatism. Yale, 1965. 65-15102

5404. Pottinger, Garrel Shane. A theory of implications. Pittsburgh, 1972. 73-13202

5405. Pousson, Leon. The totalitarian philosophy of education. Catholic U., 1944.

5406. Powell, Francis D. A Thomistic evaluation of James Wilson and Thomas Reid. Georgetown, 1951.

5407. Powell, John W. The metaphysics of Giordano Bruno. Wisconsin, 1932.

5408. Powell, Robert George. Alternate modes of consciousness: a Whiteheadian approach. Fordham, 1974. 74-19683

5409. Power, Robert Joseph. The bases of political rights in the philosophy of John Dewey. Emory, 1964. 64-11219

5410. Praetorius, Hugh Michael. Escape from the evil demon: a discourse on the Cartesianism of phenomenology. Claremont, 1969. 70-9832

5411. Prall, David Wight. A study in the theory of value. Berkeley, 1919.

5412. Prasad, Rajendra. A non-cognitivist analysis of moral language: a study of meaning and justification. Michigan, 1957. 58-1451

5413. Pratt, Grace Kipp. An analysis and comparison of the concept of social-self-realization in the reconstructionist and ethical culture philosophies. N.Y.U., 1959. 60-1100

5414. Pratt, James Bissett. Historical illustrations of the psychology of religious belief. Harvard, 1905.

5415. Pratt, James Richard. Standards of criticism in the visual arts. Brown, 1961. 63-1454

5416. Pratt, Ronald L. The notion of person in the writing of Gabriel Marcel. Catholic U., 1970. 70-10573

5417. Pray, Ruth Willis. The neo-platonic element. Chicago, 1925.

5418. Preer, George T. Materialism in the philosophy of Pietro Pomponatius. Virginia, 1938.

5419. Premo, Blanche Lillie Kolar. Wittgenstein's notion of description: from logic to grammar. Marquette, 1974. 75-14995

5420. Prendergast, Thomas Love. Matter in the physical world of Descartes. Syracuse, 1968. 69-370

5421. Prentice, Rev. Robert. The psychology of love according to St. Bonaventure. St. Bonaventure, 1950.

5422. Presler, Judith Louise. A philosophical examination of Epicurus' atomism. Oklahoma, 1973. 73-23927

5423. Press, Gerald Alan. The development of the idea of history in antiquity. Cal., S. Diego, 1974.
74-23971

5424. Press, Howard Edwin. The aesthetic basis of Whitehead's philosophy. Columbia, 1967. 71-6241

5425. Preston, Arline F. Primitivism in French literature of the 16th century. Johns Hopkins, 1951.

5426. Preston, M. Different theories of beauty. Cornell, 1880.

5427. Preston, Robert A. Causality and the Thomistic theory of knowledge. Catholic U., 1960.

5428. Preus, Anthony Axel. Problems in explanation in Aristotle's biology. Johns Hopkins, 1968.
68-16463

5429. Preuss, Peter Siegfried. The individual in community. Toronto, 1971.

5430. Prevots, Claude Henry. The semantics of legal reasoning. Wisconsin, 1961. 61-5974

5431. Price, Bruce William. Kant's conceptions of intuition, judgments of perception and experience. Rochester, 1974. 74-22621

5432. Price, Connie Barnett Crank. Consciousness and history in Bergson's philosophy. Penn St., 1972.
73-20116

5433. Price, Jeffrey Thomas. Language and being in Wittgenstein's *Philosophical* *investigations*. Penn St., 1969. 70-19451

5434. Price, Kingsley Blake. Metaphysics in relation to ethics: a study of Hume. Berkeley, 1946.

5435. Price, Marjorie Spear. Essentialism and the doctrine of natural kinds. N.Y.U., 1974. 74-30031

5436. Price, Robert George. Plato's *Cratylus* and contemporary analysis. Yale, 1963.

5437. Price, Ross Eugene. The philosophies of Ralph Tyler Flewelling and Edgar Sheffield Brightman: a comparison and a critique. Southern Cal., 1966.
67-2118

5438. Priest, Ward Curtiss. The need and value of restructuring human communication systems: towards the HCS. R.P.I., 1972.
72-30227

5439. Priestley, Christopher Douglas Craig. Nagarjuna's argument for the emptiness of all beings. Toronto, 1972.

5440. Prigge, Norman K. The meaning of epistemologically ideal statements. Cal., S. Barbara, 1974.

5441. Primack, Maxwell. Francis Bacon's philosophy of nature. Johns Hopkins, 1962.

5442. Prins, Tunis. A study in the problem of fact. Southern Cal., 1938.

5443. Pritchard, Michael Scott. The sense of justice. Wisconsin, 1968.
63-5346

5444. Probst, Joseph Stanislaus. Reason, experience, and natural law. Fordham, 1948.

5445. Procter, Thomas Hayes. Faith and knowledge in religion. Harvard, 1916.

5446. Proctor, George Lewis. Propositions, facts, and immediate experience. Virginia, 1957.
57-4247

5447. Prosch, Harry, Jr. The current impasse of ethics. Chicago, 1955.

5448. Proudfoot, Charles Merrill. God treated as an unobservable entity in scientific theory. Kansas, 1971.
71-27198

5449. Proulx, Fernande (Sr. St. Jean-Elzéar). Le Marxisme et le rapport de la pensée de l'être. Laval, 1965.

5450. Provence, Donald Lee. Is seeing believing? Stanford, 1968.
69-271

5451. Provine, Robert Calhoun. The voluntarism of William James: an historical and critical study. Brown, 1933.

5452. Pruitt, Sylvia Ann. An inquiry into the ethical implications of Whitehead's metaphysics. Emory, 1970.
70-22888

5453. Przezdiecki, Joseph John. The passivity of the possible intellect according to Thomas of Sutton: study and texts. Toronto, 1952.

5454. Pugh, John Kennedy. An ontology of human acting: person and community in the philosophy of Joseph de Finance, S.J. Marquette, 1975. 76-8649

5455. Pujol, Rev. Augustin M. The hylomorphic teachings of William of Ockham. St. Bonaventure, 1962.

5456. Puligandla, Ramarkrishna. An examination of the Copenhagen interpretation of quantum theory. Rice, 1966. 66-10371

5457. Puls, Sr. Mary Sarto. The personalistic theism of Borden Parker Bowne. Marquette, 1965. 67-3635

5458. Punzo, Vincent Christopher. Royce on the problem of individuality. St. Louis, 1963. 64-4266

5459. Purdy, Laura Martha. A critical analysis of Francisco de Vitoria's Law of peace. Stanford, 1974. 75-6908

5460. Purkiser, Westlake T. Some concepts of the datum in American realism. Southern Cal., 1948.

5461. Purnell, Frederick, Jr. Jacopo Mazzoni and his comparison of Plato and Aristotle. Columbia, 1971. 72-10457

5462. Purtill, Richard L. Explanation, predication and confirmation. Chicago, 1965.

5463. Pustilnik, Jack. Process and causality: Whitehead's reply to Hume. Columbia, 1958. 59-739

5464. Putnam, Mthr. Caroline Canfield. Beauty in the Pseudo-Denis. Catholic U., 1960.

5465. Putnam, Hilary. The meaning of the concept of probability in application to finite sequences. U.C.L.A., 1951.

5466. Putz, Carl Hampton. The nature of scientific laws. Pittsburgh, 1970. 71-10556

5467. Pyun, Hae Soo. On the metaphysics of F.J.E. Woodbridge. Columbia, 1966. 69-15578

- Q -

5468. Quest, Charles Edward. Rationality. Claremont, 1967. 68-10535

5469. Quine, Willard Van Orman. The logic of sequences: a generalization of Principia mathematica. Harvard, 1932.

5470. Quinn, Charles Francis, III. An analysis of the concept of constructive categoricity. Notre Dame, 1971. 71-19084

5471. Quinn, Dennis Patrick. An examination of Kant's treatment of transcendental freedom. Notre Dame, 1968. 69-4077

5472. Quinn, John. St. Bonaventure and the notion of Christian philosophy in modern scholarship; an introduction to St. Bonaventure and the Divine Immutability. Toronto, 1966.

5473. Quinn, Rev. John Michael. The doctrine of time in St. Thomas Aquinas; some aspects and applications. Catholic U., 1961.

5474. Quinn, Michael Sean. Rules and the moral life. Pittsburgh, 1973. 74-18418

5475. Quinn, Philip Lawrence. Duhemian conventionalism. Pittsburgh, 1970. 71-10557

5476. Quinn, Warren Scott. Excellence and moral virtue. Michigan, 1968. 69-12215

5477. Quintanilla, Luis. Bergsonisme et politique. Johns Hopkins, 1938.

5478. Quittmeyer, Ernest Martin. Ethics of American laws of inheritance and bequest. Yale, 1904.

5479. Qureshi, Tufail Ahmed. The Cartesian modes and levels of doubt: a phenomenological description. Buffalo, 1973. 73-19228

- R -

5480. Raab, Francis Vincent. A criterion of necessary truth. Yale, 1952.

5481. Rabbin, Harvey Gabriel. Philosophy and a science of man. Cal., S. Cruz, 1973.

5482. Rabenstein, William Louis. The problem of teleology in relation to the views of Bosanquet, Royce, B. Russell, and S. Alexander. Cornell, 1934.

5483. Rabinovitch, Nachum L. Probability and statistical inference in ancient and medieval Jewish literature. Toronto, 1971.

5484. Rabinowitz, Margula. The methodological principles of Sir Isaac Newton. Pennsylvania, 1960.
60-3682

5485. Rabinowitz, Rea E. Meaning and structure in the visual arts and music. Brandeis, 1974.
74-28008

5486. Rachels, James Webster, Jr. Butler's theory of moral agency. No. Carolina, 1967. 68-2223

5487. Radcliff, Peter Edward, Jr. The paradigm case argument as an existence proof. U. of Washington, 1958. 58-7373

5488. Radest, Howard Bernard. Toward a philosophy of culture (a study of Felix Adler's view of education.) Columbia, 1971. 71-23615

5489. Radford, Robert Thomas. Freedom and explanation: a critique of Melden's action theory. Texas, 1970.
71-179

5490. Radner, Daisie Missouri Crumling. Causality: a study of seventeenth century philosophy. Minnesota, 1969. 70-15794

5491. Radner, Michael. Philosophical implications of recent work of Cohen and Scott in the foundations of mathematics. Minnesota, 1968. 69-6842

5492. Raemers, Sidney A. A critical examination into the alleged ontologism of Orestes A. Brownson. Notre Dame, 1929.

5493. Raff, Charles. Knowledge and memory. Brown, 1967.
68-1487

5494. Rafie, Marcel. Des sciences dites humaines. (Edition critique de la Sociologie d'Emile Durkheim.) Montreal, 1974.

5495. Raghavan, Maithili. Are meta-ethical theories normatively neutral? Michigan, 1964. 64-6739

5496. Rago, Henry. The philosophy of esthetic individualism. Notre Dame, 1941.

5497. Ragusa, Thomas J. The substance theory of mind and contemporary functionalism. Catholic U., 1937.

5498. Raico, Ralph. The place of religion in the liberal philosophy of Constant, Tocqueville, and Lord Acton. Chicago, 1971.

5499. Ralston, Harold Jameson. The concept of purpose in the philosophy of Professor C. Lloyd Morgan. Iowa, 1930.

5500. Ramberan, Osmond George. Faith, language and the problem of evil: in recent analytic philosophy. McMaster, 1974.

5501. Ramer, Ronald Irving. A classical utilitarian theory of distributive justice. Syracuse, 1973.
74-10170

5502. Ramige, Eldon Albert. Contemporary concepts of time and the idea of God. Iowa, 1933.

5503. Ramirez, Augustine. Unconscious drives and human freedom in Freud's psychoanalysis. Catholic U., 1955.

5504. Ramirez, Joel Celedonio. The personalist metaphysics of Xavier Zubiri. Georgetown, 1969.
70-5920

5505. Ramm, Bernard Lawrence. An investigation of some recent efforts to justify metaphysical statements derived from science with special reference to physics. Southern Cal., 1950.

5506. Ramm, Hartmut. The political philosophy of Regis Debray: between Lenin and Guevara. Florida St., 1974. 75-12667

5507. Ramsdell, Edward Thomas. Pragmatic elements in the epistemology of Borden P. Browne. Boston U., 1932.

5508. Ramsdell, Robert Duane. Brightman's view of the person and educational theory. Boston U., 1967.
67-13331

5509. Ramsden, Elizabeth G. A discussion of the issues in the theory of knowledge involved in the controversy between John Dewey and Bertrand Russell. Bryn Mawr, 1951. 4520

5510. Ramsey, John Tyler. Studies in Asconius. Harvard, 1975.

5511. Ramsperger, Albert Gustav. Physics and metaphysics. Berkeley, 1928.

5512. Rand, Benjamin. Consciousness and immortality. Harvard, 1885.

5513. Randall, Albert B., Jr. Hope: an exploration of Camus, Marcel and intimacy. Oklahoma, 1973.
73-26323

5514. Ranken, Nani Lengyel. The cognitive significance of ethical theories. Yale, 1960.

5515. Ranly, Rev. Ernest Willibald. Scheler's phenomenology of community. St. Louis, 1964. 64-13480

5516. Ransdell, Joseph Morton. Charles Peirce: the idea of representation. Columbia, 1966. 67-9367

5517. Rao, Pappu Surya Sundara Rama. H.L.A. Hart on law and morality. So. Illinois, 1968. 69-6300

5518. Rapaczynski, Andrzej. Reflection and the structure of Hegel's system. Columbia, 1974. 75-5241

5519. Rapaport, Elizabeth. Moral weakness. Case, 1971.
72-95

5520. Rapchak, John Wallace. The origins of the philosophy of history. Penn St., 1967. 68-8737

5521. Rapp, Richard John. The concept of God in the philosophy of A.N. Whitehead, dealing specifically with the problem of the superjective nature. Duquesne, 1969. 70-10147

5522. Rappaport, Steven Dodson. G.E. Moore's sense-datum theory. Toronto, 1972.

5523. Rashid, Muhammad Harun-Ar. Alexander's theory of value and its foundations. Missouri, 1972.
73-21433

5524. Rasmussen, Dennis Fletcher. Poetry and truth: an inquiry into their relation. Yale, 1970.
71-46

5525. Rasmussen, Maxine Konig. The concept of communication in the existential philosophy of Karl Jaspers. No. Dakota, 1973. 74-4159

5526. Rasmussen, Paul Erik. Descartes' world hypothesis. So. Illinois, 1969. 7C-7308

5527. Ratanakul, Pinit. The self is freedom: a critical study of Jean-Paul Sartre's philosophy of freedom. Yale, 1970. 71-47

5528. Ratner, Joseph. Spinoza on God. Columbia, 1930.

5529. Ratte, Rena Josephine. George Berkeley's theory of language. Duke, 1959. 6C-1256

5530. Rattray, Robert Fleming. Samuel Butler and the philosophy of nature. Harvard, 1913.

5531. Ratzsch, Delvin Lee. God, freedom and Plantinga. Massachusetts, 1975. 76-5386

5532. Rau, Catherine Dunn. Plato's views on art. Berkeley, 1945.

5533. Rauch, Leo. Intentionality and its development in the phenomenological psychology of Edmund Husserl. N.Y.U., 1968. 68-13138

5534. Rawlings, Margaret B. Coleridge as a philosophical critic. Bryn Mawr, 1935.

5535. Rawls, John Bordley. A study in the grounds of ethical knowledge, considered with reference to judgments on the moral worth of character. Princeton, 1950. 11003

5536. Rawson, Freeman Leigh, III. Set-theoretical semantics for a fragment of elementary mathematical language. Stanford, 1973. 74-6532

5537. Rayfield, David Leon. Practical reasoning and the relation between decision and action. Duke, 1967.
68-2739

5538. Raynor, Owen Nicholas. Philosophical doubt. Virginia, 1961. 61-4564

5539. Read, M.S. English evolutionary ethics. Cornell, 1895.

5540. Read, Waldemar. John Dewey's conception of intelligent social action. Chicago, 1897.

5541. Reagan, Charles Ellis. Freedom and determinism: a critical study of certain aspects of this problem in the light of the philosophy of Paul Ricoeur. Kansas, 1967. 68-618

5542. Reagan, James Thomas. The material substrate in the Platonic dialogues. St. Louis, 1960. 61-772

5543. Reardon, Rev. John J. Selfishness and the social order. Catholic U., 1943.

5544. Reaven, Sheldon Joseph. Aspects of holism in languages and theories. Berkeley, 1975. 76-15350

5545. Reba, Marilyn Anderson. Rationality and altruism. No. Carolina, 1973. 74-15387

5546. Reck, Andrew Joseph. Substance and some philosophers. Yale, 1954.

5547. Redding, Earl Wallace. Aesthetic, religious, and moral intuition in the philosophy of Alfred North Whitehead. Miami, 1969. 70-11203

5548. Redding, Rev. James F. The virtue of prudence in the writings of St. Thomas Aquinas. Fordham, 1950.

5549. Redmon, Robert Bruce, Jr. The ontological significance of semantical methods. No. Carolina, 1969. 70-12100

5550. Redmond, Daniel Clyde. Causation and the explanation of actions. Wisconsin, 1974. 74-22136

5551. Redpath, Peter A. The ontological status of time in the Commentary on the sentences, the Commentary on the physics, and the Summa theologiae of Thomas Aquinas. Buffalo, 1974. 74-20028

5552. Reed, David Allan. The genesis of negativity. Yale, 1960.

5553. Reed, Homer B. Morals of monopoly and competition. Chicago, 1912.

5554. Reed, Margaret McLeish Schipper. Practical relevance, neutrality, and normative ethical theory: an essay in ethical method. Texas, 1971. 72-11410

5555. Reed, Thomas McHugh. Certainty. Texas, 1967. 67-8150

5556. Reeder, Paul A. The instrumental theory of judgment. Syracuse, 1931.

5557. Reeves, Alan Leslie. Referential opacity. Berkeley, 1970. 71-9901

5558. Reeves, Clement. Paychotherapy in search of theoretical foundations: the ontological approach of Rollo May. Ottawa, 1974.

5559. Reeves, Gene Arthur. Our knowledge of God and the nature of God in the philosophies of Gabriel Marcel and Paul Tillich. Emory, 1963. 64-4551

5560. Reeves, George C. The philosophy of Tommaso Campanella with special reference to his doctrine of the sense of things and of magic. Indiana, 1935.

5561. Reeves, M. Francis. God and history in the thought of Paul Tillich. Boston U., 1967. 67-13287

5562. Regan, Teresa N. (Sr. Frances Carmel). A study of the *Liber* *de* *spiritu* *et* *anima*; its doctrine, sources and historical significance. Toronto, 1949.

5563. Regan, Thomas Howard. The commendation-thesis. Virginia, 1966. 66-15194

5564. Regester, John Dickinson. Immediate intuition in the New Rationalism of Albert Schweitzer. Boston U., 1928.

5565. Regis, Edward, Jr. Aristotle's conception of the metaphysical individual. N.Y.U., 1972.
73-11757

5566. Reichenbach, Bruce Robert. The cosmological argument. Northwestern, 1968. 69-1917

5567. Reichert, Donald Henry. The philosophy of freedom and education in the thought of Jacques Maritain. Ohio St., 1966. 67-6359

5568. Reid, Charles Lloyd. The epistemological value of the concept of the given. Duke, 1960. 6C-6038

5569. Reid, Joel Otto. Existentialism in black American literature. Claremont, 1974. 74-20112

5570. Reid, John Robert. A naturalistic theory of value. Berkeley, 1936.

5571. Reid, Stanley Bonneau. The role of logical form in propositions about existence. Berkeley, 1931.

5572. Reidenbach, Clarence. A critical analysis of patriotism as an ethical concept. Yale, 1918.

5573. Reidy, Sr. Jeanne. Value language analysis and Carl Rogers' psychotherapy: two approaches to questions about the human person. Notre Dame, 1969.
69-9454

5574. Reidy, Martin Francis. Aristotle's doctrine concerning applied mathematics. Toronto, 1968.

5575. Reif, Sr. Mary Richard. Natural philosophy in some early seventeenth century scholastic textbooks. St. Louis, 1962.   64-3764

5576. Reilly, Rev. Francis Eagan. The method of the sciences according to Charles Sanders Peirce. St. Louis, 1959.   60-353

5577. Reilly, George C. The psychology of St. Albert the Great. Catholic U., 1934.

5578. Reilly, James Patrick. The divisions of being in Thomas of York; study and text. Toronto, 1951.

5579. Reilly, Rev. John Patrick. Cajetan's notion of existence. St. Louis, 1961.   61-6487

5580. Reilly, Richard Paul. The possibility of moral weakness: an essay on the metaphysics and psychology of morals. Cal., S. Barbara, 1972.   73-19153

5581. Reilly, William Francis, Jr. The pragmatism of William James as a religious philosophy. Fordham, 1961.   62-1039

5582. Reilly, Rev. William Leo. Metaphysical abstraction according to Joseph Marechal, S.J. Fordham, 1957.

5583. Reiman, Jeffrey Howard. Time and the epoche of Husserl. Penn St., 1968.   69-14561

5584. Reinehr, Merle Jerome. Particles and waves in contemporary physics. So. Illinois, 1975.
76-13281

5585. Reiner, William B. The value of cause and effect analysis in developing ability to recognize cause and effect relationships. N.Y.U., 1942.
73-8739

5586. Reinkraut, Richard Henry. The limits of empiricism: the epistemological status of religious discourse. Connecticut, 1974.   73-28519

5587. Rein'l, Robert Lincoln Coffin. Intuition and analysis in Bergson's theory of knowledge. Harvard, 1940.

5588. Reintiz, Eva. A study in the early philosophy of Karl Jaspers. Johns Hopkins, 1961.

5589. Reis, Lincoln. The predicables and the predicaments in the *Totius summa logicae Aristotelis*. Columbia, 1936.

5590. Reisner, Edward Hartman. Religious values and intellectual consistency. Columbia, 1915.

5591. Reiss, Lester Joseph. Some main principles of naturalism. Boston U., 1967. 67-13289

5592. Reiter, Michael Alan. Legal reasoning as applied to the interpretation of statutes. Wisconsin, 1969. 70-3675

5593. Reith, Herman. The Marxist dialectics of nature. Laval, 1946.

5594. Reither, William Harry. The ethics of Joseph Butler. Ohio St., 1931.

5595. Reitzner, Rev. Melvin Kenneth. Arthur O. Lovejoy's critique of idealism. St. Louis, 1972. 72-24006

5596. Rembert, George Andrew, Jr. A critical study of "Dreaming" by Norman Malcolm and a defense of the traditional view of the constituents of dreams. Cornell, 1973. 74-6339

5597. Remick, Oscar Eugene. Value in the thought of Paul Tillich. Boston U., 1966. 66-11324

5598. Remsberg, Robert G. Wisdom and science at Port-Royal and the Oratory; a study of contrasting Augustinianisms. Columbia, 1941.

5599. Renner, O.J. Natural rights. Cincinnati, 1918.

5600. Rensma, Patricia Ann. Eros and wholeness in the thought of Spinoza and Hegel. Penn St., 1970. 71-21793

5601. Rescher, Nicholas H. A reinterpretation of the philosophy of Leibniz in the light of his physical theories. Princeton, 1951.

5602. Resnick, Lawrence. H.H. Price's analysis of the nature of concepts. Cornell, 1956.

5603. Resnik, Michael David. Frege's methodology: a critical study. Harvard, 1964.

5604. Restuccia, Paul Philip. Marx's concept of alienation. So. Illinois, 1968. 69-1761

5605. Reuman, Robert Everett. An examination of value theory in the light of the bifurcation of fact and value. Pennsylvania, 1949. 3096

5606. Reuscher, John Alfred. Kant's philosophy of space. Fordham, 1969. 69-16239

5607. Reutemann, Br. Charles L. The Thomistic concept of pleasure as compared with hedonistic and rigoristic philosophies. Catholic U., 1953.

5608. Reynolds, Paul Arthur. Emergent evolution and the nature of mind. Cornell, 1930.

5609. Rhinelander, Philip Hamilton. Rational conduct and the common good. Harvard, 1949.

5610. Rhodes, Margaret Louise. Mental disorder and irrationality. Brandeis, 1975. 75-15121

5611. Rhodes, Sheila Sack. A critique of the ethical utility of interpersonal psychology. Buffalo, 1969. 70-17361

5612. Ricci, Louis Michael. Independent existence in Royce, Perry and Husserl. Buffalo, 1970.
71-7213

5613. Rice, Lee Collins. Moral judgment in Benedict de Spinoza. St. Louis, 1967. 68-1288

5614. Rice, Robert Adams. John Priestley's materialist theory of cognition: its evolution and historical significance. Brandeis, 1969. 69-16315

5615. Rice, Roland P. Mysticism in the philosophy of William Ernest Hocking. Boston U., 1954.

5616. Rich, Gertrude V.B. Interpretations of human nature: a study of certain late seventeenth and early eighteenth century British attitudes toward man's nature and capacities. Columbia, 1935.

5617. Richards, Benjamin Armstrong. The inalienability of traditional individual rights. Yale, 1959.

5618. Richards, David Henry. Self-valuation in religious experience. Fordham, 1975. 76-4140

5619. Richards, George Samuel. Kant's theory of ethics examined with reference to his theory of knowledge and to the fundamental principles in the moral teaching of Jesus Christ. Yale, 1894.

5620. Richards, Howard C. Karl Marx: the relation of the labor theory of value to distributive justice. Cal., S. Barbara, 1974.

5621. Richards, Jerald Homer. The nature, function, and validity of religious language in the thought of Austin Farrer. Boston U., 1966.   66-11283

5622. Richards, John. The theory of types. Buffalo, 1971.
72-10509

5623. Richards, Norvin Waldemar, Jr. The concept of visualizing. Virginia, 1969.   70-8069

5624. Richards, Robert John. Wilfrid Sellars: toward a scientific explanation of man. St. Louis, 1971.
72-5321

5625. Richards, William M. A new interpretation of the Tractatus logico-philosophicus. Georgetown, 1970.   71-19332

5626. Richardson, David Bonner. Explanation of Berdyaev's philosophy of history. Toronto, 1954.

5627. Richardson, James David. A critique of Armstrong's analysis of consciousness. Boston U., 1973.
73-23512

5628. Richardson, Robert Allan. Aesthetics and freedom: a critique of Kant's analysis of beauty. Yale, 1969.   70-2793

5629. Richey, Sr. Francis Augustine. Character control of wealth according to St. Thomas Aquinas. Catholic U., 1940.

5630. Richfield, Jerome. Juridic law as a criterion of value theory. Cincinnati, 1950.

5631. Richman, Robert June. Meaning and confirmation. Harvard, 1953.

5632. Richmond, Samuel Alec. Wants, evaluations, and purposes. Michigan, 1969.   70-21774

5633. Richter, John Blain. New light on Spinoza. Missouri, 1974.   75-5789

5634. Richter, Mary Ann Carroll. The individuals which can be counted among those called persons. No. Carolina, 1973. 73-26233

5635. Richter, Paul David. Can the question, "What is art?" be answered? Rochester, 1968. 68-15856

5636. Richter, Peyton E. The metaphysical foundations of Jordan's aesthetics. Duke, 1953.

5637. Rickert, Richard Frederick. Aesthetic interpreting and describing: their functions in regard to the "transinterpretive" art of Kafka and of Zen. No. Carolina, 1972. 73-4869

5638. Rickertsen, Bryan Chris. A theory of truth and meaning: an inquiry concerning linguistic understanding. Nebraska, 1974. 75-16923

5639. Ricks, William Timothy. An examination of R.W. Beardsmore's views on moral justification. Georgia, 1975.

5640. Riddle, Chauncey Cazier. Karl Pearson's philosophy of science. Columbia, 1958. 59-1498

5641. Riddle, Glenn Keith. A critical examination of recent deontological ethical theories. Wisconsin, 1955.

5642. Ridgley, Frank Harris. Jewish ethical idealism. Pennsylvania, 1916.

5643. Riedel, Marcus Eric John. Rational criteria and moral sensitivity: a study of rules and motives in decision making. Chicago, 1967.

5644. Riedl, John O. The life and philosophy of Orestes A. Brownson. Marquette, 1930.

5645. Rieman, George Frederick, Jr. Foundations of acceptance. Pennsylvania, 1960. 61-2061

5646. Riepe, Dale Maurice. Early Indian philosophical naturalism. Michigan, 1954. 8401

5647. Ries, Clayton Benedict. Freedom and self-becoming in Karl Jaspers' existential philosophy. No. Dakota, 1973. 74-4160

5648. Rigg, Melvin Gillison. Theories of the obligation of citizen to state. Pennsylvania, 1920.

5649. Right, William K. Ethical significance of pleasure, feeling, and happiness in modern neo-hedonistic systems. Chicago, 1906.

5650. Rigterink, Roger J. Aristotle's conception of geometric objects. Wisconsin, 1973.   73-21176

5651. Riker, John Hanwell. Ethics, meta-ethics, and metaphysics: a study in Whitehead's cosmology. Vanderbilt, 1969.   70-5423

5652. Riley, Buddy Gresham. The self, self-knowledge and pragmaticism. Yale, 1965.   65-15106

5653. Ring, Agnes Elizabeth Muir. Explicability and determinism. Brown, 1975.   76-15703

5654. Ring, Louis Merrill. Kinaesthetic theory: a philosophical and historical investigation. U. of Washington, 1965.   65-15407

5655. Ringelheim, Joan. Historical reconstruction and psychoanalysis. Boston U., 1968.   68-18119

5656. Ringen, Jon D. Behavior theoretic explanation: a study of the new dualism in the philosophy of action. Indiana, 1971.   72-6828

5657. Ringer, Virginia Hartt. Conceptions of human nature and entailed conceptions of the state within the framework of the developing Anglo-American tradition. Southern Cal., 1957.

5658. Ringnalda, Murco. The empiricism of Moritz Schlick. Southern Cal., 1953.

5659. Riordan, Joseph. Form and intellect in Averroes. Toronto, 1960.

5660. Ripley, Julien A. Methodological analysis in the social sciences. Virginia, 1933.

5661. Riser, John Sherwood. The philosophical analysis of theological statements. No. Carolina, 1962.   63-3560

5662. Ritchie, Jessie Elizabeth. The concept of dialectic. N.Y.U., 1954.   11951

5663. Rivello, Sr. Joseph Roberta. An adaptation of Bernard J.F. Lonergan's heuristic structure: a response to institutional moral scotosis. Temple, 1974.   74-28189

5664. Rizik, James. Genetic accounts in Fichte and Hobbes. Harvard, 1968.

5665. Robb, James Harry Kenneth. The nature of the human soul in the *Quaestiones de anima* (Q. 1-3) of St. Thomas Aquinas; study and text. Toronto, 1953.

5666. Robb, John W. An examination of James Ward's philosophy as a basis for a philosophy of religion. Southern Cal., 1953.

5667. Robb, Kevin Walter. The Hellenic eros: a study in the transition from the oral to the Platonic mentality. Yale, 1969.

5668. Robbins, Beverly Levin. The definite article in logic and grammar. Pennsylvania, 1966.
66-4639

5669. Robbins, David Orison. Paradigmatic interpretation of Plato's ideal theory. Princeton, 1939.
3029

5670. Robbins, Dennis Alan. Towards a phenomenology of human emotion. Boston Coll., 1974. 74-14243

5671. Robert, Leo. The philosophical method of Shadworth Hodgson. Harvard, 1933.

5672. Robert, Patrice. Hylémorphisme et devenir dans Saint Bonaventure. Laval, 1936.

5673. Roberts, Br. Augustine. Max Scheler's phenomenology of person. Duquesne, 1968.

5674. Roberts, David, IV. The nature of the finite mode in Spinoza's metaphysics. Emory, 1973.
74-460

5675. Roberts, Don Davis. The existential graphs of Charles S. Peirce. Illinois, 1963. 64-6138

5676. Roberts, Dorothy Elliott. The centrality of ethics to Jean-Marie Guyau's naturalism. Berkeley, 1955.

5677. Roberts, Helen Louise Nisbet. An introduction to the terminist logic of John Buridan. Columbia, 1952. 4227

5678. Roberts, James Russell. Seventeenth century contributions to Emerson's thought. U. of Washington, 1940.

5679. Roberts, Lawrence David. Duns Scotus and the concept of human freedom. Indiana, 1969. 70-12410

5680. Roberts, Lorraine Beattie. Prolegomena to a philosophy of man. Waterloo, 1975.

5681. Roberts, Rev. Victor William. Hegelian dialectic in the light of its antecedents in Plato, Aristotle, Kant, and Fichte. Fordham, 1973. 74-2758

5682. Robertson, John Edwards. The distinction between substance and non-substance in Aristotle's metaphysics. Texas, 1975.　　76-8097

5683. Robertson, Robert E. The concept of the given in new realism and pragmatism. Texas, 1953.

5684. Robin, Richard Shale. Critical common-sensism: a study in the philosophy of C.S. Peirce. Harvard, 1958.

5685. Robins, Michael Harvey. The fact-value dichotomy: a theory of games analysis. Northwestern, 1970.　　71-1955

5686. Robins, Sidney Swaim. Hegel's pragmatism. Harvard, 1910.

5687. Robinson, Andrew H. Contingency and the modern scholastics. Laval, 1955.

5688. Robinson, Daniel Sommer. The place of inference in logical theory. Harvard, 1917.

5689. Robinson, Edward Schouten. Early Greek theories involving similarity and contrariety as reported by Plato and Aristotle. Harvard, 1932.

5690. Robinson, Franklin Edward. Jouvenel on the common good. So. Illinois, 1970.　　71-2402

5691. Robinson, Helier James. The philosophy of the suprarational. Toronto, 1966.

5692. Robinson, Jenefer Mary. Representation and expression in the arts: a study of some recent theories. Toronto, 1975.

5693. Robinson, John Alan. Causation, probability and testimony. Princeton, 1956.　　58-369

5694. Robinson, John Hayes. Seeing the world aright: a study of Ludwig Wittgenstein's pretractarian notebooks. Notre Dame, 1975.　　75-19953

5695. Robinson, John M. The *dinē* in presocratic cosmology. Cornell, 1949.

5696. Robinson, John W. The social philosophy of Georges Sorel. Boston U., 1938.

5697. Robinson, Peter. A philosophical analysis of the concept of reduction in the behavioral sciences. Boston U., 1969.　　69-18432

5698. Robinson, Richard. The province of logic; an interpretation of certain parts of Cook Wilson's State-ment and inference. Cornell, 1930.

5699. Robinson, Richard Ellsworth. A set-theoretical approach to empirical meaningfulness of measurement statements. Berkeley, 1963. 64-2125

5700. Robinson, Robert Nesbitt. The theme of joy in Thomas Traherne. Emory, 1973. 74-461

5701. Robinson, William Spencer. Perception and reference. Indiana, 1966. 67-3706

5702. Robischon, Thomas Gregory. Objective relativism in American philosophy. Columbia, 1955. 12319

5703. Robison, Andrew Cliffe, Jr. Religious experience and justified religious belief. Princeton, 1974. 74-17485

5704. Robison, John Gordon. An extensional study of deontic sentences. Pennsylvania, 1962. 62-4335

5705. Robison, Wade Lee. The limits of empiricism: on the possibility of a private language. Wisconsin, 1968. 69-986

5706. Roblin, Ronald Edward. R.G. Collingwood's philosophy of history. No. Carolina, 1969. 70-3305

5707. Robson, James Wesley. Logical constructions. Harvard, 1932.

5708. Robson, Kent Elmer. Chronicles and history. Stanford, 1974. 74-13683

5709. Rocco, Thomas Martin. The ideal observer theory of ethical statements. Catholic U., 1971. 71-25663

5710. Roche, Rev. Evans. The De primo principio of John Duns Scotus. St. Bonaventure, 1946.

5711. Roche, Mary Elizabeth (Sr. Thérèse Aquinas). Imagination in gravitational theories. St. John's, 1967. 68-3829

5712. Roche, William Joseph. The problem of attributes, of creation, and of the existence of God, in Moses Maimonides and Thomas Aquinas. Harvard, 1935.

5713. Rockefeller, Steven C. John Dewey's ethical idealism: an essay in the philosophy of religion. Columbia, 1973. 76-16367

5714. Rockey, Palmer L. The moral philosophy of Giambattista Vico. St. Louis, 1955.

5715. Rockmore, Thomas. Man as activity in Fichte and Marx. Vanderbilt, 1973.   73-25070

5716. Roda, Anthony. Cognitive structures. So. Illinois, 1969.   69-6301

5717. Rodier, David Frederick Theodore. The problem of the physical world in the philosophy of Plotinus. Vanderbilt, 1966.   66-10998

5718. Roe, Nathaniel Walker. The final and self-sufficient good: an examination of the foundations of Aristotelian ethical theory. Harvard, 1953.

5719. Roelofs, Charles Richard, Jr. Some problems in the moral philosophy of C.I. Lewis. Rochester, 1968.
   68-15857

5720. Roelofs, Howard Dykema. The nature of authority. Harvard, 1925.

5721. Roelofs, Robert T. William James' views on metaphysics: a study in the justification of belief. Michigan, 1954.   7713

5722. Rogers, Arthur K. The parallelism of mind and body from the standpoint of metaphysics. Chicago, 1898.

5723. Rogers, Benjamin Freeman, III. Foundational studies in statistical inference. Indiana, 1971.
   71-25352

5724. Rogers, Charles Thomas. A critique of axiomatic social choice theory: certain difficulties in the semantics of social choice. Indiana, 1975.
   76-11442

5725. Rogers, Donald William. Will and belief in the philosophy of William James. Yale, 1952.

5726. Rogers, Robert, Jr. The representative theory of perception. Berkeley, 1955.

5727. Rogers, Robert Gary. Meaning, modeling and explaining. Pennsylvania, 1972.   72-25663

5728. Rogers, Mthr. Vera. St. Thomas' argument from motion and its critics. Marquette, 1943.

5729. Rogers, Wiley Kim. On perception: an explication of Feuerbach's human philosophy and a development of

one of his primary themes. New School, 1970.
71-10629

5730. Rohatyn, Dennis Anthony. The logic of is and ought. Fordham, 1972. 72-20580

5731. Rohr, Michael David. Aspects of Aristotle's earlier theory of predication. Stanford, 1975.
76-5791

5732. Rohrbaugh, Lewis Guy. The energy concept; a spiritual interpretation of reality. Iowa, 1922.

5733. Rohrbaugh, Lewis H. Vectors in group change. Pennsylvania, 1939.

5734. Rohrberg, Charles Richard. The behaviorism of John Dewey. Columbia, 1975. 76-12779

5735. Rolbiecki, John J. The political philosophy of Dante Alighieri. Catholic U., 1922.

5736. Roll, Charles Richard. Morality and the law: a philosophical analysis of the relationship between law and morals. Indiana, 1971. 72-10001

5737. Rollin, Bernard Elliot. An examination of the distinction between natural and conventional meaning. Columbia, 1972. 75-12340

5738. Rolston, Howard Lee. Wittgenstein's concept of family resemblance. Harvard, 1972.

5739. Roma, Emilio L., III. Association and intentionality within the context of aesthetic meaning. Wisconsin, 1962. 63-686

5740. Romanelli, Pasquale. The philosophy of Giovanni Gentile; an inquiry into Gentile's conception of experience. Columbia, 1937.

5741. Romano, Joseph J. Aristotle's theory of principles: a rationalistic-empirical bipolarity. Bryn Mawr, 1968. 69-9057

5742. Rome, Beatrice K. The philosophy of Malebranche: a study of his integration of faith, reason, and experimental observation. Radcliffe, 1953.

5743. Rome, Sydney Chester. Bishop Berkeley and Thomas Reid: a study in the origins of Scottish realism. Harvard, 1941.

5744. Romer, Adam Laubenstein. Theism in Greek philosophy from Thales to Socrates. Pennsylvania, 1895.

5745. Rood, Harold Joe. Metaphor: a study of various theories and the place of metaphor in philosophy. Michigan St., 1974. 74-27475

5746. Rooney, Miriam Theresa. Lawlessness, law, and sanction. Catholic U., 1937.

5747. Root, Michael D. The implications of recent linguistics for the doctrine of innate ideas. Illinois, 1970. 71-5220

5748. Root, Vernon Metcalf. Alfred North Whitehead's theory of eternal objects. Yale, 1950.

5749. Rorty, Amélie Oksenberg. Self-reference and the theory of error: Descartes, Hume, and Bradley on philosophic method. Yale, 1960.

5750. Rorty, Richard McKay. The concept of potentiality. Yale, 1956. 66-9533

5751. Rosán, Laurence J. The philosophy of Proclus; the final phase of ancient thought. Columbia, 1949.

5752. Rose, Lynn Edmondson. Hypothesis and deduction in Plato's methodology. Pennsylvania, 1961. 61-3548

5753. Rose, Mary C. Three hierarchies of value: a study in the philosophies of value of Henri Bergson, Alfred North Whitehead, and Søren Kierkegaard. Johns Hopkins, 1949.

5754. Roseler, Robert Oswald. A re-interpretation of Kant's moral and educational philosophy with reference to present-day educational problems. Ohio St., 1930.

5755. Rosemont, Henry, Jr. Logic, language and Zen. U. of Washington, 1967. 68-3877

5756. Rosen, Bernard. Ethical intuitionism: a reconsideration. Brown, 1964. 65-2242

5757. Rosen, Deborah Ann. Two transcendental arguments for the logical notion of a memory trace. Stanford, 1970. 71-2826

5758. Rosenbaum, Alan Shelby. Ralph Barton Perry's philosophy of democracy. Buffalo, 1974. 74-20029

5759. Rosenbaum, Stephen Earl. Chisholm and the justification of perceptual beliefs. Illinois, 1974. 75-417

5760. Rosenbaum, Stuart Evan. Properties and categories. Brown, 1972. 73-2327

5761. Rosenberg, Alexander. Microeconomic general statements: a philosophical analysis. Johns Hopkins, 1971. 71-29180

5762. Rosenberg, Jay Frank. A study of the determinable-determinate relation. Pittsburgh, 1966. 67-5558

5763. Rosenberg, Jean R. The principle of individuation: a comparative study of St. Thomas, Scotus, and Suarez. Catholic U., 1950.

5764. Rosenberger, Harry Emerson. William James' philosophy of will. N.Y.U., 1927. 74-1281

5765. Rosenfield, Israel. A study of Freud's theory of unconscious motives. Princeton, 1967. 67-5748

5766. Rosenholm, Arthur Alvin. Explaining promises. Oregon, 1973. 74-6890

5767. Rosenkrantz, Roger Daniel. Informative inference. Stanford, 1968. 69-280

5768. Rosensohn, William Lasker. The phenomenology of Charles S. Peirce. Buffalo, 1972.

5769. Rosenstein, Leon. The subject of tragedy: plot and persona. Columbia, 1972. 72-28087

5770. Rosenstock, Gershon George. Trendelenburg's theory of knowledge. Columbia, 1958. 58-2601

5771. Rosenthal, Aaron. Knowledge and true belief: a study in reasons and causes. Pittsburgh, 1969. 70-8630

5772. Rosenthal, Abigail Laura. Hegel's humanism. Penn St., 1968. 69-9797

5773. Rosenthal, David Michael. Intentionality: a study of the views of Chisholm and Sellars. Princeton, 1968. 69-2558

5774. Rosenthal, Robert James. Conventionalism: analysis and critique of a philosophical type. Maryland, 1968. 68-16686

5775. Rosenthal, Sandra Brener. A systematic expansion of C.I. Lewis' conceptual pragmatism with reference to the philosophies of Peirce and Mead. Tulane, 1967. 67-17946

5776. Rosinger, Kurt Edward. Mathematical logic and the implicative function. Harvard, 1928.

5777. Ross, David James. Axiomatizing quantum theory. Stanford, 1973. 73-30464

5778. Ross, Geoffrey Allan. Determinism, freedom, and moral responsibility. Stanford, 1973. 73-30465

5779. Ross, Gregory A. Peirce, Strawson, and the quest for categories. Buffalo, 1970. 71-15045

5780. Ross, James Francis. A critical analysis of the theory of analogy of St. Thomas Aquinas. Brown, 1958. 58-7663

5781. Ross, John Addison. The problem of negation in recent philosophical logic. Toronto, 1947.

5782. Ross, Michael David. John Stuart Mill: a reappraisal. Columbia, 1972. 75-12341

5783. Ross, Ralph G. Scepticism and dogma; a study in the philosophy of F.H. Bradley. Columbia, 1940.

5784. Ross, Stephen David. The philosophy of experience: an analysis of the concept of experience in the philosophy of John Dewey. Columbia, 1961. 61-3904

5785. Ross, William G. Human nature and utility in Hume's social philosophy. Columbia, 1942.

5786. Rossi, Philip Joseph. Kant's doctrine of the 'fact of pure reason': the foundation for moral rationality. Texas, 1975. 75-24949

5787. Rossman, Neil I. Value judgments in history. N.Y.U., 1971. 72-3121

5788. Rossner, William L. The theory of love in the philosophy of St. Thomas Aquinas. Princeton, 1953. 8087

5789. Rosthal, Robert Bernard. Privacy and the concept of the person in Marcel and Strawson. Michigan, 1961. 61-6418

5790. Roth, John King. An appraisal of the ethics of William James. Yale, 1967. 67-9157

5791. Roth, Michael David. An examination of Plato's *Cratylus*. Illinois, 1969. 70-13465

5792. Roth, Rev. Robert Joseph. The conditions for self-realization in the philosophy of John Dewey. Fordham, 1961. 62-1041

5793. Roth, Sol. A theory of rationalism: an examination of the philosophy of Morris Raphael Cohen. Columbia, 1966. 66-12589

5794. Rothman, Robert. The place of knowledge in valuation (a comparative study of John Dewey's philosophy of value.) Michigan, 1936.

5795. Rothman, William David. Three essays in aesthetics: I. A theory of the threefold relationship of work of art, artist, and 'beholder'; II. A theory of the art of the narrative film; III. A descriptive analysis of the film "Notorious." Harvard, 1974.

5796. Rothwell, Mel-Thomas. Three foundations of ethics in Maritain, Stace, and Ramsey. Boston U., 1955.

5797. Rottmayer, William Arthur. A formal theory of perception. Stanford, 1970. 71-2828

5798. Rottschaefer, William Andrew. Ordinary knowledge in the scientific realism of Wilfrid Sellars. Boston U., 1973. 73-14172

5799. Rouleau, Sr. Mary Celeste. The place of love and knowledge in human activity according to selected texts of Saint Thomas Aquinas. St. Louis, 1961. 61-6489

5800. Rouse, David Lowry. The form and content of social life: an examination of Marx's materialism. Vanderbilt, 1974. 75-1153

5801. Rousseau, Edward L. The distinction between essence and supposit in the angel according to St. Thomas Aquinas. Fordham, 1954.

5802. Rowan, John Patrick August. St. Thomas' doctrine of peace. Toronto, 1947.

5803. Rowan, Robert James. A conception of the common good. Berkeley, 1958.

5804. Rowe, William Leonard. An examination of the philosophical theology of Paul Tillich. Michigan, 1962. 62-3258

5805. Rowell, Edward Z. Masayrk's realism and the Czech nation. Chicago, 1922.

5806. Rowland, Sr. Mary Joyce. The acts of the mind in Newman's theory of assent. St. Louis, 1962.
64-3765

5807. Rowntree, Stephen Clyde. The university in process: a critical study based on Whitehead's philosophy. Fordham, 1973. 74-2759

5808. Roy, Andrew Tod. Modern Confucian social theory and its concept of change. Princeton, 1948.
11014

5809. Roy, Dhirendra Nath. The historical sources of the pragmatic theory of truth. Iowa, 1926.

5810. Royce, Josiah. Interdependence of the principles of human knowledge. Johns Hopkins, 1878.

5811. Royse, James R. Some investigations into ramified set theory. Chicago, 1969.

5812. Ruben, David-Hillel. Relativism, rules and contemporary moral philosophy. Harvard, 1971.

5813. Rubin, Ronald Gary. Locke's theory of primary and secondary qualities. Cornell, 1973. 73-22526

5814. Rubinoff, Mervyn Lionel. The relation between philosophy and history in the thought of R.G. Collingwood. Toronto, 1964.

5815. Rubinstein, Annette T. Realistic ethics. Columbia, 1934.

5816. Ruble, Raymond Stanley. Kant's second analogy and Hume's theory of causality. Wisconsin, 1970.
71-3150

5817. Ruby, Lionel. The nature of beauty as distinguished from other aesthetic categories. Chicago, 1930.

5818. Ruchti, Warren Frederick. A solution for the problem of cotenability. Pennsylvania, 1964.
65-1387

5819. Rucker, E. Darnell. Corporate reform and economic reality: a critical study of Elijah Jordan's social theory. Chicago, 1957.

5820. Rudd, Herbert Finley. Chinese moral sentiments before Confucius; a study in the origin of ethical valuations. Chicago, 1914.

5821. Ruddick, Chester Townsend. On the contingency of natural law. Pennsylvania, 1931.

5822. Ruddick, Sara Loop. Wittgenstein on sensation statements. Harvard, 1964.

5823. Ruddick, William McConnell. The special theory of relativity and conceptual changes. Harvard, 1964.

5824. Rudinow, Joel. Objectivity and sensitivity in aesthetics. British Columbia, 1974.

5825. Rudner, Richard S. Four studies of the esthetic object. Pennsylvania, 1949.

5826. Rudolph, Arthur William. Superhistorical individuality in Nietzsche's thought. Southern Cal., 1963. 65-8903

5827. Rudolph, Gerald Allen. The affective criticism of I.A. Richards. U. of Washington, 1959. 59-3344

5828. Ruether, Rosemary Radford. Gregory of Nazianzus: rhetor and philosopher. Claremont, 1965. 66-3383

5829. Rueve, Rev. Stephen James. Francis Suarez and the natural moral law. St. Louis, 1933. 174

5830. Ruf, Henry Lawrence. Language, personal existence and religious ontology. Emory, 1964. 64-11220

5831. Ruhlen, Ralph Lester. The relationship of the economic order to the moral ideal in the thought of Maritain, Brunner, Dewey and Temple. Boston U., 1959. 59-3473

5832. Ruja, Harry. A critique of the postulational theory of the a priori. Princeton, 1936.

5833. Rukavina, Thomas. Heidegger as critic of Western thinking. Indiana, 1960. 60-2839

5834. Rumper, Herman Edward. Demythologizing and the meaning of mythic language. Cal., S. Diego, 1971. 71-26581

5835. Runkle, Gerald J.T. Reid's criticism of Hume and his reconstruction in philosophy. Yale, 1952.

5836. Runzo, Joseph John. Conceptual schemas, perception, and God. Michigan, 1974. 75-10279

5837. Russell, Anthony. The logic of question and answer and its relevance to historical thoughts according to R.G. Collingwood. Ottawa, 1973.

5838. Russell, James Michael. Self-deception. Cal., S. Barbara, 1971.   73-8105

5839. Russo, Francis Xavier. The educational philosophy of John Howland. Boston U., 1964.   64-11631

5840. Russo, Salvatore. The concept of matter in Leibniz. Cornell, 1933.

5841. Rutenber, Culbert G. The doctrine of the imitation of God in Plato. Pennsylvania, 1946.

5842. Ryan, Br. Bernard. An Aristotelian and Thomistic interpretation of certain aspects of the logic of sociology. N.Y.U., 1948.   73-8754

5843. Ryan, Cheyney Cadwalader. Value, capital and crises: a study in ideology. Boston U., 1975. 75-17

5844. Ryan, John D. The awareness of God in the thought of Paul Tillich. Drew, 1973.   73-26146

5845. Ryan, John K. Modern war and basic ethics. Catholic U., 1933.

5846. Ryan, Rev. Michael Terrence. The notion and uses of dialectic in St. Thomas Aquinas. Notre Dame, 1962.   62-4413

5847. Ryan, Br. Xavier. The metaproblematic enquiry of Gabriel Marcel. Catholic U., 1970.   70-21842

5848. Rynin, David. A study in the logic of empiricism. Berkeley, 1933.

5849. Rzadkiewicz, Rev. Arnold. The philosophical bases of human liberty according to St. Thomas Aquinas. Catholic U., 1949.

- S -

5850. Saatkamp, Herman Joseph, Jr. An explication and critical examination of George Santayana's concept of animal faith. Vanderbilt, 1972.
                                                  72-26127

5851. Sabin, Ethel Ernestine. William James and pragmatism. Illinois, 1916.

5852. Sabinash, John Anthony. St. Bonaventure's _Itinerarium mentis in Deum_: a translation with introduction and commentary. Pittsburgh, 1943.

5853. Sablica, Michael John. Christ and the idea of reconciliation in the philosophy of Hegel. Duquesne, 1973.

5854. Sacheri, Carlos Alberto. Nécessité et nature de la délibération. Laval, 1968.

5855. Sachs, David John. Ends and means, with reference to teleology in general. Princeton, 1953.
                6834

5856. Sacksteder, George W. Philosophy and the Supreme Court crises: a study in judgment. Chicago, 1953.

5857. Safier, Fred Jacob. The philosophy of Søren Kierkegaard. Harvard, 1934.

5858. Sagal, Paul Thomas. The concept of supposition and its place in the development of medieval semantology. Pennsylvania, 1967.   68-9232

5859. Sagebeer, Joseph Evans. Phenomena and noumena in the history of philosophy. Pennsylvania, 1891.

5860. Sagoff, Mark Henry. Kant's argument for the autonomy of taste. Rochester, 1970.   70-17906

5861. Sahakian, William S. The emotive ethic in contemporary British and American philosophy. Boston U., 1951.

5862. Saibel, Bernard Leon. The philosophy of George Santayana. Harvard, 1935.

5863. Said, Wadad Habib. The uniqueness and intelligibility of value. Bryn Mawr, 1951.   2785

5864. St. Amour, Jeanne-Marie. Transcendence in Teilhard and Blondel. Missouri, 1972.   73-21482

5865. St.-Edouard, Sr. Quelques problèmes sur la qualité. Laval, 1956.

5866. St. Hilaire, Sr. Mary Georgette. Precepts of natural law in St. Thomas. St. Louis, 1963.
                64-4271

5867. St.-Martin, Jeannine (Sr. St.-Martin-de-Tours). Sur le prooemium de la politique. Laval, 1964.

5868. Saint-Pierre, Bernard. La physique de la vision dans l'antiquité. Contribution à l'établissement des sources anciennes de l'optique medievale. Montreal, 1973.

5869. Sait, Una Mirrielees (Bernard). The ethical implications of Bergson's philosophy. Columbia, 1914.

5870. Salesses, William Edward, Jr. A statement of the ethical theories of pragmatism and Thomism as expressed by John Dewey and Jacques Maritain. Claremont, 1968. 68-18286

5871. Salladay, Susan. A study of the nature and function of religious language in relation to Kierkegaard's theories of subjective truth and indirect communication. Boston Coll., 1974. 74-19225

5872. Sallis, John Cleveland. The concept of world: a study in the phenomenological ontology of Martin Heidegger. Tulane, 1964. 64-13718

5873. Salmon, Wesley Charles. John Venn's theory of induction. U.C.L.A., 1950.

5874. Samson, André. Sensation et intellection des présocratiques à Aristote. Laval, 1966.

5875. Samuel, Peter Louis. An examination of John Rawls' theory of justice. Rochester, 1972. 72-28797

5876. Samuel, William Henry. External reality in the Lockian philosophy. Pennsylvania, 1893.

5877. Samuelson, Norbert Max. The problem of God's knowledge in Gersonides- a translation of and commentary to Book three of the Milhamot adonai. Indiana, 1969. 70-14970

5878. Sanborn, Patricia Flagg. Gabriel Marcel's conception of the self. Columbia, 1965. 65-9175

5879. Sanchez, Halley David. Faculty psychology and analysis of self-consciousness in the theoretical and aesthetical philosophy of Kant. Penn St., 1974. 75-9834

5880. Sandelin, Clarence Kenneth. The educational philosophy of Henry Adams: a Brahmin contribution to critical realism. Wisconsin, 1956. 19134

5881. Sanders, Steven Matthew. A theory of egoistic ethics. No. Carolina, 1974. 75-4864

5882. Sanderson, Donald George. Nietzsche and evolution. Texas, 1974. 74-14760

5883. Sandin, Robert Theodore. Axel Hägerström's philosophy of religion, with special reference to his theory of knowledge and his concept of reality. Minnesota, 1959. 60-945

5884. Sandok, Sr. Theresa H. Kierkegaard on irony and humor. Notre Dame, 1975. 75-19954

5885. Sanford, David Hawley. An examination of D.M. Armstrong's theory of perception. Cornell, 1966. 66-6076

5886. Sanford, Gertrude Virginia. A criticism of the correspondence and coherence theories of truth. Berkeley, 1929.

5887. Sankowski, Edward Tadeusz. Emotion and norm. Cornell, 1971. 72-18572

5888. Sano, Roy Isao. Neglected aspects of the mature Aristotle: a development of Jaeger's methods and theses. Claremont, 1972. 72-26244

5889. Santa Maria, Carmelo Saenz de. A history of the organization of philosophical studies in Guatemala, 1575-1769. Georgetown, 1953.

5890. Santas, Gerasimos Xenophon. The Socratic paradoxes and virtue and happiness in Plato's earlier dialogues. Cornell, 1961. 62-964

5891. Santayana, George. Lotze's system of philosophy. Harvard, 1889.

5892. Santoni, Ronald Ernest. The realism of C.J. Ducasse and J.B. Pratt: a comparison and critique. Boston U., 1961. 61-1102

5893. Sapadin, Eugene. An examination of Hume's arguments against ethical rationalism. Claremont, 1969. 70-11907

5894. Sapontzis, Steve Frederic. Merleau-Ponty and philosophical methodology. Yale, 1971. 71-31007

5895. Sargeant, Barbara Anne. Corporate theory in Thomas Hobbes. Toronto, 1974.

5896. Sargent, Charles Edward. A reexamination of the doctrine of Gall and Spurzheim in the light of recent science, with a consideration of its philosophical implicates. Yale, 1905.

5897. Sarracino, Mia Katrin. Aesthetic perception and "seeing as." Chicago, 1975.

5898. Sartorius, Rolf Edward. The justification of the judicial decision. Princeton, 1965. 65-6384

5899. Sass, Louis DeWald. The materialist theory of mind. Columbia, 1953. 6698

5900. Sasseville, Thérèse (Sr. St. Edouard). Essai d'interprétation critique de la doctrine poétique de Valéry. Laval, 1965.

5901. Sasso, James Joseph. Value consciousness in Friedrick Nietzsche. Boston U., 1970. 70-23128

5902. Satre, Thomas Ward. Action, mental acts, and linguistic abilities. Claremont, 1968. 68-18289

5903. Sattler, Rev. Henry V. A philosophy of submission. Catholic U., 1948.

5904. Saunders, Jason L. Renaissance stoicism; the philosophy of Justus Lipsius. Columbia, 1952.

5905. Saunders, John Turk. A philosophical study of memory. U.C.L.A., 1961.

5906. Sauriol, Pierre. Logique traditionnelle et logique moderne: concordances et discordances. Montreal, 1973.

5907. Savage, Charles Melvin. Work and meaning: a phenomenological inquiry. Boston Coll., 1974.
74-4171

5908. Savage, Rosa Tiampo. Nature and naturalism in John Dewey. St. Louis, 1967. 68-1292

5909. Savaria, Sr. Madeleine Gabrielle. Etienne Gilson's concept of the nature and scope of philosophy. Catholic U., 1951.

5910. Savery, Barnett. A definition of value. Harvard, 1934.

5911. Savery, William Briggs. Some fundamental ethical concepts, with special reference to the concepts of responsibility and freedom. Harvard, 1899.

5912. Savitt, Steven Frederick. Frege and Wittgenstein on identity, logic and number. Brandeis, 1971.
72-17997

5913. Savodnik, Irwin. Time and organization in theoretical biology: essay in the philosophy of biology. N.Y.U., 1970. 71-2335

5914. Sawyier, Fay Horton. Remembering particulars. Chicago, 1964.

5915. Saydah, John Roger. C.I. Lewis: a study in ethics. Columbia, 1967. 67-9370

5916. Sayegh, Fayez A. Existential philosophy: a formal examination. Georgetown, 1950.

5917. Sayles, Edward McAneney. A critical evaluation of R.G. Collingwood's views on metaphysics. U.C.L.A., 1956.

5918. Sayre, Charles A. Moral implications in the philosophy of Descartes in the light of the philosophy of Pascal. Drew, 1952.

5919. Sayre, Farrand. Diogenes of Sinope; a study of Greek cynicism. Johns Hopkins, 1938.

5920. Sayre, Kenneth Malcolm. Phenomenalism and the selective theory. Harvard, 1958.

5921. Sayre, Woodrow Wilson. The concept of individuality in political theory. Harvard, 1957.

5922. Sayward, Charles Warren, Jr. An analysis of various pragmatic predicates. Cornell, 1964. 64-13847

5923. Scales, Albert Louis. William James and John Dewey: an interpretive and critical study. Yale, 1917.

5924. Scales, Ronald Dale. Attribution and existence. Cal., Irvine, 1969. 71-4272

5925. Scally, Thomas. The role of natural justice in the philosophy of Thomas Hobbes. Boston Coll., 1971. 71-22159

5926. Scanlan, Rev. Carl David. The basic character of Cudworth's ethics. St. Louis, 1968. 69-375

5927. Scanlan, James Patrick. The concept of interest in The federalist: a study of the structure of a political theory. Chicago, 1956.

5928. Scanlon, John Daniel. Husserl's conception of philosophy as a rigorous science. Tulane, 1968. 68-15265

5929. Scanlon, Thomas Michael, Jr. A unified treatment of elementary proof theory. Harvard, 1968.

5930. Scannell, Br. Leo. Principles operative in the American and French Revolutions in the light of the doctrine on revolution of Francisco Suarez. N.Y.U., 1955. 12234

5931. Scarlett, Brian Francis. An examination of materialist theories of mind and an approach to an alternative theory. Toronto, 1974.

5932. Scarrow, David Shotwell. The origin and development of Bradley's logic. Harvard, 1959.

5933. Schacht, Richard Lawrence. The category of "alienation." Princeton, 1968.   63-8959

5934. Schachter, Jean-Pierre Adalbert. The core of Wittgenstein's Investigations: a philosophy of language. Syracuse, 1969.   70-10393

5935. Schaefer, Ronald Griffen. Concept formation. Michigan, 1974.   74-25319

5936. Schaefer, Thomas E. The meaning of Chun Tzu in the thought of Mencius. Georgetown, 1963.

5937. Schaff, Dion. Aristotle's categories. Brown, 1971.
72-8183

5938. Schaffner, Kenneth Francis. The logic and methodology of reduction in the physical and biological sciences. Columbia, 1967.   68-8618

5939. Schagrin, Morton Louis. William Whewell: philosopher of science. Berkeley, 1966.   67-5158

5940. Schaich, Paul Clifford, Jr. The dreaming world of F.H. Bradley: a metaphysical theory of perception. Yale, 1969.   70-16247

5941. Schaldenbrand, Sr. Mary Aloysius. Phenomenologies of freedom: an essay on the philosophies of Jean-Paul Sartre and Gabriel Marcel. Catholic U., 1960.

5942. Schamis, Jeffrey. Absolute rights. Chicago, 1972.

5943. Scharff, Robert Caesar. 'Erlebnis' and 'existenz': Dilthey and Heidegger on the approach to human experience. Northwestern, 1970.   71-1964

5944. Scharfstein, Ben-Ami. Roots of Bergson's philosophy. Columbia, 1943.

5945. Scharle, Thomas Warren. Axiomatization of fragments of S5. Notre Dame, 1973.   74-72

5946. Schatz, Mary Spencer. Application of an ethical theory to the problem of military conscription. Boston U., 1973.   73-14176

5947. Schaub, E.L. The primacy of the practical reason in the Jena period of J.G. Fichte's philosophy. Cornell, 1910.

5948. Schedler, George Edward. The justification of the institution of legal punishment. Cal., S. Diego, 1973. 74-1375

5949. Schedler, Norbert Oscar. Methodology in the metaphysics of theism: a philosophical analysis of the method of Austin Farrer and Ian Ramsey. Princeton, 1967. 68-2516

5950. Scheer, Richard Keith. Bertrand Russell's conceptions of meaning and vagueness of meaning. Nebraska, 1958. 58-3777

5951. Scheffler, Israel. On quotation. Pennsylvania, 1952.

5952. Schell, Edith L. (Weaver). The educational philosophy of Bernard Bosanquet. Johns Hopkins, 1961.

5953. Scherer, Donald William. A study of the teleological argument for the existence of God. Cornell, 1965. 65-14721

5954. Schermer, Marsha Rockey. On Nietzsche's purported contradictoriness: a reinterpretation of the works of Friedrich Nietzsche with an emphasis on non-assertional linguistic acts. Ohio St., 1974.
75-3187

5955. Scheu, Sr. Marina. The categories of being in Aristotle and St. Thomas. Catholic U., 1944.

5956. Scheuer, Marcellius. Philosophy of man in communism. Catholic U., 1952.

5957. Schick, Frederic. Explication and inductive logic. Columbia, 1958. 58-2475

5958. Schievella, Pat S. The philosophy of Conwy Lloyd Morgan. Columbia, 1967. 68-8619

5959. Schiff, Daniel Carl. The intention and incoherence of the *De rerum natura*. Penn St., 1973.
74-16077

5960. Schild, Willy. Purposive explanation. N.Y.U., 1969.
70-3104

5961. Schiller, Jerome Paul. I.A. Richards and the autonomy and personal relevance of poetry. Harvard, 1960.

5962. Schiller, Marvin. The alienable and inalienable: a study in political philosophy. No. Carolina, 1969.   70-21228

5963. Schilling, Sylvester P. The empirical and the rational in Hegel's philosophy of religion. Boston U., 1934.

5964. Schilpp, Paul A. A critical analysis of Kant's ethical thought of the pre-critical period. Stanford, 1936.

5965. Schindler, Stefan Donald I. Sartre contra Freud: toward a synthesis of consciousness and unconsciousness in models of human reality. Boston Coll., 1975.   75-20708

5966. Schipper, Gerrit. The empirical naturalism of John Dewey. Harvard, 1942.

5967. Schlabach, Anne V. A critical study of some problems of individualism derived from Hawthorne's novels and Emerson's Representative men. Wisconsin, 1947.

5968. Schlaeger, Margaret Clare. Jonathan Edwards' theory of perception. Illinois, 1964.   65-900

5969. Schlafer, David John. The prima facie duty thesis: Sir David Ross on the nature of moral obligation. So. Illinois, 1974.   74-18876

5970. Schlagel, Richard H. An analysis of the sense-data theories of Moore, Russell, and Broad. Boston U., 1955.

5971. Schlecht, Ludwig Frederick, Jr. The universalizability of moral judgments. Emory, 1967.   67-10304

5972. Schlegel, Edward Regis. Truth, transcendental object, and thing-in-itself in Kant's Critique of pure reason. Duquesne, 1974.   74-23631

5973. Schlosberg, Jed. Action and theatricality. Texas, 1974.   74-14762

5974. Schlosser, Brian John. Contemporary ethical naturalism. Rockefeller, 1974.

5975. Schmidt, Michael Fred. Explanation. Ohio St., 1969.
                                                         69-22201

5976. Schmidt, Paul Frederic. Perception, science and metaphysics: a study in Whitehead. Yale, 1951.

5977. Schmidt, Robert William. The domain of logic according to St. Thomas Aquinas. Toronto, 1947.

5978. Schmidtke, Charles Raymond. Bergson's meaning of continuity. Tulane, 1973. 73-25303

5979. Schmiege, Oscar John, Jr. Augustine, on perceiving the natural world. Minnesota, 1971. 72-14372

5980. Schmitt, Charles Bernard. Gianfrancesco Pico's critique of Aristotelian philosophy. Columbia, 1963. 64-5551

5981. Schmitt, Richard George. Husserl's phenomenology: reconstruction in empiricism. Yale, 1956.

5982. Schmitz, Alfred Otto. The dialectic of mystery: a study of the philosophic method of Gabriel Marcel. No. Carolina, 1963. 64-9439

5983. Schmitz, Kenneth Louis. The problem of the immortality of the human soul in the works of Cajetan (1469-1534). Toronto, 1953.

5984. Schmotzer, John Stephen. The graphic portrayal of All under heaven (T'ien-hsia): a study of Chinese world views through pictorial representations. Georgetown, 1973. 75-7867

5985. Schmucker, Larry Alan. Wittgenstein's remarks on basic views. Texas, 1970. 72-2414

5986. Schnaidman, Marvin M. The individual and society in Bernard Bosanquet's social philosophy. Columbia, 1975. 75-25719

5987. Schneewind, Jerome Borges. The nature of McTaggart's theory of appearance. Princeton, 1957.
58-7886

5988. Schneider, Erna Floretta. An analysis of contrary-to-fact conditional sentences. Yale, 1952.

5989. Schneider, Herbert Wallace. Science and social progress; a philosophical introduction to moral science. Columbia, 1920.

5990. Schneider, Rev. Marius. Max Scheler's phenomenological philosophy of values. Catholic U., 1951.

5991. Schneider, Sr. Mary Monica. Augustinian citations in Saint Bonaventure's formal treatment of knowledge. St. Louis, 1957. 58-4382

5992. Schneider, Philip Allen David. New foundations for confirmation in science. Duke, 1968. 69-3893

5993. Schneider, Richard E. Eckhart's doctrine of the transcendental perfections in God and creatures. Toronto, 1965.

5994. Schneider, Robert E. Positivism in the United States: the apostleship of Henry Edger. Columbia, 1947.

5995. Schochet, Jacob Immanuel. The psychological system of Maimonides. Waterloo, 1974.

5996. Schoedinger, Andrew Barr. Wants, decisions and human actions. Brown, 1974. 75-9237

5997. Schoeman, Ferdinand D. Human rights and utilitarian analyses. Brandeis, 1971. 71-30151

5998. Schon, Donald Alan. Rationality in the practical decision-process. Harvard, 1955.

5999. Schoolcraft, Arthur Allen. The pessimism of Windelband: its origins and development. Boston U., 1932.

6000. Schotch, Peter Kim. The semantics of modal logic: some aspects of the matrix method. Waterloo, 1973.

6001. Schouls, Peter Arthur. The problem of memory in the epistemology of some Anglo-American philosophers. Toronto, 1967.

6002. Schouwers, Pierre Edmond. Conscience libre et morale selon Maurice Merleau-Ponty. St. Louis, 1971. 72-5324

6003. Schrader, David Eugene. An analysis of the stone paradox. Massachusetts, 1975. 76-5396

6004. Schrag, Brian Eugene. Universalizability and the concept of morality. Vanderbilt, 1975.
76-119

6005. Schrecker, Anne Martin. A study of Francis Hutcheson's two ethical theories in relation to some moral philosophies of the enlightenment. Bryn Mawr, 1961. 61-6578

6006. Schrickel, Harry George. Prolegomena to a theory of value. Cincinnati, 1938.

6007. Schroeder, Frederick Maxwell. The doctrine of presence in the philosophy of Plotinus. Toronto, 1969.

6008. Schrynemakers, Arthur Hubert. Descartes' philosophical, psychological, and moral views on The passions of the soul. Notre Dame, 1960. 60-1238

6009. Schueler, George Frederick. Self-interest and altruism. Berkeley, 1973.

6010. Schufreider, Gregory J. Anselm's ontological argument. Cal., S. Barbara, 1975.

6011. Schuh, Edward Walter. A theory of inherent value. Harvard, 1953.

6012. Schuldenfrei, Richard. The nominalism of Nelson Goodman. Pittsburgh, 1972. 72-22971

6013. Schuller, Peter Michael. Karl Marx's ethical theory. Boston U., 1974. 74-20403

6014. Schultz, Rev. James Carl. From insight to metaphysics: the metaphysics of Bernard J.F. Lonergan's Insight. Notre Dame, 1972. 72-26821

6015. Schultz, Robert Allen. Reasons to be moral: the problem of justification in Kant's ethics. Harvard, 1971.

6016. Schultz, Robert Charles. Reason, philosophical intuitionism, and justification in Sidgwick's ethics. Emory, 1969. 69-19616

6017. Schulz, James Alan. McTaggart's theory of substance. Northwestern, 1974. 75-7985

6018. Schumacher, Leo S. The philosophy of the equitable distribution of wealth. Catholic U., 1949.

6019. Schumacher, Matthew. The knowableness of God. Catholic U., 1905.

6020. Schumm, George Frederick. A study in the extensions of S4. Chicago, 1975.

6021. Schuster, Cynthia Andrews. The ethical import of empiricism. U.C.L.A., 1950.

6022. Schuyler, Eugene. Title of dissertation unknown. Yale, 1861.

6023. Schwager, Robert Louis. Agency, ability, and obligation: a study of W.D. Ross's two theories of obligation. Cornell, 1968. 69-8862

6024. Schwartz, Evangeline D. Hare and his critics on universalizability in ethics. Claremont, 1967. 68-10542

6025. Schwartz, Herbert S. An Aristotelian analysis of the elements, principles, and causes of the art of music. Columbia, 1936.

6026. Schwartz, Lewis Mark. The emergence of accounts of purposive behavior within empirical philosophy. Pennsylvania, 1965. 65-5803

6027. Schwartz, Robert Allen. Preliminary studies in rules and behavior. Pennsylvania, 1967. 67-7875

6028. Schwartz, Robert John. Reduction, rephrasal, and the problem of mind. Washington U., 1975. 76-4778

6029. Schwartz, Stephen Paul. The practical syllogism and intentional action. Cornell, 1971. 71-27400

6030. Schwartz, Thomas. The collective interest. Pittsburgh, 1969. 70-18077

6031. Schwarz, David Samuel. Reference and definite descriptions. Berkeley, 1972.

6032. Schwarz, Stephen Dietrich. Reid and the justification of perception. Harvard, 1966.

6033. Schwyzer, Alison Moore. A defense of the command theory of law. Berkeley, 1974.

6034. Schwyzer, Hubert Rudolf George. The acquisition of concepts and the use of language. Berkeley, 1968. 63-13955

6035. Sclafani, Richard J. 'Art' and family-resemblances. Chicago, 1968.

6036. Scoledes, Aristotle Georgius Michale. Interpretations of determinism and indeterminism in quantum mechanics: an analysis of some major issues over determinism in microphysics. Stanford, 1964. 65-6346

6037. Scoon, Robert. Early Greek philosophy. Columbia, 1916.

6038. Scott, Benjamin D. The problem of error in American realism. Boston U., 1922.

6039. Scott, Earl Striker. An examination of John Wisdom's conception of philosophy. N.Y.U., 1975. 76-10224

6040. Scott, Rev. Frederick Joseph Down. The pragmatism of Maurice Blondel: the problem of knowledge in the perspective of action. Georgetown, 1956.

6041. Scott, George Edward. The formal and informal logics of modality. Virginia, 1961. 61-4566

6042. Scott, James Howard. Santayana's naturalistic philosophy of culture. Columbia, 1972. 72-31233

6043. Scott, Roderick. The personalistic insights in ancient Chinese philosophy. Southern Cal., 1947.

6044. Scott, Roland Waldeck. Social ethics in modern Hindu thought. Columbia, 1951. 2859

6045. Scott, Stephen Hamilton. Universals and ontological analysis. Indiana, 1970. 70-17962

6046. Scott, Theodore Kermit, Jr. The *Sophismata* of John Buridian. Columbia, 1963. 63-7432

6047. Scott, Ulric Carl, Jr. The philosophical notebooks of George Berkeley: an historical, structural, textual, and interpretive analysis. Minnesota, 1970. 70-20235

6048. Scott, Walter Gaylord. A systematization and critical analysis of William Ockham's theory of natural signs. Johns Hopkins, 1969. 72-16873

6049. Scribner, Phillip Hugh. A critical appraisal of methodological individualism. Johns Hopkins, 1966. 66-12507

6050. Scully, John Patrick Edgar. Reality and truth in Thomas of York; study and text. Toronto, 1960.

6051. Scully, Richard Edward. The ontological argument. Cincinnati, 1925.

6052. Seaman, Francis Chester. The impact of the theory of relativity on some recent philosophies. Michigan, 1951. 2445

6053. Seaton, Wallace Knight. An edition and translation of the *Tractatus de consequentiis* by Ralph Strode, fourteenth-century logician and friend of Geoffrey Chaucer. Berkeley, 1973. 75-6797

6054. Sedey, Daniel. Tense, time, and paradox: the construction of a tenseless language. Michigan, 1969. 69-18105

6055. Seeburger, Francis Frey, V. The question of being and the "reversal" of thinking in the works of Martin Heidegger. Colorado, 1973. 73-23295

6056. Seelye, Kate Chambers. Moslem schisms and sects (Al-Fark bain al-Firak), being the history of the various philosophic systems developed in Islam, by abū-Mansūr 'abd-al-Kahir ibn-Tahir al-Baghdādī (d. 1037). Columbia, 1919.

6057. Seeskin, Kenneth Robert. The concept of participation in Plato's later dialogues. Yale, 1972. 73-10

6058. Sefler, George Francis. The structure of language and its relation to the world: a methodological study of the writings of Martin Heidegger and Ludwig Wittgenstein. Georgetown, 1970. 70-23809

6059. Segal, Jerome L. John Dewey's theory of perception. Northwestern, 1972. 72-32571

6060. Segal, Jerome Michael. Alienness and agency. Michigan, 1975. 75-20443

6061. Segerberg, Karl Krister. An essay in classical modal logic. Stanford, 1971. 72-11659

6062. Seibert, Charles Henry, Jr. On being and space in Heidegger's thinking. DePaul, 1972. 72-31245

6063. Seidel, Asher Milton. Universals as qualities of material objects. Michigan, 1970. 71-15298

6064. Seidel, George Joseph. Martin Heidegger's interpretation of the pre-Socratics. Toronto, 1962.

6065. Seidensticker, William David. Peirce's theory of esthetics and normative science. Fordham, 1968. 69-2610

6066. Seifert, Gary Francis. Ramist logic and the philosophy of Hobbes. Buffalo, 1973. 73-29134

6067. Seigel, Jerrold Edward. Rhetoric and philosophy in Renaissance humanism from Petrarch to Valla: studies in the development of quattrocento thought and its classical antecedents. Princeton, 1964. 64-6286

6068. Seigfried, Charlene Haddock. The status of relations in William James. Loyola, 1973. 73-26833

6069. Self, Donnie Jordan. Value language and objectivity: an analysis in philosophical ethics. No. Carolina, 1973. 74-5973

6070. Seligman, David. Justice and the role of retribution in punishment. Columbia, 1966. 66-8532

6071. Seligman, David Ben. Bodily sensations. Duke, 1968. 68-14326

6072. Selk, Eugene Edward. Hans Reichenbach's philosophy of science and epistemology: a study of their interrelationship. Marquette, 1971. 72-5788

6073. Sellars, Roy Wood. The categories, particularly cause and space. Michigan, 1909.

6074. Sellers, William Keith. Reconciling two apparently rival theories of visual perception. Chicago, 1975.

6075. Selsam, Howard Brillinger. T.H. Green: critic of empiricism. Columbia, 1930.

6076. Seltzer, Edward C. The problem of objectivity: a study of objectivity reflected in a comparison of the philosophies of Ernst Cassirer, Jean Piaget and Edmund Husserl. New School, 1969. 70-7659

6077. Selwyn-Brown, Arthur. Psychology of evaluation. N.Y.U., 1909. 73-22393

6078. Selznick, Gertrude J. Functionalism, the Freudian theory, and the philosophy of value. U.C.L.A., 1960.

6079. Semerena, Wade Kinsey. Pragmatism and realism in the philosophy of C.S. Peirce. Miami, 1973. 74-281

6080. Senchuk, Dennis Michael. A study in Cartesiam dualism. Minnesota, 1973. 74-10582

6081. Sen Gupta, Narendra Nath. Anti-intellectualism: a study in contemporary epistemology. Harvard, 1915.

6082. Senter, Nell Walton. Civil disobedience and moral autonomy. Virginia, 1972. 72-33256

6083. Serafini, Anthony Louis. Conventions, intentions and speech acts. Syracuse, 1972. 73-19844

6084. Serene, Eileen Flanigan. Anselm's _Philosophical frag-ments_: a critical examination. Cornell, 1974. 74-17681

6085. Sesek, Rev. Raphael Alexander. Leibniz's proofs of God. Catholic U., 1964. 64-12496

6086. Sesonske, Alexander. Value and obligation: the foundations of an empiricist ethics. U.C.L.A., 1953.

6087. Sesplugues, Juan. La filosofia social de José Ortega y Gasset. Columbia, 1950. 2129

6088. Sessions, William Lad. A critical examination of dipolar panentheism. Yale, 1971. 71-31009

6089. Seubert, K. Helen. The problem of vision in Heidegger and ancient Hindu thought. Penn St., 1974. 75-19812

6090. Severens, Richard Hoxie. Ontological commitments in categorial systems. Duke, 1960. 60-6040

6091. Sewell, William Clyde. Einstein, Mach, and the general theory of relativity. Case, 1975. 75-27962

6092. Shaffer, Jerome Arthur. A study of philosophical analysis: with special reference to Russell's analysis of the external world. Princeton, 1952. 6836

6093. Shahan, Ewing Pope. Whitehead's theory of experience. Columbia, 1950.

6094. Shahan, Robert Wayne. A consideration of the evidence adduced by Berdyaev for the reality of freedom and its priority over being. Northwestern, 1970. 71-10188

6095. Shalvey, Thomas Joseph, Jr. The philosophical foundations of the role of the collective in the work of Lévi-Strauss. Georgetown, 1970. 71-4104

6096. Shanab, Robert Elias Abu. Logical positivism, operationalism, and behaviorism. Ohio St., 1970. 70-6878

6097. Shaper, Sue Z. The justification of punishment. Rice, 1974. 74-21331

6098. Shapere, A. Dudley. A study of moral deliberation. Harvard, 1957.

6099. Shapira, Michael Stewart. Some varieties of skepticism and of anti-skepticism. Berkeley, 1973.

6100. Shapiro, Daniel. Self-deception. C.U.N.Y., 1975. 76-1491

6101. Shapiro, Gary Michael. Peirce's theory of habit. Columbia, 1970. 71-6256

6102. Shapiro, Henry Lewis. Virtue and friendship in the Nicomachean ethics. Columbia, 1969. 70-7065

6103. Shapiro, Herman. Motion, time and place according to William Ockham. Columbia, 1957.

6104. Shapiro, Vivian Margolis. The philosophy and social thought of Josiah Royce. Brandeis, 1967. 67-16576

6105. Sharkey, Paul William. Hume's theory of space and time. Notre Dame, 1973. 73-24333

6106. Sharkey, Philip James. Human rights: the relationship among civil, socioeconomic and political rights. N.Y.U., 1975. 75-22924

6107. Sharma, Ved Prakash. An enquiry into the nature of aesthetic form with special reference to literature and painting. Minnesota, 1962. 63-6097

6108. Sharvy, Richard Eric. Things. Wayne St., 1969.

6109. Sharvy, Robert Lee. Delacroix's philosophy of art. Northwestern, 1952.

6110. Shaw, James Rochester. Early models for cardiac structure and function: the presocratics through the Middle Ages. Indiana, 1972. 72-30448

6111. Shaw, Jaysanker Lal. Some logical problems concerning existence. Rice, 1970. 70-23572

6112. Shaw, Stewart Arnold. Locke's concept of power. Columbia, 1967. 67-14096

6113. Shawer, Chere Ardine Winnek. Abu Bakr Muhammad Ibn Zakariya al-Razi on reason and nature. Missouri, 1973. 74-18642

6114. Shea, James Marvin, Jr. Self-deception. Cornell, 1967. 67-1411

6115. Shea, William Michael. Intelligence, intelligibility and God: an horizon analysis of the American naturalist philosophies of Frederick J.E. Woodbridge and John H. Randall, Jr. Columbia, 1973.
73-28247

6116. Shea, William Winslow. A phenomenology of the aesthetic object. Yale, 1962.

6117. Shear, Jonathan. The self and pure consciousness. Berkeley, 1972. 72-14636

6118. Shearer, Edna Aston. Hume's place in ethics. Bryn Mawr, 1915.

6119. Shearin, Josse Edwin, Jr. Concepts of action. Virginia, 1971. 72-7274

6120. Shearson, William Arrindell. The notion of encounter in existentialist metaphysics: an inquiry into the nature and structure of existential knowledge in Kierkegaard, Sartre, and Buber. Toronto, 1970.

6121. Sheehan, Robert James. The philosophy of happiness according to St. Thomas Aquinas. Catholic U., 1956.

6122. Sheeks, Russell Wayne. Intellect and will in the philosophy of Schopenhauer. So. Illinois, 1967. 67-15874

6123. Sheffer, Henry Maurice. A programme of philosophy, based on modern logic. Harvard, 1908.

6124. Shehadi, Fadlou A. Ghazali's unique unknowable God: a critical analysis of some of the problems raised by Ghazali's view of God as utterly unique and unknowable. Princeton, 1959. 59-5224

6125. Shein, Louis. A critique of Nicolai Hartmann's ethics; a study of the axiological problem and its relation to human conduct. Toronto, 1946.

6126. Shelanski, Vivien B. Teleological explanations in biology. Chicago, 1970.

6127. Sheldahl, Terry Kent. Concepts of semantic description and methods of semantic investigation. Johns Hopkins, 1967. 67-13829

6128. Sheldon, Mark Peter. An analysis of the concept of imagination with a related theory of metaphor. Brandeis, 1975. 75-24835

6129. Sheldon, Wilmon Henry. The identity of the theoretical and practical attitudes. Harvard, 1899.

6130. Shellenberger, Robert Duane. Personal identity and bodily continuity. Northwestern, 1969. 70-156

6131. Shelley, Karan Antonette Early. The universalizability of moral judgments. M.I.T., 1973.

6132. Shellhaas, Joseph Benjamin. Fouillée's ethics of idées-forces, its psychological and metaphysical bases and a critique thereof. Ohio St., 1951.

6133. Shenk, Jacob Paul. The cosmological argument in Eric L. Mascall and Milton K. Munitz. Boston U., 1972.   71-26477

6134. Shepard, Charles Kelley. The mind-brain identity theory and the problem of phenomenal properties. Texas, 1974.   74-14765

6135. Shepard, Darrell Royce. The sensibility of 'Holy Spirit.' Nebraska, 1968.   68-11569

6136. Shepard, Philip Thomas. A nominalistic construal of arithmetic. Washington U., 1969.   70-10972

6137. Shepherd, Queen Lois. Some recent conceptions of consciousness. Illinois, 1915.

6138. Sheppard, Rev. Vincent. Religion and the concept of democracy. Catholic U., 1949.

6139. Sher, George Allan. Reasons, actions, and determinism. Columbia, 1972.   72-28098

6140. Sherburne, Donald Wynn. A Whiteheadian aesthetic: some implications for aesthetics of Whitehead's mature metaphysical speculation. Yale, 1960.

6141. Sheridan, Gregory Robert. The privacy of mind: an essay on the logic of psychological statements. U.C.L.A., 1966.   67-6190

6142. Sheridan, James Francis. Paul Carus: a study of the thought and work of the editor of the Open Court Publishing Company. Illinois, 1957.   58-4838

6143. Sheriff, Wilbur Spencer. Religion and ethics. An essay in English philosophy. Pennsylvania, 1933.

6144. Sherman, Katherine Sarah. Descartes' Passions of the soul. Toronto, 1972.

6145. Sherman, Rosalyn Sylvia. The concept of interpretation in psychoanalysis. Boston U., 1968.
   68-18115

6146. Sherover, Charles M. The Kantian source of Heidegger's conception of time. N.Y.U., 1966.
   67-633

6147. Sherwin, Susan Bernice. Moral foundations of feminism. Stanford, 1974.   74-13690

6148. Shevach, David Reuel. Emotion and the unconscious. Cal., S. Diego, 1971. 71-26582

6149. Shields, Allan E. An exposition and critique of humanist voluntarism, the philosophy of F.C.S. Schiller (1864-1937). Southern Cal., 1952.

6150. Shier, John David. Scientific objectivity and moral values. Wisconsin, 1972. 72-27349

6151. Shih, Kee Soo. Paul Carus's 'positive monism' and critique of other types of monism (Mach, Haeckel, Peirce.) Temple, 1973. 73-30173

6152. Shih, Vincent Yu-Chung. A study of the concepts of Ti, T'ien, and Tao in ancient Chinese philosophy in the light of Western religious and philosophical thought. Southern Cal., 1939.

6153. Shiman, Paul Leonard. Aspects of assertive predication. Columbia, 1970. 73-8983

6154. Shimer, William Allison. Relativity in science and philosophy: a study of its history, validity, and application. Harvard, 1925.

6155. Shimony, Abner Eliezer. A theory of confirmation. Yale, 1953.

6156. Shin, Oh-Hyun. Sartre's concept of the self. Michigan, 1975. 75-29324

6157. Shipka, Thomas Albert. Social conflict and re-construction. Boston Coll., 1969. 70-12609

6158. Shircel, Rev. Cyril L. The univocity of the concept of being in the philosophy of John Duns Scotus. Catholic U., 1942.

6159. Shirk, Evelyn U. Adventurous idealism: the philosophy of Alfred Lloyd. Columbia, 1953.

6160. Shirley, Edward Salmond. A proposal for a contextualist theory of truth. Massachusetts, 1969. 69-18670

6161. Shoemaker, Robert Gardner. Reason and moral attitudes: an examination of the logic of moral discourse. Texas, 1967. 67-8157

6162. Shoemaker, Sydney Sharpless. Self knowledge and self identity. Cornell, 1958. 59-1970

6163. Shope, Robert Kinard. Wish-fulfillment and psychic energy in psychoanalytic theory. Harvard, 1966.

6164. Short, Morris Robert. Self-esteem: a study of the ethical significance of certain aspects of the dynamics of self-esteem as developed in psychiatry and Gestalt psychology. Columbia, 1953.
5206

6165. Short, Thomas Lloyd. Objectivity without a cognitive given: Peirce's philosophy of science. Texas, 1974. 74-24934

6166. Shouery, Imad Toufic. The psychological origins of Sartre's conception of freedom. Oklahoma, 1968.
68-7543

6167. Shrader, Sr. Kristin. Cybernetics and materialism. Notre Dame, 1972. 72-16272

6168. Shue, Henry Greyson. Selective objection and conscription: a search for a principle. Princeton, 1970. 71-14417

6169. Shuford, Haywood Rhyne, Jr. A behavioristic theory of signs. Brown, 1964. 65-2248

6170. Shumaker, Elmer Ellsworth. The function of knowledge. Yale, 1902.

6171. Shumaker, James David. The moral literature of Alexander Pope: a philosophical analysis. Florida St., 1969. 70-8573

6172. Shuman, Samuel I. Clarity and vagueness in language. Pennsylvania, 1951.

6173. Shute, Clarence W. The psychology of Aristotle: an analysis of the living being. Columbia, 1941.

6174. Sh-Veev, Charles Levin. The conventionalist philosophy of empirical and deductive science. Southern Cal., 1971. 72-11957

6175. Sibley, William M. An examination of Dewey's theory of knowledge. Brown, 1943.

6176. Sides, Henry Nicholson. Sense-data, knowledge, and conceptual schemes. No. Carolina, 1967.
68-2232

6177. Sidorsky, David. The nature of disagreement in social philosophy: four criticisms of liberalism. Columbia, 1962. 63-3700

6178. Sieburth, Guenter. On ancient measure. Wisconsin, 1966. 66-9181

6179. Siegel, Judith F. Logic without mentalism: a study of Quine's views. Chicago, 1975.

6180. Siegel, Tema Leah. Wittgenstein on sensation. Chicago, 1975.

6181. Siegler, Fred Adrian. An examination of attempts to find incorrigible knowledge. Stanford, 1960.
60-3833

6182. Siemens, Warren Dean. Theories of scientific change: their nature and structure. M.I.T., 1973.

6183. Sievert, Donald Edward. Austin, Wittgenstein and Strawson on mind. Iowa, 1967. 68-977

6184. Sikora, Joseph John. Object and method in the philosophy of nature and in physical science. Notre Dame, 1958. 58-1403

6185. Sikora, Richard Innes. Reason, language and choice: a critical analysis of contemporary developments in ethical theory. Berkeley, 1963. 64-2133

6186. Silber, John Robert. The highest good as the unity of form and content in Kant's ethics. Yale, 1956.

6187. Silver, Bruce Sheldon. The status of the sciences in the philosophy of George Berkeley. Colorado, 1971. 71-25873

6188. Silver, Ruth Eleanor. A critique of methodological individualism and its interpretation of societal concepts. Pennsylvania, 1969. 70-7851

6189. Silverman, David Wolf. The problem of prophecy in Gersonides. Columbia, 1974. 75-5254

6190. Silverman, Hugh Jerald. Existential ambiguity: a phenomenology of human nature. Stanford, 1973.
73-30476

6191. Silvers, Anita. Beardsley's account of critical argument. Johns Hopkins, 1967. 67-13830

6192. Silvers, Stuart. The evolutionary development of scientific method in England from Bacon to Mill-being a historical analysis of the methods of experimental investigation. Pittsburgh, 1963.
64-5956

6193. Silverstein, Harry Shevelson, III. Ethics, action, and universalisability. Chicago, 1967.

6194. Simard, Émile. L'hypothèse. Laval, 1948.

6195. Simco, Nancy Jane Davis. A critical exposition of Strawson's Individuals. Kansas, 1969. 70-11073

6196. Simec, Sr. M. Sophie. Philosophical bases for human dignity and change in Thomistic and American non-Thomistic philosophy. Catholic U., 1953.

6197. Simmonds, Kent Cooper. Philosophical comments on Symposium, 201d-7a. Ohio St., 1969. 70-6884

6198. Simmons, Edward Dwyer. The Thomistic doctrine of intellectual abstraction for the three levels of science: exposition and defense. Notre Dame, 1952. 5276

6199. Simmons, James Robert. The problem of human individuality with emphasis on the philosophy of Alfred North Whitehead. Columbia, 1955. 12069

6200. Simon, Howard Leslie. Towards a theory of legal exceptions. Minnesota, 1974. 75-12161

6201. Simon, Jerome Stephen. An examination of certain aspects of the coherence theory of truth. Brown, 1969. 70-8791

6202. Simon, Michael Arthur. Mental events and brain processes: an investigation of the identity theory. Harvard, 1967.

6203. Simon, Robert Leonard. Four concepts of equality. Pennsylvania, 1969. 69-21428

6204. Simon, Thomas William. Teleological clocks- cybernetic clouds: a philosophical analysis. Washington U., 1973. 74-13794

6205. Simonds, Roger Tyrrell. The naturalistic philosophy in classical Roman law. Yale, 1957.

6206. Simons, Leo. The doctrine of fallibilism. Columbia, 1951. 3384

6207. Simpson, John Evan. Facts. Duke, 1966. 67-9760

6208. Simpson, Kenneth Moore. The necessary and the empirical in geometry. Berkeley, 1941.

6209. Simpson, Richard Lee. Malcolm on dreaming. British Columbia, 1971.

6210. Sinclair, James Huntly. The theory of the state in Hegel's philosophy. Syracuse, 1916.

6211. Singer, Beth Judith. Order and liberty in human life: a study of Santayana's metaphysics of society. Columbia, 1967. 67-10611

6212. Singer, Edgar Arthur, Jr. The composite nature of consciousness. Pennsylvania, 1894.

6213. Singer, Irving. An approach to aesthetics through the criticism of Santayana's views. Harvard, 1952.

6214. Singer, Marcus George. Generalization in ethics. Cornell, 1952.

6215. Singer, Milton Borah. On formal method in mathematical logic. Chicago, 1940.

6216. Singh, Bhagwan B. An examination of Josiah Royce's conception of the self and the world. Buffalo, 1970. 71-7225

6217. Sinha, Ajit Kumar. The problem of appearance and reality in Sankara and Bradley. Illinois, 1955. 11538

6218. Sinha, Shukla. A critical evaluation of G.E. Moore's theory of empirical knowledge. Michigan St., 1975. 76-5645

6219. Sinisi, Vito Frederick. The semantics of reism. Berkeley, 1960.

6220. Sinks, John Douglas. Definite descriptions in a modal language. Duke, 1974. 75-2425

6221. Sipe, Robert Bernard. Toward a new society: an exploration of alienation and liberation in our technocratic society. Claremont, 1973.

6222. Sipfle, David Arthur. Dimensions of freedom: freedom and humility. Yale, 1958.

6223. Sircello, Guy Joseph. An examination of Ernst Cassirer's philosophy of language. Columbia, 1966. 69-567

6224. Sirridge, Mary Jeannette. Problems of truth and reference in fiction. Ohio St., 1972. 73-11577

6225. Sist, Arthur John. Non-alienated society: an appraisal of its possibility in the light of the Sartrean problematic and of the responses of the pluralistic and participatory theories of democracy. Yale, 1971. 71-22346

6226. Sitelman, Robert. The aesthetic character of representational painting. Columbia, 1972. 73-16244

6227. Sitton, Robert McConnell. The ontological status of the work of art: three contemporary views. Duke, 1964. 64-8256

6228. Sjaardema, Hendrikus. A critical examination of the concept of understanding in the psychologies of Wilhelm Dilthey, Eduard Spranger, and Karl Jaspers. Southern Cal., 1939.

6229. Sjursen, Harold P. Kierkegaard: the individual and the public. A study in the problem of essential communication. New School, 1974. 75-7729

6230. Skagestad, Finn Peter. R.G. Collingwood's theory of presuppositions: its origins and development and contemporary philosophical significance. Brandeis, 1973. 73-32407

6231. Skidmore, Arthur Whitford, III. Studies in Peirce's theories of logic. Texas, 1968. 68-16138

6232. Sklar, Lawrence. Inter-theoretic reduction in natural science. Princeton, 1964. 65-2156

6233. Skocz, Dennis Edward. The right to private property in post-Marxian perspective. Duquesne, 1974. 75-3732

6234. Skorpen, Erling Raymond. The cognitive status of moral judgments. Yale, 1960.

6235. Skousgaard, Stephen Arthur. Self and freedom: an interpretation of the essence, existence, and symbols of human freedom based on the philosophy of Paul Ricoeur. Tulane, 1975. 76-4004

6236. Skrupskelis, Ignas Kestutis. The problem of God in the philosophy of Josiah Royce. Toronto, 1967.

6237. Skyrms, Frederick Brian. The concept of physical necessity. Pittsburgh, 1964. 66-3842

6238. Slafkosky, Alexander L. The best form of government. Laval, 1954.

6239. Slaght, Ralph Lawrence. Defeasibility and the analysis of non-basic knowledge. Pennsylvania, 1972. 73-1450

6240. Slakey, Thomas John. Aristotle's theory of perception and thinking as the reception of forms: a critical analysis. Cornell, 1961. 61-1114

6241. Slater, John Edgar. Luther's attitude toward philosophy. Pittsburgh, 1941.

6242. Slater, John Greer. A methodological study of ordinary-language philosophy. Michigan, 1961.
61-6425

6243. Slattery, Rev. Kenneth F. The Thomistic concept of the virtue of temperance and its relation to the emotions. Catholic U., 1952.

6244. Slattery, Ralph Joseph. The coherence theory of logic and the idealist theory of the state. Ohio St., 1930.

6245. Slaughter, John Wilson. On praxis: an inquiry into Marx. Drew, 1970. 70-24590

6246. Slavin, Rev. Robert Joseph. The philosophical basis for individual differences according to St. Thomas Aquinas. Catholic U., 1936.

6247. Sleeper, Ralph William. Metaphysics and the value theories of Urban, Dewey, and Perry. Columbia, 1956. 16296

6248. Sleigh, Robert Collins, Jr. An examination of Thomas Reid's account of our knowledge of the external world and other minds. Brown, 1963. 64-2009

6249. Sleinis, Edgar Evalt. Intrinsic properties of objects. Johns Hopkins, 1971. 71-21053

6250. Sleva, Rev. Victor E. The separated soul according to St. Thomas Aquinas. Catholic U., 1940.

6251. Slinger, James Warren. Language, meaning, and ordinary-language philosophy. Wisconsin, 1971.
71-9200

6252. Slivinski, Dennis Leo. Personal identity within the context of Whitehead's metaphysics. Vanderbilt, 1974. 75-1157

6253. Sloan, Phillip Reid. The history of the concept of the biological species in the seventeenth and eighteenth centuries, and the origin of the species problem. Cal., S. Diego, 1970. 70-18321

6254. Slote, Michael Anthony. Certainty and language. Harvard, 1965.

6255. Smaby, John William. On the derivation of 'ought' from 'is'. Minnesota, 1968. 69-6846

6256. Small, Kenneth Hollingshead. Uses of illocutionary acts: Alston and Searle. Chicago, 1974.

6257. Smart, Hugh R.G. The theories of space and time found in Hume's writings. Duke, 1950.

6258. Smerud, Warren Douglas. Can there be a private language? An examination of some principal arguments. U. of Washington, 1967. 67-14219

6259. Smigelskis, David Joseph. The problematic of Aristotle's metaphysical inquiry. Yale, 1969.
70-2807

6260. Smilde, Ralph Louis. Carl Gustav Carus: an examination of his natural philosophy and of his psychology. Columbia, 1967. 67-10612

6261. Smith, Carol Ann. Abstractionism: contemporary attacks and alternatives. Pittsburgh, 1972.
73-5014

6262. Smith, David Woodruff. Intentionality, noemata, and individuation: the role of individuation in Husserl's theory of intentionality. Stanford, 1970.
71-19765

6263. Smith, Dennis Stephen. The unity of Hume's _Treatise_. Catholic U., 1975. 75-21271

6264. Smith, Edward Griffin. A disagreement on the need of a sensible species in the writings of some medical doctors in the late middle ages. St. Louis, 1974. 74-24144

6265. Smith, Elizabeth Helen. Natural rights; a reconsideration. U. of Washington, 1970. 71-8547

6266. Smith, Sr. Enid. The goodness of being in Thomistic philosophy. Catholic U., 1947.

6267. Smith, Esther Diane. Aspects of human agency in the phenomenology of Paul Ricoeur. Claremont, 1975.
75-12755

6268. Smith, Mthr. Frances Antoinette. Louis Lavelle's philosophy of man: self-creation through consent to participation. Fordham, 1964. 64-8593

6269. Smith, Gerard. Freedom in Molina. Toronto, 1936.

6270. Smith, Howard Taylor. The ontological foundations of Hegel's system of science. Tulane, 1971.
72-14205

6271. Smith, H. Jeffery. Esthetic meaning. Berkeley, 1940.

6272. Smith, Harry Jason. Augustine's idea of God. Drew, 1929.

6273. Smith, Henry Bradford. The transition from "Bewusstsein" to "Selbstbewusstsein" in Hegel's phenomenology of mind. Pennsylvania, 1909.

6274. Smith, Ignatius. Classification of desires in St. Thomas and in modern sociology. Catholic U., 1915.

6275. Smith, James LeRoy. Aesthetics and art within a Whiteheadian cosmology. Tulane, 1969. 70-6428

6276. Smith, James Marvin. Punishment: its nature and justification. Brown, 1960. 62-5760

6277. Smith, James Ward. Propaedeutic value theory. Princeton, 1942. 810

6278. Smith, Janet Farrell. Theory of reference and existential presuppositions in Russell and Meinong. Columbia, 1975. 75-18442

6279. Smith, Sr. Joanmarie. John Dewey and the ideal community. Fordham, 1971. 71-26996

6280. Smith, John E. Royce's social infinite; the community of interpretation. Columbia, 1950.

6281. Smith, John Jeffrey. Direct and indirect methods of teaching morals: a historical and psychological study. Yale, 1915.

6282. Smith, John Leigh. Plato and the paradox of false statements: a study of the *Euthydemus* and the *Sophist*. Virginia, 1975. 75-26021

6283. Smith, John Milton. A comparison and criticism of the educational philosophies of Plato and John Dewey. Iowa, 1941.

6284. Smith, Joseph W., Jr. An exploration of the problem of faith and reason through a study of philosophical and Biblical doctrines. Virginia, 1948.

6285. Smith, Kenneth Ray. Dialectical conceptions of the spirit: Hegel, Kierkegaard, and Nietzsche. Yale, 1972. 73-14

6286. Smith, Laurence Christian. Social science and values. Nebraska, 1951.

6287. Smith, Malcolm Barry Estes. A critical study of the emotive theory of ethics. Cornell, 1969.
70-534

6288. Smith, Mary Ann Wrynn. Scientific laws and necessity. Michigan St., 1973. 74-6132

6289. Smith, Mary Joan. Positivism and situated identity. N.Y.U., 1971. 72-13405

6290. Smith, Nicholas Dabney. Plato's similes of light in the Republic: a reinterpretation. Stanford, 1975. 75-25609

6291. Smith, Ralph D. The idea of God in the philosophy of Aristotle. American U., 1934.

6292. Smith, Richard Allen. Collingwood, phenomenology, and absolute presuppositions. Purdue, 1975.
76-595

6293. Smith, Richard Campbell. Time distinctions in contemporary philosophy. Yale, 1960.

6294. Smith, Richard Lee. The self, behavior, and causation. U.C.L.A., 1971. 72-13652

6295. Smith, Richard Lee. Continuity and change: an essay in the philosophy of science. Yale, 1975.
75-24602

6296. Smith, Robert Carl. A critical analysis of religious and philosophic issues between Buber and Jung. Temple, 1961.

6297. Smith, Robert Lawrence, Jr. The syntax and semantics of ERICA. Stanford, 1972. 72-30707

6298. Smith, Robin A. Plato's dialectic from the standpoint of Aristotle's first logic. Claremont, 1974. 74-7909

6299. Smith, Robin Sommers. An analysis of the concept of truth. Chicago, 1965.

6300. Smith, Br. Sixtus Robert. A Thomistic theory of the liberal arts. Laval, 1947.

6301. Smith, Steven Albert. Satisfaction of interest and the concept of morality. Harvard, 1972.

6302. Smith, Thomas Vernor. Philosophic bases of the American doctrine of equality. Chicago, 1922.

6303. Smith, Vincent E. The philosophical frontiers of physics. Catholic U., 1947.

6304. Smith, William. Leibnitz. Syracuse, 1885.

6305. Smith, William Aloysius, Jr. Giovanni Gentile on the existence of God. St. John's, 1967.
68-3819

6306. Smith, William Corbett. A study in reference. Princeton, 1975. 76-18247

6307. Smithson, Rulon Nephi. The evolution of the historical method of Augustin Thierry: a study in social and political consciousness. Columbia, 1970.
71-6260

6308. Smits, Henry. Some aspects of the ontological argument. Missouri, 1971. 71-30691

6309. Smokler, Howard Edward. Scientific concepts and philosophical theory: an essay in the philosophy of W.K. Clifford. Columbia, 1959. 59-4092

6310. Smokler, Irving Alan. Theoretical phenomenalism. Michigan, 1972. 73-11262

6311. Smook, Roger Wayne. The paradox of identity. Maryland, 1971. 71-23982

6312. Smoot, William Robertson, II. A critical study of the ethical theory of Jean-Paul Sartre. Northwestern, 1973. 73-30728

6313. Smucker, Jan Arden. A study of the problem of determining ontological commitments in Wittgenstein's *Tractatus*. Michigan St., 1969. 70-15136

6314. Smullyan, Arthur Francis. Evidence, memory, and induction. Harvard, 1941.

6315. Smyth, Anastasia Marjorie Mary. The nature and role of prudence according to the philosophy of St. Thomas Aquinas. Toronto, 1944.

6316. Smyth, Richard Andrew. Kant's theory of reference. Indiana, 1961. 61-4487

6317. Smythe, Thomas Wayne. A materialist conception of personal identity. Michigan, 1971. 72-4982

6318. Snapper, John William. A dual abstract ontology: a study in Frege. Chicago, 1974.

6319. Snare, Francis Eugene. Should I be moral? Michigan, 1970. 70-4198

6320. Sneath, Elias Hershey. A critical examination of Scottish realism. Yale, 1890.

6321. Snedden, James L. Arnold. A critical examination of the systematic philosophy of William E. Hocking. Buffalo, 1956. 57-1383

6322. Sneed, Joseph Donald. The projection postulate and quantum mechanical measurement. Stanford, 1964. 65-2900

6323. Snell, George Boyd. Personalism as an aspect of modern philosophy. Toronto, 1938.

6324. Snoeyenbos, Milton Henry. Art theory. Minnesota, 1975. 75-21092

6325. Snow, Adolph Judah. Matter and gravity in Newton's physical philosophy; a study in the natural philosophy of Newton's time. Columbia, 1926.

6326. Snow, Robert Emerson. The problem of certainty: Bacon, Descartes, and Pascal. Indiana, 1967. 68-7243

6327. Snyder, Albert Aaron. The appeal to ordinary use: a study in philosophical methodology. Cornell, 1966. 67-3795

6328. Snyder, Donald Paul. Causation, predication and modal logic. Duke, 1964. 64-11209

6329. Snyder, John Julius. The mode of science and the modes of demonstration proper to the metaphysics of St. Thomas Aquinas. Toronto, 1969.

6330. Snyder, Lee Regis. Phenomenological analysis of passive synthesis. Buffalo, 1975. 76-9119

6331. Snyder, Peter Vandervoort. An analysis of P.H. Nowell-Smith's Ethics. Massachusetts, 1969. 70-3180

6332. Snyder, William Stover. Whitehead's theories of perception: an epistemological source of speculative philosophy. Princeton, 1955. 57-2181

6333. So, Hung-Yul. Causal explanation of human action. Michigan, 1974. 75-10297

6334. Sobel, Jerry Edward. Heidegger's conception of the world. Harvard, 1974.

6335. Sobel, Jordan Howard. "What if everyone did that?" Michigan, 1961. 61-2796

6336. Sober, Elliott R. Simplicity. Harvard, 1974.

6337. Sobers, David Lee. Kant's justification of the possibility of judgments of taste. Rochester, 1967. 67-13650

6338. Soccio, Douglas John. A philosophical analysis of Oscar Wilde's esthetic morality. Washington U., 1975. 75-4780

6339. Soghoian, Richard J. G.E. Moore's critique of naturalistic ethics. Columbia, 1970. 70-23465

6340. Soler, Jorge Leoncio. The psychology of Iacopo Zabarella (1533-1589). Buffalo, 1971. 72-255

6341. Soles, Deborah Hansen. Epistemological accounts of predication. Johns Hopkins, 1975. 75-1550

6342. Soll, Albert Ivan. Hegel's search for absolute knowledge. Princeton, 1966. 66-13354

6343. Sollazzo, Gary James. Ryle on the concept of thinking. Maryland, 1973. 74-264

6344. Solomon, Manson Julius. Ethical justification. Columbia, 1973. 73-28251

6345. Solomon, Robert Charles. Unconscious motivation. Michigan, 1968. 68-7731

6346. Solomon, William David. Moral neutrality and contemporary ethical theory. Texas, 1972. 73-522

6347. Somerville, Rev. James M. Bond in being; the vinculum in Leibniz and Blondel. Fordham, 1954.

6348. Sommers, Frederic Tamler. An empiricist ontology: a study in the metaphysics of Alfred North Whitehead. Columbia, 1955. 15750

6349. Sommese, Rebecca Rooze. Cartesian categories in twentieth-century philosophy of mind. Yale, 1973. 73-29251

6350. Son, Le Minh. Teaching: a logical analysis and an epistemological investigation. Ohio St., 1971. 72-15299

6351. Sontag, Frederick Earl. Perfection and possibility. Yale, 1952.

6352. Soper, Ernest Philip. The "acceptability" of law: an analysis of the concept of law based on the legal theory of Professor H.L.A. Hart. Washington U., 1972. 73-5066

6353. Soper, William Wayne. The self and its world in Ralph Barton Perry, Edgar Sheffield Brightman, Jean-Paul Sartre and Søren Kierkegaard. Boston U., 1962. 62-3616

6354. Sorantin, Erich. The problem of musical expression. Vanderbilt, 1932.

6355. Sosa, Ernest. Directives: a logico-philosophical inquiry. Pittsburgh, 1964. 66-3844

6356. Sosensky, Irving. John Dewey's theory of warranted assertability. Columbia, 1955. 13990

6357. Spade, Paul Vincent. The mediaeval liar: a study of John Buridan's position on the paradox, with a catalogue of the *Insolubilia* literature of the middle ages. Toronto, 1972.

6358. Spader, Peter Henry. The realization of value: a study in the philosophy of Max Scheler. Columbia, 1969. 70-7072

6359. Spae, Joseph John. Ito Jinsai, a philosopher, educator and sinologist of the Tōkugawa period. Columbia, 1948.

6360. Spangler, George Alfred. Aristotle on change: the importance of being something. Alberta, 1974.

6361. Spargo, Sr. Emma Jane Marie. The category of the aesthetic in the philosophy of St. Bonaventura. Fordham, 1950.

6362. Sparkman, Kathleen Palmer. Theories of the public: local, national and international. Columbia, 1960. 61-872

6363. Sparling, Kathryn Wyndham. Early Natsume Soseki images and patterns of the absolute. Harvard, 1974.

6364. Spector, Marshall. Theory and observation: an examination of some problems in logical empiricism. Johns Hopkins, 1963.

6365. Spelman, Elizabeth Victoria. Other minds: issues of knowledge and language. Johns Hopkins, 1973. 74-10450

6366. Speltz, Rev. George H. The importance of rural life according to the philosophy of St. Thomas Aquinas. Catholic U., 1944.

6367. Spencer, James Calvin, Sr. Edmund Husserl's conception of the transcendental: a critical analysis. Buffalo, 1974. 74-20034

6368. Spencer, John R. The philosophy of logic of Hugh Maccoll. McGill, 1972.

6369. Spencer, Mary Dale Foster. A logic for moral decision. Texas, 1970. 71-194

6370. Spencer, Theodore James. The problem of individuation. Iowa, 1975. 76-13447

6371. Spencer, Willard Wylie. Our knowledge of other minds: a study in mental nature, existence, and intercourse. Yale, 1925.

6372. Spero, Shubert. The significance and justification of religious belief. Case, 1971. 71-22852

6373. Spickler, Stuart Francis. Shadworth H. Hodgson: a British anticipation of phenomenology. Colorado, 1968. 68-14402

6374. Spiegel, Claude Richard. The metaethics of David Hume. Cincinnati, 1969. 70-468

6375. Spiegler, Gerhard Ernst. Between relativism and absolutism: a study of problematic dimensions in the Dialektik and Dogmatik of Friedrich Schleiermacher. Chicago, 1962.

6376. Spieler, David Arthur. Is disembodied existence logically impossible? Michigan, 1972. 73-11265

6377. Spielman, Stephen Martin. The logical structure of probability. Pennsylvania, 1967. 68-9242

6378. Spinnenweber, Andrew Earl. Practical knowledge in the thought of St. Thomas Aquinas. Duquesne, 1971. 72-31716

6379. Spiro, Lawrence M. The Freudo-Marxism of Herbert Marcuse. Columbia, 1973.

6380. Spiro, Solomon Joseph. The principles of Judaism according to Rabbi Simon ben Zemah Duran. Yeshiva, 1970. 71-13740

6381. Spitzer, Adele Ruth. The unity of Plato's theory of art. Yale, 1962.

6382. Spivey, Mark Allan. Prehensions. No. Carolina, 1971. 71-21003

6383. Sponga, Rev. Edward J. Process and spirit, the dialectic of universal dynamism in Hegel and Blondel. Fordham, 1955.

6384. Spongberg, Viola Hildur. The philosophy of Erik Gustaf Geijer. N.Y.U., 1944. 73-22430

6385. Sprague, Rosamond K. Parmenides, being, and the theory of types. Bryn Mawr, 1953.

6386. Sprague, Wayne L. The community and the individual in the later philosophy of Josiah Royce. Boston U., 1953.

6387. Springer, Jon Randall. The moral argument for the existence of God in the thought of W.R. Sorley. So. Illinois, 1972. 73-6247

6388. Springer, William C. The world and the word in Merleau-Ponty: towards an existential epistemology and an ontology of the human body. Rice, 1967. 67-13125

6389. Sprinkle, Henry Call. Concerning the philosophical defensibility of a limited indeterminism; an enquiry based upon a critical study of the indeterministic theories of James, Renouvier, Boutroux, Eddington, Bergson and Whitehead. Yale, 1929.

6390. Sprintzen, David Allen. Revolt, dialogue and community: a study in the thought of Albert Camus. Penn St., 1968. 68-15154

6391. Sprohge, Hans Dieter. The role of reason in the cosmology of Kant's first *Critique*. Buffalo, 1974. 75-7803

6392. Squadrito, Kathleen Marie. A defense of Locke's theory of sensitive knowledge. Washington U., 1973. 73-24906

6393. Stabile, Katherine E. The origin of the problems of the medieval noetic: Aristotle or Alexander of Aphrodisias? Fordham, 1974. 74-25126

6394. Stacer, Rev. John Regis. Hocking's widening empiricism. Tulane, 1970. 70-24552

6395. Stack, George Joseph. Berkeley's theory of perception. Penn St., 1964. 65-6768

6396. Stack, Michael Francis. Hume and the external world. Duke, 1971. 71-24207

6397. Stadler, Ingrid Hess. An explication of Kant's analysis of beauty. Radcliffe, 1959.

6398. Stafford, Rev. Robert H. The morality of universal military conscription in peacetime. Catholic U., 1952.

6399. Stafford, Sue Perrott. Language, mind, and brain: some philosophical implications of the theories of Noam Chomsky. Connecticut, 1973. 73-9823

6400. Stafford, William Tecumseh, Jr. Teleology and purpose in recent Anglo-American philosophy. Southern Cal., 1964. 64-7612

6401. Stahl, Gary Hudnut. Relativism, induction, and criticism. Columbia, 1964. 65-4587

6402. Stahl, Gerry. Marxian hermeneutics and Heideggerian social theory: interpreting and transforming our world. Northwestern, 1975. 75-29759

6403. Stahl, John Thomas. The notion of probability in the theistic argument of F.R. Tennant. Boston U., 1967. 67-13263

6404. Stahl, Roland C., Jr. The influence of Bergson on Whitehead. Boston U., 1950.

6405. Stalker, Douglas Frank. Deep structure. No. Carolina, 1974. 75-4872

6406. Stallknecht, Newton Phelps. Bergson's idea of creation. Princeton, 1930.

6407. Stalnaker, Nan Younger. Dewey's criticisms of traditional empiricism. Yale, 1973. 73-29254

6408. Stalnaker, Robert C. Historical interpretation. Princeton, 1965. 65-13173

6409. Stam, James Henry. The question of the origin of language in German thought, 1756-1785. Brandeis, 1964. 64-12874

6410. Stamatakos, Bess Makris. Plato's theory of number. Michigan St., 1975. 75-12527

6411. Stamey, Joseph Donald. Christian ethics and violent conflict: the "Just War" as an ethical model. Boston U., 1968. 63-18145

6412. Stanage, Sherman Miller. The role of the "overlap" in Collingwood's philosophy. Colorado, 1959. 60-1046

6413. Standley, Gerald Brent. Study in the correspondence of perceptions. Buffalo, 1955. 11858

6414. Stanley, Philip Edwin. Hume's doctrine of necessary connection. Harvard, 1928.

6415. Stanley, Richard Arthur. Studies in negation. Virginia, 1968. 68-18236

6416. Stanley, Robert Lauren. A basis for logic in natural deduction. Harvard, 1951.

6417. Stannard, Jerry Willmert. The psychology of the passions in the Old Stoa. Illinois, 1958. 58-1743

6418. Stanton, William Lawrence. Anomalous monism and the mental *qua* mental. Princeton, 1975. 76-22607

6419. Stanway, Ross Allison. A comparative study of the theories of truth in Bradley and Joachim. Toronto, 1966.

6420. Stark, Craig Latimer. The idea of God in the late dialogues of Plato. Princeton, 1970. 70-23642

6421. Starkey, Lawrence Harry. A philosophical critique of F.R. Tennant's empirical approach to theism in the light of current science. Southern Cal., 1960. 60-4488

6422. Starr, David Edward. *Ousia* and *Dasein*: an ontological investigation of Aristotle and Heidegger. Boston U., 1972. 72-25335

6423. Starsky, Morris Joseph. The ontological problem of *Oratio obliqua*. Michigan, 1968. 68-7735

6424. Start, Lester J. Kierkegaard and Hegel. Syracuse, 1953.

6425. Statman, Richard. Structural complexity of proofs. Stanford, 1974. 74-27119

6426. Staudenbaur, Craig Anthony. The metaphysical thought of Henry More: its sources and development. Johns Hopkins, 1961.

6427. Stavrides, Maria Margareta. The concept of existence in Kierkegaard and Heidegger. Columbia, 1952. 4239

6428. Stawinski, Arthur Walter. Ludwig Wittgenstein and the perceptual foundations of knowledge. Northwestern, 1973. 73-30732

6429. Stearns, Isabel S. The nature of the individual. Bryn Mawr, 1938.

6430. Stearns, J. Brenton. Gabriel Marcel's repudiation of idealism. Emory, 1961. 62-38

6431. Stecker, Robert Andrew. Moral sense theories. M.I.T., 1975.

6432. Steel, Margaret. The structure of language: Chomsky and Quine. W. Ontario, 1974.

6433. Steel, Thomas Jamison. Some definitions concerning knowing how. Brown, 1973. 74-3077

6434. Steelman, Edmund H. The Aristotelian influence in neo-Thomism. Temple, 1946.

6435. Stegeman, Beatrice Ann. The art of science. So. Illinois, 1967. 68-3920

6436. Steger, Evelyn Ecker. The verbum cordis according to St. Thomas Aquinas. Catholic U., 1967. 67-17137

6437. Steibel, Gerald Lee. John Dewey's philosophy of democracy applied in a critique of classic liberalism. Columbia, 1951. 3118

6438. Steiger, Henry William. A philosophical investigation of the doctrine of Christian science. Boston U., 1946.

6439. Stein, George Philip. The ways of meaning in the arts. Columbia, 1953. 6714

6440. Stein, Howard. An examination of some aspects of natural science. Chicago, 1958.

6441. Stein, Ronald H. A critical examination of the ethical thought of Dr. Samuel Clarke. Buffalo, 1972. 72-20849

6442. Stein, Stanley Martin. The ontological status of social institutions. Calgary, 1973.

6443. Stein, Waltraut Johanna Hedwig. Intersubjectivity and schizophrenia. Northwestern, 1963. 64-2279

6444. Steinberg, Alan Martin. Disembodied consciousness. Cornell, 1974. 74-29940

6445. Steinberg, Eric Matthew. Hume's attitude toward common sense. Columbia, 1974. 75-16141

6446. Steinbock, Bonnie. Moral reasons and motivation. Berkeley, 1974.

6447. Steiner, Mark Jay. On mathematical knowledge. Princeton, 1972. 72-24704

6448. Steinhardt, Leigh D. The variable in its relation to semantic problems. Radcliffe, 1940.

6449. Steinkraus, Warren E. The given in certain epistemological theories since 1920. Boston U., 1952.

6450. Stell, Lance Keith. Man, needs, and justice: Marx's critique of the division of labor. Michigan, 1974. 75-825

6451. Stelzer, John Herbert. Some results concerning subjective probability structures with semiorders. Stanford, 1967. 68-6492

6452. Stengren, George L. Human intellectual knowledge of the material singular according to Francis Suarez. Fordham, 1965. 65-14186

6453. Stenner, Alfred Jackson. Paradox, prediction and self-vitiating hypotheses. Michigan St., 1963. 64-965

6454. Stenson, Sten Harold. A history of Scottish empiricism from 1730 to 1856. Columbia, 1952. 4240

6455. Stepelevich, Lawrence S. Henri Bergson's concept of man: an exposition and critique. Catholic U., 1963. 63-7974

6456. Stephens, Ira Kendrick. Criticism as a philosophical method. Harvard, 1927.

6457. Stephens, John Alan. The origins of ideas fundamental in the mathematical and physical sciences. Southern Cal., 1950.

6458. Stephens, Kenneth D. The theory of action. Claremont, 1971. 71-21672

6459. Stephens, Robert Goodall. The return of intuitionism in present-day ethics. Yale, 1935.

6460. Stephens, Walter S. Berdyaev's doctrine of man. Chicago, 1962.

6461. Sterba, James Paul. A theory of distributive justice. Pittsburgh, 1973. 74-18434

6462. Stergiades, John William. Urban's theory of value and its relation to ethical obligation. Marquette, 1974. 75-15001

6463. Sterling, Colleen Grimm. Reason, space and reality in the philosophy of Emile Meyerson. Bryn Mawr, 1954. 10692

6464. Stern, Herold S. The question of a value-free social science. N.Y.U., 1969. 70-3114

6465. Stern, Irwin Lawrence. Determinism and morality. Harvard, 1968.

6466. Stern, Kenneth. Minds: mine and others'. Yale, 1960.

6467. Stern, Leah Jacobs. The transcendental object in the Critique of pure reason. Rochester, 1971. 72-772

6468. Stern, Raphael George. Truth and meaning. N.Y.U., 1975. 76-10230

6469. Sternfeld, Robert. Contemporary philosophies of experience: philosophic method in Dewey, Bradley, and Husserl. Chicago, 1948.

6470. Stevens, Caroline T. Interconnections among philosophy, science, and social practice: B.F. Skinner and Carl Rogers, a case study. Missouri, K.C., 1974. 76-11502

6471. Stevens, Edward Ira. Freedom, determinism, and responsibility: an analysis and a Whiteheadian interpretation. Vanderbilt, 1965. 65-10486

6472. Stevens, Rev. Edward Vincent. G.H. Mead on the moral self. St. Louis, 1965. 65-14665

6473. Stevens, Eldon Lloyd. Kierkegaard's categories of existence. Colorado, 1964. 65-4274

6474. Stevens, John Coolidge. Charles Taylor's theory of teleological explanation. Chicago, 1974.

6475. Stevens, Pearl Ray. The idea of God in the philosophy of Paul Tillich. Nebraska, 1961. 61-5385

6476. Stevens, William Louis. Property: its definition and justification. Chicago, 1972.

6477. Stevenson, Charles Leslie. The emotive meaning of ethical terms. Harvard, 1935.

6478. Stevenson, John Graham. Aristotle's conception of metaphysics: the scope and province of first philosophy as revealed in the first part of Metaphysics Γ. Chicago, 1975.

6479. Stewart, Calvin George. Hume's theory of the passions. U. of Washington, 1974. 74-29505

6480. Stewart, David Alexander. Independence in American new realism; an idealist's survey. Toronto, 1939.

6481. Stewart, Donald Lee. Man and fidelity: a study in Marcel. Hawaii, 1969. 70-9984

6482. Stewart, Douglas James. Nature and purpose: a study of Greek teleological theories. Cornell, 1964.

6483. Stewart, John David. Paul Ricoeur's phenomenology of evil. Rice, 1965. 65-10357

6484. Stewart, Malcom Fisk. The limits of theology as determined by the empirical criterion of meaningfulness. Iowa, 1941.

6485. Stewart, Michael Alexander. Plato's investigations into language, with special reference to Cratylus. Pennsylvania, 1966. 66-4656

6486. Stewart, Robert Brown. The principle of indifference, paradoxes, and a priorism in theories of induction. Indiana, 1972. 73-12350

6487. Stich, Elizabeth Ann. A chronological analysis of Rawls' principles of justice. Minnesota, 1974. 75-12167

6488. Stich, Stephen P. Grammars, psychological theories and turing machines. Princeton, 1968. 69-10525

6489. Stine, Gail Caldwell. Quantification in knowledge and belief contexts. Harvard, 1969.

6490. Stine, Russell Warren. The doctrine of God in the philosophy of Fichte. Pennsylvania, 1943.

6491. Stine, William David. The a priori in John Dewey's theory of inquiry. Harvard, 1969.

6492. Stith, Richard Taylor, III. A theory of respect. Yale, 1973. 74-11923

6493. Stith, Robert Charles. A phenomenological interpretation of Wittgenstein. Duquesne, 1972.
72-29452

6494. Stiver, James LeRoy. Presupposition, implication, and necessitation: a critique of and alternative to Van Fraassen's presuppositional logic. No. Carolina, 1972. 73-4877

6495. Stock, Hyman. The methods of Descartes in the natural sciences. Columbia, 1931.

6496. Stocker, Michael Adam Gerber. Supererogation. Harvard, 1966.

6497. Stockwell, Bowman Foster. The philosophy of Miguel de Unamuno. Boston U., 1933.

6498. Stohrer, Rev. Walter John. The role of Martin Heidegger's doctrine of *Dasein* in Karl Rahner's metaphysics of man. Georgetown, 1968. 68-12812

6499. Stokes, Ella H. The conception of a kingdom of ends in Augustine, Aquinas and Leibniz. Chicago, 1910.

6500. Stokes, Marion Boyd, Jr. Clarity, vagueness and knowledge. Boston U., 1940.

6501. Stokes, Thomas John. William of Ockham's doctrine of science. Toronto, 1961.

6502. Stokes, Rev. Walter Elliott. The function of creativity in Whitehead's metaphysics. St. Louis, 1960. 61-779

6503. Stoll, Marion Rush. Whewell's philosophy of induction. Bryn Mawr, 1929.

6504. Stolnitz, Murray Jerome. The emotionalist philosophy of art. Harvard, 1949.

6505. Stone, Murray Paul. Perception and aesthetic enjoyment. Wisconsin, 1974. 74-19940

6506. Stone, Robert Vandiver. The self as agent-in-the-world: an alternative to Husserl's and Sartre's accounts of the ego. Texas, 1972. 74-5363

6507. Stone, Wendell Cornell. The principle of contradiction. Yale, 1931.

6508. Storck, John. Man and civilization. An inquiry into the bases of contemporary life. Columbia, 1929.

6509. Storer, Morris Brewster. The roots of moral obligation. Harvard, 1937.

6510. Storer, Thomas F. The epistemological significance of linguistic analysis. Iowa, 1947.

6511. Stormer, Gerald Douglass. The early Hegelianism of R.G. Collingwood. Tulane, 1971.   71-20231

6512. Storrs, Margaret. The relation of Carlyle to Kant and Fichte. Bryn Mawr, 1929.

6513. Stott, Gilmore. A theory of dual obligation. Princeton, 1951.   5170

6514. Stough, Charlotte Lucille. The Greek sceptics. Berkeley, 1966.   66-3704

6515. Stoutland, Frederick Maynard. The structure of historical knowledge. Yale, 1959.

6516. Stover, Robert Capner. An introduction to Wilhelm Dilthey's philosophy of experience. Columbia, 1953.   6719

6517. Strandberg, Josiah Robert Woodrow. Some metaphysical questions about parts and wholes. Brown, 1975.   76-15723

6518. Strasser, Michael William. Saint Thomas' critique of Platonism in the Liber de causis. Toronto, 1963.   63-8099

6519. Stratton, John Reginald. Analysis and individuals; an examination of the notions of a picture, objects and sense in Wittgenstein's Tractatus. Toronto, 1969.

6520. Stratton, Jon David. The Hegelian motif in Heidegger's thought on language. So. Illinois, 1972.   73-6248

6521. Stratton, Melville Juliand. The immanent and the transcendent in Husserl's Cartesian meditations. Buffalo, 1970.   71-7228

6522. Straumanis, Joan Cole. A pronominal analysis of proper names. Maryland, 1974.   75-17906

6523. Straus, Reed. The anarchist argument: an analysis of three justifications of anarchism. Columbia, 1973.   74-17907

6524. Street, Charles Larrabee. Individualism and individuality in the philosophy of John Stuart Mill. Columbia, 1926.

6525. Streveler, Paul Andrew. The problem of future contingents from Aristotle through the fifteenth century, with particular emphasis upon medieval views. Wisconsin, 1970.   70-24823

6526. Strickler, Nina. The problem of the absolute: a study in Spinoza, Hegel and Wittgenstein. DePaul, 1973.   73-28663

6527. Strike, Kenneth Arthur. An analysis of the concept of motivation in its role in the explanation of human behavior. Northwestern, 1968.   69-1953

6528. Stripling, Scott Randall. The picture theory of meaning: an interpretation of Wittgenstein's Tractatus logico-philosophicus. Penn St., 1975.   75-17229

6529. Stroh, Guy Weston. An analysis of Santayana's ontology and epistemology in the light of his distinction between essence and existence. Princeton, 1957.   58-7893

6530. Stroll, Avrum. The emotive theory of ethics. Berkeley, 1951.

6531. Stromberg, Rev. James. An essay on experimentum. Laval, 1966.

6532. Stromberg, Wayne Hodgson. Conceptual confusions in the Gestalt psychology of visual perception. Cal., S. Diego, 1975.   75-19639

6533. Strong, Anna L. Consideration of prayer from the standpoint of social psychology. Chicago, 1908.

6534. Strong, Edward W. Procedures and metaphysics; a study in the philosophy of mathematical-physical science in the sixteenth and seventeenth centuries. Columbia, 1937.

6535. Stroud, Barry Greenwood. Two conventionalistic theories of logical truth. Harvard, 1962.

6536. Struckmeyer, Frederick Raymond. The moral values in art. Boston U., 1967.   67-13265

6537. Strug, Cordell Thomas. William James and the Gods: a peek at the conceptual underbelly of the Varieties of religious experience. Purdue, 1973.   73-28147

6538. Stuart, Henry Waldgrave. Valuation as a logical process. Chicago, 1900.

6539. Stuart, James Donald. Kant's refutation of Berkeley's idealism. Cincinnati, 1970. 71-1547

6540. Stucky, Elizabeth J. Basic data and prima facie physical objects. Duke, 1955.

6541. Stulberg, Joseph Benjamin. Legal reasoning and utilitarianism. Rochester, 1975. 75-22781

6542. Stump, Eleonore Annerose. Boethius' De topicis differentis. Cornell, 1975. 76-9565

6543. Stunkel, Kenneth Reagan. Indian ideas and western thought during the romantic age: a critical study. Maryland, 1966. 67-2373

6544. Sturgeon, Nicholas Lee. Nonnaturalism, noncognitivism and reasons: a study in the ethical theory of Charles L. Stevenson. Princeton, 1972. 72-18791

6545. Sturm, Fred Gillette. Existence in search of essence: Farias Brito's philosophy of spirit. Columbia, 1961. 62-1930

6546. Sugiura, Sadajiro. Hindu logic in China and Japan. Pennsylvania, 1898.

6547. Suiter, Richard. Competence and generative semantics. Chicago, 1972.

6548. Suits, Bernard Herbert. The aesthetic object in Santayana and Dewey. Illinois, 1958. 58-1744

6549. Sukale, Michael Hermann. Four studies in phenomenology and pragmatism. Stanford, 1971. 72-6007

6550. Sulkow, Martin. An inquiry into certain proofs of the doctrine of personal immortality. New School, 1958.

6551. Sullivan, Arthur F. Religion in Santayana's philosophy of the spirit. Fordham, 1960.

6552. Sullivan, Celestine James. A theory of essence: chiefly that of George Santayana. Berkeley, 1931.

6553. Sullivan, Daniel Joseph. The function of rules in moral reasoning. McGill, 1973.

6554. Sullivan, Denis Francis. C.S. Peirce: on the foundations of human knowledge. Fordham, 1975. 75-18932

6555. Sullivan, Edward. The divine ideas according to
William of Ockham; study and text. Toronto, 1951.

6556. Sullivan, Rev. Emmanuel Francis. The analogy of instrumental causality in Thomistic metaphysics.
Catholic U., 1964. 65-5548

6557. Sullivan, Rev. Emmanuel J. Christian Wolff's concept of the possible. Catholic U., 1971.
71-25243

6558. Sullivan, Frank Russell, Jr. Faith and reason in
Kierkegaard. Boston U., 1973. 73-23519

6559. Sullivan, Rev. Henry Joseph. The new psychology.
Georgetown, 1956.

6560. Sullivan, Rev. James Bacon. First principles in
thought and being. Catholic U., 1939.

6561. Sullivan, Paul Robert. Ontic aspects of cognition
in poetry. Georgetown, 1961.

6562. Sullivan, Rev. Robert Jerome. The formation of Alfred Schutz's category of relevance: the fundamental category of the sociology of knowledge.
Boston Coll., 1975. 75-15746

6563. Sullivan, Roger Joseph. The primacy of practical
reason. Texas, 1973. 75-4492

6564. Sullivan, Thomas Dennis. The problem of universals
in the later Ludwig Wittgenstein. St. John's,
1969. 70-1356

6565. Sullivan, Wilbur Mark. The logic of the Peri ermē
neias , ascribed to Apuleius of Madaura. Stanford,
1964. 64-9851

6566. Sullivan, William Michael. The process social paradigm and the problem of social order. Fordham,
1971. 71-26997

6567. Summers, James A. St. Thomas and the universal.
Catholic U., 1956.

6568. Sumner, Leonard Wayne. Normative ethics and metaethics. Princeton, 1965. 66-5015

6569. Sun, George Chih-Hsin. Chinese metaphysics and
Whitehead. So. Illinois, 1971. 72-22491

6570. Sun, Siao-Fang. Semiotical analysis of the language
of science. Chicago, 1958.

6571. Sundaram, Krishnamoorthy. Phenomenological description and scientific theorizing. Buffalo, 1975.
75-18849

6572. Sunne, Dagny G. Some phases in the development of the subjective point of view during the post-Aristotelian period. Chicago, 1903.

6573. Suppe, Frederick Roy. The meaning and use of models in mathematics and the exact sciences: a study in the structure of exact scientific theories. Michigan, 1968. 68-7739

6574. Suppes, Patrick C. The problem of action at a distance. Columbia, 1950. 2135

6575. Supple, Joseph M. Dialectics in experimental biology. Laval, 1942.

6576. Surber, Jere Paul. Language, time, and system: an examination of Hegel's conception of language. Penn St., 1974. 74-28987

6577. Suri, Surindar Singh. The philosophy of mind of George Herbert Mead. Northwestern, 1953.
6247

6578. Susseles, Ida Schaeffer. Burke Aaron Hinsdale as educator. N.Y.U., 1939. 73-3446

6579. Sussman, Alan N. Ordinary language considered as an observation language for Freudian theory. Chicago, 1974.

6580. Suter, Ronald. Solipsism as a case study in philosophical methodology. Stanford, 1967. 67-11073

6581. Suter, Rufus Orlando, Jr. The philosophy of Jonathan Edwards. Harvard, 1932.

6582. Sutfin, Edward J. The philosophy of St. Anselm of Canterbury. Loyola, 1939.

6583. Sutton, Kenneth Ray. John Elof Boodin's creationism. New Mexico, 1969. 71-3940

6584. Sutton, Paul W., Jr. The role of fact in moral judgment. Johns Hopkins, 1955.

6585. Sutula, John August. Fatalism (arguments in support of the position that whatever occurs must occur.) Ohio St., 1974. 75-11433

6586. Swabey, William Curtis. The philosophy of Malebranche. Cornell, 1919.

6587. Swain, Marshall William. The logic of epistemic rationality. Rochester, 1967. 67-8979

6588. Swan, Peter J. The equality of man in the philosophy of St. Thomas Aquinas. Toronto, 1946.

6589. Swann, George Rogers. Philosophical parallelisms in six English novelists. Pennsylvania, 1929.

6590. Swanson, Joe William. Some aspects of the doctrine of emergence. Harvard, 1959.

6591. Swartz, Norman Manuel. Contingent identity. Indiana, 1971. 72-6838

6592. Swartz, Robert Jason. Perception, sense-experience, and ordinary language. Harvard, 1963.

6593. Sweeney, Charles Leo. Divine infinity in the writings of Saint Thomas Aquinas. Toronto, 1954.

6594. Sweeney, Robert Daniel. A study of Max Scheler's philosophy of value. Fordham, 1962. 62-3777

6595. Sweet, Albert Milton. A semantic explication of metaphysical analogy. Emory, 1961. 62-39

6596. Sweet, Mary Dolores Hammitt. Unity, determinism, and the universe. Missouri, 1969. 69-16106

6597. Sweigart, John Winfield, Jr. The epistemological status of ethical statements for David Hume and C.I. Lewis. Pennsylvania, 1959. 59-4664

6598. Swenson, Esther Cornelius. Toward philosophical dialogue as philosophy of culture. Northwestern, 1960. 60-6582

6599. Swenson, Meredith Jane. Privacy and necessity: an essay on some central themes in contemporary philosophy of mind. N.Y.U., 1974. 74-30051

6600. Swertfeger, Floyd F. The Système de philosophie of Pierre Sylvain Règis; a study in the history of Cartesianism. Virginia, 1928.

6601. Swift, Morrison Isaac. The ethics of idealism, as represented by Aristotle and Hegel. Johns Hopkins, 1885.

6602. Swing, Thomas Kaehao. Kant's transcendental logic. Yale, 1965. 66-1111

6603. Swiniarski, John. Theories of supposition in medieval logic: their origin and their development

from Abelard to Ockham. Buffalo, 1970.
71-7229

6604. Switalski, Bruno. William of Auvergne, De trinitate (Chs. I-XIII); text and study. Toronto, 1966.

6605. Switzer, Sr. Harriet Kern. The role of receptivity in the philosophy of action of Maurice Blondel. Fordham, 1968. 69-2617

6606. Syfers, James Winans. The ontology and epistemology of the Critique of pure reason. Iowa, 1963.
64-7948

6607. Sykes, Richard Dodgson. The doctrine of substance in the logical works of Aristotle. Princeton, 1960. 60-5060

6608. Sylvester, Robert Peter. An examination of the ethical philosophy of G.E. Moore. Northwestern, 1963. 64-2532

6609. Synan, Edward Aloysius. The Logica attributed to Richard of Campsall; study and texts. Toronto, 1952.

6610. Sytkowski, Pamela Riesen. Physis, nomos, and eleutheria: the concept of nature and the development of Greek political theory. Marquette, 1975.
76-8653

6611. Szabados, Bela. Self-deception and its paradoxes. Calgary, 1972.

6612. Szathmary, Arthur. Relativistic criteria in aesthetics. Harvard, 1943.

- T -

6613. Taeusch, Carl Frederick. An analysis of the categorical judgment. Harvard, 1920.

6614. Taft, Julia J. Woman movement from the point of view of social consciousness. Chicago, 1913.

6615. Tait, Foster Eliott. The problem of data in fact and value contexts. Pennsylvania, 1965. 66-4657

6616. Tait, William Walker. The theory of partial recursive operators. Yale, 1959.

6617. Takahashi, Takeicki. The symptomatic function and value of synthetic moral judgment. Chicago, 1927.

6618. Takei, Franklin Shunji. Existence and the New Being: a study of Paul Tillich's theological system. Penn St., 1966. 66-10479

6619. Talbert, Earnest L. Dualism of fact and idea in its social implication. Chicago, 1909.

6620. Talbot, E.B. The nature of Fichte's fundamental principles with special reference to its relation to the individual consciousness. Cornell, 1898.

6621. Talbot, Rev. Edward Francis. Knowledge and object. Catholic U., 1932.

6622. Talbott, Thomas Bradley. Fatalism and the timelessness of truth. Cal., S. Barbara, 1974. 75-21638

6623. Talbutt, Palmer Cummins, Jr. The emotive interpretation of metaphysics. Duke, 1961. 62-2008

6624. Taliaferro, Robert C. The Aristotelean theory of movement with a translation from the Greek of the treatises on place and on the vacuum of John Philoponus of Alexandria. Virginia, 1936.

6625. Tallarico, James Joseph. The nature and role of the philosophical presupposition of the law of inertia from Aristotle to Newton. Toronto, 1970.

6626. Tallmadge, Guy Kasten. Philosophical implications of American humanism. Wisconsin, 1936.

6627. Tallon, Hugh Joseph. The concept of self in British and American idealism. Catholic U., 1939.

6628. Talmage, Ronald Roy. Cognitive models in Leibniz' metaphysics and philosophy of science. St. Louis, 1974. 75-26331

6629. Tam, Ping Kwan. Are there rules of acceptance in inductive logic? An evaluation of Carnap's arguments against rules of acceptance. Pittsburgh, 1971. 71-24360

6630. Tamme, Sr. Anne Mary. A critique of John Dewey's theory of fine art in the light of the principles of Thomism. Catholic U., 1956.

6631. Tamthai, Mark Gustaaf. Analytic components of empirical theories: an application of formal methods in philosophy of science. Indiana, 1975. 76-2898

6632. Tanenzapf, Sol. Emotivism and its critics: an analytic study of an ethical theory. Yale, 1967. 68-5859

6633. Tang, Yueh. Affective factors in perception. Harvard, 1920.

6634. Tanner, Amy E. Association of idea. Chicago, 1898.

6635. Tapke, Peter Frank. Moral motivation in recent ethical theories. Harvard, 1960.

6636. Tapper, Bonno. The objective validity of values. Iowa, 1928.

6637. Tapscott, Bangs Leslie. Proper names: how they are and what they mean. U. of Washington, 1968.
69-1221

6638. Tartaglia, Philip Orazio. Some difficulties in the construction of a theory of natural language. N.Y.U., 1966. 67-640

6639. Tassi, Aldo Giacomo. The political philosophy of the American Revolution: 1763-1776. Fordham, 1970.
71-8742

6640. Taube, Mortimer. Causation, freedom and determinism: an attempt to solve the causal problem through a study of its origins in seventeenth century philosophy. Berkeley, 1935.

6641. Taurek, John Michael. Determinism and moral responsibility. U.C.L.A., 1972. 73-10486

6642. Taylor, Charles Senn. The friendship of art and science: an inquiry into Nietzsche's writings before Zarathustra. Boston Coll., 1974. 74-19227

6643. Taylor, Craig Elliot. An essay on the possibility of inference. Illinois, 1974. 75-447

6644. Taylor, Darrell DeWayne. Husserl and Merleau-Ponty and the problem of the cultural studies. Southern Cal., 1966. 66-7083

6645. Taylor, Frank Simmons. The right and the good in the ethics of Henry Sidgwick. Boston U., 1969.
69-18416

6646. Taylor, Harry M. Coleridge's statement and defense of the evangelical faith as ultimate metaphysics. Drew, 1938.

6647. Taylor, James Carson. Perception and empirical knowledge. U.C.L.A., 1942.

6648. Taylor, John Francis Adams. Perception and nature: a monograph on Whitehead. Princeton, 1940.
3052

6649. Taylor, Joseph. The Aristotelian concept of natural philosophy. Laval, 1948.

6650. Taylor, Paul Warren. The verification of value judgments in naturalistic theories of ethics. Princeton, 1951.   5171

6651. Taylor, Richard C. The analysis of judgment situations. Brown, 1951.

6652. Taylor, Stephen Eugene. Free will and determinism: a defense of libertarianism. Ohio St., 1971.
                                                72-15309

6653. Taylor, Wallace Bruce, II. The meaning of time in physics and daily life. U.C.L.A., 1953.

6654. Taylor, William Edington. The ethical and religious theories of Bishop Butler. Toronto, 1903.

6655. Taylor, William James. Aristotle's psychology of cognition. Yale, 1901.

6656. Tebaldi, David Anthony. Thomas Reid's refutation of the "Way of ideas." Rutgers, 1974.   74-27662

6657. Teeter, Lura S. Some aspects of aesthetic judgment. Radcliffe, 1950.

6658. Teghrarian, Souren. Meaning and convention. Buffalo, 1970.   71-15050

6659. TeHennepe, Eugene Kenneth. Ordinary language philosophy: historical perspectives. Northwestern, 1969.   70-171

6660. Teitelman, Michael Louis. Mill's theory of liberty. Princeton, 1972.   72-18793

6661. Tejera, Victorino. Philosophy and the art of poetry: a survey of some contemporary relations among poetic criticism, philosophy and poetry. Columbia, 1956.   16911

6662. Teller, Paul Richard. Problems in confirmation theory. M.I.T., 1970.

6663. Telles, Lawrence. Some problems in the concept of a theory of education. C.U.N.Y., 1973. 73-22747

6664. Teloh, Henry Andrew. The ontology of Plato's *Hippias major*. Wisconsin, 1972.   72-23078

6665. Temin, Marc K. Sentential state theories and their state languages. Princeton, 1973.   73-18785

6666. Temko, Philip Oppleman. Rules of language. Stanford, 1968. 69-8280

6667. Tempelmeier, Ernest Stefan. The raven paradoxes and epistemological problems of confirmation theory. Temple, 1972. 72-22152

6668. TenBroeke, James. A comparison of the views of Hartmann and Lotze concerning the self-consciousness of the absolute. Yale, 1891.

6669. Teng, Chin-Kao. The philosophy of life of the ancient Taoists. Chicago, 1928.

6670. Ten Hoor, Marten. A critical estimate of the philosophy of George Santayana. Michigan, 1921.

6671. Tenzis, Louis. Ralph Waldo Emerson's approach to God. Loyola, 1970.

6672. Teo, Wesley Kheng-Hua. Heidegger on *Dasein* and Whitehead on actual entities. So. Illinois, 1969.
70-447

6673. Terrell, Dailey Burnham. Ethics, language and ontology: a study of the implications of Franz Brentano's *Sprachkritik* for ethical theory. Michigan, 1956. 56-3964

6674. Terrell, Huntington. The concept of a moral judgment. Harvard, 1956.

6675. Terrenal, Quentin C. *Causa sui* and the object of intuition in Spinoza. Catholic U., 1975.
75-13039

6676. Terris, Martin Frederick. Authority and rights in the university. Georgia, 1974. 75-2661

6677. Teschner, George Albert. The relation of man to transcendence in the philosophy of Kierkegaard. New School, 1975. 76-5997

6678. Teske, Rev. Roland John. The identity of things and of selves in the metaphysics of F.H. Bradley. Toronto, 1973.

6679. Tétreau, Richard David. The agent intellect in Meister Dietrich of Freiberg; study and text. Toronto, 1966.

6680. Thackray, Edgar. A comparative study of sense perception in Greek philosophy. Harvard, 1907.

6681. Thalberg, Irving Grant, Jr. Believing in a moral principle. Stanford, 1960.   60-2414

6682. Thalberg, Suzanne McCormick. Lying. Stanford, 1963.   63-6447

6683. Thalheimer, Alvin. The meaning of the terms: "existence" and "reality." Johns Hopkins, 1918.

6684. Thalheimer, Ross. A critical examination of the epistemological and psychophysical doctrines of Bertrand Russell. Johns Hopkins, 1929.

6685. That, Le Manh. The philosophy of Vasubandhu. Wisconsin, 1974.   74-18961

6686. Thau, Stewart. Linguistic acts and the concept of meaning. Michigan, 1969.   69-18120

6687. Thayer, H.S. The logic of pragmatism. Columbia, 1952.

6688. Thayer, Vivian Trow. A critique of the ethical philosophy of Benedict de Spinoza. Wisconsin, 1922.

6689. Thedick, Mary C. The inductive method of Francis Bacon. Radcliffe, 1947.

6690. Thibadeau, Eugene Francis. An interpretation of Wittgenstein's later (1929-1951) philosophy of mathematics. N.Y.U., 1973.   73-19451

6691. Thibault, Herve J. Creation and metaphysics: a genetic approach to existential act. Marquette, 1967.   68-498

6692. Thie, Sr. Marilyn Clare. Whitehead on a rational explanation of religious experience. Georgetown, 1974.   75-59

6693. Thielemann, Leland James. The tradition of Hobbes in eighteenth-century France. Columbia, 1950.   2489

6694. Thobe, Urban Albert. The independence of Aristotle's doctrine of the principles of absolute being from his theory of elements. Notre Dame, 1967.   67-13605

6695. Thomas, Carla Ruth. The philosophical anthropology of Wilhelm von Humboldt. Buffalo, 1970.   71-6123

6696. Thomas, Deborah Rose. The individuation of minds. Brown, 1973.   74-3082

6697. Thomas, George Bryson, Jr. Knowing how: a study of the concept of a human ability. Harvard, 1963.

6698. Thomas, George Finger. The nature and metaphysics of value in recent philosophy. Harvard, 1929.

6699. Thomas, James Alwin. Truth, translation, and ontological commitment. Washington U., 1973.
73-24912

6700. Thomas, James Andrew. The philosophical anarchism of William Godwin: his philosophy of man, state and society. Southern Cal., 1964. 64-13511

6701. Thomas, James Doyle. The self between east and west: concepts of self in Mead, Jung and Mahayana Buddhism. Claremont, 1974. 74-14893

6702. Thomas, James Ellison. The problem of religious discourse: linguistic analysis and the phenomenology of language. Claremont, 1972. 72-30549

6703. Thomas, John Edward. Analogy and the meaningfulness of religious utterances. Duke, 1964. 64-11691

6704. Thomas, John Joseph. God and logic in the ontological argument. Miami, 1973. 74-282

6705. Thomas, Mary Edith. Medieval skepticism and Chaucer; an evaluation of the skepticism of the 13th and 14th centuries of Geoffrey Chaucer and his immediate predecessors. Columbia, 1950.

6706. Thomas, Norman L. Existential pragmatism, a treatise in ethics. Claremont, 1970. 70-11919

6707. Thomas, Sid Barm, Jr. Acquaintance and complex objects in Bertrand Russell's early work. Wisconsin, 1961. 61-3175

6708. Thomas, Stephen Naylor. Philosophical model-building and the philosophy of mind. M.I.T., 1968.

6709. Thomas, William John. Church's thesis and philosophy. Case, 1972. 72-18744

6710. Thomasma, David Charles. A critical exploration of pre-conceptual knowledge. Catholic U., 1972.
72-21805

6711. Thomason, Sr. Adelaide. An explanation and application of the law of contrast in Charles Hartshorne's panentheism. Fordham, 1969. 69-16241

6712. Thomason, Jacqueline M. Observation, indeterminacy, and ontological relativity: an examination of the philosophy of W.V. Quine. Massachusetts, 1973.
74-8640

6713. Thomason, Richmond Hunt. Studies in the formal logic of quantification. Yale, 1965. 66-1113

6714. Thompson, Clifford Griffith. The ethics of William Wollaston. Yale, 1919.

6715. Thompson, Constance Marion. Aristotle's doctrine of dynamis and energeia with special reference to some aspects of evolution. Toronto, 1931.

6716. Thompson, Frank Wilson. Indeterminacy and relativity in language theory. Harvard, 1973. 74-20155

6717. Thompson, George L. Weaver. Intellectualizing: philosophic inquiry in the group process. Cincinnati, 1968. 69-6363

6718. Thompson, Golden O. The philosophical problem of the definition of matter in twentieth-century thought. Boston U., 1951.

6719. Thompson, Helen B. Psychological norms in men and women. Chicago, 1900.

6720. Thompson, Josiah Donald, Jr. The lonely labyrinth: a study in the pseudonymous works of Søren Kierkegaard, 1843-1846. Yale, 1964.

6721. Thompson, Manley Hawn, Jr. The pragmatic philosophy of C.S. Peirce. Chicago, 1942.

6722. Thompson, Raymond Duane. Maritain and Tillich: art and religion. Boston U., 1962. 62-4552

6723. Thompson, Richard James. The ethics of Abelard. Toronto, 1940.

6724. Thompson, Samuel Martin. A study of Locke's theory of ideas. Princeton, 1931.

6725. Thompson, Thomas Henry. Criticism and esthetics. Iowa, 1952. 4111

6726. Thompson, Tyler. Lotze's conception of the self. Boston U., 1950.

6727. Thompson, William Burton. Faith and reason in the theology of Henry Nelson Wieman. Michigan, 1971.
71-23892

6728. Thompson, William J. A sociological study of a denominational group of church officers. N.Y.U., 1910. 74-1299

6729. Thoms, Bert. Predications of value. Johns Hopkins, 1950.

6730. Thornton, Robert Ambrose. Measurement, concept formation and principles of simplicity: a study in the logic and methodology of physics. Minnesota, 1946.

6731. Thrane, Gary Alan. Seeing: a modern assessment of Berkeley's theory of vision. Chicago, 1973.

6732. Thro, Linus John. The critique of St. Thomas in the Reportata parisiensia and the orientation of the Scotistic metaphysics. Toronto, 1948.

6733. Tibbetts, Eleanor Elizabeth. Free will in consciousness. Pennsylvania, 1894.

6734. Tibbetts, Paul Edison, Jr. Preception, action, and reality in the writings of George Herbert Mead. Purdue, 1973. 74-5058

6735. Tice, John Keyser. Everett Hall's aesthetic theory. No. Carolina, 1967. 68-6773

6736. Tice, Terence Nelson. Ideology old and new: historical-analytical background for use of the concept "ideology" in scholarly discourse, with systematic bibliography. Michigan, 1970. 70-21803

6737. Tiebout, Harry M., Jr. Philosophy and psychoanalysis: theories of human nature and conduct in Freud's psychology. Columbia, 1951. 3387

6738. Tiedeman, Kent Hallett. Personal knowledge: the epistemology of Michael Polanyi. Cincinnati, 1971. 72-1448

6739. Tienson, John Leander. Quantified epistemic logic. Illinois, 1969. 70-13518

6740. Tietz, John Herman. J.L. Austin's "ifs and cans" and the incompatibility of free will and determinism. Claremont, 1966. 67-9530

6741. Tigner, Steven Samuel. The nature of Plato's theory of anamnesis. Michigan, 1968. 69-12256

6742. Tilden, Nancy Lee. An analysis of metaphor. Berkeley, 1952.

6743. Tilghman, Benjamin Ross. The aesthetic object and its relation to aesthetic experience. U. of Washington, 1960. 59-5477

6744. Tilley, Ethel. The problem of identity in Henri Bergson's philosophy. Boston U., 1936.

6745. Tillman, Frank A. Truth and meaning: some concepts at issue in contemporary Anglo-American analytic philosophy. Columbia, 1958. 59-1504

6746. Tillman, Mary Katherine. Wilhelm Dilthey's descriptive psychology. New School, 1974. 75-867

6747. Tillman, Rev. Stanley Carl. The principle of contiguity: its meaning and value as applied by Saint Thomas to the powers of man. St. Louis, 1954.

6748. Titchener, John McLellan. The concept of the sense-datum in the perceptual essays of G.E. Moore. Ohio St., 1967. 67-2551

6749. Titiev, Robert Jay. Some model-theoretic results in measurement theory. Stanford, 1969. 70-1620

6750. Titus, Mark Edmond. Aesthetic orders: a theory of the arts. Emory, 1971. 72-3044

6751. Tivnan, Edward F.X. The moral psychology of Plato's Republic. Princeton, 1974. 75-23244

6752. Tlumak, Jeffrey Stewart. Skepticism and transcendental arguments. Massachusetts, 1975. 76-5402

6753. To, Thi Anh. Eastern and western cultural values: conflict or harmony? U.S. Int'l, 1972.
72-23507

6754. Tobin, Richard James. Judging the avant-garde: originality and value in the arts. Wisconsin, 1975.
75-19097

6755. Todd, Donald David. Austin and sense-data. British Columbia, 1967.

6756. Todd, Quintin Robert. James, Whitehead, and radical empiricism. Penn St., 1969. 70-7249

6757. Todd, William Lewis, Jr. An image theory of meaning. Michigan, 1959. 60-1799

6758. Todes, Samuel Judah. The human body as the material subject of the world. Harvard, 1963.

6759. Todrank, Gustave Herman. The empirical evidence for Brightman's theistic cosmology. Boston U., 1956.
56-1987

6760. Toland, William Gipsy. The later Wittgenstein and classical pragmatism: a critical appraisal. No. Carolina, 1967.
68-6774

6761. Tollefsen, Olaf Philip. Verification procedures in dialectical metaphysics. Georgetown, 1970.
70-23811

6762. Tollen, William. The concept of equality in modern political theory. A study in the philosophy of the state. Pennsylvania, 1934.

6763. Tolley, William Pearson. The idea of God in the philosophy of St. Augustine. Columbia, 1930.

6764. Tolmachoff, Innokently, Jr. Plekhanov's understanding of Marxism. Virginia, 1972.
72-33388

6765. Tomas, Vincent Anthony. The criticism of literature. Brown, 1941.

6766. Tomasic, Thomas Michael. William of Saint-Thierry: toward a philosophy of intersubjectivity. Fordham, 1972.
73-1495

6767. Tomberlin, James Edward. God and other minds: an examination of Alvin Plantinga's philosophy of religion. Wayne St., 1972.
73-12609

6768. Tomeh, George J. Reason and revelation in Islam with particular reference to al-Ghazzali and Averroes. Georgetown, 1951.

6769. Tominaga, Thomas Toyoshi. A Wittgensteinian inquiry into the confusions generated by the question "What is the meaning of a word?" Georgetown, 1973.
74-1444

6770. Tomkins, Silvan S. Conscience, self-love and benevolence in the system of Bishop Butler. Pennsylvania, 1934.

6771. Tompkins, David Beveridge. The individual and society; a comparison between the views of the Enlightenment and those of the nineteenth-century. N.Y.U., 1914.
73-20896

6772. Tompkins, Robert Richard. An analysis of inference necessary for a complete classical elementary number theory. Penn St., 1965.
66-4866

6773. Toner, Jules Joseph. The notion of spiritual nature according to St. Thomas Aquinas. Toronto, 1952.

6774. Toness, Alfred. Aspects of the problem of the past. Chicago, 1931.

6775. Tong, Lik Kuen. Context and reality: a critical interpretation of Whitehead's philosophy of organism. New School, 1968. 7C-7662

6776. Tong, Rev. Paul K.K. The formal logic of St. Albert the Great. Catholic U., 1963. 64-1072

6777. Toolan, Rev. David S. The problem of evil and the mystic's way to God: a study of William Ernest Hocking. S.M.U., 1974. 75-15187

6778. Tooley, Michael James. A defense of the cognitive significance of experimentally transcendent theological statements. Princeton, 1968. 69-10526

6779. Tooley, Rodelia Josephine Hapke. Willard Van Orman Quine: translational indeterminacy. Stanford, 1974. 74-27033

6780. Toon, Mark. The philosophy of sex according to St. Thomas Aquinas. Catholic U., 1954.

6781. Topazio, Virgil W. The background and development of D'Holbach's moral philosophy. Columbia, 1951.
3339

6782. Torgerson, Jon Norman. On tensed and tenseless discourse. Nebraska, 1971. 72-16020

6783. Tormey, Alan Joseph. The concept of expression: a study in philosophical psychology. Columbia, 1968. 71-17625

6784. Tormey, Judith Farr. Relevance in ethics. Columbia, 1970. 71-6269

6785. Tornay, Stephen Chak. William Ockham's philosophy. Chicago, 1934.

6786. Torrell, Eugene. La connaissance prophétique dans le manuscrit de Douai 434. Édition critique, étude littéraire des textes et commentaire de la O.481. Montreal, 1973.

6787. Torres, José A. Philosophic reconstruction and social reform in John Dewey and José Ortega y Gasset. Chicago, 1954.

6788. Tougas, Sr. Miryam. The relation of existence to the subject of metaphysics in the philosophy of St. Thomas. Catholic U., 1961. 62-993

6789. Toussaint, Bernard John. The interpretation of the "self" in the early Heidegger. DePaul, 1971. 72-19700

6790. Tovey, Barbara Schinnerer. Locke's theory of identity. Massachusetts, 1975. 75-16609

6791. Tovey, George Vernon. Francis Bacon, the reformer of learning. Columbia, 1950. 1755

6792. Tovey, Peter. The axiom of complementation. M.I.T., 1974.

6793. Tovo, Jerome Charles. The experience of causal efficacy in Whitehead and Hume. Indiana, 1964. 64-12095

6794. Tower, C.V. The relation of Berkeley's later to his earlier idealism. Cornell, 1898.

6795. Townsend, Dabney Winston, Jr. Religion and history: a phenomenological investigation of the common basis of literature and theology. Emory, 1970. 71-9016

6796. Townsend, Harvey Gates. The principle of individuality in the philosophy of Thomas Hill Green. Cornell, 1913.

6797. Tracy, George Edward. On the nature of symbol: as set out in the theology of Karl Rahner, S.J. Boston Coll., 1974. 74-18262

6798. Trageser, Gertrude A. Criticism of John Dewey's Quest for certainty. Fordham, 1934.

6799. Tragesser, Robert S. A phenomenological analysis of elementary mathematical evidences. Rice, 1968. 68-15668

6800. Trainor, Jennie Mary Rosaleen. Thomas Jefferson on freedom of conscience. St. John's, 1966. 66-10563

6801. Tramel, Stephen Gerard. The significance of libertarianism: an essay on freedom and causation. Nebraska, 1970. 71-3662

6802. Trant, Edward Joseph. The critical realism of G.E. Moore. Fordham, 1961. 62-1044

6803. Trap, William Martin. Divine personality, a study in the philosophy of religion. Michigan, 1925.

6804. Trask, Ida M. The development of William James's philosophy. Southern Cal., 1936.

6805. Traub, Donald Francis. Gabriel Marcel's 'concrete approaches' to society. Boston Coll., 1973.
73-21726

6806. Traub, Esen Ortac. The socio-political dimension of Merleau-Ponty's phenomenology. Bryn Mawr, 1973.
74-8961

6807. Travers, David Morris William. On Brentano's Psychology from an empirical standpoint. Ohio St., 1972. 72-21023

6808. Travis, Charles Stephen. Innate ideas. U.C.L.A., 1967. 68-3286

6809. Travis, Janet Louise. A critical examination of the uses of evolutionary theory in philosophical arguments. Boston U., 1970. 70-23142

6810. Travis, Larry Evan. A logical analysis of the concept of stored program: a step toward a possible theory of rational learning. U.C.L.A., 1966.
66-11964

6811. Treacy, Charles Jeremiah. Plato's doctrine of evil. Toronto, 1941.

6812. Treash, Gordon Spencer. Actuality and social order: Whitehead's theory of societies. Emory, 1968.
69-5243

6813. Trebilcot, Joyce. First problems in emotions. Cal., S. Barbara, 1970.

6814. Tredwell, Robert Fertig. The concept of judgment in the Critique of pure reason. Yale, 1960.

6815. Trenholme, Russell Shannon. An analysis of causation. Princeton, 1974. 75-20670

6816. Trentman, John Allen. Simple supposition and ontology: a study in the fourteenth-century logical theory. Minnesota, 1964. 65-162

6817. Trevas, Robert Joel. The ethical theory of Hastings Rashdall. Maryland, 1971. 71-23985

6818. Triplett, Janet Clari-Marvel. John Dewey: a critical analysis of the interdependence of knowledge and action. New Mexico, 1972. 72-30740

6819. Trivers, Howard. Time and history, with special reference to Hegel's Vernunft in der geschichte. Harvard, 1941.

6820. Trivus, Sidney. Space, time and measure: a study in the philosophy of David Hume. U.C.L.A., 1974.
                75-2011

6821. Trott, Elizabeth Anne. Experience and the absolute. Waterloo, 1971.

6822. Troxell, Eugene E. A critical analysis of C.I. Lewis' views on logical necessity. Chicago, 1966.

6823. Troyer, John Gordon. Color: a philosophical study. Harvard, 1971.

6824. True, Rev. Isaac David Ray. Whitehead on truth. St. Louis, 1972.   72-24027

6825. Trueblood, David Elton. The differentiae of man: an historical and analytical study of theories concerning the uniqueness of man in nature. Johns Hopkins, 1934.

6826. Truitt, Willis Harrison. Social theory and the foundations of aesthetic culture: a critique of and contribution to the Marxian theory of art. Boston U., 1969.   69-18414

6827. Ts'ai, Yung-ch'un. The philosophy of Ch'eng I: a selection of texts from the complete works edited and translated with introduction and notes. Columbia, 1950.   1756

6828. Tsanoff, R.A. Schopenhauer's criticism of Kant's theory of experience. Cornell, 1910.

6829. Tseu, Rev. Augustine T. The ethical doctrine of Mo-Tze. Loyola, 1948.

6830. Tsugawa, Albert Genyo. The moral philosophy of Lord Kames. Michigan, 1958.   58-3740

6831. Tubbs, Walter Elmer, Jr. Towards a structural concept of intention: a philosophical and neuro-psychological inquiry. Drew, 1969.   70-1092

6832. Tucker, Robert Charles. The self and revolution: a moral critique of Marx. Harvard, 1958.

6833. Tulloss, Rodham Elliott. Some complexities of simplicity: concerning the grades of simplicity of recursively enumerable sets. Berkeley, 1971.

6834. Tumulty, Peter John, Jr. A study in the ethics of
William James. Notre Dame, 1974.   75-1861

6835. Tung, Gea. Metaphor and analogy in the I ching.
Claremont, 1975.   76-15791

6836. Tuomela, Raimo Heikki. Auxiliary concepts within
first-order scientific theories. Stanford, 1969.
70-10538

6837. Turbayne, Colin M. Constructions versus inferences
in the philosophy of Bertrand Russell. Pennsylvania, 1950.

6838. Turley, Peter Thomas. Peirce on the laws of nature.
Fordham, 1967.   67-11504

6839. Turley, Robert S. Determinism in Freudian psychoanalytic theory. Notre Dame, 1964.   65-4708

6840. Turnbull, Robert George. An examination of C.D.
Broad's moral philosophy. Minnesota, 1952.
4888

6841. Turner, Charles Carlton. The meaning of God in the
philosophy of William James. Drew, 1972.
72-28874

6842. Turner, Ingrid Jacqueline. Maurice Merleau-Ponty:
the philosophy of language. Columbia, 1974.
75-7542

6843. Turner, Joseph. The methodology of James Clerk Maxwell. Columbia, 1953.   6725

6844. Turner, Karon Jack. Mind as a principle of order in
the philosophy of C.S. Peirce. Missouri, 1972.
73-21494

6845. Turner, Walter Henry. The concept of casus in the
philosophy of St. Thomas Aquinas. Toronto, 1941.

6846. Turner, William Stephen, III. A logical and epistemological critique of contemporary nominalism with
regard to the problem of universals. Emory, 1960.
61-1458

6847. Turquette, Atwell Rufus. A study and extension of
M-valued symbolic logics. Cornell, 1943.

6848. Tursman, Richard Allen. Nietzsche's view of science
and art. Illinois, 1965.   65-3684

6849. Tweedale, Martin Middleton. John of Rodynton on knowledge, science and theology. U.C.L.A., 1965.
65-12698

6850. Tweedie, Donald F., Jr. The significance of dread in the thought of Kierkegaard and Heidegger. Boston U., 1954.

6851. Tweyman, Stanley. Reason and conduct in the philosophy of David Hume and in the philosophies of his predecessors. Toronto, 1972.

6852. Twohill, Sr. M. Dominic. The background and St. Thomas Aquinas' reading of the De divinis nominibus of the pseudo-Dionysius. Fordham, 1960.

6853. Twomey, Rev. John E. The general notion of the transcendentals in the metaphysics of St. Thomas Aquinas. Catholic U., 1958.

6854. Tybor, Arthur Francis. The doctrine of soul in John of Jandun's Quaestiones de anima. Toronto, 1967.

6855. Tye, Michael John. A critical examination of two contemporary linguistic metaphilosophies. Buffalo, 1975. 76-9128

6856. Tymoczko, Andrew Thomas. Indeterminacy of translation: variations on a theme. Harvard, 1972.

6857. Tyrrell, Rev. Bernard James. Bernard Lonergan's philosophy of God. Fordham, 1972. 72-20585

6858. Tyrrell, Rev. Francis M. The role of assent in judgment: a Thomistic study. Catholic U., 1948.

6859. Tzu, Lien Chao. The problem of subjectivity and objectivity in moral judgment as treated in pragmatism. Chicago, 1929.

- U -

6860. Uchenko, Andrew Paul. The logic of events. Berkeley, 1928.

6861. Uchii, Soshichi. The confirmation of causal laws. Michigan, 1971. 72-5000

6862. Udell, Sr. Mary Gonzaga. A theory of criticism of fiction in its moral aspects. Catholic U., 1941.

6863. Uehling, Theodore Edward, Jr. The notion of form in Kant's Critique of aesthetic judgment. Ohio St., 1965. 65-13286

6864. Uemura, Joseph Norio. A critique of the case for small community. Columbia, 1958. 59-1506

6865. Uffelmann, Hans Werner. Towards an ontology of social relations. Northwestern, 1967.   67-15353

6866. Uhl, Lenom Leander. Attention: a historical summary of the discussions concerning the subject. Johns Hopkins, 1889.

6867. Uhler, Kathleen Louise. A clarification of Edmund Husserl's distinction between phenomenological psychology and transcendental phenomenology. Georgetown, 1975.   76-16328

6868. Ullian, Joseph Silbert. Explorations in recursive function theory. Harvard, 1957.

6869. Ulm, Melvin Stephenson. Indeterminacy of translation and theories of truth. Ohio St., 1975.
    76-3582

6870. Ulrich, Dolph Edward. Matrices for sentential calculi. Wayne St., 1968.   71-2997

6871. Ulrich, Lawrence Paul. The concept of man in Teilhard de Chardin. Toronto, 1972.

6872. Ulrich, William R. Reference and propositional identity. Cornell, 1974.   74-26329

6873. Umana, John. On the logic of ethical egoism. Michigan, 1975.   75-20466

6874. Umphrey, Stewart Price. Plato's Laches. New School, 1973.   74-163

6875. Unangst, Margaret R. Notes and commentary on Giordano Bruno's Ash Wednesday supper. Pennsylvania, 1936.

6876. Underhill, Lee. The problem of evil in the philosophy of Alfred North Whitehead. Drew, 1957.

6877. Underhill, Robert Lindley Murray. The logic of the moral concepts. Harvard, 1916.

6878. Underwood, Byron Edward. Kierkegaard's category of the concrete individual. Harvard, 1966.

6879. Unhjem, Arne. Justification in the development of Tillich's philosophy. Boston U., 1964.
    64-11595

6880. Unsoeld, William Francis. Mysticism, morality, and freedom: the role of the vital impetus in Bergson's theory of ethics. U. of Washington, 1959.
    59-3350

6881. Uritus, Ronald Michael. Cognition and action in Bergson's ethics. St. Louis, 1972. 74-4587

6882. Urquhart, Alasdair Ian Fenton. The semantics of entailment. Pittsburgh, 1973. 73-27174

6883. Utzinger, John Grantham. The phenomenological appeal to moral experience: a study of Mandelbaum's moral philosophy. U. of Washington, 1959.
60-876

- V -

6884. Vaccaro, Vincent Thomas. Agent causality in the understanding of human action. Virginia, 1973.
73-24978

6885. Vachon, Louis Albert. Les preuves naturelles de l'existence des substances séparées. Laval, 1948.

6886. Vader, Michael G. Schelling's metaphysics of indifference. Yale, 1971. 71-31024

6887. Vail, Loy Maugh. Heidegger and the ontological difference. Yale, 1964.

6888. Valberg, Eugene. Rationality and self-deception. Buffalo, 1973. 73-29146

6889. Valberg, Jerome Jacob. Agency: some metaphysical problems concerning the concept of action. Chicago, 1966.

6890. Valentine, Eugene John. Two concepts of human acting in history in the writings of Karl Marx. Michigan St., 1975. 76-5661

6891. Valentine, John Marshall. Operative intentionality, motility, and the act of speaking: a critique of the behaviorist/transcendentalist model of perceptive behavior. Vanderbilt, 1974. 75-12788

6892. Valenzuela, Raymond A. The emerging concern for transcendent values in Spanish American philosophy. Drew, 1955.

6893. Valone, James Joseph. The phenomenology of Alfred Schutz: toward a philosophy of the social sciences. Boston Coll., 1975. 75-21281

6894. Van Antwerp, Charles Edgar. Crazy Dave, the skeptic who knew too much. Oregon, 1971. 72-14769

6895. Vance, Robert Dale. Reference and intentionality. Duke, 1966. 67-9764

6896. Van Cleve, James Lewis. The role of the given in empirical knowledge. Rochester, 1974. 74-14417

6897. Vanden Burgt, Robert Joseph. Philosophical roots of the finite God theories of William James and Edgar Sheffield Brightman. Marquette, 1968. 69-3332

6898. Van De Pitte, Frederick Patrick, Jr. The anthropological basis of Kant's philosophy. Southern Cal., 1966. 66-10552

6899. Van De Pitte, Margaret Magdalene. The epistemological function of an affective principle in the phenomenology of intersubjectivity. Southern Cal., 1966. 66-10553

6900. Van Der Bogert, Frans. On some pragmatic conditions of reasonable induction. Cornell, 1973. 74-6324

6901. Vanderhoof, Frank Marshall. Theologico-political treatise by Benedict de Spinoza; translated with introduction and notes. Columbia, 1952. 4599

6902. Vander Lugt, Gerrit T. Emergent evolution. A critical analysis. Michigan, 1928.

6903. Vander Lugt, William. The concrete universal as a logical principle. Michigan, 1932.

6904. Vander Nat, Arnold. First-order indefinite and generalized semantics for weak systems of strict-implication. Pittsburgh, 1974. 74-26820

6905. Vander Veer, Garrett Lowell. Bradley's theory of the self. Yale, 1961.

6906. Vander Weel, Richard. Definition and demonstration: a study in Aristotle's posterior analytics. Laval, 1969.

6907. Van De Vate, Dwight, Jr. The formalization of certain Aristotelian concepts. Yale, 1956.

6908. Van De Veer, Albert Donald. The causal explanation of action. Chicago, 1968.

6909. Van de Walle, William Edwin. The nature of explanation. Harvard, 1926.

6910. Van Domelen, Sr. Mary Ermelinda. The philosophical method of Edgar Sheffield Brightman. St. Louis, 1961. 61-6497

6911. Van Dyk, John. The value of the commentaries on Peter Lombard's Sentences for the history of medieval philosophy: an inquiry and an assessment. Cornell, 1975. 76-9574

6912. Van Dyke, Martin. Augustine's views of human nature. Princeton, 1924.

6913. Van Evra, James Woodson. A history of some aspects of the theory of logic, 1850-present. Michigan St., 1967. 67-1692

6914. Van Fraassen, Bastiaan Cornelis. Foundations of the causal theory of time. Pittsburgh, 1966. 66-13481

6915. Van Hook, Jay Martin. Paul Tillich's conception of the relation between philosophy and theology. Columbia, 1966. 67-812

6916. Van Inwagen, Margery Naylor. Descartes' three versions of the ontological argument. Rochester, 1969. 70-2919

6917. Van Inwagen, Peter Jan. An essay on the freedom of the will. Rochester, 1969. 69-14798

6918. Van Iten, Richard James. The British empiricists and the problem of universals. Iowa, 1964. 64-11055

6919. Van Leeuwen, Hendrik Gerrit. The problem of certainty in English thought from Chillingworth to Locke. Iowa, 1961. 61-1938

6920. Van Loo, Elizabeth Dorinda Downes. Jung and Dewey on the nature of artistic experience. Tulane, 1973. 73-25307

6921. Van Marter, Leslie Edward. Categories as a non-arbitrary finite system of mutually irreducible simple entities: a study based on comparative analysis of Aristotle, Kant, and Charles Sanders Peirce. Chicago, 1964.

6922. Vannatta, Thomas Auld. A study of polarities in the philosophy of Georg Simmel. Ohio St., 1949.

6923. Van Neste, Victor F., Jr. Geach's analysis of referring phrases. Boston U., 1974. 74-14228

6924. Vannoy, Russell Columbus. Are intentions causes? Rochester, 1973.   73-25860

6925. Van Riper, Benjamin Whitman. Some views of the time problem. Chicago, 1912.

6926. Van Rosen, Beatrice. The constant and variable elements of art and aesthetic response. Pennsylvania, 1939.

6927. Van Sant, George Montgomery. The problem of negation and negative statements. Virginia, 1958.
   58-5549

6928. Van Saun, Walter. Development of St. Augustine's idea of God. Cincinnati, 1929.

6929. Van Steenburgh, Elston Wells. A philosophical analysis of metaphor applied to George Berkeley's theory of meaning. Michigan, 1960.   60-2580

6930. Van Steere, Douglas. Critical realism in the religious philosophy of Baron Friedrich von Hügel. Harvard, 1931.

6931. Van Til, Cornelius. God and the absolute. Princeton, 1927.

6932. Van Tuinen, Jacob. The phenomenological ethics of Max Scheler. Michigan, 1936.

6933. Van Wesep, Henry. Gorgias of Leontini. A review and an interpretation. Princeton, 1917.

6934. Van Wyk, Herbert S. The philosophic views of James Orr. N.Y.U., 1942.   73-8806

6935. Vargas, Br. S. Alfonso. Psychology and philosophy of teaching according to traditional philosophy and modern trends. Catholic U., 1944.

6936. Varion, George. The doctrine of one personal God due to the Semetic family. Syracuse, 1895.

6937. Varnedoe, Samuel Lamartine, Jr. A critical examination of Berkeley's doctrine of ideas and its role in his philosophy. Pennsylvania, 1967.
   67-7880

6938. Varney, Mary Rosalind. Perception and error in Aristotle's psychology. Johns Hopkins, 1970.
   70-26698

6939. Varnum, Daniel Porter. Implication and causation. Harvard, 1925.

6940. Vartanian, Aram. Diderot and Descartes; the role of Cartesian ideas in the growth of scientific naturalism in 18th century France. Columbia, 1951.
2866

6941. Vaska, Vootele. The concept of being in the philosophy of Teichmüller. Columbia, 1964. 67-10392

6942. Vass, Dewey Houston. Plato's philosophy of education. Chicago, 1929.

6943. Vater, Michael George. Schelling's metaphysics of indifference. Yale, 1971. 71-31024

6944. Vaughan-Wilkes, Kathleen. Mind undermined: a defence of psycho-physical functionalism. Princeton, 1974. 75-6684

6945. Vaught, Carl Gray. Contemporary conceptions of the nature and existence of God: a study of Tillich and Hartshorne. Yale, 1966. 66-15032

6946. Veatch, Henry Babcock, Jr. The nature of moral justification. Harvard, 1936.

6947. Veazie, Walter. Empedocles' psychological doctrine in its original and its traditional setting. Columbia, 1922.

6948. Veblen, Thorstein B. The ethical grounds of a doctrine of retribution. Yale, 1884.

6949. Vélez-Saenz, Jaime. The doctrine of the common good of civil society in the works of St. Thomas Aquinas. Notre Dame, 1951.

6950. Veltman, Désiré Theodore. The system of the categories of science, their objective status and ontological significance. Yale, 1928.

6951. Venable, Bruce Elwood. The structure of mysticism and ontology in Plotinus. U. of Washington, 1975.
76-17672

6952. Vendler, Zeno. Facts and laws. Harvard, 1959.

6953. Venturella, Robert Eugene. A critical analysis of Herman H. Horne's interpretation of John Dewey's Democracy and education. Oklahoma, 1973.
73-26328

6954. Verdi, John Joseph. Illusion and illocution: J.L. Austin's Sense and sensibilia. Southern Cal., 1975. 76-5259

6955. Verene, Donald Phillip. An examination of Ernst Cassirer's philosophy of symbolic forms. Washington U., 1964. 65-6829

6956. Verges, Frank Gust. The argument from perceptual illusion. Cal., S. Diego, 1970. 70-22309

6957. Vermazen, Bruce James. Semantic theories in recent linguistics. Stanford, 1967. 67-17521

6958. Vernon, Thomas Sidney. The metaphysical role of ideas in the philosophy of Descartes. Michigan, 1963. 64-900

6959. Versényi, Laszlo Gaspar. Heidegger's theory of truth. Yale, 1955.

6960. Vertin, Joseph Michael. The transcendental vindication of the first step in realist metaphysics, according to Joseph Marechal. Toronto, 1973.

6961. Vetter, Sr. Patricia Louise. The theory of community in Charles S. Peirce. St. Louis, 1968.
68-14085

6962. Vexler, Felix. Studies in Diderot's esthetic naturalism. Columbia, 1922.

6963. Vial, Fernand Louis. Une philosophie et une morale du sentiment; Luc de Clapiers, Marquis de Vauvenargues. Michigan, 1934.

6964. Vician, Thomas Allen, Sr. The crisis of the personal: an historical investigation into the foundations of the problem of the self in modern philosophy. Claremont, 1971. 71-21670

6965. Vick, George Robert. Kant's doctrine of existence as a predicate. Southern Cal., 1968. 69-5074

6966. Vickers, John Michael. A critical examination of Frank Ramsey's theory of value and belief. Stanford, 1962. 62-5526

6967. Vidrine, Marshall Ross. The role of analogies in scientific discovery. Duke, 1975. 76-8786

6968. Vielkind, John N., Jr. Philosophy, finitude, and wholeness: a dialogue with Plato's *Charmides*. Duquesne, 1974. 74-21042

6969. Vier, Rev. Peter. Evidence and its function according to John Duns Scotus. St. Bonaventure, 1951.

6970. Vigorito, John Victor. Time in the philosophy of Gabriel Marcel. Colorado, 1968. 68-14232

6971. Vingoe, Robert Henry. F.H. Bradley and his critique of pragmatism. Toronto, 1953.

6972. Vinnedge, Hewitt B. Philosophic influence in medieval civilization. Marquette, 1928.

6973. Visgak, Charles Anthony. The physiological theory of the emotions as the foundation for the moral judgment of the individual according to William James. Duquesne, 1972. 73-4666

6974. Vision, Gerald Allan. The requirement to universalize moral judgments. Michigan, 1968. 68-7750

6975. Visker, Rev. Rudolphus Hinderikus. Moral theory and values in Louis Lavelle. St. Louis, 1968.
69-387

6976. Visvader, John Anthony. The other-minds problem. Minnesota, 1967. 68-7401

6977. Vitale, John. Kant and Hume on the a priori validity of the causal principle. Wisconsin, 1972.
72-23768

6978. Vivas, Eliseo. Some aesthetic problems. Wisconsin, 1935.

6979. Vlach, Frank. 'Now' and 'then': a formal study in the logic of tense anaphora. U.C.L.A., 1973.
73-28997

6980. Vlastos, Gregory. God as a metaphysical concept. Harvard, 1931.

6981. Voelkel, Theodore Swallen. Heidegger and the problem of circularity. Yale, 1971. 72-135

6982. Vogel, Arthur Anton. The Aristotelian theory of explanation and some recent criticisms. Harvard, 1952.

6983. Vogel, Manfred Henry. An examination of some of the basic aspects of Feuerbach's philosophy and his critique of religion, with an English translation of his Grundsätze der philosophie der zukunft. Columbia, 1964. 64-9912

6984. Vogel, Rev. Murel Raymond. The philosophy of Father Claude Buffier, S.J. Fordham, 1945.

6985. Volkomener, Sr. Mary Theophane. Thomistic ethics and anthropological data: some possible contributions of empirical materials to moral science. St. Louis, 1960.

6986. Vollmer, Philip. The dialectical method of Socrates. Pennsylvania, 1893.

6987. Vollrath, John Frederick. Actions and events. Indiana, 1967. 68-7227

6988. Von Bretzel, Philip Kinsey. Conventionalism, constructivism, and logical necessity. Michigan, 1973. 74-3743

6989. Von Dohlen, Richard Frederick. A case study in the explication of unclear theories in the social sciences: the relationship of values to freedom in the social theory of Talcott Parsons. Boston U., 1973. 73-14186

6990. Von Domarus, Gunter Walter Eilhard Alfred. The logical structure of the mind. Yale, 1930.

6991. Von Eckardt, Ursula Maria. The inalienable right to the pursuit of happiness: the meaning of the concept examined in the Declaration of Independence and related texts. New School, 1953.

6992. Von Frank, James Harold. Synthetic necessity. No. Carolina, 1972. 72-24857

6993. von Hippel, Caren Lynn Saaz. Piaget's work in early child development as it relates to Chomskian psycholinguistics. Michigan, 1971. 72-15032

6994. Von Jess, Wilma C. Gundersdorf. The divine attributes in the thought of Saint Augustine. Boston Coll., 1971. 71-26655

6995. Vonk, Paul Kenneth. The concept of divine revelation in the philosophy of religion. Duke, 1951.

6996. Von Oech, Roger V. The philosophy of man in the thought of Ernst Cassirer. Stanford, 1975. 76-5825

6997. Von Schoenborn, Alexander. Being, man and questioning: an ontological prolegomenon to Heidegger's existentialism. Tulane, 1971. 71-27310

6998. Vorsteg, Robert Herman. Philosophical explications of meaning. Ohio St., 1969. 70-19376

6999. Vos, Arvin Gene. St. Augustine's view of created reality. Toronto, 1970.

7000. Vos, Kenneth Duane. The contribution of Edmond Cahn, H. Richard Niebuhr and John Macmurray to the ethics of responsibility. Columbia, 1972.
73-9052

7001. Voskuil, Duane Martin. Whitehead's metaphysical aesthetic. Missouri, 1969. 70-3027

7002. Voss, Stephen Horton. What it is to have an impression. Stanford, 1968. 69-8292

7003. Vreeland, Br. Cosmas Gregory. Royce on will and the loyalty principle. St. Louis, 1964. 64-13447

7004. Vycines, Vincent. Earth and gods: problems of Heidegger's late philosophy. Duquesne, 1958.

- W -

7005. Waber, William Frederick, Jr. The roles of reason and sentiment in Hume's doctrine of the social virtues. Johns Hopkins, 1959.

7006. Wacker, Jeanne. Feeling in art and formalism in aesthetics. N.Y.U., 1955. 14998

7007. Wade, Donald Vance. The concept of individuality in Søren Kierkegaard. Toronto, 1944.

7008. Wade, William Lignon. A comparison of the *De magistro* of Saint Augustine with the *De magistro* of Saint Thomas. St. Louis, 1935. 188

7009. Wadelton, George Alfred. The existence of abstract entities. Princeton, 1951. 11050

7010. Wadia, Pheroze S. Seeming and being: a critical examination of Professor A.J. Ayer's philosophy of perception. N.Y.U., 1968. 69-8009

7011. Wagner, Carl Roland. The savage transparence. Yale, 1952.

7012. Wagstaffe, Sr. M. Joseph. The Thomistic philosophy of culture and the virtue of art. Catholic U., 1952.

7013. Wainwright, William Judson. Religious feelings and religious statements. Michigan, 1961. 61-6448

7014. Wakin, Malham M. The logic of obligation. Southern Cal., 1959. 59-4404

7015. Waks, Leonard Joseph. Understanding as an educational aim. Wisconsin, 1968. 63-9145

7016. Wald, Albert W. The foundations of St. Anselm's first ontological argument. Berkeley, 1972.

7017. Walden, Phyllis Ann. A philosophical investigation of loneliness. Missouri, 1972. 73-21843

7018. Waldman, Carol Louise High. Intention, motive and valuation. Bryn Mawr, 1972. 73-5901

7019. Waldman, Theodore. A re-examination of the notion of consent and political obligation. Berkeley, 1956.

7020. Waldner, Ilmar. Interpersonal utility comparisons. Stanford, 1969. 70-10543

7021. Waldo, Charles Ives, III. Concepts, the self, and empiricism. Kansas, 1969. 70-11085

7022. Walhout, Donald. Objectivity and value. Yale, 1952.

7023. Walker, John Mark. Aesthetic theory and the concept of expression. Brown, 1967. 68-1512

7024. Walker, Kendrick Wayne. A critical examination of D.M. Armstrong's materialistic theory of mind. Southern Cal., 1974. 75-6452

7025. Walker, Merle G. The problem of being in Plato. Radcliffe, 1936.

7026. Walker, Vern Robert. An information theoretic account of truth conditions for third-person claims concerning the perception of objects. Notre Dame, 1975. 75-13106

7027. Wall, Angela Kane. Carnap and the solution of the paradoxes of analysis. Vanderbilt, 1970. 70-16440

7028. Wall, George Bernard. The implications of cultural anthropology for the question: what is the basis of moral obligation? Southern Cal., 1965. 65-10110

7029. Wall, Thomas Francis. Intentionality and analogy theory of thinking. Boston Coll., 1970. 70-24613

7030. Wallace, Edith O. The notes on philosophy in the
Commentary of Servius. Columbia, 1938.

7031. Wallace, James Donald. Pleasure: its objects and its
relation to action. Cornell, 1963. 64-1048

7032. Wallace, John Roy. Philosophical grammar: a study of
classical quantification theory, the theory of
sense and reference, and the logic of sortal predicates. Stanford, 1964. 64-13652

7033. Wallace, Kenneth Douglas. The epistemological basis
for Ernst Cassirer's philosophy of science and its
application to spatial theory. Fordham, 1974.
74-19694

7034. Wallace, Richard John. Transworld identity: an essay
in the semantic foundations of modal logic. Rutgers, 1974. 75-8454

7035. Wallace, Robert William. A re-examination of the
cogito argument in the light of recent criticism.
Syracuse, 1970. 70-15224

7036. Wallenmaier, Thomas Eugene. An explication of the
physiological concept of function. Michigan St.,
1973. 74-6163

7037. Wallis, Wilson Dallam. Individual initiative and
social compulsion. Pennsylvania, 1915.

7038. Wallraff, Charles Frederic. Max Scheler's theory of
moral obligation. Berkeley, 1939.

7039. Wallwork, Ernest Edward, Jr. The moral philosophy
of Emile Durkheim. Harvard, 1971.

7040. Walsh, Daniel Cyril Clark. The metaphysics of ideas
according to Duns Scotus. Toronto, 1934.

7041. Walsh, Dorothy. The objectivity of the judgment of
aesthetic value. Bryn Mawr, 1935.

7042. Walsh, George Vincent. The concept of the terminating judgment in C.I. Lewis's theory of empirical
knowledge. Princeton, 1952. 11052

7043. Walsh, Harold Trueman. The philosophy of science of
William Whewell. Michigan, 1960. 60-6947

7044. Walsh, Rev. James Francis. The influence of the philosophers of the Reformation on the concept of
moral law. Fordham, 1935.

7045. Walsh, James Jerome. Aristotle's conception of
       Akrasia. Columbia, 1960.   60-3155

7046. Walsh, John Henry. A fundamental ontology of play
       and leisure. Georgetown, 1968.   69-2083

7047. Walsh, Joseph Leo. Revolutionary violence in Merleau-
       Ponty, Marx and Engels: a critical comparison.
       Brandeis, 1975.   75-24841

7048. Walsh, Rev. Joseph Michael. The principle "Bonum est
       diffusivum sui" in St. Bonaventure: its meaning
       and importance. Fordham, 1958.

7049. Walsh, Margaret Ann. Foundational sexuality: the
       chiasm of masculine and feminine. Duquesne, 1972.
                                           73-14579

7050. Walsh, Samuel W.J. Hegel's philosophical psychology
       of the individual. Boston U., 1951.

7051. Walter, Edward F. The problem of a justification of
       normative ethics. N.Y.U., 1968.   69-8011

7052. Walters, James Henry. Knowledge: a study of some
       conditions. Wisconsin, 1971.   72-2663

7053. Walters, Kenneth William. The role of transcendence
       in possible existence. Northwestern, 1971.
                                           72-7853

7054. Walters, William Harvey. Predication and unsaturation:
       an essay on Frege's philosophy of logic. Massa-
       chusetts, 1975.   75-27558

7055. Walther, Eric. The beginning of philosophy: three
       modern views. Yale, 1965.   66-1118

7056. Walther, Sandra Sue. Bare particulars, form, and con-
       tent: a structural analysis of Gustav Bergmann's
       ontology. Yale, 1966.   66-15034

7057. Walton, Delvy Craig. *De la recherche du bien*: a study
       of Malebranche's science of ethics. Claremont,
       1965.   66-3390

7058. Walton, Douglas Neil. The meaning of 'can': a study
       in the philosophy of language. Toronto, 1972.

7059. Walton, Kendall Lewis. Conceptual schemes: a study
       of linguistic relativity and related philosophical
       problems. Cornell, 1967.   68-4654

7060. Walton, William Merland. The person in the writings
       of St. Thomas Aquinas. Toronto, 1947.

7061. Wambari, Benson Kaguongo. The concept of alienation: its application to emergent African states. Massachusetts, 1973. 74-8653

7062. Wand, Bernard. Hume's theory of social and moral motivation. Cornell, 1953.

7063. Wang, Hao. An economical ontology for classical arithmetic. Harvard, 1948.

7064. Wanjohi, Gerald Joseph. La philosophie de l'évolution chez Theodosius Dobzhansky. Montreal, 1973.

7065. Ward, Benjamin Frank, Jr. Aim, decision, adventure: an inquiry into Whitehead's metaphysics of creative purpose. Yale, 1972. 73-382

7066. Ward, Frederick Champion. Mind in Whitehead's philosophy. Yale, 1937. 67-2749

7067. Ward, Leo. St. Thomas' theory of moral values. Catholic U., 1929.

7068. Warganz, Joseph Francis. A re-examination of Thomistic arguments for immortality in the light of Pietro Pomponazzi's De immortalitate animae. St. John's, 1968. 68-11260

7069. Wargo, Robert Joseph John. The logic of Basho and the concept of nothingness in the philosophy of Nishida Kitaro. Michigan, 1972. 73-11291

7070. Warmbrod, William Kenneth. The relevance of linguistic studies to philosophy. No. Carolina, 1970. 71-11764

7071. Warner, Clifford Terry. The explanation of human action: an essay towards a theory. Yale, 1967. 68-6865

7072. Warnock, John Dorrance. Some characteristics of English thinking, as shown in the development of science and philosophy. Yale, 1899.

7073. Warren, Edward Willard. The concept of consciousness in the philosophy of Plotinus. Johns Hopkins, 1961.

7074. Warren, Howard Boniwell. Irving Babbitt and Paul Elmer More: a comparison. Drew, 1940.

7075. Warren, J. Natura agit propter finem. Laval, 1954.

7076. Warren, Lawrence Edwin. An historical and critical sketch of eschatology. Drew, 1927.

7077. Warren, Mary Anne. The new epiphenomenalism. Berkeley, 1974.

7078. Warren, Thomas Bratton. God and evil: does Judeo-Christian theism involve a logical contradiction? Vanderbilt, 1969.   70-5470

7079. Warren, William Preston. Pantheism in neo-Hegelian thought. Yale, 1929.

7080. Warther, Mary A. The transcendental notion of supposit with special reference to the material supposit and its quantity. Catholic U., 1954.

7081. Wartofsky, Marx William. Denis Diderot and Ludwig Feuerbach: studies in the development of materialist monism. Columbia, 1952.   4250

7082. Washburn, Michael Clyde. The problem of self-knowledge and the evolution of the critical epistemology: 1781-1787. Cal., S. Diego, 1970.
71-3866

7083. Washell, Richard Francis. A study in the logic of Albert the Great. Toronto, 1969.

7084. Washio, Shogoro. A criticism of the realism of G.E. Moore and B. Russell. Harvard, 1911.

7085. Wass, Meldon Clarence. God infinite and the Summa fratris Alexandri. St. Boneventure, 1962.

7086. Wasserman, Steven B. Moral justification. Yale, 1974.   74-26356

7087. Wasserstrom, Richard Alan. Toward a theory of legal justification. Michigan, 1960.   60-2584

7088. Wassmer, Rev. Thomas A. A phenomenological study of the guilt experience in the light of modern ethics and value theory. Fordham, 1954.

7089. Waterfall, Donald Ernest. Plato and Aristotle on Akrasia. Princeton, 1969.   70-14246

7090. Waterhouse, Joseph Bryant. Perception and existence. U.C.L.A., 1971.   72-2934

7091. Waterman, Mina. Voltaire, Pascal and human destiny. Columbia, 1942.

7092. Waters, Anthony Harry. Alienation in the philosophy of Jean-Paul Sartre. Missouri, 1975.   76-7559

7093. Waters, Thomas Bruce. Physical and psycho-physical causation in the light of recent philosophical discussion. Ohio St., 1935.

7094. Watson, Edith McL. Regulative and constitutive principles with reference to the philosophy of Vaihinger. Radcliffe, 1937.

7095. Watson, Gary L. The nature of responsibility. Princeton, 1972. 73-9658

7096. Watson, George H. A critical analysis of the philosophic methodology of Rudolph Carnap. Southern Cal., 1948.

7097. Watson, James Raymond. Martin Heidegger's attempt to ground metaphysics: the time-character of being. So. Illinois, 1973. 74-6293

7098. Watson, John B. Animal education. Chicago, 1903.

7099. Watson, Lawrence William. A study of the origins of formal logic in Husserl's Formal and transcendental logic. DePaul, 1973. 73-19070

7100. Watson, Richard Allan. Simon Foucher and the Cartesian way of ideas. Iowa, 1961. 61-5620

7101. Watson, Sarah Martha. James's pragmatism and its relations to Fascism. Ohio St., 1942.

7102. Watson, Walter. Nature and action. Chicago, 1958.

7103. Wattles, Jeffrey Hamilton. Hegel's philosophy of organic nature. Northwestern, 1973. 73-30754

7104. Waxman, Meyer. The philosophy of Don Hasdai Crescas. Columbia, 1920.

7105. Weatherford, Roy Carter. Probability and certainty in C.I. Lewis' epistemology. Harvard, 1972.

7106. Weaver, Irvin W. The social philosophy of The federalist. Boston U., 1953.

7107. Weaver, Oliver Cornelius, Jr. Duty and purpose in the ethical theory of Joseph Butler. Northwestern, 1952.

7108. Webb, Clifford Wellington. Space and time in the philosophies of Kant and Bergson. Toronto, 1956.

7109. Webb, George Philip. Aristotle's theory of action. U. of Washington, 1969. 70-8504

7110. Webb, Judson Chambers. Mentalism, mechanism, and metamathematics. Case, 1974. 74-22100

7111. Webb, Rodman Bukeley. The presence of the past: John Dewey and Alfred Schutz on the genesis and organization of experience. Rutgers, 1974. 75-17369

7112. Weber, Alden O. An analysis of perception. Cornell, 1936.

7113. Weber, Anna M. Is value attributive or psychological? A study of three realists. Cornell, 1950.

7114. Weber, Fredric M. An existential interpretation of contemporary trends in philosophy of science. Northwestern, 1973. 73-30757

7115. Weber, Frederick Palmer. Contradiction and the triadic pattern in Hegel's logic. Virginia, 1940.

7116. Weber, Sr. Mary Florian. An immanent interpretation of five Platonic dialogues: Apology, Crito, Phaedo, Timaeus, and Laws X. Catholic U., 1968. 69-9091

7117. Weber, Renée Oppenheimer. Individual and social being in Heidegger's Being and time. Columbia, 1966. 67-845

7118. Weber, Rev. Robert Paul. Contemporary theories of the artificial synthesis of life. Catholic U., 1966. 67-1274

7119. Weber, Shierry Jo Meyer. Aesthetics, liberation, and reflection: a study in the history of critical thought. Cornell, 1975. 75-27877

7120. Weber, Stephen Lewis. Proofs for the existence of God: a meta-investigation. Notre Dame, 1969. 70-7896

7121. Webering, Rev. Damascene. Theory of demonstration according to William Ockham. St. Bonaventure, 1953.

7122. Webster, Florence. The nature of life; a study in metaphysical analysis. Columbia, 1922.

7123. Webster, Glenn Albert. R.G. Collingwood's conception of philosophy. U. of Washington, 1967. 67-14231

7124. Webster, William Earl. A theory of diatonic musical scores. Pennsylvania, 1971. 72-6248

7125. Weddle, Perry David. On Plato's doctrine of ideas. Nebraska, 1967. 68-758

7126. Wedeking, Gary Alan. A critical examination of command logic. Washington U., 1969. 69-22566

7127. Wedemeyer, Karl Heinz. The social philosophy of Dietrich Bonhoeffer. Boston U., 1969. 69-18719

7128. Weedon, William S. Persuasion. Virginia, 1936.

7129. Wegener, Charles W. The problem of the practical. Chicago, 1950.

7130. Wei, Sidney K. International relationship in China and its ethical, social and political interpretation. Chicago, 1920.

7131. Weidin, Vernon E., Jr. Aristotle's argument for the necessity of substance in light of his theory of predication. Chicago, 1971.

7132. Weierich, André Jean. The relationship of Teilhard de Chardin's law of complexity/consciousness to the mechanism/vitalism debate in biology. Oregon St., 1971. 71-14033

7133. Weigle, Luther Allan. A historical and critical study of Kant's *Antinomy* *of* *pure* *reason*. Yale, 1905.

7134. Weiher, Rev. Charles Frederick. Foundations of an abstractionist theory of natural number. Notre Dame, 1960. 60-3732

7135. Weil, Vivian Max. Basic actions: a component analysis. Illinois, Chi., 1972. 73-9238

7136. Weinberg, Albert K. The desire for self-approbation in human motivation. Johns Hopkins, 1931.

7137. Weinberg, Arthur Myron. The artist and the social philosopher: the debate between art and morality in mid-nineteenth century France. Columbia, 1951. 3398

7138. Weinberg, Carlton B. Mach's empirio-pragmatism in physical science. Columbia, 1937.

7139. Weinberg, Julius Rudolph. Logical positivism of the Viennese circle. Cornell, 1935.

7140. Weiner, Martin Harvey. A theory of desires. Stanford, 1972. 73-4620

7141. Weiner, Neal Orlove. The divided line: the converting art, and the dramatic structure of Plato's Republic. Texas, 1969. 69-15882

7142. Weingard, Robert. Physics and times. Wisconsin, 1969. 70-3738

7143. Weingartner, Rudolph Herbert. Experience and culture: the philosophy of Georg Simmel. Columbia, 1959. 60-2029

7144. Weinstein, Scott. Some applications of Kripke models to formal systems of intuitionistic analysis. Rockefeller, 1975.

7145. Weinstock, Jerome Arthur. An essay on freedom of action. Johns Hopkins, 1969. 69-21057

7146. Weinzweig, Marjorie Joan Smolensky. Phenomenological criticisms of the sense-datum concept. Berkeley, 1970. 71-9952

7147. Weir, Walter Daniel. An examination of hedonism. Harvard, 1956.

7148. Weisberg, David Evelyn. Aristotle on akrasia. Michigan, 1971. 72-5008

7149. Weisberg, Harold. The concept of institution and the ontology of history. Columbia, 1962. 64-9215

7150. Weiss, Abner. Rabbi Loew of Prague: theory of human nature and morality. Yeshiva, 1969. 69-21024

7151. Weiss, Arthur. Introduction to the philosophy of art. Berkeley, 1909.

7152. Weiss, Charles. The metaphysical implications of modern physics. N.Y.U., 1931. 73-20932

7153. Weiss, Donald David. A new contractarianism: a critique of Rawls' theory of justice. Princeton, 1971. 71-25959

7154. Weiss, Donald Herbert. George Herbert Mead's personality theory: a comparison with that of Sigmund Freud and with neurophysiology. Tulane, 1964. 65-2526

7155. Weiss, Frederick Gustav. Hegel's conception of truth: an interpretation and criticism. Virginia, 1974. 74-23307

7156. Weiss, Paul. Logic and system. Harvard, 1929.

7157. Weiss, Raymond Lincoln. Wisdom and piety: the ethics of Maimonides. Chicago, 1966.

7158. Weiss, Stephen Edward. The Sorites antinomy: a study in the logic of vagueness and measurement. No. Carolina, 1973. 74-5982

7159. Weissman, Stanley Norman. Foundations of a theory of translation for natural languages. Columbia, 1965. 66-6963

7160. Weiswurm, Alcuin A. The nature of human knowledge according to St. Gregory of Nyssa. Catholic U., 1952.

7161. Weitz, Morris. The method of analysis in the philosophy of Bertrand Russell. Michigan, 1943.

7162. Welch, Cyril. A phenomenological analysis of the occurrence of meaning in experience. Penn St., 1964. 64-13423

7163. Welch, E. Parl. Max Scheler's philosophy of religion; a study in phenomenology. Southern Cal., 1934.

7164. Welch, Livingston. Imagination and human nature. Columbia, 1935.

7165. Weld, Hiram C. Some types of personalism in the United States. Boston U., 1944.

7166. Welker, David Dale Roy. Semantic contrast. Michigan, 1968. 68-13429

7167. Wellbank, Joseph Harris. The use of reason in ethics: E.S. Brightman, C.I. Lewis, and S.E. Toulmin. Boston U., 1965. 65-11232

7168. Weller, Eric John. Causality and agency: a study in the concept of an act. Rochester, 1964.
 64-9250

7169. Wellman, Carl Pierce. The objective validity of moral judgments. Harvard, 1954.

7170. Wellmuth, John James. Epistemological foundations of formal logic. Michigan, 1941. 330

7171. Wells, Donald Arthur. The influence of Hegel on Marx and T.H. Green in the philosophy of the state. Boston U., 1946.

7172. Wells, Edgar Franklin. Josiah Royce's theory of the internal and external meaning of ideas. Harvard, 1941.

7173. Wells, Harry K. Process and unreality; a criticism of method in Whitehead's philosophy. Columbia, 1950.

7174. Wells, Kenneth E. Thai Buddhism, its rites and activities. Columbia, 1940.

7175. Wells, Norman Joseph. The distinction of essence and existence in the philosophy of Francis Suarez. Toronto, 1955.

7176. Wells, Ronald Vale. Three Christian transcendentalists: James Marsh, Caleb Sprague Henry, Frederic Henry Hedge. Columbia, 1942.

7177. Wells, Rulon Seymour, III. The correspondence of language to fact. Harvard, 1942.

7178. Wells, Wesley Raymond. A behavioristic study of religious values. Harvard, 1917.

7179. Wellwood, David Philip. Language, ontology, and relativity. Georgia, 1975.   76-6459

7180. Welsh, Paul. Dewey's theory of inquiry. Cornell, 1948.

7181. Welton, Donn Curtis. The temporality of meaning: a critical study of the structure of meaning and temporality in Husserl's phenomenology. So. Illinois, 1973.   74-6252

7182. Wen, Hsi-tseng. The status of man in Neo-Confucianism. Southern Cal., 1954.

7183. Wendt, Harman G. Max Dauthendey, poet-philosopher. Columbia, 1936.

7184. Wengert, Robert George. The tenability of intensions. Toronto, 1971.

7185. Wenkart, Henriette. Santayana's philosophy of matter and of mind. Harvard, 1970.

7186. Wentura, David Franklin. Technology and human values, east and west. C.I.A.S., 1974.   75-17542

7187. Wentworth, Elizabeth. The problem of the methodological autonomy of history with reference to certain modern western thinkers. Southern Cal., 1959.
   59-2618

7188. Wenz, Peter Samuel. George Berkeley's attack on the doctrine of abstract ideas. Wisconsin, 1971.
   71-28373

7189. Werhane, Patricia Hogue. Language and private phenomena. Northwestern, 1969. 70-181

7190. Werkmeister, William H. Dreisch's philosophy: an exposition and a critical analysis. Nebraska, 1927.

7191. Werner, Baldur Erich. Foundations of temporal modal logics. Wisconsin, 1974. 74-22150

7192. Werner, Louis. The game-analogy. Harvard, 1972.

7193. Werner, Richard W. The metaphysical foundations of Plato's ethics. Rochester, 1974. 74-22639

7194. Wernick, Sidney William. The a priori factor in moral judgments. Harvard, 1938.

7195. Werth, Lee Frederick. Tense and temporality. Waterloo, 1972.

7196. Wertheimer, Roger. The significance of sense. Harvard, 1969.

7197. Wertz, Spencer Keifer. Humean models of historical discourse. Oklahoma, 1970. 70-23012

7198. Wessels, Linda Ann. Schrödinger's interpretations of wave mechanics. Indiana, 1975. 75-11464

7199. West, Charles M. The nature of the Aristotelian intellect. Laval, 1951.

7200. West, Charles Raymond, Jr. Nietzsche's concept of amor fati. Columbia, 1957. 58-4715

7201. West, Elinor Jane Maddock. The Promethean ethic in the Protagoras. Columbia, 1967. 67-14107

7202. West, Henry Robison. Act-utilitarianism and rule-utilitarianism. Harvard, 1965.

7203. Westley, Richard John. The doctrine of individuation in the philosophy of Gilbert de la Porrée. Toronto, 1954.

7204. Weston, Thomas Spengler. The continuum hypothesis: independence and truth-value. M.I.T., 1974.

7205. Westphal, Frederick Allen. Our knowledge of immediate experience and the use of mental predicates in ordinary language. Northwestern, 1963.
64-5882

7206. Westphal, Merold Edwood, Jr. The unity of reason in Hegel's Phaenomenologie. Yale, 1967. 67-8431

7207. Wettersten, John Russell. Towards a scientific psychology: a Popperian approach. Boston U., 1970.
70-22382

7208. Wetzel, Charles Robert. A critical evaluation of John Dewey's theory of inquiry. Nebraska, 1962.
63-26

7209. Whalley, Michael James. On the question of the perceivability of a causal link between particular events, with special reference to the research of Albert Michotte. Cornell, 1975. 76-12900

7210. Whallon, Robert Edward. Metaphysical theories of the freedom of the will. Harvard, 1945.

7211. Wheatley, James Melville Owen. Contemporary British phenomenalism: an inquiry into its meaning and justification. Toronto, 1957.

7212. Wheeler, Arthur Murray. The concept of rationality in the ethics and value theory of Clarence Irving Lewis. Wisconsin, 1958. 53-7550

7213. Wheeler, Mthr. Mary Cecelia. Philosophy and the Summa theologica of St. Thomas Aquinas. Catholic U., 1956.

7214. Wheeler, Michael Orvan. Natural law theory and the concept of a rule. Arizona, 1971. 71-25134

7215. Wheeler, Samuel Crane, III. The logical form of ethical language: radical translation, morals and the good. Princeton, 1970. 71-14426

7216. Wheelwright, Philip Ellis. The concepts of liberty and contingency in the philosophy of Charles Renouvier. Princeton, 1924.

7217. Whiddon, Frederick Palmer. Anselm's ontological argument and representative later interpretations. Emory, 1963. 64-188

7218. Whisner, William Noel. An analysis of the cognitivist-non-cognitivist controversy. Texas, 1970.
70-18309

7219. Whitbeck, Caroline Ann. The treatment of space and time in the general theory of relativity. M.I.T., 1970.

7220. Whitchurch, Irl Goldwin. The philosophical bases of asceticism in the Platonic writings and in pre-Platonic tradition. Cornell, 1921.

7221. White, Arthur Albert, Jr. Paternalism. Virginia, 1974. 74-29215

7222. White, Carl Milton. Meaning and instrumentalism. Cornell, 1933.

7223. White, Clifford Dale. Indications for ethics in the concepts of guilt and shame in certain psychiatric theories. Boston U., 1963. 63-6584

7224. White, David Allen. Heidegger and the language of poetry. Toronto, 1973.

7225. White, David Cowden. The historical reason in the thought of José Ortega y Gasset. Drew, 1958.

7226. White, David Edmund. Natural theology in Bishop Butler's Analogy of religion. Cornell, 1973. 74-10222

7227. White, Hugh V. The concept of consciousness in the philosophy of René Descartes. Stanford, 1935.

7228. White, James Eadie. Cartesian privacy and the problem of other minds. Colorado, 1968. 68-14407

7229. White, Michael Joe. Speech act theory: a critical assessment. Cal., S. Diego, 1974. 74-27569

7230. White, Morton G. The origin of Dewey's instrumentalism. Columbia, 1943.

7231. White, Nicholas Perry. Aristotle on non-substance. Harvard, 1970.

7232. White, Peter John. A study of the psychology of cognition in John Locke's Essay. York, 1972.

7233. White, Sarah Parker. A moral history of women. Syracuse, 1935.

7234. White, Stephen S. A comparison of the philosophies of F.C.S. Schiller and John Dewey. Chicago, 1938.

7235. White, Stephen Wayne. The equality principle: problems and interpretations. Georgia, 1971. 72-11058

7236. White, Thomas I. A study of the influence of Plato and Aristotle on Thomas More's Utopia. Columbia, 1974. 76-30169

7237. Whitehill, James Donald. Homo suicidens, an envisionment of self-nihilation as a human way of being: mediations of vision in models, paradigm, and images. Drew, 1970. 70-17782

7238. Whitelaw, John Douglas. The idea of poverty as virtue, and its role in the historical development of the church according to some writings of Petrus Ionnis Olivi (1248-1298). Toronto, 1970.

7239. Whiteside, David Edward. An analysis of the concept of alienation in Karl Marx's early writings. Michigan, 1971. 72-15045

7240. Whiteway, Lloyd Miller. The concept of conscience in the ethical theory of Bishop Joseph Butler. Temple, 1972. 73-8894

7241. Whitman, Merrill Jay. Judicial discretion. Michigan, 1973. 73-24715

7242. Whitney, Hugh. Development of the Aristotelian idea of God in the philosophy of Saint Thomas Aquinas. Harvard, 1936.

7243. Whitney, Jill April. The ethical significance of anger. Yale, 1971. 71-17163

7244. Whitney, William T. Lotze's conception of reality, with reference to the possible contradiction between his ontological and psychological criteria. N.Y.U., 1908. 74-1303

7245. Whittemore, Robert Clifton. Panpsychism and the function of God. Yale, 1953. 64-11385

7246. Whittier, Duane Hapgood. Jordan's metaphysic of language and aesthetic meaning: a preliminary study. Illinois, 1961. 62-695

7247. Wholey, Joseph Skeffington, Jr. Decidable theories. Harvard, 1962.

7248. Wick, Warner A. Metaphysics and the new logic. Chicago, 1941.

7249. Wicke, Lloyd C. Comparative philosophies of history and their metaphysical assumptions. Drew, 1938.

7250. Wickersham, John Paul. De primo et ultimo instanti: a problem of indeterminacy in medieval physics. St. Louis, 1973. 74-24156

7251. Wickey, Norman Jay Gould. British idealism and the philosophy of religion. Harvard, 1923.

7252. Wiebe, Richard Penner. Abstract entities in the philosophy of Rudolf Carnap. Berkeley, 1965. 65-3209

7253. Wiebenga, William Martin. Wittgenstein's theory of meaning. Yale, 1966. 66-15037

7254. Wieck, David Thoreau. Comic as an aesthetic concept. Columbia, 1961. 61-3911

7255. Wiederhold, Albert Georg. Formative influences on dialectic materialism. Stanford, 1941.

7256. Wiederhold, Hermann. The relations between Nietzsche's and Kant's philosophies. Boston U., 1941.

7257. Wiedmann, August Karl. Romanticism and its continued heritage in Kandinsky and German expressionism. Northwestern, 1971. 71-30984

7258. Wieman, Henry Nelson. The organization of interests. Harvard, 1917.

7259. Wieman, Robert Morgan. The social criteria of value. Berkeley, 1955.

7260. Wiener, Norbert. A comparison between the treatment of the algebra of relatives by Schroeder and that by Whitehead and Russell. Harvard, 1913.

7261. Wienpahl, Paul deVelin. Language, definition and ethics. U.C.L.A., 1945.

7262. Wierenga, Edward Ray. Three theories of events. Massachusetts, 1974. 75-6110

7263. Wiersma, Sheri Louise. Intentionality and the emotions. Brown, 1971. 72-8201

7264. Wiesner, Naphtali A. Faith and suffering: a study of the impact of concentration camp experiences on moral and religious attitudes. New School, 1951.

7265. Wiggins, Forrest Oran. The moral consequences of individualism. Wisconsin, 1938.

7266. Wilbanks, Jan Joseph. Hume's theory of imagination. Ohio St., 1964. 65-3942

7267. Wilbur, James Benjamin, III. Prescription, attitudes and imperatives. Columbia, 1954.

7268. Wilcox, John Thomas. Some limitations to ethical relativity in Stevenson's emotivism. Yale, 1960.

7269. Wild, John Daniel. The science and metaphysics of symbolism. Chicago, 1926.

7270. Wilder, Hugh Thompson. Toward a naturalistic theory
of meaning. W. Ontario, 1973.

7271. Wildt, Sr. Carol Marie. Julian Huxley's conception
of evolutionary progress. St. Louis, 1973.
74-24157

7272. Wilensky, Sara O. Mishnato shel Yizhak Arama be-mis-
geret ha-pilosofiah ha-Pilonit: the teaching of
Isaac Arama in the framework of Philonic philosophy. Radcliffe, 1951.

7273. Wiles, Ann McCoy. Plato's theory of forms: a critical analysis. Virginia, 1974.   74-23321

7274. Wilkerson, Rev. Jerome Francis. The concept of friendship in the *Nicomachean ethics* of Aristotle.
Catholic U., 1963.   63-8065

7275. Wilkins, Burleigh Taylor. Natural law, human nature,
and natural rights in Edmund Burke: a study in the
history of ideas. Princeton, 1965.   65-12332

7276. Wilkinson, George David. John B. Stallo's criticism
of physical science. Columbia, 1951.   2561

7277. Wilkinson, John. A pragmatic analysis of communication. Chicago, 1954.

7278. Wilkinson, Winston Albert. Does knowledge imply belief? Syracuse, 1972.   73-9579

7279. Will, Frederick L. Formal and material truth. A
criticism of idealistic logic. Cornell, 1937.

7280. Will, Samuel F., Jr. Victor Cousin's esthetics.
Yale, 1954.

7281. Willard, Dallas Albert. Meaning and universals in
Husserl's *Logische untersuchungen*. Wisconsin,
1964.   64-13935

7282. Willard, Laurence Bricard. An interpretation of
positivism. N.Y.U., 1940.   73-3487

7283. Willer, Charles E. Pragmatic elements in Kant's
philosophy. Chicago, 1912.

7284. Williams, Bert Charles. Berdyaev's philosophy of
history. Boston U., 1949.

7285. Williams, Clifford E. 'Now', interchangeability
without a change of truth value, and time. Indiana, 1972.   72-15936

7286. Williams, Clifford John. The epistemology of John Watson. Toronto, 1966.

7287. Williams, Donald Cary. A metaphysical interpretation of behaviorism. Harvard, 1928.

7288. Williams, Ernie Milton, Jr. The logical structure of aesthetic discourse. Florida St., 1971.
72-9221

7289. Williams, Forrest Wilbur. Art and knowledge of nature. Northwestern, 1957. 58-370

7290. Williams, Frank Canon Scientific explanation by covering laws. Duke, 1969. 70-20292

7291. Williams, Frederick William. The doctrine of natural rights in the United States (1780-1790). N.Y.U., 1941. 73-20949

7292. Williams, Gardner. The role of pleasure in the theory of value. Michigan, 1929.

7293. Williams, George. The problem of annihilation versus immortality: an examination of ontological and ethical questions concerning death. Buffalo, 1970.

7294. Williams, Judy Carol. The philosophical significance of the notion of seeing-as. Cal., Davis, 1974.
74-29351

7295. Williams, Kenneth Raynor. The ethics of Thomas Jefferson. Boston U., 1962. 62-5545

7296. Williams, Martha Elaine. The problem of man and his justification in the philosophy of Friedrich Nietzsche. Bryn Mawr, 1959. 59-6992

7297. Williams, Michael James. Phenomenalism. Princeton, 1973. 74-9734

7298. Williams, Milton Howard. A study of meaning. Cornell, 1937.

7299. Williams, Paul Eshelman. A study in Hegel's method. Cornell, 1938.

7300. Williams, Peter Colburn. The principle of reciprocity. Harvard, 1973.

7301. Williams, Ronald Guy. The logical forms of evaluative sentences: some deep-structural models of evaluative discourse. Stanford, 1975. 75-25630

7302. Williams, Sterling Price. The conception of reason in Sidgwick's ethics. Chicago, 1918.

7303. Williams, Thomas Raymond. The ideal observer theory in ethics. Indiana, 1972.   73-9786

7304. Williamson, Elizabeth. The concept of possibility in its philosophical applications. Chicago, 1931.

7305. Williamson, James Hunter. A critique of the monadology of Leibniz. Yale, 1942.

7306. Williamson, Robert Boatwright. The ambiguity of dikaiosyne in Plato's Republic. Virginia, 1967.   63-3131

7307. Willing, Anthony. Aristotle on paradoxes of accidence. Massachusetts, 1975.   75-16614

7308. Wills, Russel Milton. The structure of experience. U. of Washington, 1972.   73-3804

7309. Wilmot, Patrick Francis. Student revolt, decolonization and the master-slave relation. Vanderbilt, 1972.   73-14540

7310. Wilsey, Elwyn Donald. Roman world philosophy, the unity of empire, religion, and law in the conception of a system of the world. Columbia, 1931.

7311. Wilshire, Bruce Withington. Natural science and phenomenology: William James' Principles of psychology as a search for reconciliation. N.Y.U., 1966.   68-10127

7312. Wilson, Augusta Manie. The principle of the ego in philosophy with special reference to its influence upon Schlegel's doctrine of "ironie." N.Y.U., 1908.   73-20956

7313. Wilson, Curtis A. William Heytesbury: medieval logic and the rise of mathematical physics. Columbia, 1953.

7314. Wilson, Daniel Hughes. Field-theoretic consciousness. Kansas, 1975.   76-16795

7315. Wilson, David Hawxhurst. The objectivity versus the subjectivity of value. Harvard, 1931.

7316. Wilson, Emmett, Jr. Causality and human action. Harvard, 1966.

7317. Wilson, Fred Forster, Jr. Studies in analyticity. Iowa, 1965.   66-3510

7318. Wilson, George McGahey, Jr. The nature of the natural numbers. Cornell, 1972. 73-7161

7319. Wilson, Gordon Anthony. Dymorphism and the metaphysical unity of man in Quodlibeta magistri Henrici Goethals a gandavo doctoris solemnis: socii sorbonici: et archdiaconi tornacensis cum duplici tabella. Tulane, 1975. 76-4008

7320. Wilson, Hugh Van Rensselaer. Ethical aspects of reward. Chicago, 1932.

7321. Wilson, Judith Diane. E.H. Gombrich and beyond: a study of Ernst Hans Gombrich's views on pictorial imagery and of their implications for identification of the distinctive features of pictorial works of art. Wisconsin, 1974. 74-18964

7322. Wilson, Kirk Dallas. The logical grammar of Kant's twelve forms of judgment: a formalized study of Kant's table of judgments. Massachusetts, 1972. 72-19480

7323. Wilson, Margaret Hodge Dauler. Leibniz' doctrine of necessary truth. Harvard, 1965.

7324. Wilson, Neil Leslie. Individuals, qualities and language. Yale, 1952.

7325. Wilson, Patrick Garland. On interpretation and understanding. Berkeley, 1961.

7326. Wilson, Peter Alan. Psychologism in Hume. Duke, 1974.

7327. Wilson, Rev. Russell. The modes of abstraction according to St. Thomas Aquinas. Georgetown, 1949.

7328. Wilson, Tom Bullock. Frederick J.E. Woodbridge, interpreter of Greek philosophy. Arkansas, 1964. 64-10080

7329. Wilson, Warren Kent. Are modal statements really metalinguistic? Pittsburgh, 1969. 70-4272

7330. Wimsatt, William Church. Modern science and the new teleology I- the conceptual foundations of functional analysis. Pittsburgh, 1971. 72-7880

7331. Win, Khin Maung. Some philosophical problems in contemporary Burma: a study in the comparative philosophy of culture. Yale, 1959. 70-11475

7332. Windt, Peter Yale. Three types of philosophy of language: a preliminary investigation. U. of Washington, 1967. 68-3889

7333. Wingard, Gordon George, II. Rights and practical prescriptions. Syracuse, 1970. 71-11004

7334. Wingell, Albert Edward. The relationship of intellect and will in the human act according to St. Thomas Aquinas. Toronto, 1966.

7335. Winkler, Earl Raye. The ontological argument: a critique of St. Anselm's Proslogion II and III. Colorado, 1971. 72-6498

7336. Winn, Clifton Charles. A monadic universe. Harvard, 1931.

7337. Winnie, John Arthur. A formal theory of propositions. Minnesota, 1970. 71-18841

7338. Winslade, Ann Garry. Visualizing. Maryland, 1970. 71-12165

7339. Winslade, William Joseph. A study of the existence and nature of relations. Northwestern, 1967. 67-15372

7340. Winston, Alexander P. The concept of human freedom in Bergson and James. U. of Washington, 1949.

7341. Winston, Kenneth Irwin. Critique of an analysis of formal justice. Columbia, 1970. 71-6276

7342. Winter, Judith Bass. Motivational and countermotivational explanations of behavior in Freudian psychoanalytic theory. Yale, 1968. 69-8456

7343. Winter, Michael Frederick. Lived time in Husserl and Whitehead: a comparative study. Northwestern, 1975. 75-29784

7344. Wintersteiner, Gail S. Can science progress? A critique of Sir Karl Popper's philosophy. Boston U., 1973. 73-14191

7345. Winthrop, Henry. A theory of behavioral diffusion (a contribution to the mathematical biology of social phenomena.) New School, 1953.

7346. Wisadavet, Wit. Sartre's and the Buddhist's concept of man. Indiana, 1963. 64-5509

7347. Wisan, Richard Norman. The world in words: on the relation between the meaning of terms and the nature of things; with special reference to an evaluation of English ordinary-language philosophy. Columbia, 1955. 15753

7348. Wisdom, William Asbury. Necessary and contingent truth in the philosophy of Gottfried Wilhelm Leibniz. Bryn Mawr, 1966. 67-40

7349. Wise, Ralph Eugene. Irrational man and the modern dilemma: an inquiry into the world and thought of Paul Elmer More and Reinhold Niebuhr. Syracuse, 1963. 64-5669

7350. Wise, Stephen Seymour. The improvement of the moral qualities; an ethical treatise of the eleventh century by Solomon ibn Gabirol, printed from an essay on the place of Gabirol in the history of the development of Jewish ethics. Columbia, 1901.

7351. Wiseman, Charles Michael. Epistemic logic: an examination of the logics of Von Wright, Chisholm, and Hintikka. Columbia, 1969. 70-7095

7352. Wiseman, Mary. The interpretation of the categorical imperative in the ethics of C.I. Lewis. Columbia, 1974. 75-12371

7353. Wiseman, William J.J. Subjectivity in the existential method of Søren Kierkegaard. Temple, 1948.

7354. Withers, John William. Euclid's parallel postulate: its nature, validity, and place in geometric systems. Yale, 1904.

7355. Witter, Charles Edgar. Pragmatic elements in Kant's philosophy. Chicago, 1913.

7356. Wojciechowski, Edward Casimir. Vladimir Soloviev's doctrine of the absolute. Notre Dame, 1963. 63-7333

7357. Wojciechowski, Jerzy. Le problème du mouvement. Laval, 1952.

7358. Wojick, David Eugene. Conceptual change and meaning sameness in science and philosophy. Pittsburgh, 1974. 74-19444

7359. Wolf, Robert George. Ernst Cassirer's concept of scientific law. St. Louis, 1970. 71-21432

7360. Wolf, Rev. Theodore John. The function of qualities in substantial change according to Saint Thomas Aquinas. St. Louis, 1945.

7361. Wolfe, Sr. Mary Joan of Arc. The problem of solidarism in St. Thomas Aquinas; a study in social philosophy. Catholic U., 1938.

7362. Wolfenstein, Martha. Taine's philosophy of art: a study in sociological aesthetics. Radcliffe, 1939.

7363. Wolff, Robert Paul. The role of mental activity in the *Treatise of human nature* and the *Critique of pure reason*. Harvard, 1957.

7364. Wolgast, Elizabeth Hankins. Scepticism and the proof of an external world. U. of Washington, 1955.
13008

7365. Wolstein, Benjamin. Experience and valuaticn, a study in John Dewey's naturalism. Columbia, 1949.

7366. Wolter, Rev. Allan B. The transcendentals in the metaphysics of Duns Scotus. Catholic U., 1946.

7367. Wolters, Richard Mark. Wittgenstein's ontology in his early works. Massachusetts, 1974. 74-15052

7368. Wolterstorff, Nicholas Paul. Whitehead's theory of individuals. Harvard, 1957.

7369. Wolz, Heinrich Georg. The role of the will in the philosophy of René Descartes. Fordham, 1946.

7370. Womack, H. Lynn. The mission of America (1815-1860), an historical study of an idea. Johns Hopkins, 1955.

7371. Wong, Yeu-Quang. The relation between G.E. Moore's ethics and epistemology. So. Illinois, 1971.
72-5404

7372. Woo, Esther. An evaluation of Hartshorne's critique of the notion of absolute being in classical tradition. Fordham, 1974. 74-19695

7373. Wood, Allen William. Kant's moral religion. Yale, 1968. 69-8457

7374. Wood, Richard Arlan. An inquiry into the *Treatise*. Nebraska, 1968. 68-11573

7375. Wood, Richard James. The theory of forms in Plato's late dialogues. Yale, 1965. 66-1126

7376. Wood, Robert Earl. *I and thou*: an analysis of the ontological foundations of Martin Buber's thought. Marquette, 1967. 68-499

7377. Wood, Sanford Watts. Christian politics and civil philosophy: an interpretation of Hobbes's *Leviathan*. Vanderbilt, 1968. 68-18005

7378. Wood, Thomas Eugene. Empiricism and current linguistic theory. Berkeley, 1975. 76-15438

7379. Woodhouse, Mark Burr. Personal identity and individuation with reference to the theories of H.D. Lewis and Sydney Shoemaker. Miami, 1970. 70-18169

7380. Woodruff, Paul Bestor. Two studies in Socratic dialectic: the Euthyphro and the Hippias major. Princeton, 1973. 74-9738

7381. Woodruff, Peter Worthing. Foundations of three-valued logic. Pittsburgh, 1969. 70-216

7382. Woods, Earl Robert. The existence of God as knowable by reason according to William of Ockham. Fordham, 1971. 71-27003

7383. Woods, John Hayden. Entailment and paradoxes of strict implication. Michigan, 1966. 66-6745

7384. Woods, Martin Thomas. The concept of agent intelligence in Aristotle: a solution in accordance with the traditional problem of the one and the many. Southern Cal., 1966. 66-10558

7385. Woodward, Beverly Anne. Commitment to nonviolence: a theory of action and politics. New School, 1972. 72-27891

7386. Woodward, Sr. Mary Irene. Metaphysics and the glory of God. Catholic U., 1967. 67-7323

7387. Woody, John Melvin. The dialectic of freedom. Yale, 1964.

7388. Woody, Susan Minot. An inquiry into the status and significance of universality in law. Yale, 1963.

7389. Woofenden, William Ross. Swedenborg's philosophy of causality. St. Louis, 1970. 71-21433

7390. Workman, Allen J. An inquiry into sources of aesthetic in pre-Socratic philosophy. Southern Cal., 1951.

7391. Workman, John Rowe. The evolution and meaning of agathos in the philosophy of Plato. Princeton, 1944. 3071

7392. Workman, Rollin Wallace. A comparison of the theories of meaning of John Dewey and Oxford ordinary language philosophers with some attention to that of F.C.S. Schiller. Michigan, 1958. 58-3753

7393. Worley, John Harland. Hume's theory of ideas. Northwestern, 1967. 68-3239

7394. Wortham, Charles Warfield. John Locke's philosophy of language and its relation to his theory of knowledge. Columbia, 1967. 67-10619

7395. Woznicki, Andrew Nicholas. The metaphysical foundation of the order of being in St. Thomas Aquinas. Toronto, 1967.

7396. Wren, Thomas Edward. Moral obligation and the structure of human action. Northwestern, 1969. 70-185

7397. Wright, Clarence Elmer. A cautious defense of teleology. Indiana, 1969. 69-22042

7398. Wright, John Eugene, Jr. Responsibility as an ethical norm in the thought of Erik H. Erikson. Southern Cal., 1973. 73-31687

7399. Wright, John Prentice. Mind and external existence: an analytical-historical study of a problem of Humean metaphysics. York, 1975.

7400. Wright, Philip B. Space, time and mind. Claremont, 1968. 68-18299

7401. Wright, Richard Allen. Toward a theory of indefinite reference. Illinois, 1973. 74-12258

7402. Wright, Theodore Francis. The human and its relation to the divine. Harvard, 1891.

7403. Wright, Walter Ernest. Self and absolute in the philosophy of Fichte. Vanderbilt, 1971. 71-29337

7404. Wu, Joseph Sen. The problem of existential import in Dewey's theory of propositions. So. Illinois, 1967. 67-15883

7405. Wu, Kathleen Gibbs Johnson. A new formalization of the logic of knowledge and belief. Yale, 1970. 70-26841

7406. Wu, Kuang-ming. Existential relativism. Yale, 1965. 65-1127

7407. Wu, Lawrence Ching-Fang. Prediction and explanation in the behavioral sciences. Texas, 1975. 75-14537

7408. Wubnig, Judith. A study of the relationship between morality and rationality in Kant's critique of aesthetic judgment. Yale, 1963. 64-7149

7409. Wuori, Gerald Kauno. Imagination, mind and history in R.G. Collingwood's philosophy of man. Purdue, 1973. 74-15262

7410. Wurzburger, Walter Samuel. Brentano's theory of a priori judgments. Harvard, 1951.

7411. Wycoff, William Alfred, Jr. The new rationalism of Fung Yu-Lan. Columbia, 1975. 75-27475

7412. Wyman, Eva May. The experimental problem of "instinct" and "intelligence." Pennsylvania, 1931.

7413. Wynne, Mthr. Alice Mary. The bearing of St. Thomas' doctrine of substantial union on the science of ethics. Fordham, 1934.

7414. Wyschgorog, Michael. Kierkegaard and Heidegger; the ontology of existence. Columbia, 1954.

- X -

7415. Xenakis, Jason Byron. A non-reductionist interpretation of Plato's ethics. Harvard, 1953.

- Y -

7416. Yaffe, Martin David. The new thinking of Franz Rosenzweig. Claremont, 1969. 69-8941

7417. Yake, John Stanley. John Stuart Mill and Plato. Buffalo, 1970. 71-7236

7418. Yalden, Maxwell Freeman. Language and cognition: an examination of the hypothesis that language influences habitual perception and thought. Michigan, 1956. 57-2182

7419. Yalden-Thomson, David C. Hume's moral philosophy in the *Treatise of human nature*. McGill, 1949.

7420. Yamamoto, Seisaku. The philosophy of pure experience. Emory, 1961. 63-3987

7421. Yamamoto, Yutaka. Contractualism and the problem of justification in ethics. Michigan, 1973.
74-15895

7422. Yamasaki, Beatrice Takiko. William Duff and the concept of 'Original genius.' Bryn Mawr, 1962.
63-2388

7423. Yanal, Robert John. Truth and the aesthetic appreciation of works of fiction. Illinois, Chi., 1975.
76-10536

7424. Yandell, Keith Edward. Metaphysical systems and decision procedures. Ohio St., 1966. 66-15158

7425. Yardan, Rev. John Louis. Demonstration of fact in philosophy and science. Catholic U., 1965.
65-9217

7426. Yartz, Francis Joseph. Order and moral perfection in the philosophy of St. Thomas Aquinas. St. Louis, 1968. 69-386

7427. Yarvin, Herbert. Some Cartesian questions. Brown, 1973. 74-3096

7428. Yeargain, Scott A., III. Freedom in Being and nothingness. Missouri, 1970. 71-3392

7429. Yee, Richard Wing. The problem of the immortality of the human soul in the works of Pietro Pomponazzi. Toronto, 1966.

7430. Yeghiayan, Eddie. Hume's theory of moral sentiments. Cal., Irvine, 1974. 75-11038

7431. Yetman, David Albert. Criteria: an essay in the philosophy of language. Arizona, 1972. 72-30382

7432. Yezzi, Ronald David. The application of mathematics to concepts in physics: four theories. Sc. Illinois, 1968. 69-6323

7433. Ylvisaker, Richard Stalland. Pure reason: a study of the foundations of the metaphysics of F.H. Bradley. Minnesota, 1966. 67-7807

7434. Yoes, M.G., Jr. Some problems of intensionality. Pennsylvania, 1965. 65-13407

7435. Yoos, George E. An analysis of three studies of pictorial representation: M.C. Beardsley, E.H. Gombrich, and L. Wittgenstein. Missouri, 1971.
71-30699

7436. Yoshida, Ronald Mamoru. Von Neumann's proof and hidden variables. U. of Washington, 1971.
72-7441

7437. Yost, George, Jr. Sir Thomas Browne and Aristotle. Princeton, 1941. 3074

7438. Yost, Robert Morris, Jr. Locke's theory of the external world. Harvard, 1948.

7439. Young, Betty Sue. Antoine Arnauld's *Des vrayes et des fausses idées*, a criticism and translation. Cornell, 1954.

7440. Young, Charles Morton. Justice and "techne" in Plato's *Republic*. Johns Hopkins, 1973.   74-10463

7441. Young, Gary. The common-sense view of one's knowledge of other minds. Chicago, 1971.

7442. Young, George McCracken, Jr. The philosopher of the common task: a study of the life and thought of Nikolaj Fedorov. Yale, 1973.   73-29509

7443. Young, Gregory Allan. The paradoxes of confirmation: a study in the logic of confirmation. Miami, 1975.   76-12832

7444. Young, Helen Hawthorne. The writings of Walter Pater. A reflection of British philosophical opinion, 1860-1890. Bryn Mawr, 1932.

7445. Young, Iris Marion. From anonymity to speech: a reading of Wittgenstein's later writing. Penn St., 1974.   75-9863

7446. Young, James Anthony. Knowledge of good in Moore and Aquinas. Texas, 1961.   61-4730

7447. Young, John Joseph. Counterfactual and subjunctive conditionals. Virginia, 1972.   72-26271

7448. Young, John Michael. Kant's transcendental idealism and theory of objectivity. Yale, 1969.
   70-2834

7449. Young, Julian Padraic. A causal theory of action. Pittsburgh, 1972.   72-22933

7450. Young, Malcolm G. The common-sense view of one's knowledge of other works. Chicago, 1970.

7451. Young, Theodore Alfred. Change in Aristotle, Descartes, Hume and Whitehead: an essay in philosophy of nature. Indiana, 1964.   64-12107

7452. Young, Warren Cameron. Nature and naturalism in the thought of Frederick J.E. Woodbridge and John Dewey. Boston U., 1946.

7453. Young-Bruehl, Elisabeth. Freedom and Karl Jaspers' philosophizing. New School, 1974.   74-21365

7454. Yperman, Pierre. The philosophy of Alain. Claremont, 1973. 74-989

7455. Yu, David. A comparative study of the metaphysics of Chu Hsi and A.N. Whitehead. Chicago, 1959.

7456. Yu, Paul. Knowledge and the a priori. Michigan, 1973. 74-15898

7457. Yule, David. Theories of abstract implication. Harvard, 1922.

- Z -

7458. Zabeeh, Farhang. The place of meaning and reason in Hume's theory of knowledge. Berkeley, 1958.

7459. Zack, Naomi. An evaluation of the epistemology of C.I. Lewis. Columbia, 1970. 70-23473

7460. Zacks, Hannah. Perception and action in Henri Bergson and allied philosophers. Columbia, 1966. 66-8535

7461. Zaffron, Richard Harold. Scientific explanation: explanation-types and explanation-levels. Indiana, 1968. 68-13695

7462. Zagolin, Laura. Self-deception. McGill, 1975.

7463. Zahradka, Lotar. The theory of the general will and its totalitarian application. Berkeley, 1958.

7464. Zaidi, Syed Ahmed Raza. Relational metaphysics. New School, 1975. 75-25464

7465. Zaitchik, Alan Moshe. The limits of hypothetical contractualism. M.I.T., 1973.

7466. Zamoyta, Br. Casimir Stanislaus. The unity of man: St. Thomas' solution to the body-soul problem. Catholic U., 1956.

7467. Zanardi, William Joseph. Transcendental method and the crisis of historicism. Loyola, 1975. 75-22370

7468. Zandstra, Joe. Logical difficulties in the philosophy of John Ellis McTaggart. Michigan, 1934.

7469. Zaner, Richard Morris. Contributions to a phenomenology of the body. New School, 1961.

7470. Zanoni, Candido P. Logical pragamtism: the philosophy of Vailati. Minnesota, 1968. 69-1562

7471. Zartman, James Francis. Definition and open texture. Illinois, 1965. 65-7184

7472. Zawadsky, John Paul. The sources of dialectical materialism: Hegel, Marx, Engels and Lenin. Harvard, 1965.

7473. Zderad, Loretta Therese. A concept of empathy. Georgetown, 1968. 68-12814

7474. Zedler, Beatrice H. St. Thomas' critique of Avicennianism in the De potentia Dei. Fordham, 1947.

7475. Zeigler, Gregory Moncure. Aristotle's views on akrasia. U.C.L.A., 1973. 73-18656

7476. Zeigler, Harley Herschel. Some aspects of the concept of unconscious purpose in modern philosophy. Boston U., 1940.

7477. Zeiler, Sr. M. Judith. From contingency to hope (Merleau-Ponty's phenomenological philosophy in its impact upon his religious thought.) Duquesne, 1968.

7478. Zeldin, Mary-Barbara K. Kant's doctrine of moral freedom. Radcliffe, 1950.

7479. Zeller, Dennis Edward. The limits of freedom. Texas, 1975. 76-14541

7480. Zellner, Harold Marcellars. The logic of imperatives. Miami, 1971. 72-12897

7481. Zeltner, Philip Miles. The aesthetic philosophy of John Dewey. Buffalo, 1974. 75-1532

7482. Zemach, Eddy Mordekai. The boundaries of the aesthetic domain. Yale, 1965. 65-9736

7483. Zeman, Joseph Jay. The graphical logic of C.S. Peirce. Chicago, 1964.

7484. Zenzen, Michael John, Jr. Aesthetic experience and corporeal being-in-the-world: an aesthetic theory founded on the phenomenological ontology of M. Merleau-Ponty. R.P.I., 1973. 74-5161

7485. Zerby, Lewis Kenneth. Hans Kelsen's Reine rechtslehre. Iowa, 1945.

7486. Zeuschner, R.B. The thought of the Ch'an (Zen) master Ho-tse Shen-hui and the conflict between the northern and southern schools of Ch'an Buddhism. Hawaii, 1975.

7487. Zeyl, Donald John. *Geneis* and *onsia* in the metaphysics of Plato. Harvard, 1972.

7488. Ziegler, Howard J.B. Frederick Augustus Rauch; American Hegelian. Columbia, 1950.   2362

7489. Ziegler, William John, Jr. The legal and political theories of Oliver Wendell Holmes. Notre Dame, 1969.   69-18520

7490. Ziff, Robert P. The notion of a work of art with special reference to the esthetic theory of R.G. Collingwood. Cornell, 1952.

7491. Zimmerman, Gabriel Aaron. John Laird on the autonomy of ethics. St. Louis, 1969.   70-20430

7492. Zimmerman, Marvin. A defense of the verifiability principle. N.Y.U., 1958.   61-2603

7493. Zimmerman, Michael Edward. The concept of self in Martin Heidegger's *Being and time*. Tulane, 1974.   74-20780

7494. Zimmerman, Philip William. Freedom and determinism: as treated in the philosophy of contemporary physics. N.Y.U., 1972.   72-26627

7495. Zimmerman, Robert Lloyd. Kant, Schiller, and Hegel: a study in metaphysical aesthetics. N.Y.U., 1962.   62-5389

7496. Zink, Sidney. A critique of the ethical theory of John Dewey. Cincinnati, 1941.

7497. Ziyadah, Ma'an. The theory of motion in Ibn Bajjah's philosophy. McGill, 1973.

7498. Zoecklein, Walter Otto. The ontological commitments in stoic logic. Cal., S. Diego, 1969.   69-19703

7499. Zonneveld, Rev. Leo J. The notion of Christian philosophy according to Maurice Blondel. Catholic U., 1968.   69-9105

7500. Zuckerstaetter, Rudolf. Schopenhauer's objections to Kant's moral philosophy. Harvard, 1970.

7501. Zuniga, Joaquin Alberto. Practical criticism and metacriticism. Berkeley, 1973.

7502. Zweig, Arnulf. Theories of real definition: a study of the views of Aristotle, C.I. Lewis, and Wittgenstein. Stanford, 1960. 60-2417

7503. Zweig, Marilyn Broadribb. Dispositional and non-dispositional properties and predicates. Rochester, 1963. 63-7786

INDEX

Abbagnano, N., 3769
Abbott, F.E., 914
Abelard, P., 4201
abortion, 2534, 2699, 4548, 4934
Abraham Ibn Daud, 169
absolute, 314, 433, 1584, 6526, 6821, 6931, 7356, 7403
abstract entities, 362, 2326, 2592, 4435, 7009, 7252
abstract ideas, 4516, 7188
abstraction, 756, 1946, 3455, 3959, 4251, 5582, 6198, 6261, 7327
accident, 729, 2096
accounting, 137
Achillini, A., 4450
Ackermann, R., 2545, 5274
acrasia, 4742
action, 140, 149, 211, 216, 304, 381, 385, 413, 416, 546, 651, 672, 684, 797, 959, 989, 998, 1159, 1218, 1229, 1273, 1384, 1394, 1481, 1514, 1734, 2002, 2394, 2415, 2443, 2458, 2695, 2846, 3171, 3211, 3467, 3640, 3808, 3849, 3964, 4030, 4060, 4079, 4107, 4237, 4241, 4308, 4332, 4363, 4481, 4504, 4557, 4567, 4574, 4704, 4879, 4933, 4971, 4985, 5044, 5192, 5276, 5489, 5537, 5550, 5656, 5902, 5973, 5996, 6029, 6119, 6333, 6458, 6574, 6734, 6818, 6889, 6987, 7071, 7102, 7109, 7135, 7168, 7317, 7334, 7396, 7449
active intellect, 1123
Adam, 4741
Adams, H., 5880
ad hoc hypotheses, 3873
adhyasa, 716
Adler, F., 5488
aesthetics, 23, 57, 112, 147, 231, 671, 776, 892, 924, 1049, 1058, 1150, 1157, 1223, 1227, 1701, 1824, 1980, 1996, 2072, 2273, 2572, 2680, 2824, 2855, 2903, 3002, 3032, 3059, 3300, 3348, 3517, 3620, 3693, 3762, 3812, 3834, 3851, 3905, 3930, 3931, 3943, 3965, 4111, 4198, 4347, 4355, 4483, 4488, 4679, 4721, 4847, 4916, 5163, 5239, 5268, 5339, 5388, 5415, 5426, 5485, 5496, 5635, 5637, 5692, 5739, 5795, 5825, 5897, 6107, 6116, 6226, 6227, 6271, 6324, 6439, 6504, 6505, 6612, 6657, 6725, 6743, 6750, 6926, 6978, 7023, 7041, 7119, 7151, 7288, 7289, 7321, 7482;
adjustment in, 824; Alain, 3320; Alexander, S., 3946; ancient philosophy, 325; Aquinas, T., 917, 4900; Augustine, 480, 1083; beauty, 928, 1083, 1705, 5041, 5817; Bonaventure, 6361; Bosanquet, B., 5100; Bullough, E., 5313; Burke, E., 4687; Collingwood, R.G.,

3348, 4621, 5302, 7490; Cousin, V., 7280; Croce, B., 1718, 1957, 2937, 4856; Delacroix, H., 6109; Dewey, J., 2937, 4446, 6548, 6630, 6920, 7481; Diderot, D., 2208; and epistemology, 926, 2210; Gill, E., 3441; Goethe, J., 642; Goodman, N., 3245; Greek, 141; Hall, E., 6735; Hegel, G., 2811, 3591, 7495; Heidegger, M., 2439, 3894; Herder, J.G., 1624; history of, 3554; Humboldt, W., 4362; Hume, D., 2653; Hutcheson, F., 2653, 3634; Jarvis, J., 3027; Japanese, 5112; Jordan, E., 5636, 7246; Jung, C.G., 5325, 6920; judgment in, 3226, 6754; Kant, E., 1362, 1773, 1868, 2378, 2424, 3402, 3591, 3634, 4021, 4316, 4416, 4908, 5302, 5628, 5860, 6337, 6397, 6863, 7408, 7495; Kames, H., 3167; Langer, S., 802, 2216, 3732; linguistic method in, 1338; literature, 103; Leontiev, K., 5155; Lewis, C.I., 5162; Lukacs, G., 1589; Maimon, S., 4416; Maritain, J., 2700; Marx, K., 6826; Merleau-Ponty, M., 5359, 7484; Moritz, C.P., 1886, Nietzsche, F., 139, 432, 6848; objectificational, 116; objectivity in, 5824; Ortega y Gasset, J., 3311; Peirce, C.S., 6065; photography, 4707; Plato, 919, 2243, 3300, 4772, 5532, 6381; Prall, 477; pre-Kantians, 693; pre-Socratics, 7390; reaction terms, 966; reason in, 2254; Richards, I., 491; Santayana, G., 179, 198, 6213, 6548; Schiller, F., 7495; Schopenhauer, A., 26, 3591; self in, 156; Shaftesbury, 2332; Shi Too, 1230; Tagore, R., 2243; Taine, H., 7362; truth in, 1493; values in, 191, 6536;

Whitehead, A.N., 5424, 6140, 6275, 7001; Zeising, A., 731
Africa, 5060
Agassiz, L., 885
aitia, 815
Alain, 3320, 7454
Alan of Lille, 5402
al-Balighah, 3346
Alberdi, J.B., 5218
Albertus Magnus, abstraction, 3455; agent intellect, 4596; god, 1039; illumination, 3455; logic, 1266, 6776, 7083; motion, 4148; prudence, 5236; psychology, 5577; substantial form, 3862
Alexander of Aphrodisias, 1337, 6393
Alexander Sermoneta, 1766
Alexander, F.M., 4139
Alexander, H.B., 1326
Alexander, S., 3386, 5523; aesthetics, 3946; ethics, 3625; mind, 2462; naturalism, 4114; nature, 4037; space, 1543; teleology, 5482; time, 1543; value, 1378, 2626
Al-Ghazzali, 4381, 4848, 6768
alienation, 1873, 2034, 3773, 4546, 4802, 5604, 5933, 6221, 6225, 7061, 7092, 7239
Allport, G., 1268, 2802, 3485
Al Raqqad, 323
Alston, 6256
altruism, 4620, 4844, 5545, 6009
ambiguity, 1831
American philosophy, 334, 1541, 2623, 3275, 4213, 5702
analogy, 844, 1569, 1703, 2768, 4490, 5780, 6595
analyticity, 353, 730, 794, 818, 876, 977, 1602, 2320, 3118, 3207, 4442, 5374, 5376, 7317
anarchy, 3, 3268, 6523
Anatoli, J., 2450
Anaxagoras, 1151

Anaximander, 1742
angels, 1244, 5801
anger, 516, 7243
animal rights, 512
animism, 144
Anselm, St., 1641, 2005, 2286, 3014, 3723, 5378, 6010, 6084, 6582, 7016, 7217
anthropology, 1245, 1789, 2421, 5267, 7028
anti-semitism, 3895
Antonius Andreae, 608
anxiety, 631
aphasia, 1654
appearance, 136, 537
a priori, 1036, 2490, 2760, 3219, 4062, 4336, 5164, 5394, 5832, 7194, 7456
Apuleius of Madaura, 6565
Aquinas, T., 321, 405, 587, 1745, 2271, 2606, 3105, 3734, 4639, 4740, 4857, 5002, 5092, 5846, 6436, 6732, 6852, 7008, 7474; absolute, 901; abstraction, 4251, 6198, 7327; accident, 729, 2096; action, 3604, 4481, 7334; aesthetics, 917, 4900; agent intellect, 979; agriculture, 4162; altruism, 4620; analogy, 5780; angels, 1243, 5801; Aristotle, 2918, 3030, 3442; Aristotelianism, 2840; authority, 2091; beauty, 1705; becoming, 6694; being, 176, 1976, 2672, 3121, 4427, 5003, 5955, 7395; belief, 400; body, 126; casus, 6845; causality, 1963, 2487, 3621, 4028, 4089, 4493, 4655, 5427; certitude, 2342, 2549; chance, 3312; change, 1122; cognition, 664; conaturality, 3399; conscience, 3459; creation, 2163; definition, 165; desire, 6274; economics, 5629; education, 3180, 4869; emotion, 3326; epistemology, 5427; essence, 4784, 5082; ethics, 405, 495, 559, 3192, 4709, 4815, 5118, 5241, 7413, 7426; evil, 1327, 1554; existence, 2284, 3098, 3610, 6788;
finality, 5010; form, 2403; free will, 1466, 4723; friendship, 677, 4644; God, 297, 778, 994, 1690, 2265, 2316, 3408, 5031, 5712, 5728, 6593, 7242; good, 2928, 7446; habitus, 609; happiness, 167, 1573, 6121; hope, 1578; illumination, 2912; immortality, 7068; individual, 6246; individuation, 3178, 5763; intellect, 404, 1166, 3437, 3955, 7334; judgment, 199; knowledge, 4236, 5799, 6378; labor, 3501; law, 3107, 3534, 3660; liberty, 5849; life, 2284; logic, 5977; love, 5788, 5799; man, 236, 929, 3955, 6588, 6747, 7466; mathematics, 133; matter, 2403, 3030; metaphysics, 1642, 2543, 4368, 4709, 4986, 6329, 6556, 6788; mind, 4955; natural law, 388, 632, 5866; nature, 1717, 4095, 4380, 4458; necessity, 3064; obedience, 4235; ontology, 4424; optimism, 4170; order, 3337; passions, 254; perfection, 521; person, 7060, 2091; phantom, 1184; physics, 280, 4777; Plato, 973, 6518; pleasure, 5607; political philosophy, 1715, 1814, 2008, 2569, 3303, 3354, 4078, 4199; possible intellect, 2151; property, 4167; prudence, 847, 4235, 5548, 6315; psychology, 5013, 5033; punishment, 2177; quality, 1575; rational soul, 663; reason, 4420; relation, 2668, 3357, 3639; religion, 658; self-determination, 2343; sensation, 3437, 3443, 3582; sex, 6780; shame, 2832; social philosophy, 677, 1347, 2041, 2998, 4294, 4836, 5108, 5166, 6366, 6949, 7361; soul, 3742,

5665, 6250; spirit, 6773; substance, 556, 5269; substantial forms, 1037, 2312, 4597; suicide, 4979; Summa theologica, 7213; teleology, 6499; Tertia via, 3583; time, 5473, 5551; transcendence, 6853; truth, 4295; universals, 1158, 3587, 6567; utopianism, 3828; value, 176, 639, 7067; virtues, 495, 3952, 5306; vis cogitiva, 940, 3579; will, 254, 7334; wisdom, 5043; worship, 2345
Arabic philosophy, 1945, 3892, 6056, 6113
Arendt, H., 3563
Aristophanes, 980
Aristotle, 2776, 2812, 2955, 3442, 4444, 4991, 5096, 5293, 5461, 5888, 6298, 6393, 6422, 6907, 6982, 7307, 7437; abstraction, 4251; action, 3640, 7109; akrasia, 7045, 7089, 7148, 7475; analogy, 1669; Aquinas, T., 4779; being, 154, 498, 782, 3136, 3185, 4575, 5955; biology, 182, 1804, 2716, 4130, 5428; categories, 507, 1186, 3699, 4029, 5309, 5937, 6921; causality, 4089, 4493; change, 3640, 6360, 7360, 7451; choice, 2115; cognition, 6655; concept, 2628; definition, 3805, 6906, 7502; education, 3180, 3740; emotion, 5371; energeia, 514; entelektheia, 514; epsitemology, 3065; error, 6938; eternity, 1474; ethics, 168, 1630, 2260, 3192, 3643, 3928, 4279, 5718, 6102, 6601; evil, 1283; evolution, 6715; existence, 3185; final cause, 2465; freedom, 1311; friendship, 4644, 6102, 7274; gravity, 3668; heroes, 1471; individual, 5565; infinite, 1825; intellect, 7199, 7384; knowledge, 3707, 3866, 4608; language, 1186, 2529, 3780; logic, 458, 1759, 4349, 4635, 5589; mathematics, 133, 157, 2591, 5574, 5650; matter, 3030; mean, 3377; memory, 557; metaphor, 1147; metaphysics, 1937, 2325, 3252, 3461, 4152, 4368, 5682, 6259, 6478; Meteorologica, 1337; movement, 313, 6624; music, 6025; nature, 659, 1426, 6649; necessity, 3697; number, 148; opposition, 228; perception, 6240, 6938; Perihermenias, 2231; Physics, 1054, 2918, 3743; physis, 4000; Plato, 148, 1143, 5058; Platonism, 2881; pleasure, 319; poetry, 5058; politics, 2569, 5212; possibility, 1474; predication, 513, 4776, 5731; principles, 5741; prudence, 5083; psychology, 6173; relation, 2668; responsibility, 679; Rhetoric, 1374; science, 4240; sense-perception, 533, 2969, 3970; soul, 723, 1038, 1151, 2781; spirit, 6773; substance, 5682, 6607, 7130, 7231, 7360; substantial form, 2733; syllogism, 2635; time, 3715; truth, 2791; universals, 3587
Armstrong, D.M., 4058, 4806, 5627, 5885, 7024
Arnauld, A., 1287, 3663, 7439
Arrow, K., 3891
art, 184, 1227, 1789, 1933 2893; creativity in, 2809; emotion in, 535; expression in, 992; and Hegel, 2006, and knowledge, 3239; and language, 1001
Asconius, 5510
assent, 291, 1047, 5806, 6858
assertion, 2608, 3788, 4356, 5134, 6356
association, 2315, 6634
astronomy, 3590, 3962
atheism, 955, 1813
Athenagoras, 4061

490

atomism, 412, 481, 5159, 5297, 5422
atonement, 2405
attention, 4700, 6866
Atticus, 3879
Augustine, St., 2223, 2266, 2799, 2807, 3304, 5006, 6994, 6999, 7008; aesthetics, 480; beauty, 1083; Confessions, 3091; creation, 803, 2265, 5114, 6999; education, 3180, 3484; epistemology, 779, 1341, 4456, 4744, 4861; essence, 2729; ethics, 787; faith, 1237, 3914; freedom, 1156, 1311, 4209; free will, 2921; God, 2265, 4137, 6272, 6763, 6928; judicium, 791; man, 4137, 6912; metaphor, 1147; nature, 3010; necessity, 4209; perception, 5979; political philosophy, 459, 2168; rationes seminales, 638, 4232; reason, 1237, 3914; science, 5598; sensation, 2238, 3582; sense knowledge, 1120; sin, 583; soul, 5030; stoicism, 3007; superbia, 4291; teleology, 6499; time, 891; truth, 1597, 4746; wisdom, 5598; wonder, 5598
Aurobindo Ghose, 349, 774, 1614, 2009, 3062, 3617, 3674, 3829
Austin, J.L., 1643, 1942, 1954, 2380, 3626, 4618, 5101, 6740, 6954; epistemology, 3710; sense-data, 473, 1882, 6755; truth, 382, 4448
authenticity, 691, 2470, 3429
authority, 235, 595, 696, 845, 1680, 2091, 3615, 3733, 4310, 5720
autonomy, 780
Avenarius, R., 862, 1345
Averroes, 835, 1123, 2325, 4381, 5659, 6768
Averroism, 4126
Avicenna, 4705, 7474; good, 3199; logic, 323, 3540; miracles, 204
awareness, 3883
Ayer, A.J., 473, 983, 1882, 1942, 3235, 3276, 7010

Babbitt, I., 4266, 7074
Bachmanns, I., 3022
Bacon, F., 1477, 4076, 5266, 5441, 6326, 6689, 6791
Bacon, R., 1809, 3637
Baconthorpe, J., 1920
bad faith, 547
Baeumker, C., 565
Baier, K., 4624
Bagavad Gita, 3854
Bakunin, M., 2654
Baldwin, J.M., 3016, 4660
Balfour, A.J., 360
Bañez, D., 3983
Banfi, A., 5337
Barfield, 1511
Barth, K., 89, 4653
Bartley, W.W., 2705
Bautain, L., 3055
Bayle, P., 1417
Beardsley, M.C., 6191, 7435
Beardsmore, R.W., 5639
beatitude, 808
becoming, 257, 1125, 3090, 6694
behavior, 214, 1418, 1949, 2022, 2173, 2533, 2704, 2911, 3068, 3469, 3523, 4228, 4512, 5020, 5231, 6027, 6294
behaviorism, 553, 1637, 2396, 2437, 3003, 4146, 4970, 5734, 6096, 6169, 7287, 7407
being, 233, 804, 859, 1059, 2334, 2757, 2787, 2796, 5106, 5327, 5439; Aquinas, T., 1976, 2672, 3121, 4427, 5003, 5955, 6266, 7395; Aristotle, 498, 782, 3136, 4575, 5955; Blondel, M., 6347; Boethius, 1976; Cajetan, T., 4273; Capreolus, 1620; Duhem, P., 5078; Duns Scotus, J., 6158; Eckhart, 4786; Ficino, M., 1239; Hartshorne, C., 7372; Heidegger, M., 242, 318, 2581, 2956, 3355, 3894, 4337, 4428, 6055, 6062, 6997, 7097,

7117; Hervaeus Natalis, 81; Leibniz, G., 6347; Ortega y Gasset, J., 3400; Parmenides, 6385; Plato, 1022, 3480, 3664, 4479, 4697, 7025; Royce, J., 2099, 4531; Suarez, F., 1012, 1530; Teichmüller, 6941; Tillich, P., 4930; Thomas of York, 2264, 5578; Ulrich of Strasbourg, 1238, 5014; Whitehead, A.N., 2090; Wittgenstein, 5433
belief, 150, 346, 372, 400, 798, 993, 1017, 1314, 1401, 1849, 1933, 1991, 2116, 2279, 2319, 2364, 2452, 2933, 3424, 3533, 3847, 3920, 4030, 4122, 4508, 4543, 4912, 5059, 5242, 5725, 5771, 7278, 7405
Ben Asher, B., 4566
Benedict of Assignano, 1529
Beneke, F.F., 1289
Bentham, J., 1934, 2425, 2732, 4172, 5016
Berdyaev, N., 223, 1635, 1738, 1794, 2438, 3334, 3456, 4984, 5332, 5626, 6094, 6468, 7284
Bergmann, G., 1360, 4054, 4669, 7056
Bergson, H., 1173, 4031, 5248, 5944, 5978, 6404; action, 7460; causality, 1544; change, 1544; consciousness, 5432; creation, 6406; duration, 1544, 5183; élan vital, 3386; ethics, 54, 1767, 1782, 2224, 5869, 6880, 6881; evolution, 4268; experience, 4257; finality, 2259, 2900; freedom, 4627, 4719, 7340; God, 1672; history, 5432; identity, 6744; intuition, 2599, 3754, 4627, 5587; liberty, 945; matter, 4469; metaphysics, 504, 4271, 4719; mortality, 4652; perception, 3233, 7460; person, 4928; personalism, 5258; political philosophy, 5477; pragmatism, 2192; religion, 1767, 4680; space, 7108; time, 7108; value, 5753; world, 1066
Berkeley, G., 2182, 2330, 3221, 3314, 3361, 3734, 4534, 4945, 6047, 6731; abstraction, 756, 3959; empiricism, 1247; epistemology, 884; ethics, 1278, 3095, 5070; idealism, 978, 1546, 2598, 4134, 6539, 6794; ideas, 6937, 7188; image, 1512; immaterialism, 626, 1965; language, 915, 1278, 2373, 5529; mathematics, 336; meaning, 1003, 6929; nature, 3120; notions, 5174; objects, 1682; perception, 6395; realism, 5743; relativity, 3790; science, 715, 6187; senses, 2969; signs, 4193; substance, 606, 3519; truth, 3024; universals, 1009; utilitarianism, 3704
Bernard of Clairvaux, 810, 1720, 5017
Bernardus Sylvestris, 4145
Berthier, G.F., 3771
Bhartrhari, 51
Binswanger, L., 4878
biology, 488, 2167, 3119, 3198, 3623, 3846, 5366, 5913, 6575; Aristotle, 182, 1804, 2716, 4130, 5428; Darwin, 4130; epistemology, 1817; ethics, 3929; history of, 903; teleology in, 494, 1423, 4120, 6126; Weismann, A., 4130
black culture, 5123
black protest, 621
blaming, 1222
Blanshard, B., 1170, 2087, 3096, 3276, 4094, 5249
Blondel, M., 916, 2379, 3211, 3804, 4890, 5864, 6040, 6347, 6383, 6605
Blood, B.P., 4377
body, 122, 140, 149, 269, 4994, 5161, 6758, 7469; Aquinas, T., 122; Descartes, R., 1004, 3037; Merleau-Ponty, M., 308, 437, 1185, 1851, 2691,

6388; Whitehead, A.N., 2691
Boehme, J., 76, 690, 4823
Boethius, 27, 1976, 2097, 5039, 5092, 6542
Bohr, N., 4027, 4174
Bolivar, S., 5149
Bonaventure, St., 3324, 4317, 5472, 5672, 5852; aesthetics, 6361; causality, 5086; conscience, 2820; creation, 633; epistemology, 1449; evil, 3556; God, 4445; good, 3556, 7048; illumination, 2912; knowledge, 5991; love, 5421; man, 5057; ontology, 101; psychology, 5033; social philosophy, 1540
Bonhoeffer, D., 3066, 7127
Bonner, H., 558
Boodin, J.E., 3016, 6583
Bosanquet, B., 344, 877, 996, 1987, 2234, 2970, 3721, 4011, 4724, 4920, 5100, 5482, 5952, 5986
Boss, M., 4394
Bostrom, C.J., 369
Bowne, B.P., 2150, 3815, 4373, 5309, 5457, 5507
Boyle, R., 554, 1403, 1746, 2042, 5116
Bradley, F.H., 610, 3483, 4177, 5749, 5783, 5940, 6217, 6469, 6905, 6971; ethics, 170, 647, 1179, 2706; existence, 2234; experience, 4217; freedom, 4290; good, 1302; judgment, 740, 3155; logic, 3321, 5104; man, 4138; metaphysics, 376, 408, 3307, 6678, 7433; reality, 2234; relations, 1440; religion, 1179; self, 2970, 3417, 4875; thought, 2234; truth, 6419; universals, 1768
Bradwardine, T., 1399, 4109, 4803
Brandt, R., 254
Brecht, B., 435
Bremond, H., 938
Brentano, F., 2033, 4636, 7410; ethics, 357, 4093, 6673; ontology, 2188; psychology, 1917, 6807
Breton, A., 4980

Bridgman, P.W., 3593
Brightman, E.S., 305, 474, 2246, 3570, 4183, 4632, 4785, 5437, 5503, 6353, 6759, 6897, 6910
Brito, F., 6545
Broad, C.D., 2103, 2297, 2340, 2589, 3083, 3089, 3696, 3819, 4043, 4997, 5970, 6840
Brooks, P., 2736
Brown, N.O., 3251
Brown, T., 3251
Brownson, O., 1467, 2643, 4108, 4554, 4695, 4922, 5492, 5644
Brunet, C., 574
Brunner, E., 450, 803, 846, 4962, 5831
Bruno, G., 2097, 2524, 5209, 5407, 6875
Brunschvicg, L., 1861
Buber, M., 303, 309, 3180, 4691, 4770, 6296, 7376
Buddhism, 1065, 1071, 1534, 1606, 2601, 3236, 3372, 6701, 7174, 7346, 7486
Buffier, C., 4367, 6984
Buffon, G.L., 1962
Bullough, E., 5313
Bultmann, R., 2631
Buridan, J., 4646, 5677, 6046, 6357
Burke, E., 4687, 7275
Burley, W., 3549
Butler, J., 2765, 4750, 6770, 7226; ethics, 970, 3859, 4112, 4977, 5486, 5594, 6654, 7107, 7240
Butler, S., 5530
Butterfield, H., 1765

cabala, 526
Cajetan, T., 4273, 5579, 5983
Calkins, M.W., 2496
Cambridge Platonists, 215, 3714
Campanella, T., 581, 5560
Campbell, C.A., 11, 2153, 2874
Camus, A., 1919, 2476, 5513, 6390; man, 472; society, 472

493

can, 7058
Capreolus, J., 1620
Carlyle, T., 4880, 6512
Carnap, R., 748, 876, 1368, 1602, 3294, 3902, 4553, 4972, 6629, 7027, 7096, 7252
Carnell, E.J., 305
Carritt, E.F., 4048
Cartesianism, 207
Carus, P., 6142, 6151
Caso, A., 44, 2558, 5218
Cassirer, E., 3403, 6555; concept, 301, 1993; culture, 5289; epistemology, 3073, 7033; history, 1536, 4242; language, 6223; man, 6996; meaning, 3963; mind, 2462; myth, 1182, 1326; objectivity, 6076; reference, 3963; science, 7033, 7359; symbols, 3678; value, 3678
categorical imperative, 2943, 5401
categories, 1610, 3169, 3362, 3896, 4260, 5105, 5760; Aristotle, 507, 3669, 4029, 5309, 5937, 6921; Bowne, B.P., 5309; James, W., 5364; Kant, E., 4102, 5309, 6921; Mill, J.S., 1212; category mistakes, 1943, 4407; Ockham, W., 4029; Peirce, C.S., 364, 881, 1969, 4002, 4102, 5779, 6921; Spencer, H., 5364; Strawson, P.F., 5779; Whitehead, A.N., 2426
causality, 21, 48, 74, 541, 612, 685, 755, 935, 998, 1007, 1407, 1442, 1490, 2026, 2098, 2200, 2457, 2607, 3005, 3047, 3068, 3096, 3332, 3543, 3672, 3849, 3850, 3991, 4411, 5037, 5120, 5230, 5335, 5490, 5550, 5585, 5693, 6073, 6254, 6294, 6333, 6640, 6815, 6861, 6884, 6908, 6939, 7093, 7168, 7209, 7316, 7389; Aquinas, T., 1963, 2487, 3621, 4028, 4089, 4493, 4655, 5427; Bergson, H., 1544; Bonaventure, St., 5086; Cavalcanti, G., 497; Ducasse, C.J., 3111; Hume, D., 366, 1638, 5816, 6793, 6977; Kant, E., 4712, 5816, 6977; Lamprecht, S., 1208; Ockham, Wm. of, 828; Peter of Auvergne, 1784; Taylor, R., 317; Whitehead, A.N., 1696, 3140, 6793
certainty, 1425, 1618, 2342, 2407, 2549, 2977, 3179, 3444, 3552, 3606, 4053, 4088, 4623, 5385, 5555, 6326, 6919
Cervantes, 1482
Chaadayev, P.I., 4747
chance, 1173, 2689, 3312, 6705
change, 181, 1122, 1544, 3640, 5102, 6360, 7451
character, 1855, 3147
chemistry, 564, 3695
Cheng, I., 6827
Chicherin, B., 2473
Chinese philosophy, 5984, 6043, 6152, 6359
Chisholm, R., 571, 4058, 5759, 5773, 7351
choice, 840, 3947, 4983, 5135, 5724
Chomsky, N., 1899, 2039, 3494, 4626, 6399, 6432, 6993
Christian Science, 6438
Chrysippus, 2472
Chuang Tzu, 1072
Chu Hsi, 7455
church, 6709
Cicero, 1060, 1177, 2885, 3974, 4451, 5136
cinema, 2724, 3092, 4202
civil disobedience, 438, 1134, 1967, 3430, 6082
civilization, 3589, 4639, 6508
Clapiers, L. de, 6963
Clarke, S., 4066, 6441
classes, 172, 1008, 2171, 3006
Clifford, W.K., 6309
coercion, 1792
cogito, 98, 207, 7035; Descartes, R., 368, 2223, 4083; Hintikka, J., 4083; Merleau-Ponty, M., 858
cognition, 384, 664, 2420, 3449, 5270, 5716, 6655,

7232, 7418
Cohen, F.S., 3629
Cohen, H., 4506
Cohen, M.R., 1421, 3786, 4258, 5491, 5793
Coleridge, S.T., 5534, 6646
Collingwood, R.G., 1539, 3654, 6230, 6292, 6412, 6511, 7123; action, 2394; aesthetics, 3348, 4621, 5302, 7490; history, 1580, 3042, 4439, 4897, 5706, 5814, 5837; logic, 1352; man, 4412, 7409; metaphysics, 1389, 2062, 2130, 5917; reality, 1878
color, 6823
comedy, 5171, 7254
commands, 7126
commitment, 509
common sense, 66, 1178, 2967, 3189, 3600, 3646, 4367, 4749, 4973
communication, 171, 930, 1388, 1556, 2746, 2910, 3196, 3904, 4849, 5023, 5390, 5438, 5525, 6229, 7277
communism, 1668, 5956
community, 3690, 5429, 6864; Dewey, J., 6279; Macmurray, J., 3779; Marcel, G., 4549; Marx, K., 4495; Peirce, C.S., 1587, 6961; Royce, J., 4959, 6280, 6386; Scheler, M., 5515
complementation, 6792
computers, 4670
Comte, A., 1509, 2595, 4798, 4811
conaturality, 3399
concepts, 104, 219, 252, 262, 301, 775, 823, 1052, 1993, 2011, 2628, 4713, 5067, 5197, 5602, 5935, 6034, 7021, 7059
Condillac, E. de, 982
confirmation, 13, 2697, 3706, 6155, 6662, 6667, 7443
conflict, 3138
Confucianism, 173, 1080, 1097, 1526, 3085, 3395, 3688, 4633, 4753, 5808, 7182
Conrad, J., 373

Conrad-Martius, H., 2773
conscience, 770, 2497, 2820, 3129, 3278, 3459, 6770, 6800, 7240
consciousness, 177, 1233, 1465, 1902, 2384, 2992, 4515, 5512, 6117, 6137, 6212, 6444, 7314; altered states of, 3471; Armstrong, D., 5627; Berdyaev, N., 5332; Bergson, H., 5432; computer, 4670; Descartes, R., 7227; Fichte, J.G., 3845; Hume, D., 38; Husserl, E., 4816; Jaspers, K., 5332; Kant, E., 4514; Merleau-Ponty, M., 4816; Nicholas of Cusa, 1026; Plotinus, 7073; Ramanuja, 1107; Sartre, J.-P., 469, 540, 1233, 3451, 4211, 4816, 5965; Teilhard de Chardin, P., 1391, 3956, 7132; Vygotsky, L.S., 436; Whitehead, A.N., 4968, 5408
conscription, 5946, 6168, 6398
consequences, 387
consistency, 4280
constatives, 796
contingency, 3509, 3903, 4066, 4484, 5687, 6525
continuity, 407, 1081
contractualism, 7465
contradiction, 1979, 6507
contrary to fact, 5988
convention, 4246
conversion, 5128
Copernicus, N., 2723
cosmological argument, 1258, 1376
cosmology, 83, 502, 666, 839, 2719, 3568, 4075, 4990, 5091, 5651, 5695, 6133, 6759
counter-factuals, 2745, 3271, 3712, 4090, 7447
courage, 561
Cournot, A.A., 2075, 2258, 4491
Cousin, V., 7280
creation, 633, 2107, 2500, 3450, 4909, 6691; Aquinas, T., 2163, 2265; Aristotle,

2265; Augustine, 803, 5114;
  Bergson, H., 6406; Brunner,
  E., 803; Giles of Rome, 964;
  Gregory of Nyssa, 2789; Plato, 803
creativity, 348, 719, 855,
  1254, 1420, 2809, 3062,
  3080, 6502
Crescas, H., 7104
criminology, 1340, 2232, 2291,
  2502, 2941, 4379
crisis, 3546
criteria, 1491, 1562, 2518,
  3143
Croce, B., 1014, 1584, 1718,
  1957, 2135, 2501, 2937,
  4564, 4856
Crombie, I.M., 2554
Cudworth, R., 4539, 5926
culture, 3561, 4639, 5289,
  6042, 6598, 6644, 6753,
  7012, 7143, 7331
Cumberland, R., 961
custom, 3855
cybernetics, 3409, 6167
cynicism, 5919

Dante Alighieri, 5735
Darwin, C., 515, 531, 4130
Dauthendey, M., 7183
Davidson, T., 571, 912
death, 1121, 2685, 3804, 5381
Debray, R., 5506
decision, 2895, 3202, 3318,
  3728, 5537, 5643, 5998, 7424
deduction, 2814, 6416
definition, 8, 165, 338, 714,
  1051, 1074, 1577, 2142,
  3805, 6906, 7471, 7502
Deism, 2847, 3544, 3797, 4690
Delacroix, F., 6109
deliberation, 741, 5854
democracy, 296, 1785, 2714,
  3875, 3891, 3967, 4092,
  4153, 4833, 5027, 5758,
  6138, 6225, 6437
Derrida, 92
Descartes, R., 454, 830, 1041,
  2217, 2901, 3122, 3270,
  3361, 3919, 4710, 4765,
  5147, 5526, 5749, 6008,
  6144; body, 1004, 3037;
  certainty, 4726, 6326;
  change, 7451; <u>cogito</u>, 368,
  2223, 2420, 4083; con-
  sciousness, 7227; dualism,
  6080; error, 4417; ethics,
  1415, 5918; existence,
  1393; experience, 1163;
  God, 4296, 5015, 6916;
  ideas, 6958; intention,
  3462; language, 3227;
  man, 2052; material substance, 292; metaphysics,
  749, 1293, 2555, 3327;
  mind/body, 536; other
  minds, 7228; physics,
  4296; realism, 1280, 5081;
  scepticism, 1377, 4813;
  science, 982, 1241, 2015,
  6495, 6940; self, 4417;
  space, 4819; substance,
  2038; time, 1518; will,
  7369
descriptions, 1028
desire, 1101, 1220, 7140
detachment, 3872
determinism, 69, 361, 453,
  679, 855, 933, 939, 1025,
  1139, 1475, 2236, 2801,
  2836, 2905, 2914, 2987,
  3542, 4033, 4067, 5653,
  6036, 6139, 6596, 6640,
  6641, 6652, 6740, 6839,
  7494
Dewey, J., 119, 335, 640,
  843, 1779, 1994, 2584,
  2816, 3497, 3595, 4139,
  5036, 5318, 5734, 5923,
  6356, 6469, 6798, 6953,
  7234, 7404; aesthetics,
  2937, 4446, 6548, 6630,
  6920, 7481; communication,
  171; contemplation, 962;
  control, 1294; community,
  6279; democracy, 6437;
  education, 45, 788, 2902,
  3493, 6283; empiricism,
  6407; epistemology, 109,
  1631, 2944, 5509; ethics,
  53, 245, 703, 761, 787,
  1099, 1381, 2456, 2469,
  2688, 3019, 3703, 3822,
  4156, 4227, 4478, 4502,
  4563, 5168, 5831, 5870,
  7496; experience, 452,
  2692, 4217, 5784, 7111;
  freedom, 1653, 2063,
  4947; free-will, 447;

good, 1371, 2928; individual, 2269; inquiry, 705, 6491, 7180, 7208; instrumentalism, 962, 7230; knowledge, 6175; language, 985; liberalism, 4282; logic, 117, 701, 3067, 4011, 5024; man, 1884, 4390; Marxism, 4949; metaphysics, 2000, 2257, 3461, 6247; method, 568; naturalism, 5966, 7365; nature, 430, 2065, 5908, 7452; perception, 6059; political philosophy, 594, 1648, 3468, 5409; pragmatism, 4010, 5027; realism, 1075; reason, 965; religion, 18, 1895, 5713; science, 1689, 2527; self, 3822, 4476, 5050, 5792; social philosophy, 446, 1987, 2118, 2269, 3213, 4967, 5540, 6787; truth, 1941, 2324, 4950; utilitarianism, 2178; value, 1798, 1872, 2137, 2649, 4952, 5794, 6247
dialectic, 3503
dialectical materialism, 7255, 7472
Diderot, D., 2208, 3966, 4076, 6940, 6962, 7081
Dietrich of Freiberg, 6679
Dilthey, W., 2074, 2474, 4321, 4708, 5362, 5942, 6228, 6516, 6746
ding-an-sich, 1731, 2931, 4592, 4851, 5972
Diogenes of Sinope, 5919
Dionysius the Aeropagite, see Pseudo-Dionysius
discovery, 3691, 4289, 4331
distinction, 1837
divided line, 265
Döblin, A., 3512
Dōgen, 3506
Donne, J., 1200
Dooyeweerd, H., 1183
Dostoyevsky, F., 1619, 1919
doubt, 3241, 5479, 5538
Douglas, W., 3652
drama, 57
dreams, 1778, 5298, 5596, 6209
Dreisch, H., 7190
Dresser, H.W., 113

dualism, 552, 2666, 2904, 3116, 6080
Ducasse, C., 3111, 5892
Duff, W., 7422
Duhem, P., 958, 1787, 1995, 3305, 4042, 5078, 5475
Duméry, H., 1334, 1547
Duncan, H., 171
Duns Scotus, J., 929, 1839, 2489, 2756, 2861, 4366, 4463, 5079, 5679, 5710, 5763, 6158, 6732, 6969, 7040, 7366
Durkheim, E., 171, 4925, 5494, 7039
duty, 3465, 4063, 4164, 5286

Eckhart, M., 4359, 4665, 4786, 5993
economics, 266, 351, 1896, 2034, 2613, 3948, 4754, 4958, 5386, 5553, 5629, 5761, 5895, 6018
Edger, H., 5994
education, 161, 244, 249, 320, 799, 1270, 1275, 1398, 1657, 1918, 2023, 2059, 2070, 3274, 3773, 3821, 3824, 3944, 5284, 5305, 5405, 6350, 6663, 6676, 6810, 6935, 7015, 7098; Adams, H., 5880; Adler, F., 5488; Agassiz, L., 885; Aquinas, T., 3180, 4869; Aristotle, 3740; Augustine, 3484 Bentham, J., 4172; Bergson, H., 2155; Bosanquet, B., 5952; Brightman, E., 5508; Confucius, 1097; Dewey, J., 45, 788, 2902, 3492, 6283; ethical culture, 234; and ethics, 5201; Hegel, G., 4072; Heidegger, M., 3492; Hinsdale, B., 6578; Howland, J., 5839; humanism and, 1127, 4599; Kant, E., 5754; Kierkegaard, S., 3675; Maritain, J., 5567; Nietzsche, F., 2946; Pace, E., 653; Peters, R., 4828; Plato, 1118, 6283, 6942; Skinner, B.F., 5132;

Tolman, E., 3741; and value, 1202; Whitehead, A.N., 3298, 4662, 5807; Wittgenstein, L., 4100
Edwards, J., 134, 331, 635, 1226, 3026, 4846, 5968, 6581
Egidius Colonna, 1814
ego, 274, 3029, 3451, 6506, 7312
ego-centrism, 923
Einstein, A., 294, 4612, 4883, 6091
Eliade, M., 80
emanation, 2016
emergent evolution, 2205, 2728, 2991
Emerson, R.W., 2287, 2508, 3343, 4558, 5678, 5967, 6671
emotion, 738, 1167, 2275, 3028, 3149, 3680, 4071, 4408, 5670, 5887, 6148, 6813, 7263; Aquinas, T., 3326; Aristotle, 5371; James, W., 3616; Russell, B., 3616; Ryle, G., 3616; Sartre, J.-P., 1998
emotivism, 1528
empathy, 7473
Empedocles, 1151, 5047, 6947
empiricism, 155, 174, 352, 1247, 3054, 3711, 3902, 4718, 5198, 5848, 6075, 6364, 6394, 6407, 6454, 6756, 7378
energy, 4694, 5021, 5732
Engelbert of Admont, 2129
Engels, F., 4243, 7047
entailment, 396, 3200, 6882
Epicharmus, 4573
Epicurianism, 2382, 4383, 4485, 5422
epiphenomenalism, 78, 1829, 7077
epistemology, 367, 411, 1168, 1464, 1583, 2430, 2566, 2850, 2958, 3174, 3189, 3206, 3705, 4047, 4119, 4369, 4385, 4748, 4957, 5368, 5440, 5568, 5810, 6081, 6449, 6510, 6587, 7082; and aesthetics, 926, 2210; Aquinas, T., 5427; Aristotle, 1235, 3065;

Augustine, 779, 1341, 4456, 4746, 4861; Austin, J.L., 3710; Berdyaev, N., 1635; Berkeley, G., 884; Bernard of Clairvaux, 810; and biology, 1817; Bonaventure, St., 1449; Bowne, B.P., 5507; Broad, C.D., 2589; Bruno, G., 5209; Butterfield, H., 1765; Campanella, T., 581; Cassirer, E., 3073, 7033; definition, 8; Dewey, J., 109, 1631, 2944, 5509; and economics, 2613; Edwards, J., 1226; Epicurean, 2382; ethical models in, 833; Four, V. du, 4080; Gassendi, P., 1842; Godfrey of Fontaine, 4792; Gregory of Nyssa, 7160; Hägerström, A., 5883; Hegel, G., 1678, 6342; Henry of Ghent, 739; Hicks, G., 773; Hobbes, T., 551, 3256; Hobhouse, L.T., 5383; Hugh of St. Victor, 3569; Hume, D., 599, 655, 879, 884, 1501, 4578, 7458; Husserl, E., 879, 4578; James, W., 1312, 3367; judgment, 2986; Kant, E., 1443, 4339, 4358, 4606, 5350; Lewes, G., 2044; Lewis, C.I., 1274, 1751, 2671, 2977, 7042, 7105, 7459; Locke, J., 884, 2541, 4671, 7394; Lossky, N., 3608; Lotze, R., 3653; Maritain, J., 5068; Mill, J.S., 2888, 4294; Mead, G.H., 2064, 3287; monism, 3811; Moore, G.E., 2894, 3571, 3779, 4289, 6218, 7371; naturalism, 3802; negation, 1160; neuroepistemology, 131; Newman, J., 1392; Nietzsche, F., 655; Norris, J., 4698; operationalism, 1625; Origen, 1502; Peirce, C.S., 2468, 2944, 4896, 6554; phenomenalism, 1694; Piaget, J., 3065; Plato, 743, 812, 897, 1235, 1277, 2580,

3170, 3877, 4852; Poincaré, H., 5223; Polanyi, M., 4008, 6738; Quine, W., 2806, 5316; Reichenbach, H., 6070; Reid, T., 356, 3739; Reinach, A., 673; Royce, J., 1138, 1691, 3421; Russell, B., 3240, 5509, 6684; Santayana, G., 2567, 4717, 6529, 6670; Sartre, J.-P., 1654; Schleiermacher, F., 649, 4358; Schlick, M., 3887; and science, 3397; Sellars, R., 586; Spencer, H., 2771; Spinoza, B., 4, 4466; Suarez, F., 3861, 6542; Trendelenberg, A., 5770; Veblen, T., 1305; Watson, J., 7286; Whewell, W., 2888; Whitehead, A., 549, 2304, 3807, 6332; William of Auvergne, 899; Wittgenstein, L., 6428
epoché, 5000
equality, 875, 1232, 1257, 2003, 2181, 5022, 6203, 6302, 6762, 7235
Erasmus, D., 3578
Erikson, E., 7398
eros, 124, 1405
error, 3413, 4417, 6038, 6938
eschatology, 7076
essence, 271, 1558, 1914, 2959, 3983; Aquinas, T., 4784, 5082; Aristotle, 2729; Locke, J., 289, 4106; Santayana, G., 2875, 6552; Spinoza, B., 2361; Suarez, F., 7175
essentialism, 251, 1321, 1363, 3036, 4019, 4222, 5435
eternity, 724, 1246, 1474, 2335, 4239
ethics, 163, 248, 466, 467, 660, 758, 968, 1359, 1508, 1658, 1780, 1827, 1830, 1892, 1975, 2028, 2131, 2190, 2278, 2546, 2609, 2678, 2818, 2882, 2942, 2984, 3075, 3125, 3133, 3182, 3184, 3261, 3514, 3535, 3803, 3858, 4005, 4014, 4063, 4136, 4288, 4311, 4370, 4397, 4587, 4674, 4845, 4876, 4887, 4975, 4999, 5026, 5054, 5055, 5072, 5271, 5282, 5345, 5367, 5377, 5393, 5396, 5447, 5474, 5476, 5514, 5519, 5535, 5539, 5554, 5580, 5611, 5649, 5709, 5815, 5911, 5915, 6143, 6301, 6319, 6335, 6346, 6369, 6431, 6641, 6681, 6784, 6985, 7028, 7088, 7194, 7303; and aesthetics, 693, 1913; Albertus Magnus, 1427; Alexander, S., 3625; Aquinas, T., 404, 495, 559, 3192, 4709, 4815, 5118, 5241, 7413, 7426; Aristotle, 168, 1630, 2260, 3192, 3643, 3928, 4279, 5718, 6102, 6601; Augustine, 787; Ayer, A.J., 983; Baier, K., 4624; Baldwin, J., 4660; Beardsmore, R., 5639; Ben Asher, B., 4566; Bergson, H., 54, 1767, 1782, 1968, 2224, 5869, 6880, 6881; Berkeley, G., 1278, 3095, 5070; and biology, 3929; Blanshard, B., 5249; Bradley, F., 170, 647, 1179, 2706, 5932; Brandt, R., 245; Brentano, F., 357, 4093, 6673; Brightman, E., 7167; Broad, C.D., 3696, 4048, 6840; Brunner, E., 846, 5831; Bruno, G., 5209; Buridan, J., 4646; Butler, J., 970, 3859, 4112, 4977, 5486, 5594, 6654, 7107; Cambridge Platonists, 215; Carritt, E., 4048; Chinese, 5820; Cicero, 5136; Clarke, S., 6441; Clapiers, L., 6963; cognitivism, 2341, 7218; conciliation, 3794; Confucianism, 3085, 3688; contextualism, 2805; Cudworth, R., 5926; Cumberland, R., 961; definition in, 2086; deliberation, 6098; deontological, 115,

4048, 5641; Descartes, R., 1415, 5918; determinism, 6465; Dewey, J., 53, 245, 703, 761, 787, 1099, 1381, 2456, 2469, 2688, 3019, 3595, 3703, 3822, 4156, 4227, 4502, 4563, 5168, 5831, 5870, 7496; Durkheim, E., 4925, 7039; and economics, 226, 5553; and education, 50, 5201, 6281; egoism, 3340, 3730, 4810, 5881, 6873; emotivism, 522, 983, 3510, 4660, 5861, 6287, 6477, 6530, 6632, 6973, 7268; empiricism, 2198, 5142, 6021, 6086; and epistemology, 961; Erikson, E., 7398; Euripedes, 984; and evolution, 1082, 1567, 4268; Ewing, A., 442, 2713; existentialist, 186, 2482, 6706; expressivism, 2359; field theory, 2784; Findlay, J., 2017; Fouillée, A., 6132; Freud, S., 687, 1456, 2140, 3278; Garnett,A., 442; Gentile, G., 2361; Greek, 3655; Green, T., 170, 2735, 3466; Guyau, J., 4392, 5676; Hare, R.M., 87, 206, 760, 1396, 2193, 2451, 2845, 2858, 2935, 3749, 4624, 6024; Hart, H., 5517; Hartmann, E., 3152; Hegel, G., 1077, 6601; Hilliard, 2544; Hindu, 1093, 6044; Hobbes, T., 2317, 3031; Hobhouse, L.T., 3425, 3923; d'Holbach, P., 6781; Homer, 4140; Hume, D., 46, 135, 599, 711, 761, 948, 1155, 1348, 1663, 1805, 2122, 2506, 2838, 3095, 3101, 3515, 3520, 5893, 6118, 6597, 7419, 7430; Hutcheson, F., 511, 692, 1295, 1632, 3229, 6005; Huxley, J., 4190; idealism, 2868, 5051; ideals in, 3394; individualism, 1375, 7265; intuitionism, 170, 759, 1406, 2146, 2831, 4682, 5756, 6459; James, W., 661, 878, 2256, 3385, 5790, 6834; Jaspers, K., 5130, Jefferson, T., 7295; Jewish, 4350; Jordan, E., 1318; judgement, 555, 2060, 2100, 2542, 2712, 2790, 4787, 6234; justification in, 544, 1788, 2136, 2876, 3248, 3624, 4361, 4642, 4940, 6015, 6016, 6344, 6584, 6617, 6674, 6946, 7050, 7086, 7169, 7421; Kames, H., 6830; Kant, E., 77, 218, 272, 468, 542, 1164, 1179, 1317, 1926, 2353, 2538, 2674, 3135, 3624, 3792, 4634, 4812, 5619, 5754, 5786, 5964, 6015, 6186, 7478, 7500; Kierkegaard, S., 1179, 1685, 3106, 4234, 5273; Kohlberg, L., 4660; Laird, J., 7491; Lavelle, L., 6975; law, 1790, 2162, 2922, 3755, 4699, 5478, 5736; Levinas, E., 220; Lewis, C.I., 1053, 1495, 2688, 2798, 4069, 5184, 5719, 6597, 7167, 7212, 7352; linguistic philosophy, 768, 2677, 3470; Locke, J., 3095, 3751, 5025; Loew of Prague, 7150; and logic, 1301, 1832, 6877, 7215, 7261; Lossky, N., 4873; Lotze, R., 4688; Luther, M., 3848; Lyons, D., 2353; Maimonides, M., 2455, 7157; Malebranche, N., 7057; man, 3848; Mandelbaum, M., 6883; Maritain, J., 4017, 4894, 5796, 5831, 5870; Martineau, J., 725, 2909; Marx, K., 6013; Marxism and, 2774; Mead, G., 763; meta-ethics, 895, 1854, 2093, 2165, 2915, 3448, 4206, 5495, 6568; method in, 1100; Mill, J.S., 3359, 4426; mind/body and, 256; Moore, G.E., 255, 760, 1634, 1921, 2713, 3135, 3526, 6608, 6802, 7371; Moritz, C., 1886; motivation in, 332, 6446, 6635;

Murdoch, I., 3104; Murphy, A., 713; naturalism, 206, 766, 1221, 2688, 2696, 3302, 3510, 3765, 4684, 5075, 5360, 5974, 6339, 6550; negation in, 519; Niebuhr, H., 1469, 4478; Niebuhr, R., 1469, 4017, 7000; Nietzsche, F., 49, 703, 1510, 4264, 4938; non-cognitivism, 4434, 5412, 6544; non-naturalism, 4755, 6544; normative ethics, 3622, 3709, 6568, 7051; norms, 393; Nowell-Smith, P., 4773, 6331; objectivism, 443, 1441; objectivity in, 4751, 6150; Ockham, W., 1148, 2166, 4168; Pascal, B., 5918; Peirce, C.S., 4809; Pepper, S., 5142; Perry, R., 378, 2688, 3650; and personality, 180, 5343; pessimism, 3677; phenomenalism, 6883; phenomenology, 4917; Piaget, J., 4660; Plato, 3300, 4323, 5235, 7193, 7201, 7415; Pletho, G., 288; pluralism, 1664; Pope, A., 6171; positivistic, 43, 2447; pragmatism, 6859; preceptive, 530; pre-Kantian, 693; prescriptivism, 1826, 2106, 2442, 3112, 3230, 7267; Price, R., 1406, 2831, 3801, 4017, 5240, 5243; Prichard, H., 4048; psychology and, 2497; Ramsey, I., 5796; Rashdall, H., 6817; rationality in, 290, 492, 711, 761, 923, 1024, 1150, 1199, 1487, 1750, 2254, 2662, 2727, 2800, 2870, 5288, 6161, 6185, 6553, 7167; reflective thinking in, 188; relativism, 388, 1076, 3183, 4127, 4745, 5262, 5812; and religion, 1179, 2046, 2481; Renouvier, C., 2432; renunciation, 1413; Ricoeur, P., 1140; romantic, 508; Rosmini-Serbati, A., 771; Ross, W., 340, 442, 1921, 2713, 4048, 5969; Royce, J., 2213; Russell, B., 47, 4227; Santayana, G., 78, 2445, 4796; Sartre, J.-P., 2193, 3295; Scheler, M., 1555, 2949, 4801, 6932, 7038; Schopenhauer, A., 26, 7500; Schweitzer, A., 3940; Shaftesbury, 692, 2512, 4085, 5133; Sellars, R., 2548; Sidgwick, H., 427, 2076, 3495, 3793, 6016, 6645, 7702; Singer, M., 2353, 2648, 4624; situation, 1743, 1841; Smith, A., 3177, 4192; Smith, T., 3650; as social, 3124; Solomon ibn Gabirol, 7350; Sorley, W., 442; Spencer, H., 4293, 4684; Spinoza, B., 618, 1735, 4938, 5008, 5613, 6688; Stace, W., 5796; Stevenson, C., 522, 2385, 3526, 6544, 7268; Stoic, 341, 864, 4247; subjectivism, 1441, 3317; Temple, W., 2548, 5831; Toulmin, S., 1797, 7167; universalizability, 543, 1700, 1845, 2346, 2416, 2648, 2935, 3340, 5971, 6004, 6024, 6131, 6193, 6214, 6974; Urban, W., 6462; values in, 58; Vico, G., 5714; Vives, J., 3650; war, 5845; Westermarck, E., 5262; Whitehead, A., 390, 1750, 3231, 4631, 4809, 5452, 5651; William of Auvergne, 5034; Wittgenstein, L., 2618, 2731, 3208; Wollaston, W., 6714; Ziff, P., 3526; Zubiri, X., 1860
ethical culture, 234, 5413
ethology, 3339
Eucken, R., 1032
Euclid, 7354
Euripides, 984
euthanasia, 573
evaluative language, 118, 6077
events, 571, 2240, 4333, 6860, 6987, 7262
evidence, 1017, 2033, 2871,

3725, 3888, 4398, 5206, 6969
evil, 34, 720, 1612, 2642, 2899, 3607, 4863, 5500, 7078; Aquinas, T., 1283, 1327, 1554; Bonaventure, St., 3556; Brightman, E., 4183; Ferré, N., 4183; Hocking, W., 6777; Hume, D., 700; James, W., 4181; Kant, E., 700, 2159; Leibniz, G., 700, 1327; Plato, 6811; Plotinus, 1327; Ricoeur, P., 6483; Sartre, J.-P., 4963; Whitehead, A., 6876
evolution, 244, 374, 527, 2515, 3119, 4505, 4570, 4805, 5113, 5609, 6809, 6902; Aristotle, 6715; Darwin, C., 515; Dobzhansky, T., 7064; and ethics, 1082, 1567; Goethe, J., 769; Huxley, J., 7271; Kant, E., 769; Leibniz, G., 769; Nietzsche, F., 5882; Peirce, C.S., 1870; and religion, 1846, 3826; Spencer, H., 277, 4805; Teilhard de Chardin, P., 500, 515
Ewing, A.C., 442, 2713
existence, 183, 233, 342, 866, 1593, 2018, 2226, 2740, 2833, 2929, 4319, 4421, 4593, 5095, 5571, 5579, 5612, 5924, 6111, 6376, 6683, 7053, 7090, 7406; Aquinas, T., 3610, 6788; Bosanquet, B., 2234; Bradley, F.H., 2234; Brito, F., 6545; Descartes, R., 1393; Giles of Rome, 4860; Heidegger, M., 6427, 7414; Hocking, W., 232, 4074; Jaspers, K., 2480; Kant, E., 6965; Kierkegaard, S., 3263, 6427, 6473, 7414; Santayana, G., 2445; Suarez, F., 7175; Tillich, P., 4842, 6618
existentialism, 249, 650, 2988, 3098, 3180, 4123, 5569, 5916, 6120, 6706
existenz, 2381, 5073
experience, 859, 3172, 4157, 4304, 4907, 5446, 7162, 7205, 7308, 7420; Avenarius, R., 862; Bergson, H., 4257; Blanshard, B., 2087; Bradley, F.H., 4217; Brightman, E., 2246; Descartes, R., 1163; Dewey, J., 453, 2692, 4217, 5784, 7111; Dilthey, W., 5943, 6516; Edwards, J., 4846; Gentile, G., 5740; Heidegger, M., 5943; Hodgson, S., 954, 3918; James, W., 1004, 1445, 5216; Kant, E., 854, 3449, 6828; Köhler, W., 1152; Lewis, C.I., 2246; Radhakrishnan, S., 162; Schopenhauer, A., 6828; Whitehead, A.N., 421, 2087, 4217, 4365, 6093
explanation, 425, 670, 712, 959, 1490, 1955, 2989, 3058, 3508, 3522, 5960, 5975, 6909, 6982
expression, 6783
expropriation, 94
extension, 3164, 4953

fact, 64, 2267, 5004, 5442, 6207, 7177, 7425
faculty psychology, 2772, 4397, 5879
fair play, 4898
faith, 79, 333, 1237, 1279, 1328, 1522, 1687, 1856, 2088, 2280, 3528, 3555, 3914, 4132, 4358, 4680, 4855, 4895, 5385, 5445, 6284, 6558
family resemblance, 4853, 5738, 6035
Fanon, F., 4154, 5088
Farrer, A., 2113, 2874, 5621, 5949
fascism, 754, 7101
fatalism, 590, 902, 2703, 6585, 6622
fate, 1139
Federalist, The, 5927, 7106
feeling, 2517, 3001, 3267
Feigl, H., 4059
feminism, 4354, 4472, 6147, 6614, 7233

Ferré, N., 4006, 4183
Feuerbach, L., 4142, 5729, 6983, 7081
Feyerabend, P., 821, 1733, 3791
Fichte, J.G., 737, 1888, 3000, 3001, 3162, 3845, 5664, 5715, 5947, 6490, 6512, 6620, 7403
Ficino, M., 1239
fictional entities, see theoretical entities
fideism, 3771
field theory, 2784
finality, 261, 2259, 2465, 2900, 5010
Finance, J. de, 5454
Findlay, J.N., 2017
finitude, 907
Fite, W., 843
Flake, O., 483
Flewelling, R., 5437
Fodor, J., 3938
force, 3566
form, 2936; Aquinas, T., 2403; Plato, 287, 668, 919, 2829, 7273, 7375
formalism, 506, 3487, 7006
Foucher, S., 7100
Fouiliée, A., 6132
Four, V. du, 4080
Fox, G., 3586
Francis of Meyronnes, 905
Frank, P., 3158
freedom, 39, 239, 865, 972, 1027, 1104, 1570, 1601, 1639, 1836, 1912, 2029, 2607, 2740, 2761, 2914, 3296, 3334, 3368, 3499, 3521, 3985, 4305, 4370, 5628, 5778, 5911, 6002, 6222, 6640, 7145, 7387, 7479; Arendt, H., 3563; Aristotle, 1235, 1311; Augustine, 1156, 1311, 4209; Berdyaev, N., 2438, 4984, 6094; Bergson, H., 4627, 4715, 7340; Blondel, M., 2379; Bradley, F.H., 4298; Bradwardine, T., 4109; Camus, A., 1919; Dewey, J., 1653, 2063, 4947; Dostoyevsky, F., 1919; Douglas, W., 3652; Duns Scotus, J., 5679; Freud, S., 5503;

Gandhi, 4189; Gide, A., 1919; Heidegger, M., 3881; Hobbes, T., 2836; James, W., 1974, 7340; Jaspers, K., 3949, 5647, 7453; Kant, E., 1311, 2159, 2993, 4117, 4453, 5286, 5471; Leibniz, G., 1479; Locke, J., 3476; Marcel, G., 5941; Maritain, J., 3716, 5567; Merleau-Ponty, M., 3525; Molina, L., 6269; Plantinga, A., 5531; Plato, 1235, 1311; and psychoanalysis, 545; Ricoeur, P., 5541, 6235; Russell, B., 3605; Santayana, G., 78; Sartre, J.-P., 184, 825, 1310, 2043, 2078, 2702, 3881, 5527, 5941, 6166, 7428; Scheler, M., 2431; Schelling, F., 2615; Schleiermacher, F., 28; Siewerth, G., 3541; social freedom, 114; Stace, W., 3605; Whitehead, A.N., 5011, 5380
free-will, 451, 741, 939, 2212, 2363, 2660, 2801, 2987, 3023, 3071, 3266, 3585, 5062, 6652, 6733, 6740, 6917, 7210; Aquinas, T., 1466, 4723; Augustine, 2921; Campbell, C., 11; Dewey, J., 447; Fichte, J., 737; Schopenhauer, A., 4872
Frege, G., 418, 818, 2211, 2608, 2814, 3181, 3580, 4388, 4825, 5603, 5912, 6318, 7054
Freher, D., 4823
Freud, S., 942, 1606, 4780, 6078, 6579, 6737, 7342; anxiety, 631; conscience, 3278; death, 5381; determinism, 6839; ethics, 687, 1456, 2140, 3278; freedom, 5503; laughter, 1144; man, 1256, 2140, 3835; mind, 2360; personality, 601, 7155; religion, 1582; shame, 2832; symbolism, 4630; unconscious, 1724, 4980, 5765, 5965

friendship, 677, 2117, 4644,
    6102, 7274
Fromm, E., 4904
Frye, N., 4771
Fuller, L.L., 5237
function, 3351, 4064, 4388,
    4937, 6868, 7036
functionalism, 757, 1245,
    1633, 3523, 6078
Fung yu-Lan, 7411
future, 1180, 2350, 2587,
    3527

Gabirol, Solomon ibn, 7350
Galen, 1831
Galileo Galilei, 2641, 2723,
    3405, 4296
games, 5685, 7192
Gandhi, M., 1749, 3617, 4189,
    4638
Garnett, A., 442
Gassendi, P., 1842, 5159
Gauthier, 1309
Geach, P.T., 920, 6923
Geijer, G., 6384
generic statements, 1455
genesa, 3768
Genet, J., 4036
genetic fallacy, 5200
genius, 420
Gentile, G., 2135, 2361, 2759,
    3020, 4868, 5740, 6305
geography, 4468
geometry, 2398, 3100, 5094,
    5650, 6208
Gerard, A., 1045
Gerasenus, N., 3255
Gersonides, 36, 5877, 6189
gestalt theory, 1874, 4300,
    6164
Geulincx, A., 1293
Geyser, J., 4993
Gide, A., 1919
Gilbert de la Porrée, 7203
Giles of Rome, 964, 1265,
    4026, 4860
Gill, E., 3441
Gilson, E., 5909
Gioberti, V., 5042
given, 126, 2777, 5683, 6896
gnosticism, 3456, 3648
God, 409, 630, 1450, 1612,
    2251, 2763, 2842, 2964,
    2976, 3149, 4099, 4357,
    4404, 4465, 4766, 5048,
    5340, 5375, 5448, 5502,
    5836, 6019, 6931, 6936,
    6980, 7078, 7085, 7120;
    7245, 7335, 7387, 7402;
Albertus Magnus, 1035;
American philosophy, 246,
    302, 1877, 4213; analytic
    philosophy, 1055; Anselm,
    St., 1641, 2286, 3723,
    4351, 6010, 7016, 7217;
Aquinas, T., 297, 778,
    994, 1690, 2265, 2316,
    3408, 5031, 5712, 5728,
    6593, 7242; Aristotle,
    2265, 6291; Augustine,
    4137, 6272, 6763, 6928;
Avicenna, 3199; Berdyaev,
    N., 223; Bergson, H.,
    1672; Boethius, 27; Bona-
    venture, St., 4445; Bright-
    man, E., 3570, 6897;
Clarke, S., 4066; cosmolo-
    gical argument, 1258,
    1376, 5566; Descartes, R.,
    4296, 5015, 6916; Eck-
    hart, M., 5993; Emerson,
    R., 302, 6671; Fichte, J.,
    6490; as finite, 253, 2105;
Galileo, 4296; Gentile, G.,
    6305; Gersonides, 5877;
Gregory of Nyssa, 2883,
    4195; Hartshorne, C.,
    1354, 2308, 3908, 6945;
Hegel, G., 1124, 4640;
Heidegger, M., 5277; Henry
    of Ghent, 1753; Herder, J.,
    831; as immutable, 994;
James, W., 2105, 6841, 6897;
John Scotus Erigena, 3627,
    4147; Kant, E., 311, 3396;
language about, 1723, 2659;
Leibniz, G., 4066, 5015,
    6085; Locke, J., 4066;
Lonergan, B., 6857; Loss-
    ky, N., 3420; Maimonides,
    M., 2316, 5712; Marcel,
    G., 5234, 5559; Martineau,
    J., 461; modal argument,
    29; neo-Hegelianism, 3114;
Nicholas of Cusa, 4418;
Ockham, W., 27, 4520,
    7382; ontological argument,
    322, 1386, 1616, 1641,
    2152, 2286, 2540, 3014,

3074, 3745, 3758, 3908,
4351, 4863, 5015, 6010,
6051, 6308, 6704, 6916,
7016, 7217; Plantinga, A.,
4003, 5531, 6767; Plato,
2101, 6420; Randall, J.H.,
6115; Royce, J., 1795;
Schelling, F., 2511;
Sciacca, M., 4342; Sertillanges, A., 871; Sorley,
W., 461, 6387; Spinoza, B.,
3325, 4486, 5015, 5528;
Stoics, 1437; Suarez, F.,
1728; teleological argument, 1358, 5953; Tennant,
F., 297, 461; Thomas of
York, 4348; Tillich, P.,
882, 1354, 4256, 5559, 5561,
5844, 6475, 6945; Ward, J.,
461; Whitehead, A.N., 732,
1267, 1542, 2105, 2854,
4171, 5521; Wittgenstein,
L., 484; Woodbridge, J.,
6115
Godamer, H., 2331
Godfrey of Fontaines, 1306,
4792
Godwin, W., 1154, 6700
Gödel, K., 947
Goethe, J., 642, 769
golden rule, 97
Goldmann, L., 4533
Gombrich, E.H., 7435
good, 42, 460, 1114, 1473,
1698, 1970, 2040, 2370,
2377, 2787, 3261, 5256,
5609, 5803; Aquinas, T.,
2928, 7446; Bonaventure,
St., 3556, 7048; Bradley,
F.H., 1302; Dewey, J., 1371,
2928; Green, T.H., 1302;
Hobhouse, L.T., 3647; Kant,
E., 299; Mill, J.S., 5173;
Moore, G.E., 7446; Peirce,
C.S., 5315; Plato, 1667,
7391; Plotinus, 3381; Sidgwick, H., 1302
Goodman, N., 2808, 3245, 3457,
6012
Gorgias of Leontini, 6933
gravity, 2641, 3668, 5711,
6325
Greek philosophy, 268, 538,
724, 2869, 3655, 3898,
5689, 5744, 5874, 6037,
6482, 6514, 6572, 6610,
6680, 7328
Green, T.H., 170, 893, 950,
1115, 1302, 2735, 3265,
3466, 3481, 3865, 4239,
4449, 4654, 6075, 6796,
7171
Greene, G., 3698
Gregory of Nazianzus, 5828
Gregory of Nyssa, 2789,
2883, 4195, 7160
Gregory of Rimini, 4165
Grice, H.P., 371
Grote, J., 2283, 4163
guilt, 4696, 7088, 7223
Guyau, M.J., 4392, 5676

habit, 379, 2195, 6101
Hägerström, A., 5883
Hall, E., 4260, 6735
hallucination, 1697, 2112,
2907, 4223
Hamann, J.G., 4581, 5038
Hamilton, W., 910, 4255,
5121
Hampshire, S., 3542, 3562
Han Fei, 3753
happiness, 167, 654, 1095,
1219, 1573, 5649, 5890,
6121
Hare, R.M., 87, 206, 760,
1396, 2145, 2193, 2451,
2845, 2858, 2935, 3749,
4624, 6024
harmony, 1411
Harris, W.T., 4091
Hart, H.L.A., 306, 5517,
6352
Hartman, R.S., 3382
Hartmann, E. von, 896, 1486
Hartmann, N., 2833, 3601,
3785, 5175, 6125, 6668
Hartshorne, C., 1354, 2308,
3203, 3908, 4094, 6711,
6945, 7372
Hauriou, M., 2507, 2830
Hawthorne, N., 5967
Hayim ben Isaac, 3746
Hedge, F.H., 7176
hedonism, 517, 2194, 2544,
2947, 4096, 7147
Hegel, G.W.F., 151, 441,
2135, 2509, 3932, 4091,
4253, 4315, 4387, 5215,

5273, 5304, 5348, 5518, 5600, 5772, 5853, 6383, 6424, 7299; absolute, 6526; action, 5044; aesthetics, 2811, 3591, 7495; art, 2006; consciousness, 3331, 3638, 6273; dialectic, 870, 1681, 1739, 2270, 3994, 4185, 5681; education, 4072; Egypt, 5046; epistemology, 857, 1678, 6342; estrangement, 3993; ethics, 1077, 6601; finality, 2797; freedom, 1758, 2063; God, 1124, 4640; Greece, 3330; harmony, 1411; history, 1307, 2698, 3015, 6819; language, 1282, 1548, 6576; logic, 575, 1416, 1644, 3968, 7115; man, 258, 1322; mind, 2528, 4220; nature, 7103; negation, 987, 2550; neo-Hegelianism, 3114; notion, 1463; Phenomenology of the spirit, 14, 1719, 2215, 2356, 3638, 6273, 7206; power, 5296; pragmatism, 5686; psychology, 7050; relation, 2668; religion, 4399, 4609, 5089, 5963; science, 656, 6270; self-determination, 121; society, 4110; state, 4686, 6210, 7171; thought, 5122; time, 5122, 6819; truth, 809, 4285; value, 3700; will, 4297

Heidegger, M., 2239, 2577, 3829, 4394, 5833, 6089, 6422, 6981, 7004; aesthetics, 2439, 3894; authenticity, 691, 2470, 3429; being, 242, 318, 2581, 2956, 3355, 3894, 4337, 4428, 6055, 6062, 6997, 7097, 7117; dasein, 6498, 6672; death, 2685, 5381; dread, 6850; education, 3493; eternal recurrence, 4306; existence, 6427, 7414; experience, 5943; freedom, 3881; God, 5277; ground, 783, 952; history, 3750; intersubjectivity, 4637; Kant, E., 1133, 1711, 4731, 6146; language, 604, 4337, 4428, 6058, 6520; life, 4187; love, 5250; meaning, 683; metaphysics, 1537, 1903, 2504, 5141, 7097; mitsein, 1875; Nietzsche, F., 3079, 3662; nihilism, 1960; nothing, 1225; ontology, 2288, 2338, 4931, 6887; overcoming of philosophy, 62; poetry, 7224; possibility, 2927; pre-Socratics, 6064; self, 2891, 3702, 4306, 6789, 7493; social philosophy, 6402; space, 6062; technology, 3033; time, 4431, 4603, 6146, 7097; truth, 4285, 6959; world, 5872, 6334

Heine, H., 110
Heisenberg, W., 4027
Hellenistic philosophy, 82, 1566, 5667
Helmholtz, H.L. von, 3323
Hempel, C.G., 3294
Henry of Ghent, 739, 1753
Heraclitus, 1925, 3282, 5047, 5069, 5211
Herder, J.G., 831, 1624, 2187
hermeneutics, 1263, 3081, 3082
Herodian, 4927
Heroditus, 3898
Hersey, J., 2368
Hertz, H.R., 1290
Herveus Natalis, 1958
Hesiod, 2617
Hick, J., 667, 4006
Hicks, G.D., 773, 4058
Hilbert, D., 418
Hildreth, R., 5347
Hilliard, 2544
Hinsdale, B.A., 6578
Hintikka, J., 4083, 7351
historical consciousness, 1414
history, 1561, 1636, 1843, 2114, 3190, 3799, 3818, 4817, 4820, 5150, 5154, 5181, 5355, 5423, 5520, 5708, 6408, 6515, 6795, 7149, 7187, 7249, 7467; Augustine, 891; Berdyaev,

N., 5626, 7284; Bergson, H., 5432; Bultmann, R., 2631; Cassirer, E., 1536, 4242; Collingwood, R.G., 1580, 3042, 4439, 4897, 5706, 5814, 5837; concepts in, 1052; Cournot, A., 2258; cyclic theory of, 5; Dilthey, W., 5362; evidence in, 1252; explanation in, 32, 820, 1214, 1240, 1372, 2258, 2436, 3502, 3683, 3990, 3996, 4919; Hegel, G., 1307, 2698, 3015, 6819; Heidegger, M., 3750; Hume, D., 2675, 3981, 7197; Jaspers, K., 2650; Kant, E., 224; Löwith, K., 2650; Marx, K., 2170, 2235, 6890; meaning in, 3906; Mounier, E., 944; Nietzsche, F., 1251, 3750; Peirce, C.S., 4600; history of philosophy, 784; Scheler, M., 1555; Taine, H., 3328; Thierry, A., 6307; Thucydides, 1204; Tillich, P., 4065, 5226, 5561; Toynbee, A., 1315, 4242; Tröltsch, E., 1438; truth in, 3209; value neutrality in, 5787; Vico, G., 5203; Voegelin, 4242; Whitehead, A.N., 75
Hobbes, T., 1192, 1272, 2398, 5074, 5664, 6066, 6693; common good, 72; determinism, 2836; economics, 5895; ethics, 2317, 3031; epistemology, 551, 3256; essence, 271; freedom, 2836 idea, 271; justice, 5925; language, 1887; man, 2896; mind, 551; natural law, 164, 3262; nature, 3256; obligation, 164, 4542; political philosophy, 72, 2738, 3031, 7377; state, 4686
Hobhouse, L.T., 1002, 3387, 3425, 3647, 3923, 4932, 5383
Hocking, W.E., 232, 2004, 2067, 2337, 2357, 3080, 4074, 5615, 6321, 6394, 6777
Hodgson, S.A., 954, 3918, 5671, 6373

Holbach, P.-H. d', 5246, 6781
holism, 898, 5222, 5544
Holmes, O.W., 7489
Holy Spirit, 6135
Homer, 3898, 4140, 5069
Hooke, R., 1057
Hooker, R., 4194
hope, 435, 1578, 4827, 4982, 5292
Horne, H., 6953
Howison, G.H., 3796
Howland, J., 5839
Hsiung Shih-li, 1071
Hsün Tzu, 1102, 1754
Hugel, F. von, 1454, 4208, 6930
Hugh of St. Victor, 3569
humanism, 1127, 1175, 1971, 3500, 3864, 4266, 4599, 4921, 5005, 5772, 6067. 6626
Humboldt, W. von, 4362, 6695
Hume, D., 130, 282, 1662, 1726, 1865, 1879, 2872, 3414, 4171, 4372, 4443, 5463, 5749, 5835, 6263, 6414, 6445, 6820, 6851, 7326, 7374; aesthetics, 2653; belief, 346, 400; causation, 48, 366, 612, 1638, 5816, 6793, 6977; change, 7451; consciousness, 38; determinism, 933; empiricism, 3711; epistemology, 599, 655, 879, 884, 1501, 4578, 7458; ethics, 46, 135, 599, 711, 761, 948, 1155, 1348, 1663, 1805, 2122, 2506, 2838, 3095, 3101, 3515, 3520, 5434, 5893, 6118, 6597, 7419, 7430; evil, 700; history, 2675, 3981, 7197; ideas, 7393; image, 1512; imagination, 2376, 2454, 3770, 3953, 7266; language, 1333; logic, 4016; meaning, 3309; metaphysics, 3461, 3981, 5434, 6374, 7399; mind, 5213, 7363; miracles, 40, 1699; motivation, 7062; natural theology, 2887; nature, 1871;

necessity, 419; objects, 3299; passions, 6479; perception, 2825; political philosophy, 599, 1155, 4789, 7005; relations, 1679, 2464; religion, 838, 3244, 4265, 4552, 4838, 4866; scepticism, 3488, 3869, 4320; self, 166, 2601, 4875; social philosophy, 5785; space, 2302, 6105, 6257; substance, 212; superstition, 2383; teleology, 3078; theology, 3490; time, 6257; universals, 1066; world, 6396
humor, 5191, 5884
Hu Shih, 5036
Husserl, E., 92, 321, 906, 1549, 1714, 2032, 3018, 4215, 5099, 5125, 5341, 5348, 5928, 5981, 6469, 6644, 6867; Cartesian meditations, 207; concept, 775; consciousness, 4816; contingency, 3509; ego, 274, 3029, 6506; epistemology, 4578; epoché, 5000; evidence, 3888; existence, 5612; given, 2777; Hume, 879; individuation, 6262; intentionality, 4301, 5533, 6262; intersubjectivity, 85, 1428; logic, 208, 2461, 4118, 4544, 7099; language, 1428; mathematics, 3097; meaning, 7281; method in, 3784; objectivity, 6076; other minds, 1721, 4733; perception, 1741, 1747; political philosophy, 3507; presence, 2196; reduction, 274, 598; space, 3475; time, 722, 3083, 5583, 7181, 7343; transcendental, 6367; universals, 1073, 7281; world, 827, 3565
Hutcheson, F., aesthetics, 2653, 3634; ethics, 511, 693, 1295, 1632, 3229, 6005
Huxley, J., 3936, 4190, 7271
Huxley, T.H., 531
hylomorphism, 5455, 5672

hypothesis, 197, 295, 4706, 6194

Ibn Bajjah, 7497
Ibn Tufayl, 2813
I-Ching, 6835
idealism, 25, 1067, 2514, 2629, 4250, 5348, 5595, 6627; Berkeley, G., 978, 1546, 2598, 4134, 6539, 6794; Bradley, F.H., 3483; Brunschvicg, L., 1861; ethics, 2868, 5051; Kant, E., 4134, 6539; Marcel, G., 6430; Moore, G.E., 3483, 3992; Ortega y Gasset, J., 1640; Perry, R., 3992; Pringle-Pattison, A.S., 5287; Sellars, R., 4797; Ward, J., 4134
ideals, 4629
ideas, 271, 1073, 1287, 2057, 4082, 4339, 6937, 6958, 7100, 7125, 7172, 7393
identity, 300, 413, 1822, 1990, 2244, 2707, 2851, 2930, 3898, 4375, 4604, 5285, 5912, 6311, 6591, 6744, 6790, 7379
ideology, 3458, 3599, 4547, 5843, 6736
ignorance, 1043
illocutionary acts, 988, 6256
illumination, 2912, 3455
images, 104, 136, 422, 990, 1512, 2393, 3689
imagination, 2376, 2454, 2459, 2565, 2828, 2898, 3533, 3558, 3619, 3770, 3953, 4321, 5053, 6128, 7164, 7266
immortality, 127, 1281, 1496, 1629, 3748, 5512, 5983, 6550, 7068, 7293, 7429
imperatives, 1096, 4761, 7480
implication, 714, 2880, 3128, 5143, 5193, 5404, 5776, 6494, 6904, 6939, 7383, 7457

impressions, 7002
incorrigibility, 5032
indeterminism, 909, 2010, 2689, 3719, 4981, 6389, 7250
Indian philosophy, 1488, 2562, 2714, 2769, 2849, 2899, 3113, 3548, 4447, 4473, 5646, 6044, 6546
individual, 471, 850, 857, 1370, 1451, 1588, 2269, 2578, 3939, 4023, 4276, 4345, 4860, 5429, 5458, 5565, 5826, 6199, 6246, 6429, 6771, 6796, 6878, 7007, 7037, 7324, 7368
individual (metaphysical concept of), 175, 359, 2252
individualism, 751, 1318, 2148, 2664, 4086, 4115, 4335, 4513, 4702, 5222, 5967, 6049, 6188, 6524
individuation, 1141, 1169, 3178, 4149, 4970, 5077, 5333, 5763, 6370, 6696, 7203, 7379
indoctrination, 431
induction, 35, 295, 678, 922, 1103, 1197, 1367, 1812, 2202, 2602, 2863, 3322, 3380, 3633, 4913, 4939, 5372, 5873, 5957, 6314, 6401, 6486, 6503, 6900
inertia, 6625
inference, 2971, 4015, 4398, 4782, 5723, 5767, 6643
infinity, 530, 925, 1825, 2303, 2524, 2552
Ingarden, R., 4226
Inge, W., 2141
innate ideas, 1899, 5747, 6808
instinct, 225, 3291, 3957, 4212, 7412
institutions, 3168
instrumentalism, 50, 962, 1692, 4252, 4676, 5036, 7222, 7230
intellect, 1166, 3549, 3955, 6122, 7199, 7334, 7384
intelligence, 404, 1069, 1563, 3612
intention, 385, 546, 1811, 3166, 3806, 3933, 6831, 6924, 7018, 7184

intentionality, 160, 592, 927, 1560, 3356, 3438, 3539, 3614, 3628, 3867, 3903, 4301, 4327, 4352, 4386, 5019, 5533, 5773, 6895, 7029, 7263, 7434
interest, 406, 2583, 6301
interpretation, 3081, 4441, 4457, 4725, 4758, 7325
intersubjectivity, 1764, 2418, 2743, 2973, 4313, 6443, 6766, 6899; Fichte, J., 3000; Husserl, E., 85, 1428; Kant, E., 4637; Merleau-Ponty, M., 3526; Sartre, J.-P., 805
introspection, 2103
intuition, 1531, 1627, 2410, 2599, 3291, 3909, 4627, 5148, 5326, 5547, 5587
intuitionism, 170, 402, 1406
Iqbal, M., 309
irrationalism, 2686, 5188
Isaac Arama, 7272
Isaac ibn Farhi, 4501
Isocrates, 3898

Jaeger, W., 5888
James, W., 335, 1497, 1693, 2274, 3701, 3773, 4013, 4263, 5188, 5301, 5451, 5923, 6756, 6804, 7311; belief, 400, 5725; categories, 5364; consciousness, 540; emotion, 3616; epistemology, 1312, 3367; ethics, 661, 878, 2256, 3385, 5790, 6834; evil, 4181; experience, 1064, 1445, 5216; faith, 4132; freedom, 1974, 7340; God, 2105, 6841, 6897; individual, 4343; life, 4132; man, 1088; metaphysics, 1800, 4788, 5721; mind, 4275; monism, 4390; personal identity, 347; pragmatism, 661, 5581, 5851, 7101; rationality, 358; realism, 2292, 2751; relations, 6068; religion, 503, 1922, 3878, 4275, 4680, 4918, 5581, 6537;

self, 347, 1447; time, 540;
truth, 2324; will, 5725,
5764; will to believe,
2351
Japanese philosophy, 3545,
5112
Jarves, J.J., 3027
Jaspers, K., 1850, 2480,
2650, 2689, 3079, 3371,
3856, 3949, 5073, 5130,
5332, 5525, 5588, 5647,
6228, 7453
Jefferson, T., 1232, 3594,
3950, 5190, 6800, 7295
Jewish philosophy, 169, 530,
826, 1532, 1628, 1840,
2280, 2289, 2412, 3733,
4020, 4350, 4506, 5483,
5642, 6380
Jiva Goswami, S., 643
Joachim, 6419
John, St., 4032
John of Damascus, 33
John of Jandun, 4126, 6854
John of St. Thomas, 863,
2841, 4704
John of Salisbury, 1814,
2877, 3534, 4400
John of the Cross, St., 3763
John the Scot, 4082
John Scotus Erigena, 1756,
3627, 4147
Johnstone, H.W., 2974
Jordan, E., 1318, 2816, 2830,
4808, 5636, 5819, 7246
Jouvenel, 5690
joy, 5700
judgment, 524, 1591, 1730,
2100, 3577, 3816, 3920,
4262, 5556, 6613, 6651,
6858; Aquinas, T., 199;
Bradley, F.H., 3155; Dewey,
J., 4502; Kant, E., 2619,
3954, 6814, 7322; Sartre,
J.-P., 394
Jung, C.G., 5325, 6296, 6701,
6920
Jungius, J., 200
justice, 240, 957, 1084,
1727, 2734, 3194, 3383,
4424, 5443, 6070, 6461,
7341; Bradley, F.H., 740;
distributive, 614; Hobbes,
T., 5925; Leibniz, G.,
4790; Plato, 360, 1188,
7440; Rauschenbusch, W.

583; Rawls, J., 178, 1297,
1862, 2333, 2827, 4756,
4862, 5259, 5875, 6487,
7153; Rommen, H., 583;
Tillich, P., 583; utili-
tarianism, 2349, 5501
justification, 15, 87, 2242,
2923, 3232, 4121, 4589,
4642, 5204, 5275, 5356,
6879

Kalomiti, M., 1702
Kames, H.H., 3167, 6830
Kandinsky, V., 7257
Kant, E., 1483, 1820, 2187,
2295, 2479, 3297, 3314,
3827, 3932, 4695, 4890,
5348, 5379, 5398, 5431,
6512, 7133, 7448; aesthetics, 1362, 1773, 1868,
2378, 2424, 3402, 3591,
3634, 4021, 4316, 4416,
4908, 5302, 5628, 5860,
6337, 6397, 6863, 7408,
7495; altruism, 542; analyticity, 818; a priori,
4062; categorical impera-
tive, 2943; categories,
5309, 6921; causation,
4712, 5816, 6977; cogni-
tion, 3449; consciousness,
5879; Critique of pure reason, 5352, 6391, 6467,
6606; ding-an-sich, 2931,
3386, 4592, 4851, 5972;
dualism, 3116; duty, 5286;
education, 5754; epistemology, 1443, 4339, 4358,
4606, 5350; ethics, 77,
218, 272, 468, 1164, 1179,
1317, 1926, 2353, 2538,
2674, 3135, 3792, 4634,
4812, 5619, 5754, 5786,
5964, 6015, 6186, 7478,
7500; evil, 700, 2159;
evolution, 769; experience,
854, 3449, 6965; faith,
3555, 4358, 4895; freedom,
1311, 2159, 2993, 3296,
4117, 4453, 5284, 5471,
5628; geography, 4468;
God, 299; happiness, 1219;
Heidegger, M., on, 1133,
1711, 4731; history, 224;
hope, 5292; idealism,

4134, 6539; ideas, 4339; intuition, 3116; judgment, 2619, 3954, 6814, 7322; logic, 6602; man, 6898; mathematics, 735, 818, 4050; metaphysics, 2593, 2822, 3135; mind, 5213, 7363; obligation, 2972; personality, 3281; political philosophy, 2694; pragmatism, 7283, 7355; psychology, 1317, 1623; realism, 4601; reason, 3555; religion, 311, 1179, 1509, 1922, 2102, 3767, 3844, 7374; scepticism, 4494; <u>schemata</u>, 913; science, 1509, 3836; second analogy, 4498; self, 1193, 4461; self consciousness, 4515; sensation, 2080; space, 1216, 2634, 5606, 7108; subject, 5247; subjectivity, 2925; suicide, 4979; teleology, 3665, 4318; theology, 2197, 2611, 3490, 4022; time, 854, 7108; transcendental, 485, 3341, 4974, 6467

Katz, J., 3938
Kaundabhatta, 1605
Kautsky, K., 4243
Kelsen, H., 539, 4685, 7485
Kierkegaard, S., 1453, 1783, 2857, 3290, 3567, 3618, 3958, 4210, 4253, 4303, 4334, 4387, 4403, 4607, 4770, 5085, 5253, 5857, 6424, 6720; communication, 830, 6229; dread, 6850; education, 3675; ethics, 1179, 1685, 3106, 4234, 5273; existence, 3263, 6427, 6473, 7414; faith, 1687, 6558; Hegel, G., 151; humor, 5191, 5884; individual, 6878, 7007; particulars, 1260; religion, 1106, 1179, 1922, 2404, 3284, 4824; repetition, 4244; self, 6353; social philosophy, 4870; subject, 5247; subjectivity, 7353; suffering, 3491; time, 2681; transcendence, 2313, 6677; truth, 3011, 3276, 3398, 5871; values, 1769, 2467, 5753; verification, 974

Kilwardby, R., 2693, 3308
King, Jr., M.L., 837
knowledge, 21, 91, 150, 1017, 1821, 1891, 2066, 2391, 2579, 2737, 3656, 3707, 3810, 3866, 4122, 4236, 4304, 4479, 4555, 4608, 4626, 4716, 5018, 5145, 5228, 5799, 5991, 6170, 6181, 6378, 6500, 6621, 7052, 7456
Köhler, W., 1153
Kohnstamm, P., 5361
Korn, A., 3499
Kotarbinsky, T., 3574
Kripke, S., 4222, 7144
Kuhn, T., 365, 903, 967, 1733, 3791

labor, 3501, 3927, 5620, 6450
Lacan, J., 279
Laird, J., 3096, 7491
Lalande, A., 4913
Lamprecht, S., 1208
Langer, S.K., 802, 1326, 2216, 5165
language, 1460, 1468, 1610, 1748, 1757, 2084, 2352, 2709, 2766, 2910, 2990, 3100, 3159, 3187, 3333, 3472, 3510, 3642, 3910, 3938, 3973, 4047, 4689, 4744, 4853, 4885, 4972, 5065, 5202, 5220, 5324, 5747, 5755, 5830, 6034, 6172, 6254, 6409, 6638, 6666, 6716, 6957, 7159, 7179, 7189, 7324, 7332, 7378, 7431; Aristotle, 1186, 2529, 3780; and art, 1001, 1013; Berkeley, G., 1278, 5524; Brentano, F., 6673; Carnap, R., 1368; Cassirer, E., 6223; Chomsky, N., 2039, 6432, 6993; Dewey, J., 985; evaluative language, 4871; formal language, 3160; Frege, G., 3181, 4825; grammar, 496, 1523, 2263, 4496, 5668, 6405, 6488, 7032; Hamann,

J., 4581; Hegel, G., 1282, 1548, 6576; Heidegger, M., 604, 4337, 4428, 6058, 6520; Hobbes, T., 1887; Hume, D., 1333; Husserl, E., 1429; linguistic force, 222; Locke, J., 1887, 4858, 7394; Mead, G., 985; Merleau-Ponty, M., 2186, 3188, 4625, 6842; and mind, 4024; natural languages, 3547; and ontology, 129; Plato, 2228, 3315, 6485; pre-linguistic apprehensions, 327; private, 4070, 5705; Quine, W., 6432; recursive grammar, 142; Reichenbach, H., 4272; Rosenzweig, F., 3056; Russell, B., 1285, 2652, 4046; Sapir, E., 976; signs, 807; silence, 4830; tenses, 652, 1176, 6054, 7195; and theology, 1161, 2591; transformational grammar, 1523, 5065; value, 869; Wheelwright, P., 985; Whorf, B., 976, 5061; Wittgenstein, L., 152, 566, 969, 1408, 1660, 2726, 3069, 3661, 4595, 5433, 5934, 6058, 6769

Lao Tzu, 3922, 3977
Laski, H.J., 3977
laughter, 1144
Lavelle, L., 6268, 6975
law, 591, 963, 1195, 1211, 1325, 1527, 1790, 1992, 2157, 2372, 2995, 3247, 3333, 3584, 3855, 4092, 4101, 4307, 4568, 4899, 5346, 5430, 5592, 5630, 5746, 5856, 5948, 6033, 6200, 7087, 7241, 7388; Aquinas, T., 3107, 3534, 3660; authority, 845, 1680, 3733; Bentham, J., 3732; Cohen, F., 3629; and ethics, 2922, 3755, 4699, 5478, 5736; Field, S.J., 2399; Fuller, L., 5237; Hart, H., 306, 5517, 6352; Hauriou, M., 2830; international, 3686; Jewish, 2412, 3733; John of Salisbury, 3534; Jordan, E., 2830, 4808; Kelsen, H., 539, 4685; Léon, L. de, 3641; Nuremberg trials, 3360; Plato, 1585, 3279; positivism, 4035; Reinach, A., 673; responsibility, 637, 1209, 2092; Roman, 6205; Ross, A., 2516; Spinoza, B., 389; Stoic, 1330; Suarez, F., 3107
Leibniz, G.W., 1600, 4056, 6304, 7305; appetition, 90; Aristotle, 5373; being, 6347; The Best, 1242; evil, 700, 1327; evolution, 769; expression, 3694; freedom, 1478; God, 4066, 5015, 6085; identity, 2125; individuation, 4149; justice, 4790; logic, 5001; matter, 5840; metaphysics, 1242, 2655, 2783, 5001; nature, 4346, 5601; necessity, 2048; optimism, 4170, 5176; perception, 2375; possibility, 4467, 5328; Schleiermacher, F., 28; science, 982, 6628; space, 2001; teleology, 6499; truth, 7323, 7348; will, 3162
leisure, 395, 3971, 7046
Lenin, V.I., 645, 3842, 4243
Léon, L. de, 3641
Leon, M., 3137
Leontiev, K.N., 5155
Lequier, J., 686
LeSenne, R., 1412
Lesniewski, S., 947, 3404, 3644
Lessing, G.E., 93, 809
Lévinas, E., 220, 2563, 3702
Lévi-Strauss, C., 6095
Lévy-Bruhl, L., 1173
Lewes, G.H., 2044, 3349
Lewis, C.I., 312, 1042, 2246, 4203, 4308, 5775, 6822, 7502; aesthetics, 5162; epistemology, 1274, 1751, 2671, 2977, 7042, 7105, 7459; ethics, 1053, 1495, 2688, 2798, 4069, 5184,

5719, 6597, 7167, 7212, 7352; induction, 1103; and Kant, 623; logic, 2299, 3175; meaning, 3489, 4180; mind, 3110; practical reason, 4278; truth, 1684; value, 1005, 2246, 4462, 2752
Lewis, H.D., 7379
liberalism, 1986, 2620, 2764, 2792, 3387, 4258, 4282, 6177
liberation, 3937
libertarianism, 4393, 6652, 6801
liberty, 1034, 2792; Aquinas, T., 5849; Bergson, H., 945; Bradwardine, T., 4109; Croce, B., 1014; Mill, J., 747, 1257, 6660; Renouvier, C., 7216
life, 841, 1379, 2164, 2474, 3837, 3852, 4187, 7118, 7122
limit, 2019, 3736
linguistic philosophy, 52, 648, 768, 1040, 1338, 2305, 2890, 3363, 3840, 6242, 6251, 6327, 6855
Lipsius, J., 5904
literature, 600, 1811, 2938, 3347, 3573, 3698, 4771, 5257, 6224, 6589, 6765, 6795, 6862, 7423, 7501
Lloyd, A., 6159
Locke, A., 4432
Locke, J., 2398, 2708, 2847, 2982, 3122, 4535, 5876, 6724, 7438; certainty, 6919; cognition, 7232; composition theory, 852; epistemology, 884, 2541, 4671, 7394; essence, 289, 4106; ethics, 3095, 3751, 5025; faith, 4681; freedom, 3476; God, 4066; identity, 2897, 4214, 6790; image, 1512; language, 1887, 2373, 4858, 7394; logic, 3460; meaning, 2051; metaphysics, 3460; method, 120; mind, 1146, 3447; mind/body, 3447; obligation, 950; perception, 5151; political philosophy, 1382, 1446, 3504, 3751, 3800, 4654, 5025; power, 534, 6112; property, 1446; realism, 2786; religion, 2682; religious toleration, 888; qualities, 5813; Sargeant, J., 628; scepticism, 2996; soul, 4455; substance, 289; universals, 1006
Lodge, O., 1296
Loew of Prague, 7150
Löwith, K., 2650
logic, 676, 1010, 1035, 1137, 1236, 1329, 1339, 1369, 1424, 1774, 1952, 2120, 2161, 2466, 2561, 2647, 2741, 3025, 3094, 3788, 3899, 3935, 4034, 4191, 4249, 4410, 4413, 4588, 4589, 4611, 4649, 4839, 5119, 5189, 5214, 5384, 5668, 5707, 5755, 5906, 6041, 6215, 6423, 6739, 6870, 7156, 7170, 7248, 7279, 7503; Albertus Magnus, 1266, 6776, 7083; Aquinas, T., 5977; Arabic, 323; argumentation, 569; Aristotle, 458, 1759, 2635, 4349, 4635, 5589; Avicenna, 3540; Babarella, G., 1838; Boolean, 5049; Bosanquet, B., 344, 4011; Bradley, F., 3321, 5104, 5932; Broad, C.D., 2340; Buddhist, 1534; Carnap, R., 748, 6629; Chinese, 2709, 3087; Chisholm, R., 7351; Collingwood, R.G., 1352; conditionals, 560, 694; constants, 4524; conventionalism, 2328; decision, 3202; definition, 714, 1577; deontic logic, 1342, 2966; Dewey, J., 117, 701, 3067, 4011, 5024; directives, 6355; entailment, 396, 1806; Epicurean, 4383; and ethics, 1301, 7215, 7261; extension, 2180; external logic, 100; finite, 111; form, 1435, 3756; Frefe, G., 5912, 7054; Gentile, G., 3020; Greek, 1404, 6565;

Hegel, G., 1416, 1644, 3968, 7115; Heidegger, M., 1978; Hintikka, K., 7351; history of, 620, 706, 873, 943, 1025, 1647, 1766, 2709, 3087, 6604, 6816, 6913, 7313; Hume, D., 4016; Husserl, E., 208, 2461, 4118, 4544, 7099; hypothesis, 295, 1355; imperatives, 1097; Indian, 6546; induction, 295, 678, 1197, 1367, 1812, 2202, 3045, 4536; instantial sentences, 386; intensional logic, 293, 1781, 2636, 3364; Kant, E., 6603; Lebesque, H., 2229; Leibniz, G., 5001; Lewis, C.I., 2299, 3175; Locke, J., 3460; Lotze, R., 4011; MacColl, H., 6368; many-valued, 1308, 4471, 4540, 7381; Mill, J., 1364, 2176, 2963, 3432, 3685, 4294, 4320, 6000, 6061, 6220, 6328, 7034, 7191, 7329; modal logic, 251, 323, 710, 2094, 3553, 3776, 4540, 5093; multi-vocal sentences, 1915; negation in, 519, 5781; non-existence, 1205; paradoxes, 1303; Paulus Pergulersis, 728; Peirce, C.S., 482, 697, 843, 3464, 3603, 4550, 6231, 7483; Plato, 4219; predicables, 2959; Pseudo Scotus, 4155; Quine, W., 887, 1847, 6179; reflexive statements, 593; Reid, T., 4389; Russell, B., 3342, 4954, 5056; Sorites, 7158; Stoic, 4438, 7498; symbolic, 2047, 6847; tense-logic, 1176, 1191, 4097, 6979; terms, 4437; verification, 138; Wilson, C., 5698; Wittgenstein, L., 5912; Von Wright, 7351
logical positivism, 7139
logicism, 399
<u>logos</u>, 584, 1608, 2843
loneliness, 7017
Lonergan, B., 580, 1263, 1656, 2061, 3180, 3561, 3778, 4423, 5663, 6014, 6857
Lorenz, K., 3339
Lossky, N.O., 3420, 3608, 4873
Lotze, R.H., 3653, 4011, 4688, 5891, 6668, 6726, 7244
love, 1253, 1395, 2590, 3439, 3645, 5133, 5250, 5421, 5788, 5799
Lovejoy, A.O., 5124, 5595
loyalty, 1448
Lubbock, P., 4805
Lu Hsiang-shan, 3088
Lukacs, G., 1589
Lull, R., 190
Luther, M., 1604, 3848, 6241
Lutheranism, 3944
lying, 1983, 6682
Lyons, D., 2353

MacColl, H., 6368
Mach, E., 3237, 6091, 7138
Macintosh, D.C., 2494, 4711
MacMurray, J., 3222, 3779, 4274, 4901
macrocosm/microcosm idea, 1259
McTaggart, J.M., 5987, 6017, 7468
Madhyamika, 1004
Magni, V., 4360
Maimon, S., 4416
Maimonides, M., 2316, 2455, 2779, 5395, 5712, 5995, 7157
Maine de Biran, 2089, 2670
Maistre, J. de, 951
Malcolm, N., 68, 5596, 6209
Malebranche, N., 1020, 1287, 1293, 1726, 1947, 2182, 3057, 3164, 3577, 3919, 4143, 4848, 5742, 6586, 7057
man, 161, 1332, 2294, 2617, 3044, 3419, 3663, 3782, 4237, 4329, 4667, 4781, 5005, 5048, 5323, 5481, 5616, 5657, 5680, 6191, 6196, 6825, 7319; Allport, G., 2802; Aquinas, T.,

236, 929, 3955, 6588, 6747, 7466; Berdyaev, N., 6460; Bergson, H., 6455; Bonaventure, St., 5057; Bradley, F., 4138; Bremond, H., 938; in Buddhism, 7346; Camus, A., 472; Cassirer, E., 6996; Cicero, 3974; Collingwood, R.G., 4412, 7409; communism, 1668, 5956; Confucianism, 7182; Dewey, J., 1884, 4391; Duns Scotus, J., 929; Eckhart, M., 4665; and ethics, 1436; Freud, S., 1256, 2140, 3835; Godwin, W., 6700; Hegel, G., 1324; Hobbes, T., 2896; Hsün Tzu, 1102; Humboldt, W., 6695; Hu Shih, 5036; James, W., 1088; Jefferson, T., 5194; Kant, E., 6898; Lavelle, L., 6268; Malebranche, N., 1020; Marcel, G., 2285, 3084; Marcuse, H., 472; Marx, K., 403, 734, 1813, 2762, 2848, 5715; Montaigne, M., 4464; Niebuhr, R., 3050, 7349; Nietzsche, F., 7296; Ortega y Gasset, J., 4068; Pascal, B., 1019; Rahner, K., 6498; Ricoeur, P., 3151; Romero, F., 5180; Rousseau, J., 2434; Sartre, J.-P., 2043, 4390, 7346; Scheler, M., 4537, 4841; Sellars, R., 5624; Skinner, B.F., 472; Teilhard de Chardin, P., 6871; Tillich, P., 4401; time, 1313; Whitehead, A., 4175, 5194
management, 2388
Mandelbaum, M., 6883
manifest destiny, 7370
Mann, T., 662
Mantuani, P., 3204
Marcel, G., 2225, 2355, 3273, 3814, 5416, 5513, 5847, 6481; community, 4549; depth, 4204; experience, 1021; freedom, 5941; God, 5234, 5559; hope, 4982; idealism, 6430; intersubjectivity, 4313; man, 2285, 3084; mystery, 3345, 5982; person, 5789; self, 1550, 5878; social philosophy, 6805; time, 6970
Marcuse, H., 472, 1451, 1576, 3393, 6379
Maréchal, J., 629, 3219, 5582, 6960
Maritain, J., 795, 1596, 1927, 2700, 2817, 3411, 3716, 4017, 4556, 4894, 5068, 5567, 5796, 5831, 5870, 6723
Marsh, J., 7176
Marsilius of Padua, 1814, 2323
Martineau, J., 461, 725, 2909
Marx, K., 1866, 2276, 2654, 2711, 3393, 3752, 4580, 5045, 5620, 6245, 6832; action, 3980, 4933; aesthetics, 6826; alienation, 5604, 7239; atheism, 1813; community, 4495; economics, 2034; ethics, 6013; Greece, 3330; history, 2170, 2235, 6890; history, 2170, 2235, 6890; individual/society, 1588; labor, 6450; man, 403, 734, 1813, 2762, 2848, 5715; materialism, 2170, 5800; nature, 2848, 5593; political philosophy, 3070; power, 5296; religion, 4243; self-determination, 121; society, 4110; state, 7171; value, 1344; violence, 7047
Marxism, 108, 2433, 2690, 3937, 4949, 5312, 5449, 6379, 6764; Banfi, A., 5337; ethics, 2774; Feuerbach, L., 4142; methodology in, 189; political philosophy, 5016
Masaryk, T., 5805
Mascall, E., 5291, 6133
Maslow, A., 3485
mass, 3636
master/slave, 7309
material substance, 292
materialism, 1201, 2073,

2170, 2294, 4176, 4617,
5418, 5614, 5800, 6167,
7024
mathematics, 202, 1033, 1111,
2493, 2582, 2965, 3598,
4043, 4729, 4839, 5195,
5384, 5394, 5491, 5536,
6136, 6447, 6573, 6799,
7063, 7110; Aquinas, T.,
133; Aristotle, 133, 157,
2591, 5574; Berkeley, G.,
336; Brouwerian algebra,
3538; certainty in, 3552;
Euclid, 7354; Frege, G.,
818; Gerasenus, N., 3255;
Husserl, E., 3097; Kant,
E., 735, 818, 4050; negation in, 519; Plato, 767,
4579; Russell, B., 4837,
5469, 7260; Schroeder, E.,
7260; truth in, 194, 1350,
2663; Weyl, H., 4081;
Whitehead, A., 5469, 7260;
Wittgenstein, L., 2775,
3496, 3572, 3890, 6690
matter, 213, 544, 981, 1135,
1353, 1417, 1437, 2016,
2403, 2875, 3030, 4369,
4469, 5420, 5840, 6718,
7185
Matthew of Acquasparta, 384
Maxwell, J.C., 2327, 6843
May, R., 5558
Mazzoni, J., 5461
Mead, G.H., 829, 1665, 3286,
5775; action, 1394, 6734;
communication, 171; epistemology, 2064, 3287; ethics, 763; language, 985;
meaning, 3415; metaphysics,
1116; mind, 1867, 3478,
6577; objects, 617; perception, 3287, 6734; personality, 7155; perspective,
59; rationality, 3358;
self, 1165, 1284, 1550,
2758, 3478, 3942, 4693,
6472, 6701; social philosophy, 2301, 2730, 3016;
time, 1394
meaning, 12, 64, 499, 800,
1369, 1611, 1874, 1944,
2014, 2191, 2448, 2491,
2573, 2906, 3187, 3217,
3602, 3706, 3870, 3961,
3978, 4492, 4668, 4689;
Ayer, A., 3234; Berkeley,
G., 1003, 6929; Blanshard,
B., 4094; Cassirer, E.,
3963; coherence, 2390;
Dewey, J., 7392; Heidegger,
M., 683; Hellenistic philosophy, 82, 1566; Hume,
D., 3309; Husserl, E.,
7281; Lewis, C.I., 3489,
4180; Locke, J., 2051;
Mead, G.H., 3415; Mill, J.,
3963; Plato, 4697; and
pragmatism, 1675; Russell,
B., 5950; Schiller, F.,
7392; Whitehead, A., 2531;
Wittgenstein, L., 3837,
4728, 5004, 7253
meaninglessness, 1910, 3759
measurement, 2309, 2585,
3335, 4843, 5699
mechanics, 24, 1057, 1290,
3566, 7198
mechanism, 6, 2515, 3670,
7110
mediation, 3220
Meinong, A., 282, 2837,
6278
Melanchthon, P., 2932
Melden, A.I., 5489
memory, 84, 105, 456, 557,
849, 1190, 1904, 2321,
4113, 4764, 4799, 4874,
4892, 5493, 5757, 5905,
6001, 6314
Mencius, 5936
mental acts, 373, 3724,
4386
mental illness, 2232, 2502,
4737, 5610, 6443
mentalism, 4840, 7110
Merleau-Ponty, M., 462, 946,
1954, 2778, 4044, 4484,
5894, 6644; aesthetics,
5359, 7484; body, 308,
437, 1185, 1851, 2691,
6388; cogito, 858; concept, 775; consciousness,
4816; Descartes, R., 4710;
expression, 5177; freedom,
3525; individual, 4023;
intentionality, 4352; intersubjectivity, 3525;
language, 1462, 2186,
3188, 4625, 6842; ontology,

1651, 2175; perception, 2637, 3061; religion, 7477; self, 3134; sexuality, 4200, 4625; social philosophy, 6806; space, 2691; subjectivity, 463, 2185; time, 2691, 3123; violence, 3766, 7047
Meslier, J., 1971
metaphor, 440, 1147, 2640, 2749, 3104, 5745, 6128, 6742, 6929
metaphysics, 65, 122, 793, 1018, 1593, 2526, 2639, 2980, 3052, 3338, 3705, 4105, 4173, 4584, 4602, 4835, 4944, 4994, 5126, 5511, 6517, 6534, 6623, 6691, 6761, 6889, 7424, 7464; Aquinas, T., 1642, 2543, 3064, 4368, 4709, 4986, 6329, 6557, 6788, 7319, 7386; Aristotle, 1937, 2325, 3252, 3461, 4152, 4368, 5682, 6259, 6478; Aurobindo Ghose, 774; Averroes, 835, 2325; Berdyaev, N., 1794; Bergson, H., 504, 4271, 4719; Bosanquet, B., 996; Bowne, B., 3815; Bradley, F.H., 376, 408, 3307, 6678, 7433; Bruno, G., 5407; Chinese, 6569; Chu Hsi, 7455; Coleridge, S., 6646; Collingwood, R., 1389, 2062, 2130, 5917; creativity, 719; Descartes, R., 749, 1293, 1618, 3327, 5307; Dewey, J., 200, 2257, 3461, 6247; Duns Scotus, J., 2861, 6732, 7040; Emmet, E., 4027; existence, 183; existentialism, 650, 6120; Frege, G., 3580; Geulincx, A., 1293; Hartshorne, C., 4094; Heidegger, M., 1132, 1537, 1903, 2504, 5141, 7097; Hocking, W., 2357; Hume, D., 3461, 3981, 5434, 6374, 7399; idealism, 25; Indian, 349; individuals, 175; James, W., 1800, 4788, 5721; judgment, 2986; Kant, E., 2593, 2822, 3135; Leibniz, G., 1242, 2655, 2783, 5001; Locke, J., 3460; Lonergan, B., 6014; Lotze, R., 4688; Malebranche, N., 1293; Marechal, J., 629, 6960; Maritain, J., 795; Mead, G., 1116; Mill, J.S., 4294; Moore, G., 6426; Newton, I., 856; Ockham, W., 4368; Peirce, C.S., 3017, 4675; Perry, R., 6247; Plato, 523, 749, 3833, 6178, 7487; pragmatism, 3034; Ragunatha, 5400; and religion, 1110, 2754; Renouvier, C., 310, 2917; Royce, J., 5090; Schopenhauer, A., 2783, 3999; Smith, G., 2387; Spinoza, B., 475, 1431, 3214, 4864, 5674; Strawson, P.F., 3473; Suarez, F., 1530, 4818; Thomistic, 123, 2226; thought, 657; Urban, W., 5357; Whitehead, A.N., 1108, 2397, 2605, 3452, 3461, 5452, 6348, 6502; Wittgenstein, L., 2296, 3580; Woodbridge, F., 5467; Zubiri, F., 5504
method in philosophy, 476, 3433
Meyerson, E., 1995, 2948, 3737, 4336, 6463
Michotte, A.E., 7209
Mill, J.S., 2255, 2764, 4255, 4720, 4880, 5782, 7417; categories, 1212; empiricism, 3454; epistemology, 2888, 4294; equality, 1257; ethics, 3359, 4426; good, 5173; individualism, 6524; liberty, 747, 1257, 6660; logic, 1364, 2175, 2963, 3432, 3685, 4294, 4320; meaning, 3963; metaphysics, 4294; nature, 485; political philosophy, 960, 4769; psychology, 3359; reference, 3963; religion, 5225; science, 752, 4830; social philosophy, 1030, 3885, 4769; universals, 1972; utilitarianism, 489, 747, 3671, 4378

Mills, C.W., 956
mind, 1292, 1494, 1883, 2124, 2156, 2597, 3218, 3246, 3356, 3447, 4722, 5497, 5608, 5899, 6349, 6599; Alexander, S., 2462; Aquinas, T., 4955; Armstrong, A., 7024; Cassirer, E., 2462; Chomsky, N., 6399; Cohen, M., 1568; Descartes, R., 536, 2555, 7228; Edwards, J., 134; Freud, S., 2360; group mind, 2821; Hegel, G., 2528, 4220; Hobbes, T., 551; Hume, D., 5213, 7363; James, W., 4275; Kant, E., 5213, 7363; language, 4024; Lewis, C., 3110; Locke, J., 1146; Mead, G., 1867, 3478, 6577; other minds, 681, 1721, 2233, 2449, 3108, 3240, 3536, 3915, 4003, 4009, 4254, 4406, 4715, 4733, 6365, 6371, 6466, 6767, 6976, 7228, 7441; parallelism, 5722; Peirce, C.S., 4159, 6844; physicalism, 392; Piaget, J., 4452; Plantinga, A., 6767; Polanyi, M., 3161; privileged access, 4141, 4715; Ryle, G., 31, 4559; Santayana, G., 3718, 7185; Sartre, J.-P., 4559; Sellars, R.W., 1568, 1819; Strawson, P., 6183; Ward, J., 5264; Whitehead, A., 4806, 7066; Wittgenstein, L., 102, 4715, 6183; Woodbridge, F., 1568
mind/body, 74, 256, 1319, 1496, 1890, 3048, 3498, 3889, 3897, 4055, 4577, 5052, 5115, 5137, 5264, 5294, 5334, 5722, 5931, 6028, 6141, 6708, 6944, 6990; identity, 613, 1194, 1213, 1898, 2027, 2123, 2930, 3021, 3376, 3559, 4049, 4964, 5098, 6134, 6202
Minkowski, E., 4532
miracles, 40, 204, 326, 1699, 3825, 4298, 4774
modality, 1776

models, 627, 1435, 1776, 2422, 3412, 6573
modernism, 3917
Molina, E., 6269
monads, 7336
monism, 2769, 2892, 3237, 4390, 4454, 4517, 4821, 6151, 6418, 7081
Montague, W.P., 3440, 5124
Montaigne, M., 4464, 4956
Montesquieu, C., 4040
Montgomery, E., 3418
Moore, G.E., 2661, 4177, 5331; and Berkeley, 978; common sense, 2967; epistemology, 2894, 3571, 3739, 4289, 6218, 7371; ethics, 255, 760, 1634, 1921, 2713, 3135, 3526, 6608, 6802, 7371; good, 7446; idealism, 978, 3483, 3992; Kant, E., 3135; man, 7349; metaphysics, 2553, 3135; method, 510, 1189; necessity, 3195; perception, 2535; realism, 3912, 4203, 7084; sense-data, 473, 5522, 5970, 6748; value, 1005
More, H., 4238, 6426
More, P.E., 4480, 7074
More, T., 1551, 7236
Morgan, C.L., 5499, 5958
Morgan, L.H., 4805
Moritz, C.P., 1886
Morris, G.S., 3285
Morse, J., 4736
mortality, 4652
Moses of Narbonne, 3176
motion, 3260, 3319, 4148
motivation, 1419, 1606, 6527, 7062, 7136, 7342
motives, 755, 2712, 3808, 3933, 5632, 5765, 7018
MoTze, 4497, 6829
Mounier, E., 944
movements, 4107, 7357
Mumford, L., 1835
Munitz, M.K., 6133
murder, 2289
Murdoch, I., 3104
Murphy, A.E., 713
music, 259, 745, 1586, 1709, 2710, 2747, 2782, 2952, 3880, 4173, 4739, 6025, 6354, 7124

mystery, 2951, 3345, 5982
mysticism, 230, 413, 1145,
 1939, 2676, 2889, 3611,
 5365; Aurobindo Ghose,
 1614; Bissett, J., 4208;
 Blood, B.P., 4377; Böhme,
 J., 76; Döblin, A., 3512;
 Eckhart, M., 4359; Fox,
 G., 3586; Hocking, W.,
 5615, 6777; Hügel, 4208;
 Ibn Tufayl, 2813; Inge,
 D., 2141; Nyaya Vaiśesika,
 4208; Otto, R., 1614;
 Plotinus, 6951; Stace, W.,
 2392; Underhill, E., 1614;
 William of Thierry, 3998
myth, 1182, 1326, 1843,
 2631, 2823, 2962, 5834

Nagarjuna, 3143
names, 1288, 1617, 1844,
 4622, 4666, 5317, 6522,
 6637
Natalis, H., 81
nativism, 203
Natsume-Soseki, 6363
naturalism, 206, 374, 1716,
 1729, 1908, 1986, 2127,
 2536, 4114, 4250, 4614,
 4732, 5591, 5646, 5966,
 6205, 7270, 7365
natural kinds, 3960, 5435
natural law, 164, 276, 975,
 1244, 1670, 2029, 2460,
 3154, 3193, 3262, 3916,
 4477, 4759, 5338, 5444,
 5821, 5829, 7044, 7214;
 Aquinas, T., 388, 632,
 5866; Brunner, E., 846;
 Burke, E., 7275; Ockham,
 W., 918; Plato, 5097;
 Suarez, F., 5930; del Vecchio, 455
natural rights, 30, 1661,
 4216, 5035, 5599, 6265,
 6991, 7275, 7291
nature, 2237, 2374, 3010,
 3857, 4037, 4267, 5007,
 5334, 5575, 6113, 7102,
 7289; Aquinas, T., 1717,
 4095, 4380, 4458; Aristotle, 659, 1426, 6649; Bacon, F., 5441; Boyle, R.,
 1403; Butler, S., 5530;

Cicero, 1060, 3974; Cohen,
 M., 1568; Dewey, J., 430,
 2065, 5908, 7452; Edwards,
 J., 134; Hegel, G., 7103;
 Heraclitus, 5211; Hobbes,
 T., 3256; Hume, D., 1871;
 Kant, E., 842; Leibniz,
 G., 4346, 5601; Marx, K.,
 2848, 5593; Mill, J.S.,
 486; Newton, I., 3120;
 Peirce, C.S., 6838; Plato,
 5369; Plotinus, 1552;
 Santayana, G., 1729, 2875;
 Scotus Erigena, J., 3627;
 Woodbridge, F., 1568, 7452
necessity, 1385, 1828, 2386,
 2408, 3118, 3217, 3995,
 4324, 4440, 6237, 6288,
 6822, 6988, 6992; Aquinas,
 T., 3064; Aristotle, 3697;
 Augustine, 4209; Hume, D.,
 419; Leibniz, G., 2048;
 logic, 397, 714; Moore, G.,
 3195; Spinoza, B., 4103;
 Wittgenstein, L., 2409
negation, 519, 987, 1160,
 1627, 2550, 2608, 3649,
 4160, 4447, 5552, 5781,
 6415, 6927
neo-Platonism, 2612, 2803,
 5006, 5417
neo-Scholasticism, 3353,
 4178, 6434
Newman, J.H., 1674; assent,
 1047, 5806; belief, 400;
 certitude, 4088; epistemology, 1392; faith, 1856
Newton, I., 856, 1771, 2503,
 3120, 3566, 3687, 3731,
 3795, 5156, 5484, 6325
Nicholas of Cusa, 925, 1026,
 1756, 4418, 5077
Niebuhr, R., 837, 3050, 3280,
 4017, 4478, 7000, 7349
Nietzsche, F., 483, 1673,
 3079, 3662, 3681, 3727,
 5157, 5954, 6642, 7200;
 aesthetics, 139, 432, 6848;
 Christianity, 567; education, 2946; epistemology,
 655; eternal return, 4306;
 ethics, 49, 703, 1510,
 4264, 4938; evolution,
 5882; history, 1251, 3750;
 individual, 5826;

individualism, 4513; man, 7296; music, 259; nihilism, 5172; overman, 1264, 4509; play, 2954; science, 6848; Socrates, 1483; tragedy, 4331, 5314; values, 2467, 3391, 5901; will-to-power, 2559; Zarathustra, 1801
Nifo, A., 4314
nihilism, 1380, 1960, 2748, 5172, 5303
nominalism, 1815, 3823, 4201, 5221, 6012, 6846
non-being, 3588, 5167
non-existence, 1205
Norris, J., 4698
nothingness, 603, 1225, 3375, 7069
nous, 2869
Nowell-Smith, P.H., 4773, 6331
number, 172, 238, 298, 418, 806, 4822, 5912, 6410, 6772, 7134, 7318
Numenius of Apamea, 2612
Nyaya-Vaisesika, 4208

Oakeshott, M., 1, 1234
obedience, 4234
object, 617, 684, 762, 999, 1365, 3853, 4151, 4384, 4672, 4891, 6249, 6540
objectivity, 1572
obligation, 209, 267, 285, 426, 582, 595, 615, 950, 1153, 1215, 1276, 1402, 1508, 1517, 1836, 2181, 2224, 2532, 2630, 2860, 2972, 3184, 3597, 3632, 4135, 4196, 4356, 4462, 4523, 4542, 4674, 4876, 6023, 6509, 6513, 7014, 7019, 7028, 7396
occasionalism, 4848
Ockham, W. of, 27, 387, 828, 918, 1148, 2166, 2195, 2231, 4029, 4168, 4368, 4463, 4520, 4664, 5455, 6048, 6103, 6501, 6555, 6785, 7121, 7382
oneness, 1613
ontology, 129, 233, 505, 1092, 1203, 1316, 1386, 3369, 3644, 3658, 3823, 4454, 7179; Abbagnano, N., 3769; Aristotle, 4424; Bergmann, G., 4054; Bonaventure, 101; Brentano, F., 2188; Broad, C., 4997; Carnap, R., 4972; Goodman, N., 2808; Heidegger, M., 2288, 2338, 4931; Merleau-Ponty, M., 1651, 2175; Plato, 6664; Plotinus, 6951; Randall, J., 4732; Russell, B., 4269, 4619; Santayana, G., 753; Sartre, J.-P., 1603, 4865, 5005; and science, 1113; Strawson, P.F., 2646; Tillich, P., 4732; Whitehead, A.N., 2304, 3772, 4353, 4503
ontological argument, 322, 1386, 1616, 1641, 2152, 2286, 2540, 3074, 3745, 3758, 3908, 4351, 4538, 4863, 5015, 6010, 6308, 6704, 6916, 7016, 7217
ontological commitment, 2417, 3969
ontologism, 5252
open question argument, 760
operationalism, 6096
opinion, 1172
optics, 4616, 5868
optimism, 4170, 5176
order, 971, 1320, 2087, 3337
origin, 1502
Orr, J., 6934
Ortega y Gasset, J., 1722, 7225; aesthetics, 3411; being, 3400; historicism, 3435; idealism, 1640, ideology, 61; man, 4068; perspective, 59; political philosophy, 5029; reality, 250; reason, 2245; social philosophy, 6087, 6787
other, 1461
Otto, R., 1614, 3336, 4628, 4680
ought, 525, 1452, 1677, 1988, 5084, 5730, 6255
overman, 1264

Pace, E.A., 653
pacifism, 1981, 2983
Pai-Chang Huai-Hai, 1171
pain, 330, 777, 2498, 4545, 4988
Panofsky, E., 4499
panpsychism, 921, 2358, 3806, 7245
pantheism, 1932, 3113, 6088, 6711, 7079
paradox, 1834, 2610, 6453
paraphrase, 4976
Parmenides, 1925, 2908, 4760, 6385
Parsons, T., 216, 1159
particulars, 1260, 5299, 5914
Pascal, B., 1019, 1149, 4560, 5918, 6326, 7091
passions, 254
past, 4613, 6774
Pater, W., 7444
paternalism, 7221
patriotism, 5572
Patrizi, F., 680
Paul, St., 3145, 3951
Paulus Pergulersis, 728
peace, 5459, 5802
Pearson, K., 1621, 5640
Peirce, C.S., 688, 1525, 1714, 1953, 3651, 4804, 5318, 5516, 5576, 5675, 5684, 5768, 5775, 6079; aesthetics, 6065; belief, 4543, 5059; categories, 364, 881, 1969, 2160, 4002, 5779, 6921; community, 1587, 6961; continuity, 407; decision theory, 2895; deduction, 2814; empiricism, 764, 789; epistemology, 2468, 2944, 4896, 6554; ethics, 4809; evolution, 1870; firstness, 1162; good, 5315; habit, 6101; Hegel, G., 5304; history, 4600; individual, 3939; induction, 1103; instinct, 225, 3291; logic, 482, 697, 834, 3436, 3603, 4550, 6231, 7483; metaphysics, 3017, 4675; method, 1432, 1744, 3102; mind, 4159, 6844; nature, 6838; novelty, 2520; perception, 2810, 3072; person, 2770; possibility, 2927, 4594; pragmatism, 1909, 2444, 5403, 6721; realism, 95, 576, 1909; reason, 225; science, 225, 1995, 6165; signs, 2055, 2530; theology, 159; thirdness, 4529; truth, 2324; values, 2978, 3939
Pepper, S., 624, 1286, 3924, 4647, 5142
perception, 39, 229, 330, 993, 1356, 1977, 2109, 2441, 2644, 2934, 2994, 2997, 3077, 3250, 3287, 3834, 4150, 4233, 4261, 4343, 4371, 4398, 4415, 4767, 4829, 4885, 4923, 4996, 4998, 5063, 5069, 5450, 5701, 5726, 5797, 5836, 5979, 6074, 6332, 6413, 6532, 6592, 6633, 6647, 6734, 6891, 6956, 7026, 7090, 7112; Aquinas, T., 3970; Aristotle, 5069, 6240, 6938; Armstrong, D., 5885; Ayer, A.J., 7010; Bergmann, G., 1360; Bergson, H., 3233, 7460; Berkeley, G., 6395; Bradley, F., 5940; Broad, C.D., 3819; causality in, 736; Chisholm, R., 5759; Dewey, J., 6059; Edwards, J., 5968; Feuerbach, L., 5729; Hamilton, W., 910; Hume, D., 2825; Husserl, E., 1741, 1747; Leibniz, G., 2375; Locke, J., 5151; Merleau-Ponty, M., 2637, 3061; Moore, G., 2535; Peirce, C., 2810, 3072; Piaget, J., 2414; Plato, 4743; Price, H., 3210; psychology of, 702; Reid, T., 910, 1459, 1930, 2519, 3153, 6032; Stout, G., 3913; Whitehead, A.N., 4641, 6648
perfection, 589, 6351
Perry, R.B., 378, 1581, 1986, 2688, 3201, 3650, 3992, 4462, 4654, 5612, 5758, 6247, 6353

person, 417, 911, 989, 1059,
 1357, 1390, 1513, 1655,
 2322, 2486, 2843, 2968,
 4077, 4276, 4905, 5634;
 Aquinas, T., 7060; Berdy-
 aev, N., 2438; Bergson,
 H., 4928; Brightmann, E.,
 474; Buber, M., 309; in
 Buddhism, 3372; in Christianity, 832; Emerson, R.,
 4558; Finance, J. de,
 5454; Hampshire, S.,
 3562; Hartmann, N., 3601;
 Howison, G., 3796; Iqbal,
 M., 309; MacMurray, J.,
 3222; Marcel, G., 5789;
 Maritain, J., 4556;
 Peirce, C.S., 2770; Richard of St. Victor, 1335;
 Rogers, C., 5573; Sartre,
 J.-P., 4727; Strawson,
 P., 2488, 3562, 5789;
 Sturzo, L., 4511; Suzuki,
 D., 309; Tillich, P., 474;
 Whitehead, A., 2227
personal existence, 721,
 3843, 5830
personal identity, 132, 196,
 269, 347, 1136, 2551,
 2897, 3051, 3198, 3551,
 4039, 4214, 5344, 6130,
 6252, 6317
personalism, 253, 3283,
 4179, 4711, 5258, 5416,
 5504, 6043, 6323, 7165
personality, 19, 195, 1207,
 1433, 2499, 2734, 2970,
 3095, 3735, 4527; Allport,
 G., 1268; Aquinas, T.,
 2091; and ethics, 180,
 5343; Freud, S., 601, 7153;
 Kant, E., 3281; Mead, G.,
 7153; Perry, R., 1581;
 Renouvier, C., 2432; Temple, W., 5139
perspectives, 59, 3729
pessimism, 470, 2849, 3677,
 3682
Peter of Auvergne, 1784,
 4645
Peter of Spain, 4778
Peters, R.S., 4828
Petrus Ionnis Olivi, 7238
Petrus Thomae, 682
phantom, 1184

phenomena/noumena, 5859
phenomenalism, 1304, 1694,
 2203, 2725, 3225, 5920,
 6310, 7211, 7297
phenomenology, 1961, 3870,
 4734, 4944, 5410, 6373,
 6549
phenomenon, 1876
Philo Judaeus, 490, 605,
 826
physicalism, 392, 2079,
 3628, 5052
physics, 56, 280, 1399,
 1409, 2219, 2248, 2616,
 4283, 4296, 4777, 5164,
 5511, 5584, 6303, 7142,
 7152, 7250, 7432, 7494
Piaget, J., 684, 2414, 3065,
 4452, 4660, 6076, 6993
Pico, G., 5980
piety, 2742
pindar, 398
Plantinga, A., 4003, 5531,
 6767
Plato, 1607, 2435, 2752,
 3781, 4882, 5461, 5542,
 5669, 5841, 6298, 7116,
 7220, 7417; aesthetics,
 325, 919, 2243, 3300,
 4772, 5532, 6381; aitia,
 815; akrasia, 7089; anamnesis, 6741; Aquinas, T.,
 on, 973; being, 1022,
 3480, 3664, 4479, 4697,
 7025; causality, 3657;
 Charmides, 1217, 2999,
 3893, 6968; cosmology,
 193, 666, 4075; Cratylus,
 579, 5317, 5436, 5791;
 creativity, 803, 1420;
 dikaiosyne, 7306; divided
 line, 265, 7141; educa-
 tion, 1118, 6283, 6942;
 epistemology, 743, 812,
 897, 1235, 1277, 2580,
 3170, 3656, 3877, 4479,
 4852; ethics, 3300, 4323,
 5235, 7193, 7201, 7415;
 euthydemus, 6282; euthe-
 phro, 3038, 7380; evil,
 6811; falsehood, 562;
 freedom, 1235, 1311;
 forms, 287, 668, 919,
 2829, 7273, 7375; God,
 2101, 6420; happiness,

5890; ideas, 1073, 7125; individualism, 2664; instrumentalism, 501; intuition, 5326; justice, 363, 1188, 7440; katharsis, 1897; Laches, 6874; law, 1585, 3279; Laws, 1118; language, 1462, 2228, 3315, 6485; limitation, 2019; logic, 4219; logos, 584, 1608; love, 5133; Lysis, 324, 1217; mathematics, 767, 4579; meaning, 4697; memory, 557; Meno, 5310; metaphysics, 523, 749, 3833, 6178, 7487; method, 107, 5752; mimesis, 3760; motivation, 1419; myth, 2962; names, 5317; natural law, 5097; nature, 5369; non-being, 3588, 5167; number, 148, 6410; ontology, 6664; opinion, 3650; Parmenides, 287, 1054, 2111, 2314, 4219, 4697; participation, 5217, 6057; perception, 4743, 5069; Phaedo, 1704, 2574; Phaedrus, 192, 286, 817; Philebus, 60, 596, 1498, 4075; philia, 1770; poetry, 2311, 5058; political philosophy, 2007, 4184; predication, 3390, 4775; Protagoras, 2429, 4569, 7201; psychology, 3684; punishment, 1061; quality, 596; reality, 3757; Republic, 363, 1118, 1188, 4479, 5329, 6290, 6751; Rhetoric, 1885; social philosophy, 754; Socrates, 355; Sophist, 1022, 3480, 3164, 4697, 6282; soul, 88, 286, 523, 1271, 1516, 7429; Statesman, 4591; suicide, 4979; Symposium, 3144, 6197; Theaetetus, 812, 897, 1298, 1608, 2077; Timaeus, 193, 666, 1143, 5369; time, 2367; truth, 3480; universals, 616; virtue, 1434, 3170, 5890; wonder, 3659
Platonism, 215, 490, 2298, 2881, 4823, 4956, 5373

play, 2954, 7047
pleasure, 319, 1235, 4545, 4643, 5283, 5607, 5649, 7031, 7292
Plekhanov, G., 6764
Pletho, G., 288
Plotinus, 263, 1327, 1552, 2016, 2238, 2484, 2530, 2862, 3381, 3439, 4338, 5717, 6007, 6952, 7073
pluralism, 96, 1664, 3613, 4602
poetry, 222, 800, 949, 1015, 1224, 1713, 1762, 2058, 2581, 2683, 2720, 2817, 2916, 3046, 3142, 3215, 4001, 4522, 5058, 5524, 5900, 5961, 6561, 6661, 7224
Poincaré, H., 5223
Polanyi, M., 2665, 3161, 4008, 6738
Polin, R., 2651
political philosophy, 696, 780, 1472, 1680, 1795, 1814, 2395, 2576, 2886, 3416, 3524, 4047, 4305, 4310, 4881, 5648, 5867, 5921, 5962, 6238, 6362, 7385; American, 235, 6639; Aquinas, T., 1715, 1814, 2008, 2569, 3303, 3354, 4078, 4199; Aristotle, 2569, 5212; Augustine, 459, 2168; Aurobindo Ghose, 3674; Bentham, J., 5016; Bergson, H., 5477; Bosanquet, B., 877, 3721; Brown, N.O., 3251; Brownson, O., 4108; Cervantes, 1482; Chinese, 5397; Chinese, 5397; Collingwood, R., 4897; Croce, B., 2501; Dante, 5735; Debray, R., 5506; Dewey, J., 594, 1648, 3468, 5409; equality, 875, 6762; Federalist Papers, 5927; Gentile, G., 2361; Godwin, W., 1154; Greek, 6610; Green, T., 1115, 4654; Han Fei, 3753; Hobbes, T., 72, 2738, 3031, 7376; Hocking, W., 2004; Holmes, O., 7489; Hooker, R., 4194;

Hume, D., 599, 1155, 4789, 7005; Husserl, E., 3507; Jefferson, T., 1232; Kant, E., 2694; Laski, H., 1034; Levinas, E., 220; and linguistic philosophy, 648; Locke, J., 1382, 1446, 3504, 3751, 3800, 4654, 5025; majority rule, 792; Marsilius of Padua, 1814; Marx, K., 3070; Marxist, 5016; Mill, J.S., 960, 4769; Oakeshott, M., 1, 1234; obligation in, 285, 2630, 4703; Perry, R.B., 4654; Plato, 2007, 4184; pluralism, 5295; power, 1881; Puffendorf, S., 4203; Reuther, W., 4281; Rousseau, J., 2209; Russell, B., 2788; Santayana, G., 3; social contract, 9; Spinoza, B., 1735, 4902, 6901; Suarez, F., 5930; theology and, 3884; Thomistic, 2547; Vitoria, F. de, 1011; wealth, 4582; Whitehead, A.N., 1078
Pomponazzi, P., 5418, 7068
Pope, A., 6171
Popper, K., 171, 365, 2667, 2705, 2863, 3860, 4553, 7207
Porter, N., 3205
Posidonius, 1818
positivism, 1292, 1369, 4277, 4811, 6289, 7282
possibility, 283, 786, 1228, 1474, 1964, 2427, 2927, 4467, 5328, 6351, 6557, 7304
postulation, 3378
potentiality, 1458, 5021, 5750
poverty, 7238
power, 153, 1881, 2945, 5296, 6112
practical reason, 15, 1309, 1439, 1535, 2218, 3726, 4278, 4658, 6563
pragmatism, 909, 2192, 2419, 2444, 2471, 3034, 3407, 3868, 4735, 5066, 5683, 5922, 6549, 6687; Blondel, M., 6040; Bowne, B., 5507; Bradley, F.H., 6971; Dewey, J., 4010, 5027; ethics, 6859; Kant, E., 7283, 7355; Hegel, G., 5686; James, W., 661, 5581, 5851; justice, 3194; meaning in, 550, 1675; Peirce, C., 1909, 4675, 5403, 6721; religion, 2281, 4284; Royce, J., 708; truth, 2024, 2324; Wittgenstein, L., 6760
Prall, 477
Pratt, J.B., 4208, 5892
prayer, 6533
predestination, 3228
predication, 513, 2339, 2924, 3390, 4207, 4775, 4776, 4951, 5731, 6153, 6341
presence, 237, 1316, 1400, 2196
pre-Socratics, 1255, 5695, 6064, 7220, 7390
prestige, 4188
presupposition, 1565, 2560, 3249, 4128, 5392, 6230, 6292
Price, H.H., 3210, 5602
Price, R., 1406, 2831, 3801, 4018, 5240, 5243
Prichard, H.A., 4048, 4767
Priestley, J., 5614
primary-qualities, 578, 695
primitivism, 5425
Pringle-Pattison, A.S., 461, 5287
private-language, 2036, 4376, 6258
probability, 328, 372, 941, 1484, 1676, 2172, 2815, 3223, 3428, 4382, 4553, 4594, 5066, 5465, 5483, 5693, 6377
process, 1086, 6383
Proclus, 5751
profit, 351
progress, 605, 1573, 2622, 3831, 4084
promises, 5766
proof, 424, 5487, 5929, 6425
properties, 4057
property, 30, 94, 1446,

2154, 4167, 5131, 5160, 5260, 6233, 6476
prophecy, 6786
propositions, 247, 479, 822, 1137, 1250, 2267, 4834, 4889, 4948, 5391, 7337, 7405
Protagoras, 1336
proto-meaning, 1506
providence, 2750
prudence, 660, 799, 847, 1500, 2307, 2998, 4235, 5083, 5236, 5548, 6315
Pseudo-Denis, 5464
Pseudo-Dionysius, 1756, 6852
Pseudo-Grosseteste, 4230
Pseudo-Scotus, 4155
psychiatry, 2354
psychoanalysis, 545, 601, 942, 1062, 1068, 4394, 4409, 5503, 5558, 5655, 6145, 6163, 6737, 6944, 7223, 7342
psychologism, 4116
psychology, 772, 829, 848, 1035, 1332, 2035, 2780, 4943, 5187, 6559, 6719, 7207; abnormality in, 733; Albertus Magnus, 5577; Allport, G., 3485; Aquinas, T., 5013, 5033; Aristotle, 6173; Bonaventure, 5033; Brentano, F., 1917, 6807; defense mechanisms, 1911; Dilthey, W., 6746; explanation in, 3550; Freud, S., 4780; Hegel, G., 7050; Kant, E., 1317, 1623; Maimonides, 5995; Maslow, A., 3485; Meyerson, E., 3737; Mill, J., 3359; Plato, 3684; Rogers, C., 3485; Sartre, J.-P., 5009, 5387; Schopenhauer, A., 3999; Spinoza, B., 1775; Taylor, C., 5311; Zabarella, J., 6340
public, 4924
Pufendorf, S. von, 4302
punishment, 819, 957, 1061, 1967, 2143, 2177, 2291, 2413, 3370, 4678, 5346, 5948, 6070, 6097, 6276
purpose, 74, 125, 1248, 2835, 3467, 5499, 5632, 6026, 6400, 7065, 7476
Pythagoras, 1742, 5069

qualities, 596, 1575, 2440, 3035, 5813, 5865
quantification, 342, 710, 2411, 2575, 4402, 4510, 6489, 6713
quantity, 790, 1008
quantum mechanics, 210, 611, 1009, 1323, 1905, 1923, 2020, 2095, 2571, 3813, 3901, 4027, 4590, 4946, 5456, 5777, 6036, 6322
Quidort, J., 2852
Quine, W.V.O., 1669, 2973, 2985, 4222, 4981, 6432; analyticity, 2320; epistemology, 2806, 4716, 5316; logic, 887, 1847, 6179; number, 258; ontology, 2679, 3969; regimentation, 991; translation, 370, 1485, 2717, 4650, 6779; truth, 1553
quotation, 4004, 5951

racial memory, 3329
racism, 2762
Radhakrishnan, 162, 4158
radicalism, 1109
Raghunatha, 5400
Rahner, K., 1615, 6498, 6797
Ramanuja, 1107, 3815
Ramsey, F.P., 6966
Ramsey, I., 1210, 4131, 5796, 5949
Ramsey, P., 5111
Randall, J.H., 3474, 4732, 6115
randomness, 4701
Rashdall, H., 6817
rationalism, 145, 2217, 3012, 3054, 3057, 5564, 5793, 7411
rationality, 358, 2804, 3313, 3358, 5468
rationes seminales, 638, 4232, 5320
Rauch, F.A., 7488

Rauschenbusch, W., 583
Rawls, J., 178, 1297, 1862,
  2333, 2827, 4756, 4862,
  5259, 5875, 6487, 7153
realism, 1924, 1931, 2629,
  2873, 2961, 3013, 3197,
  4129, 4384, 4459, 4576,
  4583, 4969, 5182, 5221,
  5297, 5460, 6038, 6320,
  6480, 7084; Abelard, P.,
  4201; Armstrong, D.,
  4058; Bergmann, G., 4669;
  Berkeley, G., 5743; Brownson, O., 2643; Descartes,
  R., 1280, 5081; Dewey, J.,
  1075; Ducasse, C., 5892;
  James, W., 2293; Locke,
  J., 2786; meaning in, 550;
  Moore, G., 3912; Peirce,
  C.S., 95, 576, 1909; Pratt,
  J., 5892; Pringle-Pattison, A., 5287; Reid, T.,
  1973, 3740; in science,
  627; Sellars, W., 5798
reality, 91, 177, 2306,
  3236, 6683; Berdyaev, N.,
  233; Bosanquet, B., 2234;
  Bradley, F., 2234; Broad,
  C.D., 2297; Collingwood,
  R., 1878; Greene, T., 3265;
  Ortega y Gasset, J., 250;
  Plato, 3757; Russell, B.,
  4046; Unamuno, M., 250;
  Whitehead, A.N., 3243
reason, 225, 707, 965, 1231,
  1237, 1722, 1848, 2144,
  2245, 2939, 3555, 3914,
  4161, 4420, 4656, 4962,
  5117, 5124, 5688
reconstructionism, 1142
reduction, 274, 5697, 5938
reference, 146, 275, 300,
  377, 798, 1090, 1383,
  2014, 2523, 3157, 3288,
  3841, 3963, 4327, 4421,
  4757, 4992, 5219, 5255,
  5557, 5701, 6031, 6224,
  6278, 6306, 6316, 6872,
  6895, 7401
reflexive arguments, 3513
Régis, P.-S., 6600
Reichenbach, H., 890, 3798,
  4272, 5232, 6072
Reid, T., 1763, 2522, 5406,
  5835, 6656; common sense,
  66, 3289, 4367; epistemology, 356, 3739; logic,
  4389; other minds, 6248;
  perception, 910, 1459,
  1930, 2519, 3153, 5063,
  6032; realism, 1973,
  5743; substance, 606
Reinach, A., 673
reism, 6219
relations, 868, 1440, 2464,
  2668, 2693, 2867, 3232,
  3357, 3639, 4041, 4677,
  4730, 5040, 5186, 6068,
  7339
relativism, 1916
relativity, 143, 2121, 2505,
  3373, 3388, 3790, 4371,
  5153, 5823, 6052, 6091,
  6154, 7179, 7219
religion, 248, 1397, 2452,
  2477, 2525, 3486, 3812,
  3907, 4144, 4287, 4659,
  4827, 5159, 5363, 5445,
  5498, 5590, 5830, 6138,
  6143, 6372, 6428, 6795,
  6803, 6995, 7178, 7251,
  7258, 7264; American
  philosophy, 246, 1444;
  Aquinas, T., 658; Bergson,
  H., 1767; Bosanquet, B.,
  4920; Boström, C., 369;
  Brightman, E., 4632;
  Buddhism, 7174; Butler,
  J., 7226; Comte, A.,
  1509, 2595; creativity in,
  718; Dewey, J., 18, 1895,
  5713; Dooyeweerd, H.,
  1183; Duméry, H., 1547;
  Emerson, R., 2287, 3343;
  Engels, F., 4243; Eliade,
  M., 80; and ethics, 1179,
  2046, 2481; and evolution,
  1846, 3826; Farrer, A.,
  5621; Feuerbach, L., 6983;
  Fox, G., 3586; Freud, S.,
  1582; functionalism, 757;
  Green, T., 2735; Häger-
  ström, A., 5883; Hart-
  shorne, C., 3203; Hegel,
  G., 4399, 4609, 5089,
  5963; Heine, H., 110;
  Hicks, J., 667; Hocking,
  W., 2336; Hügel, F.V.,
  6938; Hume, D., 838, 3244,
  4265, 4552, 4838, 4866;

and idealism, 2514; James, W., 503, 1922, 2751, 3878, 4275, 4918, 5581, 6537; Kant, E., 311, 1179, 1509, 1922, 2102, 2197, 3767, 3844, 7374; Kierkegaard, S., 1106, 1179, 1922, 2404, 3284, 5085; Lenin, V., 4243; Lessing, G.E., 93; and linguistic philosophy, 4663; Macintosh, D., 2494; Maritain, J., 6722; Merleau-Ponty, M., 7477; and metaphysics, 1110, 2754; Mill, J., 5225; Niebuhr, R., 3280; Ockham, W., 4168; Otto, R., 4628; Plantinga, A., 6767; Platonism in, 2298; and pragmatism, 2281, 4284; psychology of, 5265, 5414; Rahner, K., 1615; Ramsey, I., 4131; Randall, J., 3474; Royce, J., 433, 4221; Santayana, G., 3366, 5117, 6551; Scheler, M., 7163; Schleiermacher, F., 17, 429, 750, 1646, 4961; Shaftesbury, 2512; Spencer, H., 2595; Spinoza, B., 4197; and state, 851; symbols in, 874, 2104; Thomism, 1262; Tillich, P., 2104, 2539, 3343, 6722, 6915; truth in, 1592, 2179; Ucken, 1499; values in, 3921; Ward, J., 5666; Wesley, J., 1816; Wieman, H., 1262, 2494; Wittgenstein, L., 6692; Wobbermin, G., 4918
religious consciousness, 3518
religious experience, 315, 409, 2287, 3336, 4006, 4680, 5080, 5375, 5618, 5703, 6692
religious knowledge, 2355, 2751, 3424, 4585, 5399, 5445, 5661
religious language, 99, 241, 337, 880, 931, 1023, 1210, 1314, 1521, 1598, 2539, 2853, 3132, 3139, 4225, 5210, 5586, 6702, 6703, 7013
Remy de Gourmont, 1366
Renouvier, C.B., 310, 907, 2432, 2917, 4013, 7216
renunciation, 1413
respect, 6492
responsibility, 11, 343, 371, 637, 679, 1209, 1836, 1906, 2082, 2092, 2291, 2502, 2521, 2844, 2941, 2979, 2981, 3063, 3103, 3446, 3521, 4379, 4521, 5778, 5911, 7095, 7398
retribution, 3997, 4678, 6948
Reuther, W., 4281
revelation, 89, 315, 1736, 2823, 4653, 6995
revolt, 2744
revolution, 548, 4154, 4309
Richard of Campsall, 6609
Richard of St. Victor, 1335
Richards, I.A., 491, 5827, 5961
Ricoeur, P., 607, 1140, 1346, 3151, 5541, 6235, 6267, 6483
rig veda, 1594
right reason, 864
rights, 893, 4449, 5617, 5942, 5997, 6106, 7333
Rilke, R.M., 1224, 2685
ritual, 2879
Rodynton, J. of, 6849
Rogers, C., 3485, 5573, 6470
Rogers, W., 4702
romanticism, 508, 6543
Romero, F., 1299, 5180
Rommen, H., 583
Rorty, A., 1829
Rosenzweig, F., 3056, 7416
Rosmini-Serbati, A., 771
Ross, A., 2516
Ross, W.D., 340, 442, 1921, 2713, 4048, 5969, 6023
Rostand, J., 391
Rousseau, J.J., 950, 2209, 2434, 4686
Royce, J., 1476, 1550, 2537, 3224, 3283, 7172; absolute, 433; being, 2099, 4531; community, 4959, 6280, 6386;

epistemology, 1138, 1691, 3421; ethics, 2213; existence, 5612; faith, 4855; God, 1796, 3216, 6236; individuals, 2578, 4345; individuation, 5333; interpretation, 3754; metaphysics, 5050; pragmatism, 708; religion, 433, 4221; self, 1331, 4693, 6216; social philosophy, 1997, 2301, 6104; teleology, 5482; theology, 904; time, 2483; will, 3505, 7003
rules, 585, 672, 811, 2241, 3738
Russell, B., 1807, 2183, 2204, 2594, 2610, 4177, 4883, 5272, 6092, 6707, 6837, 7161; analysis in, 1189, 2268; atomism, 412, 481; belief, 2319; descriptions, 1030; emotion, 3616; empiricism, 2344; epistemology, 3234, 5509, 6684; ethics, 47, 4227; idealism, 3483; identity, 2125; language, 1285, 2652, 4046; logic, 3342, 4954, 5056; mathematics, 4837, 5469, 7260; meaning, 5950; monism, 4821; nature, 4037; ontology, 4269, 4619; political philosophy, 2788; realism, 2961, 7084; reality, 4046; reconstructionism, 1142; reference, 6278; relation, 5186; sense-data, 5970; social philosophy, 1595, 4906; teleology, 5482; value, 1206
Ryle, G., 31, 319, 1063, 2103, 2904, 2974, 3089, 3616, 4559, 6343

Saccheri, G., 1880
St.-Simon, C.-H. de, 3782
salvation, 2638, 3607
Santayana, G., 843, 2567, 2570, 3034, 3529, 3596, 4555, 5850, 5862; aesthetics, 179, 198, 6213, 6548; culture, 6042;

epiphenomenalism, 78; epistemology, 2445, 4717, 6529, 6670; essence, 2875, 6552; ethics, 3, 78, 4796; existence, 2445; freedom, 78; materialism, 1201; matter, 2875, 7185; mind, 3718, 7185; nature, 1730, 2875; ontology, 753; politics, 3; pragmatism, 2192; reason, 4161, 5117; religion, 3336, 3366, 5117, 6551; scepticism, 1928; social philosophy, 6211
Sapir, E., 976
Sartre, J.-P., 1524, 2563, 4036, 4325, 4580, 6225; alienation, 7092; art, 184; atheism, 955; bad faith, 547; choice, 3947; consciousness, 469, 540, 1233, 3451, 4211, 4816, 5965; ego, 3451, 6506; emotion, 1998; epistemology, 1654; ethics, 2193, 3295, 6312; evil, 4963; freedom, 184, 825, 1310, 2043, 2078, 2702, 3881, 5527, 5941, 6166, 7428; intersubjectivity, 805; judgment, 394; love, 1395; man, 2043, 4390, 7346; mind, 4558; ontology, 1603, 4865, 5009; person, 4727; psychology, 5009, 5387; responsibility, 2082; self, 166, 6156, 6353; sincerity, 2149; social philosophy, 3293; time, 540; value, 3212, 4561
satisfaction, 20
scepticism, 434, 860, 995, 1928, 1936, 2658, 2737, 2793, 2940, 2996, 3488, 3869, 4320, 4406, 4494, 4813, 5245, 6099, 6514, 6705, 6752, 7364
Scheler, M., 1253, 1555, 2207, 2431, 3434, 3601, 4537, 4841, 5280, 5515, 5673, 7163; ethics, 1555, 2949, 4801, 6932, 7038; value, 5980, 6358, 6594

Schelling, F.W.J., 577, 809, 1627, 2511, 2615, 2823, 2826, 4433, 6886, 6943
Schiller, F., 1864, 1938, 3330, 7495
Schiller, F.C.S., 7, 6149, 7234, 7392
schizophrenia, 6443
Schlegel, F. von, 7312
Schleiermacher, F.D.E., 17, 28, 649, 750, 1646, 4358, 4961, 6375
Schlick, M., 3387, 5658
Schopenhauer, A., 26, 90, 259, 470, 1121, 2783, 2848, 3591, 3999, 4494, 4513, 4615, 4872, 6122, 6828
Schroeder, E., 7260
Schrödinger, 7198
Schütz, A., 1349, 6562, 6893, 7111
Schweizer, A., 3940, 5564
Sciacca, M.F., 2318, 4342, 4868
science, 266, 859, 1571, 1893, 1929, 2068, 2214, 2389, 3431, 3934, 4794, 4936, 4960, 5007, 5238, 5505, 5899, 5938, 6435, 6440, 6457, 6534, 6631, 6730, 6749, 6950, 6967, 7114, 7290, 7344, 7425, 7432; Aristotle, 4240, 4738; Augustine, 5598; Bacon, F., 1477; Berkeley, G., 715, 6187; Cassirer, E., 7033, 7359; certitude, 1425; change in, 3630, 4605, 4978, 6182, 6295, 7358; Comte, A., 1509; concepts in, 813; Condillac, E., 982; confirmation, 5992; conventionalism, 6174; creativity in, 3832; definition in, 1051; Descartes, R., 982, 1240, 1618, 2015, 6495, 6940; Dewey, J., 1689, 2527; Diderot, D., 6940; Duhem, P., 958, 1995, 5078; Einstein, A., 294; epistemology of, 1869, 3060; explanation in, 22, 185, 641, 1117, 1430, 1966, 2030, 2369, 3695, 4425, 4888, 5156, 5462, 7461; Feigel, H., 4059; Feyerabend, P., 821, 1733, 3791; Frank, P., 3158; geometry in, 10; Hare, R.M., 2145; Hegel, G., 6270; history of, 3590, 3636, 3795, 4425, 5102, 6192; idealization in, 307; Jaspers, K., 1850; Kant, E., 1509, 3836; Kuhn, T., 1733, 3791; language in, 890, 3631, 6570; law in, 278, 2641, 3798, 4888, 5466, 6288, 7359; Leibniz, G., 982, 6628; logical-empiricism, 445; Lonergan, B., 580; Mach, E., 7138; Maxwell, J., 2327; method in, 221, 704, 781, 2603, 2722, 3115, 3379, 3537, 3673, 3795, 3832, 4987, 5322, 6184, 6192; Meyerson, E., 1995, 4336; Mill, J.S., 752, 4800; models in, 5087, 6573; Newton, I., 3687, 5156; Nietzsche, F., 6848; objectivity in, 4248, 4651; observation in, 4205, 4651; Ockham, W., 6501; and ontology, 1113; operationalism, 3631; paradigms in, 5208; Pearson, K., 5640; Peirce, C., 225, 1995, 6165; Poincaré, H., 5223; Popper, K., 3860; rationality in, 290, 2920; realism, 1989; Reichenbach, H., 890, 6072; simplicity in, 16, 1024, 1666; Stallo, J., 7276; symmetry in, 221; teleology in, 7330; and theology, 3130; theory in, 3117, 3294, 3860, 3903, 4888, 6232, 6571, 6836; Vinci, L. da, 1046; Weber, M., 3477; Whewell, W., 4052, 5244, 5939, 7043; Whitehead, A., 718, 1999, 3720, 5127
Searle, J.R., 5134, 6256
secularism, 658
seeing, 3191

self, 86, 156, 727, 1564, 1852, 2237, 2453, 3165, 3338, 3986, 4487, 5652, 6117, 6294, 6627, 6964, 7021; Bosanquet, B., 2970; Brightman, E., 6353; Bradley, F., 2970, 3417, 4875, 6905; Buddhism, 2601; Campbell, C., 2153, 2874; Descartes, R., 4417; Dewey, J., 3822, 4476, 5050; Farrer, A., 2874; Fichte, J., 7403; Heidegger, M., 2891, 6789, 7493; Hocking, W., 2067; Hume, D., 166, 2601, 4875; James, W., 347, 1447; Jung, C., 6701; Kant, E., 1193, 4461; Kierkegaard, S., 6353; Lotze, R., 6726; Maine de Biran, 2089; Marcel, G., 1550, 5878; Mead, G., 1165, 1284, 2758, 3478, 3942, 4693, 6472, 6701; Merleau-Ponty, M., 3134; Perry, R., 6353; Plotinus, 4338; Ricoeur, P., 6235; Royce, J., 1331, 4693, 6216; Sartre, J.-P., 166, 6156, 6353; social self, 466; Strawson, P., 2510; Tennant, F., 2496; Thoreau, H., 2221; Ward, J., 2496; Whitehead, A., 2169, 3298, 3839, 4875
self-deception, 756, 1737, 3874, 5389, 5838, 6100, 6114, 6611, 6888, 7462
self-determination, 121, 2343
self-development, 1609, 2189, 3820, 5792
self-evidence, 2478
self-identity, 1410, 2018, 6162
self-interest, 3581
selfishness, 5543
self-knowledge, 597, 1063, 1414, 3089, 3787, 4025, 4854, 6162, 7082
self-love, 3310, 6164
self-reference, 625, 4942
Sellars, R.W., 586, 1568, 1819, 2301, 2548, 4507, 4797
Sellars, W., 121, 2564, 2777, 3041, 3096, 3156, 3163, 4436, 5356, 5624, 5773, 5798
semantics, 1270, 1511, 2222, 2926, 3128, 3494, 3938, 3941, 4328, 4414, 4551, 4846, 4966, 5549, 5858, 6127, 6448, 6957, 7166
semiotics, 5146
Seneca, 2721
sensation, 174, 684, 1120, 1336, 2080, 2238, 2297, 2579, 2969, 3427, 3437, 3443, 3582, 4643, 6071, 6180, 6392, 6680
sense-data, 4, 214, 772, 785, 2031, 2725, 3272, 3564, 3972, 4223, 4470, 4672, 5144, 5169, 5329, 5351, 5970, 6176, 7146; Aristotle, 533; Austin, J., 473, 1882, 6755; Ayer, A., 473, 1882; Moore, G.E., 473, 5522, 6748
Sergeant, J., 628
Sertillanges, A.D., 871
Servius, 7030
sets, 806, 2171, 2545, 4471, 4657, 4768, 5274, 5536, 5811
Sextus Empiricus, 995
sexuality, 2621, 4200, 4625, 6780, 7049
Shaftesbury, Third Earl of, 692, 2332, 2512, 4085, 5138
shame, 2832, 7223
Shih T'ao, 1230
Shoemaker, S., 4229, 7379
Sibley, F.N., 2272
Sidgwick, H., 427, 1302, 2076, 3495, 3793, 4915, 6016, 6645, 7302
Siewerth, G., 3541
signs, 2055, 2530, 2785, 2994
Simmel, G., 6922, 7143
Simon ben Zemah Duran, 6380
simplicity, 6336, 6833
sin, 853, 2433, 3049
Singer, M., 2353, 2648, 4624
singulars, 689, 3774, 3871, 4951, 4989

Skinner, B.F., 472, 1261, 5132, 6470
Smart, J.J.C., 2707, 4964
Smith, A., 3177, 3948, 4192
Smith, G., 2387
Smith, J.E., 4006, 4832
Smith, T.V., 3650
social change, 837, 1791, 5808
social contract, 9, 1940, 2365
social philosophy, 720, 726, 1109, 1249, 1786, 2718, 2739, 2953, 3053, 3423, 3925, 3945, 4101, 4166, 4212, 4893, 4941, 5989, 6157, 6177, 6188, 6442, 6566, 6614, 6619, 6865, 7130, 7137, 7345; Aquinas, T., 677, 1347, 2041, 2998, 4294, 4836, 5108, 5166, 6366, 6949, 7361; Aurobindo Ghose, 3617; Bonhoeffer, D., 7127; Bosanquet, B., 1987, 4920, 5986; Camus, A., 472; Croce, B., 1014; Dewey, J., 446, 1987, 2118, 2269, 3213, 4967, 5540, 6787; Gandhi, M., 3617; Gentile, G., 2759; Godwin, W., 1154; Hegel, G., 4110; Heidegger, M., 6402; Hobhouse, L., 1002; Hume, D., 5785; Jefferson, T., 3950; Jordan, E., 5819; Kierkegaard, S., 4870; King, M., 837; Marcel, G., 6805; Marcuse, H., 472, 1576; Maritain, J., 1927, 3716; Marx, K., 4110; Marxist, 2690; Mead, G., 2301, 2730, 3016; Merleau-Ponty, M., 6806; Mill, J., 1030, 3885, 4769; Niebuhr, R., 837; Ortega y Gasset, J., 5029, 6087, 6787; Perry, R.B., 378; Plato, 754; Popper, K., 2667; Royce, J., 1997, 2301, 6104; Russell, B., 1595, 4906; St.-Simon, H., 3783; Santayana, G., 6211; Sartre, J.-P., 3293; Schutz, A., 6893; Sellars, R., 2301; Skinner, B.F., 472; Sorel, G., 5696; Thoreau, H., 2221; Veblen, T., 1305; Weber, M., 3679; Whitehead, A., 6812
social science, 443, 1470, 1951, 4714, 4995, 5660; Duhem, P., 1787; language in, 478; measurement in, 3900; objectivity in, 644, 1222; value, 71, 6286, 6464; Winch, P., 5342
socialism, 5140
Socinus, 4475
sociology, 2085, 2687, 3982, 5494, 5842, 6274
sociology of knowledge, 1112, 3975, 6562
Socrates, 355, 953, 1480, 6986
solipsism, 465, 574, 3039, 6580
Soloviev, V., 7356
Sommers, 1889
Sorel, G., 5382, 5696
Sorley, W.R., 442, 461, 6387
soul, 528, 1907, 2081, 4562, 4994, 5251, 5319; Aquinas, T., 663, 3742, 5665, 6250; Aristotle, 1038, 2781; Augustine, 5030; Cajetan, T., 5983; Giles of Rome, 4026; John of Jandun, 5854; Locke, J., 4455; Merleau-Ponty, M., 437; Moses of Narbonne, 3176; Plato, 88, 286, 523, 1271, 1516, 7429; Thomas of York, 889; William of Auvergne, 5263
space, 2, 699, 744, 1216, 1543, 1740, 1840, 1900, 2001, 2012, 2174, 2262, 2302, 2634, 2657, 2691, 2975, 3146, 3475, 4322, 4436, 4602, 4612, 4807, 4819, 5606, 6051, 6073, 6105, 6257, 7108, 7400
Spanish philosophy, 3306
Spanish-American philosophy, 6892
species, 1962, 6253
speculative philosophy, 487

speech acts, 499, 1351, 2380, 4218, 4618, 5354, 6083, 7229
Spencer, H., 277, 2595, 2771, 3936, 4051, 4293, 4684, 4805, 5364
Spengler, O., 1823
Spinoza, B., 450, 717, 1192, 2250, 2819, 2865, 3575, 3932, 4231, 4292, 4433, 5600, 5633, 6675; absolute, 6526; attributes, 3479; cognition, 2420; epistemology, 4, 4466; essence, 271, 2366; ethics, 618, 1735, 4938, 5008, 5613, 6688; God, 3325, 4486, 5015, 5528; idea, 271; imagination, 2454; law, 389; metaphysics, 475, 1431, 3214, 4864, 5674; necessity, 4103; particulars, 1260; politics, 1735, 4902, 6901; psychology, 1775; religion, 4197, 4824; substance, 1982; time, 1518; truth, 4374; value, 475
sport, 3667, 4500
Spranger, E., 6228
Stace, W.T., 2392, 5796
Stallo, J.B., 7276
state, 780, 4686, 6210, 6244, 7171
Stein, E., 321
Stern, W., 5361
Stevenson, C.L., 522, 1309, 2385, 3526, 4462, 4752, 6544, 7268
Stillingfleet, E., 997
Stirner, M., 1588
Stoicism, 341, 864, 1330, 1437, 1710, 2484, 2513, 3007, 4247, 4438, 5904, 6417, 7498
Stout, G.F., 144, 3913
Strawson, P.F., 1941, 2204, 2261, 2488, 2510, 2523, 2646, 3249, 3473, 3562, 4229, 4448, 4673, 5779, 5789, 6183, 6195
Strong, A.H., 2884
Strong, C.A., 921, 3557
structure, 125, 1174
Sturzo, L., 1645, 4511

style, 1013
Suarez, F., 840, 1012, 1530, 1728, 1745, 3107, 3861, 4179, 4818, 5763, 5829, 5930, 6452, 7175
subject, 5247
subjectivism, 3789, 4598, 5148, 6572
subjectivity, 463, 1400, 2185, 2925, 3548, 7353
sublime, 1084, 5233
submission, 5903
substance, 861, 1504, 1740, 1945, 2119, 2264, 4079, 4104, 4182, 4791, 4969, 5546, 6885; Abraham Ibn Daud, 169; Aquinas, T., 556, 5269, 7360; Aristotle, 5682, 6607, 7131, 7231; Berkeley, G., 606, 3519; Descartes, R., 2038; Hume, D., 212; Locke, J., 289; McTaggart, J., 6017; Reid, T., 606; Spinoza, B., 1982
substantial form, 1037, 1265, 2733, 3862, 4597
suffering, 1457, 3491, 7264
Sufism, 4705
suicide, 573, 4979, 7237
Sullivan, H.S., 829
Sumner, W.G., 4345
Sun Yat-sen, 1131
supererogation, 115, 3150, 6496
superstition, 2383
supposit, 7080
suprarational, 5691
Suzuki, D., 309
Swedenborg, E., 3544, 7389
symbol, 1939, 2058, 2104, 2124, 2292, 2491, 2673, 5370, 5399, 6797, 7269; Cassirer, E., 3678; Freud, S., 4630; Langer, S., 2216; Tillich, P., 4930; Urban, W., 874
symbolic interaction, 383
synonymy, 730, 3666
system, 4364

Tagore, R., 2243
Taine, H., 3328
Talmud, 4350

Taoism, 1079, 1098, 4926,
  6152, 6669, 7362
Tappan, H.P., 5281
Tarde, G. de, 2687
Taylor, A.E., 4430
Taylor, C., 5311, 6474
Taylor, P.W., 4126
Taylor, R., 316
technology, 986, 2025,
  2950, 3030, 7186
Teichmüller, 6941
Teilhard de Chardin, P.,
  270, 872, 5103; consciousness, 1391, 3956, 3132;
  eros, 124; evolution, 500,
  515; man, 6871; transcendence, 5864; value, 2626
teleology, 83, 2437, 2765,
  2797, 5482, 5855, 6204,
  6400, 6474, 6482, 6499,
  6727, 7397; biology, 494,
  1423, 4120, 6126; Dilthey,
  W., 2074; Kant, E., 3665,
  4318
temperament, 195
temperence, 6243
Temple, W., 2548, 3722,
  5139, 5831
Tennant, F.R., 297, 867,
  2496, 3336, 6403, 6421
tense, 1176, 3352
tension, 1772
theism, 34, 1334, 2290,
  2526, 4125, 5229, 5291,
  5457, 5744, 5949, 6403,
  6421
theology, 1094, 1708, 2158,
  2886, 3130, 6484; Bultmann,
  R., 2631; Hume, D., 2887,
  3490; John of St. Thomas,
  863; Kant, E., 2611, 3490,
  4022; and language, 1161,
  2596, 6778; Pascal, B.,
  4560; Peirce, C., 159;
  Royce, J., 904; Tillich,
  P., 1180, 4027, 4312,
  5804; Wittgenstein, L.,
  3863
theoretical entities, 883,
  894, 2856
theosophy, 3692
Thierry, A., 6307
thing, 4586, 6108
thinking, 375, 801, 1683,
  2517, 4762, 6343

Thomas de Bungeye, 5179
Thomas of Sutton, 5453
Thomas of York, 889, 2264,
  2500, 4348, 5578, 6050
Thomism, 123, 201, 2226,
  3531, 4270, 6266
Thoreau, H.D., 2221
thought, 657, 1799, 2234,
  2632, 5122
Thucydides, 1204
Tillich, P., 2645, 2685,
  3979, 4065, 4732, 5226;
  being, 4930; existence,
  4842, 6618; God, 882,
  1354, 4256, 5559, 5561,
  5844, 6475, 6945; history,
  5561; justice, 582; man,
  4401; person, 474; reality, 474; religion, 2104,
  2539, 3343, 6722, 6915;
  revelation, 89; theology,
  1180, 4027, 4312, 5804;
  value, 5597
time, 2, 67, 401, 439, 464,
  588, 676, 698, 855, 1105,
  1246, 1740, 1803, 1900,
  2012, 2045, 2098, 2174,
  2220, 2236, 2251, 2334,
  2335, 2767, 2839, 3056,
  3238, 3259, 3719, 3976,
  4186, 4322, 4602, 4807,
  4903, 5308, 5502, 6293,
  6653, 6914, 6925, 7142,
  7400; Alexander, S.,
  1543; Aquinas, T., 5473,
  5551; Aristotle, 3715;
  Augustine, 891; Bergson,
  H., 7108; Descartes, R.,
  1518; Green, T., 4239;
  Hegel, G., 5122, 6819;
  Heidegger, M., 4326, 4431,
  4603, 6146, 7097; Hume,
  D., 6257; Husserl, E.,
  722, 5583, 7181, 7343;
  Kant, E., 854, 7108; Kierkegaard, S., 5232; logic
  of, 1313, 2262; Marcel,
  G., 6970; Mead, G., 1394;
  Merleau-Ponty, M., 2691,
  3123; Plato, 2367; Reichenbach, H., 5232; Royce,
  J., 2483; Spinoza, B.,
  1518; Whitehead, A.N.,
  2684, 2691, 3090, 3911,
  4326, 4431, 7343

Toland, J., 1793, 1932
Tolman, E.C., 3741
Tolstoy, L., 259, 1510, 3713
totalitarianism, 5405, 7463
touch, 1519, 1984
Toulmin, S., 1797, 7167
Toynbee, A., 1315, 1823, 4242
tragedy, 1859, 5769
Traherne, T., 5700
transcendence, 1515, 2282, 2313, 3817, 4290, 4423, 4993, 5864, 6367, 6521, 6677, 6853, 7366
transcendental argument, 3076, 3436
transcendentalism, 1085, 1129, 1467, 2402, 2508, 4677, 7176
translation, 370, 592, 1485, 1610, 2300, 2717, 2866, 2926, 4650, 5076, 6699, 6779, 6856, 6869, 7159
transsubjectivity, 201
Trendelenburg, A., 5770
Troeltsch, E., 1438
truth, 440, 553, 814, 1473, 1686, 2014, 2056, 2201, 2236, 2701, 3157, 3253, 3254, 3258, 3344, 3401, 3527, 3870, 4419, 4525, 5199, 5330, 5524, 5638, 6224, 6299, 6468, 6622, 6699, 6745, 6869, 7204; aesthetics, 1493; Aristotle, 2791, 4575; Aquinas, T., 4294; Augustine, 1597, 4746; Austin, J., 382, 4448; Ayer, A., 3234, 3276; Berkeley, G., 3024; Blanshard, B., 3776; Bradley, F., 6419; coherence, 3492, 5886, 7201; contextualism, 6160; convention, 12, 6535; correspondence, 1706, 2588, 2600, 3592, 4073, 5227, 5886; Croce, B., 4564; Dewey, J., 1941, 2324, 4950; Hegel, G., 809, 4285; Heidegger, M., 4285, 6959; Hervaeus Natalis, 1958; James, W., 2324; Jaspers, K., 2480, 3856; Kierkegaard, S., 974, 3011, 3276, 3398, 5871;
Leibniz, G., 7323, 7348; Lessing, G., 809; Lewis, C.I., 1684; mathematical, 1350; necessary, 900, 1684, 2247, 2408, 3744, 5071, 5480, 7323, 7348; Peirce, C., 2324, 4543; Plato, 3480; pragmatic theory, 5809; pragmatism, 2024, 2324; Quine, W.V.O., 1553; realism, 1559; Schelling, F., 809; semantics of, 457; Spinoza, B., 4374; Stoicism, 1760; Strawson, P.F., 1941, 4448; Whitehead, A.N., 6824; Wittgenstein, L., 4728
Tsanoff, R.A., 5124
Tucker, A., 2765
Tucker, R.D., 3268
Tylor, E.B., 4805
types, 1574, 3169, 5622, 6385

Ucken, 1499
Ulrich of Strasbourg, 1238, 1948, 3876, 5014
Unamuno, M., 250, 2018, 6497
unconscious, 279, 1062, 1220, 1486, 1626, 1724, 2132, 3787, 4980, 5765, 5965, 6148, 6345, 7476
Underhill, E., 1614
understanding, 3350, 4457, 6228
unity, 5038
universals, 359, 675, 742, 1387, 1579, 3410, 3445, 3988, 4098, 4182, 4528, 4814, 6045, 6063, 6846, 6903, 6918; Aquinas, T., 1158, 3587, 6567; Aristotle, 3587; Berkeley, G., 1006; Bradley, F., 1768; Frege, G., 2211; Hume, D., 1006, 1073; Husserl, E., 7281; Locke, J., 1006; Mill, J., 1972; Plato, 616; Sellars, W., 3156; Wittgenstein, L., 1950, 6564
universalizability, 4886

unknowable, 3838
Upanishads, 3113, 3316, 3854
Upham, T.C., 3071
Urban, W.M., 874, 3043, 5357,
 6247, 6462
usury, 3269
utilitarianism, 41, 55, 264,
 2329, 2349, 2586, 3717,
 4087, 4096, 5347, 5997,
 6541, 7202; Bentham, J.,
 2425; Berkeley, G., 3704;
 Dewey, J., 2178; ethics,
 345, 1935, 4859; justice,
 5501; Mill, J., 489, 747,
 3671, 4378; obligation,
 267
utopianism, 3022, 3828

vagueness, 570, 3406, 3609
Vaihinger, H., 7094
Vailati, G., 7470
Valery, P., 5900
validation, 4914, 5224
value, 163, 261, 517, 669,
 971, 1126, 1254, 1489,
 1810, 2037, 2126, 2246,
 2370, 2624, 2627, 2651,
 2947, 3257, 3264, 3277,
 3363, 3576, 3708, 3810,
 3957, 3987, 4045, 4202,
 4277, 4489, 4614, 4661,
 4721, 4795, 4850, 5254,
 5290, 5336, 5411, 5570,
 5605, 5863, 5910, 6006,
 6011, 6069, 6277, 6286,
 6538, 6615, 6636, 6698,
 6729, 7022, 7113, 7259,
 7292, 7315; Alexander, S.,
 1378, 2626, 5523; Aquinas,
 T., 176, 639, 7067; Bergson, H., 5753; Brightman,
 E., 2246, 4785; Caso, A.,
 44, 2558; Cassirer, E.,
 3678; Dewey, J., 1798,
 1872, 2137, 2649, 4952,
 5794, 6241; and education,
 1202; and evolution, 2205;
 Freud, S., 6078; Hartmann,
 N., 2833; Hegel, G., 3700;
 intrinsic, 709, 934, 1005;
 Kierkegaard, S., 1769,
 2467; and language, 869,
 7301; Lewis, C.I., 4462,
 4752; Locke, A., 4432;

Marx, K., 1344; Mumford,
 L., 1835; Nietzsche, F.,
 2467, 3391, 5901; Parker,
 D., 4462; Peirce, C.S.,
 2978, 3939; Pepper, S.,
 1286; Perry, R., 3201,
 4462, 6241; Ramsey, F.,
 6966; Romero, F., 1299;
 Russell, B., 1206; Sartre,
 J.-P., 3212, 4561; Scheler, M., 5990, 6358, 6594;
 Spengler, O., 1823; Spinoza, B., 475; Stevenson,
 C., 4462, 4752; Taylor,
 A., 4430; Teilhard de
 Chardin, P., 2626; Urban,
 W., 6462; Vasconcelos, J.,
 44, 2558; Veblen, T.,
 1622; Wiemann, H., 2960;
 Whitehead, A., 1545, 1802,
 2495, 2833, 3298, 3882,
 3939, 4565, 4571, 4785,
 5358, 5753
value-neutrality, 71
Van Fraassen, 6494
Vasconcelos, J., 44, 2558
Vasquez, G., 3777
Vasubandhu, 106, 6685
Veblen, T., 1305, 1492,
 1622, 4805
Vecchio, G. Del, 455
Venn, J., 5873
vera causa, 3392
verification, 138, 2290,
 5152, 6761, 7492
Vico, G., 5203, 5714
Vinci, L. da, 1046
violence, 3374, 3426, 3766,
 4572, 5088, 7047
virtue, 158, 1306, 2400,
 3004, 3747, 3952, 4259,
 5306; intellectual, 665;
 Plato, 1434, 3170, 5890
Viterbio, J. de, 5320
Vitoria, F. de, 1011, 2614,
 5459
Vives, J.L., 3650, 4965
Voegelin, 4242
Voltaire, F., 2049, 3797,
 3926, 7091
voluntarism, 4474, 5451,
 6149
Von Neumann, J., 7436
Von Wright, G., 7351
Vorillon, W., 636
Vygotsky, L.S., 435

Walter of Chatton, 5012
war, 1688, 2133, 2365, 4518, 5111, 5845, 6411
Ward, J., 461, 921, 2496, 4134, 5264, 5666
Ward, L., 4345
Warren, E., 875
Watson, J., 7286
Watts, I., 1505
Weber, M., 3477, 3679
Weissmann, A., 4130
weltanschauung, 3482
Wesley, J., 1816
Westermarck, E.A., 5262
western thought, 444
Weyl, H., 4081
Whewell, W., 2888, 4052, 5244, 5939, 6503, 7043
Whitehead, A.N., 227, 1030, 1652, 2054, 2253, 4056, 4526, 4883, 5976, 6404, 6569, 6775, 7173; action, 1384; actual occasion, 3093, 6672; aesthetics, 5424, 6140, 6275, 7001; being, 2090; body, 2691; categories, 2426; causation, 1696, 3140, 6793; change, 7451; concept, 301; consciousness, 4968, 5408; creativity, 3062, 3386, 6502; education, 4662, 5807; epistemology, 549, 2304, 3807, 6332; eternal objects, 3453, 4460, 5748; ethics, 390, 1750, 3231, 4631, 4809, 5452, 5651; evil, 6876; existence, 2833; experience, 421, 2087, 4217, 4365, 6093; extension, 4953; freedom, 5011, 5380; God, 732, 1267, 1542, 2105, 2854, 4171, 5521; history, 75; Hume, D., 5463; Indian philosophy, 3764; individual, 3939, 6199, 7368; intentions, 1384; intuition, 5547; language, 1956, 2426, 5061; man, 4175, 5194; mathematics, 5469, 7260; meaning, 2531; metaphysics, 1108, 2397, 2605, 3452, 3461, 5452, 5651, 6252, 6348, 6502, 7455; method, 2531; metric structure, 3984; mind, 4806, 7066; nature, 4037; negative prehensions, 1269; novelty, 2520; ontology, 2304, 3772, 4353, 4503; order, 2087; panpsychism, 2358, 3806; perception, 4641, 6332, 6648; person, 2227; personalism, 5258; pluralism, 96; political philosophy, 1078; pragmatism, 2192; prehensions, 6382; propositions, 2753; purpose, 7065; reality, 3243; religion, 1545, 5080; science, 718, 1999, 3720, 5127; social philosophy, 6812; space, 2691; subjectivism, 4598; time, 2684, 2691, 3090, 3911, 4431, 7343; truth, 6824; ultimate, 2110; value, 1545, 1802, 2495, 2833, 3298, 3882, 3939, 4565, 4571, 4785, 5358, 5753
Whorf, B.L., 976, 5061
Wieman, H.N., 1262, 2494, 2960, 6727
Wild, J., 1533, 3389
Wilde, O., 6338
will, 416, 1207, 1373, 1503, 1538, 4297; Aquinas, T., 254, 7334; Descartes, R., 7369; Edwards, J., 331, 3026; Fichte, J., 737, 3126; James, W., 5725, 5764; Leibniz, G., 3162; Ricoeur, P., 1346; Royce, J., 3505, 7003; Schopenhauer, A., 90, 6123
William of Auvergne, 899, 5034, 5263, 6604
William of St.-Thierry, 3998, 6766
Wilson, C., 5698
Wilson, J., 5406
Winch, P., 5342
Windelband, W., 5999
Winters, Y., 4771
wisdom, 266, 3989, 5043, 5598
Wisdom, J., 3127, 6039

Wittgenstein, L., 448, 1777, 1833, 1899, 1959, 1978, 2199, 2330, 2498, 2608, 3676, 4692, 5261, 5419, 5985, 6493, 7445; absolute, 6526; analyticity, 2320; being, 5433; common sense, 2967; criteria, 3143; definition, 7502; education, 4100; ethics, 2618, 2731, 3208; excluded middle, 4169; explanation, 2755; family resemblances, 5738; God, 484; immortality, 127; infinity, 2552; knowledge, 6428; language, 152, 493, 566, 969, 1408, 1660, 2726, 3069, 3661, 4595, 5433, 5934, 6058, 6769; life, 3837; logic, 5912; mathematics, 2775, 3496, 3572, 3890, 6690; meaning, 936, 3761, 3837, 4728, 5004, 7253; metaphysics, 2296, 3580; mind, 102, 4715, 6183; necessity, 2409; notebooks, 5694; number, 5912; ontology, 7367; *Philosophical investigations*, 2401, 4422; picture theory, 936, 6528, 7435; pragmatism, 6760; private experience, 1291, 4012; private language, 329, 2053; sensations, 785, 5822, 6180; theology, 3863; *Tractatus*, 73, 152, 2795, 4422, 4429, 4610, 4728, 5178, 5625, 6313, 6519; truth, 4728; universals, 1950, 6564
Wobbermin, G., 4918
Wolff, C., 839, 1320, 6557
Wollaston, W., 6714
Woodbridge, F.J.E., 1568, 1908, 2752, 2919, 5467, 6115, 7328, 7452
work, 5907
world, 827, 1066, 1091
worship, 2345
Wu-Ch'eng, 2277

Xenophanes, 1853

yoga, 449, 2237

Zabarella, J., 1838, 6340
Zea, L., 1198
Zeising, A., 731
Zen, 5755
Zeno, 4133, 6952
Ziff, P., 3526
Zubiri, X., 1860, 5504

Ref
Z
7125
B38

NOV 1 9 1980